PEOPLE in Time and Place

EASTERN HEMISPHERE

AUTHOR

Dr. Kenneth S. Cooper
Professor of History, Emeritus
George Peabody College for Teachers
Vanderbilt University
Nashville, TN

SERIES CONSULTANTS

Dr. James F. Baumann
Professor and Head of the
Department of Reading Education
College of Education
The University of Georgia
Athens, GA

Dr. Theodore Kaltsounis
Professor of Social Studies Education
College of Education
University of Washington
Seattle, WA

LITERATURE CONSULTANTS

Dr. Ben A. Smith
Assistant Professor of Social Studies Education
Kansas State University
Manhattan, KS

Dr. John C. Davis
Professor of Elementary Education
University of Southern Mississippi
Hattiesburg, MS

Dr. Jesse Palmer
Assistant Professor, Department of Curriculum and Instruction
University of Southern Mississippi
Hattiesburg, MS

SILVER BURDETT GINN

MORRISTOWN, NJ • NEEDHAM, MA
Atlanta, GA • Dallas, TX • Deerfield, IL • Menlo Park, CA

SERIES AUTHORS

Dr. W. Frank Ainsley, Professor of Geography, University of North Carolina, Wilmington, NC

Dr. Herbert J. Bass, Professor of History, Temple University, Philadelphia, PA

Dr. Kenneth S. Cooper, Professor of History, Emeritus, George Peabody College for Teachers, Vanderbilt University, Nashville, TN

Dr. Claudia Crump, Professor of Elementary Social Studies Education, Indiana University Southeast, New Albany, IN

Dr. Gary S. Elbow, Professor of Geography, Texas Tech University, Lubbock, TX

Roy Erickson, Program Specialist, K–12 Social Studies and Multicultural Education San Juan Unified School District, Carmichael, CA

Dr. Daniel B. Fleming, Professor of Social Studies Education, Virginia Polytechnic Institute and State University, Blacksburg, VA

Dr. Gerald Michael Greenfield, Professor and Director, Center for International Studies, University of Wisconsin — Parkside, Kenosha, WI

Dr. Linda Greenow, Associate Professor of Geography, SUNY — The College at New Paltz, New Paltz, NY

Dr. William W. Joyce, Professor of Education, Michigan State University, East Lansing, MI

Dr. Gail S. Ludwig, Geographer-in Residence, National Geographic Society, Geography Education Program, Washington, D.C.

Dr. Michael B. Petrovich, Professor Emeritus of History, University of Wisconsin, Madison, WI

Dr. Norman J.G. Pounds, Former University Professor of History and Geography, Indiana University, Bloomington, IN

Dr. Arthur D. Roberts, Professor of Education, University of Connecticut, Storrs, CT

Dr. Christine M. L. Roberts, Professor of Education, University of Connecticut, Storrs, CT

Parke Rouse, Jr., Virginia Historian and Retired Executive Director of the Jamestown-Yorktown Foundation, Williamsburg, VA

Dr. Paul C. Slayton, Jr., Distinguished Professor of Education, Mary Washington College, Fredericksburg, VA

Dr. Edgar A. Toppin, Professor of History and Dean of the Graduate School, Virginia State University, Petersburg, VA

GRADE LEVEL WRITERS/ CONSULTANTS

Sheila Allen
Sixth-Grade Teacher, Mount Hebron School, Upper Montclair, NJ

Susan Colford
Sixth-Grade Teacher, Booker Arts Magnet Elementary School, Little Rock, AK

Edward Graivier
Sixth-Grade Teacher, Pleasant Ridge School, Glenview, IL

Lisa Johnson
Sixth-Grade Teacher, Conrad Ball Middle School, Loveland, CO

ACKNOWLEDGMENTS

Page 56: From *Gods, Graves, and Scholars* by C.W. Ceram. Translated by Edward B. Garside. Used courtesy of Alfred A. Knopf, Inc.

Page 73: From *The Children's Homer: The Adventures of Odysseus and the Tale of Troy* by Padraic Colum. Copyright 1918 by Macmillan Publishing Co. and renewed 1946 by Padraic Colum and Willy Pogany. Reprinted by permission of the publisher.

Page 117: "Good Samaritan" from the *New American Bible with Revised New Testament*, Copyright © 1986, 1970 by the Confraternity of Christian Doctrine, Washington, D.C., is used with permission. All rights reserved.

Page 143: Copyright © 1984 by Leonard Everett Fisher. Reprinted by permission of Macmillan Publishing Co.

Page 240: From *The Diary of a Young Girl* by Anne Frank. © 1952 Otto H. Frank. © 1967 Doubleday & Co., Inc. Used by permission of the publisher.

Page 288: Copyright © 1968 by Esther Hautzig. Reprinted by permission of Harper & Row, Publishers, Inc.

Pages 294–295: Adapted from "Clever Manka" in the *Shepherd's Nosegay: Stories from Finland and Czechoslovakia* by Parker Fillmore, copyright 1950 and renewed 1986 by Harcourt Brace Jovanovich, Inc. Reprinted by permission of the publisher.

Page 367: From *Traveller's Prelude: Autobiography 1893–1927*, by Freya Stark. Used by permission of John Murray (Publishers), Ltd.

Page 445: From *African Proverbs* by Charlotte & Wolf Leslau. Used by permission of Peter Pauper Press.

Page 456: From *Tales from an Ashanti Village* by Peggy Appiah. © 1966 Pantheon Books, a division of Random House, Inc. Used by permission of the publisher.

Page 524: From *The Travels of Marco Polo Book II*. Translated by Manuel Komroff. Used by permission of Liveright Publishing Corporation.

Page 551: From *Modern Japanese Haiku and Anthology* compiled and translated by Makoto Ueda. © 1976 University of Toronto Press. Reprinted by permission of the University of Toronto Press.

Pages 573–574: Copyright © 1984 by Elsie Roughsey. Reprinted by permission of Penguin Books, Australia, Ltd.

Page 583: From *Kon-Tiki* by Thor Heyerdahl. Used by permission of Simon & Schuster, Inc.

ISBN 0-382-20941-9   1 2 3 4 5 6 7 8 9 – RRD – 99 98 97 96 95 94 93 92

CONTENTS

Unit

3

THE FORMER SOVIET UNION AND EASTERN EUROPE

CHAPTER  GEOGRAPHY OF THE FORMER SOVIET UNION AND EASTERN EUROPE   **282–301**

Visiting a Vast Empire
The Lands of Eastern Europe
More Nationalities Than Countries
CHAPTER REVIEW: PUTTING IT ALL TOGETHER

CHAPTER *11* HISTORY OF RUSSIA AND EASTERN EUROPE   **302–321**

The Middle Ages in Russia and Eastern Europe
In the Time of the Czars
The Russian Revolution
CHAPTER REVIEW: PUTTING IT ALL TOGETHER

CHAPTER *12* THE FORMER SOVIET UNION AND EASTERN EUROPE TODAY   **320–348**

Communist Rule in the Soviet Union
The Collapse of Soviet Communism
  and the U.S.S.R.
Poland and Czechoslovakia
Southeastern Europe

 LITERATURE *Dracula*
by Bram Stoker   **345**

CHAPTER REVIEW: PUTTING IT ALL TOGETHER

UNIT 3 REVIEW: COOPERATIVE LEARNING   **349**

Understanding Time Zones   **350–351**
Making Comparisons   **352–353**

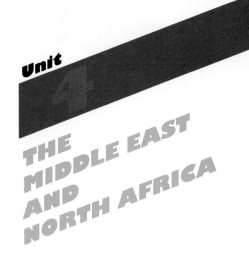

Unit

THE MIDDLE EAST AND NORTH AFRICA

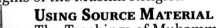 

Unit
5

AFRICA SOUTH OF THE SAHARA

Unit 7

AUSTRALIA, NEW ZEALAND, AND THE PACIFIC ISLANDS

RESOURCE SECTION

ATLAS

TIMELINES

GRAPHS

TABLES

CHARTS

DIAGRAMS

SPECIAL FEATURES

USING SOURCE MATERIAL

LITERATURE

CITIZENSHIP AND AMERICAN VALUES

SOCIAL STUDIES

LANGUAGE ARTS

MAP SKILLS HANDBOOK

Knowing how to work with maps is a social studies skill that everyone must have. You can't learn history and geography without being able to read maps. Maps, however, have uses that go beyond what you are learning in school.

Watch the nightly news. How many times are maps used? The next time you are in the library, take a copy of a weekly newsmagazine and count the number of maps that accompany the articles. Are maps used in any advertisements in the magazine? Keep a record over a week of all the times you see or use a map.

As you study the Eastern Hemisphere this year, you will be using map skills that you already have. You will also be learning some new map skills. All the map skills you will need appear in this Map Skills Handbook. Study the lesson titles on these pages to see which skills you will learn.

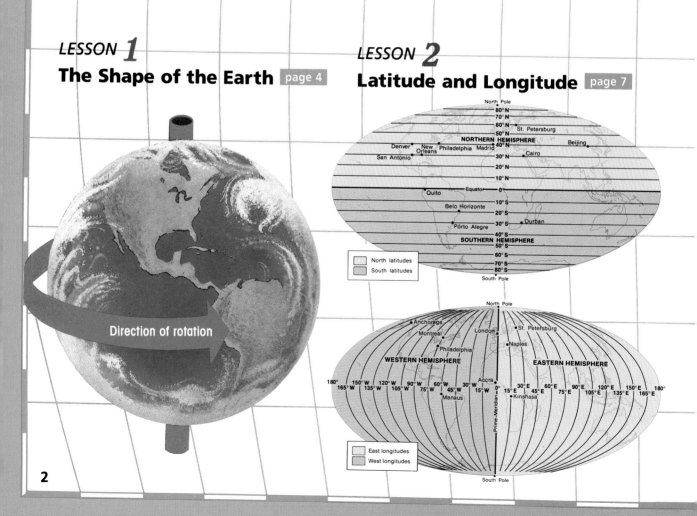

Direction of rotation

North Pole
80° N
70° N
60° N · St. Petersburg
50° N
NORTHERN HEMISPHERE 40° N · Beijing
Denver · New Philadelphia Madrid
Orleans
San Antonio 30° N · Cairo
20° N
10° N
· Quito Equator 0°
10° S
Belo Horizonte
20° S
Pôrto Alegre 30° S · Durban
40° S
SOUTHERN HEMISPHERE 50° S
60° S
70° S
80° S
South Pole

North latitudes
South latitudes

North Pole
· Anchorage London · St. Petersburg
Montreal · Naples
· Philadelphia
WESTERN HEMISPHERE EASTERN HEMISPHERE
Accra
180° 150° W 120° W 90° W 60° W 30° W 0° 30° E 60° E 90° E 120° E 150° E 180°
165° W 135° W 105° W 75° W 45° W 15° W 15° E 45° E 75° E 105° E 135° E 165° E
· Manaus · Kinshasa
South Pole

East longitudes
West longitudes

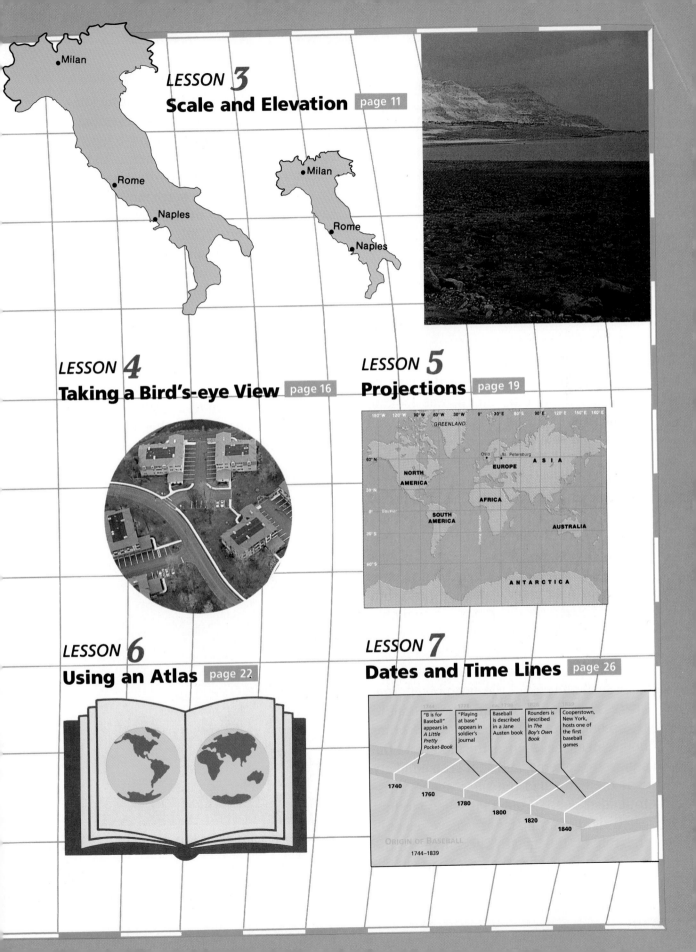

Milan

Rome

Naples

Milan

Rome

Naples

GREENLAND

60° N

NORTH
AMERICA

EUROPE

ASIA

Oslo St. Petersburg

AFRICA

30° N

0° Equator

SOUTH
AMERICA

AUSTRALIA

30° S

60° S

ANTARCTICA

180° W 120° W 90° W 60° W 30° W 0° 30° E 90° E 120° E 160° E. 160° E

"B is for
Baseball"
appears in
*A Little
Pretty
Pocket-Book*

"Playing
at base"
appears in
soldier's
journal

Baseball
is described
in a Jane
Austen book

Rounders is
described
in *The
Boy's Own
Book*

Cooperstown,
New York,
hosts one of
the first
baseball
games

1740

1760

1780

1800

1820

1840

ORIGIN OF BASEBALL
1744–1839

The Shape of the Earth

THINK ABOUT WHAT YOU KNOW

Imagine that you are an astronaut looking down on the earth from space. Describe what you see.

STUDY THE VOCABULARY

sphere   **axis**
orbit   **hemisphere**

FOCUS YOUR READING

What is the shape of the earth?

A. The Earth Is a Sphere

Over 2,000 years ago in the land of Macedonia, the king, Philip, was looking for the best teacher in all of Greece for his 13-year-old son, Alexander. Philip thought that his friend Aristotle might be willing to teach Alexander. Aristotle, famous for his teaching and learning, agreed to become Alexander's teacher. He schooled Alexander in many subjects, including information about the earth.

We do not know exactly what Aristotle taught Alexander about the earth, but many of Aristotle's writings are available to us today. Aristotle wrote that the earth was shaped like a **sphere**, that is, a round ball. We know that this is true because we have seen pictures of the earth taken from space. How could Aristotle have come to this conclusion? He noted that other bodies in space, such as the moon and the sun, were spheres, and so it seemed likely that the earth had the same shape. Aristotle also pointed out that when we first catch sight of a ship far at sea, we see only the top of the mast. The curve of the earth's surface hides the lower parts of the ship from view until it comes closer.

B. What We Know About the Earth

Movement of the Earth   Aristotle knew more about the earth than most people of his time did. Since then we have learned much more about our planet. Aristotle mistakenly thought the earth stood still. We now know that the earth moves in two ways. The earth **orbits**, or revolves around, the sun. Did you know that we are moving at almost 67,000 miles (107,803 km) an hour? This is the speed at which the earth revolves around the sun. The earth takes $365\frac{1}{4}$ days to make one revolution around the sun.

At the same time, the earth also rotates on its **axis**. The earth's axis is an imaginary line that runs through the middle of the earth from the North Pole to the South Pole. The tilt of this axis never changes as the earth orbits the sun.

THE EARTH'S AXIS

North Pole

Direction of rotation

South Pole ← Axis

The earth spins on its axis, an imaginary line that goes through the center of the earth.
► Through which two points on the earth does the axis pass?

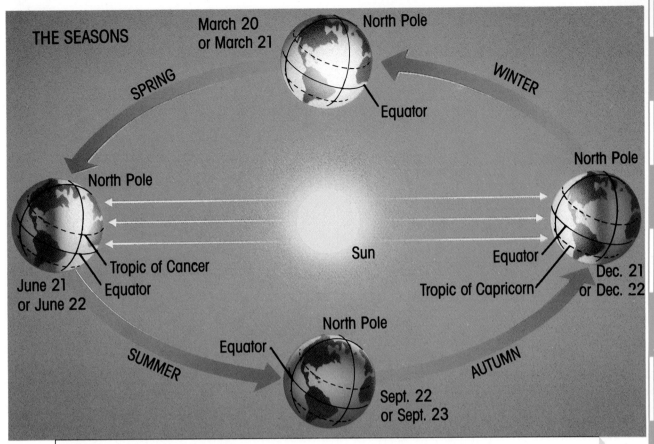

THE SEASONS

March 20
or March 21

North Pole

SPRING

Equator

WINTER

North Pole

North Pole

Sun

Tropic of Cancer

Equator

Equator

Tropic of Capricorn

Dec. 21
or Dec. 22

June 21
or June 22

North Pole

Equator

SUMMER

AUTUMN

Sept. 22
or Sept. 23

The tilt of the earth as it orbits, or travels around, the sun is the cause of our seasons.
▶ Which dates mark the start of winter in the Northern Hemisphere?

Change of Seasons The change of seasons is caused by both the revolving of the earth and the tilt of the earth's axis. Look at the diagram on this page. On June 21 or 22 the northern part of the earth is tilted toward the sun. This is the first day of summer and the longest day of the year for the area north of the Equator. The term *Equator* is used to name an imaginary line that circles the earth halfway between the North and South poles.

The Equator divides the earth into two equal halves. The Greek word for "half" is *hemi;* therefore, half the earth's sphere is called a **hemisphere**. The Equator divides the earth into two hemispheres,

called the Northern Hemisphere and the Southern Hemisphere.

For the Southern Hemisphere, June 21 or 22 is the first day of winter and the shortest day of the year. On this day, the southern part of the earth is tilted as far away from the sun as it ever gets. Half a year later, on December 21 or 22, summer begins in the Southern Hemisphere and winter begins in the Northern Hemisphere. During this half-revolution around the sun, the tilt of the earth causes a change in seasons from one extreme to the other.

Size and Shape Aristotle also thought that the earth was larger than it is in fact.

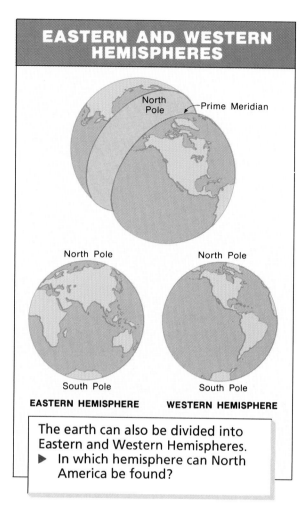

NORTHERN AND SOUTHERN HEMISPHERES

North Pole

Equator

NORTHERN HEMISPHERE   SOUTHERN HEMISPHERE

North Pole

South Pole

The Equator divides the earth into two hemispheres.
▶ What are the names of these two hemispheres?

EASTERN AND WESTERN HEMISPHERES

North Pole — Prime Meridian

North Pole   North Pole

South Pole   South Pole

EASTERN HEMISPHERE   WESTERN HEMISPHERE

The earth can also be divided into Eastern and Western Hemispheres.
▶ In which hemisphere can North America be found?

Today we know that the actual distance around the earth at the Equator is 24,902 miles (40,067 km), which is much smaller than many of the stars of our universe. We also know that the earth is not perfectly round, as Aristotle believed. The distance around the earth at the Equator is about 42 miles (68 km) greater than the distance around the poles.

Because of improvements in science and technology, we know more about the earth than Aristotle could have imagined. This year you will have an opportunity to learn more about the earth and its people.

LESSON **1** REVIEW

THINK AND WRITE

A. In what way was Aristotle correct in his ideas about the earth?
B. What do we know about the earth that Aristotle did not know?

SKILLS CHECK

THINKING SKILL

Look at the diagram on page 5. Which days of the year mark the first days of spring and summer in the Northern Hemisphere?

LESSON 2

Latitude and Longitude

THINK ABOUT WHAT YOU KNOW

Imagine that you and your family will be driving to Orlando, Florida for a visit. Discuss ways that your family could find out how to get from your home to Orlando.

STUDY THE VOCABULARY

grid	meridian
latitude	Prime Meridian
parallel	International
longitude	Date Line

FOCUS YOUR READING

How are lines of longitude and latitude used on a map?

A. A Geographical Mistake Leads Columbus to the Americas

The Greek scholar Claudius Ptolemy (KLAW dee us TAHL uh mee) did not believe that geography should include "chatter about people." Perhaps that is why we know so little about the author of one of the world's first geography books. We do know that Ptolemy lived in Egypt nearly 500 years after the time of Aristotle.

People were still studying Ptolemy's geography book more than 1,300 years later, when Christopher Columbus arrived in the Americas. In his book, Ptolemy explained that the earth is a sphere. But Ptolemy mistakenly thought that the earth was smaller than it is in fact. As a result of studying Ptolemy's book, Columbus believed the sailing distance from Europe west to the coast of Asia was much shorter. He did not realize that Asia actually lay more than halfway around the earth.

When Columbus set sail in 1492, he was not prepared for such a long trip. But, of course, he did not sail on to Asia. Instead, he reached another large mass of land that we now know as the Americas. So we can say that Ptolemy's error led to the voyage of Columbus. Few mistakes have ever had such far-reaching results.

B. Ptolemy Put a Grid on His Map

Ptolemy's Map Ptolemy wanted to give "a picture of the known world." By a "picture," he meant a map. As a matter of fact, Ptolemy might well have entitled his geography book "Instructions for Drawing Maps"! Even though Ptolemy made some mistakes in his book, we still follow some of his directions. For example, he located north at the top of the map, east on the right, south on the bottom, and west on the left. Most maps, including the ones found throughout this book, still show directions in this manner.

This map of what is now Ireland, Great Britain, and northern France was drawn by Ptolemy.
▶ Do you think this map is accurate?

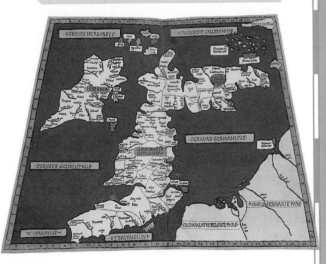

7

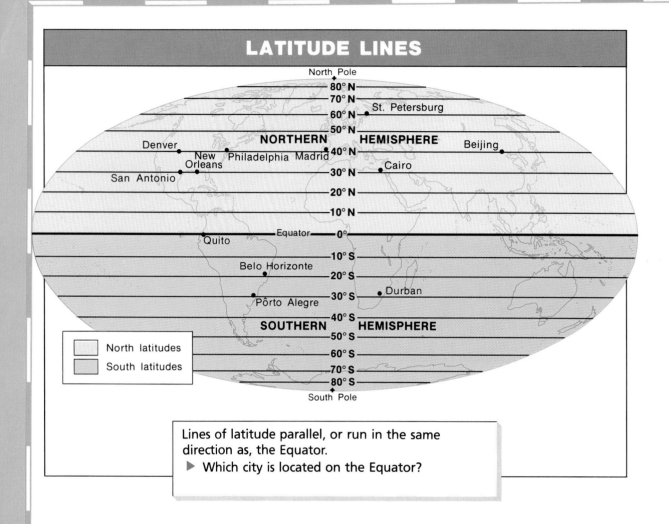

LATITUDE LINES

Lines of latitude parallel, or run in the same direction as, the Equator.
▶ Which city is located on the Equator?

Ptolemy instructed that maps should have a network of intersecting lines, called a **grid**, to locate places. He called the horizontal lines across the map **latitude**, which means "wide," because his map of the known world was wider than it was tall. Lines of latitude are also called **parallels** because they parallel, or run in the same direction as, the Equator. Like the Equator, these lines form whole circles around the earth. If you trace a parallel on a globe with your finger, your finger will always be the same distance from the Equator as it moves around the globe.

Measuring Distances The parallels measure distances in degrees from either side of the Equator toward the poles. The Equator is numbered 0° latitude. There are 90 degrees between the Equator and the North Pole, and 90 degrees between the Equator and the South Pole. We think of having a parallel for every degree. This is why we say there are 90 parallels north of the Equator and 90 parallels south of it. To make maps easier to read, mapmakers usually do not draw every parallel on maps.

The vertical lines on a map that run between the North and the South poles are lines of **longitude**, a word meaning "long." These lines are also called **meridians**. Each meridian crosses the Equator and all other lines of latitude. There are 360 meridians, or one for each degree in a circle. Meridians

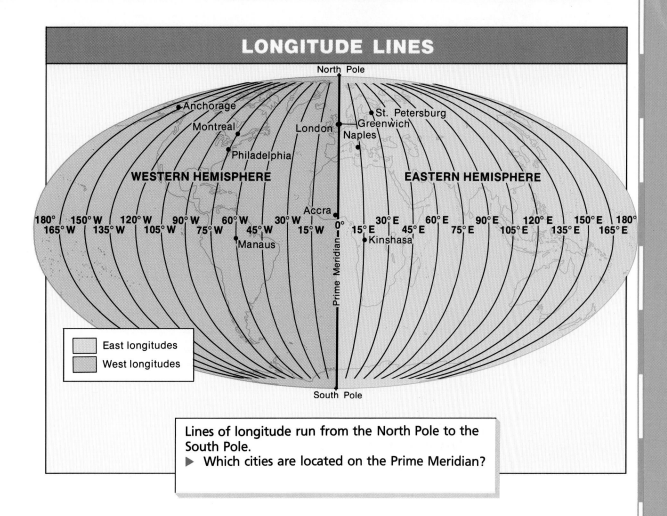

LONGITUDE LINES

North Pole

Anchorage
Montreal
Philadelphia
London
St. Petersburg
Greenwich
Naples

WESTERN HEMISPHERE

EASTERN HEMISPHERE

| 180° | 150° W | 120° W | 90° W | 60° W | 30° W | | 30° E | 60° E | 90° E | 120° E | 150° E | 180° |
| 165° W | 135° W | 105° W | 75° W | 45° W | 15° W | 0° 15° E | 45° E | 75° E | 105° E | 135° E | 165° E |

Accra

Manaus

Kinshasa

Prime Meridian

☐ East longitudes
☐ West longitudes

South Pole

Lines of longitude run from the North Pole to the South Pole.
▶ Which cities are located on the Prime Meridian?

are numbered from the **Prime Meridian**. This imaginary line runs through Greenwich, England. Meridians are counted east and west from the Prime Meridian, which is numbered 0° longitude.

Exactly halfway around the world is the 180° meridian, or what is known as the **International Date Line**, the point at which each day begins. The Prime Meridian and the International Date Line divide the earth into two hemispheres, the Eastern and the Western hemispheres.

C. Using a Map Grid

People have learned much more about making maps since the time of Ptolemy. But today we make use of longitude and latitude lines for the same reason that he did — they make it easier to locate places! Knowing the longitude and latitude of any place on the earth will enable you to find that place on a map. For example, look at the map called Using Latitude and Longitude on page 10. To find St. Petersburg, formerly Leningrad, on that map, put one finger on the line of latitude marked 60°N. Put a finger of your other hand on the line of longitude marked 30°E. Now move your two fingers along those lines until your fingers meet. The city of St. Petersburg is located at the spot where the two lines cross each other. The short way to write these facts is 60°N/30°E. You do

USING LATITUDE AND LONGITUDE

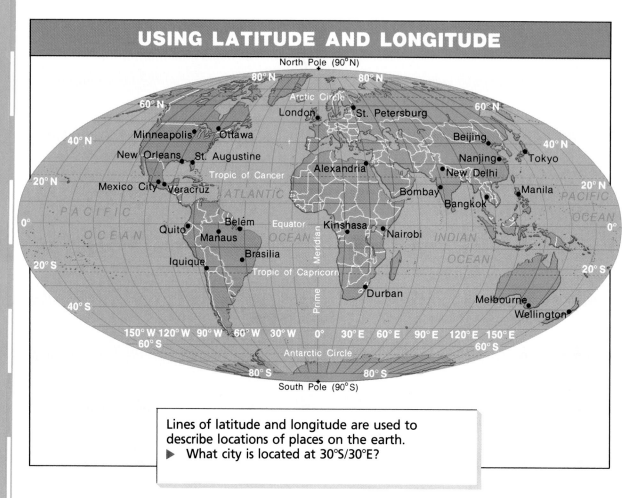

Lines of latitude and longitude are used to describe locations of places on the earth.
▶ What city is located at 30°S/30°E?

not need to write out the words *latitude* or *longitude*. That is because only latitude lines are counted north and south, and only longitude lines are counted east and west.

Sometimes the places you are looking for are not found exactly on points where lines of longitude and latitude cross. When this happens, you have to *estimate*, or figure generally, where those places are.

Using the map above, find the city of New Delhi (DEL ee), India. You will see that New Delhi is not exactly on any line of latitude or longitude. You have to estimate the latitude and longitude. New Delhi is between 20° and 30° north latitude and betwen 70° and 80° east longitude. What would you estimate New Delhi's latitude and longitude to be?

LESSON 2 REVIEW

THINK AND WRITE

A. How did Ptolemy's mistake lead Columbus to the Americas?

B. What are the two kinds of lines that form the grid that Ptolemy drew on his maps?

C. Why are grids placed on maps?

SKILLS CHECK

MAP SKILL

Look at the Using Latitude and Longitude map on this page. Find the latitude and longitude for the following cities: Durban, New Orleans, and Veracruz.

Scale and Elevation

What ways can you think of to measure the distance from your house to your school?

STUDY THE VOCABULARY

odometer   altitude
scale   contour line
elevation

FOCUS YOUR READING

How are scale and elevation shown on maps?

A. Measuring Distances Long Ago

Lack of Accurate Instruments In Ptolemy's time, people had no truly accurate way to measure long distances. They could measure a short distance, such as the size of a room, with a cord or rod, as we do with a tape measure or a yardstick. But they could not stretch a cord across a sea or from one city to another. The lack of accurate instruments was one reason for Ptolemy's mistake about the size of the earth.

Ptolemy knew that he could not depend on what sailors or overland travelers told him. If he asked a sailor how far he had come, the sailor would likely say the distance was a three-day sail. But how far could he sail in a day? It depended on the wind and the speed of the boat. Measuring land journeys was not much better. A merchant who had traveled with a caravan of camels or donkeys would also measure distance by days on the road. The merchant would say it was a five-day trip between cities. But animals do not always move at the same speed. Sometimes they get stubborn and do not move at all.

Marching armies provided a somewhat better way to measure distances on land. A troop of soldiers would usually march at about the same pace each day. A three-day march probably was a bit more accurate than a three-day camel caravan trip. But a day's march did not really give the distance unless the soldiers counted paces, and it is doubtful if troops ever counted each step.

A New Invention A Roman engineer invented a type of **odometer** (oh DAHM ut-ur). An odometer is an instrument that tells how far one has traveled. His invention used a wheel fastened to a frame that could be pushed like a wheelbarrow. On the frame he put a device that dropped a small ball into a box with each turn of the wheel. Afterward he would multiply the

This push odometer was invented by a Roman engineer.
▶ Do you think this was a good way of measuring distance?

11

Most cars have a speedometer to measure speed and an odometer to measure distance.
▶ How many miles has this car traveled?

distance around the wheel by the number of balls in the box to figure the distance the frame had been pushed. It is doubtful whether this push odometer was ever widely used.

B. Measuring Distances Today

Finding Distances Today it is much easier to find out how far you have traveled. For example, look on the dashboard of a car. Most cars today have both a speedometer and an odometer. The speedometer tells how fast you are going; the odometer tells you how far you have traveled. Odometers are but one of the instruments we have today to measure distances on the surface of the earth.

Another way to find the distance from one place to another is to use a map. When reading a map, you can estimate distances between places by using **scale**. Scale

THE METRIC SYSTEM OF MEASUREMENT

In this handbook you have learned that the distance around the earth is 24,902 miles, which is about the same as 40,067 kilometers. Kilometers and miles are both units of measure used to express distance or length. One kilometer and a little more than half a mile are about the same distance. A kilometer is a unit of measure in the metric system. The system is called metric because its standard unit of length is the meter.

The metric system is used for measuring distance. It is also used for measuring such things as weight, capacity, and temperature. The metric system is in use or is being introduced in the world's major countries except the United States.

We have used in this book both customary measurements that are in general use in the United States and metric measurements. When a customary measurement appears, it is followed in parentheses ( ) by the metric measurement that is about equal to it. Inches are changed to centimeters (cm), feet and yards to meters (m), miles to kilometers (km), and acres to hectares (ha). Pounds are changed to kilograms (kg), and quarts to liters (L). Degrees Fahrenheit (°F) are changed to degrees Celsius (°C).

shows the relationship between distances on a map and real distances on the earth's surface. Without a scale a person using a map would have no way of knowing the real distance.

Using Scale A map can be drawn to many different scales. The scale line on a map shows how much an inch (or centimeter) on the map stands for in real distances on the earth. The two maps below show the country of Italy. But each map is drawn to a different scale. Put a ruler under the scale line of the map on the left. One inch stands for about 200 miles (322 km). Now measure how many inches there are between the city of Milan and the city of Naples. There are about 2 inches. To find out how many actual miles (or km) there are between these two cities, multiply 2 × 200 (or 2 × 322). You will see that the distance between Milan and Naples is about 400 miles (644 km). Follow the same steps with the other map. The number of inches (or cm) is different from the number in the map on the left. However, when you use the scale for each map to figure the miles (or km) on the earth's surface, the distance between the two cities is the same.

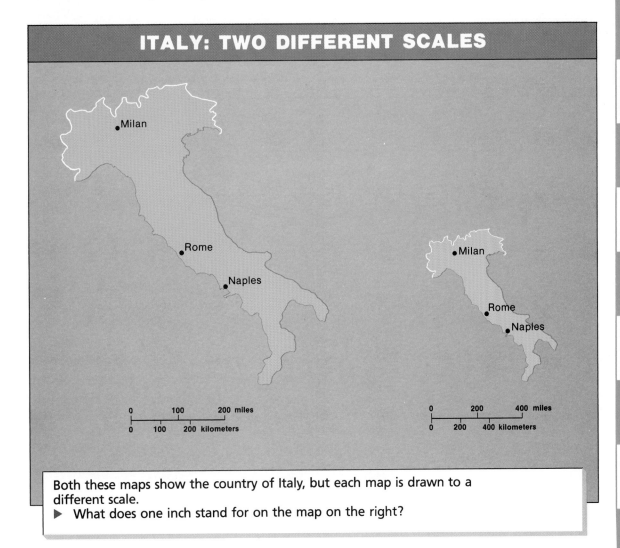

ITALY: TWO DIFFERENT SCALES

Both these maps show the country of Italy, but each map is drawn to a different scale.
▶ What does one inch stand for on the map on the right?

C. Showing the Land's Elevation

Measuring Heights Maps can be used not only to measure distances on the earth's surface but also to measure the different heights of the land. As you know, the surface of the earth is uneven. Ptolemy showed mountains on his early map, but they are little more than drawings. You would never know from looking at Ptolemy's map that some mountains are two or three times taller than others. But Ptolemy is not to be blamed. In his time there were no ways to measure the height, called **elevation** or **altitude**, of places. There is

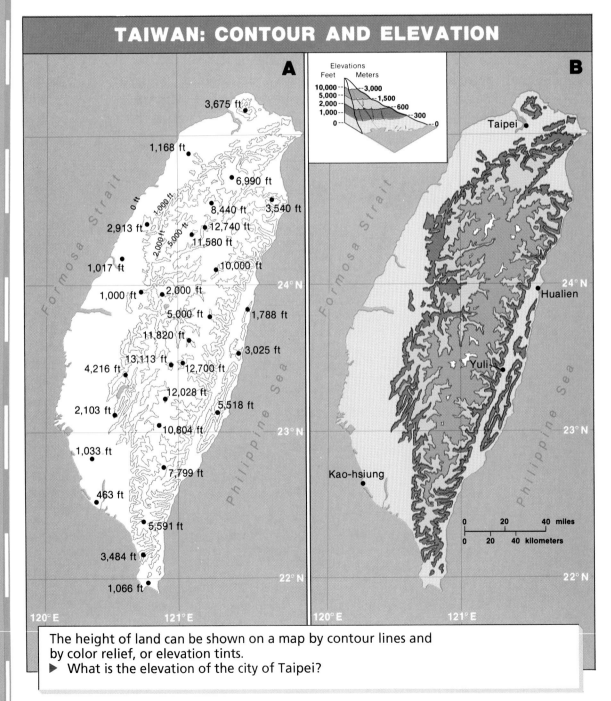

TAIWAN: CONTOUR AND ELEVATION

The height of land can be shown on a map by contour lines and by color relief, or elevation tints.
▶ What is the elevation of the city of Taipei?

The shore of the Dead Sea, more than 1,300 feet (396 m) below sea level, is covered with salt deposits.
▶ Where is the Dead Sea?

10,000 feet (3,048 m) above sea level. The elevation of the earth's land surface varies greatly. The highest mountain peaks are over 29,000 feet (8,839 m), but there are also places that are well below sea level. For example, the shore of the Dead Sea, between the countries of Israel and Jordan, is more than 1,300 feet (396 m) below the level of the sea. The difference between the highest and lowest elevations is more than 5 miles (8 km). Such differences are important facts about the earth and are shown on some maps.

Showing Elevation One good way to show the height of the land is to use **contour lines**. All points along one contour line are exactly the same distance above the level of the sea. Map A on page 14 shows the contour lines of the island country of Taiwan.

Another way to show the height of land is with a color relief map. Look at Map B of Taiwan on page 14. The different colors shown in the map key stand for different ranges of elevation. Light green shows land that is between sea level and 1,000 feet (300 m). Land that is between 1,000 feet and 2,000 feet (300 m and 600 m) above sea level is orange. Land shown in the same color may have hills, valleys, and mountains. But the elevation of all land shown in that color is within the range shown on the map key.

no doubt, though, that people knew there were differences between low hills and high mountains. People certainly must have known that the higher you climb over a mountain pass, the more difficult it becomes to breathe.

Today we measure elevation from the average height of the sea, or *sea level*. For example, if a mountain is 10,000 feet (3,048 m) high, the top of the mountain is

LESSON **3** REVIEW

THINK AND WRITE

A. Why was it difficult to get accurate measurements of land and sea distances during Ptolemy's time?
B. How do maps show distance?
C. What are two ways that land elevation is shown on a map?

SKILLS CHECK

MAP SKILL
Look at the elevation map of Taiwan on page 14. What is the elevation of the city of Yuli?

15

Taking a Bird's-eye View

What would be included on a map of your neighborhood?

cartographer   satellite

How do pictures taken from above the earth help people make better maps of the earth's surface?

A. Taking Pictures of the Earth

New Mapmaking A Frenchman known simply as Nadar was famous for his photographs of people. But in 1858 he decided that he would photograph a much larger subject. He would take a picture of a whole village, not the people of the village but the village itself. To do this, he had to get well above his subject. Nadar packed his bulky camera into the basket of a hot-air balloon, ascended about 250 feet (76 m) over a village near Paris, and snapped the picture. This was the first step toward a new kind of mapmaking.

Mapmakers During World War I, airplane pilots acted as scouts and took pictures of battlefields from their airplanes. After the war, aerial photographs came into use in making maps. Using the photographs taken from an airplane flying directly above the surface of the earth enabled **cartographers**, or people who make maps, to make detailed maps of the earth's surface.

Compare the picture on page 17 with the map of the same place, shown on the bottom of page 17. You will notice that the

photograph and the map do not necessarily show all the same things. Can you find anything in the photograph that is not shown on the map? Maps also use symbols, and the key tells what each symbol stands for. Symbols stand for real places on the earth. Mapmakers pick out the most important features of a photograph and use symbols to show them. Can you find the buildings in the photograph? Try to find those same buildings on the map.

Cartographers must make careful measurements to ensure that their maps are accurate.
▶ What tools do you see here?

FROM PHOTOGRAPH TO MAP

	Parking lots		Roads		Pond		Other land
	Buildings		Trees		River		

The photograph and the map show the same area, but the map shows the area differently. The map uses symbols to represent the most important features in the photograph.
► What do the orange symbols on the map represent in the photograph?

This picture of the United States was taken from a satellite. Satellite images help cartographers to make accurate maps.
▶ What color tells you where the bodies of water are in this picture?

B. A New View of the Earth

When astronauts went into space, they saw the earth as no one had ever seen it before. Through television and photographs, they have shared this view with us. In 1963, astronaut Gordon Cooper orbited the earth 22 times. He took many pictures of the earth's surface. His pictures of cloudless desert areas were remarkably clear and revealed features of the earth's surface that did not exist on the best maps at that time.

In the 1970s the United States launched unmanned **satellites** designed to send back to earth pictures of the earth's surface. A satellite is an object made to travel around the earth. By fitting 569 of these views together, it was possible to produce a picture map, or *photomosaic,* of the United States. Satellite photographs now help us make maps like one that Ptolemy asked for many centuries ago—"a picture of the known world."

LESSON **4** REVIEW

THINK AND WRITE

A. How do photographs taken from directly above the earth's surface help to make better maps?

B. How has exploration of space helped cartographers make better maps?

SKILLS CHECK

WRITING SKILL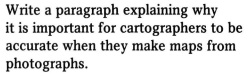

Write a paragraph explaining why it is important for cartographers to be accurate when they make maps from photographs.

Projections

THINK ABOUT WHAT YOU KNOW

Take a look at a globe and a flat map of the world. Can you think of any instances when the flat map would be more useful to you than the globe?

STUDY THE VOCABULARY

projection   **distortion**

FOCUS YOUR READING

Why is projection important in map-making?

A. Drawing a Round Earth on a Flat Map

In 1492, Martin Behaim (BAY hym) of Nuremberg, Germany, made a globe that the people of his town called "Behaim's earthapple." It is the oldest existing globe. A globe is the best representation of the earth, but even a globe has some drawbacks. To show places on an easy-to-read scale, a globe would have to be quite large. Besides, how could you get a globe into a book? Because of these and other reasons, we also need flat maps of the earth.

Drawing the spherical earth on a flat sheet is an old problem for mapmakers. Throughout the years, mapmakers have tried to solve this problem by using different map **projections**. A projection is a way to show a drawing of the earth on a flat surface. No one kind of projection serves all purposes, so different projections have been developed to meet different needs.

B. A Map for Travelers and Sailors

Early Mapmaking One of the most famous map projections was invented over 400 years ago by a man named Gerardus Mercator (juh RAHR dus   mur KAYT ur). Mercator used his knowledge of mathematics and geography and his skill as an engraver to become a mapmaker. At that time, mapmaking was a very popular business. With the exploration of the Americas, the demand for maps increased. Mercator printed the first map that carried the names of both the continents of North America and South America. He also made a map that showed that Asia and North America were separate continents.

Martin Behaim's "earthapple," completed in 1492, is the oldest globe in existence.
► Why was *earthapple* a good name for Behaim's globe?

19

A New Projection Because of the growing interest in exploration and long journeys overseas, Mercator's maps had a new projection. On his maps, Mercator drew the parallels of latitude and the meridians of longitude as straight lines meeting at right angles. Look at the map below to see the Mercator projection.

Sailors found the Mercator projection useful because it showed directions clearly. On his maps, north and south were always up and down, and east and west were always right and left. This makes it easy to see that if you sailed straight west from Oslo, Norway, you would miss the coast of the United States.

The Mercator projection was, and still is, useful for figuring the course of a ship at sea, but like all projections, there is some **distortion**, or error, in the way the map shows the earth. To show longitude as straight lines, lands on either side of the Equator must be stretched in size. The greater the distance from the Equator, the greater the stretching must be. Greenland is a good example of this problem. On the Mercator projection, Greenland must be stretched so much that it appears as big as South America. Actually, South America is eight times as large as Greenland. Look at the map below and find Greenland and South America.

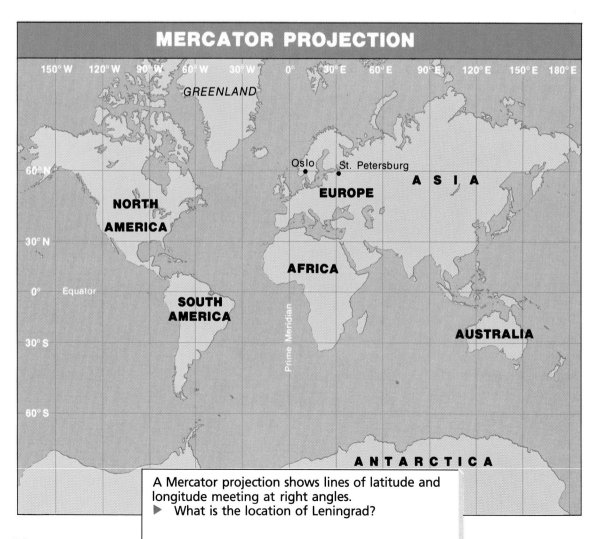

A Mercator projection shows lines of latitude and longitude meeting at right angles.
▶ What is the location of Leningrad?

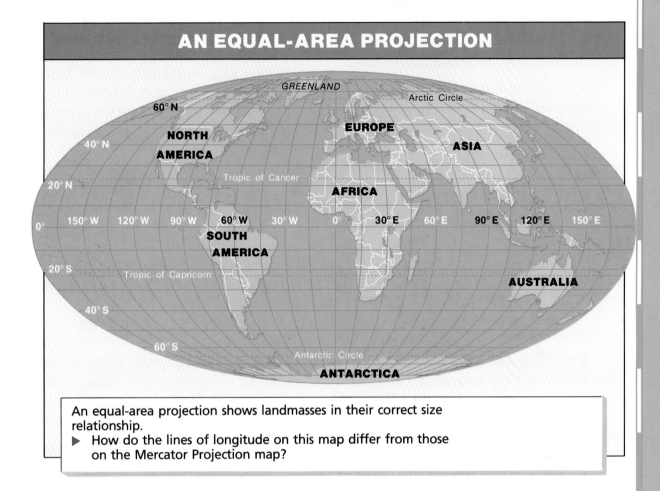

AN EQUAL-AREA PROJECTION

An equal-area projection shows landmasses in their correct size relationship.
► How do the lines of longitude on this map differ from those on the Mercator Projection map?

C. A Projection That Shows True Sizes of Land Areas

Most maps that are made today, including most maps used throughout this book, use equal-area projection. A map using equal-area projection shows land and water sizes accurately, but the shapes of the land are distorted. The lines of longitude are curved to show the curve of the earth's surface.

Equal-area projection maps serve most of our map-reading purposes better than maps using the Mercator projection. Although no one projection serves all purposes, maps are still very important tools in helping us learn about our world.

LESSON **5** REVIEW

THINK AND WRITE

A. Why do mapmakers have a problem making a flat map of the world?

B. What are the advantages and disadvantages of the Mercator projection?

C. Why do most maps made today use equal-area projection?

SKILLS CHECK

MAP SKILL

Look at the two maps on pages 20 and 21. Explain the differences between a map that uses the Mercator projection and a map that uses equal-area projection.

Using an Atlas

What kinds of information can you get from reading a map?

atlas	humidity
isthmus	precipitation
climate	population density

What is an atlas?

A. Named After a Mythical Giant

When Mercator published a book of maps, he named his book after a mythical bearded giant named Atlas. According to an old Greek myth, Atlas had disobeyed the gods. As punishment Atlas was made to stand and hold up the heavens. Some statues and pictures, like the one on this page show Atlas holding the sphere of heaven in his hands over the earth.

Mercator's Atlas became so well-known that people came to call any collection of maps an **atlas**. Today we still call a collection of maps an atlas. This book's Atlas can be found in the back of the book on pages 610–629.

Atlases, like dictionaries and encyclopedias, are reference books. We usually do not read a reference book all the way through from beginning to end. Instead, we turn to it when we want some specific information. You may find it interesting, and very helpful, to look through the Atlas in this book to discover the kinds of maps it contains. As you use this book throughout the year, you will find questions that refer to the Atlas.

B. Some Maps Let You See the Entire World

A look at a world map shows how much of the earth's surface is covered by the four oceans. Can you name the earth's four oceans from looking at the map on the next page? If you named the Pacific, Atlantic, Indian, and Arctic oceans, you are correct. The Pacific Ocean is by far the largest and deepest. It is nearly twice as large as the second largest ocean, the Atlantic. Ice covers much of the Arctic Ocean, which centers on the North Pole. No boundaries between the oceans appear on the map, because each ocean is but a part of one continuous body of water.

The world map will also enable you to locate the seven continents. These seven large bodies of land are Asia, Africa, Europe, Australia, North America, South America, and Antarctica. Locate Europe

This statue of Atlas stands in Rockefeller Center in New York.
▶ What is Atlas shown holding in this statue?

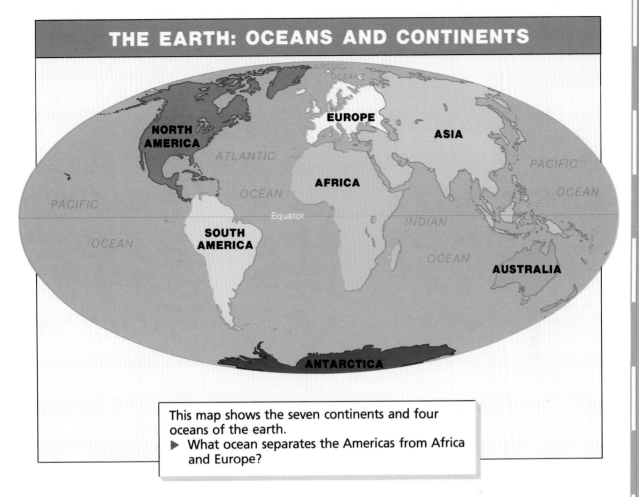

THE EARTH: OCEANS AND CONTINENTS

NORTH AMERICA

EUROPE

ASIA

ATLANTIC

PACIFIC

OCEAN

AFRICA

PACIFIC

OCEAN

Equator

SOUTH AMERICA

INDIAN

OCEAN

OCEAN

AUSTRALIA

OCEAN

ARCTIC OCEAN

ANTARCTICA

This map shows the seven continents and four oceans of the earth.
▶ What ocean separates the Americas from Africa and Europe?

and Asia on the map above. Notice that these two continents are one huge land mass. We sometimes call this land *Eurasia*, a combination of Europe and Asia.

Some continents are connected by a narrow strip of land, called an **isthmus** (IHS mus). Africa is attached to Eurasia by an isthmus, as North America is attached to South America. Australia and Antarctica are the only two continents wholly separated from the others.

C. Physical and Political Maps

In your Atlas you will find two maps for each continent. One is called a political map; the other is a physical map. Political maps show the nations, or countries, that have separate governments. Political

maps also usually give the locations of capitals and other important cities. Political maps of individual countries show the political divisions within those countries.

A physical map represents the natural features of the land. Important natural features are often labeled. Look at the physical map of North America on page 621. Find the Rocky Mountains on that map.

Sometimes, political and physical maps may be combined to make one map. Such a map makes clear the relationship between natural features and political boundaries. Look at the map of Australia and New Zealand on page 626. The Murray River serves as part of the political boundary between the Australian territories of Victoria and New South Wales.

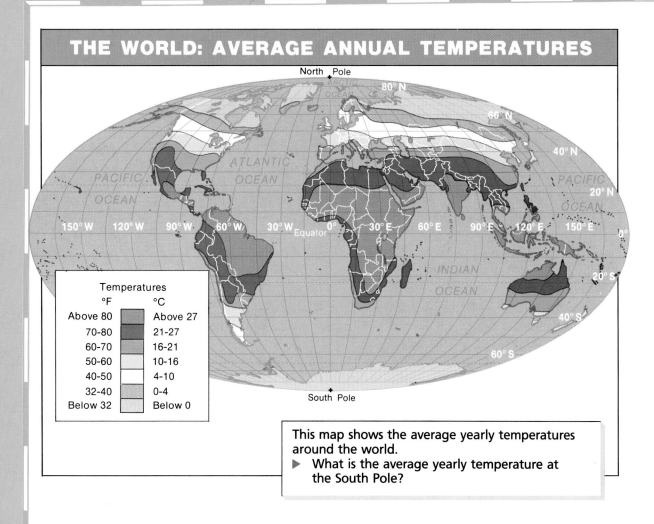

THE WORLD: AVERAGE ANNUAL TEMPERATURES

Temperatures

°F	°C
Above 80	Above 27
70-80	21-27
60-70	16-21
50-60	10-16
40-50	4-10
32-40	0-4
Below 32	Below 0

This map shows the average yearly temperatures around the world.
▶ What is the average yearly temperature at the South Pole?

D. An Atlas Can Have Many Other Kinds of Maps

Weather Maps Can you imagine television weather reporters not using maps when they give weather reports? Newspapers, too, often print daily weather maps. Those who report the weather use maps because maps are the clearest and quickest way to present facts about the weather over a country or region.

Maps can also be used to show information about the **climate** of a place. Climate is the normal or usual pattern of weather for a place over a period of time. As you can see from the map above, some climate maps show temperatures. Like weather maps, climate maps may also show the amount of dryness or dampness in the air, which is known as **humidity**, and the amount of **precipitation** a place gets. Precipitation is moisture that falls on the earth's surface in the form of rain, snow, sleet, or hail. Weather maps give you this information for a few particular days, whereas climate maps present average yearly statistics.

Other Maps There is almost no limit to the different types of facts that can be presented on maps. You can learn about the plant life of an area from a vegetation map. A vegetation map, such as the one shown on page 25, shows where there are forests, grasslands, and deserts. The Atlas at the

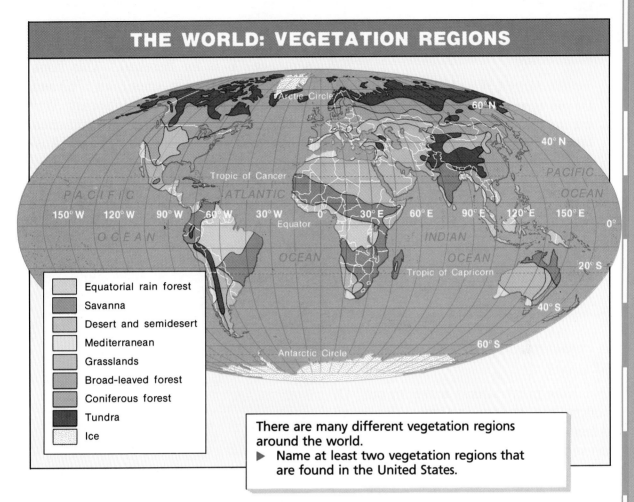

THE WORLD: VEGETATION REGIONS

Legend:
- Equatorial rain forest
- Savanna
- Desert and semidesert
- Mediterranean
- Grasslands
- Broad-leaved forest
- Coniferous forest
- Tundra
- Ice

There are many different vegetation regions around the world.
► Name at least two vegetation regions that are found in the United States.

back of this book contains other types of maps. The **population density** map shows where the largest number of people live in the world. Population density is determined by the average number of people who live on a square mile (sq km) of land.

By looking at a resource map, you can quickly get facts about where there are mineral deposits such as coal, tin, and iron ore. Maybe Mercator was correct in thinking that holding a book of maps is like having the universe in your hands!

LESSON **6** REVIEW

THINK AND WRITE

A. Why is a collection of maps called an atlas?

B. What are the names of the four oceans and seven continents?

C. What is the difference between a political map and a physical map?

D. What are some other kinds of maps that can be found in an atlas?

SKILLS CHECK

MAP SKILL

Look at the temperature map on page 24. What is the average yearly temperature at 40°N/90°W?

Dates and Time Lines

THINK ABOUT WHAT YOU KNOW

Do you agree or disagree with the following statement: "Learning dates is important to learning about the past"?

STUDY THE VOCABULARY

anno Domini   **circa**
century   **time line**
decade

FOCUS YOUR READING

How are dates and time lines used to learn about the past?

A. Questioning the Origins of Baseball

How many strikes make an out? Of course, the answer is three. Almost all Americans can answer that question because baseball is America's national game. How long have people been playing baseball? The answer to that question is not so easy. In fact, it has been the subject of a great debate.

Many people believe that baseball grew out of an old English game called rounders. Among those who believed that baseball was started in America was A. G. Spalding, a businessman and former baseball player. He formed a special commission to investigate the origin of baseball. The commission reported that baseball was invented by a man named Abner Doubleday and that one of the first baseball games was played at Cooperstown, New York, in 1839.

Some people doubt the Doubleday story and point out that long before the year 1839 various writings mentioned baseball. For example, *A Little Pretty Pocket-Book*, a children's alphabet book published in 1744 in England, used the sentence "B is for Baseball." This book was later published in America in 1762 and 1787. An American Revolutionary War soldier at Valley Forge in 1778 mentioned "playing at base" in his journal. Jane Austen, a famous English author, spoke of baseball in a book written about 1798. *The Boy's Own Book*, published in 1828, does not mention baseball, but the description

The game of baseball has been a popular American pastime for over a hundred and fifty years.
▶ How can you tell this is a baseball game from long ago?

of rounders sounds a great deal like a description of baseball.

The debate about the origin of baseball brings out the importance of dates. There is no doubt that Abner Doubleday was a real person or that he taught at a military school in Cooperstown, New York. The question is whether he invented a new game in 1839. The answer for that depends largely on dates. Dates, like maps, make it possible to have more exact knowledge about the people, lands, and events of the world. Maps tell us where; dates tell us when.

B. How Years Are Numbered

Numbering Years   The year 1839 could have been numbered differently. We could say that the game at Cooperstown was played 63 years after the Declaration of Independence was signed in 1776. But for dates to be useful to us, they must be counted from the same point.

The point from which most dates are counted was first decided by a man who lived in Rome. He was named Dionysius (dye uh NISH us) the Little. We do not know much about this man, not even why he was called Dionysius the Little. We do know that he began the practice of numbering the years from the birth of Jesus Christ. Dionysius first began to do this in the year he called A.D. 525. The letters A.D. stand for the Latin term **anno Domini** (AH-noh DOH mee nee), which in the English language means "in the year of the Lord."

Dionysius' System   Today most of the world uses the system Dionysius invented. When we write that the Cooperstown game was played in 1839, we mean that it was played one thousand eight hundred thirty-nine years after the birth of Christ. In practice we rarely use the letters A.D. when dating an event that occurred after Christ's birth.

The years before the birth of Christ are numbered backward from his birth. For example, the year before A.D. 1 was 1 B.C. The letters stand for "before Christ." The year before 1 B.C. was 2 B.C., and so on. When referring to dates before the birth of Christ, the higher the number, the earlier the year. For example, Aristotle lived from 384 B.C. to 322 B.C. The letters B.C. are always used with dates that show time before the birth of Christ.

C. Other Ways to Date Events

One Hundred Years Sometimes we date events by a period of 100 years, called a **century**. We count centuries in the same way we count years—that is, before and after the birth of Christ. The years from 1 to 100 make up the first century A.D. We live in the 1900s, the twentieth century. The year 2000 will still be in the twentieth century, but when the year 2001 arrives, we will enter the twenty-first century. Centuries before the birth of Christ are numbered like years before the birth of Christ. For example, the years 1 B.C. to 100 B.C. are considered the first century B.C.

A CENTURY HAS 100 YEARS

Years	Centuries
2001 – 2100	21st century
1901 – 2000	20th century
1801 – 1900	19th century
1701 – 1800	18th century
1601 – 1700	17th century
1501 – 1600	16th century
1401 – 1500	15th century
1301 – 1400	14th century
1201 – 1300	13th century
1101 – 1200	12th century
1001 – 1100	11th century
901 – 1000	10th century
801 – 900	9th century
701 – 800	8th century
601 – 700	7th century
501 – 600	6th century
401 – 500	5th century
301 – 400	4th century
201 – 300	3rd century
101 – 200	2nd century
1 – 100	1st century

A century is a period of 100 years by which we sometimes date events.
► Which year will begin the 21st century?

It is especially useful, and often easier, to remember the century in which a person lived rather than to remember the years of his or her birth and death. For example, Aristotle lived in the fourth century B.C., while Mercator, who was born in 1512 and died in 1594, lived in the sixteenth century. In which century was the Cooperstown baseball game played?

Ten Years We can also speak of dates in ten-year periods of time, called **decades**. We often speak of a decade, such as the 1920s or the 1970s, when we refer to events that took place over a period of several years. For example, we can say that the first manned space flights occurred in the 1960s. It was during that decade that we first started to explore space. What decade are you living in now?

Sometimes it is impossible to know the exact year of an event, but we may know *about* when the event happened. For example, we do not know the exact year that Jane Austen wrote the book in which she mentioned baseball. In such a case we write the abbreviation *ca.* or *c.* before the date. These letters stand for the Latin word **circa**, which means "about." We know that Jane Austen's book was written about 1798, so we date the writing of the book as ca. 1798.

D. Using Time Lines

Just as we can show different places on a map, we can show a series of events on a **time line**. A time line, like a map, has a scale, but the scale represents years rather than distances.

Look at the time line on the next page. It lists some of the dates related to the possible origin of baseball. This time line has a scale that runs from left to right.

A time line makes it easy to see the order of events over a period of time.

▶ How many years does this time line cover?

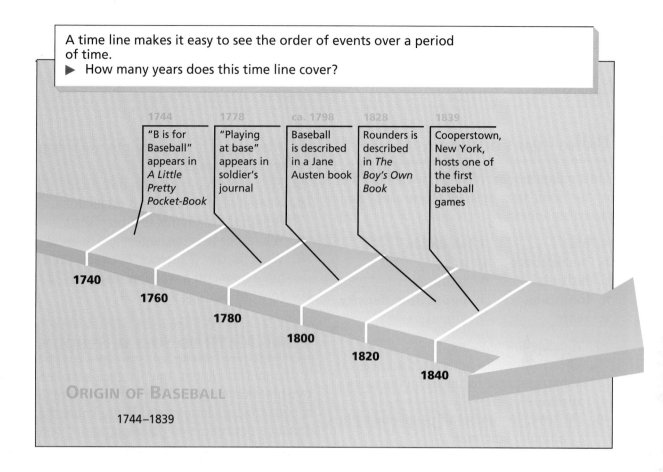

1744	1778	ca. 1798	1828	1839
"B is for Baseball" appears in *A Little Pretty Pocket-Book*	"Playing at base" appears in soldier's journal	Baseball is described in a Jane Austen book	Rounders is described in *The Boy's Own Book*	Cooperstown, New York, hosts one of the first baseball games

1740   1760   1780   1800   1820   1840

ORIGIN OF BASEBALL

1744–1839

Each segment on this time line equals 20 years. The whole time line represents 100 years, from 1740 to 1840. Some events and their dates are named above the time line, and a black line leads to each event's date on the time line.

This time line makes it easy to see the order of events dealing with the origin of baseball. For example, you will notice by looking at the time line that the book *A Little Pretty Pocket-Book* was written many years before the game at Cooperstown was played. About how many years were there between the writing of Jane Austen's book and the Cooperstown game? Throughout this book, you will find time lines to help you understand when things happened.

LESSON 7 REVIEW

THINK AND WRITE

A. Why are dates important to the discussion of the origin of baseball?
B. Explain how we number years.
C. What is the difference between a century and a decade?
D. What kind of information can be shown on a time line?

SKILLS CHECK

THINKING SKILL

Make a time line showing some important events in your life, such as the year you were born and the year you started school.

MAP SKILLS HANDBOOK REVIEW

USING THE VOCABULARY

On a separate sheet of paper, write the letter of the term that best matches each numbered statement.

a. axis
b. hemisphere
c. latitude
d. longitude
e. scale

f. elevation
g. atlas
h. isthmus
i. population density
j. climate

1. A collection of maps
2. The relationship between distances on a map and real distances on the earth's surface
3. The average number of people living in a particular land area
4. An imaginary line running through the center of the earth from the North Pole to the South Pole
5. A narrow strip of land connecting two continents
6. Vertical lines on a map
7. A place's normal pattern of weather
8. Half the earth's sphere
9. The height of the land
10. Horizontal lines across a map

REMEMBERING WHAT YOU READ

On a separate sheet of paper, answer the following questions in complete sentences.

1. In what two ways does the earth move?
2. What causes the change of seasons?
3. Why is it sometimes necessary to estimate latitude and longitude?
4. Why would it be difficult to use a map without a scale?
5. From where is elevation measured?
6. Name two common map projections.
7. What information is in a map key?
8. Which ocean is the largest and deepest?
9. What is the difference between a climate map and a weather map?
10. In what century was 1789?

TYING MATH TO SOCIAL STUDIES

In the metric system, the distance between two places is measured in kilometers. A mile is equal to 1.61 kilometers. If you know the distance between two places in miles, you can figure it out in kilometers. To convert miles to kilometers, multiply the distance in miles by 1.61. Convert the distances between New York and these world cities to kilometers: Cairo—5,602 miles; Hong Kong —8,054 miles; Mexico City—2,094 miles.

THINKING CRITICALLY

On a separate sheet of paper, answer the following questions in complete sentences.

1. Which factor affects climate more— latitude or longitude?
2. How does climate affect people's lives?
3. Name five reasons why people use maps.
4. Compare the length of longitude lines on a Mercator projection with the length of those on an equal-area projection map.
5. Why do we need a standard system of time measurement?

SUMMARIZING THE HANDBOOK

On a separate sheet of paper, copy the graphic organizer shown below. Beside the main idea of each lesson, write three statements that support the main idea.

HANDBOOK THEME

Maps and globes provide a wealth of information about people and the earth. To interpret maps, it is necessary to understand scale, symbols, latitude, longitude, and projections.

LESSON 1

We have learned much about the earth since the days of Aristotle.

1. Shaped like sphere   2.   3.

LESSON 2

Maps help us locate places.

1. Latitude lines   2.   3.

LESSON 3

There are many ways of measuring land and sea distances.

1. Different scales   2.   3.

LESSON 4

Taking pictures of the earth has helped people make more accurate maps.

1. Bird's-eye view   2.   3.

LESSON 5

Projections are a way of showing a drawing of the earth on a flat surface.

1. Mercator's maps   2.   3.

LESSON 6

Maps provide many different kinds of information.

1. Political divisions   2.   3.

LESSON 7

Dates and time lines help us learn about the past.

1. A.D. and B.C.   2.   3.

COUNTRIES OF THE
EASTERN HEMISPHERE

	FLAG	TOTAL AREA	POPULATION AND DENSITY	ECONOMY	MAJOR EXPORT
AFGHANISTAN ASIA ★ **Kabul**		250,775 sq mi 649,507 sq km	14,800,000 59 per sq mi 23 per sq km		Natural Gas
ALBANIA EUROPE ★ **Tiranë**		11,100 sq mi 28,749 sq km	3,200,000 288 per sq mi 111 per sq km		Crude Oil
ALGERIA AFRICA ★ **Algiers**		896,588 sq mi 2,322,163 sq km	24,900,000 28 per sq mi 11 per sq km		Crude Oil
ANDORRA EUROPE ★ **Andorra la Vella**		180 sq mi 466 sq km	49,000 272 per sq mi 105 per sq km		NA
ANGOLA AFRICA ★ **Luanda**		481,351 sq mi 1,246,699 sq km	8,500,000 18 per sq mi 7 per sq km		Crude Oil
AUSTRALIA AUSTRALIA **Canberra** ★		2,967,909 sq mi 7,686,884 sq km	16,800,000 6 per sq mi 2 per sq km		Coal
AUSTRIA EUROPE ★ **Vienna**		32,375 sq mi 83,851 sq km	7,600,000 235 per sq mi 91 per sq km		Machinery
BAHRAIN ASIA ★ **Manama**		255 sq mi 660 sq km	500,000 1,961 per sq mi 757 per sq km		Petroleum
BANGLADESH ASIA ★ **Dacca**		55,126 sq mi 142,776 sq km	114,700,000 2,081 per sq mi 803 per sq km		Jute
BELGIUM EUROPE ★ **Brussels**		11,781 sq mi 30,513 sq km	9,900,000 840 per sq mi 324 per sq km		Chemicals
BENIN AFRICA ★ **Porto-Novo**		43,483 sq mi 112,621 sq km	4,700,000 108 per sq mi 42 per sq km		Footwear
BHUTAN ASIA ★ **Thimbu**		16,000 sq mi 41,440 sq km	1,500,000 94 per sq mi 36 per sq km		Cement

■ Agriculture □ Industry ■ Services □ Not Available

32

	FLAG	TOTAL AREA	POPULATION AND DENSITY	ECONOMY	MAJOR EXPORT
BOTSWANA AFRICA **Gaborone**		219,916 sq mi 569,582 sq km	1,200,000 5 per sq mi 2 per sq km		Diamonds
BRUNEI ASIA **Bandar Seri Begawan**		2,226 sq mi 5,765 sq km	300,000 135 per sq mi 52 per sq km		Crude Oil
BULGARIA EUROPE **Sofia**		42,823 sq mi 110,912 sq km	9,000,000 210 per sq mi 81 per sq km		Machinery
BURKINA FASO AFRICA **Ouagadougou**		105,869 sq mi 274,201 sq km	8,700,000 82 per sq mi 32 per sq km		Cotton
BURUNDI AFRICA **Bujumbura**		10,759 sq mi 27,866 sq km	5,500,000 511 per sq mi 197 per sq km		Coffee
CAMBODIA ASIA **Phnom Penh**		68,898 sq mi 178,446 sq km	6,800,000 99 per sq mi 38 per sq km		Rubber
CAMEROON AFRICA **Yaoundé**		183,591 sq mi 475,501 sq km	10,800,000 59 per sq mi 23 per sq km		Crude Oil
CAPE VERDE ISLANDS AFRICA **Praia**		1,557 sq mi 4,033 sq km	400,000 257 per sq mi 99 per sq km		Fish
CENTRAL AFRICAN REPUBLIC AFRICA **Bangui**		240,376 sq mi 622,574 sq km	2,800,000 12 per sq mi 4 per sq km		Diamonds
CHAD AFRICA **N'Djamena**		495,752 sq mi 1,283,998 sq km	4,900,000 10 per sq mi 4 per sq km		Cotton
CHINA ASIA **Beijing**		3,691,502 sq mi 9,560,990 sq km	1,100,000,000 298 per sq mi 115 per sq km		Crude Oil
COMOROS AFRICA **Moroni**		863 sq mi 2,235 sq km	400,000 463 per sq mi 179 per sq km		Cloves

■ Agriculture ☐ Industry ▨ Services ☐ Not Available

33

COUNTRIES OF THE
EASTERN HEMISPHERE

	FLAG	TOTAL AREA	POPULATION AND DENSITY	ECONOMY	MAJOR EXPORT
Congo AFRICA **Brazzaville**		132,047 sq mi 342,002 sq km	2,200,000 17 per sq mi 6 per sq km		Crude Oil
Cyprus EUROPE **Nicosia**		3,572 sq mi 9,251 sq km	700,000 196 per sq mi 76 per sq km		Clothing
Czechoslovakia * EUROPE **Prague**		49,371 sq mi 127,871 sq km	15,600,000 316 per sq mi 122 per sq km		Machinery
Denmark EUROPE **Copenhagen**		16,629 sqmi 43,069 sq km	5,100,000 307 per sq mi 118 per sq km		Food
Djibouti AFRICA **Djibouti**		8,880 sq mi 22,999 sq km	400,000 45 per sq mi 17 per sq km		Livestock
Egypt AFRICA **Cairo**		386,900 sq mi 1,002,071 sq km	54,800,000 142 per sq mi 55 per sq km		Crude Oil
Equatorial Guinea AFRICA **Malabo**		10,825 sq mi 28,037 sq km	400,000 37 per sq mi 14 per sq km		Cocoa
Estonia EUROPE **Tallinn**		18,370 sq mi 47,578 sq km	1,500,000 82 per sq mi 32 per sq km		NA
Ethiopia AFRICA **Addis Ababa**		471,775 sq mi 1,221,897 sq km	49,800,000 106 per sq mi 41 per sq km		Coffee
Fed. States of Micronesia OCEANIA ** **Kolonia**		825 sq mi 2,137 sq km	87,000 105 per sq mi 41 per sq km		Coconut Oil
Fiji OCEANIA **Suva**		6,938 sq mi 17,969 sq km	800,000 115 per sq mi 45 per sq km		Sugar
Finland EUROPE **Helsinki**		130,128 sq mi 337,032 sq km	5,000,000 38 per sq mi 15 per sq km		Paper

34 * Recent changes in Czechoslovakia are discussed on page 340. ** The term Oceania refers to the region of scattered islands in the Pacific Ocean.

■ Agriculture □ Industry □ Services □ Not Available

	FLAG	TOTAL AREA	POPULATION AND DENSITY	ECONOMY	MAJOR EXPORT
FRANCE EUROPE ★ Paris		212,918 sq mi 551,458 sq km	56,100,000 263 per sq mi 102 per sq km		Chemicals
GABON AFRICA ★ Libreville		102,317 sq mi 265,001 sq km	1,100,000 11 per sq mi 4 per sq km		Crude Oil
GAMBIA AFRICA ★ Banjul		4,003 sq mi 10,368 sq km	800,000 200 per sq mi 77 per sq km		Groundnuts
GERMANY EUROPE Berlin ★		137,838 sq mi 357,000 sq km	78,700,000 571 per sq mi 220 per sq km		Machinery
GHANA AFRICA Accra		92,100 sq mi 238,539 sq km	14,600,000 159 per sq mi 61 per sq km		Cocoa
GREECE EUROPE ★ Athens		50,944 sq mi 131,945 sq km	10,000,000 196 per sq mi 76 per sq km		Fruits
GUINEA AFRICA ★ Conakry		94,925 sq mi 245,856 sq km	7,100,000 75 per sq mi 29 per sq km		Bauxite
GUINEA-BISSAU AFRICA Bissau		13,948 sq mi 36,125 sq km	1,000,000 72 per sq mi 28 per sq km		Groundnuts
HUNGARY EUROPE ★ Budapest		35,919 sq mi 93,030 sq km	10,600,000 295 per sq mi 114 per sq km		Machinery
ICELAND EUROPE Reykjavik		39,702 sq mi 102,828 sq km	300,000 8 per sq mi 3 per sq km		Fish
INDIA ASIA New Delhi		1,229,424 sq mi 3,184,208 sq km	835,000,000 679 per sq mi 262 per sq km		Tea
INDONESIA ASIA ★ Jakarta		779,675 sq mi 2,019,358 sq km	184,600,000 237 per sq mi 91 per sq km		Crude Oil

■ Agriculture   □ Industry   ▨ Services   □ Not Available   35

COUNTRIES OF THE
EASTERN HEMISPHERE

	FLAG	TOTAL AREA	POPULATION AND DENSITY	ECONOMY	MAJOR EXPORT
IRAN — ASIA — Tehran		635,932 sq mi 1,647,064 sq km	53,900,000 85 per sq mi 33 per sq km		Crude Oil
IRAQ — ASIA — Baghdad		168,927 sq mi 437,521 sq km	18,100,000 107 per sq mi 41 per sq km		Crude Oil
IRELAND — EUROPE — Dublin		26,600 sq mi 68,894 sq km	3,500,000 132 per sq mi 51 per sq km		Machinery
ISRAEL — ASIA — Jerusalem		7,992 sq mi 20,699 sq km	4,500,000 563 per sq mi 217 per sq km		Diamonds
ITALY — EUROPE — Rome		116,313 sq mi 301,251 sq km	57,600,000 495 per sq mi 191 per sq km		Machinery
IVORY COAST — AFRICA — Abidjan		124,508 sq mi 322,463 sq km	12,100,000 97 per sq mi 38 per sq km		Cocoa
JAPAN — ASIA — Tokyo		143,619 sq mi 371,973 sq km	123,200,000 858 per sq mi 331 per sq km		Machinery
JORDAN — ASIA — Amman		37,737 sq mi 97,739 sq km	4,000,000 106 per sq mi 41 per sq km		Phosphates
KENYA — AFRICA — Nairobi		224,960 sq mi 582,646 sq km	24,100,000 107 per sq mi 41 per sq km		Coffee
KIRIBATI — OCEANIA — Bairiki		332 sq mi 860 sq km	63,848 192 per sq mi 74 per sq km		Copra
KUWAIT — ASIA — Kuwait		6,200 sq mi 16,058 sq km	2,100,000 339 per sq mi 131 per sq km		Crude Oil
LAOS — ASIA — Vientiane		91,428 sq mi 236,799 sq km	3,900,000 43 per sq mi 16 per sq km		Timber

■ Agriculture ☐ Industry ▨ Services ☐ Not Available

	FLAG	TOTAL AREA	POPULATION AND DENSITY	ECONOMY	MAJOR EXPORT
LATVIA — EUROPE — Riga		25,400 sq mi / 65,786 sq km	2,700,000 / 106 per sq mi / 41 per sq km		NA
LEBANON — ASIA — Beirut		3,949 sq mi / 10,228 sq km	3,300,000 / 836 per sq mi / 323 per sq km		Services
LESOTHO — AFRICA — Maseru		11,716 sq mi / 30,344 sq km	1,700,000 / 145 per sq mi / 56 per sq km		Diamonds
LIBERIA — AFRICA — Monrovia		43,000 sq mi / 111,370 sq km	2,500,000 / 58 per sq mi / 22 per sq km		Iron Ore
LIBYA — AFRICA — Tripoli		679,358 sq mi / 1,759,537 sq km	4,100,000 / 6 per sq mi / 2 per sq km		Crude Oil
LIECHTENSTEIN — EUROPE — Vaduz		62 sq mi / 161 sq km	30,000 / 484 per sq mi / 187 per sq km		Machinery
LITHUANIA — EUROPE — Vilnius		25,174 sq mi / 65,201 sq km	3,700,000 / 147 per sq mi / 57 per sq km		NA
LUXEMBOURG — EUROPE — Luxembourg		999 sq mi / 2,587 sq km	400,000 / 400 per sq mi / 155 per sq km		Steel
MADAGASCAR — AFRICA — Antananarivo		226,657 sq mi / 587,042 sq km	11,600,000 / 51 per sq mi / 20 per sq km		Cloves
MALAWI — AFRICA — Lilongwe		45,193 sq mi / 117,050 sq km	8,700,000 / 193 per sq mi / 74 per sq km		Tobacco
MALAYSIA — ASIA — Kuala Lumpur		128,727 sq mi / 333,403 sq km	17,400,000 / 135 per sq mi / 52 per sq km		Crude Oil
MALDIVES — ASIA — Malé		115 sq mi / 298 sq km	200,000 / 1,739 per sq mi / 671 per sq km		Fish

■ Agriculture □ Industry ▨ Services □ Not Available

37

COUNTRIES OF THE
EASTERN HEMISPHERE

	FLAG	TOTAL AREA	POPULATION AND DENSITY	ECONOMY	MAJOR EXPORT
MALI — AFRICA ★ **Bamako**		478,652 sq mi 1,239,709 sq km	8,900,000 19 per sq mi 7 per sq km		Cotton
MALTA — EUROPE **Valletta**		122 sq mi 316 sq km	400,000 3,279 per sq mi 1,266 per sq km		Clothing
MARSHALL ISLANDS — OCEANIA ★ **Majuro**		4,500 sq mi 11,655 sq km	31,041 7 per sq mi 3 per sq km		Coconut Oil
MAURITANIA — AFRICA **Nouakchott** ★		397,955 sq mi 1,030,703 sq km	2,000,000 5 per sq mi 2 per sq km		Iron Ore
MAURITIUS — AFRICA ★ **Port Louis**		720 sq mi 1,865 sq km	1,100,000 1,528 per sq mi 590 per sq km		Sugar
MONACO — EUROPE **Monaco** ★		0.73 sq mi 2 sq km	29,000 39,726 per sq mi 15,338 per sq km		NA
MONGOLIA — ASIA ★ **Ulan Bator**		604,247 sq mi 1,565,000 sq km	2,100,000 4 per sq mi 2 per sq km		Livestock
MOROCCO — AFRICA ★ **Rabat**		172,413 sq mi 446,550 sq km	25,600,000 148 per sq mi 57 per sq km		Phosphates
MOZAMBIQUE — AFRICA **Maputo** ★		297,846 sq mi 771,421 sq km	15,200,000 51 per sq mi 20 per sq km		Fish
MYANMAR — ASIA **Rangoon**		261,789 sq mi 678,034 sq km	40,800,000 156 per sq mi 60 per sq km		Teak
NAMIBIA — AFRICA **Windhoek** ★		317,887 sq mi 823,327 sq km	1,800,000 6 per sq mi 2 per sq km		Diamonds
NAURU — OCEANIA **Yaren** ★		9 sq mi 22 sq km	8,042 946 per sq mi 365 per sq km		Phosphates

38

■ Agriculture □ Industry ▨ Services □ Not Available

	FLAG	TOTAL AREA	POPULATION AND DENSITY	ECONOMY	MAJOR EXPORT
NEPAL ASIA **Katmandu** ★		54,362 sq mi 140,798 sq km	18,700,000 344 per sq mi 133 per sq km		Textiles
NETHERLANDS EUROPE **Amsterdam**		14,140 sq mi 36,623 sq km	14,700,000 1,040 per sq mi 401 per sq km		Chemicals
NEW ZEALAND OCEANIA **Wellington**		103,736 sq mi 268,676 sq km	3,400,000 33 per sq mi 13 per sq km		Lamb
NIGER AFRICA ★**Niamey**		459,073 sq mi 1,188,999 sq km	7,400,000 16 per sq mi 6 per sq km		Uranium
NIGERIA AFRICA ★**Abuja**		356,669 sq mi 923,773 sq km	115,300,000 323 per sq mi 125 per sq km		Crude Oil
NORTH KOREA ASIA **Pyongyang** ★		46,609 sq mi 120,717 sq km	22,500,000 483 per sq mi 186 per sq km		Metals
NORTHERN MARIANAS OCEANIA **Saipan** ★		184 sq mi 477 sq km	19,000 103 per sq mi 40 per sq km		Coconut Oil
NORWAY EUROPE ★**Oslo**		125,049 sq mi 323,877 sq km	4,200,000 34 per sq mi 13 per sq km		Crude Oil
OMAN ASIA ★**Muscat**		82,000 sq mi 212,380 sq km	1,400,000 17 per sq mi 7 per sq km		Crude Oil
PAKISTAN ASIA **Islamabad**		310,403 sq mi 803,944 sq km	110,400,000 356 per sq mi 137 per sq km		Cotton
PAPUA NEW GUINEA OCEANIA **Port Moresby**		182,700 sq mi 473,193 sq km	3,900,000 21 per sq mi 8 per sq km		Gold
PHILIPPINES ASIA ★**Manila**		115,651 sq mi 299,536 sq km	64,900,000 516 per sq mi 217 per sq km		Electronics

■ Agriculture ☐ Industry ◻ Services ☐ Not Available

39

COUNTRIES OF THE
EASTERN HEMISPHERE

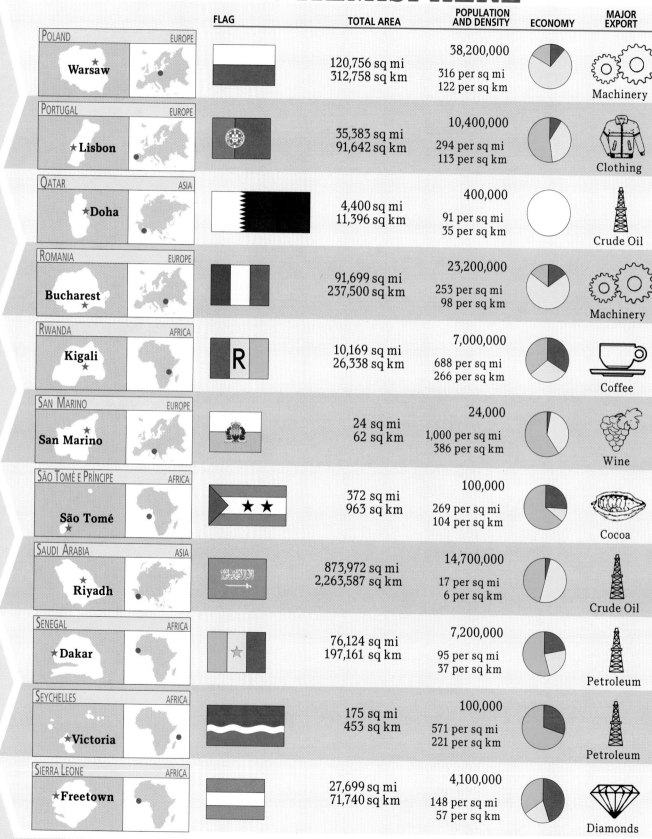

	FLAG	TOTAL AREA	POPULATION AND DENSITY	ECONOMY	MAJOR EXPORT
POLAND — EUROPE — Warsaw		120,756 sq mi / 312,758 sq km	38,200,000 / 316 per sq mi / 122 per sq km		Machinery
PORTUGAL — EUROPE — ★ Lisbon		35,383 sq mi / 91,642 sq km	10,400,000 / 294 per sq mi / 113 per sq km		Clothing
QATAR — ASIA — ★ Doha		4,400 sq mi / 11,396 sq km	400,000 / 91 per sq mi / 35 per sq km		Crude Oil
ROMANIA — EUROPE — Bucharest ★		91,699 sq mi / 237,500 sq km	23,200,000 / 253 per sq mi / 98 per sq km		Machinery
RWANDA — AFRICA — Kigali ★		10,169 sq mi / 26,338 sq km	7,000,000 / 688 per sq mi / 266 per sq km		Coffee
SAN MARINO — EUROPE — San Marino		24 sq mi / 62 sq km	24,000 / 1,000 per sq mi / 386 per sq km		Wine
SÃO TOMÉ E PRÍNCIPE — AFRICA — São Tomé ★		372 sq mi / 963 sq km	100,000 / 269 per sq mi / 104 per sq km		Cocoa
SAUDI ARABIA — ASIA — ★ Riyadh		873,972 sq mi / 2,263,587 sq km	14,700,000 / 17 per sq mi / 6 per sq km		Crude Oil
SENEGAL — AFRICA — ★ Dakar		76,124 sq mi / 197,161 sq km	7,200,000 / 95 per sq mi / 37 per sq km		Petroleum
SEYCHELLES — AFRICA — ★ Victoria		175 sq mi / 453 sq km	100,000 / 571 per sq mi / 221 per sq km		Petroleum
SIERRA LEONE — AFRICA — ★ Freetown		27,699 sq mi / 71,740 sq km	4,100,000 / 148 per sq mi / 57 per sq km		Diamonds

■ Agriculture □ Industry ▨ Services □ Not Available

	FLAG	TOTAL AREA	POPULATION AND DENSITY	ECONOMY	MAJOR EXPORT
SINGAPORE — ASIA — Singapore		225 sq mi 583 sq km	2,700,000 12,000 per sq mi 4,633 per sq km		Petroleum
SOLOMON ISLANDS — OCEANIA — Honiara		15,220 sq mi 39,420 sq km	300,000 20 per sq mi 8 per sq km		Copra
SOMALIA — AFRICA — Mogadishu		246,154 sq mi 637,539 sq km	8,200,000 33 per sq mi 13 per sq km		Livestock
SOUTH AFRICA — EUROPE — Pretoria		471,445 sq mi 1,221,043 sq km	38,500,000 82 per sq mi 32 per sq km		Gold
SOUTH KOREA — ASIA — Seoul		38,022 sq mi 98,477 sq km	43,100,000 1,134 per sq mi 438 per sq km		Ships
FORMER SOVIET UNION* — EUROPE/ASIA — Moscow		8,649,512 sq mi 22,402,236 sq km	289,000,000 33 per sq mi 13 per sq km		Crude Oil
SPAIN — EUROPE — Madrid		194,881 sq mi 504,742 sq km	39,200,000 201 per sq mi 78 per sq km		Motor Vehicles
SRI LANKA — ASIA — Colombo		25,332 sq mi 65,610 sq km	16,900,000 667 per sq mi 258 per sq km		Tea
SUDAN — AFRICA — Khartoum		967,500 sq mi 2,505,825 sq km	24,500,000 25 per sq mi 10 per sq km		Cotton
SWAZILAND — AFRICA — Mbabane		6,705 sq mi 17,366 sq km	800,000 119 per sq mi 46 per sq km		Sugar
SWEDEN — EUROPE — Stockholm		173,665 sq mi 449,792 sq km	8,500,000 49 per sq mi 19 per sq km		Machinery

*The dissolution of the Soviet Union in 1991 is discussed on page 331-336.

■ Agriculture □ Industry ■ Services □ Not Available

COUNTRIES OF THE
EASTERN HEMISPHERE

	FLAG	TOTAL AREA	POPULATION AND DENSITY	ECONOMY	MAJOR EXPORT
SWITZERLAND — EUROPE ★Bern		15,941 sq mi 41,287 sq km	6,600,000 414 per sq mi 160 per sq km		Chemicals
SYRIA — ASIA **Damascus**		71,498 sq mi 185,180 sq km	12,100,000 169 per sq mi 65 per sq km		Crude Oil
TAIWAN — ASIA ★**Taipei**		13,887 sq mi 35,967 sq km	20,000,000 1,440 per sq mi 556 per sq km		Machinery
TANZANIA — AFRICA **Dar es Salaam**		364,943 sq mi 945,202 sq km	26,300,000 72 per sq mi 28 per sq km		Coffee
THAILAND — ASIA **Bangkok**		198,455 sq mi 513,998 sq km	55,600,000 280 per sq mi 108 per sq km		Rice
TOGO — AFRICA **Lomé**		21,853 sq mi 56,599 sq km	3,400,000 156 per sq mi 60 per sq km		Phosphates
TONGA — OCEANIA **Nukualofa**		270 sq mi 699 sq km	96,448 357 per sq mi 138 per sq km		Coconut Oil
TUNISIA — AFRICA **Tunis** ★		63,378 sq mi 164,149 sq km	7,900,000 125 per sq mi 48 per sq km		Crude Oil
TURKEY — ASIA ★**Ankara**		301,380 sq mi 780,574 sq km	55,400,000 184 per sq mi 71 per sq km		Clothing
TUVALU — OCEANIA **Funafuti** ★		9 sq mi 23 sq km	8,229 914 per sq mi 353 per sq km		Copra
UGANDA — AFRICA **Kampala** ★		91,134 sq mi 236,037 sq km	17,000,000 187 per sq mi 72 per sq km		Coffee

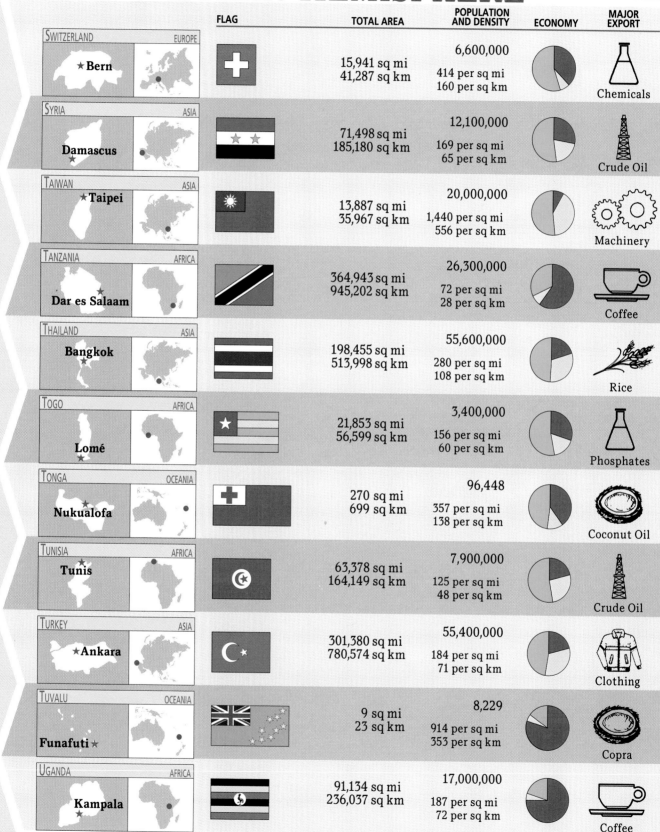

■ Agriculture □ Industry ▪ Services □ Not Available

	FLAG	TOTAL AREA	POPULATION AND DENSITY	ECONOMY	MAJOR EXPORT
UNITED ARAB EMIRATES — ASIA / ★ Abu Dhabi		32,278 sq mi / 83,600 sq km	1,700,000 / 53 per sq mi / 20 per sq km		Crude Oil
UNITED KINGDOM — EUROPE / London ★		94,598 sq mi / 245,009 sq km	57,300,000 / 606 per sq mi / 234 per sq km		Crude Oil
VANUATU — OCEANIA / Port Vila ★		5,700 sq mi / 14,763 sq km	200,000 / 35 per sq mi / 14 per sq km		Copra
VATICAN CITY — EUROPE / Vatican City ★		0.17 sq mi / 0 sq km	1,000 / 5,882 per sq mi / 2,271 per sq km		NA
VIETNAM — ASIA / ★ Hanoi		130,468 sq mi / 337,912 sq km	66,800,000 / 512 per sq mi / 198 per sq km		Clothing
WESTERN SAMOA — OCEANIA / ★ Apia		1,097 sq mi / 2,841 sq km	200,000 / 182 per sq mi / 70 per sq km		Coconut Oil
YEMEN — ASIA / ★ San'a		203,850 sq mi / 527,972 sq km	10,100,000 / 50 per sq mi / 19 per sq km		NA
FORMER YUGOSLAVIA * — EUROPE / Belgrade ★		98,766 sq mi / 255,804 sq km	23,700,000 / 240 per sq mi / 93 per sq km		Chemicals
ZAIRE — AFRICA / ★ Kinshasa		905,063 sq mi / 2,344,113 sq km	34,900,000 / 39 per sq mi / 15 per sq km		Copper
ZAMBIA — AFRICA / Lusaka ★		290,585 sq mi / 752,615 sq km	8,100,000 / 28 per sq mi / 11 per sq km		Copper
ZIMBABWE — AFRICA / ★ Harare		150,820 sq mi / 390,624 sq km	10,100,000 / 67 per sq mi / 26 per sq km		Tobacco

*The dissolution of the former Yugoslavia is discussed on page 341.

■ Agriculture □ Industry ▨ Services □ Not Available

43

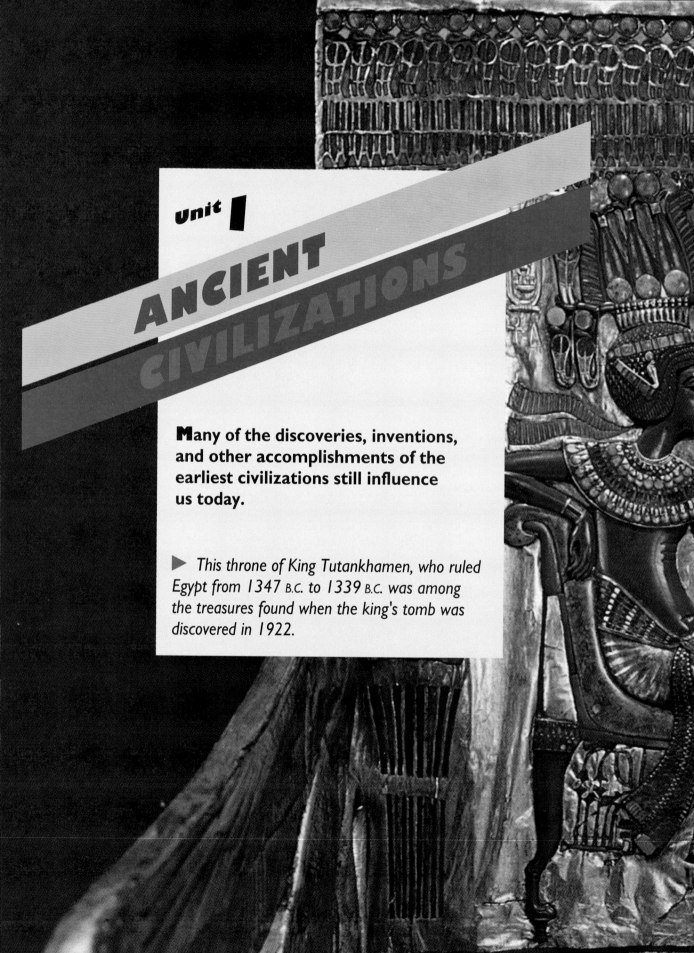

Unit 1

ANCIENT CIVILIZATIONS

Many of the discoveries, inventions, and other accomplishments of the earliest civilizations still influence us today.

▶ *This throne of King Tutankhamen, who ruled Egypt from 1347 B.C. to 1339 B.C. was among the treasures found when the king's tomb was discovered in 1922.*

CHAPTER 1

ANCIENT CIVILIZATIONS IN THE MIDDLE EAST AND EGYPT

History provides a picture of past cultures. The people of early civilizations in the Middle East and Egypt left behind cities, ancient monuments, and rich cultures that still influence our lives.

The Origin of Civilization

Imagine that you have a machine that can bring ancient peoples into modern time. How do you think their lives today would differ from their lives in ancient times?

STUDY THE VOCABULARY

civilization	dike
archaeologist	irrigate
cuneiform	ziggurat
pictograph	

FOCUS YOUR READING

What makes a civilization?

A. Civilizing a Wild Man

Long ago, people in Mesopotamia told a tale about a wild man named Enkidu who lived with the animals. Mesopotamia was the land between the Tigris and Euphrates rivers in the country now called Iraq. According to the story, Enkidu roamed the grasslands with herds of wild cattle and gazelles and came to the rivers only to drink. When a hunter dug pits to trap the animals, Enkidu filled them in. At first the hunter was puzzled, but one day he caught sight of the hairy man at a watering place. The hunter went to see his wise old father and asked for advice. His father told him to go to Uruk (OO ruk), the city ruled by the mighty Gilgamesh (GIHL-guh mesh), and ask for a beautiful woman. Such a woman would know how to deal with the wild man.

The hunter did as his father advised. He went to Gilgamesh's city and found a beautiful woman who went with him to the watering place, where they hid. After two days, Enkidu and the animals came to

drink. As soon as the woman saw Enkidu, she stepped from her hiding place. The animals immediately fled, but Enkidu stood still and gazed at her. He was so struck by the woman's beauty that instead of running away, he walked up to her. She asked him, "Why do you live with the animals? You are a human being. You have a mind. Come with me."

The woman led Enkidu to a camp of shepherds who offered them bread. Enkidu did not know what the bread was, so the woman told him, "Eat the bread, Enkidu. This is food for humans." Enkidu tasted the bread and then continued to eat until he was full.

Enkidu and the woman stayed with the shepherds for a time. He kept watch over the flocks of sheep. Then the wild man who had protected the hunted animals became a hunter. He killed lions, wolves, and other wild animals that preyed on the sheep.

One day the woman said to Enkidu, "Let us both now go to Uruk, the city of King Gilgamesh, whose strength none can match."

Enkidu went with her but boasted, "I will challenge Gilgamesh to a fight, for I, too, am a strong one!" The woman warned, "Gilgamesh has greater strength than you, and he never rests."

When Enkidu met Gilgamesh in Uruk, the two strong men grappled in combat, smashing doors and shaking walls. Gilgamesh finally overcame Enkidu, but he then took Enkidu's hand and offered to be a friend. Never had the mighty Gilgamesh met another whose strength was nearly as great as his own. Gilgamesh and Enkidu became friends and shared many adventures. The story of those adventures is one of the oldest stories in the world.

B. Characteristics of Civilization

The story of Enkidu is, of course, only a story. It is not history. It is an imaginary tale about how a human being made a friend and became civilized, that is, how he learned to live in a **civilization**. A civilization is a way of living. The word *civilization* comes from the Latin word for *city*. But the development of cities was only one of the characteristics of a civilization. Another characteristic of a civilization is the development of specialized skills and different occupations. For example, as people became better farmers, it was not necessary for everyone in a community to cultivate the soil. Some people could work by making pots, jewelry, weapons, or tools. Other characteristics of a civilization include organized governments, religions, the development of trade, and the keeping of written records.

It is the exchange of ideas that makes writing so important for civilization. Writing makes it much easier for the ideas of one person to be passed on to another. Writing makes it possible to learn from people who are dead. Can you think of something you have read that was written by someone no longer living? The Constitution of the United States was written by persons who are no longer living.

C. A Book Buried Beneath Ruins

People in Mesopotamia told the story of Gilgamesh and Enkidu long before anyone wrote it down. We do not know exactly when it was first written, but we do know that there was a copy in a library

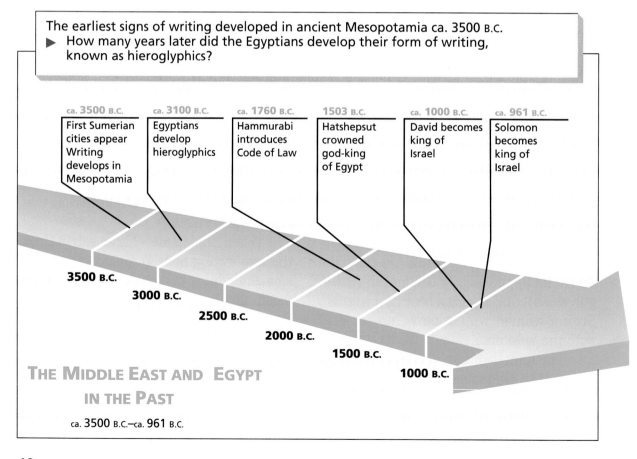

The earliest signs of writing developed in ancient Mesopotamia ca. 3500 B.C.
► How many years later did the Egyptians develop their form of writing, known as hieroglyphics?

ca. 3500 B.C.	ca. 3100 B.C.	ca. 1760 B.C.	1503 B.C.	ca. 1000 B.C.	ca. 961 B.C.
First Sumerian cities appear Writing develops in Mesopotamia	Egyptians develop hieroglyphics	Hammurabi introduces Code of Law	Hatshepsut crowned god-king of Egypt	David becomes king of Israel	Solomon becomes king of Israel

3500 B.C.
3000 B.C.
2500 B.C.
2000 B.C.
1500 B.C.
1000 B.C.

THE MIDDLE EAST AND EGYPT
IN THE PAST
ca. 3500 B.C.–ca. 961 B.C.

Archaeologists unearthed the ancient city of Nineveh in the 1850s. The ruins of this capital city are located in the present-day country of Iraq.
▶ How did the archaeologists move the stone statues?

destroyed in 612 B.C., more than 2,600 years ago.

The story of Gilgamesh was one of thousands of writings in a library at Nineveh (NIHN uh vuh) in northern Mesopotamia. In 612 B.C. an enemy army captured Nineveh and destroyed many buildings, including the library. Along with other writings, the story of Gilgamesh lay buried beneath the ruins until **archaeologists** dug them up in 1850. Archaeologists study ancient times and peoples by finding the remains of cities, tombs, buildings, and the like. How could a book lie buried so long and not have rotted away? It was not a book printed on paper. The story was written on 12 clay tablets. The words had been formed by marks on each clay tablet before it hardened. The marks, made by the tip

of a wedge-shaped stick, are known as **cuneiform** (kyoo NEE uh form) characters. *Cuneiform* means "wedge-form."

D. The Development of Writing

Keeping Records The development of writing was important to the beginning of civilization in Mesopotamia. People needed to keep records. When one person borrowed barley from another, the lender wanted a record of how much he had lent. Barley is a grain used in making some cereals. Before a shepherd took sheep to graze on the grasslands, the owner wanted to have a record of how many sheep were in the flock.

The first records were very simple. A drawing of an ox head scratched on a bit of

49

flattened clay with six marks meant "six oxen." A drawing of a barley stalk stood for the word *barley*. A picture sign that stands for a word is called a **pictograph**.

The first pictographs looked somewhat like the things they represented. But as time went on, people did not bother to draw line pictures of oxen or barley. Instead they made marks simply by pressing the end of their wedge-shaped writing stick into the clay. This was the way that cuneiform writing began. As you can see by looking at the chart below, the cuneiform characters came to look less and less like pictures.

Cuneiform Writing Pictographs were useful for making records, but they were not a true system of writing. To write a story, you need words that express action, such as *walk*, *talk*, *fight*, *hunt*. People began to make marks for actions rather than things. They made the cuneiform character for a thing connected with the action. For example, the character for foot meant "walk"; the character for mouth stood for "talk."

Writing was developed still more when characters came to be used for sounds. In time, the character for barley came to stand for the syllable *she* rather than for the grain. By using characters for syllables, people could write any word they could say. This type of cuneiform writing made it possible for the story of Gilgamesh to be written.

E. The Beginning of Cities

City Life Writing also made it possible for us to know many things about ancient civilizations. Mesopotamia did not have an ideal climate. Summers were very hot. Temperatures often climbed above 100°F (38°C) during the long summer, which lasted from early May through September. Almost no rain fell during the hot months. Some rains fell during the cooler winter and spring months, but the average yearly rainfall was less than 6 inches (15 cm).

Although summer was a time of drought in Mesopotamia, the Tigris and Euphrates rivers often flooded the land during the spring. Melting snow in the northern mountains sent waters rushing downstream, spreading over the lowland between the rivers.

Here is where city life began. A people we call the Sumerians built their cities in

DEVELOPMENT OF EARLY WRITING			
Meaning	Pictograph	Cuneiform Early	Later
Barley			
Fish			
Ox			
Bird			
Eat			
Walk/Stand			

Early writing began with the drawing of pictures that stood for objects.
▶ Why weren't pictographs a true system of writing?

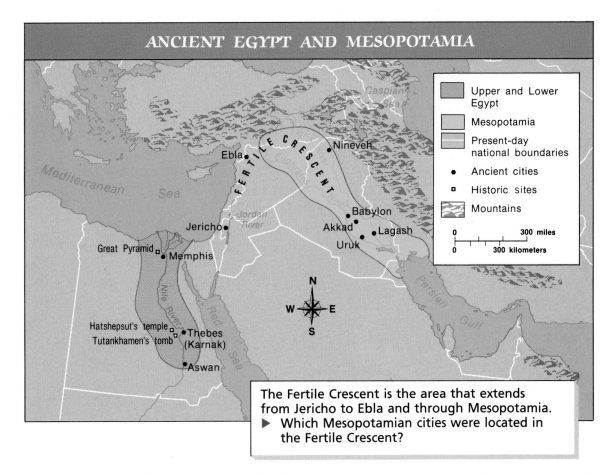

ANCIENT EGYPT AND MESOPOTAMIA

Legend:
- Upper and Lower Egypt
- Mesopotamia
- Present-day national boundaries
- ● Ancient cities
- □ Historic sites
- Mountains

0 ——— 300 miles
0 ——— 300 kilometers

The Fertile Crescent is the area that extends from Jericho to Ebla and through Mesopotamia.
▶ Which Mesopotamian cities were located in the Fertile Crescent?

Mesopotamia ca. 3500 B.C. Uruk, the city in the story of Gilgamesh, was a Sumerian city. It is certain that Gilgamesh was an early ruler, but it is doubtful that he had all the adventures described in the story.

Farming The Sumerians learned to make use of the spring floods. They built **dikes**, walls to hold back floodwater from their homes and fields. They dug canals and ditches to drain water into reservoirs, which were storage ponds. When the floodwater went down, the Sumerians used water from the reservoirs to **irrigate**, or bring water to, their fields during the summer months.

It took a lot of work to build dikes, ditches, and reservoirs, but the result was more food. By using the water during the dry summer, the Sumerians were able to grow two crops a year. Farmers not only had enough food for themselves and their families, but they produced a surplus, more than they needed.

Trading Since everyone did not have to work to raise food, some people could work at other jobs. These people erected buildings, made pottery, wove fine cloth, and worked at other crafts. A small number were overseers who directed the work of other workers.

People who spent their time doing one kind of work traded their products for other goods that they needed or wanted. The potter traded pots for the weaver's cloth, and both exchanged their products for food. In ancient times, as now, civilization depended on the exchange of goods as well as ideas.

F. Walls for Protection

The Sumerians surrounded their cities with thick walls to protect themselves from enemies. Warfare is as old as civilization, and fighting was very common in ancient times. In fact, for many centuries, cities in many parts of the world had walls for protection.

Houses and shops were closely packed together within the walls of a Sumerian city. In times of danger a city became very crowded. Farmers from villages flocked in for protection.

The largest structure in a city was a solid brick platform called a **ziggurat**. A temple for the god of the city stood on the ziggurat. Priests had charge of the temple and conducted services thought to please the god. The Sumerians believed that the safety of a city depended on its god. Wars between cities were considered to be like wars between the gods.

G. The Need for Laws

Settling Disputes The Sumerians built the first cities in Mesopotamia. Other peoples followed their example. Cities increased in number and grew in size. As a result of wars, the rulers of some cities extended their power over others. Sargon the great of Akkad brought all of Sumer and the northern half of Mesopotamia under his rule ca. 2300 B.C. Later the rulers of Babylon conquered and ruled all of Mesopotamia. Babylon was famous for its wealth and entertainments. People still sometimes refer to a rich and pleasure-loving city as "a Babylon."

People living and working together closely needed ways of settling disputes. King Hammurabi, who ruled Babylon from ca. 1792 B.C. to 1750 B.C., ordered that laws be carved on a stone pillar. He had the

Stone statues of Sumerian worshipers (inset) were found in temples at the top of ziggurats.
▶ What did the Sumerians use to build their ziggurats?

The Oriental Institute Museum, University of Chicago

pillar placed in a public place so that all might know the laws of the city.

Hammurabi's Laws The laws of Hammurabi required that people be responsible for their actions. A person had to pay for any damages done to the property of others. If one man's boat ran into another's boat and sank it, he had to pay for both the boat and the goods it carried. If a man's ox killed another, he had to pay for the dead ox.

Some of Hammurabi's laws were based on the rule "An eye for an eye, a tooth for a tooth." According to this rule,

> *If a man puts out the eye of a noble, his eye shall be put out; if a man breaks the bone of a noble, his bone shall be broken; if he knocks out the tooth of a noble, his tooth shall be knocked out.*

"An eye for an eye" is an old and harsh rule. It applied only if the injured person was of the highest, or noble, class. If the injured person belonged to a lower class, the penalty was the payment of silver. This practice is much more like the present-day practice of paying damages to the person who has been injured.

The stone carving of Hammurabi's code contains a picture of the sun god demanding new laws (inset).
▶ Where did Hammurabi rule?

Musee du Louvre, France

LESSON **1** *REVIEW*

THINK AND WRITE

A. How did the life of Enkidu change after he met the woman?

B. Why was writing so important for the development of civilization?

C. Why was the book with the story of Gilgamesh not destroyed in 612 B.C.?

D. What kinds of characters were used in the development of writing?

E. How were the Tigris and Euphrates rivers important to the building of cities?

F. What was the purpose of building walls around a city?

G. How were the laws of Hammurabi like or unlike those of today?

SKILLS CHECK

MAP SKILL

Look at the map of ancient Egypt and Mesopotamia on page 51. What two rivers were important bodies of water for the ancient cities of Mesopotamia?

Egypt—The Land of the Nile

THINK ABOUT WHAT YOU KNOW

What do you think of when someone mentions ancient Egypt?

STUDY THE VOCABULARY

mummy	delta
oasis	pharaoh
silt	pyramid

FOCUS YOUR READING

Why is Egypt called the land of the Nile?

A. Belzoni the Giant

A New Job About 180 years ago, Belzoni the Giant was amazing crowds at English fairs and circuses with feats of strength. Posters showed a tall, bearded man carrying 11 people perched on an iron harness. Belzoni also played Sampson in a famous story taken from the Bible. He pulled down scenery pillars on stage to show how Sampson destroyed his enemies in their temple. It must have been quite a show.

Giovanni Belzoni was an inventor as well as a strongman. He designed a machine for raising water from irrigation ditches. In 1815 he went to Egypt, hoping to interest the Egyptian ruler in his invention. Belzoni failed to do so, but he found a new job. People in Europe at that time had become interested in collecting ancient objects from such lands as Egypt. The British representative in Egypt hired Belzoni to collect things for the British Museum.

The representative knew that the head of a giant statue had fallen off and lay in the sand up the Nile River at Thebes. The statue was of Ramses II, an ancient ruler, but it was then mistakenly called "young Memnon." The representative sent Belzoni to get the statue's head and ship it to England.

The head was large; it weighed over 7 tons (6,350 kg). Even a strongman could not lift such a weight. But Belzoni got it moved to a barge on the Nile River.

Discovering Treasures Securing the stone head aroused Belzoni's interest in ancient Egypt. He was probably more of a treasure hunter than an archaeologist. A true science of archaeology had not yet been developed, but Belzoni did make some important discoveries. He found the buried entrance to the tomb of Seti I, a ruler who died over 3,000 years ago. The tomb had been cut nearly 1,000 feet (305 m) through rock at the base of a mountain. Seti's body had long ago been removed, but much remained that told about life in ancient Egypt at the time Seti had lived. There were wooden statues, furniture, and marvelous wall paintings that showed people in ancient times.

detail, © 1991 The Metropolitan Museum of Art, Rogers Fund, (12.182.132c)

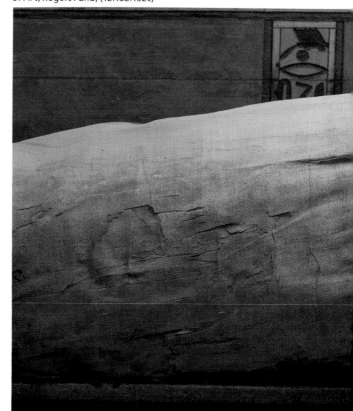

When Belzoni returned to England, he opened an Egyptian exhibit. Crowds paid to see two rooms built to resemble Seti's tomb. They viewed statues, coins, ancient writings that no one could yet read, and a **mummy**. A mummy was a body treated for burial with preservatives and wrapped in airtight cloth bandages to keep it from decaying. The mummy probably attracted the most attention. Here were the remains of an Egyptian who had lived centuries ago.

B. Fertile Land Along the Nile

The Nile Egypt is a desert land crossed by the Nile River, the world's longest river. The narrow valley watered by the Nile has been called "one long, drawn-out **oasis**." An oasis is fertile land in a desert.

The Nile rises in the mountains and highlands of East Africa and flows north to

Egyptian mummies were carefully wrapped in linen and placed in painted coffins.
▶ What kept them from decaying?

the Mediterranean Sea. Melting snows and spring rains cause the river to rise in Egypt during the summer and spread over land along the river. Belzoni made use of the summer flood to float the barge on which he loaded the statue's head.

The flood brought tons of **silt** downstream, giving the water a muddy look. Silt is fine particles of soil carried in water. As the floodwater went down, it left a layer of fertile silt along the Nile Valley. The river also deposited silt where it emptied into the sea. Over the years the deposits built up the land at the river's mouth. The built-up land is called a **delta**, because it looks somewhat like the three-cornered Greek letter delta (Δ) turned upside down.

Farming The Egyptians took advantage of the yearly flood to grow crops in the desert. When the floodwater went down in late summer, farmers scattered grain on the damp land and drove herds of goats across the fields to push the seeds into the soil. By the time the fields dried, the grain was ready to harvest.

The Egyptians irrigated land that was not reached by the flood. They built dams to hold back the water and later let it out to irrigate fields of melons, cucumbers, onions, and other vegetables. Irrigating fields took much hard work, but the Egyptian farmers were able to grow two or even three crops a year. Like the farmers of Mesopotamia, Egyptian farmers produced a surplus of food.

C. Ruling the Land of the Nile

Many people had to work together to make the kind of life the ancient Egyptians had. It was the **pharaohs** (FAR ohz), or kings, and their many officials who ruled the land.

Howard Carter found the tomb of the pharaoh Tutankhamen. Hidden deep within the tomb were rooms filled with magnificent treasures (inset).
▶ What objects were found there?

The Egyptians served the pharaohs because they regarded them as gods. They believed that the rise and fall of the Nile depended on serving the god-kings. The pharaohs provided a government, which is necessary in any land where numbers of people live and work together. The pharaohs' officials settled disputes and enforced laws. They told farmers when to expect the summer flood. They saw to it that surplus grain was stored for later use.

Menes (MEE neez) was the first pharaoh whose name we know, although we do not know much more about him. The Egyptians said that he united the Nile Valley and the Nile Delta into one kingdom ca. 3100 B.C. The pharaohs ruled Egypt for 2,000 years after Menes. No other form of government has ever lasted so long.

D. The Tomb of King Tut Is Found

Nervously Carter lit a match, touched it to the candle, and held it toward the hole. As his head neared the opening—he was literally trembling with expectation and curiosity—the warm air escaping from the chamber beyond the door made the candle flare up. For a moment Carter, his eyes fixed to the hole and the candle burning within, could make out nothing. Then, as his eyes became gradually accustomed to the flickering light, he distinguished shapes, then their shadows, then the first colors. Not a sound escaped his lips; he had been stricken dumb. . . . Finally [he was asked] "Can you see anything?" Carter, slowly turning his head, said shakily: "Yes, wonderful things."

Carter found three layers of coffins in King Tut's tomb. The photographs above show Carter cleaning the coffins and separating them from one another.
▶ Of what material was Tut's coffin made?

The passage you just read on the previous page is from a book titled *Gods, Graves, and Scholars*. This book is about famous archaeological finds, such as the one made in 1922 by the British archaeologist Howard Carter. Carter had been searching for years to find the tombs of ancient Egyptian pharaohs.

What made Howard Carter's find so important is not the pharaoh who was buried in it but the contents of the tomb. Carter had discovered the tomb of a boy-king named Tutankhamen (too tahng-KAH mun), who ruled Egypt in the middle of the fourteenth century B.C. Today we commonly call this pharaoh King Tut. His rule was very short, only nine years, and he died before he was 20 years old. But he is best known of all the Egyptian pharaohs because of Howard Carter's discovery.

What were the "wonderful things" that Carter found in the tomb of King Tut? There was Tut's coffin made of solid gold. This coffin was neatly fitted into a second coffin, and the second coffin was carefully fitted into a third. There were also all sorts of things that the boy-king could use in his next life. For example, there was the king's throne, statues of servants to wait on him, and furniture for him to use. There was also a statue of King Tut that stands over 5 feet (1.5 m) tall. Even a toy box and painting set from his childhood had been placed in the tomb.

The ruins of many pyramids stand near the Nile River. Each pyramid was constructed to protect the body of an Egyptian king. Thousands of workers built the pyramids without any machinery or iron tools.
▶ On what kind of land are these pyramids built?

The most famous of the pharaohs' tombs are the **pyramids** (PIHR uh mihdz). They are stone structures enclosing a small burial room, which once contained a pharaoh's mummy.

The Egyptians built a number of pyramids, but the three largest and most famous stand on the desert at Giza, near present-day Cairo. The largest is the Great Pyramid, built ca. 2500 B.C. Today it would cover nearly ten football fields. It is about 450 feet (137 m) high, but before some of the topmost stones were torn away, it rose to 482 feet (147 m).

LESSON 2 *REVIEW*

THINK AND WRITE

A. What kinds of things did Belzoni bring back to England from Egypt?
B. How did the Nile River help the farmers grow a surplus of crops?
C. What services did the government of the pharaohs provide to the Egyptians?
D. Why was the discovery of King Tut's tomb so important?

SKILLS CHECK

WRITING SKILL

Pretend you are an archaeologist who discovered the tomb of an Egyptian pharaoh. Write a paragraph in which you describe what you saw inside the tomb, and how you felt as you made your discovery.

The Civilization of the Egyptians

THINK ABOUT WHAT YOU KNOW

Imagine you discovered an ancient civilization. Explain how you would attempt to learn about the people.

STUDY THE VOCABULARY

Coptic   **papyrus**
hieroglyphics   **scribe**

FOCUS YOUR READING

What do we learn from writings about life in ancient Egypt?

A. Learning an Ancient Language

A few years before Belzoni was entertaining at fairs and circuses, a scientist, Jean Fourier (foor YAY), visited a school in Grenoble, France. Fourier had been in Egypt with the French army, and he told the students about the marvels he had seen in that land. One student, 11-year-old Jean-François Champollion (shahn paw-LYOHN), was fascinated by Fourier's remarks. Jean showed such interest that Fourier invited the boy to his home to see the collection of things he had brought back from Egypt.

Jean went to Fourier's house, where he carefully examined the various ancient objects. Some scraps of Egyptian writing especially interested him, and he asked, "Can anyone read them?" When Fourier answered that no one could, Jean announced, "I am going to do it. In a few years I will be able to, when I am grown."

Jean's boast was a bold one. Many great scholars had puzzled over the ancient Egyptian language without success. True, Jean was good at languages. He had

taught himself to read before he was 5, and a few years later he began to learn Latin and Greek. At the age of 13, Jean began to study **Coptic**, an Egyptian language no longer used except in the services of the Egyptian Christian Church. Some scholars thought that Coptic had come from the ancient language of the Egyptians. Jean thought that learning the Coptic language might provide a key to understanding this ancient language.

B. The Rosetta Stone

A piece of black stone about the size of a small coffee table provided the key to the language puzzle. Some French soldiers had found the stone, in 1799, buried near the city of Rosetta on the Nile Delta.

Three types of writing had been carved on the Rosetta Stone. One was

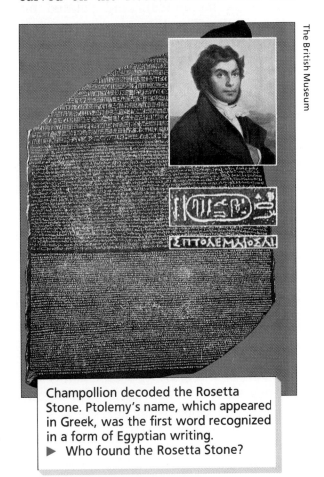

The British Museum

Champollion decoded the Rosetta Stone. Ptolemy's name, which appeared in Greek, was the first word recognized in a form of Egyptian writing.
▶ Who found the Rosetta Stone?

Greek, the other two were different types of Egyptian.

Scholars could read the Greek, but for more than 20 years, they had puzzled in vain over the Egyptian characters. They knew that one form of Egyptian writing, known as **hieroglyphics** (hye ur oh GLIHF-ihks), was that carved on many ancient buildings. They guessed that the hieroglyphic characters were pictographs, but they did not know the meaning of the marks, which looked like birds, snakes, feathers, and other objects.

Jean Champollion finally solved the puzzle. He discovered that although hieroglyphic characters had once been pictographs, they also stood for sounds in later times. This discovery provided the key to reading the ancient language. Scholars then worked out the meaning of the words carved on monuments and painted on tomb walls. The key to the language opened the way to learning much more about Egyptian civilization.

C. A Woman God-King

Being able to read the language made it possible for archaeologists to learn much more from the ruins they dug up. When they uncovered the tomb temple of Hatshepsut (hat SHEP soot), they learned about a remarkable woman who had ruled as a god-king.

Hatshepsut had been married to King Thutmose II (thoot MOH suh) who died young, leaving a small stepson Thutmose III. For a short time Hatshepsut ruled for the young boy, but she soon set him aside and ruled in her own name. Hatshepsut was crowned king, not queen. Some of her statues show her wearing a false beard. Like the god-kings before her, she was declared to be the child of a god.

Hatshepsut ruled the land from 1503 B.C. to 1482 B.C. She built temples and raised monuments that bore her name. Like earlier rulers, she began building her tomb temple while she was still alive. From the temple walls, scholars learned that Hatshepsut's ships brought back gold, ivory, perfumes, sweet-smelling trees, and live animals.

When Thutmose III grew up, he became ruler. We do not know how this came about, but we do know that he wanted to remove Hatshepsut's name from history. He had her name chiseled from temple

Hatshepsut ruled ancient Egypt as a king, not as a queen.
▶ Why, do you think, did Hatshepsut take the title of king?

walls, and he had walls built to cover carvings on her monuments. The walls later fell down, so that we are able to know at least part of this remarkable woman's story.

D. Paper from the Nile

Making Paper The Egyptians fortunately did not have to do all their writing on stone. They also wrote on sheets of a paperlike material called **papyrus** (puh-PYE rus). Papyrus is a tall reed that grows in the Nile Valley. Egyptians dried stalks of papyrus and cut them into thin strips. They hammered the strips together to form a single sheet on which they wrote with brush and ink. They used a cursive form of writing, which was simpler than the hieroglyphic characters.

Ancient Writings Sheets of papyrus are not as durable as the clay tablets of the Mesopotamians, but a surprisingly large number have survived. Among those writings that have survived is a schoolbook for young people learning to be **scribes**. Most people did not know how to write in ancient times. Scribes had the job of writing letters and copying records.

The schoolbook for scribes was in the form of letters. These letters contained advice for both students and their teachers. Students should "turn their hearts to books during the day and read during the night." Students who failed to do so might end up working on an irrigation ditch rather than at a scribe's desk. One letter stated that a student who refused to study was like a lazy donkey and should be treated like one. The teacher should beat such a student.

Some surviving writings are more entertaining than the schoolbook. The

FROM PAPYRUS TO PAPER

1. Gather reeds.
2. Cut off outside bark.
3. Cut reed into strips.
4. Soak strips in water.
5. Crisscross two layers of strips.
6. Pound wet strips into paper.

Ancient Egyptians made an early form of paper, called papyrus, from a reed that grew along the Nile River.
▶ What was used to make papyrus?

Egyptians, no doubt, told many stories that we can never know. But some of the stories written on papyrus have been found, and scholars can read them. For example, one story tells of a sailor who was shipwrecked and cast upon a desert island. Luckily he found fig trees on the island and was able to catch fish and fowls. He knew how to make fire by friction. He whirled a stick in a piece of dry wood until it smoldered. Have you ever read or heard of a story something like this?

E. "The Book of the Dead"

When the pyramids were built, the Egyptians believed that only the god-kings and those who served them lived after death. In later times they came to believe that life after death was for all people. They thought that the gods judged each person and decided whether he or she should be rewarded or punished.

To guide a person after death, scribes copied scrolls, which were placed in tombs. These scrolls are called The Book of the Dead, and a number of them have been found. The scrolls contain magic spells, advice on how to address the gods, and hymns, or songs, to the gods. Perhaps the most interesting part of The Book of the Dead reveals Egyptian ideas about the wrongs that a good person avoided. The Book of the Dead states that when a person faces the gods, he or she should be able to say truthfully,

I have not committed evil.
I have not stolen.
I have not robbed.
I have not been covetous [greedy].
I have not told lies.

These ideas might seem familiar. Today we teach that stealing, lying, and greediness are wrong.

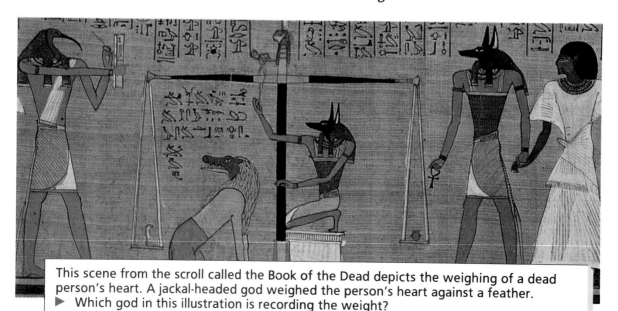

This scene from the scroll called the Book of the Dead depicts the weighing of a dead person's heart. A jackal-headed god weighed the person's heart against a feather.
► Which god in this illustration is recording the weight?

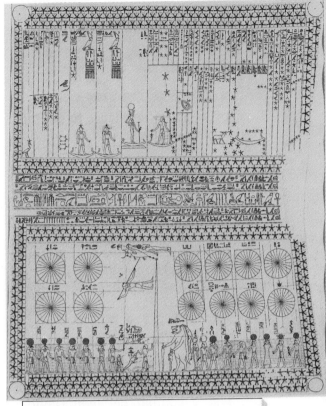

Ancient peoples measured years by watching the moon. They based their calendar year on moon months. A moon month is the time from one new moon to another, a period of 29 1/2 days. Twelve moon months make a lunar year of 354 days. To keep the seasons and this short year together, the Mesopotamians added an extra month every two or three years.

The ancient Egyptians based their calendar year on the sun year, known as a solar year. As we now know, a solar year is the time it takes the earth to orbit, or move around, the sun. The Egyptians did not realize that the earth moved, but they were able to measure the solar year accurately by careful observation of the stars.

A solar year has 365 1/4 days. The Egyptian calendar year had 12 months of 30 days each and 5 extra holidays following the last month. This makes a year of 365 days, still 1/4 of a day less than the solar year. Today we base our calendar on the solar year, and we add an extra day every fourth year, which we call leap year. The Egyptians did not have a leap year, but they knew that their calendar year differed

This Egyptian calendar, based on the sun, dates from about 1500 B.C.
► How many months did the Egyptian calendar year have?

from the solar year. Because of their careful observation of the stars, they knew what the difference was each year.

LESSON **3** *REVIEW*

THINK AND WRITE

A. What did Champollion decide to do when he was a schoolboy?
B. Why was the Rosetta Stone a key to learning about ancient Egypt?
C. What was unusual about the god-king Hatshepsut?
D. What sort of writings have been found on papyrus?
E. What does The Book of the Dead reveal about Egyptian ideas concerning wrongdoing?

F. How did the Egyptian way of measuring a year differ from that of the Mesopotamians?

SKILLS CHECK

THINKING SKILL

In the schoolbook for scribes it said, "A youth has a back and pays attention only when beaten, for the ears of the young are on their backs." What do you think this advice means?

Ancient Israel

A. A Battle with a Giant

Ancient histories tell about many wars and battles. One of the most famous battles was a combat between David, a shepherd boy, and Goliath, a man so big that he was called a giant. David was an Israelite; Goliath was a Philistine. About 3,000 years ago the Israelites and the Philistines were at war. David's older brothers had joined the Israelite army led by King Saul, but David was too young. David had remained at home, where he served as keeper of his father's sheep.

One day David's father told him to take some supplies to his brothers who were with King Saul. When David reached the Israelite camp, he found the two armies facing each other, ready for battle. The huge Goliath stood in front of the Philistines and dared the Israelites to send one man to fight him in single combat. "If he be able to fight with me, and to kill me, then we will be your servants: but if I prevail against him, then shall you be our servants."

When none of Saul's army stepped forward to meet Goliath, David said that he would battle the huge Philistine. King Saul warned David that he was too young to fight such a large and experienced warrior. But David insisted that he was not afraid. Seeing that he was determined, Saul offered David his own sword and armor. David refused to take them, saying that the heavy armor would only hinder him. Instead David armed himself with only a sling and five small stones.

When Goliath saw David, he sneered that he would soon feed the boy to the birds. David said nothing. He stepped forward, whirled his sling, and let a stone fly. It hit Goliath right on the forehead and stunned him. He stumbled and fell to the ground. Then David rushed up and killed him with Goliath's own sword.

The story of David and Goliath is a famous biblical story.
▶ What scene from the story does this picture illustrate?

B. David, King of Israel

David became a hero to the Israelites. He became so popular that King Saul grew jealous and quarreled with him. At one time he had to flee to the hill country in order to escape. But after Saul's death, David became king. Saul was the first of Israel's kings, David the second, and his son Solomon was the third.

But King David is probably the best-known ruler of the ancient Middle East, yet his kingdom was not large. Israel was only about the size of Vermont. Much of the land is hilly, and summers are very dry.

David captured the city of Jerusalem and made it his capital, but it was not yet a great city. He built no great temples or tombs like those of the Egyptian pharaohs. Yet David's name is better known than those who built the Great Pyramids. David's fame has lasted because his story is told in a book — the Jewish Bible, which the Christians call the Old Testament.

C. Ancient Writings Tell of Israel's History

The Bible The Bible is a collection of writings that cover subjects, including law, history, and poetry. All these writings, or books, were written in ancient times. For Jews and Christians the books of the Bible are religious writings. But writers of other religious views also study them, just as they study other ancient writings.

Some books of the Bible give a history of Israel both before and after the time of David. They tell that Abraham, **ancestor** of the Israelites, had once lived in Mesopotamia. An ancestor is a person from whom a family or group is descended. According to the Bible, Abraham and his household moved west to the land that later would become Israel.

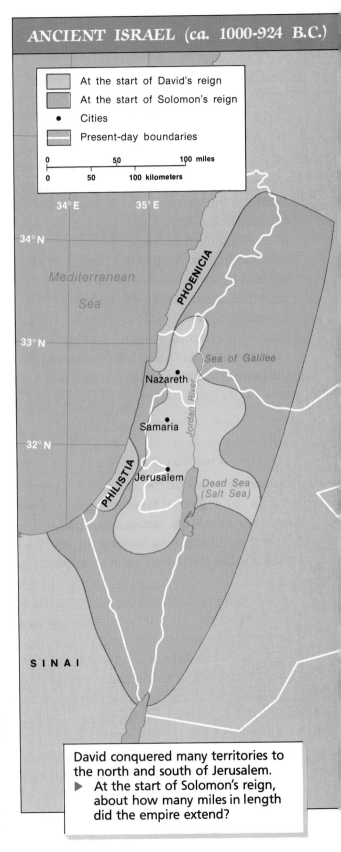

ANCIENT ISRAEL (ca. 1000-924 B.C.)

At the start of David's reign
At the start of Solomon's reign
• Cities
Present-day boundaries

0   50   100 miles
0   50   100 kilometers

34°E   35°E
34°N
Mediterranean Sea
PHOENICIA
33°N
Sea of Galilee
Nazareth
Jordan River
Samaria
32°N
PHILISTIA
Jerusalem
Dead Sea (Salt Sea)
SINAI

David conquered many territories to the north and south of Jerusalem.
▶ At the start of Solomon's reign, about how many miles in length did the empire extend?

The Bible also relates that in a time of famine, some of Abraham's descendants went to Egypt, where one of them, Joseph, had become a high official of the pharaoh. For a time the Israelites lived freely in Egypt, until an unfriendly pharaoh enslaved them.

Moses After hundreds of years, a man named Moses emerged as a great leader among the Israelites. The Israelites escaped from Egypt under the leadership of Moses. For a number of years, they lived as wanderers in the desert. Those were important years in their history. During that time the great leader Moses taught the Israelites that their God had given them their laws. Among the laws were the Ten Commandments. After the time of Moses, the people of Israel settled in the land that was to bear their name.

D. The Wise King Solomon

Solomon's Wisdom Solomon, David's son, became king of Israel ca. 961 B.C. His name is nearly as famous as that of his father. Solomon was known for his wisdom. It was said that "he was wiser than all men."

A famous story was told to show Solomon's wisdom. The story relates that two women came before the king, each claiming to be the mother of the same baby. The two women lived in the same house, and both had given birth to babies on the same day. One baby had died during the night, and its mother arose and silently exchanged the dead baby for the living one. When the other mother awoke, she realized what had happened, but the mother of the dead baby claimed the living child as her own and refused to give it up.

According to the Jewish Bible, God gave Moses and the Israelites a set of laws to live by.
▶ What are the laws called that were given to Moses?

When the two women and the baby came before King Solomon, he called for a sword. He said that since the women could not agree, he would have the baby cut in two so that each could have half. When the true mother heard the king's decision, she cried out, "Give her the living child, only do not kill him!" But the false mother said, "Let it be neither hers nor mine, so cut it in

I am the Lord your God,....You shall have no other gods before me.

You shall not make for yourself an idol in the form of anything....

You shall not misuse the name of the Lord your God....

Remember the Sabbath day by keeping it holy....

Honor your father and your mother....

You shall not murder.

You shall not commit adultery.

You shall not steal.

You shall not give false testimony against your neighbor.

You shall not covet your neighbor's house...., or anything that belongs to your neighbor.

two." The wise king now knew which was the real mother, and he returned the child to her arms.

Solomon's Temple Solomon the Wise was also known as Solomon the Builder. He wished to make Jerusalem a truly splendid city. He erected great public buildings and a grand palace with fine royal apartments. These magnificent structures served to establish the authority of the laws and government of Israel. But the most important structure of all was the temple. Built of large stones and costly woods brought from other lands, the temple was a holy place for the people of Israel.

In later times, Israel's enemies captured Jerusalem and destroyed Solomon's temple. Not even the ruins of Solomon's temple remain. Yet we know quite a lot about the building, because the Bible contains a detailed description of it. In this case, ancient writings have proved more durable than stone.

LESSON **4** REVIEW

THINK AND WRITE

A. How was David able to overcome Goliath?

B. Why is David probably the best-known king of the ancient Middle East?

C. What does the Bible tell about Abraham, Joseph, and Moses?

D. How do you know that Solomon was wise?

SKILLS CHECK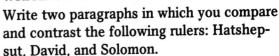

WRITING SKILL

Write two paragraphs in which you compare and contrast the following rulers: Hatshepsut, David, and Solomon.

USING THE VOCABULARY

civilization	delta
archaeologist	pharaoh
pictograph	hieroglyphics
ziggurat	papyrus
mummy	ancestor

On a separate sheet of paper, write the word from the list above that best completes each sentence.

1. A Sumerian temple stood on a solid brick platform called a _____.
2. Built-up land at the mouth of a river is a _____.
3. Egyptians made paper from reeds called _____.
4. A body treated for burial and wrapped in airtight cloth bandages is a _____.
5. An _____ is a person from whom a family or group is descended.
6. A picture sign that stands for a word is called a _____.
7. The word _____ comes from the Latin word for city.
8. An _____ studies ancient times and peoples by finding the remains of cities, tombs, and buildings.
9. A king of ancient Egypt was called a _____.
10. Egyptian pictographs carved on buildings are called _____.

REMEMBERING WHAT YOU READ

On a separate sheet of paper, answer the following questions in complete sentences.

1. What are five characteristics of a civilization?
2. What kinds of characters were used to write the story of Gilgamesh?
3. How did the Sumerians get water for the crops they planted?
4. What did King Hammurabi establish in Babylon?
5. How did the yearly floods help people who lived along the Nile River?
6. Why was archaeologist Howard Carter's discovery important?
7. What archaeological discovery provided the key to reading ancient Egyptian writing?
8. What is The Book of the Dead?
9. Whom did David fight against to become a hero?
10. What collection of writings tells about ancient Israel?

TYING LANGUAGE ARTS TO SOCIAL STUDIES

Imagine that you are a news reporter in the United States in the year 4300. Your task is to write about an archaeological discovery just made near where you live. Archaeologists have uncovered a city that they believe was an active city in the twentieth century. In your newspaper article, describe five items that have been dug up. Try to explain what the purpose of each item may have been way back in the twentieth century.

THINKING CRITICALLY

On a separate sheet of paper, answer the following in complete sentences.

1. Why, do you think, is it important to learn about ancient civilizations?
2. What reasons are there for having laws besides as ways of settling disputes?
3. Why would you have wanted or not wanted to help discover King Tut's tomb?
4. What kinds of symbols would you use to make up your own written language? Explain.
5. Why might people other than Christians and Jews study the Bible?

SUMMARIZING THE CHAPTER

Copy this graphic organizer on a separate sheet of paper. Under the main heading for each lesson, write three key words or phrases that support the main idea.

CHAPTER THEME

Many characteristics of modern civilization have their roots in ancient Middle Eastern and Egyptian civilizations.

LESSON 1

A civilization has specific characteristics.

1. Cities
2. _____
3. _____

LESSON 2

Egypt is called the land of the Nile.

1. Has fertile land
2. _____
3. _____

LESSON 3

We have learned from writings about ancient Egypt.

1. Rosetta Stone
2. _____
3. _____

LESSON 4

Some famous leaders came from ancient Israel.

1. David
2. _____
3. _____

CHAPTER 2

ANCIENT GREECE

The Greek civilization developed along the eastern Mediterranean Sea. Greek achievements in architecture, such as the Parthenon on the Acropolis, drama, and government enrich our lives today.

Myths and History

Tell why studying history is important.

epic   **myth**

What is the difference between myth and history?

A. Greece and Troy at War

The story of the Trojan War was told by a blind poet named Homer. Homer was the greatest of the Greek poets. He described the Trojan War and the years that followed in two **epics**, the *Iliad* (IHL ee ud) and the *Odyssey* (AHD ih see). An epic is a long narrative poem about great heroes and their deeds. His epics tell of the role of the gods and goddesses during the war and in the years that followed.

Troy was a rich city on the Asian coast of the Aegean (ee JEE un) Sea, in the country now known as Turkey. At the time of the war, Greece was divided into a number of separate groups, each with its own government and laws.

The war began because of a quarrel over Helen, the beautiful wife of the Greek king of Sparta. Paris, the son of the Trojan king, had heard of Helen's beauty. Paris had visited the Spartan king and had carried off his host's wife. The angry king called upon other Greeks to join him in a war against the city of Troy. Many Greek warriors took to their ships and set sail for the coast of Asia.

The war was quickly begun but not quickly ended. For ten years the Greeks battled the Trojans on the plains before the walls of Troy. Many brave warriors fell in the bloody conflict, but the Greeks could not break through the walls of Troy. To learn more about Homer's tale, read the literature selection on page 73.

B. Greek Gods and Goddesses

According to Homer's account, gods and goddesses played a large part in the Trojan War. The Greeks believed that gods and goddesses never grew old and were more powerful than humans. The gods and goddesses took part in all sorts of human affairs. They had favorites whom they helped and protected. They sent misfortunes on those who displeased them or aroused their anger.

The most important gods and goddesses dwelt on Mount Olympus, the highest mountain in Greece. Each god or goddess had particular powers. For example, Zeus (zyoos) was supposed to rule the gods on Olympus. Zeus had two brothers —Poseidon (poh SYE dun), god of the sea, and Hades, god of the underworld. Hera, wife of Zeus, was the goddess of marriage, and Hestia, her sister, protected homes.

Aphrodite (af ruh DYT ee), the beautiful goddess of love, caused the quarrel between the Greeks and the Trojans. She helped Paris kidnap Helen and so aroused the Spartan king's demand for war. Athena (uh THEE nuh), goddess of both war and wisdom, aided the Greeks, as did Poseidon. Ares (AIR eez), god of battle, encouraged the Trojans.

C. Mixing Myth and History

History's Importance The story of the Trojan War as told by Homer and other poets is not totally accurate. We do not believe that gods took part in the war. The poets mixed **myths** into their accounts.

Greek gods and goddesses played an important role in ancient Greece. Each had a special function or job.
▶ Who was the god or goddess of music?

GREEK GODS AND GODDESSES

Myths are stories about the origins and doings of the gods. They attempt to explain how and why things happen. History is an account of what did happen. Myths may be interesting — sometimes more interesting than history — but they do not necessarily tell what really happened.

Myths may be based partly on history. Was there a city of Troy that was destroyed by attackers? This was the question Heinrich Schliemann (HYN rihk SHLEE mahn), a German boy, asked his father. Heinrich listened to his father tell of buried cities and ancient heroes, especially those of the Trojan War. The boy usually took the side of the Trojans, because he thought the Greeks had wronged

them. He once asked if any ruins of Troy remained, and he was disappointed when his father said that Troy had disappeared.

On Christmas in 1829, Heinrich received a history book with a picture showing the great walled city of Troy in flames. His father explained that the picture was based on the artist's imagination. When Heinrich asked if Troy might have had such great walls, his father said that it probably had. That was enough for Heinrich. He insisted, "If such walls once existed, vast ruins of them must remain, but they are hidden away beneath the dust of ages." His father thought this was doubtful, but Heinrich declared that some day he would dig up those walls.

FROM:

The Adventures of Odysseus and the Tale of Troy

By: Homer — translated by Padraic Colum
Setting: Ancient Troy

Homer was a blind poet who lived sometime between 800 B.C. and 700 B.C. His epics, the *Iliad* and *Odyssey*, describe the Trojan War and the travels of Odysseus. These epics, originally written in Greek, have been translated into many different languages. This excerpt is based on the story of the Trojan horse.

*A*nd then Odysseus devised the means by which we took Priam's [the Trojan king's] city at last. He made us build a great Wooden Horse. We built it and left it upon the plain of Troy and the Trojans wondered at it greatly. And Odysseus had counselled us to bring our ships down to the water . . . and to make it seem in every way that we were going to depart from Troy in weariness. This we did, and the Trojans saw the great host sail away from before their City. But they did not know that a company of the best of our warriors was within the hollow of the Wooden Horse, nor did they know that we had left a spy behind to make a signal for our return.

The Trojans wondered why the great Wooden Horse had been left behind. And there were some who considered that it had been left there as an offering to the goddess, Palla Athene, and they thought it should be brought within the city. Others were wiser and would have left the Wooden Horse alone. But those who considered that it should be brought within prevailed; and, as the Horse was too great to bring through the gate, they flung down part of the wall that they might bring it through. The Wooden Horse was brought within the walls and left upon the streets of the city and the darkness of the night fell.

73

Uncovering Troy It was many years before Heinrich Schliemann undertook his search for the city of Troy. He was 46 when he finally began exploring the Asian coast of the Aegean Sea. He was in his 50s when he excavated the site of an ancient fortified city. Schliemann mistakenly believed that he was excavating Homer's Troy. It was later learned that he had indeed found the site of Troy, but that he had dug through the ruins of Homer's Troy to those of still earlier times. Since Schliemann's excavation, the remains of Homer's Troy have been correctly identified and studied. We now know that there was a city of Troy and that it was destroyed by fire about the time of Homer's heroes. We also know that in those times the ancestors of the Greeks attacked cities on the coast of Asia. These are facts of history that Homer mixed with myths about the gods and goddesses.

D. Writing History

Long after the time of Homer, armies from Asia invaded Greece. Three times between 499 B.C. and 479 B.C., the Persians attacked the Greeks in Europe. The emperor of the Persians ruled the largest empire the world had yet known. The conquest of Greece would make it still larger.

Herodotus (hih RAHD uh tus) wrote the history of the Persian Wars. He was a Greek, but he was very fair to the Persians.

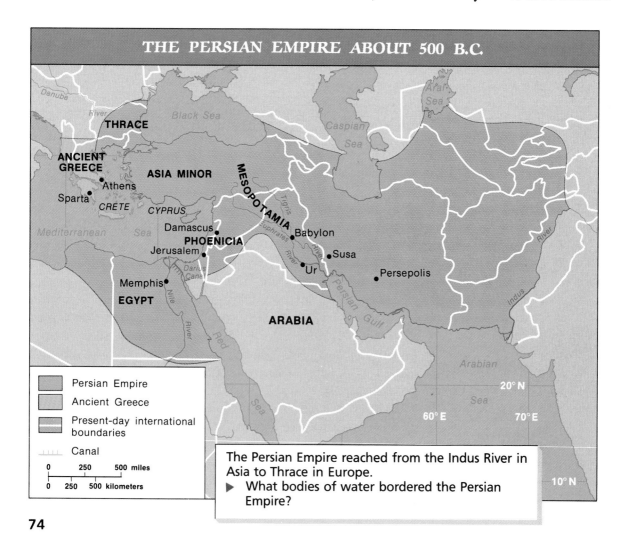

THE PERSIAN EMPIRE ABOUT 500 B.C.

Persian Empire
Ancient Greece
Present-day international boundaries
Canal

| 0 | 250 | 500 miles |
| 0 | 250 | 500 kilometers |

The Persian Empire reached from the Indus River in Asia to Thrace in Europe.
▶ What bodies of water bordered the Persian Empire?

74

He wrote to preserve the record of the "great and wonderful achievements of both our own [Greeks] and the Asian peoples."

The main subject of Herodotus' history was the Persian Wars, but he covered much more than the conflicts. He described most of the peoples and the lands ruled by the Persians. These lands reached from the Mediterranean Sea to India. Since this empire covered so much of the known world, Herodotus' book was almost a world history and geography.

Herodotus had traveled widely throughout the Persian Empire. His reports about what he had actually seen are believable. But Herodotus does tell some tall tales about faraway lands that he had not visited. He reports that in some places there are flying snakes, dog-headed men, and cattle that walk backward as they graze. They do so because they have long pointed horns that bend forward. Were they to walk forward as they nibbled grass, their horns would get stuck in the ground.

Such tales are hardly history, and Herodotus did not necessarily believe them. He admits, "I merely record the story without guaranteeing the truth of it." When he reports that the Persian magicians calmed a storm at sea by putting a spell on the wind, he adds, "Of course, it may be that

Herodotus was the first Greek historian.
▶ What was the main subject of his writings?

the wind just naturally dropped."

Homer mixed myth and history. Herodotus sometimes mixed history and fictional, fanciful tales. It is doubtful that he fooled many Greeks of his time. He certainly does not fool readers today. We have little trouble separating history from fancy in Herodotus' work. But the tall stories make the book more fun to read.

LESSON **1** REVIEW

THINK AND WRITE

A. According to Homer, what was the cause of the Trojan War?
B. What were the powers of the major Greek gods and goddesses?
C. Why do we think that Homer's account of the Trojan War was based partly on history?
D. What different types of subjects did Herodotus write about?

SKILLS CHECK

MAP SKILL

Compare the map of the Persian Empire on page 74 with that of the Eurasia political map in the Atlas. Make a list of at least five modern countries that are located within the land once ruled by the Persian emperor.

The Cities of Greece

THINK ABOUT WHAT YOU KNOW

Think about what it would be like to live in a country where the people could not vote or participate in the government of the country. How, do you think, would life be different than it is in the United States?

STUDY THE VOCABULARY

despot	democracy
strait	monarchy
city-state	jury
oligarchy	alliance

FOCUS YOUR READING

What was the difference between the cities of Sparta and Athens, and why did they go to war?

A. Protection from a "Wooden Wall"

A Hidden Message "You shall be safe behind the wooden wall!" That was the oracle's message to the Athenians in the summer of 480 B.C. An oracle is a place or person that a god uses to reveal hidden knowledge. The Athenians, like all Greeks, believed that oracles gave messages from the gods. The Athenians had asked the oracles for advice because a great danger threatened their city. Xerxes (ZURK seez), the Persian emperor, had invaded Greece with a huge army and fleet. Efforts to stop the Persians at Thermopylae (ther MAHP-uh lee), a mountain pass, had failed. By land and sea, the Persians moved toward the city of Athens. They took Athens and burned it. All the men, women, and children of Athens escaped to the nearby island of Salamis.

The Athenians were puzzled over the oracle's words. That was the trouble with oracles; their messages were like riddles. What was the "wooden wall"? Some Athenians recalled that a wooden wall had at one time surrounded the Acropolis (uh-KRAHP uh lis), the high hill in the midst of the city. They said that the oracle meant for them to defend the city from the Acropolis. Themistocles (thuh MIHS tuh kleez), the boldest of the Athenian leaders, insisted, "The wooden wall is your ships." He persuaded the Athenians to abandon the city and withdraw to nearby islands. They would depend on their fleet of wooden ships for protection.

Battle of Salamis Themistocles realized that the Persians had far more ships than the Athenians. But he believed that the

A Greek army of 6,000 fought the Persians at Thermopylae.
► What weapons did these armies fight with in the battle of Thermopylae?

Athenians would have a chance if they could fight in the narrow bay of Salamis, which they knew so well. To get the Persians to enter the bay and attack, Themistocles played a trick worthy of Odysseus. He sent a Greek posing as a deserter into the Persian camp. The Greek told the Persians that the Athenians planned to slip out of the bay of Salamis during the night. The Persians believed the Greek and sailed into the narrow waters.

Xerxes was sure that he would witness a great victory. He had a seat placed on a hill above the shore so he could watch. What he saw when the battle began did not please him. Confusion spread among the Persians as their ships crowded into the narrow, unfamiliar bay. They got in each other's way. Some Persian ships wrecked on the rocks as the Athenian ships skillfully darted between them. By the end of the battle, the Persians had lost the greater part of their fleet. Xerxes had witnessed a great victory, a victory of the Athenians!

Left without many ships, Xerxes returned to Asia, leaving an army in northern Greece. The next year the Greeks defeated the remaining Persian forces at the battle of Plataea. However, the battle in the bay of Salamis proved to be the turning point of the war.

B. Fighting the Persians

The Greeks were fighting to protect their country from the Persians. Persia was a foreign land ruled by one all-powerful person called a **despot** (DES put). A despot is a person who rules with total and unlimited control. The Greeks rightly feared such a ruler, because they knew that despots often abused their great powers. Herodotus tells of such an abuse in his history of the war.

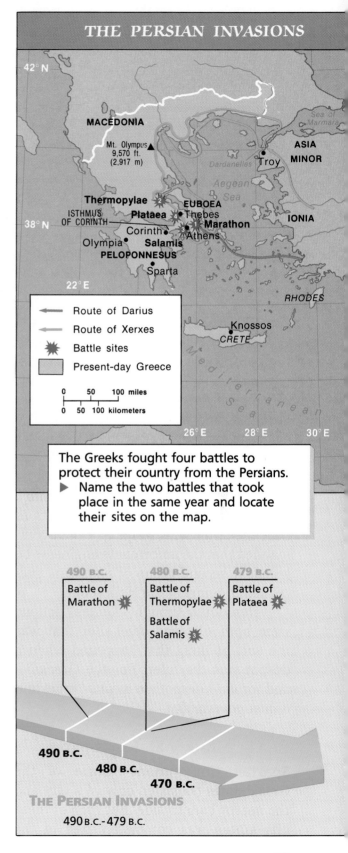

THE PERSIAN INVASIONS

The Greeks fought four battles to protect their country from the Persians.
▶ Name the two battles that took place in the same year and locate their sites on the map.

490 B.C. — Battle of Marathon
480 B.C. — Battle of Thermopylae / Battle of Salamis
479 B.C. — Battle of Plataea

THE PERSIAN INVASIONS
490 B.C.–479 B.C.

This drawing depicts the bridge of boats that Xerxes ordered to be built across the Hellespont.
▶ How were these boats used to build a bridge?

When Xerxes prepared to invade Greece, he ordered his engineers to build a bridge of boats across the Hellespont (HEL-us pahnt). The Hellespont was the **strait**, or narrow waterway, connecting the Aegean Sea and the Sea of Marmara. The Hellespont is now called the Dardanelles (dahr duh NELZ). A swift current flowed through the strait, and the first bridge of boats broke. The Persian despot fell into a violent rage. He ordered his servants to beat the strait with whips. He then commanded that the unfortunate engineers be killed. A second group of engineers succeeded in bridging the Hellespont.

Herodotus thought Xerxes' actions were both silly and cruel. But that was the sort of thing that happened when a despot was the ruler. For the Greeks—and for us—despotism means "cruel and unjust government."

C. The Military State of Sparta

Spartan Government Some of the Greek states consisted only of a city and the nearby countryside. But each of these **city-states** was completely free of the others. They had different types of governments. Some city-states were ruled by a small group. The Greeks called this type of government an **oligarchy** (AHL ih gahr-kee). In other city-states, such as Athens, government was by the people, which the Greeks called **democracy**. A king ruled Macedonia (mas uh DOH nee uh), in northern Greece. Government of a kingdom by one ruler was known as a **monarchy**. We still use these Greek words for forms of government. We call the government of the United States a democracy.

Military Life Sparta was a free city, but individual Spartans had little freedom to live as they liked. From the time a Spartan boy was seven, he trained to be a soldier. Boys lived together in military troops. Young men in charge of the troops taught the boys the skills that would make them strong, vigorous warriors. The boys learned to use spears and swords, and to live in the open in all kinds of weather.

When a man married, he continued to live with his fellow fighting men for another ten years. Only after that was he free to live with his family.

Spartan girls grew up in their own homes, but the city did not forget them. It was expected that they would become the wives and mothers of warriors, so they had to take part in vigorous sports that would make them strong. The girls also learned to manage household affairs.

Spartan laws discouraged everything that might take people's attention away from the military life. Sparta did not welcome visitors from other cities, and few Spartans were allowed to travel. The city's leaders feared that citizens might become interested in other ways of life.

For much the same reason, Spartans took no part in business. Outsiders carried

The military was a large part of the life of a Spartan male.
▶ What did Spartan soldiers wear to protect themselves in combat?

D. Democracy in Athens

Pericles Pericles (PER uh kleez) was the leader of Athens for 30 years. He was neither a monarch nor a despot. The Athenians elected him year after year. Pericles proudly declared that Athens was a democracy. In Athens, power was "in the hands of the many rather than the few."

Pericles was right in calling Athens a democracy at that time. As compared with other ancient governments, the government of Athens *was* democratic. But it would not seem democratic today. When Pericles spoke of government by the people, he should have said government by the citizens. Not all of the people who lived in Athens were citizens. Being a citizen was like belonging to a family; it depended on birth. Only the child of a citizen could be a citizen. Children who were born in Athens and lived there all their lives were not considered citizens if their parents had come from other places.

on trade for the city. Not that there was much trade. The Spartans bought no fine clothing or rare foods. They prided themselves on their simple lives.

Even in sports the Spartans did not forget military training. The games they played were soldiers' games.

Why did the Spartans think it so important to have a strong army? They believed that they needed to have a strong army largely because they were afraid. The Spartans had a large number of slaves called *helots*, who worked their land. Since there were fewer Spartans than helots, the Spartans lived in fear of a slave revolt. It has been said that fear of their slaves enslaved the Spartans.

The Granger Collection

The Age of Pericles was the greatest period of ancient Athenian history.
▶ What type of government did Athens have under Pericles?

79

Citizens' Roles Athens seems undemocratic to us today because women had no voice in the city's affairs. Even women who were citizens could take no part in the government. Politics in Athenian democracy was for male citizens only.

Pericles said that all the citizens should take an active part in the politics of the city. But not all citizens could take part. If all 40,000 male citizens had shown up for the assembly, there would have been no room for them at the meeting place, which could seat only 6,000. Of course, that was quite a large group to discuss and decide matters anyway.

A citizen might also serve for a year on the Council of Five Hundred, which had charge of the city's day to day business. Members of the council were chosen by lot, that is, by drawing names, rather than by election. This was democratic in that every citizen had an equal chance to have his name drawn.

The Athenians selected their **juries** by lot, as we do. A jury is a group of people called into court to give a verdict, or decision, in a dispute. Athenian juries were much larger than ours. One jury would have hundreds of members. Since cases were decided by a majority of votes, the jurors did not all have to be in agreement as in American juries.

Slavery Perhaps the most undemocratic thing about Athens was slavery. Like the Spartans, the Athenians had slaves, though their slaves did not make up so large a part of the population. Slavery was common in ancient times. Some of the slaves were enemies who were captured rather than killed in battle. Other people were slaves by birth; their parents had been slaves.

E. Sparta and Athens Are Rivals

The Delian League Because the city-states were independent, they found it difficult to act together for any long period of time. After turning back the Persian invasion, Athens formed the Delian (DEE lee-un) League, an **alliance** with other Greek cities. An alliance is supposed to be a partnership, but in fact, the city-state of Athens soon ruled the league. Sparta, fearful of Athens' growing power, formed another league.

When some of the cities in the Delian League tried to withdraw, Athens forced them to stay a part of the league. These cities then complained that the alliance that they had formed had turned into an Athenian empire.

Rivalry between Sparta and Athens led to the Peloponnesian War.
▶ Why has this war been called a struggle of the elephant and the whale?

Sparta was more powerful on land, but Athens controlled the sea. The war, known as the Peloponnesian (pel uh puh NEE-shun) War, has been called a struggle of the elephant and the whale.

Both Athens and Sparta tried to get Persian support during the deadly Peloponnesian War. The Persians, happy to see the Greeks fighting among themselves, supplied the Spartans with money for ships. Once the Spartans had a fleet, they defeated the Athenians in 405 B.C.

The end of the Peloponnesian War did not mean a long period of peace in Greece. Quarrels continued among the cities for another half century.

A History Book Thucydides (thoo SIHD-ih deez) of Athens wrote a history of the Peloponnesian War. He started writing at the beginning of the war because he thought it would be a great war and worth writing about more than any war of earlier times. Although Thucydides was an Athenian, he was more interested in writing an accurate account than in defending Athens. Thucydides wanted to record exactly what happened during the Peloponnesian War. Unlike Herodotus, Thucydides did not mix history and fictional stories. His only aim was to tell what happened. Thucydides wrote one of the world's finest histories.

Peloponnesian War The growing power of Athens aroused Spartan fears. War broke out between Sparta and Athens in 431 B.C. In the struggle that followed,

LESSON **2** *REVIEW*

THINK AND WRITE

A. What two opinions did the Athenians have about the meaning of the oracle?
B. Why did the Greeks dislike despotism?
C. What was the life of a Spartan like?
D. What was undemocratic about the government of Athens?
E. What caused the Peloponnesian War?

SKILLS CHECK

MAP SKILL

Look up *Athens* in the Gazetteer to find the latitude at which it is located. Turn to the map of North America in the Atlas. List cities in the United States that are near the same latitude.

DIRECT VS. INDIRECT DEMOCRACY

As you learned in the last lesson, the Greek city-state of Athens developed a democratic system of government. All the citizens of Athens met in one place to make laws and other important decisions. This form of democracy is known as direct democracy because the citizens participated directly in the making of decisions. The system worked well because Athens was a small community.

The United States also has a democratic form of government. But there are so many people in the United States that it would be impossible for all of them to assemble in one place. Therefore, our citizens elect representatives — the members of Congress — to make laws and important decisions. This system is called indirect democracy because citizens do not directly participate in the everyday workings of government.

Does this mean that citizens in our country are no longer involved in national decisions after they elect their representatives? Of course not. Citizens vote for people who will best represent their views. Good citizens have an obligation to monitor the work of these representatives. People can write to their elected officials to let them know how they feel about certain

President George Bush addresses the United States Congress in 1990.

issues. When citizens are unhappy with the way in which they are being represented, they can vote for new representatives in the next election. In this way, elected officials are responsible for listening to the concerns of the public.

Thinking for Yourself

Answer the following questions on a separate sheet of paper.

1. What do you think are the benefits and problems of an indirect democracy?
2. Why is it important that elected representatives listen to the concerns of the people they represent?
3. What are some ways to let your representatives know your point of view on certain issues?
4. Write a letter to your local or state representative. Express your concerns about an issue that interests you or choose one of the following issues: pollution, hunger, or homelessness.

Alexander the Great

THINK ABOUT WHAT YOU KNOW

What characteristics, do you think, make a ruler great?

STUDY THE VOCABULARY

colony   culture

FOCUS YOUR READING

Who was Alexander the Great, and what did he accomplish?

A. The Value of Observation

It happened one day when Alexander's father, King Philip II of Macedonia, was offered the opportunity to buy a horse called Bucephalus (byoo SEF uh lus). The name means "bull-headed." Philip decided to take a look at the horse, and Alexander went along. Bucephalus appeared to be easily frightened. As soon as anyone approached, he kicked up a fuss. Not even the most experienced riders could get on him. Philip was angry at the trader for trying to sell him an unruly animal. But Alexander shook his head and sighed, "What a fine horse you are losing, just because your men do not know how to handle him."

The king, not pleased at all by his son's remark, burst out, "I suppose you could handle him better than your elders!"

"I certainly could."

Irked by his son's boldness, Philip offered to make a bet. If Alexander could ride Bucephalus, he could have the horse. If he failed, he would have to pay an amount equal to the price of the horse. Alexander readily took the bet.

Philip did not know that Alexander was applying a lesson learned from his teacher, Aristotle. When Alexander was young, Aristotle had taught him the importance of observing, that is, paying careful attention to what you see. But Aristotle probably never guessed that his teaching would help Alexander win a horse.

Young Alexander had observed that Bucephalus had been frightened by his own shadow. When Alexander approached the horse, he spoke softly, took hold of the bridle, and gently turned Bucephalus toward the sun so that he could not see his shadow. As soon as the horse calmed down a bit, Alexander leaped lightly upon his back, taking care not to pull the rein too hard. Bucephalus took off at full gallop. Those who watched thought the king's son would surely be killed. But Bucephalus seemed to sense that he had met his master. After a run across the field,

Alexander and his horse Bucephalus saw many a battle together.
▶ Why, do you think, was Bucephalus Alexander's favorite horse?

Alexander turned the horse about and trotted back to the starting point.

Bucephalus became Alexander's favorite horse. In later years, he carried Alexander through battles in far-off lands. At least a dozen times, Alexander owed his life to the strength and spirit of his horse. It was quite an unexpected result from Aristotle's teaching.

B. Greece Controlled by a Macedonian King

Although the city of Macedonia was in northern Greece, many Greeks considered the Macedonian people backward farmers and shepherds.

Philip took advantage of the quarrels among the Greek city-states. He formed a well-trained and powerful army. Backed by his army, he extended his power over them. By 338 B.C. the king of Macedonia controlled all of Greece.

Philip planned to invade Asia, which was still ruled by the Persian emperor. The Greeks had long talked about invading the Persian Empire. Such a war would pay back the Persians for Xerxes' invasion of Greece so many years before. But Philip never led an army into Asia. He was murdered in 336 B.C. before he could do so.

Alexander became king when he was only 20 years old. The Greeks, who had opposed Philip, thought they could now throw off Macedonian rule, since the new king was "a mere boy." But Alexander was well prepared and proved them wrong by capturing the city of Thebes (theebz). As a warning to others, Alexander destroyed Thebes. He left only one house standing— that of the poet Pindar. By his treatment of Thebes, Alexander wished to show that he was both a powerful military leader and a lover of Greek poetry.

C. Alexander's Conquests

Building an Empire After making sure that the Greeks accepted his leadership, Alexander launched the long-discussed war against Persia. He crossed the Hellespont, where Xerxes had long ago built a bridge of boats. He reminded the Greeks that their ancestors had once fought on the Asian coast at Troy. Alexander led his troops to the site of ancient Troy and camped on the plain where Homer's warriors had fought.

Alexander freed the Greek cities in Asia from Persian rule, but he did not stop there. He moved east and defeated the Persian army, even though they outnumbered the Greeks. Alexander moved down the east coast of the Mediterranean into

Alexander the Great was one of the greatest military geniuses of the ancient world.
▶ How had Alexander won his place in history as Alexander the Great?

Egypt. He went on to conquer the lands of the Middle East. Not content to stop, he led his army east to the Indus River, in what is now Pakistan. He wanted to go still further, but his weary troops refused. Alexander yielded and marched back to Babylon. It is easy to understand why. They had conquered the largest empire the world had ever known. Even though he was not yet 30, Alexander had won his place in history as Alexander the Great.

Alexander did more than conquer. He also planted Greek **colonies** in Egypt and the Middle East. A colony is a settlement of people living in a new territory while being ruled by the government of another country. These colonies were ruled by

Greece. The colonies took the form of Greek cities, many named Alexandria. The most famous Alexandria was in Egypt, on the delta of the Nile River. This city still bears its founder's name.

Bucephalus Captured Bucephalus accompanied Alexander on the invasion of Asia. Once near the Caspian Sea, a band of horse thieves captured the conqueror's favorite horse. Alexander was so upset that he sent out messengers who announced that unless Bucephalus was returned unharmed, the Greeks would destroy every village in the region. The thieves hurriedly returned Bucephalus to his master. The horse had not been harmed, but he was

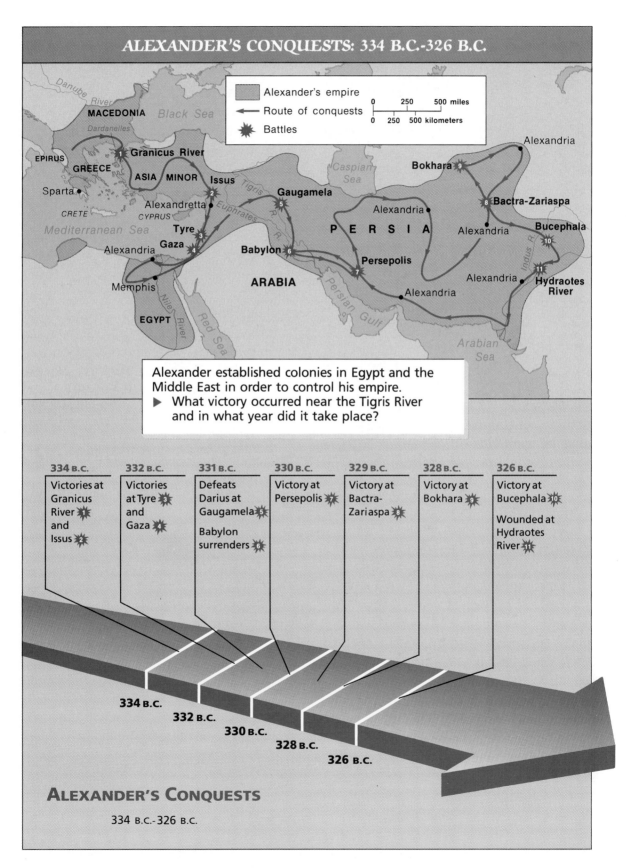

ALEXANDER'S CONQUESTS: 334 B.C.–326 B.C.

Alexander's empire
Route of conquests
Battles

0 250 500 miles
0 250 500 kilometers

MACEDONIA
Black Sea
Danube River
Dardanelles
EPIRUS
GREECE
ASIA MINOR
Granicus River ①
Issus ②
Sparta
CRETE
CYPRUS
Alexandretta
Mediterranean Sea
Tyre ③
Gaza ④
Alexandria
Memphis
ARABIA
EGYPT
Nile River
Red Sea
Gaugamela ⑤
Tigris R.
Euphrates R.
Babylon ⑥
Caspian Sea
PERSIA
Persepolis
Persian Gulf
Alexandria
Alexandria
Bokhara ⑨
Bactra-Zariaspa ⑧
Alexandria
Bucephala ⑩
Indus R.
Hydraotes River ⑪
Alexandria
Arabian Sea

Alexander established colonies in Egypt and the Middle East in order to control his empire.
▶ What victory occurred near the Tigris River and in what year did it take place?

334 B.C.	332 B.C.	331 B.C.	330 B.C.	329 B.C.	328 B.C.	326 B.C.
Victories at Granicus River ① and Issus ②	Victories at Tyre ③ and Gaza ④	Defeats Darius at Gaugamela ⑤ Babylon surrenders ⑥	Victory at Persepolis ⑦	Victory at Bactra-Zariaspa ⑧	Victory at Bokhara ⑨	Victory at Bucephala ⑩ Wounded at Hydraotes River ⑪

334 B.C.
332 B.C.
330 B.C.
328 B.C.
326 B.C.

ALEXANDER'S CONQUESTS
334 B.C.–326 B.C.

growing old. When he died, Alexander named one of the colonial cities Bucephala in honor of his horse. Alexander never returned to Greece. He seems to have planned to rule his empire from ancient Babylon, in Mesopotamia. We will never know how well the conqueror would have ruled, because Alexander died in Babylon in 323 B.C., at the age of 32.

D. Greek Culture

Spreading Culture   After Alexander's death, several of his generals carved out of his empire kingdoms for themselves. His boyhood companion Ptolemy became king of Egypt. Ptolemy's family ruled Egypt for about 300 years. The famous queen Cleopatra was the last member of Ptolemy's family to rule.

Alexander had planted colonies partly to control the empire and partly because he wanted to spread Greek **culture** in other lands. A people's culture is made up of their language, ideas, arts, and general way of life.

The Greek kings who ruled after Alexander continued his plan of spreading Greek culture in Egypt and the Middle East. Government officials used the Greek language, as did many of the business people in the cities.

Gymnasiums   Much life in the Greek cities was centered in the gymnasiums. Today we use that word to mean a place for athletic exercises and playing such games as basketball and volleyball. The Greek gymnasiums were places for athletic training, but they were also places where people could gather for discussions and reading. Some gymnasiums had libraries. In a Greek city a gymnasium was a place to exercise the mind as well as the body.

The ruins of Persepolis, an ancient capital of Persia, prove that Greek culture spread to the Middle East.
▶ What can you learn about Greek architecture from these ruins?

The Museum Artists and writers in the Greek cities copied Greek models. Buildings were made in the Greek style. The Ptolemys established a center for Greek culture at Alexandria in Egypt. They called it the Museum, which means "place of the muses." The muses were Greek goddesses of art and learning. For example, Calliope (kuh LYE uh pee) was a muse of poetry; Terpsichore (turp SIHK uh ree), of dance; and Clio (KLYE oh), of history. At the Museum, people studied these and other subjects. There was a great library, the largest in the ancient world. The Museum was somewhat like a modern university.

The spread of Greek culture had been Alexander's dream. He shared the belief of his teacher Aristotle that Greek culture was the best in the world. He thought that by spreading it to others, he offered them a great gift.

The Museum in Alexandria, Egypt, was a learning center of Greek culture.
▶ How does the Museum resemble a library of today?

LESSON **3** *REVIEW*

THINK AND WRITE

A. Why was Alexander able to ride Bucephalus?
B. How were Philip II and Alexander able to control all of Greece?
C. What lands did Alexander conquer?
D. How and why was Greek culture spread?

SKILLS CHECK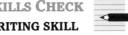

WRITING SKILL

Alexander the Great was a great leader. Choose someone who you think is a great leader today and write a paragraph explaining why you chose that person.

89

Greek Achievements

The first Olympic Games were held in Greece. How many sports can you name that are played in the Olympic Games today?

philosophy **amphitheater**

What were some important Greek achievements?

Socrates, a Greek philosopher, is one of the most admired people in history.
▶ For what work was Socrates admired?

A. The Search for a Wise Man

Socrates (SAHK ruh teez) of Athens was a philosopher. That was not his business, for **philosophy** is not a business or trade. Philosophy is "the love of wisdom."

Socrates had a great desire to understand things. He spent much time talking to people and asking them questions. He was one of the world's great teachers.

A friend of Socrates once asked the oracle at Delphi, "Who is the wisest of the Greeks?" The oracle answered that it was Socrates. When Socrates heard of the oracle's answer, he was deeply puzzled. He knew that he was not wise. What did the oracle mean? Socrates decided to search for someone wiser and then go to the oracle and say, "Here is one wiser than I."

Socrates first sought out a politician who was thought to be wise by many, a view that the politician himself fully shared. As Socrates listened to the politician, he soon decided that this was by no means a wise man.

Socrates questioned other politicians and found them no wiser. He then visited some poets. He asked them to explain passages from their own poems. He learned that although the poets could say many fine things, they did not truly understand their meaning.

At last, Socrates questioned skilled craftworkers. They certainly knew a great deal about their crafts, but they made the same mistake as the poets. "Because they were good workers, they thought they also understood every other subject."

Socrates admitted that his questioning had not made him a popular man, but he kept on. As a true lover of wisdom, he must find out the meaning of the oracle. In the end, he concluded that what the oracle meant was this: If you would be wise, be like Socrates, who knows that he knows nothing.

Socrates did not stop his questioning with his search for the wise man. He spent many hours asking people about matters that they thought they understood. He led his students to examine their beliefs and ideas. He told them, "The unexamined life is not worth living."

Some Athenians thought Socrates' questions upset the beliefs of his students. When some of the students took part in the overthrow of the Athenian government, they said that Socrates was to blame. After the old government was restored, Socrates was brought to trial before a large Athenian jury. The majority voted him guilty and condemned him to death. He died in 399 B.C. after drinking hemlock poison.

B. The Search for Knowledge and Wisdom

Socrates did not write about his teachings. We know of them from dialogues written by Plato, his most famous student. Plato's dialogues are like plays in which Socrates and others have speaking parts.

Some years after Socrates' death, in 387 B.C., Plato started a school near Athens, called the Academy. In time, the name of Plato's school was used by many schools and centers of learning.

Among those who came to Plato's Academy was a young man from Macedonia named Aristotle. He remained in Athens until Plato's death. As you have already read, he later returned to Macedonia to become Alexander's teacher. Aristotle started teaching in a grove known as the Lyceum (lye SEE um). He had the habit of walking up and down the paths of the Lyceum while teaching, so his followers were nicknamed "the walkers."

Aristotle told the students who walked about with him, "All men by nature desire to know."

Plato (center left) and Aristotle (center right) are shown in the *School of Athens,* by Raphael.
▶ How can you tell that the painting shows a center for learning?

Even if this is not true of everyone, it was certainly true of Aristotle. He studied and wrote about politics, poetry, and philosophy. Later, Aristotle became known as the philosopher. He was called "the master of them that know."

C. Built to Delight the Eye

The Parthenon When the Athenians returned after the battle of Salamis, they found their city in ruins. Scarcely a building or house was left standing. The Athenians set about rebuilding the city with stronger walls and finer buildings. Pericles, the leader of the democracy, persuaded the people to build a city "to cheer the heart and delight the eye."

One of the greatest works of architecture was the Parthenon (PAHR thuh nahn), the temple of Athena, goddess of the city. The Parthenon stood on the Acropolis, a high rocky hill, so it could be seen from all parts of the city. The Parthenon is one of the best-known buildings of all time. Thousands of people each year climb the Acropolis to see the ruins that are still there. People from all over the world

The ruins of the Parthenon attract many visitors each year. This statue of Athena stands in Toronto, Canada.
▶ Of what materials is the statue made?

recognize the columned structure, shown below on page 92.

Phidias (FIHD ee us), the greatest of Greek sculptors, was in charge of carving the statues that decorated the outside of the Parthenon. He also made the statue of Athena that stood inside the temple. This was no ordinary statue of stone. It was made of gold and ivory, and it stood 38 feet (11 m) tall. The Greeks had no electric spotlights such as we would use today. Instead, Phidias had a shallow pool of water placed in front of the statue to reflect light that came through the thin tiles of the roof. All of that gold and ivory must have made a dazzling sight.

Greek Columns Greek builders made use of many stone columns. They designed the three styles shown in the drawing. It is easy to identify each of these styles by their capitals, the top part of the columns. The capital of the Doric columns, used on the Parthenon, is quite plain. The Ionic column has a capital with scrolls, and the Corinthian capital has carved stone leaves. We still use these styles. In Washington, D.C., the Lincoln Memorial has Doric columns. The Jefferson Memorial has Ionic columns, and the columns on the Supreme Court Building are Corinthian.

D. Gods Honored Through Sports

Ancient Olympics The Greeks took sports seriously. It was a saying of the Greeks that a person should have "a sound mind in a sound body." By *sound* they meant "healthy."

Greek sporting events were part of religious festivals. Athletes believed that they honored the gods by taking part in the games. According to an old myth, Zeus,

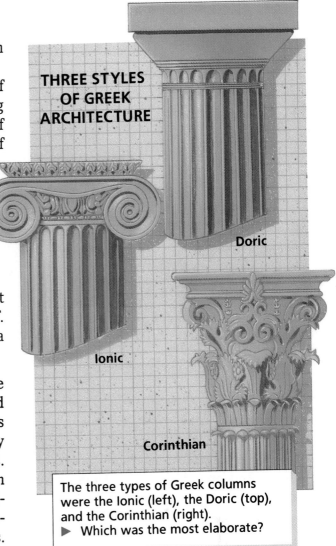

THREE STYLES OF GREEK ARCHITECTURE

Doric

Ionic

Corinthian

The three types of Greek columns were the Ionic (left), the Doric (top), and the Corinthian (right).
► Which was the most elaborate?

the greatest of the gods, had established the Olympic Games in his own honor. A temple to Zeus stood at Olympia, where the games took place every four years. In ancient times the Olympic Games were called the Olympian Games.

Athletes at the Olympian Games did not play team sports, such as football or basketball. Many of the contests were what we call track and field events. Athletes ran races, took part in jumping contests, and threw the discus and javelin. They also competed in wrestling matches. Wrestling was a popular sport. Both Plato and Aristotle mention it in their writings.

The ancient Greeks participated in many events during their Olympian Games.
▶ What event is pictured here?

124

The Olympian Games also had chariot and horse races. Chariot racing was dangerous, but crowds loved it. Horse races aroused great excitement. It was the ambition of many wealthy people to have their horse win at Olympia. It was said that 356 B.C. was a lucky year for King Philip II of Macedonia. In that year he won an important battle, his son Alexander was born, and his horse won the Olympian race.

Modern Olympics The modern Olympic Games have never been held at Olympia. The first modern games were at Athens in 1896. Since then they have been held in cities all over the world. The games have taken place every four years since 1896 except during World Wars I and II.

The Olympic Flame that is lighted at the opening ceremony of the modern games comes from ancient Olympia in Greece. Thousands of runners in cross-country relays bring the lighted torch to the host country. The last runner carries the torch into the stadium, circles the stadium, and then lights the Olympic Flame. The flame burns until the end of the games.

The modern games have no connection with religion. Their purpose is to encourage understanding and friendship among the different nations.

E. Important Events Live on Through Poems and Plays

Pindar Pindar was the poet whose house Alexander left standing at Thebes. Pindar described the purpose of his poems when he wrote, "Unsung the noblest deed will die." By this Pindar meant that people remember great deeds only when storytellers, historians, and poets tell about them. Pindar composed poems in praise of great achievements. One group of poems praised athletes who won glory at the games. Many of Pindar's poems have been lost. He may well have praised others, but the memories of their deeds have died.

Even the poems that have survived have an important part missing. Pindar's poems were composed to be sung, but the music is lost. We can only guess what they were like when Pindar sang them. But we at least have some wise sayings that he put in the poems and that do not need music. One of these sayings reads: "Not every truth is better for showing its face and often silence is the wisest thing for a man to heed."

Sappho We know only a little about another great poet, Sappho of Lesbos. She seems to have taught music and poetry to girls. Plato declared that Sappho wrote like a goddess. Unfortunately, only a few fragments of her poems survive. From these fragments we know that she wrote about friendship, love, and nature. One fragment reads: "The stars about the lovely moon hide their shining forms when it lights up the earth at its fullest." How could this idea be expressed differently?

Plays The ancient Greeks liked plays. Every Greek city had its theater, and plays were a part of religious festivals. The stories were well-known to the audiences.

The Greeks performed their plays in amphitheaters.
▶ For what events today do we use arenas similar to amphitheaters?

People came to the **amphitheaters** (AM fuh thee ut urz), or large open-air theaters, not for the stories but to hear the fine speeches of the characters in the plays. An amphitheater is a semicircular structure with ascending rows of stone seats set into a hillside. Some of these Greek plays have survived over thousands of years and are presented today.

LESSON **4** REVIEW

THINK AND WRITE

A. How did Socrates solve the riddle of the oracle's reply?
B. How did Plato and Aristotle continue the work that Socrates started?
C. What would you have seen if you had visited the Parthenon when it was first built?
D. What sports were included in the Olympian Games?
E. Who were Pindar and Sappho?

SKILLS CHECK

THINKING SKILL

Make a time line for the period from 500 B.C. to 300 B.C., using a scale of one inch (5 cm) for each 25 years. Show the following events on the time line: Battle of Salamis (480 B.C.); Alexander becomes king (336 B.C.); Death of Socrates (399 B.C.); Peloponnesian War begins (431 B.C.); Plato establishes the Academy (388 B.C.).

USING THE VOCABULARY

myth	alliance
city-state	colony
democracy	culture
monarchy	philosophy
jury	amphitheater

Each of the following sentences contains the wrong vocabulary word. On a separate sheet of paper, rewrite each sentence with the correct vocabulary word from above.

1. To the ancient Greeks, monarchy was the love of wisdom.
2. A myth is a group of people called into court to give a verdict in a dispute.
3. A Greek philosophy consisted of a city and the nearby countryside.
4. People who live in an amphitheater live in a new territory but are ruled by the government of another country.
5. A people's democracy is made up of their language, ideas, arts, and general way of life.
6. A large open-air theater is a city-state.
7. The Greeks called government by the people a monarchy.
8. A culture is a story about the origins and doings of the gods.
9. The government of a kingdom by one ruler was known as an alliance.
10. A jury is a partnership.

REMEMBERING WHAT YOU READ

On a separate sheet of paper, answer the following questions in complete sentences.

1. What poems written by Homer tell about the Trojan War?
2. What were the names and powers of five gods or goddesses?
3. What evidence is there that the city of Troy really existed?
4. In what ways did the people of Sparta have little freedom?
5. How was democracy in the city-state of Athens limited?
6. What were the accomplishments of Alexander the Great?
7. In what ways did Greek culture continue to spread after Alexander died?
8. Who were three famous ancient Greek philosophers?
9. Why did the Greeks participate in sporting events?
10. From what types of literature can we learn about the ancient Greeks?

TYING MATH TO SOCIAL STUDIES

A marathon is a 26.2-mile race. How many marathons would you have to run to cover 131 miles? If you completed only one half of a marathon, how many miles would you have run? To train for a marathon, you might run 7 miles on Monday, 15 miles on Tuesday, 9 miles on Wednesday, 5 miles on Thursday, 4 miles on Friday, and 2 miles on Saturday. What is the average number of miles you would run on those days?

THINKING CRITICALLY

On a separate sheet of paper, answer the following in complete sentences.

1. How are myths related to history?
2. Which government is best—a monarchy, an oligarchy, or a democracy? Explain.
3. Where would you have preferred to live, Sparta or Athens? Explain why.
4. What characteristic of Greek culture do you think was most valuable? Explain why.
5. How were the Olympian Games different from the modern Olympic Games?

SUMMARIZING THE CHAPTER

On a separate sheet of paper, draw a graphic organizer that is like the one shown here. Copy the information from this graphic organizer to the one you have drawn. Under each main heading write three statements that support it.

CHAPTER THEME   Many things in modern culture began in ancient Greece. Under the Greeks, Western civilization made many advances.

LESSON 1

A myth is different from history.

1. Tells about gods
2.
3.

LESSON 3

Alexander the Great was a famous leader with many major accomplishments to his credit.

1. Won a huge empire
2.
3.

LESSON 2

There were many differences between the city-states of Sparta and Athens.

1. Athens: democracy, Sparta: military
2.
3.

LESSON 4

There were many great achievements in ancient Greek culture.

1. Established philosophy
2.
3.

ANCIENT ROME

Ancient Rome was a leader in cultural development. Rome gave us great art, literature, and architecture, such as the Colosseum, whose ruins still stand in the city of Rome today.

The Republic

Imagine our country is ruled by a king. The king's powers are unlimited. How would your life be different than it is with our type of government?

STUDY THE VOCABULARY

republic	consul
patrician	dictator
plebeian	peninsula
Senate	legend

FOCUS YOUR READING

Why did the Roman city-state become a republic and the ruler of the western Mediterranean?

A. Greek Myths Borrowed by a Roman Poet

The Roman poet Virgil wrote about the ancestors of the Romans in the *Aeneid* (ee NEE ihd). Virgil based his long poem on myths borrowed from the Greeks. Gods and goddesses play important parts in the *Aeneid*. They are the gods and goddesses of the Greeks, although Virgil uses their Roman names. The chief of the gods is known as Jupiter rather than Zeus, and his wife is called Juno rather than Hera.

The *Aeneid* is a continuation of Homer's *Iliad*. Virgil recounts the adventures of Aeneas (ee NEE us), a prince of Troy. When the Greeks inside the wooden horse open the gates to Troy, Aeneas prepares to fight to his last breath. A goddess tells him to take his family and escape rather than remain and face certain death. Aeneas does as the goddess orders. He escapes to the hills, taking his small son and carrying his aged father on his back.

On the slopes of Mount Ida, Aeneas joins other Trojans who have fled the burning city. Aeneas wishes to remain on the mountain until they can return and build a new Troy on the site of the old. But his father advises the Trojans to leave the place that has such unhappy memories. He tells them to build ships and sail in search of a new homeland.

The Trojans follow the old man's advice. They cut timbers from a forest and build ships. When the ships are completed, the Trojans set sail without knowing where they are going. Aeneas receives a message in a dream from the god Apollo, who tells him to seek a new home in Italy.

In the course of their journey, the Trojans encounter a monster with the body of a large bird and the head of a woman. She warns the Trojans that they will face great hardships. They will not reach their new homeland until they are so hungry that "they will eat their tables."

The goddess Juno continues to cause trouble for the Trojans. After they set sail from Sicily, she sends a terrible storm that blows them away from Italy. But Neptune, god of the sea, calms the storm. Aeneas and the remaining Trojans make their way to the coast of North Africa.

In North Africa, Aeneas meets the beautiful Dido, queen of Carthage, and they fall in love. Aeneas remains with Dido for a year, delaying his search for the new Troy. Jupiter grows impatient and sends a messenger to remind Aeneas of his duty. When Dido discovers that Aeneas is leaving, she pleads with him to stay. He is touched by her love but tells her that when the gods command, people must obey. As Aeneas sails away, Dido kills herself.

The Trojans set sail again and this time reach the land of the Latins, in central

Italy. They leave their ships and gather in a grove of trees to eat. They do not bother to set up tables with platters on them. Instead they place meat on large slabs of bread. After gobbling the meat, they hungrily eat the slabs of bread. The son of Aeneas jokes, "We were so hungry we even ate our tables!" Then Aeneas remembers what the monster had said. He hugs his son and happily declares, "Now I know we have reached the right place!"

It is true the Trojans have reached the right place, but they have not yet reached the end of their troubles. The king of the Latins wishes to marry his daughter to Aeneas, but the other Latins oppose mixing with newcomers. A war breaks out in which many brave warriors lose their lives.

Jupiter asks Juno why she continues to trouble Aeneas. Juno sighs and agrees that she will no longer keep the Trojans from their new home in Rome. But she begs Jupiter not to let the Latins lose their name and language and become Trojans. She said "Let Rome rule the world, but let Troy perish forever." Jupiter agrees. "The Trojans will mingle with the Latins to become one people and all will be called Latins." By this myth, Virgil explained why the language of Rome was Latin.

Virgil, the greatest Roman poet, is shown in this mosaic with the spirits who inspired him.
▶ What is Virgil holding?

This bridge stretches across the Tiber River in Rome.
▶ How did Rome's location help to make it a prosperous city-state?

B. Rule by Kings Overthrown

Rome began as a city-state on the Tiber River. Its size was about the same as that of the Greek city-states. According to an old story, the first king was Romulus (RAHM yuh lus), a descendant of Aeneas.

The first Romans were a warlike people who fought fiercely against their enemies in war but quarreled among themselves in time of peace. Numa, the second king, realized that the Romans must learn peaceful ways. He told the Romans that the gods punished those who wronged their neighbors. To persuade people to respect the rules he gave them, Numa invented a story. He told the people that a goddess spoke to him. A Roman historian in later years excused Numa's story about the goddess. It was, the historian wrote, the only way he could rule "an ignorant and yet uncivilized people."

The Romans remembered Numa as a good and wise king, but later kings were neither good nor wise. Tarquin the Proud abused his powers and killed those who objected. The Romans finally drove Tarquin from the throne in 510 B.C.

C. Roman Republic Established

Citizens of Rome To take the place of the Roman king, the Romans established a **republic**. The Latin word means a government that is the "people's affair." A republic is a government in which citizens choose representatives to run the country. But not all of the people had an equal voice in the republic. Only male citizens could take any part in Roman government, and they were divided into two classes, **patricians** and **plebians** (plee BEE unz). Most of the patricians in Rome were upper-class landowners. The plebeians were the common people who made up about 90 percent of the Roman population. Being a citizen in the early Roman Republic was a matter of birth.

A Roman political leader named Cicero is shown addressing the Roman Senate.
▶ Who were the members who made up the Roman Senate?

Both patricians and plebeians could attend the large assembly, a group that elected leaders. But, the patricians controlled the assembly. Only patricians served as members of the council of elders. The Romans called this council the **Senate**. It was a body of 300 older men from which the citizens elected two **consuls** every year. A consul was one of the top officials in the republic. Having overthrown a king, the Romans did not want a single leader who ruled for life. Each consul held office for one year. Each consul had as much power as the other, so they could keep watch over and check each other.

Cincinnatus In time of emergency the Senate might choose a single leader, called a **dictator**. A dictator takes complete charge of a government. A dictator held power for six months or until the emergency had passed. The word *dictator* has an unfavorable meaning today. We think of dictators as being unjust or unreasonable. But the Romans remembered Cincinnatus, a very different kind of dictator.

Cincinnatus was plowing his field one day when several senators came to his farm and told him that the Senate had chosen him dictator. Rome needed a single leader because an enemy army threatened the city. Cincinnatus left his plow and took command of the republic. He called all the citizens to arms. He led them into battle and won a quick victory. After having done his duty, Cincinnatus returned to his farm.

Many different governments have been called republics since the time of Cincinnatus. The United States is a republic. Indeed, it can more correctly be called a "people's affair" than the ancient Roman Republic. In the United States today, all adult citizens have an equal right to vote and hold office.

D. Taking Over the Italian Peninsula

Rome was only one of a number of city-states and kingdoms on the Italian **peninsula**. A peninsula is a piece of land surrounded by water on three sides and connected to a larger piece of land. Wars between the small states were as common as wars between the cities of Greece.

Service in the army was the duty of every male citizen in the Roman Republic. Each man furnished his own weapons and equipment. Discipline was very strict. Cowards could be punished by death.

The story of Horatius (hoh RAY shus) described the ideal citizen soldier. According to the story, Horatius and two companions held back an enemy army at a bridge across the Tiber until the Romans could destroy it. As the timbers began to crack, Horatius ordered his two companions to go back. He fought alone until he heard the bridge crash into the river. He then leaped, fully armed, into the rushing river and swam safely to the other side. Horatius' bravery saved the city of Rome.

Here Horatius is shown bravely fighting the enemy to save Rome.
▶ Where did Horatius defeat the enemy army?

Every Roman citizen was in the army.
▶ What weapons is this Roman soldier holding?

The story of Horatius may only be a **legend** rather than true history. A legend is a story handed down from earlier times that may be no more than partly true. But whether legend or history, the story of Horatius at the bridge tells what Romans expected of their soldiers.

Roman soldiers may not all have been as brave and skillful as Horatius, but they did win wars. Rome defeated other states in Italy and won control of the whole peninsula. The city-state on the Tiber now ruled a whole country.

E. The Punic Wars

Carthage Rome controlled Italy, but the North African city of Carthage controlled the western Mediterranean lands. In myths, Carthage was the city of Queen Dido. In fact, Carthage was a city established by the Phoenicians (fih NIHSH unz), who came from what today is known as

Lebanon. Carthage became a prosperous and powerful city that ruled the coasts of North Africa and Spain.

Both Carthage and Rome had interests in Sicily, the large island off the tip of the Italian peninsula. The Carthaginians (kahr thuh JIHN ee unz) thought that the Romans in Sicily threatened their control of the western Mediterranean. The Romans thought the Carthaginians threatened their control of Italy. The rivalry in Sicily lead to three wars, which the Roman people called the Punic Wars. *Punic* means "Phoenician."

First Punic War   In the First Punic War, between 264 B.C. and 241 B.C., the Romans forced the Carthaginians out of Sicily. But this did not end the struggle. In the years that followed, the Carthaginian general Hannibal prepared to fight again. He trained an army in Spain, which Carthage ruled. Hannibal led his troops over the Pyrenees mountain range, through southern France, and across the Alps, the most rugged mountains in western Europe. Hannibal's forces included not only men and horses but elephants as well. Using elephants in war was an idea that Alexander's army had brought back from India. The large animals frightened troops not familiar with them, but they sometimes turned and trampled their own handlers. It was difficult to move such an army over the snow-covered Alps, but Hannibal finally reached Italy.

Second Punic War   In the Second Punic War, Hannibal defeated the Roman army, but he failed to take the walled city. After their defeat the Romans wisely showed patience. They waited until they were strong enough to send a force to attack Carthage. The Carthaginians called their best general back home, but this time Hannibal was defeated.

Hannibal crossed the Rhone River to attack the Romans.
▶ Why, do you think, did he and his men use elephants?

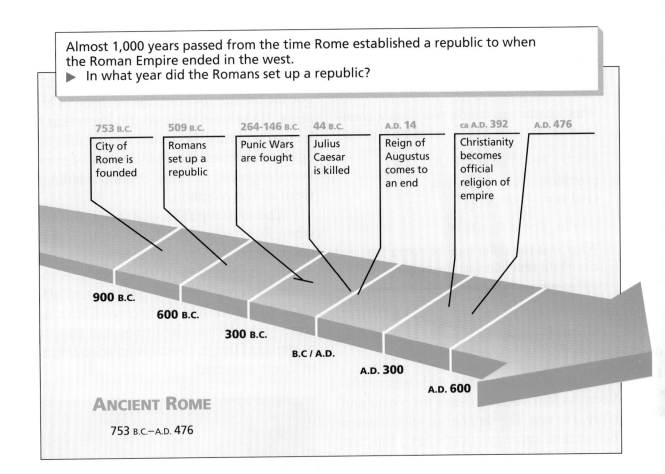

Almost 1,000 years passed from the time Rome established a republic to when the Roman Empire ended in the west.

▶ In what year did the Romans set up a republic?

753 B.C. City of Rome is founded

509 B.C. Romans set up a republic

264-146 B.C. Punic Wars are fought

44 B.C. Julius Caesar is killed

A.D. 14 Reign of Augustus comes to an end

ca A.D. 392 Christianity becomes official religion of empire

A.D. 476

900 B.C.

600 B.C.

300 B.C.

B.C / A.D.

A.D. 300

A.D. 600

ANCIENT ROME
753 B.C.–A.D. 476

Third Punic War Even after its defeat, Carthage continued to be a prosperous trading city. Cato, a Roman senator, feared that Carthage would grow strong and try to avenge Hannibal's defeat. Cato ended every speech in the Senate with the cry, "Carthage must be destroyed!" Rome waged the Third Punic War from 149 B.C. to 146 B.C. and again defeated Carthage. Cato was dead by then, but he got his way: Carthage was totally destroyed. Rome now ruled both Italy and the western Mediterranean. The map on page 110 shows the land Rome controlled after the Punic Wars.

LESSON *1* REVIEW

THINK AND WRITE

A. What was the connection between the story of Aeneas and the Trojan War?

B. Why did the Romans overthrow rule by kings?

C. Why wasn't the Roman Republic a government by all of the people?

D. What can we learn from the legend of Horatius at the bridge?

E. What was the outcome of each of the three Punic Wars?

SKILLS CHECK

WRITING SKILL

Write two paragraphs in which you compare and contrast a patrician and a plebeian.

The Empire

What characteristics do you think a country must have for it to be considered great?

province   **assassination**
civil war   **emperor**

What was the difference between the city-state republic and the empire?

A. Julius Caesar and the Roman Empire

Julius Caesar (SEE zur) was ambitious; he had a strong desire for power and glory. He was 32 years old in 68 B.C. when he became quaestor (KWES tur), the first step up the political ladder in Rome.

By the time Caesar was 41, he became consul, one of the two top officials in the republic. After a one-year term, Caesar became governor of the **province** of Gaul, a region ruled by Rome. A province is a division of a country. Gaul consisted of northern Italy and part of southern France.

Rising politicians sought to become governors of provinces because they had command of armed forces. An army enabled an ambitious politician to win both glory and wealth. The glory came from conquering new lands for Rome; the wealth came from looting the conquered.

Caesar spent nine years as governor of Gaul. He enlarged the province by conquering all of what is now France along with Belgium and Switzerland. Caesar crossed to Britain twice, but he did not add the islands to the empire.

B. Caesar—Dictator for Life

Dangerous Politics When Caesar finished his years in Gaul, his political rivals got the Senate to order him to disband his army. He refused to do so. He knew that if he had no army, he would be defenseless against his enemies. Politics had become very dangerous in Rome. Riots and killings were all too common.

The old republic had been formed when Rome was a small city-state. It was not suited to govern a far-flung empire. Yet the Romans still kept their old government, with its assembly, Senate, and officials chosen for one-year terms. Elections were often decided by bribes and threats by gangs of thugs. Caesar refused to return to Rome unarmed.

Julius Caesar was a talented, strong leader who had ambitious goals.
▶ How did Caesar enlarge the Roman Empire?

Many Romans believed Caesar ruled wisely, but some feared his power. This painting depicts the assassination of Caesar.
▶ Do you think this painting is accurate?

As Caesar led his army to Rome, his enemies, led by Pompey, fled to Greece. Pompey and Caesar had once been political partners, but they were now on opposite sides in a **civil war**, that is, a war between groups within the same city or country. This conflict between two groups of Romans divided families. Brother sometimes fought against brother.

Caesar as Dictator After making sure that he controlled Italy, Caesar led his army to Greece. In a bloody battle on August 9, 48 B.C., Caesar's troops defeated the forces that backed Pompey. Caesar went on to overcome his opponents throughout the empire. In 44 B.C. the Romans made Caesar dictator for life. They hoped that a strong leader would bring peace to Rome. One month of the year was renamed *July*, "the month of Julius," in his honor. Many people probably thought rule by a dictator was better than civil war.

Caesar had plans for a number of reforms, but he had time to carry out only a few of them. One was an improved calendar much like the one we still use. The three regular years have 365 days, but the fourth year, called a leap year, has 366.

Death of Caesar Meanwhile, Caesar's enemies whispered to others that the dictator intended to become king. They reminded the Romans that their ancestors had long ago driven a king from Rome and created the republic. Anyone wishing to become a king was an enemy. Patriotic Romans should kill a would-be king as readily as an enemy on the battlefield. On March 15, 44 B.C., the **assassination** of Caesar occurred when 60 of his enemies stabbed him to death in the Senate house. An assassination is murder by a secret or sudden attack. To learn more about the assassination of Caesar, read the literature selection on the next page.

FROM:

Julius Caesar

By: William Shakespeare
Setting: Roman Senate

The English writer William Shakespeare is one of the greatest playwrights of all time. In 1599, William Shakespeare wrote a play called *Julius Caesar*. The play takes place in ancient Rome and describes events before and after the assassination of Caesar. Brutus, a Roman general who was a friend of Caesar's, is one of the men who plots Caesar's murder. Brutus and his group of conspirators stab Caesar to death as he enters the Roman Senate.

Although Brutus believes that Caesar's death is necessary to ensure the safety of Rome, he is torn between his friendship for Caesar and his sense of duty. In this literature selection, Brutus explains to the Roman Senate why he betrayed Caesar.

Romans, countrymen, and lovers! hear me for my cause, and be silent, that you may hear: believe me for mine honour, and have respect to mine honour, that you may believe: censure [condemn] me in your wisdom, and awake your senses, that you may better judge. If there be any in this assembly, any dear friend of Caesar's, to him I say, that Brutus' love to Caesar was no less than his. If then that friend demand why Brutus rose against Caesar, this is my answer:—Not that I loved Caesar less, but that I loved Rome more. Had you

rather Caesar were living and die all slaves, than that Caesar were dead, to live all free men? As Caesar loved me, I weep for him; as he was fortunate, I rejoice at it; as he was valiant [brave], I honour him: but, as he was ambitious, I slew [killed] him. There is tears for his love; joy for his fortune; honour for his valour; and death for his ambition. Who is here so base that would be a bondman [slave]? If any, speak; for him have I offended. Who is here so rude that would not be a Roman? If any, speak; for him have I offended. Who is here so vile that will not love his country? If any, speak; for him have I offended. I pause for a reply.

C. Rome and the Emperor Augustus

Octavian Apollonia (ap uh LOH nee uh) was a Greek city on the coast of what is now Albania. It was a port and a sort of university town. Among the students there in 44 B.C. was Octavian (ahk TAY vee un), the 18-year-old grandnephew of Caesar.

When news of Caesar's death reached Apollonia, Octavian's friends urged him to flee to northern Greece and seek protection from troops loyal to Caesar. Octavian was not only Caesar's grandnephew but also his adopted son and heir. An heir is a person who is entitled to inherit property or to succeed to an office. Caesar's friends feared that those who had killed Caesar would also kill his heir.

Octavian did not take his friends' advice. Instead he returned to Rome and plunged into the struggle for power. The peace that Caesar had established was broken by another civil war. Some politicians supported Octavian because they thought he was "a mere boy" whom they could either control or set aside. However, they were quite wrong. Octavian proved to be the most able leader in the dangerous struggle, and by the year 31 B.C. he alone controlled Rome.

Ruling Rome Octavian avoided the title of king, but he was in fact a monarch. He spoke of his position as princeps, which meant "first citizen." Octavian was also the first Roman ruler to be called **emperor**, a Roman title meaning "commander." An emperor is the supreme ruler of an empire. Octavian did not do away with the old Senate, but he made sure that he controlled it. The Senate named him *Augustus*, that is, "honored." It is as the Emperor Augustus that Octavian is known in history. That name survives on our calendar along

Emperor Augustus brought order to Rome and made many improvements there for which he is remembered.
▶ What do we use today that his name appears on?

with that of Julius Caesar. The Romans named the eighth month of the year *August*, "the month of Augustus."

Emperor Augustus ruled the Roman Empire for over 40 years. Within the empire it was a time of peace. People, no doubt, welcomed peace after the civil wars. Some of the great Roman writers praised Augustus. Virgil was one of them. Virgil wrote the poem the *Aeneid* at the emperor's request.

Augustus' Accomplishments Augustus made Rome a grander city. He built large public buildings and erected monuments. Toward the end of his life, he proudly declared that he had found Rome a city of brick and had left it a city of marble.

Augustus improved the government of the provinces. Officials treated people under Rome's rule more fairly. But Augustus did not make any of his reforms quickly. His favorite saying was, "Make haste slowly." How can you say that in a different way?

D. A "New Rome" in the East

Emperors Rule Rome remained a monarchy after the death of Augustus in A.D. 14. For the next four centuries, emperors ruled the empire. Some ruled well; some ruled badly. The Romans never found a way to make sure that only able and just men became monarchs. In fact, some seemingly good men became bad rulers once they secured power.

The emperors ruled a great variety of peoples and lands. The map below shows the Roman Empire when it was at its largest. As you can see from the map, Rome ruled all of the lands surrounding the Mediterranean Sea.

Constantine Emperor Constantine ruled from A.D. 306 to 337. He built a new capital in the eastern part of the empire, which had the largest population. Constantine located the "New Rome" on the site of an

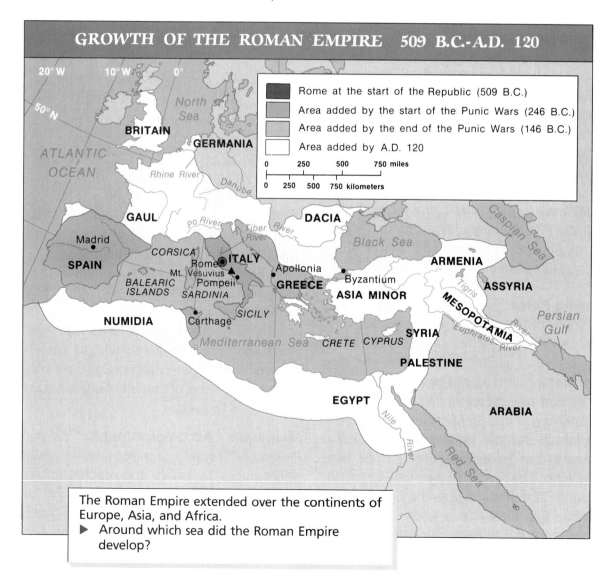

GROWTH OF THE ROMAN EMPIRE 509 B.C.-A.D. 120

Rome at the start of the Republic (509 B.C.)
Area added by the start of the Punic Wars (246 B.C.)
Area added by the end of the Punic Wars (146 B.C.)
Area added by A.D. 120

The Roman Empire extended over the continents of Europe, Asia, and Africa.
▶ Around which sea did the Roman Empire develop?

Constantine built the Hagia Sophia as a Christian church, but since 1935 it has been a museum.
▶ Where is the Hagia Sophia?

ancient Greek city called Byzantium (buh-ZAN shee um). The new city was called Constantinople (kahn stan tuh NOH pul) —"the city of Constantine." Today it is known as Istanbul.

Constantine erected fine palaces and public buildings in the new capital. He had statues and monuments moved from the old Rome to the new. Unlike old Rome, there were no temples honoring the old Roman gods in the new capital. Constantine had adopted the Christian religion; he was the first Roman emperor to do so. Constantine also built a large Christian church called Hagia Sophia, which means "Church of Holy Wisdom."

Byzantine Empire In time the Roman Empire broke apart. The emperors at Constantinople ruled less and less of what had been the empire. Finally all that was left of the empire was the city of Constantinople and a part of Greece. Historians call the empire of later times the Byzantine Empire. The name comes from the original Greek city on the Bosporus strait. The Byzantine Empire grew out of the old Roman Empire, but it existed for about a thousand years after the fall of the Roman Empire in western Europe.

LESSON **2** *REVIEW*

THINK AND WRITE

A. What positions in the Roman government did Caesar hold?
B. How did Caesar become dictator?
C. What position did Octavian come to hold?
D. What was the advantage of the site Constantine chose for the new capital?

SKILLS CHECK

MAP SKILL

Using the map on page 110, name the areas Rome had added to its empire by the end of the Punic Wars.

Life in a Roman City

Imagine that you are an archaeologist digging up ruins of an ancient Roman city. What remains of the city might you expect to find?

volcano   **gladiator**
aqueduct

What can we learn from the ruins of Pompeii?

A. The Day the Mountain Erupted

Pliny the Elder, friend of the emperor, commanded the Roman fleet. From his house on the Bay of Naples, he could look across the water toward Mount Vesuvius (vuh SOO vee us). Shortly after lunch on an August day in A.D. 79, Pliny's sister drew his attention to a strange cloud rising from Mount Vesuvius. His nephew, known as Pliny the Younger, wrote that the cloud looked "like an umbrella pine tree," with a trunk rising high in the sky and then spreading out like branches. What they were seeing was the eruption of a **volcano**, which is an opening in the earth from which melted rock, stone, and ashes are thrown out.

Pliny the Elder had a great curiosity about things in nature, so he decided he wanted to take a closer look. He ordered that a small boat be made ready so that he could sail closer to the mountain. Just as he was preparing to leave, he received a message that people living on the lower slopes of the mountain were trapped and had no way to escape except by sea. Pliny ordered a ship so that he might rescue those fleeing from the volcano.

Pliny's ship reached the shore where the people waited, but he could not sail away because the wind was blowing in the wrong direction. To reassure people, Pliny went to a nearby house where he calmly ate supper and then lay down to sleep. During the night the fall of ashes became so heavy that it was feared the house might fall in. Pliny told people it would be better to wait in the open. He advised them to tie pillows on their heads to protect them from falling stones and heavy ashes. Pliny himself lay down on the beach, where he was later found dead. He was not buried in ashes nor hit by a falling rock. Pliny the Younger thought that his uncle had been killed by gas from the volcano. Modern writers think it more likely that he died of a heart attack.

In this photograph you can see the ruins of Pompeii after Mount Vesuvius, shown in the background on the left, erupted in the year A.D. 79. The mosaic (inset) shows a painting that once decorated a wall in a Pompeian home.
▶ What can you tell about Pompeii from these ruins?

B. A City Beneath Ashes

The ashes and rocks thrown up by Vesuvius on that August day buried the city of Pompeii (pahm PAY ee). A layer from 19 to 20 feet (6 to 7 m) deep covered what had been a city of 20,000 people. Most Pompeians had fled in time, but some had not. Their bodies lay beneath the ashes.

Little was done after the eruption to uncover Pompeii. Not until 1748 did treasure hunters dig tunnels into the mound. They were seeking marble statues and other objects for wealthy buyers. Archaeologists did not begin excavating until after 1860. Since then, a large part of the city has been uncovered.

The disaster that destroyed the living city preserved the ruins of homes, baths, temples, and shops. These ruins tell a great deal about how people lived in a Roman city more than 19 centuries ago.

C. Old Ruins and Public Baths

Crowded Living Few things are as interesting to visitors to Pompeii as the ruins of houses and public baths. Pompeii had no large apartment buildings such as those in Rome, yet people had to live close together within this walled city. Houses were crowded along narrow streets that were not much wider than broad sidewalks.

Shopkeepers and their families usually lived in a room or two at the back of their shops. The houses of wealthier people had more rooms, but they, too, lived close to their neighbors. Houses did not have windows on the outside walls. Pictures of outdoor scenes were painted on the walls to make them seem larger. Rooms opened on an inner courtyard, which was only partly covered by a roof. Some of the largest homes had enclosed gardens with rooms along the sides.

City Water Some of the homes had running water. Other people could get water from flowing fountains in the streets. A water channel such as an **aqueduct**, or a stone canal, brought water to the city from a stream about 15 miles (24 km) outside the walls. Lead pipes under the street carried water to the houses and fountains.

Roman Baths The baths in a Roman city were more than places to wash up. A bath was somewhat like an athletic or health club where people met and exercised. They could relax in the steam room, take warm and hot baths, and then refresh themselves with a plunge in a cold bath.

Roman baths were where people went to socialize. Signs such as the one here advertised the baths.
▶ What purpose did the holes in the ceiling and the wall serve?

D. Making a Living in Pompeii

Farms A number of well-to-do families who lived in Pompeii owned land outside the city. They did not work on the land themselves, but they depended on their estates for their living. Farmers living in villages outside the city of Pompeii actually cared for the owner's vineyards and olive groves. Slaves also did much of the work on the land. The Romans, like the Greeks, had slaves.

Markets Farmers brought fresh fruits and vegetables to the city and sold them in the open marketplace. People who fished for a living also brought their fresh catch to the market.

Many Pompeians kept shops along the streets of the crowded city. Among other things, they sold olive oil, wine, leather goods, perfume, meat, and a fish sauce that most people liked.

Bakeries Much of the bread to supply the 20,000 inhabitants of Pompeii came from establishments which combined milling and baking. Pompeii had at least 40 bakery shops. Wheat and barley were brought directly to the bakery, where the grain was ground into flour. The large stone wheels in the bakery mills were turned by donkeys or slaves. Bakers made the flour into loaves and baked them. The bakery shops turned out at least ten different kinds of bread, not counting dog biscuits.

Making Cloth Pompeii's largest industry was making cloth. Country people spun and wove wool into rough cloth that they brought to the cloth finishing shops in the city. There workers bleached the cloth, that is, made it lighter. Then they would dye it. Judging by the size of the cloth finishers' hall, Pompeii must have had a number of people employed in this business.

E. Roman Entertainment

The largest place of amusement in Pompeii was the amphitheater. An overhead awning provided shade for at least part of the audience. People could see plays at the theater or watch variety shows with clowns, jugglers, and acrobats. People enjoyed stage shows, but they did not consider acting a respectable occupation.

The amphitheater at Pompeii could hold almost the entire population. The fact that it was so large suggests that Pompeians liked the cruel, bloody sports that took place there. Most people in the Roman world did.

The amphitheater was a place for fights between wild animals. For example, bears were forced into fighting tigers. Lions were matched against wild bulls. The animals usually fought until one had killed the other.

Gladiators also fought in the amphitheater. Gladiators were usually slaves or condemned criminals who were trained to fight with swords and other weapons to entertain the crowds. Gladiators sometimes fought wild animals; sometimes they fought each other. The fight in the arena

Gladiators fought wild beasts to amuse the crowds.
▶ What weapons did the gladiator use to defend himself?

gave the gladiators a chance to escape their fate. A skillful gladiator might win his freedom by defeating his opponent. However, the loser all too often lost his life. Such sports were one of the least attractive parts of life in a Roman city.

LESSON 3 REVIEW

THINK AND WRITE

A. From what danger was Pliny the Elder trying to rescue people?
B. Why have ruins of Pompeii been so well preserved?
C. Describe a house and a public bath in Pompeii.
D. What are some ways that people in Pompeii made a living?

E. What were some of the entertainments in Pompeii?

SKILLS CHECK

THINKING SKILL

Find *Mount Vesuvius* in the Gazetteer. What makes this volcano unique to Europe's mainland?

The Beginning of Christianity

THINK ABOUT WHAT YOU KNOW
Name ways in which we get some information from the past.

STUDY THE VOCABULARY
historical source   **parable**

FOCUS YOUR READING
How did Christianity in the Roman Empire change over the course of time?

A. Pliny the Younger and the Christians

Pliny the Younger was 17 when his uncle died on the beach near Vesuvius. He inherited his uncle's property and, following his example, became a Roman official.

Pliny the Younger wrote many letters that have been published. These letters are valuable **historical sources**. Historical sources are writings that provide information about the past.

In A.D. 110 the emperor sent Pliny to a province on the south shore of the Black Sea. This region is now part of Turkey. Pliny wrote a number of letters to the emperor, describing conditions in the province. In one letter, Pliny tells how he dealt with persons who were accused of being Christians. Christianity was one of the few religions that was against the law in the empire. The Romans allowed people to worship a wide variety of gods and goddesses so long as they also worshiped the

official gods of Rome. They considered that praying to the official gods showed loyalty to Rome. Since the Christians refused to worship the Roman gods, the emperors considered them dangerous.

Pliny wrote that when he questioned people charged with being Christians, he gave them three chances to deny it. If they did, he made them prove their loyalty by praying to the Roman gods. Pliny knew that no real Christian would do so.

The emperor replied that Pliny was doing the right thing. People had to be given a chance to prove that they were not Christians. Of course, if they refused, they had to be punished.

B. Writings About Jesus

The Christians, who were brought before Roman officials like Pliny, were followers of Jesus. Jesus had lived in the land of the Jews, which was part of the Roman Empire. Jesus wrote no books. What historians know about him comes mostly from

The Sermon on the Mount is one of the most famous speeches of Jesus.
► How do we learn about the life and teachings of Jesus?

The Granger Collection

The Granger Collection

Many of the teachings of Jesus were in the form of parables.
▶ How did the Good Samaritan help the man left to die?

the writings of his followers. The most important sources about his life and teachings are four books that Christians call the Gospels. The Gospels are included in the Christian New Testament, a part of the Christian Bible.

According to the Gospels, Jesus did not teach in a school. Jesus talked to people wherever he found them. The Gospels tell of his teaching people on a mountainside and on the shore of a lake. Jesus often spoke of the Jewish laws and prophets in his teachings. All of his early followers were Jews. Jesus often explained his teachings by telling stories called **parables**. A parable is the teaching of Jesus in story form. One of the best-known parables, printed on this page, is the story of the Good Samaritan.

A man fell victim to robbers as he went down from Jerusalem to Jericho. They stripped and beat him and went off leaving him half-dead. A priest happened to be going down that road, but when he saw him, he passed by on the opposite side.

Likewise a Levite came to the place, and when he saw him, he passed by on the opposite side. But a Samaritan traveler who came upon him was moved with compassion at the sight. He approached the victim, poured oil and wine over his wounds and bandaged them. Then he lifted him up on his own animal, took him to an inn and cared for him. The next day he took out silver coins and gave them to the innkeeper with the instruction, "Take care of him. If you spend more than what I have given you, I shall repay you on my way back."

117

Jesus spoke to his followers about the "kingdom of Heaven." Some people took this to mean that he planned to overthrow the Romans and set up a government. These people had Jesus brought before Pontius Pilate, the Roman official at Jerusalem. Jesus was tried, condemned, and put to death by being nailed to a cross. The followers of Jesus believe that he rose from the dead three days later.

C. Paul of Tarsus

A man named Paul was one of the most important early Christian leaders. Paul was a Jew from Tarsus, a city which is located in present-day Turkey. Paul left his home to go to Jerusalem to study the Jewish law.

Paul at first strongly opposed the Christians, but he had a complete change of heart. Paul of Tarsus became a Christian and traveled from city to city to spread the Christian religion. Paul went to Athens, Greece, a city where people liked to hear about new things. The book of Acts in the New Testament of the Christian Bible contains an account of what Paul said to the Athenians.

Paul kept in touch with Christians in different cities by writing letters. These

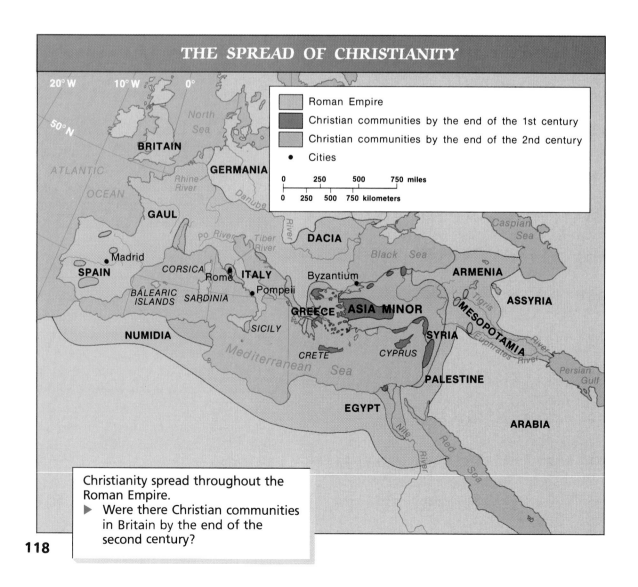

THE SPREAD OF CHRISTIANITY

Roman Empire
Christian communities by the end of the 1st century
Christian communities by the end of the 2nd century
• Cities

Christianity spread throughout the Roman Empire.
▶ Were there Christian communities in Britain by the end of the second century?

letters, called epistles, are also a part of the New Testament. They are among the sources that historians use in tracing the history of Christianity.

D. The Official Religion of the Empire

Roman laws against the Christians did not keep their religion from spreading within the empire. As you have read, Emperor Constantine became a Christian ca. 312. What caused Constantine to accept the Christian religion? The emperor himself gave a reason to the Roman historian Eusebius (yoo SEE bee us).

According to Constantine's account, in the year 312 he was preparing for a battle in which his troops were greatly outnumbered. Before the battle, Constantine believed that he had a vision in which he saw a flaming cross against the sun and a message written across the sky that said, "By this sign you will conquer." Constantine's army won the battle and, in gratitude, Constantine proclaimed religious freedom throughout the Roman Empire.

Constantine did not try to do away with all other religions, but he did give Christianity a favored place in the new capital at Constantinople. However, he did

The Granger Collection

Constantine was the first Roman emperor to convert to Christianity.
▶ What event does this painting depict?

not permit the erection of temples to the old gods. Later, ca. 392, Emperor Theodosius the Great made Christianity the official religion of the empire.

LESSON **4** REVIEW

THINK AND WRITE

A. How could people brought before Pliny prove that they were not Christians?

B. What source do historians have for the life and teachings of Jesus?

C. How did Paul of Tarsus spread Christianity?

D. How did the position of Christians change between the times of Constantine and Theodosius?

SKILLS CHECK

THINKING SKILL

You have read the parable about the Good Samaritan. What do you think Jesus was trying to teach in this parable?

Roman Achievements

Imagine that your city or town has no written laws. How would this affect the way you live?

ex post facto law   **Romance language**

What were some of the achievements of the Romans, and how do they influence our lives today?

A. A Need to Write Laws Down

In the days when Rome was a small city-state, a quarrel broke out between the patricians and the plebeians. It was a quarrel about laws. Rome at this time had no written laws. When a dispute arose between people, the law was whatever the judge said it was. Since only patricians could be judges, the plebeians complained that they were not treated fairly.

The quarrel between patricians and plebeians grew so bitter that it threatened to destroy the republic. To keep this from happening, ten leading men were chosen in 451 B.C. to collect and write down the laws. After working a year, the ten men called the citizens together and showed them ten wooden tables, or tablets, on which they had written laws. The people were partly satisfied with the ten tables, but it was pointed out that they were not complete. Some laws had not been included. Two more tables were drawn up, making twelve in all.

Some laws of the Twelve Tables, such as one declaring that a patrician could not marry a plebeian, seem unfair to us today. But the Twelve Tables were only the beginning of Roman law. The Romans in later times created different and fairer laws.

B. Just Laws for an Empire

The Twelve Tables could not serve as the laws for Rome's large empire. The empire included so many different peoples, each with their own laws and customs. To govern these different groups, the Romans had to develop a system of laws that all of the groups would accept.

Some Roman philosophers observed that all peoples wanted laws to do the

Quarrels often arose between the patricians and plebeians, the two classes of Romans, about the fairness of their laws.
▶ What did the Romans do to make the laws clear?

same thing—provide justice. But what is justice? The philosophers said that justice is giving each person what he or she deserves. How can we know what each person deserves when people come from so many different groups? The philosophers pointed out that although people differed, they all had reason and the ability to think. A just law would be one that seemed reasonable to thinking people, whatever their group. For example, it would seem reasonable that people accused of a crime should have a chance to face their accusers and defend themselves.

Some Roman laws that are based on reason have lasted longer than their empire. The Constitution of the United States contains this rule: "No **ex post facto law** shall be passed." The Latin words *ex post facto* mean that no law can be used to punish a person for something done before the law was made. This rule seemed reasonable to both the ancient Romans and the Americans who wrote the Constitution. It still seems reasonable today.

C. The Roman Alphabet

Good ideas get passed around, and an alphabet is a good idea. Each letter of an alphabet stands for one of the sounds from which words are formed. It is far easier to learn an alphabet than to memorize the hundreds of signs used in either cuneiform or ancient Egyptian writing.

The Romans borrowed the idea of an alphabet from their Italian neighbors, the Etruscans (ee TRUS kunz). But the Etruscans had not invented the alphabet; they borrowed it from the Greeks. The Greeks in turn had borrowed the alphabet from the Phoenicians.

The Phoenicians were the ones who had established Hannibal's city of Carthage,

DEVELOPMENT OF THE ROMAN ALPHABET			
Phoenician	Greek	Etruscan	Roman
↊	A	A	A
ꓱ	B		B
⅂	Γ	>	C
◁	△		D
ⴻ	E	Ǝ	E

This chart shows how each civilization that borrowed this alphabet changed it.
▶ Which letters of the Greek alphabet did the Romans change?

in North Africa. Their homeland was the land now called Lebanon, but they traded throughout the Mediterranean. It was from Phoenician traders that the Greeks learned the advantage of writing with an alphabet. The chart on this page shows the different ways in which the Phoenicians, Greeks, Etruscans, and Romans wrote *A B C D E*. Notice that the Etruscans did not have letters for *B* and *D*.

In time the Roman alphabet was used to write other languages. Today the languages of western Europe are written in the Roman alphabet. The words you are reading on this page are printed in that alphabet. It is the most widely used alphabet in the world.

D. The Language of the Romans

The alphabet was not the only thing western Europeans borrowed from the Romans. A number of them also borrowed the Latin language. As with the alphabet, the borrowers changed what they had borrowed. Spanish, Portuguese, French, Italian, and Romanian are different languages, but they all grew out of Latin. They are called **Romance languages** because they developed from the Roman tongue. Note that two of the Romance languages are the main languages of Central and South America. For that reason, those regions are known as Latin America.

English is not a Romance language, but it includes many words that come from Latin. For example, the following words used for parts of this book come from Latin words: *table*, *contents*, *unit*, *index*.

E. The Romans as Builders

Roads and Bridges The Romans were practical people. Their engineers did their best work when building useful structures, such as roads, bridges, and aqueducts. One of the oldest structures in Rome is the Cloaca Maxima, the great sewer. It was built more than 2,500 years ago, and it still drains into the Tiber River.

Roman road builders knit the empire together with more than 2,500 miles (4,023 km) of roads. Many were simply dirt or graveled roads, but important highways were paved with flat stones. Engineers built beautiful arched stone bridges across streams and deep valleys. In some places, they tunneled through mountains.

The network of roads made it possible for the Romans to move armies quickly throughout the empire. Officials could

The Granger Collection

The Pont du Gard is a Roman aqueduct in southern France.
▶ What purpose did aqueducts serve for the Romans?

travel or send messages from one part of the empire to another. The fastest travelers went on horseback or in light carriages and could cover from 40 to 50 miles (64 to 80 km) a day. That seems slow now, but it was fast for that time. People did not travel faster overland until the invention of the steam locomotive centuries later.

Roman Buildings Aqueducts, such as that at Pompeii, carried water great distances from springs and streams to cities. In some places, aqueducts ran through tunnels. In others they were supported by stone bridges, as shown on page 122.

The Romans were master builders in concrete. The great dome on the Pantheon shows their skill. It rises 71 feet (22 m) from its base and is 142 feet (43 m) across. It has stood for nearly 19 centuries. The Pantheon is used as a model for modern buildings constructed today.

The Colosseum (kahl uh SEE um) was a huge stadium that covered 6 acres (2 ha) of land and could seat about 45,000 spectators. The Romans used the Colosseum as the site of mock naval battles, fights between gladiators, struggles between men and wild animals, and other forms of public entertainment. Ruins of the Colosseum still stand in Rome today.

The Pantheon, built ca. 126, served as a temple to the Roman gods.
▶ What building in the United States has a shape similar to that of the Pantheon?

LESSON **5** REVIEW

THINK AND WRITE

A. Why did the plebeians want written laws?
B. According to Roman philosophers, what kind of laws would different peoples accept?
C. What different alphabets led to the one used in printing this book?
D. Which languages are Romance languages?

E. What are some types of structures built by the Romans?

SKILLS CHECK

WRITING SKILL

Choose one of the Roman achievements mentioned in this lesson. Write a paragraph or two describing what your life would be like without that achievement.

USING THE VOCABULARY

republic	civil war
patrician	aqueducts
Senate	gladiators
dictator	historical source
emperor	ex post facto

On a separate sheet of paper, write the word or words from above that best complete the sentences.

1. A person who takes complete charge of a government is called a _____ .
2. Octavian was the supreme ruler, or _____ , of the entire Roman Empire.
3. Writings that provide information about the past are called _____ .
4. Roman landowners who had the most power, property, and money were called the _____ class.
5. Rome changed its form of government from a monarchy to a _____ , in which people elect representatives to rule.
6. The Latin words _____ mean that no law can be used to punish a person for something done before the law was made.
7. Fighting between groups within the same city or country is called a _____ .
8. Roman professional fighters, called _____ , fought one another at public games.
9. Water was brought to the city through _____ , or stone canals.
10. The wealthy kept their voice in government by serving in the _____ .

REMEMBERING WHAT YOU READ

On a separate sheet of paper, answer the following questions in complete sentences.

1. The male citizens of Rome were divided into what two classes?
2. What two armies battled during the Punic Wars?
3. Why was Caesar assassinated?
4. What name did the Roman Senate give to Octavian?
5. Who was the first Roman emperor to adopt Christianity?
6. How did the people make a living in Pompeii?
7. Name some types of Roman entertainment.
8. From what writings have Christians learned about Jesus?
9. Name three Romance languages.
10. What types of structures did the Romans build?

TYING MATH TO SOCIAL STUDIES

The Romans used letters to represent numbers. These are the Roman numerals and their values:

I = 1	L = 50	M = 1,000
V = 5	C = 100	
X = 10	D = 500	

Write the numerical value for the following: XXX, XII, MMCCLV, LXV. Write Roman numerals for the following: 35, 58, 221, 553.

THINKING CRITICALLY

On a separate sheet of paper, answer the following questions in complete sentences.

1. The eruption of Mount Vesuvius destroyed Pompeii. What other natural occurrences can cause such destruction?
2. How was the government of ancient Rome like our government?
3. Compare the Romans' public games at the Colosseum with a modern-day sporting event.
4. What kind of a leader do you think Julius Caesar was?
5. What do you consider to be the greatest accomplishment of the ancient Romans?

SUMMARIZING THE CHAPTER

Copy this graphic organizer on a separate sheet of paper.
Beside the five questions, fill in each blank with an answer.

CHAPTER THEME	The influences of Roman government, law, religion, language, and architecture are still apparent throughout Western civilization.

LESSON 1	What were some characteristics of the Roman Republic?	1. _____ 2. _____ 3. _____
LESSON 2	What were some characteristics of the Roman Empire?	1. _____ 2. _____ 3. _____
LESSON 3	What can we learn from the ruins of Pompeii?	1. _____ 2. _____ 3. _____
LESSON 4	How did Christianity in the Roman Empire change over the course of time?	1. _____ 2. _____ 3. _____
LESSON 5	What were some of the achievements of the Romans?	1. _____ 2. _____ 3. _____

CHAPTER 4

Ancient India and China

The ancient civilizations of India and China have dominated Asia for thousands of years. Their cultures thrived with powerful rulers, kingdoms, and religious beliefs.

Cities on the Indus River

THINK ABOUT WHAT YOU KNOW

Why do you think a group of people would choose to develop a civilization near water?

STUDY THE VOCABULARY

subcontinent   nomad

FOCUS YOUR READING

How have we learned about the history of the South Asian subcontinent?

A. Cities the World Forgot

Could a book prevent war? An English writer, H. G. Wells, thought so. Wells believed that wars began because of the ways people think. He also believed that the ways people think depend on the kind of history they have learned. Wells noted that in 1919 most people knew little history except that of their own country. Wells thought that people needed to have a new kind of history. He set to work to write a book that would "tell truly and clearly the whole story of mankind so far as it is known."

Wells turned out a volume of about half a million words, which he called *The Outline of History*. He wrote of early civilizations in Mesopotamia, Egypt, Greece, Rome, and China. But his account of civilization along the Indus River in the country now called Pakistan consisted of only three short paragraphs.

Wells failed to mention the Indus cities because he could write history only "so far as it is known." In 1919, historians knew nothing of the Indus cities. Their history lay hidden beneath mounds on the plain of the Indus River.

It is true that British railroad builders had dug into one mound some years earlier. But they were not searching for an ancient city. They only wanted crumbling bricks and rubble on which to lay railroad tracks. Workers found a few carved stones, but no one had any idea that what they had dug into was the ruins of the ancient city Harappa (huh RAP uh).

B. Archaeologists Uncover Lost Cities

Shortly after Wells wrote *The Outline of History*, archaeologists started digging into a mound known as Mohenjo-Daro (moh hen joh DAHR oh). This name means "hill of the dead," but we have no idea what the place was called by the people who lived there 4,000 years ago.

The archaeologists discovered that the "hill of the dead" covered what must have been a city that existed from ca. 2300 B.C. to 1750 B.C. Archaeologists also discovered that Harappa, where the railroad builders had dug for rubble, had been a city of perhaps as many as 35,000 people ca. 2300 B.C.

Both Harappa and Mohenjo-Daro stood on river plains frequently covered by floods. Both cities had been erected on built-up platforms of earth and brick so as to be above the floods.

Since the 1920s, archaeologists have discovered the remains of a number of ancient towns and villages in Pakistan and parts of western India. These countries are located on the large peninsula that extends from southern Asia into the Indian Ocean. The peninsula is so large that it is called the South Asian **subcontinent**. It is called a subcontinent because although it is a large landmass, it is still smaller than a continent.

C. Ruins Tell a Story

A City Plan Many ancient cities grew haphazardly, that is, without any plan. But the ruins of Mohenjo-Daro tell a different story. The main streets were laid out in straight lines, forming a grid. People lived in brick houses that were much alike. Each had a bathroom with a drain in the floor. The drains connected with sewers that ran along the streets. It seems clear that someone planned and directed the building of this city. It could hardly have grown in such a regular pattern on its own.

Ancient Findings Various objects found by the archaeologists tell about games and toys of the Indus people. They had dice and stone marbles. The spots on the dice are arranged in exactly the same pattern that appears today. Among the toys there were a clay monkey that could be made to slide down a string and a clay bull that wiggled its head. A little clay cart must have looked much like a real one.

Jewelry from the ruins shows that the Indus people traded for goods from other lands. There are beads of turquoise, jade,

Artifacts discovered in the ruins of the ancient city of Harappa provided clues about the lives of the Indus people.
▶ What ancient artifacts are shown here?

and jasper. These stones are not found near the Indus plain, so the Indus people must have traded for the stones.

The ruins of the city give proof of what was grown on the land. The largest structures were granaries, buildings for storing grain. Traces of cotton fibers on a silver box show that the Indus people were the first to grow cotton.

D. Mysteries Still Remain

Religion The remains in the mounds have revealed much, yet mysteries remain. We know little about the religion of the Indus people. It is not clear what role religion played in the Indus civilization. However, a number of clay images have led historians to think that these people may have worshiped a mother goddess. The bodies of the dead were buried with their heads to the north. Was this related to their religious beliefs? We do not know.

Language The greatest unsolved mystery is the language that the Indus people spoke. Historians do not know what it was. If they knew, perhaps they could find out more about the Indus people, such as where they came from and what happened to them. It appears that they had some sort of writing. Archaeologists have found stone seals with a type of script carved on them, but no one knows how to read it. No one has found a Rosetta stone for the Indus script.

Historians are not sure what happened to the Indus cities. The cities seem to have been abandoned ca. 1700 B.C. It is possible that future discoveries will help to solve this mystery. Historians may someday be able to write much more about the Indus cities that H. G. Wells did not even know existed.

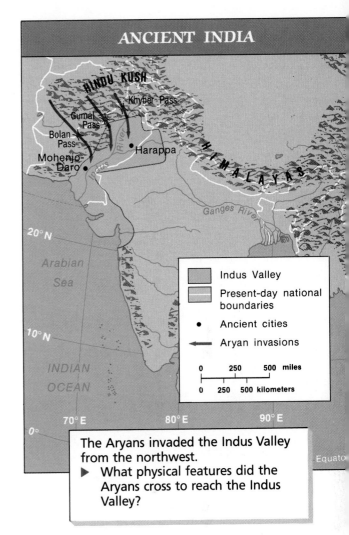

ANCIENT INDIA

Legend:
- Indus Valley
- Present-day national boundaries
- • Ancient cities
- ← Aryan invasions

0 250 500 miles
0 250 500 kilometers

The Aryans invaded the Indus Valley from the northwest.
▶ What physical features did the Aryans cross to reach the Indus Valley?

E. The Aryans on the Subcontinent

The subcontinent is set off from the rest of Asia by a mountain wall formed by the Hindu Kush and the Himalayas. Passes in the northwestern part of the Hindu Kush have served as gateways through which peoples have moved from time to time. It was through these gateways that the Aryans (ar EE unz) entered the subcontinent between 1500 B.C. and 1000 B.C.

The early Aryans were **nomads,** tribes of people who moved about with herds of goats, sheep, and cattle. Since

The warlike Aryans settled on the lands they conquered.
▶ What form of transportation did the Aryans use?

they built no cities, they left no ruins to tell their story to archaeologists. They had no written language, so they left no written sources for historians.

Most of what we know about the early Aryans comes from hymns and chants. These were not written down until much later. They were preserved in the memories of priests. In much later times the hymns were put into books called Vedas, a name that means "knowledge." The language of the Vedas is Sanskrit (SAN-skriht). Some modern languages spoken in India come from Sanskrit.

When the Aryans came through the mountain passes, they were a warlike people. They drove horse-drawn chariots into battle. The sight of galloping horses pulling armed warriors in chariots must have struck fear in the hearts of lightly armed foot soldiers.

After entering the subcontinent, the Aryans settled on the lands that they had conquered. In time, herders took up farming. Later many of the Aryans moved eastward into the plain of the Ganges River. The descendants of the Aryans became the rulers of many kingdoms in the subcontinent.

LESSON 1 REVIEW

THINK AND WRITE

A. In what ways could history that people have learned influence the ways they think?

B. How were the Indus cities protected from floods?

C. What facts did archaeologists learn from what they found in the ruins?

D. What mysteries about the Indus people remain?

E. How do we know about the early Aryans?

SKILLS CHECK

WRITING SKILL

Pretend you were one of the archaeologists who uncovered the ancient cities of Mohenjo-Daro and Harappa. Then imagine that H. G. Wells asked you to send him a report on your findings so he could continue his book *The Outline of History*. Write him a letter describing your discoveries.

Buddhism and Hinduism

If you were asked to name five things in your life that make you the happiest, what would they be?

STUDY THE VOCABULARY

ascetic   **caste**
Brahman

FOCUS YOUR READING

What were some teachings of the Buddha and of Hinduism?

A. The Suffering of a Prince

Siddhartha Gautama (sihd DAHR tuh GOUT uh muh) was the son of a king who ruled a land that included part of what is now India and Nepal. Many stories and legends have been told about Siddhartha. At the time of Siddhartha's birth, ca. 563 B.C., a priest said that Siddhartha would become either a great king or a great teacher of wisdom. If he remained in his father's palace, he would become a king. But if he learned of the suffering outside the palace and its gardens, he would become a teacher.

The king wished above all else that his son would become a great king. To keep him satisfied with life at the royal court, the king built his son several palaces. The king even tried to keep Siddhartha from seeing or hearing anything unpleasant. Gardeners even picked the flowers once they had bloomed so that the prince never saw a fading or dead blossom.

One day as he rode in his chariot, Siddhartha happened to see a weak old man. He asked his driver what had happened to the man. The driver replied,

"Such is life, he has grown old as everyone must." On another day, Siddhartha saw a man suffering from a painful illness. The prince asked his driver if others suffered from illness. Again the driver answered, "Such is life, many are ill." On a third day, Siddhartha saw the body of a dead man. When he asked if others died, the driver said, "Such is life, all must die."

B. Siddhartha's Search

Finding Contentment Prince Siddhartha thought much about what he had learned. He no longer found life within the palace rewarding. He wanted to find a

This statue of the Buddha stands in India. Buddha is the name Siddhartha's followers gave him.
▶ Of what is the statue made?

more satisfying way of life. As he was thinking, he saw an **ascetic**, a holy man who had given up all comforts and pleasures. The ascetic had no possessions, ate very little, and seemed not to notice pain. Perhaps, Siddhartha thought, this is the satisfying way of life. One night he slipped out of the palace and joined a group of ascetics living in forest caves. He adopted their way of life. He prayed, recited chants, and fasted, that is, ate very little food. He fasted so strictly that he nearly died. The other ascetics admired Siddhartha's spirit, but he was not yet content. He still had not found a satisfying way of life.

Siddhartha left the ascetics. One day he seated himself under a bo tree and vowed that he would not arise until he understood why he had failed to find a satisfying way of life. It was under the bo tree that Siddhartha received enlightenment, or understanding. He realized that in the palace and in the forest cave, he had been thinking only of himself. The way to a satisfying life is to forget yourself.

Buddha Other people came to learn from Siddhartha. He told them, "A man is not learned because he talks much; he who is patient, free from hatred and fear, is called learned." A wise person understands that "the fault of another is easily seen, but the fault of oneself is hard to see."

Siddhartha spent the rest of his long life teaching others what he had discovered. Those whom he taught called him the *Buddha,* which means "the enlightened one." His followers are called Buddhists.

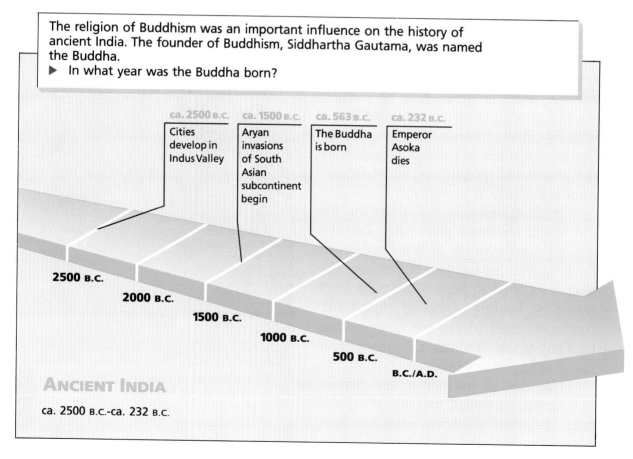

The religion of Buddhism was an important influence on the history of ancient India. The founder of Buddhism, Siddhartha Gautama, was named the Buddha.
▶ In what year was the Buddha born?

ca. 2500 B.C.	ca. 1500 B.C.	ca. 563 B.C.	ca. 232 B.C.
Cities develop in Indus Valley	Aryan invasions of South Asian subcontinent begin	The Buddha is born	Emperor Asoka dies

2500 B.C.

2000 B.C.

1500 B.C.

1000 B.C.

500 B.C.

B.C./A.D.

ANCIENT INDIA

ca. 2500 B.C.–ca. 232 B.C.

C. Asoka Spreads Buddhism

The Buddha chose to be a great teacher rather than a great king. But it was a ruler who did much to spread Buddhism in later times. Emperor Asoka (uh SOH-kuh) was the most powerful ruler on the subcontinent ca. 261 B.C. In his early years he was a warlike king who attacked and conquered a neighboring kingdom. But the death and suffering caused by the war greatly troubled Asoka. He declared that he would never again go to war.

Asoka turned to the teachings of the Buddha. He decided to relieve suffering rather than cause it. He had trees planted along roads to shade hot, weary travelers. Asoka ordered that wells be dug so that travelers could refresh themselves. He also built hospitals to care for people and for animals.

Asoka believed that his duty to his people came before everything else. He instructed his officials to keep him informed about the affairs of his people. If necessary, the officials were told to interrupt him if he was busy and awaken him if he was sleeping.

Asoka wished his people to learn of the Buddha's teachings. He built stone pillars with Buddhist teachings carved on them. Some of Asoka's pillars still stand. One pillar has the following message.

> *Father and mother must be listened to; the teacher must be respected by the pupil; and courtesy must be shown to friends, relatives, and servants.*

Asoka sent Buddhist teachers to other lands. Some went west to Alexandria in Egypt and perhaps to other Mediterranean lands. Asoka's son and daughter went to Sri Lanka, the island off the southern tip of the subcontinent. According to a

Asoka built stone pillars and had Buddhist teachings carved on them.
► What is carved on top of Asoka's pillar?

legend, they carried with them a root from the bo tree under which the Buddha had sat. They planted the tree in Sri Lanka, where some say it still grows.

D. A Religion of Many Beliefs

Hinduism Asoka did not intend that Buddhism replace other religions. Buddhism did not, in fact, become the religion of the subcontinent. The religion of most peoples in this land is called Hinduism.

Hinduism grew partly out of the religion of the early Aryans as it is described in the Vedas. The early Aryans believed in a number of gods. Like the Greeks, the Aryans thought that the gods and goddesses were like human beings except that they had greater powers and did not die.

Caste System The early Aryans were divided into four social classes: priests, called **Brahmans**; warriors and rulers; farmers and merchants; and lowly workers. These classes have been called **castes**. A person's caste depended upon birth. Each caste had its special duties.

Hinduism accepts the worship of all gods and goddesses, although some of them are considered more important than others. Hinduism teaches respect for all living creatures. Many Hindus eat only

The Aryan god Indra is shown holding symbols of his power in his many hands.
▶ On what is Indra riding?

grain and vegetables because they believe it is wrong to kill animals.

Hinduism remains the religion of most people in India, which is the largest country on the subcontinent today. When people moved from India to other lands, they took the Hindu religion with them.

LESSON 2 REVIEW

THINK AND WRITE

A. Why did Siddhartha's father try to keep him from learning about suffering?
B. Why did Siddhartha decide that he had failed to find a satisfying way of life in either the palace or the forest cave?
C. How did Asoka teach others about Buddhism?
D. What are the beliefs of Hinduism?

SKILLS CHECK

THINKING SKILL

One of the Vedas compares the castes with parts of the body. For example, the Brahmans are the mouth, and the workers are the feet. How would you explain this comparison?

The Beginnings of Early Civilization in China

THINKING ABOUT WHAT YOU KNOW

Try to write a sentence using only symbols to stand for your words.

STUDY THE VOCABULARY

**dialect   Confucianism
Pinyin**

FOCUS YOUR READING

What does the early history of China tell about Chinese ideals, writing, and government?

A. Chinese Legends

Shen-nung The Chinese in ancient times told legends about the "Good Emperors" of still earlier times. The legends did not explain exactly what happened in those times, so they were not history. The legends sought to explain the development of Chinese ideals, or goals for ways to live.

According to the legends, the Good Emperors invented civilization—better ways of living—in China. Emperor Shen-nung taught people how to use hoes and plows to cultivate crops. He also showed them the advantage of trade. As told in an old Chinese history, he had the people gather together "so they could part with goods they did not want in order to obtain goods they needed." As a result, "everyone was better off."

Huang-ti A second Good Emperor, Huang-ti (hwahng dee), was much admired for his mind. It was said that he could speak when he was only 2 months old. By the time he was 15 years old, he had mastered every subject.

Huang-ti invented boats and taught people to harness horses and oxen. He showed his people how to make bows and arrows "so they would be feared by those who intended to harm them."

Yao The legends say that a third Good Emperor, Yao, was truly a good man. He lived simply, dressing in the same rough clothing used by his subjects. He ate only plain food from a clay spoon. Yao's reign set an example of ideal harmony, that is, people living together in peace and friendship. Harmony was an ideal much praised by the Chinese teachers of later times. The legends told that Yao first brought harmony to his family and then to his kingdom. Afterward he encouraged harmony among all peoples.

In this ivory carving, two of the Good Emperors discuss a book.
► According to legends, what did the Good Emperors invent?

When Yao grew old, he decided to find the best person in the kingdom to take his place. After much searching, he heard of Shun, who showed ideal loyalty to his family. Shun's family was by no means an ideal family. His father was wicked and unfair, his stepmother was stingy and mean, and his half-brother was spoiled, lazy, and nasty. The family was so bad that it tried to kill Shun so that the half-brother would get all the family's property.

One day while Shun was painting the top of the barn, his father set fire to the building. Shun jumped, using two wide-brimmed straw hats as a parachute, and landed safely. You might think that Shun would have had nothing to do with his wicked family after that. But according to the legend, he continued to be patient and act rightly, even toward those who had wronged him. Yao decided that Shun was just the man to rule the kingdom. Of course, this is only a legend. But although it does not give us history, it does tell us about ancient Chinese ideals.

B. Writing on Shells and Bones

Like the Greeks, the ancient Chinese believed in oracles. You have read that oracles were supposed to give messages from the gods. The Chinese wrote questions for

This illustrates the legend of Shun, who showed ideal loyalty to his family.
▶ What was Shun's parachute?

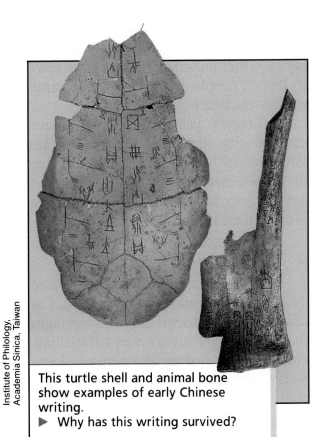

Institute of Philology,
Academia Sinica, Taiwan

This turtle shell and animal bone show examples of early Chinese writing.

▶ Why has this writing survived?

C. Chinese Writing

Early Pictographs The Chinese system of writing grew from the written characters scratched on the oracle shells and bones. Like cuneiform or Egyptian writing, the earliest Chinese characters were pictographs. The chart on this page shows the pictographs for *turtle*. As you can see, the earliest pictographs looked somewhat like a turtle. But the later ways of writing these characters changed so much that they no longer looked like pictures.

A character that stood for the name of one thing could be combined with other characters to form new words. Two characters for a tree meant "forest." The characters for dog and mouth meant "bark." The characters for the sun and moon together stood for "bright." Some characters stood for sounds rather than things.

the oracle on turtle shells and animal bones. Scratched on one shell was the question, "Should the king go to war this spring?" Another read, "Will Lady Hao be in good health after she has a baby?" There is one bone with the question "Will it rain tomorrow?" The shell or bone bearing a question was heated until it cracked. Priests then could supposedly tell the answer to the question by the way the shell or bone cracked.

Questions scratched on oracle shells and bones may not seem to be important sources of history, but they prove a significant fact. The Chinese had a written language as early as 1500 B.C. The oracle shells and bones are the oldest surviving Chinese writings. Archaeologists believe that the ancient Chinese probably also wrote on strips of wood and bamboo. But wood and bamboo rot, so such writings would have disappeared long ago.

DEVELOPMENT OF CHINESE WRITING

1 2 3 4

The earliest Chinese characters were pictographs.
▶ Which character most resembles a turtle?

Chinese Characters The many different kinds of characters made up the Chinese system of writing. To read and write, a person had to memorize a great many characters. Altogether there are nearly 50,000 characters, but most are rarely used today. However, a person must learn about 1,000 characters to read even simple material. Newspapers use between 2,000 and 3,000 characters. A dictionary for college students will have about 14,000 characters. In comparison, how many letters must you learn to read English?

Although the Chinese writing system is indeed hard to learn, it has had one advantage. People in different parts of China speak in different **dialects**, but they all use the same written characters. A dialect is a variety of the same language. Some people say *shan* for "mountain," while others say *si*. But all people can recognize the same written character.

In recent years the Chinese have made writing somewhat simpler. Characters can now be written in fewer lines, so they are easier to learn. The government has tried to have all Chinese speak the same national language.

D. Chinese Spelling

People writing in English have used different ways to spell Chinese names. The Chinese government now encourages them to use the **Pinyin** system of spelling. Pinyin is one system of writing Chinese words with our alphabet, the Roman alphabet. It is said that Pinyin shows quite accurately how the Chinese pronounce the words. For example, the Pinyin spelling for the name of one of China's great rivers is *Chang Jiang* (chahng jee AHNG). In the past it was usually spelled *Yangtze* (yang-SEE). The Pinyin spelling for the Hsi Chiang (see jee AHNG), another great river, is *Xi Jiang* (shee jee AHNG). *Huang He* (hwahng hih) is the Pinyin name for the Yellow River. It is called the Yellow River because its waters carry so much yellow soil.

Pinyin spelling is used in this book for most Chinese names. You will see as you use the book that whenever we have used the Pinyin term, we have often mentioned its older English spelling.

E. The Teachings of Confucius

The most famous person of ancient China was a man known by the name Confucius (kun FYOO shus). Confucius was a sage, a very wise man, whose greatest wish was to advise kings. He was born in

The writing on this wall shows some ancient Chinese characters, many of which are still used.

▶ Why do you think Chinese is a difficult language to learn?

In this etching, Confucius spreads his ideas for an orderly society to his followers in ancient China.
▶ Where is Confucius seated?

551 B.C., just a few years after Prince Siddhartha, but the lives of these two began very differently. Prince Siddhartha grew up in a palace. Confucius was an orphan who worked as a boy. Siddhartha left the palace because he did not want to be a king. Confucius spent years seeking to become the adviser of a king. Siddhartha sought a satisfying way of life. Confucius sought to create a good government.

Confucius was deeply troubled by conditions in China. The land was divided into a number of kingdoms. The kings fought each other and oppressed the people they ruled. Confucius believed that there could be peace and justice under a good government. But he knew there could be good government only when good people governed. Confucius searched for a king who would put his teachings into practice. He never found one, so he spent his time teaching young

men. Perhaps they would be advisers to kings in the future.

Once when Confucius and some of his students were traveling through a wild region, they came upon an old woman weeping beside a grave. Confucius asked her why she wept. She replied that a tiger had killed her only son, just as another tiger had once killed her husband. "Why do you live in this place?" asked Confucius. "Because there is no oppressive [cruel] government here," she replied. Confucius turned to his students and told them, "Remember this woman; oppressive government is worse than a tiger."

Confucius carefully observed all religious ceremonies. He taught that all should respect the gods and the "will of heaven." But Confucius did not establish a religion. He once said that he did not expect his followers to be saints, that is, holy persons. He would be satisfied if they were

ANALECTS: SAYINGS OF CONFUCIUS

Confucius, who is shown below teaching his students, used his teaching as a tool for making changes in the world around him. The goal that Confucius had for his students was that they be able to act effectively in the world. For that reason, he taught his followers how to get along with others.

The *Analects* contains the teachings of Confucius and his followers. Below are some of the sayings of Confucius taken from this book.

> To know what you know and know what you don't know is the characteristic of one who knows.

> Learning prevents one from being narrow-minded.

> A gentleman blames himself, while a common man blames others.

> A man who committed a mistake and doesn't correct it is committing another mistake.

> When asked, what do you think of repaying evil with kindness, Confucius replied: Then what are you going to repay kindness with? Repay kindness with kindness but repay evil with justice.

> A man who does not think and plan long ahead will find troubles right at his door.

> Don't criticize other people's faults, criticize your own.

> A man who brags without shame will find great difficulty in living up to his bragging.

Understanding Source Material

1. Which saying do you most agree with?
2. Which saying do you least agree with?

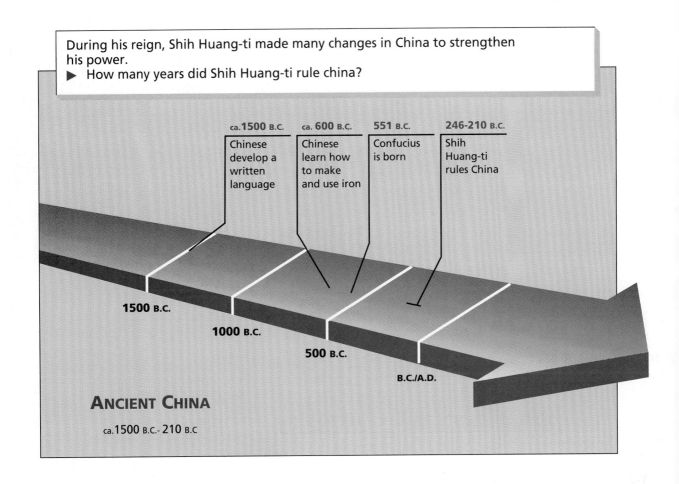

During his reign, Shih Huang-ti made many changes in China to strengthen his power.

► How many years did Shih Huang-ti rule china?

ca. 1500 B.C.
Chinese develop a written language

ca. 600 B.C.
Chinese learn how to make and use iron

551 B.C.
Confucius is born

246-210 B.C.
Shih Huang-ti rules China

1500 B.C.

1000 B.C.

500 B.C.

B.C./A.D.

ANCIENT CHINA
ca. 1500 B.C.- 210 B.C

gentlemen, that is, men who were honest, fair, and courteous. A true gentleman followed the rule, "What you do not want done to yourself, do not do to others."

Confucius and his followers probably invented the legends about the Good Emperors. They hoped that the real rulers would follow the good examples of the legendary Yao and Shun. Although Confucius never found such a king, his teachings were not forgotten. Over the years the sage had more influence than any king. For more than 2,000 years, Chinese students studied his teachings concerning the ideal gentleman. These teachings, known as **Confucianism**, became the Chinese model for official and personal behavior.

F. A Clay Army

In 1974, workers digging a well near the city of Xi'an, once known as Hsien-yang (shee en YAHNG), discovered an army — an army of clay soldiers. These were not toy soldiers but life-sized statues of men and horses that lay buried in a large underground chamber. At one time thousands of the soldiers stood four abreast along the corridors of the chamber, but the stout timbers that held up the earth-covered ceiling had collapsed long ago. Most of the statues lay in pieces when the workers uncovered them.

As archaeologists began putting the figures together, they could see how carefully the figures had been made. Even

Shih Huang-ti had a life-sized clay army made. It is said that each figure was modeled after a real soldier.

▶ Besides soldiers, what is pictured here?

more astonishing than the size and numbers of the clay figures was the fact that they were all different; no two soldiers and no two horses looked alike. Some of the soldiers wore armor and some belted robes. Some warriors had braided hair, some had hair pulled into a knot on top of their heads. Even the expressions on their faces were different.

The clay army had been armed with real weapons. The soldiers had held swords, spears, bows, and crossbows. The wooden parts of the weapons had rotted away long ago, but the bronze arrowheads, swords, and crossbow fittings lay in the ruins. The chamber also held full-sized

chariots, each hitched to four life-sized horses. Each chariot had a clay charioteer and guard.

Since 1974, two more underground chambers containing clay figures have been discovered. Altogether the three chambers contain between 7,000 and 8,000 figures of men and horses. It would have taken the labor of many people to make these figures and construct the underground chambers. Why did they do it? They were forced to work by a powerful ruler. The clay army was supposed to protect, in some magical way, the tomb of Shih Huang-ti (SHEE hwahng dee), an emperor who died over 2,300 years ago.

G. Burning Books and Building Walls

Shih Huang-ti   Shih Huang-ti was king of Ch'in, a warlike kingdom in northwestern China. Shih Huang-ti brought the whole land under his rule by conquering the other kingdoms. We still call the country he conquered *China*, which means "land of the Ch'in." Shih Huang-ti ruled China from 246 B.C. to 210 B.C.

Shih Huang-ti was by no means Confucius's ideal gentleman. In fact, he strongly opposed the sage's teachings, which he thought dangerous. Since many books contained Confucius's sayings, Shih Huang-ti ordered that all books be burned except those about useful subjects. By "useful" Shih Huang-ti meant books on farming and medicine. Fortunately, some students hid their books. Others knew their books so well that they later wrote them down from memory.

Thousands of Chinese people built the Great Wall of China.
► What were some of the steps involved in building the wall?

Among Shih Huang-ti's most important projects was the building of the Grand Canal in China.
► What else did he have built?

Great Wall   The burning of the books was only one of the steps Shih Huang-ti took to strengthen his power. He forced thousands to build projects, including his tomb. He also sent many people to work on the Great Wall. Earlier kings had built walls to protect parts of the land from the raids of horse-raiding tribes. Shih Huang-ti connected these shorter walls to form the Great Wall. Below is how Leonard Everett Fisher, in his book *The Great Wall of China*, tells how Shih Huang-ti may have described his plans for the Great Wall.

I shall build a new and mightier wall and shall join all the walls together. I shall have one long wall across the top of China. . . . It will be six horses wide at the top, eight at the bottom, and five men high. I shall build it at the edge of our steepest mountains. No Mongol . . . will be able to go around it, over it, under it, or through it. It will be the Great Wall!

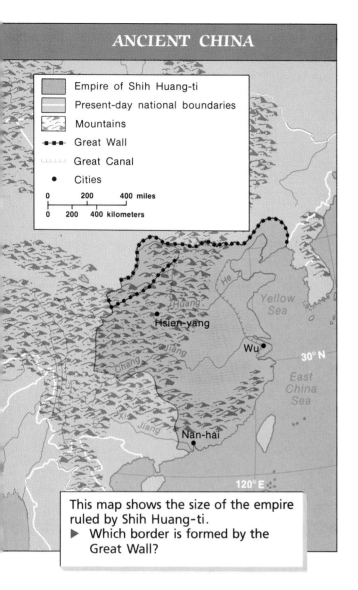

ANCIENT CHINA

▨	Empire of Shih Huang-ti
▭	Present-day national boundaries
〰	Mountains
▪▪▪	Great Wall
⊔⊔⊔	Great Canal
•	Cities

0   200   400 miles
0   200   400 kilometers

Huang
He
Yellow Sea
Hsien-yang
Jiang
Chang
Wu•
30° N
East China Sea
Xi
Jiang
Nan-hai•
120° E

This map shows the size of the empire ruled by Shih Huang-ti.
▶ Which border is formed by the Great Wall?

In later times other emperors made the wall stronger and larger. The Great Wall stretches 1,500 miles (2,413 km) across northern China, as shown by the map on this page. If such a wall were built in the United States, it would reach halfway across the country. The Great Wall is said to be the largest structure ever built. In fact, the Great Wall is the only structure made by humans that can be seen from outer space.

A Powerful Ruler Some things Shih Huang-ti did to make himself powerful probably benefited China. He directed that all should write characters in the same way so that there would be only one system of writing throughout the empire. He even ruled that wheels on carts must be placed the same distance apart. The unpaved roads were little more than cart tracks. It was easier for animals to pull carts when all followed the same tracks.

Shih Huang-ti was a very powerful ruler, but in the end there were things he could not do. He forced thousands of people to build his tomb, but the underground army of clay soldiers failed to protect it. Shortly after his death, thieves entered the tomb and robbed it.

LESSON 3 REVIEW

THINK AND WRITE

A. What ideals were taught in the legends of the Good Emperors?

B. What was the purpose of the writings on shells and bones?

C. How was character writing useful yet difficult?

D. Why does the Chinese government encourage foreign writers to use Pinyin spelling?

E. What did Confucius teach?

F. What was the purpose of Shih Huang-ti's underground army?

G. What steps did Shih Huang-ti take to strengthen his power?

SKILLS CHECK

MAP SKILL

Look at the map of ancient China on this page. Which two rivers cross the Grand Canal? Tell what body of water each of these rivers flows into.

144

USING THE VOCABULARY

On a separate sheet of paper, write the letter of the term that best matches each numbered statement.

a. subcontinent
b. nomads
c. castes
d. dialect
e. Pinyin

1. A variety of a particular language
2. Social classes of the people of India
3. A large landmass that is smaller than a continent
4. A system of writing Chinese words with the Roman alphabet
5. Tribes of people who move about with herds of goats, sheep, and cattle

REMEMBERING WHAT YOU READ

On a separate sheet of paper, answer the following questions in complete sentences.

1. What two Indus cities were uncovered by archaeologists after Wells wrote *The Outline of History*?
2. What ancient objects did archaeologists find in the ruins of Mohenjo-Daro?
3. What are the Vedas?
4. In what language are the Vedas written?
5. For what was Siddhartha searching?
6. What are the followers of Buddha called?
7. What is the religion of most of the people on the subcontinent?
8. What ruler helped to spread Buddhism?
9. Into what four classes were the early Aryans divided?
10. On what are the oldest surviving Chinese writings found?
11. What are the names of China's three great rivers?
12. What teachings have become the Chinese model for official and personal behavior?
13. Whose tomb was the clay army supposed to protect?
14. How did Shih Huang-ti strengthen his power?
15. What in China is the largest structure in the world?

TYING ART TO SOCIAL STUDIES

The caste system developed as a result of the practices of Aryan society. People were divided into four major groups. As a class, make a mural that shows people from each of the four castes. Divide into groups, with each group responsible for drawing the members of one of the castes. Decide how your mural will be organized and how you will label each of the castes. Your class can display the mural when it is completed.

THINKING CRITICALLY

On a separate sheet of paper, answer the following in complete sentences.

1. H. G. Wells wanted his book to "tell truly and clearly the whole story of mankind. . . ." Why is it important for us to have a clear record of the past?
2. How might historians describe your neighborhood if they discovered it in the year 4000?
3. What is your opinion of the caste system?
4. The ancient Chinese people were interested in knowing the future. They believed that oracles could predict the future. If people could see into the future, what would be some possible advantages and disadvantages for humanity?
5. What does the discovery of the clay army at Xi'an tell us about ancient Chinese beliefs in life and death?

SUMMARIZING THE CHAPTER

Copy this graphic organizer on a separate sheet of paper. In both columns of the chart, fill in each box with an answer. Some boxes may have more than one answer.

CHAPTER THEME	The culture, society, and early history of India and China have made a lasting impact on each country's civilization.	
ANCIENT CIVILIZATIONS	INDIA	CHINA
LEADERS		
LANGUAGES	Indus Script	
RELIGIONS		No organized religion
ARCHAEOLOGICAL DISCOVERIES		
RIVERS		Chang Jiang

COOPERATIVE LEARNING

When travelers prepare for a visit to a foreign country, they may read guidebooks. Guidebooks describe the geography and interesting places of various regions and also describe customs of people who live in those regions. How would you go about writing a guidebook?

PROJECT

Work with a group of classmates to plan and write a guidebook for time travelers. In it, you will describe one of the ancient civilizations you studied in Unit 1. Your group's guidebook might include information on ancient sporting events, temples and monuments, religious practices, languages, land features, or climate. Use your imaginations. Ask yourselves, "What would a time traveler need to know?"

Hold a group meeting to decide what information your guidebook will include. Be sure to share ideas and record group members' suggestions. Use the information in your textbook. You may also want to visit a library to gather more information.

Divide tasks among group members. Depending on the number of students in the group and the information your guidebook will include,

your group might divide tasks as follows:

● One group member could write about the important temples and monuments in the civilization.

● Another group member could write about religious practices.

● A third group member could draw pictures to illustrate what has been written for the guidebook.

● One group member could draw a map of the region and label where the important monuments and temples were built.

● Another group member could prepare a cover, title page, and table of contents for the guidebook.

PRESENTATION AND REVIEW

After your group members have met to put all your information together, present your guidebook to the rest of your class. Work together to answer any questions the other students may have about the ancient civilization your guidebook describes.

After your group has made its presentation, meet again to evaluate your project. How well did your group members work together? How could your guidebook have been improved?

REMEMBER TO:
● Give your ideas.
● Listen to others' ideas.
● Plan your work with the group.
● Present your project.
● Discuss how your group worked.

A. WHY DO I NEED THIS SKILL?

Graphs are a visual way of organizing information. They present facts in ways that are clear and easy to read. When facts are organized in a graph, it is much easier to understand the facts and to see the relationships between them.

B. LEARNING THE SKILL

There are different kinds of graphs. The most common are pie graphs, bar graphs, line graphs, and pictographs.

A pie graph is used to show and compare percentages, or parts of a whole. Each "slice" of the "pie" represents a certain percentage—a part of the whole pie.

The pie graph below shows how much of the world's total land area each of the seven continents occupies. The whole circle stands for the world's total land area, or 100 percent. Each slice stands for a continent and how much of the total land area it occupies. The pie graph also shows how the continents compare with each other in size.

A bar graph can also be used to show and compare facts. The bar graph below shows the land area of each continent in the world. The left side of the graph is divided into segments that each represent 2 million square miles. The right side of the graph has segments that each represent 5 million square kilometers.

Each bar that extends from the bottom of the graph shows the land area of a continent. For example, the land area of Asia is about 17 million square miles (44 million sq km), and the land area of Europe is about 4 million square miles (10 million sq km). By

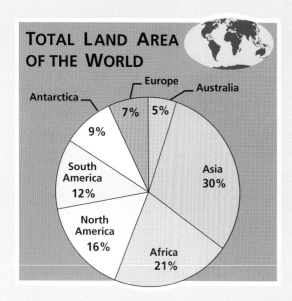

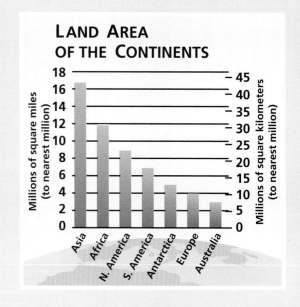

looking at the bars for these two continents, you can visualize about how many times larger Asia is than Europe.

Line graphs are used to show changes over time. The line graph on this page shows how world population has changed since the year 2000 B.C. and includes projections to the year A.D. 2000.

On left side of the graph, there are segments that represent the number of people, in billions. Along the bottom of the graph, there are segments that represent 1,000 years each.

A pictograph—a graph that uses picture-symbols—is used to show amounts, such as population figures. To see an example of a pictograph, turn to page 541 in Chapter 21. The graph on that page shows population figures for the most populated countries in the world.

C. PRACTICING THE SKILL

1. On the pie graph, what percentage of the world's land area is occupied by Asia?
2. According to the bar graph, what is the land area of the North American continent?
3. What is the land area of Antarctica?
4. How many years does each segment on the bottom line of the line graph represent?
5. What was the approximate world population in the year A.D. 1800?

D. APPLYING THE SKILL

Take a survey to find out which ice-cream flavor each student in your class likes best. Then organize your results in a pie graph.

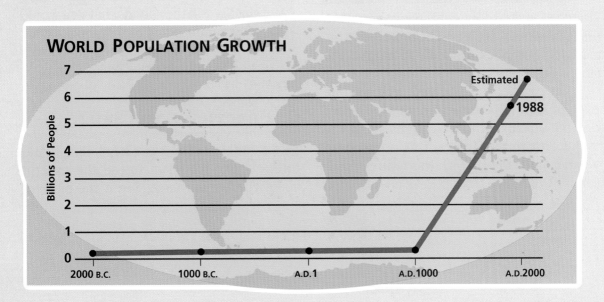

WORLD POPULATION GROWTH

A. WHY DO I NEED THIS SKILL?

This social studies textbook tells about people, places, and events of the past and present. The book presents facts — accepted or verified information — about the history of peoples of the Eastern Hemisphere.

People besides textbook authors write about historical events. These other authors might write stories, myths, poems, or plays that tell something about history. We call these writings literature, and their purpose is not so much to present facts but to entertain, excite, or inspire readers. Reading literature that deals with historical events can give you insight into the feelings, attitudes, and daily lives of the people who lived at different times in history.

B. LEARNING THE SKILL

There are several different types of literature that can relate to history. The table found on page 151 describes some of the more common types.

On page 73 of Chapter 2, you read an excerpt from *The Adventures of Odysseus and the Tale of Troy*, which tells about the fall of Troy to the Greeks. This is a modern version of the *Iliad*, which was written thousands of years ago by the Greek poet Homer.

This literature excerpt gives you a firsthand, real-life feeling for what it would have been like to be at Troy as the Greeks hid inside the wooden horse and tricked the Trojans.

You can use the following reading strategies to increase your understanding and enjoyment of literature.

- **Pretend** you are the main character in the selection; try to feel the excitement or fear she or he must have felt. For example, how would you have felt if you had been Odysseus?

- **Imagine** that you are an observer watching what is going on. For example, what would you have thought if you had been a Trojan citizen watching the Greeks deliver a huge wooden horse to your city?

- **Visualize** the event; think of the sights, the smells, and the sounds that you would have experienced. For example, what might you have seen, smelled, or heard if you had been inside the Trojan horse?

C. PRACTICING THE SKILL

Select one of the strategies for reading literature and use it as you reread the excerpt about the Trojan horse. See if the piece of literature and the actual historical event "come alive" for you. Then use the **pretend**, **imagine**, or **visualize** strategy that you have just learned about as you reread the selection from *Julius Caesar*, on page 108 in Chapter 3. How do you feel as you explain your actions to the Roman Senate?

D. APPLYING THE SKILL

Use a **pretend**, **imagine**, or **visualize** strategy as you read the other literature excerpts in this book. Perhaps you will become so interested that you will find the source of the literature and read the entire piece.

LITERATURE THAT RELATES TO HISTORY		
Type of Literature	**Characteristics**	**Example**
Historical fiction	Stories set in the past; based on real, historical events but with much information made up by the author	*Ivanhoe* p. 176
Poetry	Rhythmical writings that may or may not rhyme; makes reader imagine and understand various feelings and events	*The Adventures of Odysseus and the Tale of Troy*, p. 73
Drama	Stories intended to be performed by actors; helps audience or reader picture and be affected by events	*Julius Caesar*, p. 108
Myths, legends, and fables	Stories intended to teach a moral lesson or explain the origins of things; sometimes based on historical events but featuring fantasy or exaggeration	Anansi Tale: "How Wisdom Was Spread Throughout the World," p. 456
Diaries, journals, and biographies	Writings about real people and their experiences; written by the people themselves (diaries, journals) or by someone else (biographies)	*The Diary of a Young Girl*, p. 240

Unit 2
WESTERN EUROPE

For centuries, Western Europe has been a center of dramatic changes that have had far-reaching effects on other parts of the world.

▶ *Hundreds of years ago, powerful lords in Western Europe built castles that provided protection during attacks. Bodiam Castle, complete with a moat, still stands in Sussex, England.*

CHAPTER 5

GEOGRAPHY OF WESTERN EUROPE

The physical landscape of Western Europe includes majestic mountains, rivers, and peninsulas. The moderate climate, good soil, and valuable natural resources make Western Europe a favorable region.

The Continent and Its Climate

THINK ABOUT WHAT YOU KNOW

The region of Western Europe includes many countries with many different physical characteristics. What are some physical features in Greece and Italy that you have already studied?

STUDY THE VOCABULARY

natural resource	current
deciduous	Gulf Stream
coniferous	North Atlantic
forestry	Drift
climograph	

FOCUS YOUR READING

What are some of the physical characteristics of Western Europe?

A. The Grand Tour

The Grand Tour was a trip through Western Europe taken by a young Englishman and his tutor, or teacher. In the eighteenth century, wealthy English families often sent their sons on the Grand Tour after they had finished school. The eighteenth century, you remember, was the hundred years between 1701 and 1800.

It was thought that the Grand Tour completed a young gentleman's education. It was supposed to improve his manners and develop his mind. There were probably good reasons for attempting to do both. The manners of some young men were compared to those of wild bears, so their tutors were called bearkeepers. As for developing their minds, this task must have been difficult in some cases. One young fellow journeyed through Italy scarcely looking out the window of his coach. He was more interested in his dog and her puppies than in enjoying the beautiful Italian countryside.

The Grand Tour began with crossing the English Channel. This is the arm of the Atlantic Ocean that connects with the North Sea and separates the British Isles from the European continent. The British Isles are a large group of islands located off the west coast of Europe. The two largest islands are Great Britain and Ireland. The travelers gathered at Dover or one of the other channel ports to board a sailboat. Sometimes they had to wait several days for a favorable wind. This was before there were steamships.

The English Channel is narrow, but its waters can be rough. Some of the young tourists became so seasick that they thought they would die. Of course, they didn't, but seasickness can make a person feel miserable.

Once on shore, the students and their tutors traveled either in horse-drawn coaches or in barges called water carriages. Travel by water was much smoother than travel by coach over rough roads, and Western Europe had a number of rivers and canals. In later chapters you will read about some important waterways that are still used for shipping.

Few of the eighteenth-century tourists were interested in Western Europe's mountains. Most travelers regarded the Alps in Switzerland as a barrier to cross rather than a natural wonder to be visited. Of course, travel across the Alps was difficult 200 years ago. There were no good roads or tunnels, only steep and dangerous trails over the high passes. A coach could not be driven over these trails. Instead it had to be taken apart and loaded on the backs of pack animals, such as donkeys. A

People endured difficulties as they climbed Mont Blanc in the 1850s.
▶ Are these tourists well equipped for mountain climbing?

B. Europe: A Part of Eurasia

Europe and Asia are both called continents, although they are both located on the same great landmass. These two continents are separated by the Ural Mountains. The landmass is called Eurasia, which is a combination of *Europe* and *Asia.* Europe is a peninsula of Eurasia, as the map on pages 618–619 shows.

Even though Europe is a small continent, it has a long coastline because of its shape. Several smaller peninsulas extend into the seas from the larger peninsula of Europe. Italy is the boot-shaped peninsula of southern Europe. Spain and Portugal are on the Iberian Peninsula, which has the Atlantic Ocean on one side and the Mediterranean Sea on the other. The Balkan Peninsula of southeastern Europe is divided into six countries. Greece forms the tip. The other countries are Albania, Bulgaria, Romania, European Turkey, and Yugoslavia. In northern Europe the Arctic Circle crosses the Scandinavian peninsula, which is divided into Norway and Sweden. Jutland is a smaller peninsula in the north. Denmark is located on Jutland.

C. The Land and Water of Western Europe

Most of the lands that make up Western Europe are located on the western part of the European mainland, but some are not. Some are islands. Great Britain, Ireland, and Iceland are islands in the Atlantic Ocean. Malta and Cyprus are islands in the Mediterranean Sea. Greece is located on the continent, but it is in the southeastern part rather than the western part.

The term *Western Europe* grew out of history rather than geography. After World War II the countries of Europe were divided into two different groups. In

traveler unable to make the climb on foot could arrange to be carried on a seat hanging between two poles. But it took a team of six strong people to carry a person of average size over a steep pass. A heavier person required eight, and a truly hefty tourist needed a team of ten people.

Because of the difficulty of crossing the Alps, some tourists avoided the mountains altogether. They took a boat in southern France and sailed along the Mediterranean coast to Italy.

Europe has changed greatly since the young English gentlemen took the Grand Tour, but the rivers, seas, mountains, and plains are still there. In this chapter you will learn about them by taking your own Grand Tour through reading.

WESTERN EUROPE: PHYSICAL

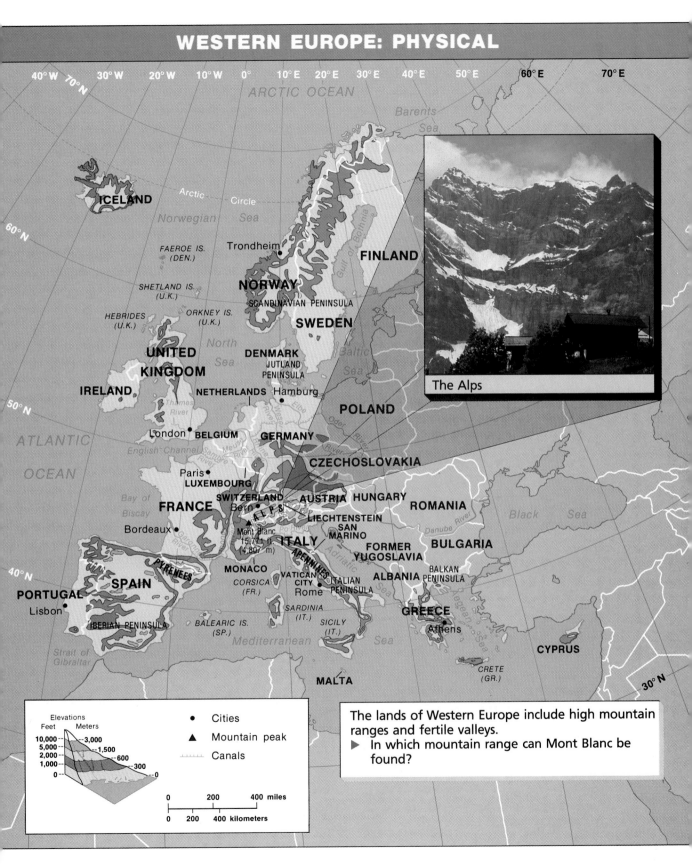

40° W 30° W 20° W 10° W 0° 10° E 20° E 30° E 40° E 50° E 60° E 70° E

70° N

ARCTIC OCEAN

Barents
Sea

ICELAND

Arctic
Circle

Norwegian
Sea

60° N

FAEROE IS.
(DEN.)

Trondheim

FINLAND

The Alps

SHETLAND IS.
(U.K.)

NORWAY

SCANDINAVIAN PENINSULA

Gulf of Bothnia

HEBRIDES
(U.K.)

ORKNEY IS.
(U.K.)

SWEDEN

North
Sea

DENMARK
JUTLAND
PENINSULA

Baltic
Sea

UNITED
KINGDOM

IRELAND

NETHERLANDS

Hamburg

50° N

Thames
River

POLAND

London

BELGIUM

GERMANY

Elbe
River

Oder
River

ATLANTIC

English Channel

Meuse R.

Weser R.

CZECHOSLOVAKIA

OCEAN

Sambre R.

Paris

LUXEMBOURG

Rhine
River

Bay of
Biscay

FRANCE

SWITZERLAND
Bern

ALPS

AUSTRIA

HUNGARY

ROMANIA

Black   Sea

LIECHTENSTEIN

Danube River

Bordeaux

Mont Blanc
15,771 ft.
(4,807 m)

Po R.

SAN
MARINO

BULGARIA

ITALY

APENNINES

FORMER
YUGOSLAVIA

40° N

PYRENEES

MONACO

Adriatic Sea

BALKAN
PENINSULA

Garonne
River

CORSICA
(FR.)

VATICAN
CITY
Rome

ITALIAN
PENINSULA

ALBANIA

SPAIN

PORTUGAL

Lisbon

IBERIAN PENINSULA

BALEARIC IS.
(SP.)

SARDINIA
(IT.)

SICILY
(IT.)

GREECE

Athens

Aegean Sea

CYPRUS

Strait of
Gibraltar

Mediterranean   Sea

CRETE
(GR.)

30° N

MALTA

Legend

Elevations
Feet   Meters

10,000 -- --3,000
5,000 -- --1,500
2,000 -- --600
1,000 -- --300
0 -- --0

● Cities
▲ Mountain peak
⋯⋯⋯ Canals

0   200   400 miles

0   200   400 kilometers

The lands of Western Europe include high mountain ranges and fertile valleys.
▶ In which mountain range can Mont Blanc be found?

Eastern Europe the Soviet Union established its government in a number of countries. The countries of Western Europe remained free of Soviet control. You will read about this division of Europe and its end in later chapters.

Because of the continent's shape, no place in Western Europe is more than 300 miles (481 km) from the sea. Ships enter the Mediterranean Sea from the Atlantic Ocean through the Strait of Gibraltar. Here only about three fourths of a mile (1 km) separates Europe from Africa. The Adriatic and Aegean seas are arms of the Mediterranean. Ships can sail from the Aegean

through the Dardanelles and Bosporus (BAHS puh rus) into the Black Sea. The North and Baltic seas provide routes to northern Europe. A look at the map on page 157 suggests why many Europeans became sailors or fishers. It has been easy to go to sea from much of Western Europe.

D. Mountains of Western Europe

Mont Blanc Dr. Michael Paccard (pak-kar) was a village physician, but he was not seeing patients on the day of August 8, 1786. Instead, he and a companion named Balmat were slowly making their way over snow and slippery ice to the top of Mont Blanc (mohn blahn) in France. No one had ever climbed Mont Blanc, the highest peak in the Alps.

In the village below the mountain, a man watched the slow progress of the climbers through his telescope. When the climbers finally reached the top of the peak, Dr. Paccard tied a handkerchief on his climbing stick and waved it so the watcher would know that Mont Blanc had been conquered.

On that August day over 200 years ago, Paccard and Balmat climbed Mont Blanc just for the thrill of doing it. Their climb is said to have marked the birth of mountaineering, mountain climbing as a sport. Many men and women took up the sport in the years that followed. The picture on this page shows what the fashionable woman of 1870 was supposed to wear when she went mountaineering.

Almost a century after Paccard and Balmat had reached the peak, Mark Twain saw Mont Blanc while touring Europe. He later wrote a travel book about his tour. The following is an excerpt from Twain's book *A Tramp Abroad*, describing Mont Blanc.

This fancy dress and stockings were considered fashionable for women mountain climbers in the 1870s.
▶ Was this outfit practical?

Mont Blanc, the highest peak in the Alps, was called the "monarch of the Alps" by Mark Twain. This photograph shows Mont Blanc rising above Chamonix Valley in France.

▶ Why, do you think, did Mark Twain refer to this mountain as the "monarch of the Alps"?

About half an hour before we reached the village . . . a vast dome of snow with the sun blazing on it drifted into view and framed itself in a strong V-shaped gateway of the mountains, and we recognized Mont Blanc, "the monarch of the Alps." With every step after that this stately dome rose higher and higher into the blue sky and at last seemed to occupy the zenith [peak.] . . . We . . . saw exquisite prismatic colors [rainbow colors] playing about some white clouds which were so delicate as to almost resemble gossamer [threadlike] webs. . . . We sat down to study and enjoy this singular spectacle.

The Alps The Alps are the largest group of mountains in Western Europe. The Alps form parts of France, Switzerland, Italy, Germany, Austria, as well as the former Yugoslavia. Waters from the Alps flow into four of Europe's major rivers: the Rhine River, the Rhone River, the Po River, and the Danube River. If you locate these rivers on the physical map on page 157, you will discover that the four rivers flow in quite different directions. The Rhone flows south to the Mediterranean Sea; the Rhine flows north to the North Sea; the Po flows into the Adriatic Sea; and the Danube follows its long route eastward to the Black Sea.

The Pyrenees The Pyrenees (PIHR uh-neez) form a mountain wall between the Iberian Peninsula and the rest of Europe. Though its peaks are not as high as those of the Alps, the Pyrenees are rugged mountains. A third range, the Apennines, has been described as the spine or backbone of the Italian peninsula. A look at the map on page 157 will show you why.

There is little chance for mountaineering on the North European Plain. This lowland area stretches from the coast of France eastward into the Soviet Union.

This wooded mountain region in Germany is called the Black Forest.
► What types of trees grow in this region?

E. Natural Resources of Western Europe

Forests The North European Plain has an abundance of good soil, only one of Europe's valuable **natural resources**. A natural resource is any material provided by nature that people use. Natural resources are not evenly distributed over the earth. Western Europe is one of the fortunate places. This region has good soil and plentiful rainfall.

At one time, forests covered most of Western Europe. Much of the forestland has been cleared for farms and cities, but there are still great forests, especially in northern Europe. Forests cover most of the Scandinavian peninsula and Finland. Even countries with large populations, such as France and Germany, have preserved some forestland. **Deciduous** (dee-SIHJ oo us) trees can be found in most of these forests. *Deciduous* comes from a Latin word that means "to fall off." The leaves of deciduous trees fall every year. Oaks, elms, and maples are examples of deciduous trees.

The Black Forest is the name given to an entire region in Germany that is a **coniferous** (koh NIHF ur us) forest. *Conifer* means "cone-bearing." Trees in coniferous forests bear cones. Evergreen trees, such as pines, firs, and spruces, are conifers. The Germans have been among the world's leaders in **forestry**, which is the science of caring for forests. Trees are grown and harvested as crops, but the amount of wood cut is never greater than the new growth.

Minerals Western Europe has deposits of various minerals, including coal, iron, lead, zinc, copper, salt, and limestone. Limestone is not a rare mineral, but it is an important one. Limestone is necessary for making concrete, which is widely used in building. Oil is also a valuable mineral. Western Europe became an important oil producer when oil was discovered offshore in the North Sea.

F. Ocean Streams and Altitude

Climate London, England, is farther north than Minneapolis, Minnesota, yet London has a milder climate. London winters are warmer and summers are cooler than those in the middle of North America. Remember that latitude measures distance from the Equator. London is 51° north of the Equator; Minneapolis is 45° north of the Equator.

The **climographs** on this page show the differences between the climates of the two cities. A climograph is a graph that shows both the average temperature and the average precipitation for a certain place. The line shows the average temperature for each month. An average temperature is halfway between the high and low temperatures. For example, if the high was 60°F (16°C) and the low was 40°F (4°C), the average temperature would be 50°F (10°C). Note that the temperature scale is on the left side of the climograph.

The bars on the climograph show the average rainfall for each month of the year. By comparing the climographs, you can see that the rainfall is more evenly distributed throughout the year in London than in Minneapolis.

A comparison of the curves of the temperature lines shows that temperatures vary more in Minneapolis than in London. Temperatures rise much higher in the summer and fall much lower in the winter in Minneapolis.

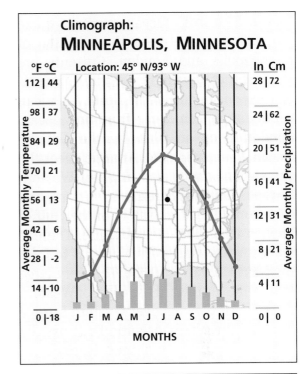

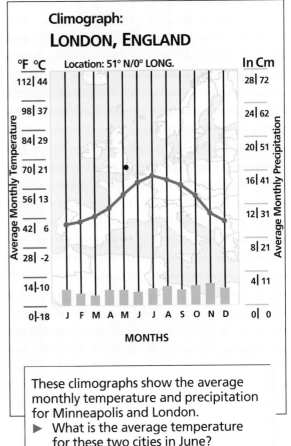

These climographs show the average monthly temperature and precipitation for Minneapolis and London.

▶ What is the average temperature for these two cities in June?

Ocean Streams Ocean **currents** make the difference between the climates of Minneapolis and London. Currents are streams that flow in the oceans. Minneapolis is in the middle of the North American continent, which is far from any ocean. London is on an island in the Atlantic Ocean. Currents in the Atlantic affect the climate of London and much of Western Europe. The **Gulf Stream** flows north and east from the warm waters of the Gulf of Mexico into the North Atlantic. There it merges with other warm currents to form the **North Atlantic Drift**. This very large stream moves toward the coast of Western Europe. Air blowing over Western Europe from off the North Atlantic Drift usually keeps winter temperatures warmer. In summer, ocean breezes cool those parts of Western Europe near the coast.

Ocean currents have less effect on places farther from the coast. Berlin, a city in Germany, is located at about the same latitude as London, but Berlin is farther from the ocean. As a result, Berlin winters are somewhat cooler.

Altitude also affects climate. Places at high elevations, such as mountains like the Alps, are cooler than are places at low

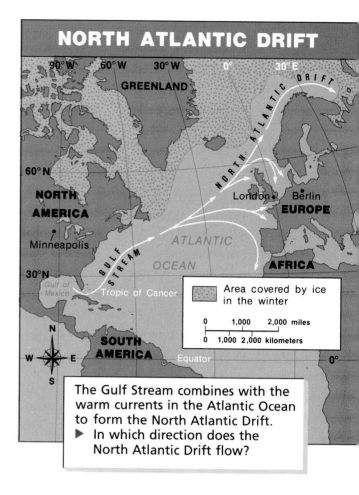

The Gulf Stream combines with the warm currents in the Atlantic Ocean to form the North Atlantic Drift.
▶ In which direction does the North Atlantic Drift flow?

elevations, like those nearer sea level. Average temperatures in the Alps generally decrease 2°F (1°C) with every 650-foot (198-m) rise in altitude.

LESSON 1 REVIEW

THINK AND WRITE

A. Why were young English gentlemen sent on the Grand Tour?

B. Why may Europe be called "a peninsula with peninsulas"?

C. Why are some European countries not located on the western part of the continent still called Western European countries?

D. What are three important groups of mountains in Western Europe?

E. Why can it be said that nature has been generous to Western Europe?

F. Why does Western Europe have a mild climate in spite of its location?

SKILLS CHECK

MAP SKILL

By looking at the physical map on page 157, you can see that Western Europe is a large region. Which four countries in the region lie the farthest north, south, east, and west?

A Variety of Peoples on a Small Continent

THINK ABOUT WHAT YOU KNOW

While on the Grand Tour, students traveled through Italy. What are some of the ancient ruins of Rome that the students may have visited?

STUDY THE VOCABULARY

rural   metropolitan
urban   area

FOCUS YOUR READING

How do you think the resources of Europe contributed to its population?

A. Students on the Grand Tour

The main purpose of the Grand Tour in the eighteenth century was to let students see the peoples and cities they had studied. Students may not have known as much as their tutors had hoped. One student wrote that his tutor "taught me a number of hard names yesterday which I tried hard to remember, but I forgot everything in ten minutes."

Those people who took the Grand Tour in the eighteenth century visited many of the places that tourists visit today. Students and tutors went to the Cathedral of Notre Dame (noh truh DAHM) in Paris. They climbed the bell tower and looked out at the size of the city. There they could try to compare the size of Paris with the size of London.

When English students visited the Palace of Versailles (vur SYE), outside Paris, they sometimes caught sight of the king. France still had a king at that time. One of the attractions of Versailles was the chance to see the king dine in public. What did students learn from this visit? One of them noted that the king held his fork in his left hand, as is the English custom.

Tourists visiting the German city of Berlin saw King Frederick II, who came to be known as Frederick the Great, reviewing his well-drilled troops. Some of the English students journeyed to Switzerland to see the estate of Voltaire (vahl TER), a famous French writer. A few managed to meet Voltaire. Those less fortunate stared through the gate, hoping to catch a glimpse of the famous man.

A visit to Italy was the high point of the Grand Tour. Students in the eighteenth century spent much time studying Latin. Tutors probably hoped that a visit to Rome would remind students of Julius Caesar

Students on the Grand Tour visited the Palace of Versailles, just as many tourists do today.
▶ Where is Versailles located?

163

and Cicero. Some students did find Rome interesting, but others were struck by its shabbiness. Many of the poorer Romans lived in shacks built amid ancient ruins. The area inside the Colosseum, where gladiators had once fought, was a crowded slum neighborhood. The great circus, where chariots had once raced, was used as a cow pasture.

Tourists in the eighteenth century, like those today, bought souvenirs to take home. Italy was the favored place to look for souvenirs. Tourists bought gold jewelry and scented soaps in Milan (muh-LAHN) and paintings in Florence. Some paintings were copies of famous works.

Others were portraits of the tourists themselves. In Venice they found all sorts of glassware, including glass models of a full-rigged ship. Venice was famous for its ships as well as its glassblowers. It was very stylish to buy ancient relics or keepsakes in Rome. Pieces of ancient statuary were preferred.

The young gentlemen who took the Grand Tour may not have learned as much as their parents and tutors had hoped. But the young men surely must have learned something about the peoples and lands of Western Europe. Otherwise, parents would hardly have continued to send their sons on the Grand Tour.

Eighteenth-century tourists often visited the city of Venice, in Italy. Venice was well known for its ships and for its glassware.
▶ What takes the place of streets in Venice?

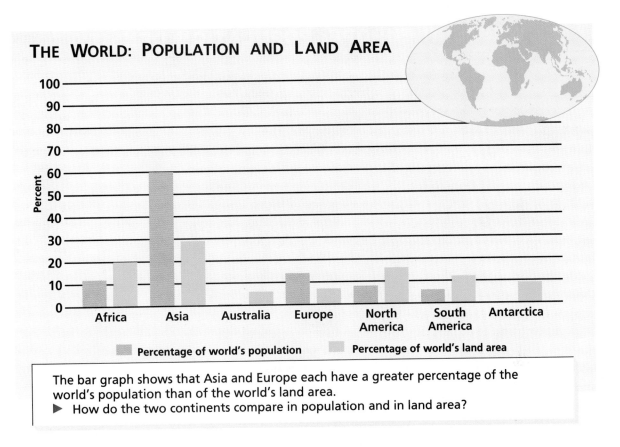

THE WORLD: POPULATION AND LAND AREA

Percent

- 100
- 90
- 80
- 70
- 60
- 50
- 40
- 30
- 20
- 10
- 0

Africa · Asia · Australia · Europe · North America · South America · Antarctica

▢ Percentage of world's population   ▢ Percentage of world's land area

The bar graph shows that Asia and Europe each have a greater percentage of the world's population than of the world's land area.
▶ How do the two continents compare in population and in land area?

B. A Small Continent with Many Faces

Ever since the eighteenth century, people have toured Europe to learn about its people and history. Such trips have been called grand tours even in later times. In 1891 a 15-year-old girl from Nashville, Tennessee, made a trip to Europe with seven other girls. She kept a diary of her trip, which she later stored in an old trunk. It was found by her grandson nearly 90 years later. It was published and given the title *A Young Nashvillian's Grand Tour: Europe in 1891.*

Europe is a small continent. Only Australia is a smaller continent. Yet Europe today has many people. Only Asia has more. The bar graph on this page shows important facts about the size of Europe and its population. The pink bars

on this graph show what percentage of the world's population lives on each continent. The blue bars show the percentage of the world's land area for each continent. By comparing the set of bars for Europe, you can see that Europe's percentage of population is greater than its percentage of land area.

We measure how many people live in an area by population density. This is the average number of people living in a square mile or square kilometer. We find the population density of a country by dividing the number of people by the total land area.

The population density of the larger Western European countries is fairly high. France has a population density of 263 persons per square mile (102 per sq km). Germany has a population density of 571 persons per square mile (220 per sq km).

165

WESTERN EUROPE: POPULATION DENSITY

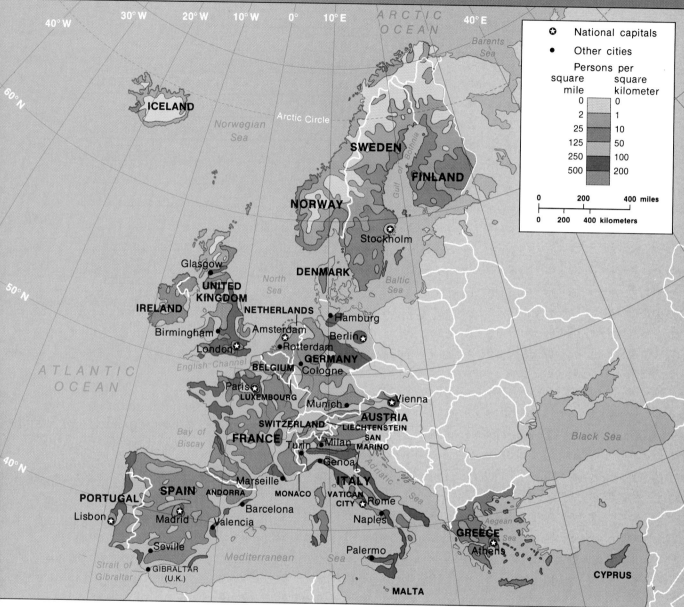

THE 25 LARGEST CITIES OF WESTERN EUROPE

London (U.K.) 6,755,000
Madrid (Spain) 3,200,000
Berlin (Germany) 3,056,000
Rome (Italy) 2,826,000
Paris (France) 2,176,000
Barcelona (Spain) 1,770,000
Hamburg (Germany) 1,592,000

Milan (Italy) 1,515,000
Vienna (Austria) 1,512,000
Munich (Germany) 1,267,000
Naples (Italy) 1,206,000
Turin (Italy) 1,035,000
Rotterdam (Netherlands) 1,025,000
Cologne (Germany) 922,000

Birmingham (U.K.) 920,000
Athens (Greece) 886,000
Marseille (France) 874,000
Lisbon (Portugal) 818,000
Valencia (Spain) 785,000
Glasgow (U.K.) 762,000
Genoa (Italy) 736,000

Palermo (Italy) 720,000
Amsterdam (Netherlands) 676,000
Seville (Spain) 672,000
Stockholm (Sweden) 653,000

About one half of the 25 largest cities of Western Europe have a population of more than 1 million.
▶ Which of the 25 largest cities are national capitals with a population greater than 1 million?

The small country of the Netherlands has the highest population density, with 1,040 persons per square mile (401 per sq km). Compare these figures with the figure for the United States, which has a population density of 69 persons per square mile (27 per sq km).

C. Western Europe's Population

The population of a country is never spread evenly over its territory. Cities have more people per square mile or kilometer than **rural**, or country, areas. Paris, the capital city of France, has a population density of 19,893 persons per square mile (7,715 per sq km), but there are parts of France with less than 125 persons per square mile (48 per sq km). The map on page 166 shows how the population density varies within the many countries of Western Europe.

Most Western Europeans live in **urban** areas, that is, in cities and towns. Over 92 percent of the British population is urban. France's city-dwellers make up 77 percent of its population. Even in the country of Sweden, which has a low population density of 49 persons per square mile (19 per sq km), 85 percent of the people live in cities.

In most Western European countries, the capital cities are also the largest cities. Rome is the largest city in Italy, Paris is the largest in France, and London the largest in England. About 30 percent of the Greek population lives in the **metropolitan area** of Athens. A metropolitan area is made up of a large city and the city's suburbs, or surrounding towns.

Western Europe still has many productive farms. But today most people live in cities. You will read more about farms in Europe in later chapters.

D. European Languages Around the Globe

Dozens of different languages are spoken in Europe. Most countries have one single national language. The French speak French, the Italians speak Italian, and so on. But several small countries have more than one official language because they use the languages of their bordering countries. Belgium has two languages, Luxembourg has three, and Switzerland has four. Because of the location and size of their countries, people in Western Europe find it useful to speak more than their own language.

All Western European countries have close neighbors. France's boundaries touch those of six other countries, and only about 20 miles (32 km) of the English

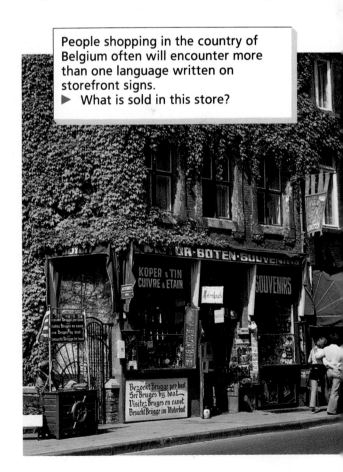

People shopping in the country of Belgium often will encounter more than one language written on storefront signs.
▶ What is sold in this store?

Channel separates France and England. Switzerland borders four countries, each with its own official language. Students in European schools spend more time studying foreign languages than American students do. For example, Swedish students begin to study a foreign language when they are in the third grade.

The use of European languages has spread far outside Europe. Nine of the 20 most widely spoken languages in the world are European. This book was written in a European language — English. Almost all of the people of North America and South America speak either English, Spanish, Portuguese, or French. English is also the language of the Australians and many others in Asia and Africa. Indeed, English is the second most widely spoken language in the world. The first is Chinese, with over a billion speakers.

E. Democratic Governments and the European Community

The Western European countries are democracies. Some, such as Italy, Germany, and France, are democratic republics. Others, such as Norway, Great Britain, and the Netherlands, have monarchs as heads of state. But the monarchs do not actually govern. The people elect representatives to make laws and govern in the monarchies as well as in the republics.

Western Europeans enjoy many democratic freedoms, such as freedom of speech, the press, and worship. Some countries have official religions, but people are free to follow other religions.

All Western European countries today have universal education, that is, schooling for all children. Almost everyone is literate, or able to read. To enjoy the full

MAJOR EUROPEAN LANGUAGES SPOKEN AROUND THE WORLD

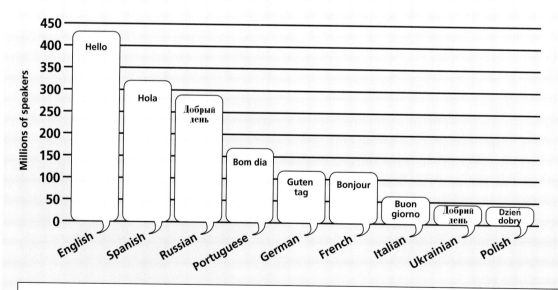

Almost half of the 20 most widely spoken languages in the world are European.
► About how many people speak English?

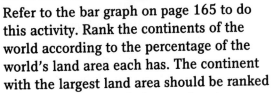

Young students in Switzerland listen to their teacher during a mathematics class. Education is extremely important in Western European countries.

▶ How is this classroom similar to your classroom?

benefits of democratic freedoms, people must be educated.

Belgium, Denmark, France, Germany, Greece, Ireland, Italy, Luxembourg, the Netherlands, Portugal, Spain, and the United Kingdom have joined the European Community (EC), with the intention of becoming a single "home" market. Eventually the countries of the EC will have a common currency, probably called the *ecu*. EC members are working toward greater cooperation on many other issues.

LESSON 2 REVIEW

THINK AND WRITE

A. In what ways was the Grand Tour in the eighteenth century like a tourist trip today?

B. How is population density figured?

C. How does a population density map tell more about where people live than a population density figure for the whole country?

D. Why do Europeans generally spend more time studying foreign languages than American students do?

E. Explain the connection between democratic freedoms enjoyed by Western Europeans and the ability to read.

SKILLS CHECK

THINKING SKILL

Refer to the bar graph on page 165 to do this activity. Rank the continents of the world according to the percentage of the world's land area each has. The continent with the largest land area should be ranked number 1. Then rank the continents according to percentage of population.

169

USING THE VOCABULARY

On a separate sheet of paper, write the word or words that best complete each sentence.

natural resource
deciduous
coniferous
forestry
climograph
current

Gulf Stream
North Atlantic
   Drift
urban
metropolitan area

1. A graph that shows both the average temperature and the average precipitation for a certain place is called a _____.

2. A stream that flows in the oceans is called a _____.

3. Cities and towns make up _____ areas.

4. The _____ flows north and east from the warm waters of the Gulf of Mexico into the North Atlantic.

5. The Latin word _____ means to "fall off."

6. Any material provided by nature that people use is called a _____.

7. The Gulf Stream merges with other warm currents to form the _____.

8. The science of caring for forests is called _____.

9. A large city and its suburbs, or surrounding towns, makes up a _____.

10. Trees in _____ forests bear cones.

REMEMBERING WHAT YOU READ

On a separate sheet of paper, answer the following questions in complete sentences.

1. What was the Grand Tour?

2. What is the name of the landmass that combines Europe and Asia?

3. Name the five peninsulas that extend into the ocean from Europe.

4. Paccard and Balmat climbed to the top of what mountain peak?

5. What is the largest group of mountains in Western Europe?

6. What mountains form a wall between the Iberian Peninsula and the rest of mainland Europe?

7. What continent is smaller than Europe?

8. What is population density?

9. What is the second most widely spoken language in the world?

10. What kind of government do the Western European countries have?

TYING LANGUAGE ARTS TO SOCIAL STUDIES

Imagine that your class is planning a Grand Tour through Western Europe. Choose a place in Western Europe you have read about or seen a picture of that you would be interested in visiting. Write a few paragraphs explaining why you think the place you have chosen should be part of the class's Grand Tour. If possible, add a picture or drawing to your paper to visualize the place you are describing. Then combine your paper with those of your classmates to make a travel brochure. With your classmates, add a title page and a table of contents to complete the brochure.

THINKING CRITICALLY

On a separate sheet of paper, answer the following questions in complete sentences.

1. Why do you think going on the Grand Tour was a good learning experience for students?
2. Why do you think forestry is important?
3. Why, do you think, do urban areas have a higher population density than rural areas?
4. Why is it useful to speak more than one language in Europe?
5. Why is it important for a country to educate all its people?

SUMMARIZING THE CHAPTER

On a separate sheet of paper, copy the graphic organizer shown below. Beside each heading write three answers to support it.

CHAPTER THEME	The blend of physical features, natural resources, and different peoples in Western Europe make it a unique region.

LAND OF WESTERN EUROPE		PEOPLE OF WESTERN EUROPE	
Mountains	1. _____ 2. _____ 3. _____	Densely Populated Countries	1. _____ 2. _____ 3. _____
Rivers	1. _____ 2. _____ 3. _____	European Languages	1. _____ 2. _____ 3. _____
Seas	1. _____ 2. _____ 3. _____	Democratic Freedoms	1. _____ 2. _____ 3. _____
Natural Resources	1. _____ 2. _____ 3. _____		

CHAPTER 6

History of Western Europe

Strong rulers, new laws, and the development of cities like Carcassone had a great impact on Europe. A system of loyalties and protection developed into a distinctive system of government.

Feudal Lords and Serfs

THINK ABOUT WHAT YOU KNOW

What things do you think of when you hear the term *castle*?

STUDY THE VOCABULARY

tax	manor
fief	economy
knight	serf
feudalism	Crusade

FOCUS YOUR READING

What were the obligations, or responsibilities, of feudal nobles and serfs during the Middle Ages?

A. King John Goes to Runnymede

King John's Reign The king was probably not in a good mood that Monday morning in 1215. It was a pleasant June day, and King John was on his way to Runnymede (RUN ih meed), a meadow along the south bank of the Thames (temz) River. But this was no royal pleasure trip. John was on his way to make peace with the nobles, who had threatened to drive him from the throne. Nobles were the people to whom the king had given land.

King John had ruled England for 16 years. His reign, or rule, had been filled with troubles—many of his own making. From the start some people had questioned his right to the throne. They believed that his nephew, Arthur, had a better claim. The question was settled when Arthur mysteriously disappeared. Some said that John had had him murdered. To this day no one knows for sure.

John's Opponents Throughout the years, John had his share of quarrels. He quarreled with the king of France, with his own nobles, and with the pope in Rome, the head of the Roman Catholic Church. Troubles with the nobles began because John had insisted that, as king, he had the power to do whatever he wished. He paid no attention to the old customs and laws of England. He forced the nobles to pay higher **taxes**. A tax is money paid to a ruler or government in return for government services. John sometimes seized the nobles' land without just cause. He also limited their right to hunt, and hunting was their main amusement.

Finally the nobles had had enough. They banded together and declared that they would make war against the king unless he accepted limits on his power. At first, John angrily refused to give in to the nobles. But he soon discovered that he had little support. He finally agreed to accept the nobles' demands. That was the reason for King John's trip to Runnymede on June 15, 1215.

B. King John Accepts the Magna Carta

When King John reached Runnymede, he entered a tent and seated himself on a throne. The nobles presented the king with a list of their demands. John gloomily put his seal on the list, showing that he accepted the demands. This list became the basis of the Great Charter, which is known by its Latin name *Magna Carta* (MAG nuh KAHR tuh).

The Magna Carta's real significance went beyond the dispute between John and his nobles. For the first time, a king of England was bound by the law. He could not do as he pleased. The king could not have unlimited power. The Magna Carta set forth rules that the king and his officials had to follow. For example, the king could not collect taxes unless the great council of the kingdom agreed to them. Royal officials could not take a freeman's horse or wagon without the owner's permission. The Magna Carta stated that the people were guaranteed a trial by jury. The king promised in the charter "to no one will we deny or delay justice." The Magna Carta was the root of many rights and liberties, and was the basic beginning of twentieth-century democracy.

John did not keep the promises made in the Magna Carta. It is doubtful that he ever intended to do so. Within a very short time, he was at war with the nobles. Fortunately the war did not last long, because the king became deathly ill. John died 16 months after putting his seal on the Magna Carta.

Mounted warriors served to protect the kings during the Middle Ages.
▶ What did the knight and his horse wear for their protection?

C. Land Granted for Services

Vassals and Knights King John had lived in a time of a medieval civilization, which historians call the *Middle Ages*. It was so named because it was the period of European history between ancient and modern times, approximately between the years 500 and 1500.

Kings during the Middle Ages did not command a strong central government like that of the Roman emperors. Instead, kings granted land, or **fiefs** (feefs), in exchange for loyalty and military service. Those who received a fief were called *vassals*. Each vassal who was given land by the king had to agree to give the king a certain number of armed men each year for his service. These men were called **knights**. A knight was a trained warrior who fought on horseback with swords and lances during the Middle Ages. To read more about knights, turn to page 176.

Government A vassal who promised knights to the king got the knights by giving them parts of his own fief. When a vassal gave land to others, he became a *lord*. The person who received the land became his vassal. These vassals, in turn, would grant parts of their fiefs to still others. Thus many of the king's vassals became lords of their own vassals. This form of government that developed in Western Europe during the Middle Ages is called **feudalism** (FYOOD ul ihz um). It was a system of government, a way of life, and a distinctive kind of society.

Feudal governments provided a way to settle disputes. Aside from that and providing some military protection, they did little else. They did not provide schools, hospitals, fire protection, or other services that governments provide today.

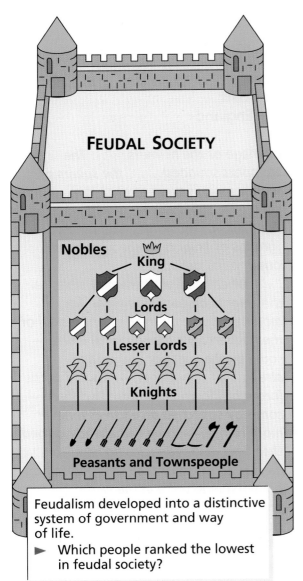

FEUDAL SOCIETY

Nobles

King

Lords

Lesser Lords

Knights

Peasants and Townspeople

Feudalism developed into a distinctive system of government and way of life.
► Which people ranked the lowest in feudal society?

D. Life on a Manor

Lords and Peasants Most nobles lived on **manors**, which were large farms or estates on their fiefs. The noble became the lord of his manor. He was responsible for governing it. The manor was the source of the noble's wealth.

The **economy** of the feudal manor was based on agriculture. Economy is the way in which natural resources and workers are used to produce goods and services. The peasants, or farm workers, were the backbone and muscle of agriculture, which was the economic foundation of feudalism. All peasants were either freemen or **serfs**. Most of them were serfs. The serf owed his labor to his lord. Serfs were not free to leave the manor without the lord's permission, but they could not be sold like slaves. The other peasants were freemen who owned or rented land from a lord. Freemen owed few, if any, obligations to a lord.

Castles and Villages The lord lived in the most important house on the manor. Powerful lords lived in castles. Perhaps you think living in a castle would be pleasant, but castles were designed for protection, not comfort. These castles were

This fifteenth-century painting shows serfs working in the fields.
► What is in the background of this feudal manor?

FROM:

Ivanhoe

By: Sir Walter Scott
Setting: Medieval England

Sir Walter Scott was born in Scotland in 1771. As an adult, he had a remarkable career as a poet, novelist, historian, and biographer. But the great success of his first narrative poem encouraged Scott to dedicate himself to literature. In fact, Scott invented a new type of literature: the historical novel.

Ivanhoe, published in 1819, is Scott's historical romantic novel about knighthood. The character Ivanhoe is a young knight who has returned from war to pit his wits, skills, and strength against a villainous knight.

In this passage, Scott describes a battle tournament between two groups of knights.

*T*he knights held their long lances upright, their bright points glancing to the sun, and the streamers with which they were decorated fluttering over the plumage of the helmets. . . . The trumpets sounded . . . the spears of the champions were at once lowered . . . the spurs were dashed into the flanks of the horses, and the two [groups of knights] rushed upon each other in full gallop.

. . . When the fight became visible, half the knights on each side were dismounted, some by the dexterity [skill] of their adversary's [opponent's] lance, — some by the superior weight and strength of opponents, which had borne [brought] down both horse and man, — some lay stretched on earth as if never more to rise, — some had already gained their feet, and were closing hand to hand with those of their antagonists [opponents] who were in the same predicament, — and several on both sides, who had received wounds by which they were disabled, were stopping their blood with their scarfs.

drafty, dirty, damp, and dim. They were usually built in hard-to-reach places. The first castles were made of wood. Later in the Middle Ages, they had thick stone walls, which were hard to attack but which kept the inside of the castles cold and damp. Small windows served well as lookouts, but they let in little sunlight. A moat, a water-filled ditch that surrounded the castle, and a heavy metal gate that protected the massive wooden door kept attackers away from the walls.

A manor also had a village, where the peasants lived. Most of the people who lived on the manor were peasants. A typical manor might have between 50 and 500 peasants. In addition to the peasant huts, a village usually had a church, a shed that served as a blacksmith shop, a mill for grinding grain, and farm fields.

Serfdom The life of a serf was a hard one. Women and girls worked in the fields with the men and boys. The serfs planted and harvested the crops. They cut hay in the summer and cut wood in the winter.

Serfs owed their lord more than work. They had to present him with gifts at certain times of the year. Nobles feasted during the holidays on the gifts from the serfs.

The lord of a manor controlled the village grain mill, bake oven, and wine or cider press. After a serf had the grain ground into meal, the lord received a share of it. When serfs baked loaves of rye bread, they gave a loaf for the lord's household.

The Magna Carta meant very little to the serfs. The king promised to respect the rights of his great vassals and certain freemen. But the charter said nothing about the serfs, who were not free.

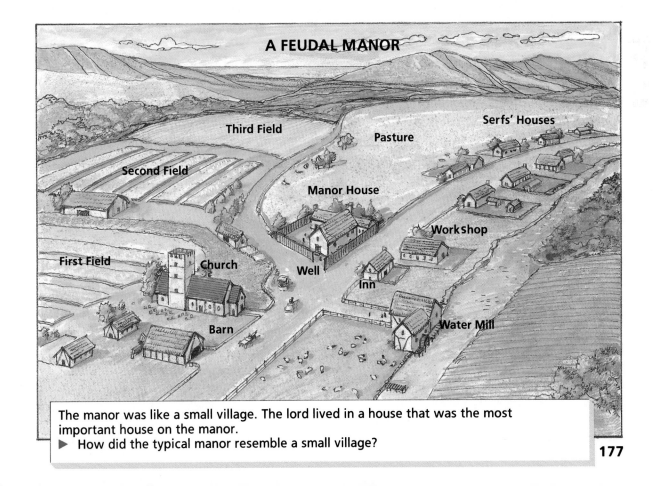

A FEUDAL MANOR

Third Field · Second Field · First Field · Church · Barn · Well · Inn · Manor House · Pasture · Serfs' Houses · Workshop · Water Mill

The manor was like a small village. The lord lived in a house that was the most important house on the manor.
▶ How did the typical manor resemble a small village?

After Richard I became king, he went off to fight in the Third Crusade.
▶ How can you tell from the engraving which man is King Richard?

E. Feudal Lords Fought "Wars for the Cross"

Feudal nobles and knights were warriors, and they had many opportunities to use their fighting skills. In 1095, Pope Urban II called upon nobles and knights to fight for the Holy Land, that part of the Middle East where Jesus had lived. The pope asked them to take part in a **Crusade** —a "war for the cross"—to free the land from Muslim control. Muslims followed the religion of Islam.

The pope told the knights that going on the Crusade was a religious duty. He also told them that it would be far better for Christian knights to fight Muslims in the Middle East than to fight each other in Europe. He also noted that there were great riches to be won in the Middle East.

The Crusade Pope Urban called for was the first in a series of Crusades during the Middle Ages. King John's brother, Richard the Lion-Hearted, led the Third Crusade in 1189. The Crusades affected both the Middle East and Western Europe.

LESSON **1** *REVIEW*

THINK AND WRITE

A. Why did the nobles threaten to rebel against King John in 1215?
B. What was the purpose of the Magna Carta?
C. Explain how the feudal system worked.
D. What duties did serfs have?
E. What was the purpose of the Crusades?

SKILLS CHECK

WRITING SKILL

Think about what it might be like to live on an American farm today. Then write a paragraph comparing this way of life with the life of a serf in the Middle Ages.

The People of the Towns and the Church

THINK ABOUT WHAT YOU KNOW

Why, do you think, do people live in towns?

STUDY THE VOCABULARY

monastery   **monopoly**
convent   **apprentice**
guild

FOCUS YOUR READING

What were the functions of the people of the church and the town?

A. Life in a Monastery During the Middle Ages

Saint Benedict During the early Middle Ages, a man later known as Saint Benedict began to live in a lonely cliffside cave near Rome. He lived there for three years, eating little else but bread that a friend lowered on a rope to his cave.

Benedict came to believe that a worthwhile life could be lived by men who lived together and worked hard. So Benedict established a **monastery**, a dwelling for monks, religious men who devote their lives to prayer and labor. For 1,400 years men went to the monastery seeking to live peaceful lives of prayer. The monastery, known as the Abbey of Monte Cassino, was the most famous one in Western Europe. The Abbey of Monte Cassino still stands today.

Caring for the sick was one of the duties of a monk during the Middle Ages.
▶ What, do you think, is in the box the monk is holding?

Daily Routine By today's standards, life in a monastery was hard. The monks got up during the night to pray. They worked long hours in the fields where they grew their own food. At certain times during the day, the monks went to church to sing and pray. Parts of each day were set aside for reading and study.

Usually the monks ate only one full meal a day. But during the summer and at times of plowing and harvest, they would have a second meal. The monks ate simply. Only the sick had meat or eggs. The monks went to bed early. At sundown it was time for evening prayers and for bed.

Nuns also lived lives full of prayer and work. They made the same kinds of

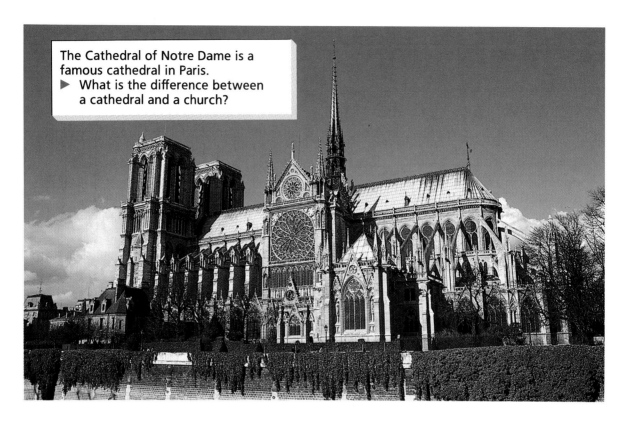

The Cathedral of Notre Dame is a famous cathedral in Paris.
▶ What is the difference between a cathedral and a church?

promises that monks made. They gave up everything they owned and never married. Nuns lived in houses called **convents**.

Helping people was part of the work in both monasteries and convents. The monks and nuns fed the poor. They gave travelers shelter for the night. They taught children, and they cared for the sick. It was a way of life very different from that of kings, queens, and knights.

B. Duties of a Village Priest

Priest's Duties The village priest was the person of the church best known to people on the manor. The priest held services in the village church, baptized babies, and taught children their religious duties. He performed marriages for the villagers in the church and conducted the services when they were buried in the churchyard.

Here is how one book described an ideal, or model, priest. He should teach children "to read, spell, and sing." He should even teach them that "their play should be honest and merry, without great noise." Of course, the book described the *ideal*, the way it should be. Actually most village children did not learn to read, and one doubts that many learned to play without great noise.

Bishop's Duties From time to time a high-ranking church official, the bishop, would visit the village church. A bishop was in charge of all the churches within a certain area.

As towns began to grow and prosper, people had more time for learning, literature, and the arts. Many young men who wanted to be priests entered schools run by bishops. The schools were located in large churches called *cathedrals*, which were often located in towns. Some of the finest and largest buildings erected in the Middle Ages were cathedrals.

C. Town Air Makes a Man Free

Travelers journeying to a town during the Middle Ages did well to arrive before sundown. If they failed to do so, they might be locked out. Many towns had walls, and the gates were closed at night. Towns built walls and gates for the same reason that feudal nobles had castles. Walls gave protection from bandits and even armies.

Houses were crowded close together within the walls of the towns. Sunlight shone only for brief periods on the narrow streets, which were only 6 to 10 feet (2 to 3 m) wide. Yet townspeople had one big advantage over people who lived on the rural manors. They did not have to labor for a lord, although the townspeople sometimes had to pay yearly taxes to a great lord. Nobles had such a need for money that they sometimes encouraged the establishment of towns by granting townspeople greater freedom. In some cases, if a serf lived for a year and a day in a town, he became free. It was said in those towns that "town air makes a man free."

This mural, entitled *The Effects of Good Government,* shows how wooden houses were crammed in next to each other so they might fit within the stone walls that encircled the town for protection.
► What kinds of activities took place in medieval towns?

D. Guilds Controlled the Town Markets

The Magna Carta stated that "all merchants shall be safe and secure in going out from England, coming into England, and going through England." However, a merchant could sell goods in a town only with the consent of its merchant **guild**. A guild was an association of people in the same business. The guild of merchants set the rules for the town market. The basic purpose of the merchant guilds was to promote the business and the personal well-being of their members.

Craft guilds were made up of people in the same trade or craft. Tailors, shoemakers, hatters, and metalsmiths all had their guilds. Each guild controlled the making and selling of its product within the town. This kind of control over the production of goods by one group is called a **monopoly**. All members of the guild had to follow the same standards. They had to use the same materials and sell their goods for the same price. The guilds did not want a free market — one in which sellers compete.

E. Guilds Controlled the Training of Workers

Pupils of Trade A young person wishing to take up a trade became an **apprentice** (uh PREN tihs), a pupil. An apprentice agreed to live and work with a master craftworker who belonged to the craft guild. An apprentice was not paid, but the master agreed to provide food and clothing as well as teach the apprentice the skills of the trade. Apprentices often lived with the master's family, above the shop. Sometimes apprentices slept in the attic.

An apprentice served four or more years, depending on the trade. A new apprentice did odd jobs requiring little skill. As time went on, more difficult skills had to be learned so that the apprentice could turn out a piece of work according to certain guild standards.

Going to Work When the period of training was completed, the apprentice became a *journeyman*. The name comes from the French word *jour*, meaning "day." A journeyman was paid for each day's work. A journeyman who wished to become a master in a guild would work for a number of years striving to produce a masterpiece. The masterpiece had to be a product made according to the very highest guild standards. A journeyman shoemaker, for example, would have to produce a very fine pair of shoes or boots.

This etching below shows members of a craft guild busily making coins during the Middle Ages.
▶ Of what guild are these workers members?

Wives commonly worked alongside their husbands in their trades, and daughters were apprenticed in the same way as their brothers. If a husband died, a woman carried on his business and craft. Many women became guild members, even members of traditional male trades. Such women were highly respected in the community. If a woman worked for a wage, however, she often received less than a man for the same work.

Guild rules for training apprentices served two purposes. The rules produced skilled workers, and they gave master craftworkers control of who could learn a trade. The masters made sure that there would not be too many workers in their line of business. This made it easier to keep prices high.

Most towns developed a town council made up of representatives of the various guilds. This council carried out many of the duties of a modern city government. Modern life as we know it today was beginning to develop.

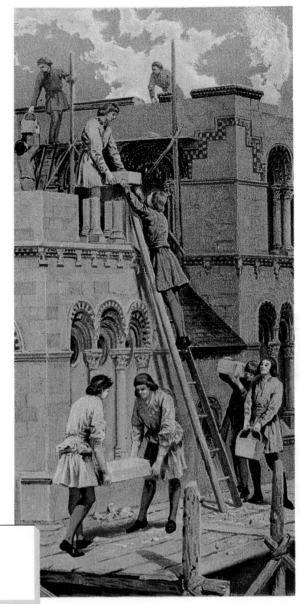

An apprentice learned a trade such as masonry, the building with stone, brick, or concrete.
▶ What materials and equipment did members of this trade guild use?

LESSON **2** REVIEW

THINK AND WRITE

A. What might the life of a monk be like?
B. What were the duties of a village priest?
C. What was the difference between the positions of a townsperson and a serf?
D. How did the guilds limit freedom?
E. What were the purposes of the apprentice system?

SKILLS CHECK

THINKING SKILL

Skim through the lesson to find five types of people who worked in towns or churches during the Middle Ages and find one characteristic for each of them. Make a chart using this information.

A Time of "Rebirth"

THINK ABOUT WHAT YOU KNOW

Tell about some thing or place that you would like to discover.

STUDY THE VOCABULARY

Renaissance   **explorer**

FOCUS YOUR READING

Why is the period of time after the Middle Ages called a time of rebirth?

A. A Rediscovery of Old Ideas

The change from the Middle Ages, or medieval history, into modern history took place gradually over many years and involved many events and developments in the arts and literature. One change was the rediscovery of the cultural heritages of ancient Greece and ancient Rome, which had become lost or forgotten during the Middle Ages. This interest in learning about the Romans and Greeks led to a birth of interest in newer types of learning. Old ideas led to new ones. Historians have used the term **Renaissance** (REN uh sahns), a French word meaning "rebirth," for this period of time following the Middle Ages.

The Renaissance started as early as the fourteenth century in Italy and then spread throughout most of Europe. The Renaissance gave Europeans new and different ideas about themselves and about the world. These ideas were expressed by writers and artists. The three best-known Renaissance artists were Leonardo da Vinci, Michelangelo, and Raphael (rahfah EL). All three of these men advanced the Renaissance style of showing nature and depicting the feelings of people.

B. Da Vinci Has New Ideas

Artist and Engineer   Leonardo da Vinci was born in 1452 in the Italian village of Vinci. The *da Vinci* in his name means "of Vinci." As a boy, Leonardo showed such an unusual ability to draw that his father took him to Florence and placed him as an apprentice in the shop of an artist.

Da Vinci was very sure of his own abilities as an artist. "I can carry out sculpture in marble, bronze, or clay, and I can do in painting whatever may be done, as well as any other [can], be he whom he may." Clearly, Da Vinci was not a modest man, yet he was not boasting. He could in fact do all these things and a great many more.

Da Vinci was an engineer as well as an artist. In 1482 he wrote to the duke of Milan, looking for a job. Leonardo said he could make devices that would be useful in war. He had an idea for a lightweight bridge that an army could easily move. He knew how to make a variety of cannons,

Da Vinci was one of the greatest painters of the Renaissance.
▶ Besides painting, what other talents did Da Vinci have?

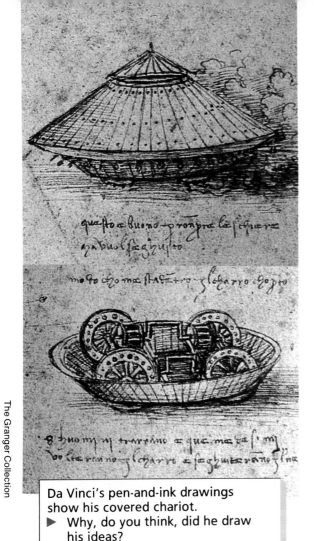

Da Vinci's pen-and-ink drawings show his covered chariot.
▶ Why, do you think, did he draw his ideas?

efforts to restore *The Last Supper* since Da Vinci's day.

Da Vinci later painted *Mona Lisa*, which has been called the most famous portrait in the world. But no one knows for sure just whose portrait it is.

The duke of Milan gave Da Vinci the job of making a huge bronze statue of a horse and rider. It would stand 23 feet (7 m) tall and would require 79 tons (72 t) of bronze. Da Vinci made a clay model, but he never cast the statue because the bronze was needed for making cannons.

Leonardo da Vinci's *Mona Lisa* is probably the most famous portrait ever painted.
▶ How did Da Vinci portray her?

including one that "could fling small stones almost like a storm." Perhaps his most unusual plan was for a cannon-firing tank, which he called a "covered chariot."

Da Vinci's Great Works Da Vinci was about 30 when he wrote his letter to the duke of Milan. The duke offered him the position of official engineer and artist. During his years in Milan, Da Vinci designed a canal and painted *The Last Supper*. He was always eager to try new things, so he used a new method of applying paint on a plaster wall for this famous painting. Unfortunately the new method did not work. The paint soon began to fade and flake off. There have been a number of

185

Michelangelo's famous *Pietà,* found in St. Peter's Church in Rome, is a marble sculpture of Mary holding the dead body of Christ on her lap.
▶ How does Christ's body appear?

C. A Man of Many Talents

Michelangelo was another man of many talents. He became a great painter, architect, and poet, though he was mainly interested in sculpture. In 1504, he sculpted the biblical hero David, who was the second king of Israel. The statue still stands in Florence, Italy.

Among Michelangelo's most famous paintings are those he painted on the ceiling of the Sistine Chapel in the Vatican. The Sistine Chapel is a famous chapel in Rome where the chief ceremonies involving the pope take place. Michelangelo lay on his back on a high scaffold, or movable platform, and covered the ceiling of the Sistine Chapel with more than 300 massive figures that show scenes from the Bible. It took four years to finish the task.

D. Raphael Saves Ancient Ruins

Raphael had come to Florence as a young man to study the works of the city's great artists, especially those of Da Vinci and Michelangelo. Raphael's paintings include a number of famous Madonnas, pictures of Mary the mother of Jesus.

In 1515, Raphael was appointed Keeper of the Remains of Rome. It was his job to save what could be saved of the remains of ancient buildings and monuments. During the Middle Ages, Rome had greatly shrunk in size. People freely used stones taken from ancient ruins to erect other buildings.

By Raphael's time, people took a very different view of the old Roman remains. They regarded the ancient Roman statues and buildings as models to be copied. Architects studied the ruins so that they could erect churches and palaces in the Roman style. Fragments of antique statues dug up from time to time became valuable. They served as models for sculptors to copy.

E. Ancient Writings Spark New Interest

Studying Latin Students during the Renaissance found a new interest in the ancient Latin writings of the Romans. There was nothing new about studying Latin. Priests and monks had done so throughout the Middle Ages. Latin was the language of the church services and the Bible in Western Europe. But some of the students during the Renaissance did not study Latin in order to become priests. They planned to become government employees or merchants. They were more interested in politics and philosophy, the love of wisdom, than religion. Students wanted to read ancient authors because some of the authors, such as Cicero (SIHS ur oh), had had the same interests they did. They also found much in the history of Greece and Rome that reminded them of the recent history of the Italian cities. Such discoveries made the ancient writings seem new.

Like the architects, students tried to copy ancient styles. They wrote letters and speeches like those of Cicero. A few students tried to write histories and biographies like those by the ancient writers.

Studying Greek Some students wanted to study the Greek language as well as Latin. After all, the Roman writers often referred to the beauty and wisdom found in Homer, Plato, and other Greek authors. If students knew Greek, they could read those works themselves.

When the city of Florence hired a Greek professor, students jumped at the chance to study with him. One of those students described his excitement at that time. He and his fellow students believed that "all knowledge comes from the Greeks." By learning Greek, they could "speak with Homer and Plato." The student said that he studied so hard during the day that he dreamed in Greek at night. It must have pleased the professor to have had a student like that.

F. Printing Makes Books Cheaper

Handwritten Books The interest in ancient writings led students to search for books that might have been forgotten. They searched in monasteries, and they visited libraries in the eastern Mediterranean lands. In the monasteries they found some dusty books that no one had read for years. In the eastern cities they found works not known in Western Europe.

Many students were eager to read the books that had been found, but only a few could do so. There were only a few copies

In this illuminated manuscript a scholar is shown teaching students Greek during the Renaissance.
► How are the students learning?

Johann Gutenberg used a printing press to print the first page of the Bible in his workshop in Mainz, Germany.

▶ How did the printing press increase learning?

of most books. The only way to make more was to copy them by hand. As a result, books were very costly. Only rulers and the rich could afford to have libraries.

Printed Cards Books did not become more plentiful until after the development of printing. The first printing was done from carved wooden blocks. The blocks were used chiefly for printing playing cards, since only 52 blocks were needed. To print an entire book by this method would require carving a separate block for each page.

Printed Books By the 1450s a German printer named Johann Gutenberg (YOH-hahn GOOT un burg) had developed a better method of printing. Gutenberg made separate metal blocks, called type, for each letter. He could spell out the words for each page with letter type and fasten them in a frame. After printing one page, the movable type could be used to set another page. Since the type was made of metal, it could be used over and over without wearing out.

The printing of books made them much cheaper, so many more people could have books. Since Gutenberg's time, millions of books have been printed. Today most schools have far more books than even the richest person could have had before Gutenberg invented movable type. You can see from the pictures on page 189 how printing has changed over time.

Printing: THEN AND NOW

1 The Chinese invented block printing around the second century A.D.

2 Scribes hand copied books throughout the Middle Ages.

3 Gutenberg first used movable type in Europe by about 1455.

4 Web-fed printing presses are commonly used today.

Printing is one of our most important means of mass communication. Advances in printing have made it possible for more people to obtain more knowledge faster and more cheaply than ever before.

▶ What invention changed the method of printing?

Christopher Columbus arrived in the New World on October 12, 1492.

▶ How can you tell from this engraving that Columbus and his crew have seen land?

G. A Time of Exploration

While some people searched for ancient books, others searched for sea routes to Asia. Christopher Columbus is perhaps the most famous **explorer** of the Renaissance. An explorer is a person who searches for new things and places. Columbus was only one of the great explorers of this period. At the same time, Vasco da Gama and Ferdinand Magellan were also making great voyages of exploration.

Much was happening during the Renaissance, and not all of it can be described as "rebirth." It was a time when people had new ideas and made new discoveries. Leonardo da Vinci had ideas for new inventions. Gutenberg produced a new way to make books that changed the world. Columbus reached land that Europeans did not know existed. After his voyage, Europeans began to explore the Americas, which they called the New World.

LESSON *3* REVIEW

THINK AND WRITE

A. Why is the period after the Middle Ages known as the Renaissance?
B. What were Da Vinci's new ideas?
C. What were Michelangelo's talents?
D. Why was Raphael appointed Keeper of the Remains of Rome?
E. Why did ancient writings spark new interest in students during the time of the Renaissance?

F. Explain the importance of Johann Gutenberg's invention.
G. Why was the Renaissance a time of discovery and rebirth?

SKILLS CHECK

THINKING SKILL

Look up the following cities in your Gazetteer: *Florence, Milan, Genoa.* Which city is a port city?

Changes in Church and Government

THINK ABOUT WHAT YOU KNOW

Choose one thing about your school that you would change if you had the chance. What would you have to do to accomplish this change?

STUDY THE VOCABULARY

Reformation   **divine right**

FOCUS YOUR READING

How were changes brought about in the church and in government?

A. A Traveler Makes Plans for a Book

Planning One Book It was a slow trip across the Alps on horseback in 1509. Desiderius Erasmus (des uh DIHR ee us ih-RAZ mus) decided that he would not waste his time trading stories with his fellow travelers. Instead, he busied his mind with plans for a little book he would write as soon as he had a chance.

Erasmus was on his way back to England after spending many years in Italy, where he studied Greek. England, however, was not his home. Erasmus was born in Rotterdam, a city in the Netherlands. He sometimes signed his name "Erasmus of Rotterdam." But he had spent little time in his native land since he first left to study.

When Erasmus reached England, he lived for a time in the house of his friend Thomas More. It was in More's house that Erasmus wrote the book he had planned while traveling. The book is entitled *The Praise of Folly*.

Erasmus' Bible Erasmus wanted very much for people to know more about the teachings of Christianity. He believed that students should use their learning to help people discover Christian teachings. He wanted students to learn Greek so that they could read the Christian New Testament in the language in which it had been written. Toward this end, he published the first printed Greek New Testament. Erasmus realized that only a few students would be able to read Greek. Since he wanted all people to read the Bible, he favored the translation of the Bible into the languages used by the commoners, or people who were not nobles.

Erasmus was a Dutch priest and a scholar in the early 1500s.
► How can you tell from this portrait that Erasmus must have been a wealthy man?

In 1517, Martin Luther wrote 95 theses, or statements, protesting abuses by the Roman Catholic Church.
► How did Luther display his protests?

B. Luther Protests Against Church Authority

The Bible's Authority Among those who made use of Erasmus' Greek New Testament was a German monk and teacher, Martin Luther. Luther's study of the Bible had led him to question some teachings of the Roman Catholic Church. People of the Church pointed out that popes had long ago condemned the ideas that Luther had adopted. Luther answered that these ideas came from the Bible and that even a pope could not condemn them.

Luther did not believe that the pope in Rome was head of the Church. Luther followed only the Bible. He insisted that the Bible provided all the guidance people needed to live a Christian life. His opponents agreed that the Bible was a book of authority, but they believed that its meaning needed to be explained.

Luther wanted the Bible to be available to all people. Only priests and students could read the Latin translation that had been used during the Middle Ages. Luther therefore translated the Bible into German, a language of the common people.

A Movement for Reform In 1521, Luther was excommunicated, or excluded, from the Roman Catholic Church. He was declared an outlaw when he would not retract, or take back, his teachings. He had become a leader of the **Reformation**, a movement to reform the Roman Catholic Church. The movement led eventually to the establishment of new churches. Followers of Luther's ideas became known as Protestants. The Protestant revolt against the authority of the pope soon spread through many parts of Europe.

C. The Reformation Divides Christians

Protestant Churches John Calvin led the Reformation in Switzerland. Like Luther, he believed in the authority of the Bible. Calvin wished to discard any church practice that was not based on the Bible.

There were a number of other Protestant leaders. They all disagreed with the Roman Catholic Church, but they also disagreed among themselves. So instead of there being one Protestant Church, there were many.

Church of England In England the Protestants won the support of King Henry VIII. The king broke away from the pope's authority and set up a Protestant church, the Church of England. Although it still

MAJOR RELIGIOUS DIVISIONS ABOUT 1600

Roman Catholic
Lutheran
Calvinist
Anglican
Orthodox
Muslim

0   200   400 miles
0   200   400 kilometers

NORWAY
SWEDEN
SCOTLAND
North Sea
Baltic Sea
DENMARK
IRELAND
POLAND
ENGLAND
RUSSIA
ATLANTIC
OCEAN
HOLY ROMAN EMPIRE
FRANCE
SWITZERLAND
OTTOMAN EMPIRE
Black Sea
PORTUGAL
ITALY
CORSICA
SPAIN
SARDINIA
Mediterranean Sea
SICILY
AFRICA

10° W   60° N   0°
50° N

Many Christians broke away from the Roman Catholic Church during the Protestant Reformation. One group of Christians set up the Anglican Church.
▶ In what country did most Anglicans live?

had its own bishops and archbishops, the Church of England, or Anglican Church, no longer accepted the authority of the pope in Rome. But some of the English disagreed with King Henry's actions. Erasmus' friend Thomas More refused to swear loyalty to the Church of England. More's refusal cost him his life. King Henry had him beheaded.

Churches Agree Quarrels between Protestants and Roman Catholics sometimes led to wars. But after many years of fighting, there remained many devoted Roman Catholics and many equally devoted Protestants in Western Europe. Both sides finally decided to live together in peace. They still did not agree about religion; they simply agreed to disagree. How would you explain what that means?

D. National Rulers Replaced Feudal Rulers

Feudalism Ends The governments of most Western European countries at the time of the Reformation differed from those of the Middle Ages. Kings no longer depended upon the services of their vassals. They paid for people to join their armies instead of calling for the knights promised by the vassals. Nobles still held high positions, but they held them "at the king's pleasure," meaning that the king could remove them whenever he wished. Rulers hired a number of officials who were commoners.

To pay for hired armies and officials, rulers collected taxes. The need for money was usually greater than the amount raised from taxes, so rulers were often in

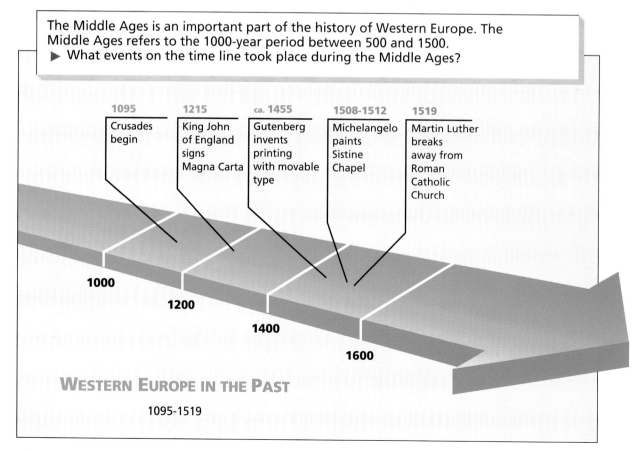

The Middle Ages is an important part of the history of Western Europe. The Middle Ages refers to the 1000-year period between 500 and 1500.
▶ What events on the time line took place during the Middle Ages?

1095 Crusades begin

1215 King John of England signs Magna Carta

ca. 1455 Gutenberg invents printing with movable type

1508-1512 Michelangelo paints Sistine Chapel

1519 Martin Luther breaks away from Roman Catholic Church

1000

1200

1400

1600

WESTERN EUROPE IN THE PAST
1095-1519

debt. Bankers who lent money became as important to governments as nobles were.

Queen Elizabeth I Monarchs were no longer just the chief feudal lords. A king or queen was the ruler of a nation. When Elizabeth I became queen of England in 1558, she realized that she needed the support of all the people. She often toured England to see her people and to be seen by them. The queen made the tours for much the same reason that political leaders today appear on television.

Elizabeth's reign became known as the Golden Age or Elizabethan Age because it was a time of great achievement in England. Writers and poets produced great works of art. English literature thrived during this period. One poet and playwright of this era, William Shakespeare, wrote some of the finest literature the world has known. You read an excerpt from his play *Julius Caesar* in Chapter 3.

King James I Although wise monarchs like Elizabeth sought the support of the people, they did not believe that the people could choose their rulers. King James I, who became king after Elizabeth's death, insisted that he ruled by **divine right**. By this he meant that his powers came from

Elizabeth I, who ruled for 45 years, saw England emerge as a world power.
► What do you think the artist tried to show about the queen?

God, not from the people. It was not until later times that the people won the right to elect their governments. You will read that story in the next chapter.

LESSON **4** REVIEW

THINK AND WRITE

A. Why did Erasmus publish a Greek New Testament?

B. What led Martin Luther to break away from the Roman Catholic Church?

C. What were some results of the Reformation?

D. How did the position of a national ruler differ from that of a feudal ruler?

SKILLS CHECK

MAP SKILL

Look at the map on page 193 to answer the following questions: In which countries did Roman Catholics live? In which countries did Lutherans live? What was the religion of the people who lived in Scotland?

WHY IS FREEDOM OF RELIGION IMPORTANT?

The First Amendment to the United States Constitution states that "Congress shall make no law respecting an establishment of religion, or prohibiting the free exercise thereof. . . . " This means the United States government cannot declare any religion to be an official religion that all citizens must follow. It also means that the people are free to choose what religion they want to practice or to choose to practice no religion at all.

In Lesson 3 of this chapter, you read about some changes in how people practiced their religions in the sixteenth century. Martin Luther was one of many people who thought that the Bible should be translated into different languages so that everyone would be able to read it. The common people began to demand that they be free to study and understand what had only been available to priests, students, and nobles.

Martin Luther and others involved in the Protestant Reformation helped to establish a number of new Christian churches, including the Lutheran Church, the Calvinist Church, and the Church of England. The members of these churches believed in the same God but chose to worship in different ways. The people who broke away from the Roman Catholic Church because they did not agree with all of its teachings were exercising their own right to freedom of religion.

Some countries still required all of their citizens to belong to official state religions. Members of various religious groups left their home in Europe and looked for a new place to live because their freedom of religion was being denied. The new place that these groups of people came to was what is now the United States.

Today, people all around the world—people from all different religious backgrounds—want to have the right to worship as they choose, openly and freely. We can all become better world citizens by respecting the beliefs of other people. If all people can peacefully "agree to disagree" about religion, perhaps we can learn tolerance, improve communication, and make the world a better place to live.

Thinking For Yourself

On a separate sheet of paper, answer the following questions in complete sentences.

1. Imagine that you are a member of a group of government officials who are writing a constitution for a new country. How would you convince the rest of the group that freedom of religion is a right that should be included in the constitution?
2. What right besides freedom of religion did Protestants exercise during the Reformation?
3. Do you think there are any people today who would give up their lives rather than give up religious freedom? Explain.
4. How do you think respecting the beliefs of other people can make you a better world citizen?
5. What do you think it would be like to live in a country where there was no freedom of religion?

USING THE VOCABULARY

knight	guild
feudalism	monopoly
serf	apprentice
Crusade	Renaissance
monastery	Reformation

From the list above, choose a vocabulary word that could be used in place of the underlined word or words in each sentence. Rewrite the sentences on a separate sheet of paper.

1. Michelangelo was an artist during the period after the Middle Ages.
2. The pope asked nobles and knights to take part in a war for the cross.
3. The association of merchants set the rules for the town markets.
4. A trained warrior fought on horseback with swords and lances.
5. A peasant bound to the land owed labor to the lord of the manor.
6. The Abbey of Monte Cassino was a dwelling for monks.
7. Each craft guild had a control over the making and selling of goods.
8. Martin Luther was a strong leader in the movement for reform in the Christian religion.
9. Vassals became lords of their own vassals under the form of government during the Middle Ages.
10. A new pupil working for a master in a guild would start by doing odd jobs.

REMEMBERING WHAT YOU READ

On a separate sheet of paper, answer the following questions in complete sentences.

1. What was the Magna Carta?
2. What were a serf's duties on a manor?
3. How did Pope Urban II convince nobles and knights to participate in a Crusade?
4. Why was the village priest the person of the church best known to people on a manor?
5. Who were the people who belonged to a craft guild?
6. How did an apprentice learn a trade?
7. Who were three important artists of the Renaissance?
8. Why did students during the Renaissance want to read the works of ancient authors?
9. Who were two important leaders of the Reformation?
10. How did the governments of most Western European countries change about the time of the Reformation?

TYING LANGUAGE ARTS TO SOCIAL STUDIES

The tournaments between knights during the Middle Ages were exciting events. Find out more about them in your school library. Working with other members of your class, write a play in which characters such as lords, ladies, and knights explain how they prepare for a tournament.

THINKING CRITICALLY

On a separate sheet of paper, answer the following in complete sentences.

1. Would you have wanted to live in a castle during the Middle Ages? Explain.
2. To what kind of job would you want to be an apprentice?
3. What person living today could be called a man or woman of many talents? Explain why.
4. Why, do you think, did people like Columbus want to discover new lands?
5. How might a government raise the money it needs without collecting taxes or getting loans from banks?

SUMMARIZING THE CHAPTER

On a separate sheet of paper, draw a graphic organizer that is like the one shown here. Copy the information from this graphic organizer to the one you have drawn. Under the main idea for each lesson, write four statements that support the main idea.

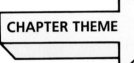
CHAPTER THEME

The way of life that developed in Western Europe during the Middle Ages changed with the growth of trade, the influences of the Renaissance and the Reformation, and the rise of national rulers.

LESSON 1

Feudal nobles and serfs had obligations.

1. _____
2. _____
3. _____
4. _____

LESSON 2

The people of the town and Church had specific functions.

1. _____
2. _____
3. _____
4. _____

LESSON 3

The period after the Middle Ages is called a time of rebirth.

1. _____
2. _____
3. _____
4. _____

LESSON 4

Changes were brought about in the Church and government.

1. _____
2. _____
3. _____
4. _____

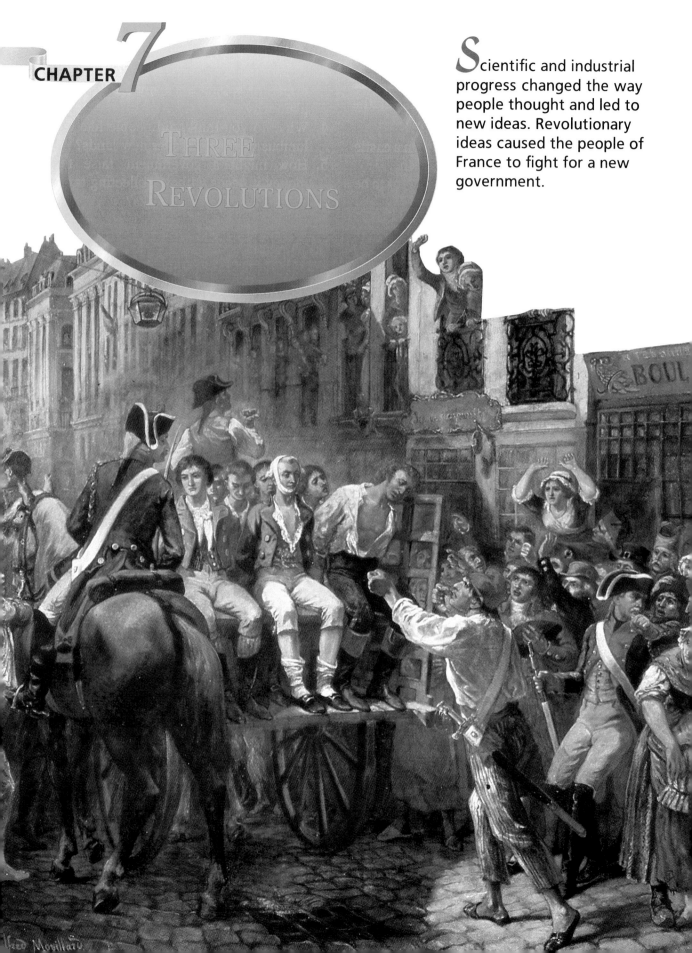

CHAPTER 7

THREE REVOLUTIONS

*S*cientific and industrial progress changed the way people thought and led to new ideas. Revolutionary ideas caused the people of France to fight for a new government.

A Revolution in Science

THINK ABOUT WHAT YOU KNOW

Imagine that you are traveling in a rocket through space. Tell what kinds of things you might see.

STUDY THE VOCABULARY

revolution   **Inquisition**
astronomy

FOCUS YOUR READING

What did Copernicus, Galileo, and other scientists do to affect the way people thought?

A. Copernicus Turns Astronomy Upside Down

Studying Space Nicolaus Copernicus lived a quiet life. He seems to have been a rather shy person who did not like to upset things. Yet upset things he did when he wrote the book *On the Revolutions of the Heavenly Bodies.*

The word **revolution** has at least two meanings. It may mean either "turning round" or "a complete change." Copernicus intended the first meaning in the title of his book. It is about the "turning round" of the earth and other planets. But the book also brought about a revolution, "a complete change," in the way people thought about the universe.

In 1497, Copernicus left Poland to study law, medicine, mathematics, Greek, and **astronomy** in Italy. Astronomy is a science that deals with the study of the stars, planets, sun, moon, and other bodies in space. In the fifteenth century, astronomy was still based on the teachings of Claudius Ptolemy (TAHL uh mee), one of the greatest astronomers and geographers of ancient times. Ptolemy believed that the earth stood still. According to him, the sun, moon, and planets revolved around the earth. However, some people did not agree with Ptolemy, and Copernicus was one of them.

Copernicus's Book After many years of observing the positions of stars and planets from a tower, Copernicus was convinced that Ptolemy was wrong. Copernicus noted that even some ancient thinkers had believed that the earth moved, rather than stood still as Ptolemy said. Copernicus spent many hours working on a book that showed that the sun is the center about which the earth and planets revolve. The book also showed that the moon moves about the earth, which constantly revolves on its axis.

Copernicus spent many years studying the stars and planets.
► How did Copernicus revolutionize astronomy?

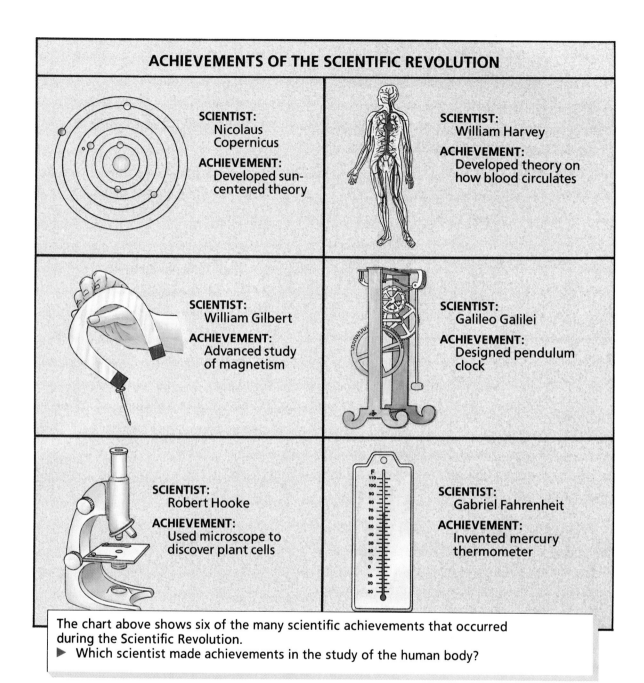

ACHIEVEMENTS OF THE SCIENTIFIC REVOLUTION

SCIENTIST:
Nicolaus Copernicus

ACHIEVEMENT:
Developed sun-centered theory

SCIENTIST:
William Harvey

ACHIEVEMENT:
Developed theory on how blood circulates

SCIENTIST:
William Gilbert

ACHIEVEMENT:
Advanced study of magnetism

SCIENTIST:
Galileo Galilei

ACHIEVEMENT:
Designed pendulum clock

SCIENTIST:
Robert Hooke

ACHIEVEMENT:
Used microscope to discover plant cells

SCIENTIST:
Gabriel Fahrenheit

ACHIEVEMENT:
Invented mercury thermometer

The chart above shows six of the many scientific achievements that occurred during the Scientific Revolution.
▶ Which scientist made achievements in the study of the human body?

After finishing his book, Copernicus put it away. Why did he not publish it? He later said that he feared "the scorn which my new opinion would bring on me." It was some time before Copernicus's friends persuaded him to write a brief summary of his ideas. He finally did so, but he would not let it be printed. Only handwritten copies were passed about.

His Ideas Spread In spite of Copernicus's effort to keep quiet, word about his ideas spread. As the shy man feared, people did make fun of him. One man scoffed, "This fool will turn the whole science of astronomy upside down." But some people who heard of Copernicus's ideas wanted to learn more, including the pope and some other Church officials.

It was a young German professor named Rheticus (RE tih kus) who finally got Copernicus to make his ideas public. After much discussion, Rheticus was allowed to publish a short summary of the book, provided he did not mention Copernicus by name.

Rheticus went to see Copernicus months later. This time Rheticus managed to get permission to publish Copernicus's book. *On the Revolutions of the Heavenly Bodies* was printed in the spring of 1543. By that time, however, Copernicus was very ill. A copy of the printed book was shown to him just before he died.

B. Galileo Tries Out His Ideas

Studying Pendulums Among those who accepted Copernicus's ideas was Galileo Galilei (gal uh LEE oh galuh LAY ee). Galileo was born in Pisa, Italy, 21 years after the publication of *On the Revolutions of the Heavenly Bodies*. As a young man he studied medicine, science, and mathematics. He went on to become a great mathematician and a famous astronomer.

Galileo's restless mind could be set working by quite ordinary incidents. For example, one day in church he noticed a lamp swinging back and forth like a pendulum. A pendulum is a weight hung so that it swings freely back and forth. He started to time each swing by counting his pulse. He discovered that regardless of how far the lamp swung, the time of each swing was the same. Galileo later discovered that the swings of a pendulum take equal time regardless of their width.

Galileo Experiments Galileo learned about pendulums by observation, or careful study, and experimentation. He tried out an idea and observed how it worked.

Aristotle, an ancient philosopher, had once said that if two objects of different weights were dropped at the same time, the heavier one would fall faster than the lighter one. Galileo tested the idea and observed that the objects of different weights reached the ground at the same time.

C. Galileo Points a Telescope Skyward

Looking at the Sky In 1609, Galileo heard that a Dutch inventor had built an instrument that made distant objects appear near. The instrument was, of course, the telescope. The government of the

Many people, such as the English poet John Milton, visited Galileo in his observatory in Italy.
▶ What instrument is used in an observatory?

Netherlands bought telescopes to be used by sea captains and military leaders. But Galileo quickly realized that telescopes could have other uses, so he made several, each more powerful than the other.

When Galileo pointed his most powerful telescope toward the sky, he saw sights that no one had ever seen before. He discovered that there were mountains and deep valleys on the moon. He saw that the Milky Way was not simply a broad band of faint light; it was made up of countless separate stars. Through the telescope he could see that the planet Jupiter had four moons that revolved around it.

Supporting Copernicus Galileo had no doubt that what he saw through the telescope provided more support for Copernicus's ideas, but not everyone trusted such observations. Some still held to the ideas of Aristotle and Ptolemy. They refused to believe that these great thinkers of ancient times could have been wrong. Some people who defended the ancient ideas held high positions in the Church at Rome. They thought Copernicus's book contained dangerous ideas, and 73 years after its publication, they finally succeeded in having it condemned as false.

To stop the spread of Copernicus's ideas, Galileo was ordered to stop writing that the earth moved. But he disregarded this order in one of his writings and was brought before the **Inquisition**, a special Church court. Threatened with severe punishments, Galileo finally swore that it was an error to say that the earth moved. There is a legend that as the old man left the court, he muttered, "But it does move." It is doubtful that he actually said this, although he may well have thought it.

This painting depicts Galileo being condemned for his writings on astronomy before the Inquisition, a special Church court.
▶ How does this courtroom compare with and differ from a courtroom of today?

Musee d' Orsay, France

D. New Instruments Improve Observation

Taking Measurements Galileo timed the swinging lamp by counting his pulse. His experiments with pendulums led to the development of more accurate clocks and watches. These instruments provided a more precise way to time an observation.

Scientific experiments required other types of accurate measurements. A German scientist, Gabriel Fahrenheit (FER-un hyt), invented a thermometer to measure temperatures. Fahrenheit put mercury into a glass tube with marked spaces. Each marked space represented a degree of temperature. One could tell if the temperature was getting warmer or colder by noting the rise or fall of the mercury.

Lenses for Seeing More Glass lenses in telescopes made it possible to observe distant planets. Lenses were also used to see objects too small for the naked eye to see. By 1674 a lens grinder in the Netherlands named Anton van Leeuwenhoek (LAY vun-hook) had a microscope so powerful that he could see microorganisms, or "little animals," in rainwater. A microorganism is any living thing too tiny to be seen without the use of a microscope.

The invention and improvement of scientific instruments were an important

Leeuwenhoek developed hundreds of lenses with powerful magnifying power.
► What two scientific instruments did his lenses improve?

part of the revolution in science. The use of instruments made it possible for more accurate observations and experiments. And observations and experiments were important in bringing about the revolution in science that changed the ways that people thought.

LESSON **1** REVIEW

THINK AND WRITE

A. How did Copernicus's idea of the universe differ from that of Aristotle and Ptolemy?

B. According to Galileo, what was the best way to learn?

C. What facts about the universe did Galileo discover by using a telescope?

D. Why were new instruments important for the development of the sciences?

SKILLS CHECK

THINKING SKILL

On one side of a sheet of paper, list the ways in which Galileo and Copernicus were alike. On the other side, list the ways in which these two scientists were different.

The Industrial Revolution

THINK ABOUT WHAT YOU KNOW

Think about the kinds of machines that you have in your home. How would your life be different if you did not have these machines?

STUDY THE VOCABULARY

Industrial   capital
   Revolution   profit
factory   free enterprise
standard of
   living

FOCUS YOUR READING

What changes resulted from the Industrial Revolution?

A. James Watt Puts Steam to Work

A Curious Boy Some of the best-known stories about famous people are hard to prove. One such story has been often told about James Watt who was born in Scotland in 1736. According to the story, one afternoon when James was a small boy, he sat in the kitchen watching a boiling tea-kettle. He discovered that when he put a spoon on the spout and stopped the steam, the steam would lift the lid. His aunt, busy with her work, paused just long enough to scold him.

"I never saw such an idle boy! For the last hour you have done nothing but watch that kettle. Go read a book or do something useful!"

We do not know whether or not James Watt did go read a book as his aunt had suggested to him. But if the story is true, that may have been the first time that James had observed the pressure of steam.

Watt Uses His Ideas When James Watt grew older, he went to London and served as an apprentice to an instrument maker. Later he returned to Scotland and took a job making and repairing equipment for science classes. One day Watt was given a model steam engine to repair. He fixed the engine, but he saw that it was not an efficient machine. He noticed that steam engines of this type worked slowly and wasted a lot of energy. He was sure that it was possible to make a much better steam engine. Watt continued to experiment until, by 1776, he was making and selling a more efficient steam engine.

The young James Watt was fascinated by steam. As an adult, he invented an improved steam engine.
▶ What sparked Watt's interest in steam?

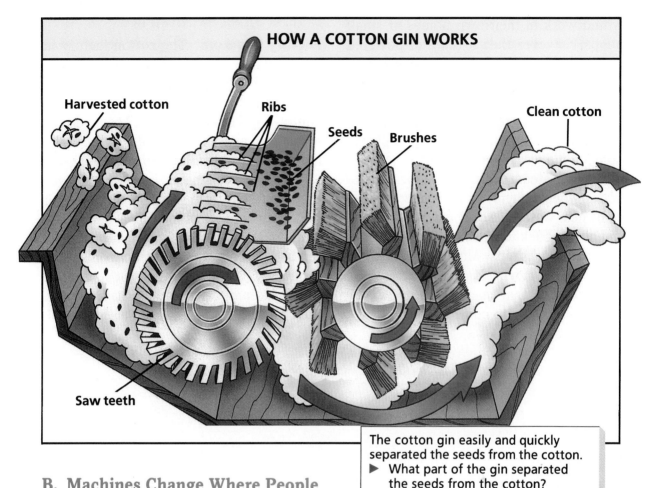

HOW A COTTON GIN WORKS

Harvested cotton

Ribs

Seeds

Brushes

Clean cotton

Saw teeth

The cotton gin easily and quickly separated the seeds from the cotton.
▶ What part of the gin separated the seeds from the cotton?

B. Machines Change Where People Work

Revolutionary Inventions Watt's steam engine was just one of the inventions that greatly changed the ways people worked. These changes brought about a revolution — the **Industrial Revolution**.

The first machines were powered by the muscles of the workers. Spinning wheels were turned by hand or foot pedal. One of the first inventions of the Industrial Revolution was a spinning machine called the spinning jenny. It increased the amount of thread that could be spun, but it was still worked by the spinner. It was not until 1769 that water power was used to work spinning machines. Water power was not used for weaving cloth until 16 years later.

The Cotton Gin As the methods for producing cloth improved, the demand increased for better ways to process the raw cotton before it went to **factories**, or buildings in which goods are manufactured. An American, Eli Whitney, visited a cotton plantation in Georgia and invented the cotton gin in 1793. This machine could clean 50 pounds (23 kg) of cotton fiber a day by separating the newly picked cotton from the seeds. This invention created a dramatic increase in the production of raw cotton for British factories.

Growth of Factories As long as people worked with hand tools or simple machines, such as a spinning wheel, they would work in their own homes or small shops. However, the use of water-powered machines changed the places where people worked. The water wheels that supplied power for the machines had to be located near waterfalls or by dams on streams. As a result, factories replaced some home workshops.

When steam engines took the place of water wheels, factories no longer needed to be near waterfalls or dams. But workers did not go back to working in their homes or small workshops. Machines had to be connected by wheels and belts to the steam engine that made them go, so the workers still had to come to the factory.

C. Machines Set the Pace

Factory Workers The cotton factory in Manchester, England, employed many children. Factories hired children because they did not have to be paid as much as adults. A girl or boy of 11 or 12 could do the job as well as a skilled hand weaver. It did not take a lot of skill to tend a machine.

Tending machines in a factory was quite different from working with tools or hand-powered machines in a shop. The workers in the cotton factory in Manchester had to follow a strict schedule. The steam engine started running at six o'clock in the morning. All workers had to be in their places by that time. At eight o'clock

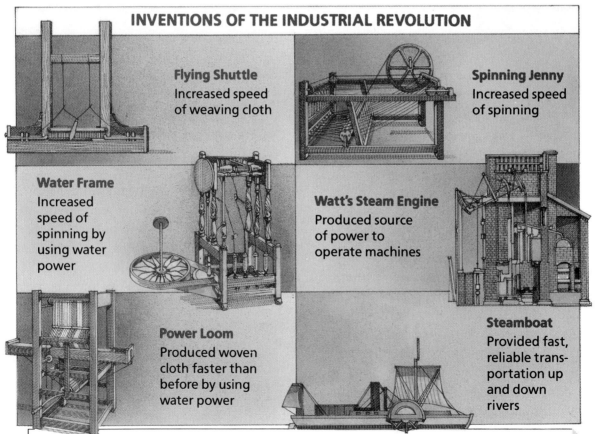

INVENTIONS OF THE INDUSTRIAL REVOLUTION

Flying Shuttle
Increased speed of weaving cloth

Spinning Jenny
Increased speed of spinning

Water Frame
Increased speed of spinning by using water power

Watt's Steam Engine
Produced source of power to operate machines

Power Loom
Produced woven cloth faster than before by using water power

Steamboat
Provided fast, reliable transportation up and down rivers

The table above shows some of the machines that were invented during the time of the Industrial Revolution.
▶ Which two inventions had to be used in a factory that was located near a waterfall or dam?

Sheffield, England, grew rapidly during the Industrial Revolution.
▶ How can you tell that Sheffield was an industrial city?

the machines were stopped while the workers ate breakfast. Half an hour later, the wheels started turning again and ran until noon. Workers could not leave their machines while the steam engine was running, so they surely must have welcomed the sound of the noon whistle.

The machines started again at one o'clock and ran until four. Workers could then take a half hour rest. Then they went back to the machines and worked until eight, when the steam engine stopped. Workers hurried to their nearby homes, because in ten hours they would have to be back in their places at the factory.

Factory Towns Workers had to live near the factories where they worked. So the growing use of steam brought with it the growth of towns and cities. Most of these towns were not attractive. The following passage is how Charles Dickens described a fictitious town during the Industrial Revolution in his novel *Hard Times.*

It was a town of machinery and tall chimneys, out of which interminable [endless] serpents of smoke trailed themselves for ever and ever, and never got uncoiled. . . . It contained several large streets all very like one another, and many small streets still more like one another, inhabited by people equally like one another, who all went in and out at the same hours, with the same sound upon the same pavements, to do the same work, and to whom every day was the same as yesterday and to-morrow, and every year the counterpart of the last and the next.

D. Machines Raise the Standard of Living

How People Lived The factory workers of Manchester lived in a crowded, smoky city, but so did people in other places. London was known for its smoky air during the Middle Ages, long before there were any factory steam engines. The city of Edinburgh in Scotland did not have factories like Manchester, but it was known as "Auld Reekie," that is, "Old Smoky."

People had to work long hours in the factories, but so did those who worked as farmers or in home workshops. Living in an industrial city did have some advantages, though. Manchester was one of the first cities in England to provide free public parks and a free public library. Businesspeople in Manchester were quicker to try new ways of living than many people who lived in old-fashioned villages and towns. Perhaps this was because they were accustomed to seeing new inventions work in the factories.

More Goods The Industrial Revolution changed how people worked and brought about a higher **standard of living**, or a measure of how well people live.

A standard of living depends on the amount of goods that makes life more comfortable and pleasant. People working in factories with machines produced far more goods than people working with tools or hand-powered machines. Commoners, those who were not nobles, could buy goods that had once been luxuries. More goods for more people was the great result of the Industrial Revolution.

E. Business People Take Risks

Money for Businesses Watt needed more than an idea to make a better steam engine. He also needed money to pay for trying out his ideas and making engines. Watt formed a partnership with Matthew Boulton, a successful businessman, who provided the **capital**. Capital can be simply defined as wealth in the form of goods or money used for making more goods.

During the Industrial Revolution some cities established parks, such as Regent's Park in Brighton, England, for people to enjoy.
► How are these people enjoying themselves?

It was a risky business venture. Watt and Boulton experimented with making and selling engines for 18 years before they made any **profit** on the engines that they sold. A profit is the financial gain after paying the costs of workers and materials to produce something.

A person who provides the capital for a business is known as a *capitalist*. It required the money of capitalists to build the factories of Manchester. Before a single yard of cloth could be produced, a capitalist had to pay for a building, buy the machines, and pay the engineers who installed them.

Risks and Opportunities Capitalists took risks, the chance of losing their money. Factories and other businesses sometimes failed to make profits. New inventions did not always work well enough to make a profit. Boulton had to wait years before he began to get his money back from Watt's invention.

Freedom to take risks was part of the new way to do business. It was quite different from the Middle Ages when guilds controlled the making and selling of goods. The masters of a guild decided who could make a product, how it was made, and its price. People now had choices about how

With Watt's idea and Boulton's capital, the two men ventured together to produce steam engines.
▶ How can you tell which piece of machinery is the steam engine?

The Granger Collection

to make and spend their money. This type of economy is called **free enterprise**. People could start businesses if they were willing to risk their money for capital. This greater economic freedom made the Industrial Revolution possible in Western European countries.

LESSON **2** REVIEW

THINK AND WRITE

A. What did James Watt learn from experiments that failed?
B. Why did the use of machines change the places where people worked?
C. Describe an average day for a factory worker.
D. What was the benefit of the Industrial Revolution?

E. Why did providing capital have its risks?

SKILLS CHECK

WRITING SKILL

Would you like to have lived during the time of the Industrial Revolution? Write a short essay discussing the reasons for your decision.

Political Revolutions

THINK ABOUT WHAT YOU KNOW

What countries can you think of that have fought civil wars?

STUDY THE VOCABULARY

Parliament   **guillotine**
constitutional
  monarchy

FOCUS YOUR READING

What brought about revolutions in England and France, and what were the results of each of these revolutions?

A. Disputes Lead to Civil War in England

Power Disputes Revolutions, or great changes, have taken place in governments from time to time. One such revolution in England was the result of the old dispute about the powers of the king. This dispute had not ended when King John granted the Magna Carta. Nearly 400 years later, King James I believed that a king received his powers from God, not from the people he ruled. Many of James's subjects disagreed. They held that a monarch, or king or queen, was bound by the ancient laws and customs, such as those included in the Magna Carta.

During the reign of James's son, King Charles I, the dispute about power led to a civil war. Charles I lost the war, and both his sons, Charles and James, fled the country. The king's foes led by Oliver Cromwell beheaded the king in 1649. Oliver Cromwell and his army ruled England after the king's death. Cromwell, called Lord Protector, exercised the powers of a dictator.

212

A Law-Making Body Most English people decided that rule by a king was better than rule by a dictator. After Cromwell's death, **Parliament** met in 1660 and invited Charles, son of the executed king, to return to England. Parliament is a law-making body made up of two groups of people. The nobles and bishops, or leaders of the Church, met as the House of Lords. Representatives of the commoners formed the House of Commons. King Charles II said that he would respect the laws of England, but he did his best to be free from Parliament's control. The dispute about royal power had not yet been settled.

When Charles II died, his brother James came to the throne. King James II insisted that the king had the power to suspend, or set aside, any law that Parliament passed. However, James's actions

In 1653, Cromwell dismissed Parliament and ruled as a dictator.
► How did the artist depict Cromwell in the drawing?

became high-handed, and he lost the support of many people who had strongly favored bringing back the rule of a king in 1660. James even lost the support of his daughter Mary, who was the wife of the Dutch ruler William of Orange.

B. A Bloodless Revolution Ends the Dispute

James Flees England In 1688 a group of English leaders decided that they could no longer put up with a king who thought he was above the law. So they invited William of Orange to come to England with an army to protect the people of England from their own king.

By now, most of King James's advisors had deserted him. He also found that he could not even count on the loyalty of his soldiers. James, remembering all too well what had happened to his father, Charles I, decided to flee the kingdom. So on a dark December night, he slipped out of the palace by a secret passageway. He took with him the Great Seal of the Kingdom. Impressions of the Great Seal were placed on all royal orders to show that they were official. James seemed to have thought that by taking the seal he would make it difficult for anyone to issue orders in his place.

James got into a small boat and started across the Thames River. Halfway across, the king dropped the Great Seal into the river. Word spread quickly that the king had fled and several watchful fishermen soon captured the king.

William and his English supporters were not pleased to learn of James's capture. William knew that it would be far better if James fled the country. He feared that holding James prisoner would cause people to sympathize with him. The

In 1689, Parliament offered the throne of England to William and Mary.
▶ How did the artist show this event in the etching?

leaders of the revolution gave James a second chance to flee. This time they made sure that no one prevented his escape.

A New Monarchy After the king had fled, Parliament declared the throne vacant. Mary was next in line for the throne, but she would accept a crown only if William was made king. Parliament finally agreed that William and Mary would be king and queen.

The Parliament that offered William and Mary their crowns also passed a Bill of Rights. This was a law setting limits on the royal power. The government of England became a **constitutional monarchy**. In a constitutional monarchy, monarchs rule according to a constitution, or basic law.

The Bill of Rights The Bill of Rights was seen as a part of England's basic law. It said that the monarchs could not suspend laws passed by Parliament. Neither could they collect taxes nor keep an army without the consent of Parliament. The election of members of Parliament would be free, and they would enjoy freedom of debate. Parts of the Bill of Rights applied to all people in the kingdom. Anyone accused of a crime had the right to a trial by jury.

In accepting the throne, William and Mary accepted the Bill of Rights. There was no longer any question about the monarchs being above the law. The long dispute had been settled by a revolution without fighting. The English have called it the Glorious Revolution because it was a bloodless revolution.

Perhaps you wonder what happened to the Great Seal that James dropped in the river. Some time later a fisherman accidently caught it in his net and brought it to the surface. Even James's last act as king was a failure.

C. France Faces Problems

France's Monarchs Unlike the Glorious Revolution, the French Revolution was not bloodless. Perhaps if the French king Louis XVI had been a better leader, things may have been different.

Louis had never wanted to be king. He was only 19 years old and his wife, Marie Antoinette (an twuh NET), was about 18 when they came to the throne in 1774. He thought himself too young for the position, which frightened him. He complained to a

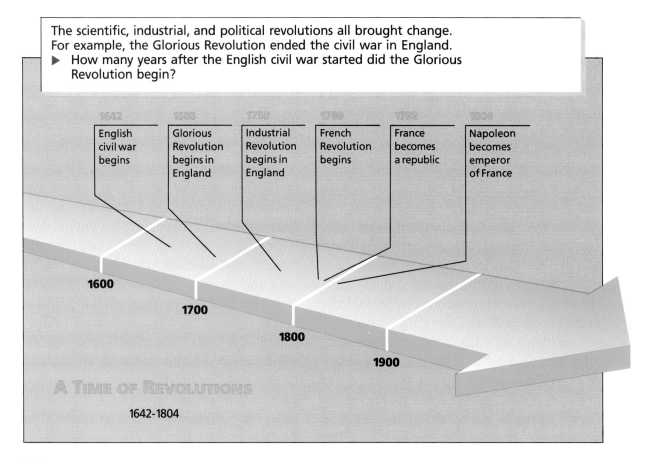

The scientific, industrial, and political revolutions all brought change. For example, the Glorious Revolution ended the civil war in England.
▶ How many years after the English civil war started did the Glorious Revolution begin?

1642 — English civil war begins
1688 — Glorious Revolution begins in England
1750 — Industrial Revolution begins in England
1789 — French Revolution begins
1792 — France becomes a republic
1804 — Napoleon becomes emperor of France

1600 1700 1800 1900

A TIME OF REVOLUTIONS
1642–1804

Louis XVI and Marie Antoinette ruled for 18 years, although neither had an interest in the monarchy.
► How do the paintings depict them as royalty?

friend, "What a burden! It seems that the universe will fall upon me!"

Marie Antoinette was not any more suited to be a queen than Louis was fit to be a king. As a young queen, she enjoyed fine clothes and going to parties. She was bored by court life, uninterested in serious matters, and lacked a good education. One of her teachers said that she was intelligent but rather lazy. "She would learn only so long as she was being amused."

Unfair Laws and Debt Louis XVI was not responsible for all the problems that France faced in 1789. But neither the king nor his people had much confidence in his ability to deal with the problems. They arose partly because of the special privileges of the nobles and the Church.

The French were not equal before the law. There were different sets of laws for the nobles and the common people. Nobles held most of the best land in France, yet they paid no taxes. Nobles held the high positions in the government. Officers in the army were nobles. Many young noble officers knew far less about warfare than the men they commanded.

Nobles also held most of the high positions in the Church. The Church owned large amounts of land, and it had its own courts and laws. The Church collected taxes from the peasants, but it paid no taxes to the king.

The storming of the Bastille marked the start of the French Revolution.
▶ What United States holiday is similar to Bastille Day?

The common people of France paid for the government, but they did not pay as much as the government spent. As a result, the king's government was deeply in debt. That was one of the most pressing problems that faced the king in 1789.

A Time for Change The special privileges of the nobles and the Church had existed since the Middle Ages. But by 1789, people were getting new ideas. A growing number had come to believe that it was time for a change. They knew that changes were possible because governments had been changed in other lands. The English had limited the powers of the king. The Americans had become independent and had set up a republic. And the American Declaration of Independence had stated that all people are created equal. If such things could happen in England and America, why not in France?

D. The Revolution Brings Changes

Violence Begins Changes came rapidly in 1789 and the years that followed. The king called representatives of the nobles and commoners together to consider new taxes. The representatives of the commoners insisted that France have a constitution that would limit royal powers.

However, some people were not willing to wait for a constitution. In Paris, many poor citizens focused their anger toward the government on the Bastille (bas TEEL), a prison-fortress within the city, where they believed hundreds of French citizens had been unjustly imprisoned. On July 14, 1789, a crowd of people in Paris took up arms and attacked the Bastille. The mob released the prisoners and destroyed the Bastille. King Louis XVI was shocked when told of what had happened. "Why, it's a revolt!" he told the official who brought him the news. The official answered, "No sire, it's a revolution."

The Monarchy Ends The attack on the Bastille was the beginning of a revolution. Great changes followed. The king's powers were limited; the nobles lost privileges; the Church lost most of its lands; and serfdom was finally abolished.

Rulers in other countries grew alarmed by the changes in France. They feared that revolution would spread, so they declared war against France. Because King Louis and Marie Antoinette were suspected of secretly favoring the foreign enemies, the monarchy was abolished. France became a republic in 1792. King Louis was tried as a traitor and put to death on the **guillotine** (GIHL uh teen), a device for beheading people. Marie Antoinette went to the guillotine the following year.

Terror Reigns Radicals now controlled the French republic. Radicals are people who want to make extreme, or very great, changes in a short amount of time. The radicals began a "reign of terror" against those suspected of opposing them. A great many people were imprisoned. More than 20,000 people were put to death by the guillotine. Finally the rule of the radicals threatened so many people that the radicals were overthrown. Their leaders, who had sent so many to the guillotine, were sent there themselves.

E. A General Becomes Emperor

A Young Dictator The overthrow of the radicals did not end changes in France. General Napoleon Bonaparte (nuh POH lee-un BOH nuh pahrt) seized control of the government in 1799.

The painting below shows King Louis XVI approaching his execution by guillotine on January 21, 1793.
▶ Where is the guillotine in this painting?

Bonaparte had risen rapidly in the army during the revolution. He was a general by the time he was 24 years old. He was only 30 when he seized control. For a few years, Bonaparte continued to call the government a republic, but he was really a dictator. In 1804 the dictator crowned himself Emperor Napoleon. France once again had a monarch.

Napoleon kept many of the changes made during the revolution. He did not bring back serfdom or give land back to the Church. All people were equal before the laws drawn up by Napoleon's order.

Napoleon's Mistake Napoleon was a very successful military leader. He defeated France's enemies on the mainland,

NAPOLEON IN EUROPE

Napoleon met his final defeat at the battle of Waterloo in 1815.
▶ In which empire did the battle of Waterloo take place?

Musee d' Orsay, France

Napoleon's troops, weakened by hunger and cold, were forced to retreat from Russia. This defeat was the beginning of Napoleon's decline.
► Do you think that Napoleon's invasion of Russia was a good idea?

although he did not conquer Great Britain. British sea power kept him from crossing the English Channel. However, Napoleon made a great mistake in 1812 when he invaded Russia. He reached and occupied Moscow, but he could not force the Russians to surrender. The French were not prepared to spend the winter in Moscow, so Napoleon had to retreat. His armies suffered terrible losses as a result of the harsh Russian winter.

France's enemies saw their opportunity. They once again united to make war against Napoleon. He met his final defeat in 1815 at Waterloo, in the country we now call Belgium. He died six years later.

LESSON 3 REVIEW

THINK AND WRITE

A. What was the cause and the result of the civil war in England?
B. What did the Glorious Revolution accomplish?
C. What problems did France face in 1789?
D. What changes did the revolution make in France?
E. How did Napoleon become an emperor?

SKILLS CHECK

MAP SKILL

After Napoleon and his troops retreated from Moscow, they marched back home to Paris, France. How many miles (km) was their trip? Use the mileage scale on the map on page 218 to estimate the distance between the two cities.

USING THE VOCABULARY

revolution
astronomy
Inquisition
Industrial
  Revolution
constitutional
  monarchy

capital
profit
free enterprise
Parliament
standard of living

On a separate sheet of paper, write the word or words from above that best complete the sentences.

1. Galileo was brought before the _____, a special Church court, because of the things he wrote.
2. Matthew Boulton provided the _____, or money or goods, so that James Watt could build and sell steam engines.
3. In a _____ a monarch rules according to a basic law.
4. In Italy, Copernicus studied _____, a science that deals with space.
5. A measure of how well people live is called a _____.
6. _____ is made up of the House of Lords and the House of Commons.
7. In a _____ economy, people have a choice about how to make and spend money.
8. The great changes in the ways people worked brought about the _____.
9. Copernicus wrote a book about the _____, or turning round, of the earth and other planets.
10. It took 18 years for Watt and Boulton to make any _____, or financial gain, on the steam engines they sold.

REMEMBERING WHAT YOU READ

On a separate sheet of paper, answer the following questions in complete sentences.

1. How did Copernicus's beliefs about space differ from Ptolemy's?
2. What did Galileo discover when he looked at the sky through a powerful telescope?
3. What was Leeuwenhoek's contribution to the Scientific Revolution?
4. Why did the invention of machines affect the growth of cities and towns?
5. How did the Industrial Revolution raise the standard of living?
6. What risks did capitalists take in providing money for businesses?
7. What were three limits set on monarchs according to the English Bill of Rights?
8. What special privileges did nobles and the Church have in France before the revolution?
9. What happened in Paris on July 14, 1789?
10. Why were Napoleon's enemies able to defeat him at the battle of Waterloo?

TYING SCIENCE TO SOCIAL STUDIES

Make a map to show the nine planets of our solar system in their orbits, or circular paths, around the sun. First look up the following planets in a science book or another reference book to find out their order from the sun: Earth, Jupiter, Mars, Mercury, Neptune, Pluto, Saturn, Uranus, Venus. Then draw the sun and the planets in their correct order in nine orbits around the sun. Be sure to label each planet.

THINKING CRITICALLY

On a separate sheet of paper, answer the following questions in complete sentences.

1. How do you think the discovery of new facts about space might change the way people think?
2. What similarities are there between the revolution in science and the revolution in industry?
3. If you had been Matthew Boulton, would you have formed a partnership with James Watt? Explain.
4. Why, do you think, was the English Parliament made up of two separate groups of people?
5. Which problems facing France in 1789 might King Louis XVI have been able to solve? Explain how.

SUMMARIZING THE CHAPTER

On a separate sheet of paper, copy the graphic organizer shown below. Beside the main idea for each lesson, write four statements that support the main idea.

CHAPTER THEME → Revolutions in science, industry, and politics changed the ways people thought, worked, and lived, and the types of governments in Western Europe.

LESSON 1

Copernicus, Galileo, and other scientists affected the way people thought.

1. _____
2. _____
3. _____
4. _____

LESSON 2

Many changes resulted from the Industrial Revolution.

1. _____
2. _____
3. _____
4. _____

LESSON 3

Revolutions in England and France resulted in political changes.

1. _____
2. _____
3. _____
4. _____

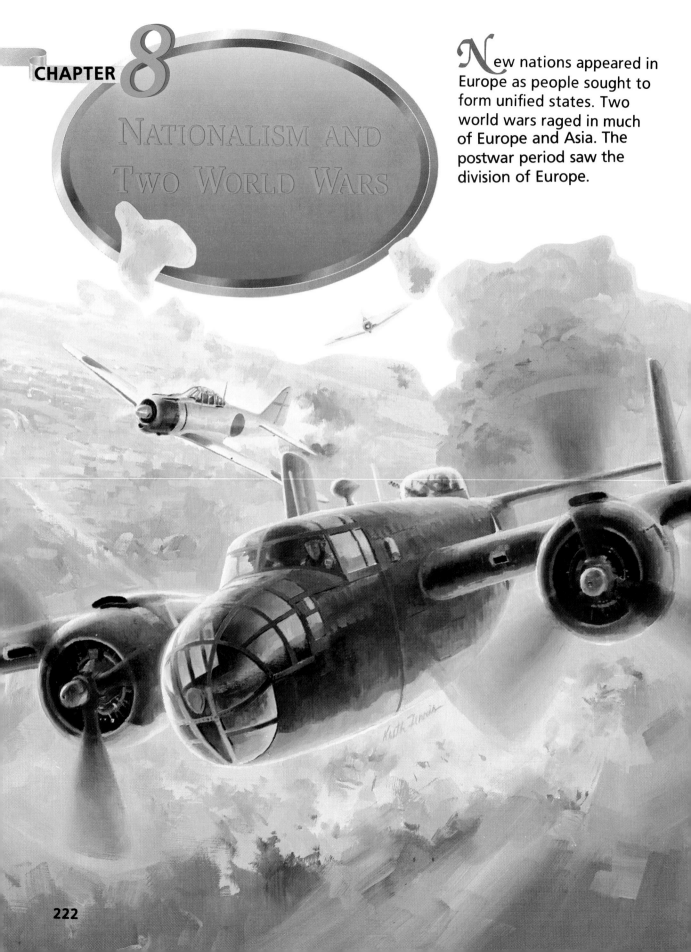

CHAPTER 8

NATIONALISM AND TWO WORLD WARS

New nations appeared in Europe as people sought to form unified states. Two world wars raged in much of Europe and Asia. The postwar period saw the division of Europe.

New Nations Appear on the Map

THINK ABOUT WHAT YOU KNOW

Imagine that each state in the United States is independent of the others. What kinds of problems or difficulties could this cause?

STUDY THE VOCABULARY

nationalism   **prime minister**
unification

FOCUS YOUR READING

How did unification occur in Italy and in Germany?

A. Giuseppe Mazzini Discovers His Duty

In 1821, when Giuseppe Mazzini (joo-ZEP pe maht TSEE nee) was 16, he met a tall, black-bearded man asking for money on the streets of Genoa, Italy. Young Mazzini could see at a glance that the tall man did not look like an ordinary beggar. He was one of the rebel soldiers who crowded into Genoa after an unsuccessful revolt against the royal government of Sardinia. Sardinia was one of the states on the Italian peninsula. Italy did not appear as a country on the map of Europe in 1821. Italy was only the name of the peninsula, which was divided into seven major states.

Loyalty and devotion to one's country is called **nationalism**. Most of the people of Italy did not have any nationalism. They did not think of themselves as Italians. They thought of themselves as belonging to a particular city or region. For example, people of Genoa called themselves Genoese; and people of Venice, Venetians.

Mazzini was troubled by his meeting with the unfortunate rebel soldier. He asked himself, did he, too, not have a duty to help to free Italy? Did he not have a duty to work for Italy's **unification**? Unification is the uniting of separate regions and cities into one nation. Mazzini realized that such a unified republic could be created only if there was a revolution.

B. Mazzini Becomes a Revolutionist

Getting Organized Mazzini decided to help unite Italy. He wrote articles for newspapers and joined a revolutionary group. The government had him exiled, or forced to leave the country, so he went to France. While in exile, he formed a group that he called Young Italy. He believed that the young people of Italy could

Giuseppe Mazzini worked for the unification of Italy.
► What actions did he take to help to unify his country?

unite their homeland if they were organized. Mazzini wrote that the members of Young Italy must teach people to think of themselves as Italians rather than Venetians or Genoese. Again and again, Mazzini told young people that they had a duty to unite Italy.

Encouraging Pride Mazzini moved to England, where he continued to work for the unification of Italy. There he established a school for poor Italian boys in London. Most of the boys worked at odd jobs. Mazzini taught the boys to read and write, and—just as important—he taught them to be proud of being Italian. Every week he spoke to them about Italy's great men and its history.

When revolution broke out in Italy in 1848, Mazzini hurried home, but the uprising failed. Mazzini could stir the hearts of the Italian people, but it took a different kind of leader to put a unified Italy on the map of Europe.

C. Cavour Puts Italy on the Map

Different Ideas Count Camillo Benso di Cavour (kah MEEL loh BAYN soh dee kah VOOR) also wanted the unification of Italy, but his ideas differed from those of Mazzini. Indeed, the two men disliked and distrusted each other. Mazzini was an exile who spent years planning unsuccessful revolutions. Cavour was an aristocrat, a member of the noble class, who made a fortune managing his family's estates. Mazzini dreamed of establishing an ideal democratic republic. Cavour thought a limited monarchy, like that of Great Britain, would be much more practical. Mazzini insisted that it would take a revolution to free Italy. Cavour believed that far more could be done through skillful politics.

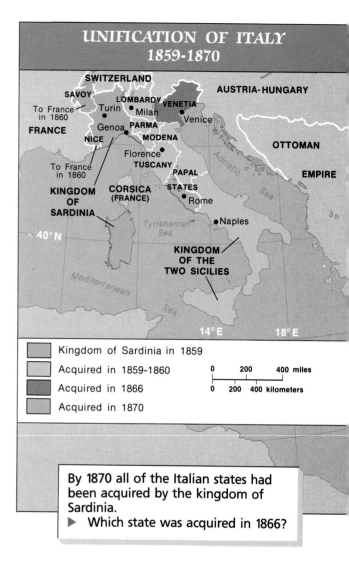

UNIFICATION OF ITALY 1859–1870

- Kingdom of Sardinia in 1859
- Acquired in 1859–1860
- Acquired in 1866
- Acquired in 1870

0   200   400 miles
0   200   400 kilometers

By 1870 all of the Italian states had been acquired by the kingdom of Sardinia.
▶ Which state was acquired in 1866?

United Italy In 1852, Count di Cavour became the **prime minister**, or chief official, of Sardinia. He wanted to combine Italy with Sardinia. Find the kingdom of Sardinia on the map above. Through wars and politics, Cavour enlarged the kingdom. One after another the Italian states united with Sardinia. Because of Cavour and Mazzini, by 1861 the king of Sardinia was declared king of Italy. The new kingdom did not yet include Venice or Rome, but they would be added within nine years. Mazzini had dreamed of a united Italy; Cavour's skill put it on the map.

Carl Schurz dreamed of a free and united Germany.
▶ Why was Schurz unhappy with life in Germany?

D. A Revolution Fails in Germany

A Student's Ideas   Italy was not the only country that struggled to become united. One morning in February 1848, a young German student, Carl Schurz (shurts), sat writing in his room. Schurz, a student at the university at Bonn, was writing a play about a German hero of earlier times. He hoped that his play would make the Germans proud of their history. Perhaps if they were proud of being Germans, their country could be united.

At the time Schurz wrote, Germany was even more divided than Italy into a number of independent states ruled by kings and nobles. Prussia was by far the largest state, but Schurz did not want a united Germany to be like Prussia. The kings of Prussia had ruled their kingdom as if it were an army. People were supposed to obey orders. Anyone who talked about freedom or democracy was viewed with suspicion. The government controlled what the newspapers printed. There were spies in the schools to report teachers or students who spoke against the ideas of the authorities.

Students like Schurz wanted Germany to be free as well as united. They dreamed of a republic in which the Germans could think and speak freely and elect their own government.

France's Example   Schurz's thoughts that February morning were suddenly interrupted when a friend burst into the room. "Don't you know what has happened? The French have established a new republic!" In 1848 the Second Republic in France had been formed.

The ideas of the French quickly spread in Germany in 1848 as they had already spread in Italy. Some people said the Germans should follow the French example. The Germans should overthrow the rulers of the separate states and form a German republic.

The Granger Collection

Germans stormed the arsenal at Berlin in 1848. They wanted democracy and unification.
▶ How are they breaking the door?

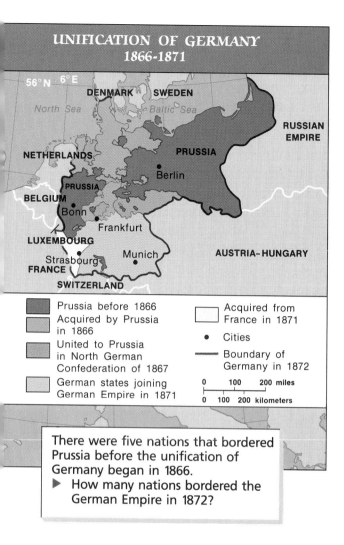

UNIFICATION OF GERMANY
1866-1871

56°N 6°E

DENMARK SWEDEN

North Sea Baltic Sea

RUSSIAN EMPIRE

NETHERLANDS PRUSSIA

Berlin

PRUSSIA

BELGIUM

Bonn

Frankfurt

LUXEMBOURG

Munich AUSTRIA-HUNGARY

Strasbourg

FRANCE

SWITZERLAND

| | Prussia before 1866 |
| Acquired by Prussia in 1866 |
| United to Prussia in North German Confederation of 1867 |
| German states joining German Empire in 1871 |

Acquired from France in 1871

• Cities

— Boundary of Germany in 1872

0   100   200 miles
0 100 200 kilometers

There were five nations that bordered Prussia before the unification of Germany began in 1866.
▶ How many nations bordered the German Empire in 1872?

A few days later the news reached the city of Bonn — an uprising had taken place in other parts of Germany. Fighting had

broken out in Berlin, the capital of Prussia. The situation grew so serious that the Prussian king agreed to give the people a voice in the government. Other German rulers followed the Prussian king's example. However, in the months that followed, the rulers did little to carry out their promises.

E. Bismarck Puts Germany on the Map

Otto von Bismarck became chancellor to the Prussian king in 1862. A chancellor has duties similar to those of a prime minister. Bismarck was an aristocrat who had little regard for democratic republics — at least for Germany. He scoffed at governments conducted "by speeches and majority votes." Power, Bismarck declared, depended on "blood and iron," that is, on military strength. Yet, Bismarck did not oppose all changes in Germany — as long as Prussia controlled the changes.

Like Cavour in Italy, Bismarck used wars and skillful politics to unite the other German states with Prussia. Bismarck wanted a unified Germany under Prussian control to be the most powerful European nation. In 1871 the king of Prussia became emperor of a united Germany.

LESSON **1** *REVIEW*

THINK AND WRITE

A. What was the political situation in Italy prior to 1821?

B. What did Mazzini do to further his dreams for Italy?

C. What was Cavour's accomplishment?

D. How was Carl Schurz's dream for Germany like Mazzini's dream for Italy?

E. What was Bismarck's accomplishment?

SKILLS CHECK

MAP SKILL

Locate the islands of Sardinia, Sicily, and Corsica on a map of present-day Europe in the Atlas. Which two are part of Italy?

World War I and Its Aftermath

THINK ABOUT WHAT YOU KNOW

Explain why you agree or disagree with the following statement: *It is good to have pride in and be loyal to your country, but taking these qualities to extremes can lead to trouble.*

STUDY THE VOCABULARY

armistice   Fascist
League of   depression
   Nations

FOCUS YOUR READING

What brought on World War I, and what were the results of the war?

A. Murder That Led to War

The Murder Site A marker on a bridge in the city of Sarajevo (sar uh YAY voh), in Bosnia, points out the place where a young man shot the archduke of Austria on June 28, 1914. Why has the site of this murder been so carefully marked? The assassination of Archduke Franz Ferdinand was just no ordinary murder. The archduke was next in line to the throne of Austria-Hungary. The death of Archduke Franz Ferdinand set off a string of events that led to the start of World War I.

The Austro-Hungarian Empire in 1914 consisted of a number of nations. The spread of nationalism among these nations threatened to tear the empire apart. In 1914, Sarajevo was the capital of Bosnia, one of the regions ruled by Austria. The majority of the people in Bosnia were Serbs. Serbian nationalists thought that Bosnia should be united with the neighboring country of Serbia.

The New York Times.

NEW YORK, MONDAY, JUNE 29, 1914.—EIGHTEEN PAGES.

HEIR TO AUSTRIA'S THRONE IS SLAIN WITH HIS WIFE BY A BOSNIAN YOUTH TO AVENGE SEIZURE OF HIS COUNTRY

The Murder Plot Gavrilo Princip (GAHR-ree loh PREENT seep), who fired the fatal shot, was a Bosnian Serb. He had fled to Serbia when he was 17 because he had taken part in a demonstration against the Austrians. During the next two years, he and other Bosnians talked of ways to free Bosnia from Austria. When he learned that the archduke would visit Sarajevo, Princip and several others plotted to attack him as a way of striking at Austrian rule.

The assassination of Archduke Franz Ferdinand led to the outbreak of World War I.
▶ Where did this event occur?

On the day of the archduke's visit, seven young men stationed themselves along the route to be taken by the archduke's motor car. Each was prepared to attack the archduke, but the plot nearly failed. At least one of the seven lost his nerve. Another decided not to shoot when he found a policeman standing behind him. One did throw a bomb, but it bounced off the archduke's car and injured two officers in the car that followed.

The whole plot would have failed had it not been for a mistake. The driver of the first car in the official procession turned into the wrong street and was stopped. As the procession backed up, the archduke's car passed close to where Princip stood. The young man was not a good shot, but he could hardly have missed at such close range. He raised his gun, turned his head, and shot, killing both Archduke Franz Ferdinand and the archduke's wife.

B. The War Begins

The Quarrel Grows All but one of those who took part in the attack were captured, but that did not end the matter. Austria charged that Serbia had encouraged the plot. The Austrians made demands that Serbia insisted no independent country could accept. The quarrel between these two countries soon involved others.

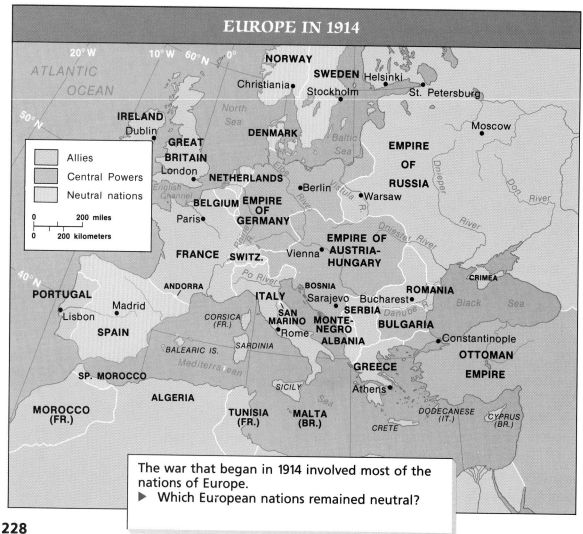

EUROPE IN 1914

The war that began in 1914 involved most of the nations of Europe.
▶ Which European nations remained neutral?

World War I soldiers dug trenches from which they defended their positions and launched attacks.
▶ What were used to support the sides of the trenches?

Both Austria and Serbia had alliances with other countries. An alliance is an agreement between nations to act together, particularly if one of them is attacked. Austria had an alliance with Germany. Serbia was an ally of Russia, which also had an alliance with France.

Other Allies Join In When Austria declared war on Serbia, Russia prepared for war. Austria asked Germany for support, and Russia called upon its ally France. Within a very short time, Germany and Austria were at war with Serbia, Russia, and France. Germany and Austria were known as the *Central Powers*. Great Britain joined France and Russia in a combination called the *Allies*. Find these countries on the map showing Europe in 1914 on page 228. Italy later entered the war on the side of the Allies.

People had good reason to call this a *world war*. The war began in Europe, but countries on other continents joined the conflict. Japan sided with the Allies, and Turkey fought on the side of the Central Powers. The British and French brought soldiers from all parts of their empires to the European battle fronts. There were troops from Canada, Australia, New Zealand, India, and different parts of Africa. The United States entered the war on the side of the Allies in 1917.

Weapons of War The murderous power of weapons played an important role in the war. Weapons gave the advantage to soldiers on the defense in battle. Machine guns could quickly cut down any troops who went over the top of their own trenches and attacked. The same land was fought over many times.

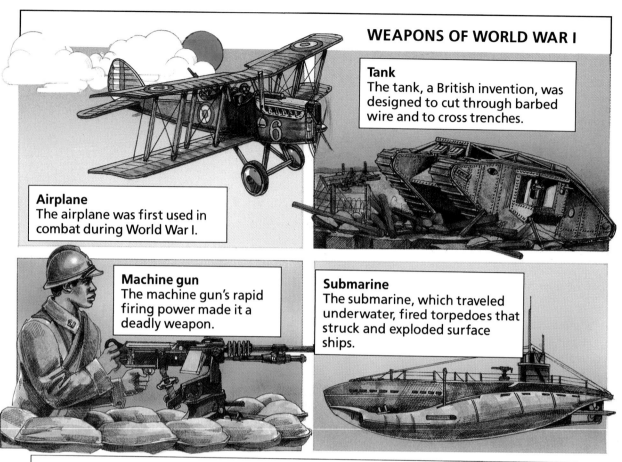

WEAPONS OF WORLD WAR I

Tank
The tank, a British invention, was designed to cut through barbed wire and to cross trenches.

Airplane
The airplane was first used in combat during World War I.

Machine gun
The machine gun's rapid firing power made it a deadly weapon.

Submarine
The submarine, which traveled underwater, fired torpedoes that struck and exploded surface ships.

The weapons of World War I enabled soldiers to fight enemies in the air, in the water, and on the land.
▶ Which weapons shown above were also vehicles of World War I?

The airplane rapidly developed as a weapon. At first, planes were used to observe the enemy, but before long, pilots were carrying pistols and shotguns. It did not take long for machine guns to be mounted on airplanes so that pilots could fight dogfights against one another in the sky.

The Germans made effective use of improved submarines, especially against the British. The German U-boats (*U* for "undersea") sank nearly 5,000 ships. Most of these ships were carrying vital materials to the Allies that were needed to continue the war.

C. The Peace Treaties Changed the Map

Fixing Blame An **armistice**, or an agreement to stop fighting, was signed on November 11, 1918. The peace treaties that followed in 1919 were drawn up by the victorious Allies, who placed the blame for the war on the Central Powers.

The Austro-Hungarian Empire was broken up. Some territory in Europe was taken from Germany, which also had to give up its overseas colonies. The treaty makers said that Germany was to blame for the war and must pay damages to the countries that had suffered great losses.

The Germans thought it was wrong to blame them for a war into which countries had been drawn by their alliances. Disputes about the payments for damages continued years after the war ended.

Terms of the Treaties The peace treaties of 1919 changed the map of Europe. You can see these changes by comparing the map below with the map on page 228. Austria and Hungary were made into separate countries. Serbia was combined with large parts of the old Austro-Hungarian Empire, including Bosnia, to form Yugoslavia. Czechoslovakia was also created from lands of the Austro-Hungarian

Empire. Part of the empire also went to Poland, which received territory from Germany and Russia as well.

The peace treaties of World War I created a new international organization called the **League of Nations**. Its purpose was to provide a peaceful way to settle disputes and to prevent future wars.

D. A Dictator Takes Power in Italy

Problems in Italy Italy was on the winning side in World War I, but the Italians faced difficulties in 1919. Many returning soldiers could not find jobs. Prices kept rising, so money became worthless. The government was deeply in debt but

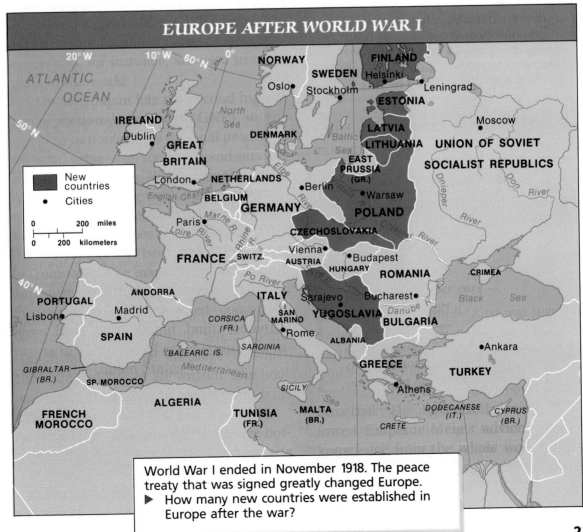

World War I ended in November 1918. The peace treaty that was signed greatly changed Europe.
▶ How many new countries were established in Europe after the war?

seemed unable to collect taxes. Many people no longer trusted their government.

An ambitious politician, a man named Benito Mussolini, took advantage of these troubled times. In 1919, Mussolini formed the first political group to be called the **Fascists**. Fascists believe in a political system that supports a single party and a single ruler, and involves total government control of political, economic, cultural, and religious activities. Mussolini organized Fascists into private military squads, called Black Shirts because of the color of their uniforms.

The New Leader Mussolini declared that Italy needed a strong leader. He spoke much about the need for action. Mussolini convinced a large number of people that he was the strong leader who could save Italy from disorder. Thousands of Black Shirts staged a "march on Rome" in 1922. The Italian king was so alarmed that he offered to make Mussolini the prime minister. However, Mussolini went on to make himself dictator, even though Italy still had a king. The Fascists called Mussolini "Il Duce" (il DOO che), which simply means "the leader."

E. Adolf Hitler and the Nazis Take Power in Germany

A German Republic After their defeat in 1918, the Germans set up a republic with leaders elected by the people. The new government had to sign the peace treaty with the victorious Allies. Most Germans honestly believed that the peace treaty was unfair because it forced them to give up German territory and pay for the losses of the war.

Some Germans, including a man named Adolf Hitler, opposed the republic from the start. Hitler was born in 1889 in Austria. At 16, he quit high school. In 1907, Hitler went to Vienna to become an art student, but he twice failed the entrance examination to the Academy of Fine Arts in Vienna. He stayed in Vienna and took odd jobs until 1914, when he volunteered in the German army and fought in World War I.

The Nazis Like many German-speaking Austrians, Hitler considered himself German. After World War I he joined a nationalist group. Hitler became the leader of this group; its members were known as *Nazis* (NAHT seez).

In 1923, Hitler and the Nazi party attempted unsuccessfully to overthrow the

The front page of this Italian newspaper shows Hitler and Mussolini together.
▶ How were these men alike?

LA TRIBUNA ILLUSTRATA

LA STORICA VISITA DEL DUCE AL FÜHRER
I due Condottieri acclamati dal grande popolo tedesco

Adolf Hitler was a charismatic leader who successfully used public rallies to promote Nazism and to gain the support of the German people. By 1933 he controlled the government of Germany.
▶ In what ways did Hitler try to appeal to the German people?

German government. Hitler was sent to prison for nine months. In prison he wrote a book titled *Mein Kampf* (myn kahmpf), which means "my battle." In this book he set forth his views about future German conquests. There were not many people outside Germany who knew about Adolf Hitler in 1924.

Hitler developed a speaking style that was truly impressive. He was an exciting speaker who talked for hours in taverns and at political meetings. He told all who listened that the German army had not lost the war. Traitors at home had betrayed the fighting men at the front. Hitler repeated over and over that Germany had lost the war because of a "stab in the back."

Hitler Gains Support Hitler had very few followers until the beginning of the world **depression** in 1929. A depression is a time when business is bad and many people are out of work. Hitler shrewdly took advantage of the bad times. He said over and over that Germany's troubles were caused by the unfair peace treaties. He promised that the Nazis would do away with the treaties and make Germany once again rich and powerful.

The Nazis and other foes of the republic created much disorder within Germany. Some Germans decided that the Nazis could bring order if they were given power. In January 1933, Hitler headed the government of Germany.

F. Hitler Becomes Germany's Dictator

Hitler Controls Germany Hitler acted quickly against all who opposed him. The Nazis outlawed all other political parties, and so Germany became a one-party state. The Nazis did not hesitate to murder their opponents. Hitler even approved the murder of Nazi party members whom he thought might cause him trouble.

Attacks on Jews Hitler attacked one whole group of Germans, the Jews. He blamed them for Germany's defeat in World War I as well as for the country's other difficulties. Hitler insisted that Jews could not be true Germans, even though their families had lived in Germany for generations. The Nazis changed the laws so that Jews were no longer citizens; they were even forbidden to fly the German flag. Universities did not accept Jews. No longer could Jewish doctors and dentists practice their professions. Many Jews lost their businesses.

On a November night in 1938, gangs directed by the Nazis attacked and burned synagogues (SIHN uh gahgz), Jewish houses of worship, and vandalized thousands of Jewish stores. Nearly a hundred

Hitler often spoke to the German people, promising them victory.
► Who, do you think, are the men in the foreground of the photo?

Jews were murdered, and thousands were thrown into prison. Unfortunately, this was only the beginning. Far more Jews were to be imprisoned and killed in the next few years.

LESSON **2** REVIEW

THINK AND WRITE

A. Why did the young Bosnian Serbs plan the death of the Austrian archduke?

B. What was the result of the assassination of the archduke?

C. What did the peace treaties do to the Austro-Hungarian Empire and to Germany?

D. Why was Mussolini able to take power?

E. What helped the Nazis rise to power?

F. What did Hitler do after he became Germany's dictator?

SKILLS CHECK

THINKING SKILL

Use the information you have learned in this lesson to make a chart comparing and contrasting two leaders of World War I, Benito Mussolini and Adolf Hitler.

World War II and What Followed

THINK ABOUT WHAT YOU KNOW

Have a discussion about something you have read, heard, or seen in movies or on television about World War II.

STUDY THE VOCABULARY

Blitzkrieg	**Axis**
genocide	**United Nations**
Holocaust	

FOCUS YOUR READING

What were the main phases of World War II in Europe?

A. World War II Begins

At War with Germany People all over Britain watched the clock on Sunday morning, September 3, 1939. They saw the hands move slowly to 11 o'clock and then past. They waited, listening to their radios for an announcement. Finally, at 11:15 A.M. they heard the prime minister, Neville Chamberlain, tell them, "This country is at war with Germany."

The war began that day because Germany had refused to stop its invasion of Poland. The attack on Poland was the latest of Hitler's moves to make Germany the most powerful country in Europe.

Hitler's Power Grows Ever since becoming dictator in 1933, Hitler had brushed aside the peace treaties of 1919. The treaties had limited the size of Germany's armed forces. Hitler began building up the army as soon as he came to power. He knew that France, with its strong military power, could stop Germany from building up its own army. If the French had threatened to march, Germany

would have had to back down. But the French did not march, so Hitler continued to assemble his military forces.

Having succeeded, Hitler paid no attention to other parts of the treaties. He sent troops into the region between the Rhine River and the French border. This, too, was against the treaties, but again the French did not act.

Germany took over Austria in 1938 to create what Hitler called Greater Germany. Germany next took over Czechoslovakia. By the spring of 1939, it was clear that Hitler wanted to do more than set aside the peace treaties of 1919; he wanted Germany to control all of Europe.

The Granger Collection

On September 1, 1939, Nazi troops invaded Poland.
▶ What event occurred as a result of this invasion?

The German air force launched a vicious attack on Great Britain.
▶ Was the German attack against Great Britain successful?

Germany Invades Poland It looked as if Poland would be Hitler's next victim. Britain and France now realized that Germany had to be stopped. Both countries declared that they would defend Polish independence. They tried to get the Soviet Union to join them. But instead the Soviet leader, Joseph Stalin, made an agreement with Hitler to divide Poland.

Hitler knew in 1939 that neither Britain nor France could send troops quickly enough to Poland to protect it from German invasion. On Friday, September 1, German troops crossed the Polish border. The British sent word on Saturday that unless the Germans agreed to stop their attack by 11 o'clock Sunday morning, Britain would declare war. The Germans did not reply, so on that September morning, World War II began.

B. German Armies Invade Europe

A Lightning War German armies rapidly overran Poland. The Germans called their attack a **Blitzkrieg** (blihts KREEG) — "lightning war." The troops had fast-moving tanks and other motorized equipment. They conquered Poland in less than three weeks.

The Blitzkrieg swept over Denmark, Norway, the Netherlands, Belgium, and France in the spring of 1940. In less than a year, Germany had defeated all its foes — except Great Britain.

Hitler considered an invasion of the British Isles. To win control over Britain, the Germans launched an air attack. The British air force battled wave after wave of German planes. If the British had lost the air battle, Hitler would have been able to send the Blitzkrieg across the English Channel. But the British air force did not lose, so Hitler gave up the idea of invading Britain at that time.

Military Airplanes:

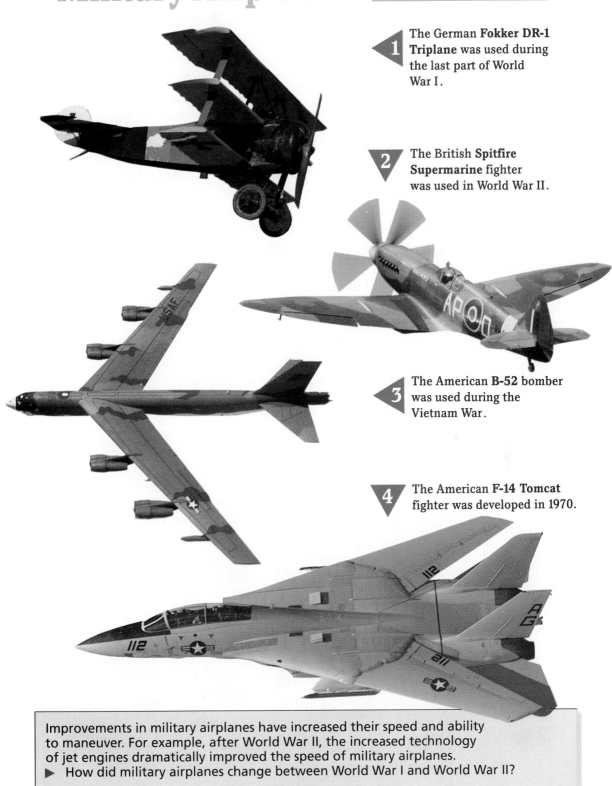

1 The German **Fokker DR-1 Triplane** was used during the last part of World War I.

2 The British **Spitfire Supermarine** fighter was used in World War II.

3 The American **B-52** bomber was used during the Vietnam War.

4 The American **F-14 Tomcat** fighter was developed in 1970.

Improvements in military airplanes have increased their speed and ability to maneuver. For example, after World War II, the increased technology of jet engines dramatically improved the speed of military airplanes.

▶ How did military airplanes change between World War I and World War II?

Attacking the Soviets Although Germany and the Soviet Union had divided Poland, neither nation's government trusted the other. So Hitler went on to invade the Soviet Union in 1941. At first the Germans advanced rapidly. They got within 20 miles (32 km) of Moscow, the Soviet capital. But the Soviets did not surrender. Hitler discovered, as Napoleon had, that it was easier to invade this large country than to defeat it. The Germans found it difficult to operate against the Soviets in the cold weather. An old Russian ruler once said that Russia had two great generals, General January and General February. These generals were on the Soviet side during the three winters of World War II. By 1944 the Soviet armies were driving the Germans from Soviet lands.

C. Nazis Spread Terror in Europe

More Attacks on Jews The Nazis persecuted the Jews in Germany before World War II. But the plight of the Jews became even worse when German armies extended Nazi power over other parts of Europe. You can read about a Jewish girl living in Nazi Europe in the literature special feature on page 240.

A large number of Jewish people fell into Nazi hands when the Germans occupied Poland and the western parts of the Soviet Union. Before attacking the Soviet Union, Hitler had told his generals that they must not only defeat the enemy but also destroy them. The Germans created special death squads to carry out this terrible task of destruction. Jews in particular were marked for death.

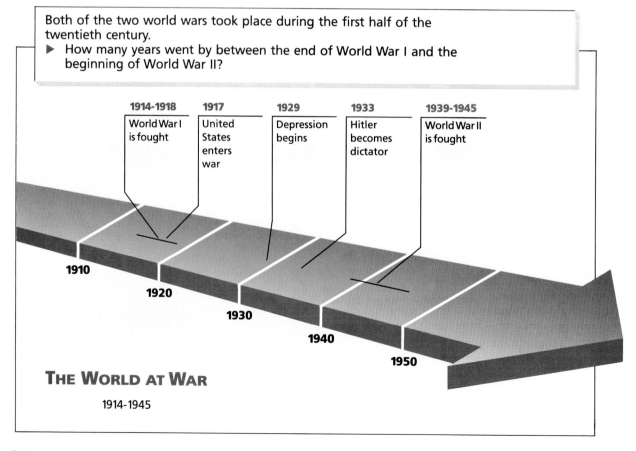

Both of the two world wars took place during the first half of the twentieth century.
▶ How many years went by between the end of World War I and the beginning of World War II?

1914-1918
World War I is fought

1917
United States enters war

1929
Depression begins

1933
Hitler becomes dictator

1939-1945
World War II is fought

1910
1920
1930
1940
1950

THE WORLD AT WAR
1914-1945

Millions of Jews were tortured and killed in Nazi concentration camps.
▶ Why are photographs like this important today?

The Death Camps The Nazis adopted a policy of **genocide**, that is, the planned killing of a whole group of people because of their race, religion, or nationality. To carry out this policy, the Nazis established special death camps with gas chambers for mass killings. The camp at Auschwitz (OUSH vihts), Poland, had a gas chamber in which 2,000 people could be killed at the same time.

Jews from all parts of Europe were taken to Auschwitz and other death camps. Altogether about 6 million Jews perished in the mass killings known as the **Holocaust**. Millions of other non-Jewish men, women, and children also were destroyed in the death camps.

Many able-bodied captives were forced to work as slave laborers. One of the captives who survived said that the Germans took far better care of their machines than of the slave laborers. The Germans cleaned and oiled the machines regularly. But a slave laborer was treated "like a piece of sandpaper which, rubbed once or twice, becomes useless and is thrown away to be burned with the waste."

D. The United States Enters World War II

At the beginning of World War II, many Americans hoped that the United States could stay out of the struggle. But when Germany overran Europe and threatened Britain, the United States sent supplies to the British.

Meanwhile, Japan had joined Germany and Italy in an alliance called the

FROM: **The Diary of a Young Girl**

By: Anne Frank
Setting: Amsterdam

A young girl, Anne Frank, and her family had moved to the Netherlands in 1933 to escape the Nazis in Germany. However, in 1942 the spread of Nazi terror throughout Europe forced Anne and her family to go into hiding in Amsterdam, the capital of the Netherlands.

It was during that time in hiding that Anne described in her diary, which she called Kitty, what daily life was like for her family and other Jews. The following passage is an excerpt from her diary, which was published as a book, *The Diary of a Young Girl.*

Wednesday, 13 January, 1943

Dear Kitty,
Everything has upset me again this morning, so I wasn't able to finish a single thing properly.

It is terrible outside. Day and night more of those poor people are being dragged off, with nothing but a rucksack [knapsack] and a little money. On the way they are deprived even of these possessions. Families are torn apart, the men, women, and children all being separated. Children coming home from school find that their parents have disappeared. Women return from shopping to find their homes shut up and their families gone.

The Dutch people are anxious too, their sons are being sent to Germany. Everyone is afraid.

And every night hundreds of planes fly over Holland [the Netherlands] and go to German towns, where the earth is so plowed up by their bombs, and every hour hundreds and thousands of people are killed in Russia and Africa. No one is able to keep out of it, the whole globe is waging war and although it is going better for the Allies, the end is not yet in sight.

. . . There is nothing we can do but wait as calmly as we can till the misery comes to an end. Jews and Christians wait, the whole earth waits; and there are many who wait for death.

Yours, Anne

Anne and her family remained in hiding until August 4, 1944, when their hiding place was discovered. Anne and the other occupants of the hiding place were arrested and sent to death camps. Anne's diary was published in 1947, two years after her death.

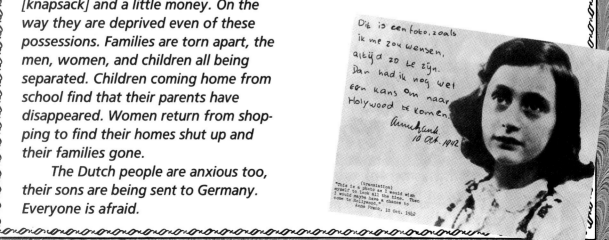

Dit is een foto, zoals ik me zou wensen, altijd zo te zijn. Dan had ik nog wel een kans om naar Holywood te komen.
Annefrank
10 Oct. 1942

(translation)
"This is a photo as I would wish myself to look all the time. Then I would maybe have a chance to come to Hollywood."
Anne Frank, 10 Oct. 1942

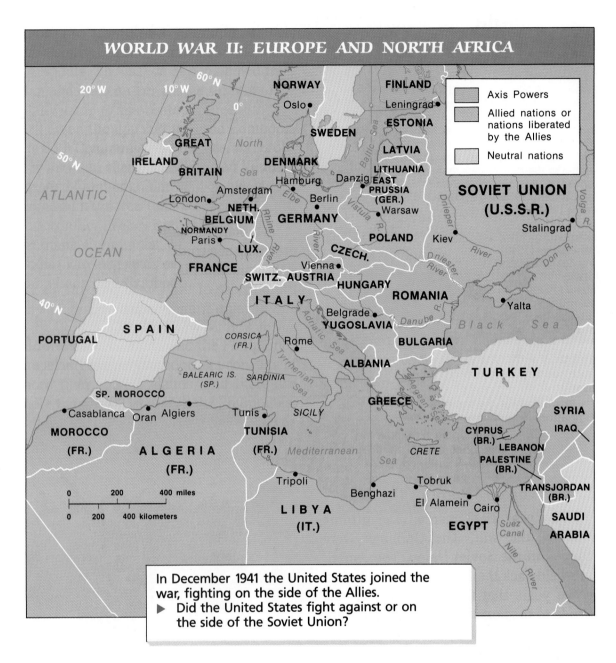

WORLD WAR II: EUROPE AND NORTH AFRICA

Legend:
- Axis Powers
- Allied nations or nations liberated by the Allies
- Neutral nations

In December 1941 the United States joined the war, fighting on the side of the Allies.
▶ Did the United States fight against or on the side of the Soviet Union?

Axis countries. When Germany defeated France, Japan took over the French colonies in Southeast Asia. The United States opposed the Japanese actions and threatened to cut off Japan's oil supplies. The Japanese launched a surprise attack against the American fleet at Pearl Harbor in Hawaii and on American bases in the Philippine Islands on December 7, 1941.

The next day the United States declared war on Japan. By doing this the United States joined the war on the side of the countries known as the Allies: France, Great Britain, and the Soviet Union. Three days later, Japan's Axis partners, Germany and Italy, declared war on the United States. During the remaining years of World War II, American forces fought both in the Pacific and in Europe.

241

THE WARRING NATIONS IN WORLD WAR II

Major Allied Nations	The Axis Nations
Australia (1939)	Albania (1940)
Belgium (1940)	Bulgaria (1941)
Brazil (1942)	Finland (1941)
Canada (1939)	Germany (1939)
China (1941)	Hungary (1941)
Czechoslovakia (1941)	Italy (1940)
Denmark (1940)	Japan (1941)
France (1939)	Romania (1941)
Great Britain (1939)	Thailand (1942)
Greece (1940)	
India (1939)	
Luxembourg (1940)	
Netherlands (1940)	
New Zealand (1939)	
Norway (1940)	
Poland (1939)	
Soviet Union (1941)	
United States (1941)	
Yugoslavia (1941)	

This table shows the year in which each country listed entered World War II.
▶ In which year did the most Allied nations enter the war?

E. The Turning Point of the War

The year 1942 marked the turning point in the war. The Germans were stopped in the Soviet Union. The Americans held back the Japanese in the Pacific. In the years that followed, the war was carried to the homelands of the Axis countries in Europe. Italy and Germany were invaded. Hitler killed himself on April 30, 1945, and Germany surrendered eight days later. The Japanese continued the war for a short time. They surrendered after the United States dropped atomic bombs on two Japanese cities, Hiroshima and Nagasaki, on August 6 and 9, 1945.

World War II was more a *world* war than World War I. World War II was fought by forces from all over the world, and it was fought in Asia, Africa, and Europe.

F. The Effects of World War II

A New Organization Even before the end of World War II, the leaders of the victorious nations began to think about a peace settlement. Plans were made for a new international organization to be called the **United Nations** (UN). It was hoped that the UN would be more successful in avoiding war than was the old League of Nations.

A plan for the United Nations was drawn up at a conference in San Francisco, California. The plan stated that it would be the purpose of the UN to promote peace and develop friendly relations among the nations of the world.

On D-Day, June 6, 1944, Allied troops invaded Normandy.
▶ How did the Allied troops arrive at Normandy?

The United Nations is headquartered in New York City.
▶ Why was the United Nations established?

Occupied Countries World War II caused other political changes. After the war the Soviet Union occupied most of the countries of Eastern Europe including Bulgaria, Romania, and Hungary, which had surrendered, and Poland and Czechoslovakia, which the Soviets had freed from Nazi control. After Germany's surrender the Soviet Union also occupied eastern Germany. The rest of Germany was divided among the United States, Britain, and France.

In 1949 the United States and the countries of Britain and France formed the nation called the German Federal Republic, or West Germany. Eastern Germany remained under Soviet control and became the German Democratic Republic, or East Germany, in that same year.

World War II caused the role of Western Europe to change. The many losses and damages in Western Europe had weakened the countries there. World affairs then were put into the hands of two superpowers, the United States and the Soviet Union. Unfortunately, the United States and the Soviet Union had different postwar aims. The Soviet Union was interested in spreading its control throughout the world. The United States, on the other hand, was determined to stop the control of the Soviet Union.

The UN had 51 members in 1945 when it started. It now has more than three times that many members. The UN has lasted longer than the old League of Nations. The United Nations has played an important part in world affairs since World War II. But it has not prevented all wars.

LESSON **3** *REVIEW*

THINK AND WRITE

A. What events led to the start of World War II in 1939?

B. What countries did Germany invade?

C. How did the Nazis spread terror in Europe?

D. Why did the United States enter the war?

E. Why was 1942 the turning point of the war?

F. What were the effects of World War II?

SKILLS CHECK

WRITING SKILL

Pretend you had kept a diary during World War II. What might a page from it say?

243

USING THE VOCABULARY

On a separate sheet of paper, write the letter of the term that best matches each numbered statement.

    a. **nationalism**
    b. **unification**
    c. **prime minister**
    d. **alliance**
    e. **armistice**
    f. **Fascist**
    g. **Blitzkrieg**
    h. **genocide**
    i. **Axis**
    j. **United Nations**

1. An agreement between nations to act together
2. An international organization formed after World War II
3. The planned killing of a whole group of people because of their race, religion, or nationality
4. A chief official
5. The Germans' "lightning war"
6. Loyalty and devotion to one's country
7. The German, Italian, and Japanese alliance during World War II
8. An agreement to stop fighting
9. The uniting of separate regions and cities into one nation
10. One who believes in a single party, a single ruler, and total governmental control of political, economic, cultural, and religious activities

REMEMBERING WHAT YOU READ

On a separate sheet of paper, answer the following questions in complete sentences.

1. What did Giuseppe Mazzini do to help work toward the unification of Italy?
2. Who was the aristocratic politician who became prime minister of Sardinia?
3. What was Otto von Bismarck's goal for Germany?
4. How did the assassination of Archduke Franz Ferdinand lead to World War I?
5. Which five countries were initially involved in World War I?
6. What international organization was created by the peace treaties after World War I?
7. What dictators came to power in Italy and Germany in the period between the two world wars?
8. Why did Adolf Hitler want Germany to invade other European countries?
9. What event led the United States to enter World War II?
10. What political changes resulted from World War II?

TYING LANGUAGE ARTS TO SOCIAL STUDIES

Pretend that you are either an Italian or a German journalist covering the national movement in your country. The unification has just been completed, and you are interviewing people at a festival celebrating the event. Write a paragraph that describes people's feelings about the unification, including what advantages there will be to living in a united country.

THINKING CRITICALLY

On a separate sheet of paper, answer the following questions in complete sentences.

1. Why, do you think, was Count di Cavour more successful than Giuseppe Mazzini in his efforts to unite Italy?
2. How, do you think, might World War I have been prevented?
3. What similarities are there in the ways that Benito Mussolini and Adolf Hitler came to power?
4. Do you think something like the Holocaust could happen in our world today? Explain why or why not.
5. What do you think an international organization like the United Nations does to try to prevent wars?

SUMMARIZING THE CHAPTER

On a separate sheet of paper, draw a graphic organizer like the one shown here. Copy the information from this graphic organizer to the one you have drawn. Under the main idea for each lesson, write three statements that support the main idea.

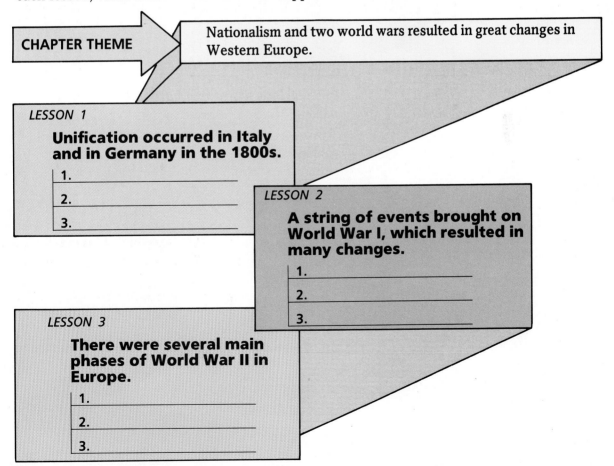

CHAPTER THEME

Nationalism and two world wars resulted in great changes in Western Europe.

LESSON 1

Unification occurred in Italy and in Germany in the 1800s.

1. _____
2. _____
3. _____

LESSON 2

A string of events brought on World War I, which resulted in many changes.

1. _____
2. _____
3. _____

LESSON 3

There were several main phases of World War II in Europe.

1. _____
2. _____
3. _____

CHAPTER 9

WESTERN EUROPE TODAY

*L*anguage, customs, and architecture are as varied in Western Europe as the landscape. Many old towns have grown into modern cities, but historic monuments and tourist attractions, such as the Eiffel Tower, have been preserved.

Switzerland, Austria, and Germany

THINK ABOUT WHAT YOU KNOW

Why is pollution a concern in many industrialized countries?

STUDY THE VOCABULARY

landlocked **raw material**
plateau **principality**
pollution

FOCUS YOUR READING

Describe the relationship between government, industry, and the environment in Switzerland, Austria, or Germany.

A. The Legend of William Tell

According to a legend, William Tell was a brave man who stood up for Swiss freedom during the Middle Ages. An old story relates that the emperor who ruled Austria and Switzerland once sent a cruel governor named Gessler to Altdorf, Switzerland. Gessler believed that the Swiss did not show him the proper respect, so he decided to teach them a lesson. The governor put his hat on a pole in the village and ordered each person passing by to bow to it. William Tell was too proud to bow to a hat, so he paid no attention.

When Gessler learned that Tell paid no attention to his order, he decided to make an example of him. He ordered Tell to shoot an apple off the head of Tell's own son. Gessler, no doubt, thought that the nervous father would kill his son, a dreadful punishment indeed! William Tell protested against the cruel order, but it did no good. So Tell picked up two arrows, placed one in his crossbow, and let it fly. His aim was perfect; the arrow split the apple in two. The disappointed Gessler asked Tell why he had picked up two arrows. The Swiss coolly replied that if he had hit his son, he would have sent the second arrow straight into Gessler's heart.

Angered by this bold reply, Gessler had Tell arrested. But the brave man soon escaped, seeking revenge on the cruel governor. Tell's opportunity for revenge came while a peasant woman pleaded with Gessler to release her imprisoned husband.

"Mercy, dear Governor!" she cried. "At last I can speak to you. . . ."

"What right have you to come to me so rudely, without asking for audience? Out of my way!" Desperately she seized his [horse's] reins. . . . "Let go of my reins or I will ride you down."

"Do so then!" She threw herself and her children on the ground before him. Gessler kicked his horse. The animal reared—and Gessler fell under its hoof, an arrow in his chest. A figure appeared on the rock above him and cried in a terrible voice: "You know the archer, Gessler! . . . You could not escape my arrow."

Gessler struggled to his feet. "William Tell . . . murderer!" he whispered harshly. "Catch him, men, that I can see him die before me." He clutched at the arrow to pull it out, but it had reached his heart. Blood came to his mouth and he fell back.

Most historians agree that the story of William Tell's shooting the apple is a legend. But it tells something important about the people who have kept the story alive. According to the legend, Tell's act led to a revolt that helped to free Switzerland. The statue of William Tell and his young son in Switzerland shows how much the Swiss have valued their freedom.

B. Tourism and Industry

Switzerland Though thousands of tourists have seen the William Tell statue, it is certainly not the main reason that they went to Switzerland. Switzerland, a small **landlocked** country is bordered by five countries. Landlocked means "having no seacoasts." Locate Switzerland on the map on the opposite page. What countries border on Switzerland?

More than half of Switzerland is covered with mountains. Most of Switzerland's 6.6 million people live on a **plateau** (pla TOH) that stretches across the middle of the country, between the mountains.

A plateau is sometimes called a tableland; it is a plain that is elevated above the surrounding land.

It is the mountains, however, that make tourism such an important industry in Switzerland. The Swiss Alps offer tourists some of the finest skiing and mountain scenery in the world. The Matterhorn is one of the most famous peaks in the Alps. It has an elevation of 14,690 feet (4,478 m). The peak, which is located on the border between Switzerland and Italy, is shown in the photograph at the bottom of this page.

Tourism is not the only important industry in Switzerland. The Swiss people

Switzerland is famous for its spectacular mountains, such as the Matterhorn (left), and for the skill and precision of its watchmakers (inset).
► What recreational activity are these tourists doing?

WESTERN EUROPE: POLITICAL

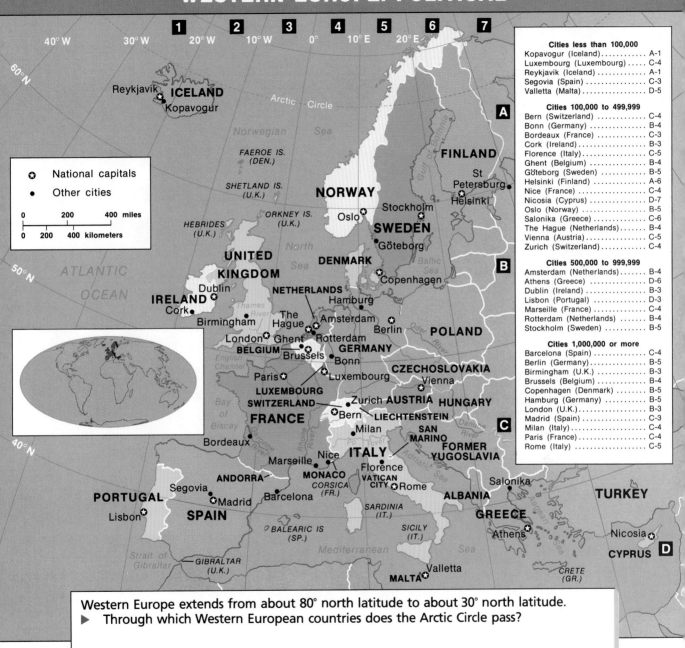

| | | | | | | |
|1|2|3|4|5|6|7|

Cities less than 100,000
Kopavogur (Iceland) A-1
Luxembourg (Luxembourg) C-4
Reykjavik (Iceland) A-1
Segovia (Spain) C-3
Valletta (Malta) D-5

Cities 100,000 to 499,999
Bern (Switzerland) C-4
Bonn (Germany) B-4
Bordeaux (France) C-3
Cork (Ireland) B-3
Florence (Italy) C-5
Ghent (Belgium) B-4
Göteborg (Sweden) B-5
Helsinki (Finland) A-6
Nice (France) C-4
Nicosia (Cyprus) D-7
Oslo (Norway) B-5
Salonika (Greece) C-6
The Hague (Netherlands) B-4
Vienna (Austria) C-5
Zurich (Switzerland) C-4

Cities 500,000 to 999,999
Amsterdam (Netherlands) B-4
Athens (Greece) D-6
Dublin (Ireland) B-3
Lisbon (Portugal) D-3
Marseille (France) C-4
Rotterdam (Netherlands) B-4
Stockholm (Sweden) B-5

Cities 1,000,000 or more
Barcelona (Spain) C-4
Berlin (Germany) B-5
Birmingham (U.K.) B-3
Brussels (Belgium) B-4
Copenhagen (Denmark) B-5
Hamburg (Germany) B-5
London (U.K.) B-3
Madrid (Spain) C-3
Milan (Italy) C-4
Paris (France) C-4
Rome (Italy) C-5

Western Europe extends from about 80° north latitude to about 30° north latitude.
▶ Through which Western European countries does the Arctic Circle pass?

have developed industries that require great skill. They became famous for making watches and clocks. They still make fine time-keeping devices, but they also produce such products as business machines and scientific instruments.

Switzerland has become an international business center. People and companies from many other countries do business with Swiss banks. A number of international companies have headquarters in Switzerland.

249

Munich, which was founded in 1158 by Duke Henry the Lion, is one of Germany's largest cities.
▶ What are some reasons that people like to visit cities?

Austria Austria is another small land-locked country located in Central Europe. There are about 7.6 million people living in Austria. Although most people live in cities and towns, they enjoy recreation in their country's many forests, lakes, and mountains. The mountain scenery in Austria draws large numbers of tourists from all over the world. There are more than 500 places to go skiing in Austria.

Germany Germany lies north of Switzerland and Austria. Germany has about twelve times more people and nearly nine times more land than does Switzerland. Unlike Switzerland and Austria, Germany is not landlocked; it has coasts on the North and Baltic seas.

Germany is one of the world's leading industrial countries. Its major products are steel, ships, vehicles, machinery, and chemicals. The country is one of the largest exporters in the world.

Tourism is important in Germany as well. Germans as well as foreigners visit cities such as Berlin, Munich, and Hamburg. The villages of the Black Forest, the castles overlooking the Rhine River, and the recreation areas of the Bavarian Alps are some other popular tourist destinations.

C. Natural Resources

Germany has many farms and gardens that supply a large part of the nation's food. Forests and woodlands cover large areas of the country. For many years the people of western Germany have been able to make use of the forests without destroying them. Trees are cut as they mature. The removal of mature trees allows space and sunlight for the growth of young trees and reduces the danger of forest fires. Unfortunately, **pollution** in the air from industries and automobiles has destroyed some of the forests, especially in eastern Germany. Pollution is the unclean condition of the earth's soil, air, and water.

The forested mountains of Austria provide industries with **raw materials.** Raw materials are natural materials that can be processed into finished products.

Some rivers are important waterways for shipping. The Rhine River is a waterway for Germany and its neighbors. Great efforts have been required to clean up rivers such as the Rhine, which have been polluted by industry.

D. Governments and Languages

Germany Divided As you have learned, after World War II the victorious Allies occupied Germany and divided it into four zones. In 1949 the United States, Britain, and France combined the three zones they occupied to form West Germany. The zone under Soviet control became East Germany. West Germany was more than twice

Hamburg is the most important industrial center in Germany.
▶ For what do you think these ships are used?

as large as East Germany. In addition, West Germany had almost four times as many people as East Germany.

Berlin, the old German capital, lay within East Germany, but it, too, was divided. West Germany held one section of the city. East Berlin became the capital of East Germany. However, Bonn, located in West Germany on the Rhine, was chosen as the capital of West Germany.

On a Sunday morning in 1961, people in Berlin awakened to the sounds of workers putting up a tall barbed-wire fence. By the end of the day a barricade 26 miles (42 km) long divided the eastern and western sections of the city. Armed East German police stood along the fence to make sure that no one tried to cut the wire or sneak through it. A concrete wall was built later to reinforce the fence through Berlin.

The Communist government of East Germany was trying to stop the movement of millions of people leaving East Germany for West Germany, especially through Berlin. But in spite of the wall and its guards, some East Germans still managed to escape to the West. Others lost their lives in the attempt. Why did people keep trying to cross to the West, even after the wall was built? One answer is for freedom. Although East Germany's formal name was the German Democratic Republic, it was *not* democratic. The Communist party ruled the country and did not allow free elections. The government owned or controlled most industries and large businesses. People had to be careful about what they said or wrote because the government did not permit free expression. When an uprising broke out during the 1950s, it was put down with the help of Soviet troops, which still occupied the country.

In West Germany, people could vote and express their ideas freely. Farmers could own the land they worked. Businesses could be owned by private individuals and companies. Freedom to do business enabled the West Germans, with the help of the United States, to rebuild their country rapidly after World War II.

Both East and West Germany became important industrial countries, but West Germany had a far higher standard of living. You may remember that the standard of living is a measure of how well people live. The standard of living in a country depends on the availability of goods that make living more comfortable and pleasant. People in West Germany had more

For nearly 30 years, East Germans were imprisoned within their country.
▶ What barriers prohibited travel in and out of East Germany?

automobiles, telephones, TV sets, and other goods. Many people, especially the young, fled East Germany for a better standard of living as well as for more freedom.

Germany United Germany was divided for 28 years. But television and radio broadcasts made the East Germans aware of West Germany's higher standard of living and of the freedoms that people enjoyed there. People in East Germany grew increasingly discontented with conditions in their own country. In the late 1980s, increasing dissatisfaction led to large demonstrations and brought about important changes.

On November 9, 1989, the border between the two Germanies was opened. Thousands of cheering people passed through the wall that had divided Berlin. The East German police, who had once shot at those trying to escape, only stood and watched the celebrating crowd. In places, the crowd knocked holes in the graffiti-covered wall that had kept families apart.

Other changes quickly followed. The Communists lost control of the government of East Germany. A free election was held in 1990. Later that year the two Germanies were united to form a single country. Berlin once again became the capital of Germany, the most populous country in Western Europe.

Unification has presented many challenges to the German government. In the

Germans rejoiced when the Berlin Wall opened in 1989. East Germans traveled freely to the West for the first time since the wall had been built.
▶ What did the opening of the Berlin Wall represent?

east, businesses must be converted to private ownership, and the standard of living must be raised. Saving the environment is a priority of the German people. Cleaning up pollution, especially in the east, is a huge task for the German government.

Austria Before World War I, Austria was part of a large empire with a monarchy and with people of many different nationalities. Today, Austria is a democratic republic made up almost entirely of German-speaking Austrians.

Switzerland Switzerland has four official languages: German, French, Italian, and Romansch (roh MAHNSH). German is by far the most commonly spoken language. Only about 1 percent of the Swiss people speak Romansch, a language that comes from the Latin of the ancient Romans. Many Swiss also speak English.

Liechtenstein Tucked between Austria and Switzerland is the tiny **Principality** of Liechtenstein (LIHK tun styn). A principality is a territory or country ruled by a prince. The whole country of Liechtenstein is smaller than Washington, D.C. Liechtenstein has a prince and a democratically elected assembly of 15 members.

This castle is typical of the many ancient buildings that still stand in Liechtenstein today.
▶ What kind of people might have lived here?

This small country has not had an army for over a century and has managed to stay out of all wars during this time. The official language of Liechtenstein is German.

LESSON *1* REVIEW

THINK AND WRITE

A. What does the William Tell legend suggest to us about the Swiss?
B. What are the important industries in Switzerland, Austria, and Germany?
C. What are some of the natural resources in Germany and Austria?
D. What governments and languages exist in Germany, Austria, Switzerland, and Liechtenstein?

SKILLS CHECK

THINKING SKILL

Divide a sheet of paper into three columns. Write one of these country names at the top of each column: *Germany, Austria, Switzerland.* Along the side of the paper, write the following topics: *Natural Resources, Government, Industry.* Make a chart by filling in the information.

The British Isles and Nordic Lands

THINK ABOUT WHAT YOU KNOW

Most countries are represented by national symbols. What symbols can you think of that represent the United States?

STUDY THE VOCABULARY

maritime climate
export
service industry

Commonwealth
  of Nations
fjord
geyser

FOCUS YOUR READING

What are the geographic features of the lands of the British Isles and of the Nordic countries?

A. Four Regions in One Kingdom

Great Britain The ancient Romans called Great Britain *Britannia* when it was part of their empire. Great Britain is the largest island of the British Isles. One Roman historian wrote that Britannia was shaped like a double-headed ax. Look at the map on this page. Perhaps if you have a good imagination, you may be able to see an ax in the shape of Great Britain.

The official name of the country today is the United Kingdom of Great Britain and Northern Ireland. But the name is often shortened to Great Britain or the United Kingdom. However, the official name tells something about the history of the country. It is called the *United* Kingdom because it unites four regions. England, Wales, and Scotland make up the island of Great Britain. Wales was united with England during the Middle Ages. Scotland became part of the United Kingdom nearly 300 years ago. At one time the United Kingdom included all of Ireland, but now only Northern Ireland is included. The term *British Isles* refers to the group of islands that includes Great Britain, Ireland, and some smaller islands.

England England is the largest region of the United Kingdom, and it has far more people than does Scotland, Wales, or

THE BRITISH ISLES: POLITICAL

- ○ National capitals
- • Other cities

0   150   300 miles
0   150   300 kilometers

Cities 100,000 to 499,999	
Belfast	B-1
Cardiff	B-2
Edinburgh	A-2
Manchester	B-2

Cities 500,000 to 999,999	
Dublin	B-1
Glasgow	A-2
Liverpool	B-2

Cities 1,000,000 or more	
Birmingham	B-2
London	B-2

Most of the United Kingdom is on the island of Great Britain.
▶ Which part of the United Kingdom is on the island of Ireland?

255

The majority of land in the British Isles is used for crops or pastures.
▶ How is this land being used?

Northern Ireland. However, England has its fine open spaces, such as the hills in the northwest and along the Pennine Chain, mountains that are sometimes called "the backbone of England."

English Channel The English Channel separates England from the European continent. In 1986 the British and French governments approved a plan to construct a tunnel under the channel. Trains will carry cars and trucks 32 miles (51 km) through this underwater tunnel. The tunnel is scheduled for completion by 1993.

B. A Green and Pleasant Land

Climate The Roman historian who thought Great Britain was shaped like an ax did not like the British climate. He was used to the sunny Mediterranean lands, and he complained that in Britannia "the sky is hidden by continual rain clouds." Actually, southeastern England does not receive much rainfall. The average yearly rainfall in London is less than it is in Rome. But in London, rain falls throughout the year; Rome usually has dry summers.

The British Isles have what is known as a **maritime climate**. *Maritime* means "having to do with the sea." A maritime climate is a climate influenced by winds blowing off the sea. Since the North Atlantic has warm currents, winters tend to be warmer than would be expected so far north. Even the Roman historian admitted that Britannia did not have extremely cold weather. He also reported that the "extreme moistness of the land" made it possible to grow most crops known to the Romans except olives. An English poet later described his homeland as "a green and pleasant land."

Land Use In Roman times forests covered most of the British Isles, but today about 80 percent of the land is used for crops or pastures. Although only a very small part of the population works on the land, the British produce about half of their country's food.

C. Working in Industries

Manufacturing Today many more British people work in industry than work on farms. As you know, the Industrial Revolution began in Great Britain. The country possessed large deposits of coal and iron ore for making steel, from which machines were constructed. Coal provided the principal source of energy in the days when steam engines turned factory wheels.

The United Kingdom still has deposits of coal, iron, tin, and other ores. Some mines have been worked for many years. As the mines became deeper, the costs of mining coal and ore increased.

Great Britain's sources of energy today include not only coal but also oil and natural gas. At one time the United Kingdom imported most of its oil. This changed with the discovery of large oil and natural gas deposits under the North Sea. The United Kingdom now **exports**, or sends to other countries, its oil.

Service Although the United Kingdom is still a manufacturing country, the number of people working in mines and manufacturing industries has been declining. Far more people work in **service industries**, or businesses that provide some kind of useful work for another business or person. Service industries provide services rather than make goods. People who fly airplanes provide service, as do those people who provide health care. Many people are employed in the tourism industry.

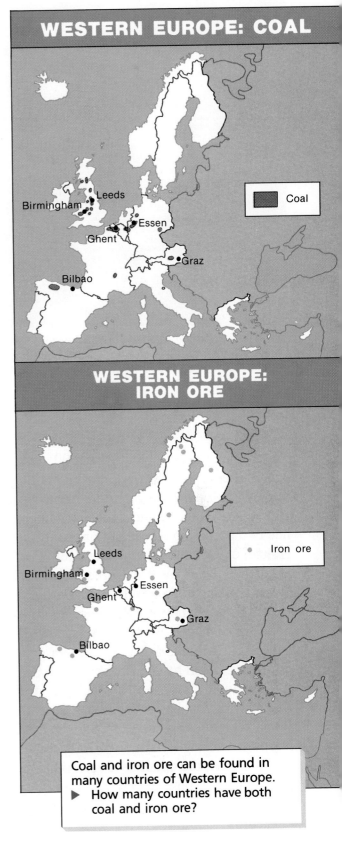

WESTERN EUROPE: COAL

Coal

Birmingham • Leeds • Essen • Ghent • Graz • Bilbao

WESTERN EUROPE: IRON ORE

• Iron ore

Birmingham • Leeds • Essen • Ghent • Graz • Bilbao

Coal and iron ore can be found in many countries of Western Europe.
▶ How many countries have both coal and iron ore?

The Parliament and Queen Elizabeth II (inset) represent the democratic monarchy of the United Kingdom. The photograph shows the Houses of Parliament and Big Ben, the great clock in the tower, on the Thames River.
▶ What is the role of the queen in the British government?

D. A Democratic Monarchy

The Glorious Revolution of 300 years ago limited the powers of the monarch. Since then the British government has become increasingly democratic. Parliament has two parts, the House of Lords and the House of Commons, but the House of Lords has little power over the making of laws. The power to govern rests with the House of Commons. Members of this house are elected by the voters, so the United Kingdom is a democracy — a government chosen by the people.

Although it is a democracy, the United Kingdom has a monarch. Elizabeth II has been queen since 1952. She receives important foreign visitors and addresses Parliament at the opening of each session. The monarch now serves as the living symbol of the country. The British national anthem is "God Save the Queen."

The United Kingdom once ruled a very large empire; it was the largest the world has ever known. It included lands on every inhabited continent. Today almost all the lands of the old empire are independent. Many have chosen to belong to the **Commonwealth of Nations**, an association of countries that were once a part of the British Empire. The Commonwealth includes such countries as Canada in North America, Kenya in Africa, India in Asia, and Australia. The monarch serves as the living symbol of the Commonwealth as well as of the United Kingdom.

E. An Island Divided

Climate If you were to cross the Atlantic Ocean from the United States to Europe by the shortest route, Ireland would be the first land you would see. Ireland, like the rest of the British Isles, enjoys a maritime climate, even though the cities of Dublin and Belfast are farther north than most Canadian cities.

A travel guidebook warns tourists going to Ireland to be prepared for some wet weather, whatever the season. Ireland receives more moisture than does most of Great Britain. The abundant moisture gives the island its nickname — the Emerald Isle, or the green island. The pastures and fields of Ireland make it a good land for raising livestock and crops. At one time the majority of the Irish people worked on the land, but today far more work in manufacturing and service occupations.

Political Differences The island is divided between the independent Republic of Ireland and Northern Ireland, which is part of the United Kingdom. The reason for the division goes far back in history. English kings conquered Ireland during the Middle Ages. Revolts broke out from time to time, so the English monarch sent a number of English and Scottish settlers to northern Ireland. Most of the settlers were of the Protestant religion, while most of the Irish were Roman Catholics.

Even though settlement in Northern Ireland took place long ago, differences between the two groups of Irish have lasted throughout the years. The Catholic Irish revolted against British rule and Ireland became independent in 1922. However, the Protestant majority in Northern Ireland chose to remain a part of the United Kingdom. Today, Northern Ireland includes a Catholic minority who want a united Ireland. Disputes about the division of Ireland continue to trouble the island.

The conflict between Catholics and Protestants in Northern Ireland has often resulted in violence.
▶ What has happened here?

F. The Nordic Countries

Norway, Sweden, and Finland, along with Denmark and Iceland, are known as the Nordic countries. The word *nordic* means "north." Norway, Sweden, and Finland all extend above the Arctic Circle. Find these three countries and the Arctic Circle on the map below. Norway extends farther north than any other country of Western Europe.

Sweden is the largest and most populous Nordic country. Most Swedes live in towns and cities located in the southern part of the country. Stockholm, the capital, is its largest city. It grew around an island fortress built during the Middle Ages.

Denmark is the smallest of the Nordic countries, but it is second only to Sweden in population. Denmark consists of the Jutland Peninsula and about 500 islands. Copenhagen, the capital, is located on the second largest island.

All the Nordic countries are democracies. Like the United Kingdom, the countries of Norway, Sweden, and Denmark are monarchies as well as democracies. The monarchs are heads of state, but elected representatives govern these countries.

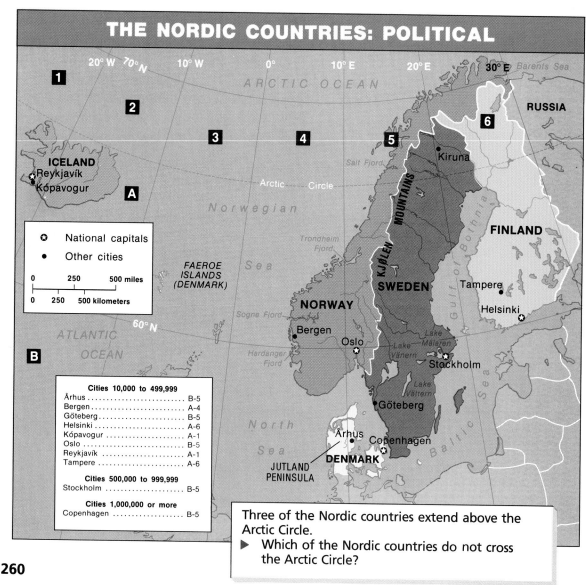

THE NORDIC COUNTRIES: POLITICAL

○ National capitals
• Other cities

0   250   500 miles
0   250   500 kilometers

Cities 10,000 to 499,999
Århus B-5
Bergen A-4
Göteberg B-5
Helsinki A-6
Kópavogur A-1
Oslo B-5
Reykjavík A-1
Tampere A-6

Cities 500,000 to 999,999
Stockholm B-5

Cities 1,000,000 or more
Copenhagen B-5

Three of the Nordic countries extend above the Arctic Circle.
▶ Which of the Nordic countries do not cross the Arctic Circle?

G. Natural Resources of the Nordic Lands

Forests Denmark does not have a lot of natural resources, but the Danes make good use of the ones that they have. Denmark has laws protecting its forests. In 1805 a law was made stating that "land which was forest must always be forest." Later laws required that a new tree must be planted for every old one cut down.

Norway, Sweden, and Finland also have large forests. Sweden's forests cover half the land. All three countries export timber. Finland's forests are the basis for its major industries exporting lumber, wood pulp, and paper along with other manufactured goods.

The Seas Although there is a limited amount of farmland in Norway, there is an abundance of marvelous scenery. It is a land of rocky mountains, glaciers, forests, and the great **fjords** (fyords). The fjords are narrow arms of the sea lying between narrow cliffs. The western coast of Norway is indented with hundreds of fjords.

The sea has been very important in Norway's history. The ancestors of the Norwegians were Vikings who raided the coasts of Europe during the Middle Ages. In later times, Norwegians made their living from the sea as fishers and sailors. The discovery of oil under the floor of the North Sea has provided Norway with additional wealth from the ocean.

The Danes also make good use of their country's location between the North and Baltic seas. Danish fishers provide large amounts of food from the seas for both home use and export.

Minerals The countries of Norway, Finland, and Sweden have important mineral deposits. Sweden's high-grade iron ore

Fjords such as this one make Norway's coast one of the most jagged in the world.
► What types of land surround the fjords?

deposits provide raw material for high-grade steel, which is used in making such products as tools and machines.

Iceland's Resources Contrary to its name, Iceland consists of more than just ice. This island has active volcanoes, fast-flowing rivers, and some grassy valleys. Cattle and sheep pasture on the grasslands. Sheep supply wool for clothing, particularly the sweaters that Iceland exports. Crops such as potatoes and turnips are grown in Iceland. Iceland's main resource is fish. Fishing is the main industry.

Despite its name, Iceland has more geysers (left) and hot springs (right) than any other country in the world.

► What is one way that the people of Iceland use these hot springs?

Iceland has hot springs and **geysers** (GYE zurz), which are fountains of steam and water that have been heated by hot volcanic rocks. When the water becomes extremely hot, it is released as steam. Water from some of the springs is used to heat buildings such as greenhouses near the Arctic Circle, where flowers, tomatoes, and other vegetables are grown. You may wonder if this country has any ice at all. Yes, glaciers cover the mountains in the southeastern part of the island.

LESSON 2 REVIEW

THINK AND WRITE

A. Which four regions make up the United Kingdom?

B. Why can Great Britain be described as a green and pleasant land?

C. In what industries do the people in the United Kingdom work?

D. What is the queen's role in governing the United Kingdom?

E. Why is Ireland a divided island?

F. Why are the countries Norway, Sweden, Finland, Denmark, and Iceland known as the Nordic countries?

G. What are some of the resources that can be found in Nordic countries?

SKILLS CHECK

MAP SKILL

Look at the map of the British Isles on page 255. What two bodies of water separate Great Britain from mainland Europe? What bodies of water separate Great Britain from Ireland? Which capital city has a million or more people? Describe its location.

LESSON 3

France and the Low Countries

THINK ABOUT WHAT YOU KNOW
What different languages can you name?

STUDY THE VOCABULARY
Mediterranean climate   bilingual

FOCUS YOUR READING
What distinctive physical features would travelers see if they visited France and the Low Countries?

Visitors to the Louvre enter the museum through a giant pyramid, which was designed by I. M. Pei and was opened in 1989.
► In what city is the Louvre?

A. Mark Twain in France

Years before Mark Twain wrote the books *The Adventures of Tom Sawyer* and *Adventures of Huckleberry Finn*, he wrote the book *The Innocents Abroad*. The book was about a trip to France with a group of tourists in 1867. In this book, Twain describes the countryside through which they traveled.

We have come five hundred miles by rail through the heart of France. What a bewitching land it is!—What a garden! Surely the leagues of bright green lawns are swept and brushed and watered every day and their grasses trimmed by the barber. . . . There are no unsightly stone walls, and never a fence of any kind. There is no dirt, no decay, no rubbish any where—nothing that even hints at untidiness—nothing that ever suggests neglect. All is orderly and beautiful— every thing is charming to the eye.

In Paris the tourists visited many of the most famous sites. Mark Twain went to the Louvre (loovr) museum, where he "looked at miles of its paintings." The Louvre has one of the world's great art collections, and contains more than a million works of art. He went on to the city of Versailles, expecting to be disappointed. He was sure that artists' paintings of the great palace and its gardens showed them "more beautiful than it was possible for any place in the world to be." But Mark Twain's doubts vanished when he saw Versailles with his own eyes. He decided that "no painter would represent Versailles on canvas as beautiful as it is in reality."

B. A Land with Variety

Climates France, the largest country of Western Europe, is a country with variety. It has hills, rolling plains, a high plateau, and rugged mountains. Both the Alps and the Pyrenees are located partly in France. The island of Corsica, in the Mediterranean, is part of France.

France has a variety of climates. The regions along the Atlantic coast have a maritime climate, somewhat like that of the British Isles. Central and eastern France are less affected by winds blowing off the ocean currents. As a result, winters are colder and summers warmer in inland Paris than in coastal Cherbourg (SHER-boorg), even though both cities are located near the same latitude. The beaches of southern France attract many vacationers because of their **Mediterranean climate**. A Mediterranean climate has cool, rainy winters and hot, dry summers. Palm, orange, and lemon trees grow in Nice (nees), a seaport located on the section of the Mediterranean coast known as the French Riviera.

The rich soil of the Rhone Valley in France is ideal for growing wine grapes.
► What is in the background?

Nine miles east of Nice lies the tiny country of Monaco, with an area of only 0.73 square miles (2 sq km). The entire country of Monaco is smaller than many American farms. It is mainly a tourist resort.

Natural Resources France has a variety of natural resources, including good soil, valuable mineral deposits, and streams used to generate electrical energy. Because of its good soil, France is able to export more food than any other Western European country. Northern France produces vegetables, grains, and more sugar beets and wheat than any country in Western Europe. Southern France has many vineyards, making the region famous for its wines.

Choropleth Maps The map on the next page shows the distribution of wheat in the countries of Western Europe. This type of map is called a *choropleth map*. It uses different colors to show the distribution of a product within a region. The colors also show how much of the product is produced by the countries in the region.

The key on the choropleth map indicates the amount of a product that each color on the map represents. For example, on this choropleth map you can see that red means a country produces 15,301 thousands of tons or more of wheat. The yellow means a country produces 0 to 1,900 thousands of tons of wheat. This choropleth map allows you to find which Western European countries produce the largest and smallest amounts of wheat, and which countries rank in between.

Governments The climates and natural resources are not the only aspects of France that vary. France has had a variety of governments since the establishment of the First Republic after the Revolution of

WESTERN EUROPE: WHEAT PRODUCTION

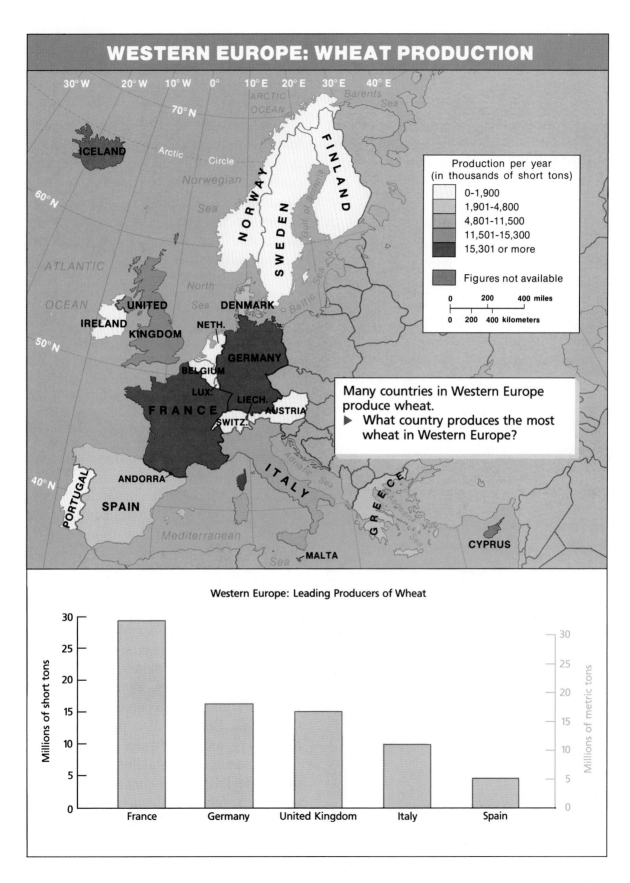

Production per year
(in thousands of short tons)

- 0-1,900
- 1,901-4,800
- 4,801-11,500
- 11,501-15,300
- 15,301 or more

Figures not available

Many countries in Western Europe produce wheat.
▶ What country produces the most wheat in Western Europe?

Western Europe: Leading Producers of Wheat

1789. As you have read, Napoleon did away with the republic and made himself emperor. Since the revolution, the French have had three kings, another emperor, and five republics, including the present Fifth Republic. The Fifth Republic, established in 1958, is a democracy.

C. The Low Countries

Just north of France lie the small countries of Belgium, Luxembourg, and the Netherlands, also known as Holland. These countries are called the Low Countries. The Netherlands is well named—its name means "low lands." Almost half the country lies below sea level. Sand dunes and dikes hold back the sea at high tide. There are also dikes along the river banks

Canals used as drainage ditches run through this grassland area in the Netherlands.
▶ For what is this land being used?

that flow across the Netherlands into the North Sea. No people have done so much as the Dutch, as Netherlanders are called, in pushing back the sea.

Located between France, Germany, and the Netherlands is Belgium. Belgium has some low, flat land that forms the coastland along the North Sea. However, Belgium also includes a hilly forested region in the southeast known as the Ardennes. The Ardennes extends from Belgium into Luxembourg.

D. Resources of the Low Countries

Land is precious in the Netherlands, because it has the highest population density of any country in Western Europe. Yet this crowded, small country has quite a lot of open space. There are green pastures and well-tended fields crossed by tree-lined roads and canals. The canals serve both as drainage ditches and as waterways for boats.

The Dutch people have learned to make good use of their land. Grass-covered dikes, and fields too moist for growing crops, are used as pastures for dairy cattle. The Netherlands exports large amounts of dairy products and a variety of other products, ranging from electric razors to cut diamonds and tulip bulbs.

Just as the Netherlands does, Belgium has a dense population. Only 3 percent of the people work on farms. Yet Belgian farms grow 85 percent of the country's food. Belgium also produces steel, machinery, and glassware.

Luxembourg is smaller than the state of Rhode Island, the smallest American state. Luxembourg's best farmland lies in the south. Its steel industry and other manufacturing industries produce goods for export through Belgium.

E. Governments and Languages

Luxembourg The Low Countries are democratic monarchies. Luxembourg's official name is Grand Duchy of Luxembourg. The term *duchy* means "a territory ruled by a duke or duchess." Like the other monarchs of Western Europe, the grand duke of Luxembourg is head of state, but the government is elected by the voters.

The people of Luxembourg have their own national language, called Letzeburgesch (LET se boor gush), but French and German are also official languages. The country's name can be spelled correctly as Luxembourg or Luxemburg. The first spelling is French; the second, German.

The Netherlands The law requires that the people of the Netherlands vote for members of parliament. Amsterdam, the largest city of the Netherlands, is the capital, but the city known as The Hague (hayg), is the seat of government. The queen lives at The Hague and the parliament meets there. The people of the Netherlands are called Dutch, since that is the language they speak.

Belgium Like the Netherlands, Belgium is a monarchy with an elected parliament. Belgium is a nation with three languages:

This magnificent building is the Peace Palace, located in The Hague.
► What kind of flower shown here is symbolic of the Netherlands?

French, German, and Flemish, a form of Dutch. Flemish is the primary language of over half of the population. The capital, Brussels, is officially **bilingual**, that is, having two languages. Flemish and French are the official languages. Students are taught in the language of their region and later study the second language.

LESSON **3** REVIEW

THINK AND WRITE

A. How did Mark Twain describe France?
B. Why is France called a land with variety?
C. Why is the term *Low Countries* a good name to describe the Netherlands, Belgium, and Luxembourg?
D. What are some of the resources in the Low Countries?
E. What governments and languages do the Low Countries have?

SKILLS CHECK

THINKING SKILL

Look at the graph on page 265. About how many times more tons of wheat does France produce than the United Kingdom? About how many times more tons of wheat does France produce than Germany? What two countries together produce about the same amount of wheat as the United Kingdom?

Countries of Southern Europe

THINK ABOUT WHAT YOU KNOW

THINK ABOUT WHAT YOU KNOW

You have already learned about Greece and Rome in ancient times. What sights from those times do you think tourists would be interested in visiting today?

STUDY THE VOCABULARY

acid rain

FOCUS YOUR READING

How do the peoples of the countries of southern Europe make use of their resources?

A. The Value of Ruins

Touring Italy   Italy is the boot-shaped peninsula that extends from the Alps mountains into the Mediterranean Sea. The country also includes the two islands of Sicily and Sardinia.

When Mark Twain reached Italy, he tried to take in all the famous sights. He went to Milan to see Leonardo da Vinci's famous painting *The Last Supper*. He went to Venice, where canals took the place of streets and where people traveled in boats called gondolas rather than in carriages and streetcars. He noted that traveling in a gondola was a lot smoother than riding in a carriage over bumpy streets. Mark Twain went on to Rome and tried to see all the famous ruins as well as the modern city. He admired the Colosseum. He observed that lizards sunned themselves on the stone seats where ancient emperors had sat watching gladiators.

Mark Twain visited Italy more than a hundred years ago, and people still go there today, partly to see the same sights.

Ruins, museums, and historic churches are among Italy's valuable resources, making tourism an important industry.

Industry and Farming   Yet it would be a mistake to think that tourism is Italy's only industry. Italy has become an important industrial country since World War II. Modern Italy has skilled workers and factories that make machinery, automobiles, shoes, and clothing. The Italians export these products all over the world. Much of the industry is located in the northern part of the country.

Besides prosperous industry, northern Italy has the most productive farmland

Italy has many skilled craftspeople who work in factories to produce some of Italy's finest products.
▶ In what type of factory is this woman working?

in the broad valley of the Po, Italy's longest river. The Po rises in the Alps and flows eastward to the Adriatic Sea. The Adriatic is an arm of the Mediterranean. Southern Italy is mostly an agricultural region, with little industry. Southern Italians grow grain, grapes, and olives, much as the ancient Romans did.

Government Many things remind us of the ancient Romans. Even Italy's government has been restored from the days of ancient Rome. Remember that the word *republic* was originally used for the government of ancient Rome. Italy, now a democratic republic, was a monarchy when it was united in the 1860s. It remained officially a monarchy until 1946, although the dictator Benito Mussolini actually ruled the country from 1925 until 1943. After World War II the Italians voted whether to keep the monarchy or establish a republic. Even the king had the right to vote in the election, but the monarchy lost.

San Marino San Marino is a very small country in the Apennines mountains of Italy. Covering only 24 square miles (62 sq km), it is even smaller than the country of Andorra. San Marino is the world's oldest existing republic. It can be well described as a "postage stamp country." It not only is very small but also receives considerable income from the sale of postage stamps.

Vatican City Vatican City is even smaller than San Marino. Vatican City is the smallest independent state in the world. It is located within the city of Rome. The pope, head of the Roman Catholic Church, is in charge of Vatican City. The Italian government agreed to the independence of Vatican City because the Roman Catholic Church is not just an Italian church.

The Rock of Gibraltar is the site of a large British military base.
▶ Why is this a good location for a military base?

B. Spain, on the Iberian Peninsula

Gibraltar At the southern tip of the Iberian Peninsula is a limestone mass known as the Rock of Gibraltar. The Iberian Peninsula is located between the Mediterranean and the Atlantic Ocean. The coast of Africa is about 14 miles (23 km) from the Rock, across the Strait of Gibraltar.

Because of its location at the narrow entrance to the Mediterranean Sea, Gibraltar has great military worth. The British acquired Gibraltar in 1704. Later they turned it into a large fort and established a military base there, which still exists.

Land and Climate Spain, Portugal, and Andorra are the countries on the Iberian Peninsula. The Pyrenees separate these countries from the rest of Europe.

Spain is the largest country on the Iberian Peninsula and the second largest in Western Europe. The greater part of

Spain is a high plateau. Madrid, the capital, is located in the middle of the central plateau. Spain has coasts on both the Atlantic Ocean and the Mediterranean Sea.

The combination of mountains, plateau, and seacoasts gives Spain a variety of climates. Snow covers the peaks in the Pyrenees. On the central plateau, summers are quite hot and dry, but in the winter, cold winds sweep across the land. The Atlantic coast has a maritime climate, so the winters are warmer and the summers are cooler than in the interior. However, Barcelona, on the Mediterranean coast, has a Mediterranean climate.

Farming and Industry The Spaniards raise wheat and other grains on the plateau. There are also large areas used as pasture, particularly for sheep, which are Spain's most important domestic animals. Oranges, lemons, limes, and olives are grown in the warmer south. Spain leads the world in the production of olives. Almonds are also an important crop.

Not so long ago many Spaniards worked on the land, but today fewer than 5 percent work in agriculture. Industry has developed rapidly in Spain. Over half the workers in Spain are employed in service industries, such as education, health care, and the military. Another important industry is manufacturing. Spain ranks among the world's leading makers of automobiles. Machinery, steel, iron, and clothing are some other important manufactured products in Spain.

Government In 1931, Spain became a democratic republic after years of being ruled by a monarch. King Alfonso XIII fled Spain in that year due to an overwhelming vote for republican government officials in the city elections. After the Spanish Civil

The dictator Francisco Franco ruled Spain from 1939 to 1975.
▶ After what war did Franco come into power?

The Granger Collection

War ended in 1939, Francisco Franco, a dictator, ruled Spain until 1975. After Franco's death, Spain established a democratic monarchy. King Juan Carlos I was made the head of state.

C. Spain's Neighbors on the Peninsula

Portugal Portugal, the second largest country on the peninsula, has its coast on the Atlantic Ocean. Lisbon, the capital of Portugal, is located farther west than any other port on the European mainland. The Portuguese have always been a seagoing people. Portuguese sailors discovered the sea route around Africa to Asia about the time that Columbus reached America.

At one time this seagoing nation ruled a large overseas empire that included lands in the continents of Africa, Asia, and South America. The Portuguese no longer rule this large empire, but their influence is still felt overseas. For example, Portuguese is the official language of Brazil, the largest country in South America.

The last Portuguese king was driven from his throne in 1910, and for many years a dictator ruled the country until he was overthrown by military officers in 1974. Portugal is now a republic with an elected government.

Andorra   Tucked away in the Pyrenees is Andorra, one of Western Europe's smallest countries. The country covers 180 square miles (466 sq km), which is less than half the area of New York City, with only about 49,000 people living there. Andorra is a principality, jointly ruled by France and Spain.

D. Ancient Ruins and Modern Pollution

Tourism   The term *Western Europe* comes from history rather than from geography. The countries that remained free from control by the Soviet Union after World War II have been called Western countries. Greece is located in Eastern Europe, but like Finland, it is considered a Western European country.

Like many other Western European countries, Greece has an important tourist industry. People are attracted by its scenery and ancient ruins. Probably no ancient structure is so famous as the Parthenon on the Acropolis at Athens.

Pollution   Athens is more than a city of ruins and museums. It is the capital of modern Greece and the country's largest city. There are many industries in the Athens area. There are also many people and automobiles. When fumes from industrial plants and automobiles mix with moisture in the air, they form **acid rain**. This is a form of air pollution that contains

These statues on the Acropolis are copies of the originals, which are now in the Acropolis Museum.
▶ Why, do you think, were the originals put into the museum?

certain chemicals that can damage trees and plants and even stone structures. Chemicals in the rain have been eating away the surface of ancient statues and carvings on stone. The Greek authorities have removed ancient statues from the Acropolis to protect them.

Farming   Greece consists of a mountainous peninsula and more than 2,000 islands, of which only about 169 are inhabited. Much of Greece is not suitable for farming; it is too rugged and rocky. Yet Greek farmers still produce wheat, olives, and grapes. The modern Greeks, like ancient Greeks, are a seagoing people.

Government   Greece has had many different forms of government since ancient times. Today, Greece is a republic in which people elect those who govern and make the laws.

E. Island Nations

Cyprus The island of Cyprus is located in the eastern Mediterranean. A large majority of Cypriots are Greeks; the minority are Turks. Disputes between the Greek majority and the Turkish minority have troubled Cyprus in recent times. Cyprus was a British colony before World War II. It became an independent republic in 1960.

In 1974 a dispute caused the Turkish government to send troops to northern Cyprus to support Turkish Cypriots. The Turks captured a large part of northeastern Cyprus, and thousands of Greek Cypriots fled to the southwestern part of the country. Since that time the island has been divided; most Greeks live in the southwest, and most Turks live in the northeast.

Farming, mining, and tourism are major industries in Cyprus. About half of the Cypriots are farmers who grow mainly citrus fruits, such as lemons and oranges. Asbestos is an important mineral on the island. Cyprus had rich deposits of copper, but the mines are now almost empty. In fact, the name *Cyprus* comes from the Greek word for "copper." Cyprus also has sandy beaches and sunny weather for tourists to enjoy.

These workers are harvesting a citrus crop in Cyprus.
► What fruit are these citrus farmers harvesting?

Malta Malta is another island nation, but it is much smaller than Cyprus. Malta is located in the middle of a narrow passage in the Mediterranean. As a result, many nations are interested in Malta as a military base. For many years the British controlled Malta because of its location, but in 1964, Malta became an independent republic. Today Malta is a member of the Commonwealth of Nations.

LESSON **4** REVIEW

THINK AND WRITE

A. Why can Italy's ancient ruins be considered a valuable resource?

B. Describe the climates and lands of Spain.

C. Which countries are Spain's neighbors on the Iberian Peninsula?

D. How have modern developments threatened ancient ruins in Athens?

E. Why are Cyprus and Malta important island nations?

SKILLS CHECK

WRITING SKILL

Pretend you are a travel agent. Which of the countries that you have just read about would you recommend to a tourist? Write a descriptive paragraph or two telling the reasons for your recommendation.

USING THE VOCABULARY

landlocked
plateau
pollution
raw materials
exports
Commonwealth of
  Nations

fjord
Mediterranean
  climates
bilingual
acid rain

From the list above, choose a term that could be used in place of the underlined word or words in each sentence. Rewrite the sentences on a separate sheet of paper.

1. The Netherlands <u>sends to other countries</u> goods such as tulip bulbs and dairy products.
2. Forests produce <u>trees</u> that can be processed into products such as paper and lumber.
3. The <u>group of countries that were once a part of the British Empire</u> includes countries such as Canada and Kenya.
4. A <u>tableland</u> is a plain elevated above the surrounding land.
5. <u>Narrow arms of the sea lying between narrow cliffs</u> are found all along the western coast of Norway.
6. France and most of Italy have <u>cool, rainy winters and hot, dry summers.</u>
7. The <u>unclean condition</u> of some of Germany's rivers has made the North Sea one of the dirtiest bodies of water in the world.
8. Students in Belgium learn to be <u>well-spoken in two languages.</u>
9. Fumes from automobiles mix with moisture in the air to form <u>air pollution.</u>
10. Austria and Switzerland are countries that are <u>surrounded entirely by land.</u>

REMEMBERING WHAT YOU READ

On a separate sheet of paper, answer the following questions in complete sentences.

1. Name three industries in Switzerland.
2. What important event in German history took place in 1990?
3. What four regions make up the United Kingdom?
4. What are the duties of the monarch of the United Kingdom?
5. Why is Ireland a divided island?
6. What countries are known as the Nordic countries?
7. What countries are known as the Low Countries?
8. What type of government do the Low Countries have?
9. Name the three countries on the Iberian Peninsula.
10. What are the two island nations in the Mediterranean Sea?

TYING HEALTH TO SOCIAL STUDIES

In many parts of the world, but especially in industrialized countries, pollution affects people's health. Pretend your class has been asked to participate in Health Awareness Week. You and your classmates have been chosen to create projects promoting the theme "Stop the Pollution." Choose a way that will allow you to best express the theme. You may make a poster, write an essay, make a speech, or choose your own idea. Dedicate the week as Health Awareness Week and share your project with the rest of the class.

THINKING CRITICALLY

On a separate sheet of paper, answer the following questions in complete sentences.

1. What are some ways that people in industrialized countries can help to eliminate their pollution problem?
2. Why, do you think, is knowing more than one language important for people who live in Western European countries?
3. Many workers in the United Kingdom are employed in service industries. Name at least five service industries in the United States.
4. Denmark has a law requiring that a new tree be planted for every one cut down. Do you think this is a good law? Explain.
5. Explain the connection between ancient history and tourism.

SUMMARIZING THE CHAPTER

On a separate sheet of paper, draw a graphic organizer that is like the one shown here. Copy the information from this graphic organizer to the one you have drawn. Under each main idea, write three statements that support it.

CHAPTER THEME

Physical features, resources, economies, and governments blend together to make the countries of Western Europe what they are today.

LESSON 1

Many resources are found in Switzerland, Austria, and Germany.

1.
2.
3.

LESSON 2

The British Isles and the Nordic countries have various geographic features.

1.
2.
3.

LESSON 3

France and the Low Countries have distinctive physical features.

1.
2.
3.

LESSON 4

The people of the countries of southern Europe make good use of their resources.

1.
2.
3.

274

COOPERATIVE LEARNING

As you learned in Unit 2, new ideas and inventions can change society. For example, the invention of the printing press put more information in the hands of more people than ever before. This made modern democracy possible. In addition, developments in agriculture, transportation, and manufacturing have altered the way people live.

Every day, new inventions change our lives. Inventors develop machines that help us do things more efficiently. Many inventors work with others. By sharing ideas, they can solve problems creatively. Similarly, you can share ideas with other students to solve a problem.

PROJECT

Work with a group of classmates to think of an invention for the future. The purpose of the invention will be to solve a problem that exists in today's society or to make people's lives easier.

The first step in the project will be brainstorming. Hold a group meeting to talk about possible inventions. Try to come up with at least ten ideas. Choose one group member to write down all your group's ideas. When you are finished

brainstorming, that person should read the list aloud and ask group members to vote on what they think is the best idea. The winner will be your group's invention.

Next, brainstorm again to discuss ways that your invention would change society. Talk about how your invention would affect people's lives. Choose one group member to take notes on your group's ideas.

Another group member should use the notes to write a short explanation of your invention and a summary of how it would affect society. Someone else in the group should draw a picture to illustrate the invention.

PRESENTATION AND REVIEW

Choose one group member to present your group's invention to the class. Then your group can answer any questions that come up and discuss with the rest of the students how your invention would improve people's lives.

Finally, hold another group meeting to evaluate your project. Did everyone in your group have a job to do? Did the group work well together? Did the class think your invention was a good one?

REMEMBER TO:
- Give your ideas.
- Listen to others' ideas.
- Plan your work with the group.
- Present your project.
- Discuss how your group worked.

A. WHY DO I NEED THIS SKILL?

The first subheading you read in Chapter 7 said "Copernicus Turns Astronomy Upside Down." This phrase conveys a piece of information, but what does it really mean? How can astronomy be turned upside down?

Copernicus disagreed with the ideas of Ptolemy, the ancient astronomer who believed that the sun, moon, and planets revolve around the earth. Thus, he "turned astronomy upside down" by advancing an idea that was the opposite of what people had believed for centuries.

As you can see, there can be a great deal of meaning behind a simple five-word phrase. But the meaning may not be obvious from the words alone. Often we must seek other facts so that we can better **interpret**, or better understand, information. Knowing how to interpret information is an important skill to learn.

B. LEARNING THE SKILL

This textbook presents a lot of information for you to interpret. One way to get the full meaning behind information is to pose questions and try to think of logical answers based on facts. You might ask yourself questions like these: Why did a particular event occur? What was the result? What picture does some information create in my mind?

In Chapter 6 you read some information about castles built during the Middle Ages. Suppose a typical medieval castle was described to you like this.

Medieval castles were usually found in hard-to-reach places. The first castles were made of wood, but later in the Middle Ages they had thick stone walls. These walls kept the inside of the castles cold and damp. The windows were very small, letting in little sunlight. A moat, a water-filled ditch, circled the castle walls on the outside. The water in the moat looked dirty.

By asking and trying to answer questions about the statements presented, you can interpret the information to discover its full meaning. For example, why were the castles built in hard-to-reach places? Why were the walls thick and made of stone? Why weren't the windows made larger to allow more sunlight to come in and reduce the dampness? What is the function of the moat around the castle? Turn back to pages 175 and 177 and reread the section about castles to find answers to these questions.

By asking questions and probing deeper into the information your social studies textbook presents, you can gain a better understanding of the facts.

C. PRACTICING THE SKILL

The following statements are from Lesson 3 of Chapter 6. Use the questioning strategy and the information in the lesson, which begins on page 184, to interpret each statement. Find facts to support the statements and write your interpretations on a separate sheet of paper.

1. This interest in learning about the Romans and Greeks led to a birth of interest in newer types of learning.
2. The Renaissance gave Europeans new and different ideas about themselves and about the world.
3. By learning Greek, they [the students] could "speak with Homer and Plato."
4. Many students were eager to read the books that had been found, but only a few could do so.
5. Much was happening during the Renaissance, and not all of it can be described as "rebirth."

The following statements are from Lesson 2 of Chapter 8, which starts on page 227. Again, use the questioning strategy that you learned about on page 276 to help you interpret the statements below. Then find facts in the lesson to support these statements and write your interpretations on a separate sheet of paper.

1. People had good reason to call this a *world war*.
2. The peace treaties of 1919 changed the map of Europe.
3. Italy was on the winning side in World War I, but the Italians faced difficulties in 1919.
4. The Italian king was so alarmed that he offered to make Mussolini the prime minister.
5. Hitler repeated over and over that Germany had lost the war because of a "stab in the back."

D. APPLYING THE SKILL

To get the most out of your social studies textbook—and all books that you read—you will need to interpret information. Think about what questions you need to raise to interpret what you read. What is the meaning behind each statement? How are the presented facts related to each other? What additional information do you need to better understand statements? Use this skill to interpret as you read this textbook.

A. WHY DO I NEED THIS SKILL?

Your social studies textbook contains a great deal of information about people, places, and events. You will find many ideas to learn and understand. Using a study-reading strategy such as **SQR** will help you identify, organize, and remember main ideas and important information.

B. LEARNING THE SKILL

SQR stands for **Survey**, **Question**, and **Read**.

Survey—When you survey, or skim over, the lesson, you will get a general idea of what the lesson is about. Begin surveying by scanning the headings, questions, and vocabulary words. Look at any pictures, maps, tables, or charts you find in the lesson. Doing this will give you a good idea of the topic of the lesson. Think about what you already know about this topic. Then see if you can make some predictions, or guesses, about what will be in the lesson.

Question—The next step is preparing a list of questions about the lesson. The FOCUS YOUR READING questions in this book will help you concentrate on the main idea of each lesson. Take another look at the vocabulary list, headings, and picture captions, and compose questions that you think deal with important ideas. You should be

able to answer your questions as you read. Write your questions on a sheet of paper or make a mental list of them.

Read—The last step is reading the lesson to find the answers to your questions. Write down the answers as you find them. Other questions may come to mind as you read. Add them to your list and try to answer them, too.

C. PRACTICING THE SKILL

Turn to page 179. You can practice **SQR** on Lesson 2 in Chapter 6, "The People of the Towns and the Church." Refer to the **USING SQR** table to help you remember the steps.

Survey the lesson, following the directions given above. Think about what you might already know about the people in the Middle Ages. Try to make predictions about the lesson.

Now make a list of questions about the lesson and write them on a sheet of paper. Leave some space after each question so you can write the answer later. You might begin by writing down the FOCUS YOUR READING question. This question is very valuable because it helps you understand the main idea of the lesson. Take another look at the vocabulary list. Make up a question for each unfamiliar word. For instance, you might write *What is a monastery?* The lesson headings can also be turned into questions. You could ask, "What was life in a monastery like during the Middle Ages?" See if you can think of five questions about this lesson.

Now you are ready to read the lesson and answer your questions. Write the answers on your paper. If you think of any more questions as you read, write those questions on your paper and look for the answers.

SQR will be especially helpful when you study for a test. Save your **SQR** questions and answers so you can use them to review the chapter.

Use **SQR** as you read the next chapter, which is about the geography of the Soviet Union and Eastern Europe. See if using **SQR** helps you to understand and remember the important ideas in that chapter. See if it is any easier to complete the Chapter Review.

D. APPLYING THE SKILL

You can use **SQR** steps to learn and understand the material in almost any subject. The **USING SQR** table will help you.

USING SQR			
Survey	• Look at headings, questions, vocabulary words, and visuals.	• Think about what you already know about the topic.	• Make predictions about the lesson topic.
Question	• Think about the questions already in the lesson.	• Use vocabulary words, headings, and other lesson features to prepare your own questions.	• Make predictions about the lesson content.
Read	• Read to answer your questions.	• Write down the answers or say them to yourself.	• Ask and answer any other questions that come to mind as you read.

Unit **3**

THE FORMER SOVIET UNION AND EASTERN EUROPE

The vast area of the former Soviet Union and Eastern Europe, which extends from Europe into Asia, has great diversity in its geography and in the many ethnic groups who live in the countries that make up this region.

▶ *The colorful domes of St. Basil's Cathedral are one of the most recognized landmarks of Moscow, Russia.*

CHAPTER **10**

GEOGRAPHY OF THE FORMER SOVIET UNION AND EASTERN EUROPE

The former Soviet Union and Eastern Europe stretch from the Baltic Sea to the Pacific Ocean. Much of the region is an extension of the North European Plain, interrupted by mountains that serve as a boundary between Europe and Asia.

Visiting a Vast Empire

THINK ABOUT WHAT YOU KNOW
Imagine that you are the ruler of an empire so large that you could never visit all of the lands you rule. How would you find out what is happening in the outer reaches of your empire?

STUDY THE VOCABULARY

tributary	**continental climate**
crest	**taiga**
tundra	**steppe**
permafrost	**time zone**

FOCUS YOUR READING
What are the geographic characteristics of the former Soviet Union?

A. Humboldt Visits Russia

A Smart Man When Alexander von Humboldt visited the Russian empire in 1829, he told the wife of the Russian ruler that diamonds would be found in the Ural Mountains. Sure enough, a short time later a 14-year-old boy working in a Urals gold mine found a diamond. It was the first time a diamond had ever been found in this region of the world.

How did Humboldt know that there would be diamonds in the Urals? It was not just a guess. Humboldt was a scientist and explorer who based his remark on his knowledge of geology, the science that deals with the earth's crust. Humboldt was known for his great learning in many fields. People said that he was "a man who knew everything." That was the reason a poor peasant stopped Humboldt one day and asked where he could find his stolen horse. The peasant thought surely a man who knew everything would know *that*.

The Vast Empire When Alexander Humboldt visited Russia in 1829, its empire consisted of lands in Asia and the eastern part of Europe. These lands came to be known as the Union of Soviet Socialist Republics; the name was often shortened to U.S.S.R. or Soviet Union. (As you read this chapter, you will find references to the former Soviet Union. Late in 1991 the 15 republics that made up the Union of Soviet Socialist Republics became 15 independent nations. In Chapter 12 you will learn how the collapse of the U.S.S.R. came about. The largest of these new nations is Russia, which has the largest area of any nation in the world. Russia was also the name of the empire that Alexander von Humboldt visited in 1829.)

The ruler of the Russian empire had invited Humboldt to visit the empire and to report about minerals that might be found in the Ural Mountains. Humboldt had a great curiosity and he was eager to learn all he could about the earth. He welcomed a chance to visit the vast Russian empire, which occupied such a large part of the earth's surface.

Travel across the huge empire was difficult in 1829, even for official guests. The empire stretched from the Baltic Sea across Siberia to East Asia. Since there were no railroads, Humboldt traveled in horse-drawn carriages or on river barges.

B. Large Bodies of Water

Long Rivers Humboldt traveled for three days on a sailing barge down the Volga River. Unfortunately, the wind blew from the wrong direction, so sailors had to row the boat along. Otherwise the barge would have traveled no faster than the slow-moving river current.

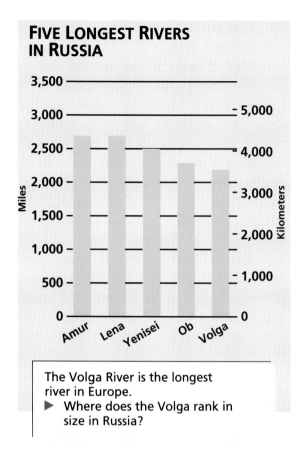

FIVE LONGEST RIVERS IN RUSSIA

The Volga River is the longest river in Europe.

▶ Where does the Volga rank in size in Russia?

The Volga is the longest river in Europe. However, it does not carry as much water as Europe's second longest river, the Danube (DAN yoob). The Volga flows about 2,200 miles (3,500 km) in a southeasterly direction from an area northwest of Moscow to the Caspian (KAS pee-un) Sea. Find the Volga River on the map on the opposite page.

Humboldt did not travel on two other important Russian rivers, the Don and the Dnieper (NEE pur). These two rivers flow south into the Black Sea. Today a canal connects the Volga and the Don. Another system of waterways connects the upper Volga with the Baltic Sea. The rivers and canals are important parts of the transportation system of the former Soviet Union, but they cannot be used during the cold winter months because they freeze.

The Yenisei (yen uh SAY) River and the Ob River are two of the largest Siberian rivers. They flow northward and empty into the Arctic Ocean.

Inland Seas The Caspian Sea, into which the Volga flows, has shores in both Europe and Asia. The Caspian is the largest inland body of water in the world. It is more than four times as large as Lake Superior, one of the Great Lakes of North America. And unlike the Great Lakes, the Caspian nas no outlet to the sea, and its waters are salty.

The Aral Sea, east of the Caspian, is another saltwater sea. In fact, it is becoming saltier. Much of the water that once flowed into the Aral Sea is now used for irrigation. As a result, the sea has greatly decreased in size. In turn, the proportion of salt has increased. The waters of the Aral Sea have become so salty that many fish can no longer live in it. This is destroying the fishing industry in the area.

Lake Baikal (bye KAWL), in eastern Siberia, is a freshwater lake with an outlet through a **tributary** of the Yenisei River. A tributary is a small stream that flows into a larger stream. Lake Baikal is more than a mile deep; it is the world's deepest lake.

C. Mountains That Separate Continents

The Urals The Ural Mountains, where Humboldt correctly said there would be diamonds, extend from north to south through much of the former Soviet Union. When Humboldt reached the Urals, he tramped about for days, collecting rock samples. What he found convinced him that the Urals were rich in minerals, including iron, copper, gold, and platinum. Because of the presence of minerals, the

THE FORMER SOVIET UNION AND EASTERN EUROPE: PHYSICAL

North Pole

ATLANTIC OCEAN

ARCTIC OCEAN

NORWAY

North Sea

Baltic Sea

FINLAND

White Sea

RUSSIA

LITHUANIA

ESTONIA

St. Petersburg

Pskov

LATVIA

NORTH EUROPEAN PLAIN

BELARUS

Moscow

MOLDOVA

UKRAINE

Dnieper

CRIMEA

Volga

Kazan

Volgograd

Don R.

TURKEY

Black Sea

GEORGIA

Mt. Elbrus 18,481 ft (5,633 m)

CAUCASUS MTS.

ARMENIA

AZERBAIJAN

TURKMENISTAN

IRAN

Don R.

Arctic Circle

SIBERIA

Yakutsk

RUSSIA

Trans-Siberian Railway

Irkutsk

Lake Baikal

Ob

KAZAKHSTAN

Aral Sea

Lake Balkhash

UZBEKISTAN

KYRGYZSTAN

TAJIKISTAN

AFGHANISTAN

Pik Kommunizma 24,590 ft (7,495 m)

MONGOLIA

CHINA

Sea of Okhotsk

Sea of Japan

Vladivostok

JAPAN

NORTH KOREA

Bering Strait

Bering Sea

Tropic of Cancer

Equator

INDIAN OCEAN

Inset

Area of Inset

GERMANY

Elbe R.

POLAND

CZECHOSLOVAKIA

AUSTRIA

SLOVENIA

HUNGARY

CROATIA

BOSNIA AND HERCEGOVINA

ITALY

Adriatic Sea

CARPATHIAN MTS.

GREAT HUNGARIAN PLAIN

Iron Gate

YUGOSLAVIA

Danube R.

ROMANIA

BULGARIA

MACEDONIA

ALBANIA

GREECE

0   100   200 miles
0   100   200 kilometers

Legend

Elevations

Feet	Meters
10,000	3,000
5,000	1,500
2,000	600
1,000	300
0	0

Land below sea level

• Cities

╌╌╌ Canals

▲ Mountain peaks

━━ Boundary of the former Soviet Union

0   300   600 miles
0   300   600 kilometers

Lake Baikal

Lake Baikal is 5,712 feet (1,741 m) deep and about 375 miles (600 km) long. In fact, it is the deepest lake in the world.
▶ In what country is Lake Baikal located?

Urals today are one of the most important industrial regions in the former Soviet Union.

The Urals are the first mountains a traveler sees when journeying eastward from the Baltic Sea. They are part of the boundary between Europe and Asia. But the Urals are not a high and rugged range like the Alps or the Pyrenees. When travelers cross the **crest**, or highest point, of the Ural Mountains, they see little to suggest that they are crossing from one continent to another.

The Caucasus   It is easier to see that the rugged Caucasus (KAW kuh sus) Mountains form a natural boundary. The Caucasus, which stretch from the Black Sea to the Caspian Sea, serve as a boundary between Europe and Asia in the south. The peaks of the Caucasus are about three times as high as the highest point of the Urals. The Caucasus are also higher than the Alps.

Mount Elbrus, the tallest Caucasus peak, is the highest mountain in Europe. But the Pamir mountains in the central Asian republic of Tajikistan, between Afghanistan and China, are even higher than the Caucasus. The highest peak in this republic is more than a mile higher than Mount Elbrus.

D. The Climates of a Vast Land

Hot and Cold   The former Soviet Union occupied one sixth of the earth's land surface, but much of this land has only limited use. Large areas are either too cold or too dry for growing crops. If you look at the map on page 287, you will see that much of the land of the former Soviet Union lies north of the Arctic Circle. You will also see that a large area of land north and east of

The Caucasus Mountains are rich in many minerals.
▶ For which two continents do these mountains serve as a boundary?

the Caspian Sea is a desert region. What other regions are shown on the vegetation map on page 287?

The arctic region is a treeless area called the **tundra**, where only mosses and low bushes can grow. The tundra receives little precipitation—usually less than 10 inches (25 cm) a year. Winters are cold and long in the arctic, but the long summer days can be quite warm or even hot. Yet the sun on long summer days thaws only the top layer of the frozen soil. A few feet below the surface, the earth remains frozen. This layer of permanently frozen earth is called **permafrost**.

THE FORMER SOVIET UNION: VEGETATION

Legend:
- Tundra
- Taiga
- Steppe
- Desert
- Mountain vegetation
- Hardwood forest

0   400   800 miles

0   400   800 kilometers

Of the six vegetation regions of the former Soviet Union, the northern forests, known as the taiga, cover the largest land area.
▶ In which region is the Aral Sea found?

Most lands in the former Soviet Union have what is called a **continental climate**, in which winters are cold and summers are hot. Unlike the maritime climate of much of Western Europe, the climate of the former Soviet Union is not greatly affected by ocean currents. Even land near the Baltic Sea is too far from the Atlantic Ocean to be much affected by its currents. St. Petersburg, a major Russian port on the Baltic, has colder winters than Oslo, Norway. Both ports are located at the same latitude, but the climate is more moderate in Oslo because it is close to the Atlantic

Ocean. Moscow, which is farther south but also farther away from the Atlantic Ocean, has even colder winters than St. Petersburg has.

Most of Siberia has great variations between summer and winter temperatures. When Humboldt traveled east of the Urals in July and August, he suffered from the heat. His discomfort was increased by having to wear a leather mask to protect his face from hordes of mosquitoes. If Humboldt had visited the same areas in January, he would have experienced very cold weather. In places where temperatures may reach 90°F (32°C) or higher in July, they can fall as low as −50°F (−46°C) in January.

Milder Climates   The Crimean (kry MEE un) peninsula, or Crimea, extends into the Black Sea. Crimea has a milder climate than most parts of the former Soviet Union. There is a lot of sunny weather in summer. Some people called the beaches of Crimea the Riviera on the Black Sea. The name suggests the French Riviera, a famous beach resort on the Mediterranean coast. However, winters in Crimea are decidedly colder than on the French Riviera.

The east coast of the Black Sea is protected by the Caucasus Mountains. It has a more truly Mediterranean climate. Citrus fruit can even be grown in this area.

The taiga, a huge forest zone, sweeps across 5,000 miles of the former Soviet Union.
▶ What kinds of trees can be found in the taiga?

E. The Forests and the Steppes

Great Forests   Although the former Soviet Union has high mountains, most of it is flat or rolling plains. It is part of the North European Plain, which extends eastward from France. Forests cover much of the land, as shown by the map on page 287. The northern forests are known as the **taiga** (TYE guh). These forests have coniferous trees, or trees with cones, such as pines. South of the taiga are the hardwood forests of trees such as maples and oaks.

As in North America, much forest land in the former Soviet Union has been cleared for farms and cities. But there are still great forests.

Treeless Steppes   South of the forests stretch the treeless plains that are called the **steppes** (steps). Humboldt compared his carriage crossing the steppes to a boat crossing a calm sea with an unbroken view of the sky. In the book *The Endless Steppe: Growing Up in Siberia,* author Esther Hautzig describes what she thought when she first saw the steppes.

The flatness of this land was awesome. There wasn't a hill in sight; it was an enormous, unrippled sea of parched and lifeless grass.

"[Father], why is the earth so flat here?"

"These must be steppes, Esther."

"Steppes? But steppes are in Siberia."

"This is Siberia," he said quietly.

If I had been told that I had been transported to the moon, I could not have been more stunned.

"Siberia?" My voice trembled. "But Siberia is full of snow."

"It will be," my father said.

A vast area of treeless plains, known as the steppes, has some of the area's richest soil.
▶ What crops are grown here?

In the former Soviet Union, wheat and other grains can be grown on the parts of the grassy steppes that receive sufficient precipitation. The dry parts of the steppes are used for grazing.

F. A Land That Had Eleven Time Zones

We measure the hours of the day by the turning of the earth. The time of day at any particular moment depends on where you are. When it is noon in London, England, it is two o'clock in the afternoon in Moscow, Russia.

Time changes with the longitude as the earth turns. Therefore the earth is divided into 24 standard **time zones**, one for each hour of the day. Some time zone boundaries zigzag so that people living in the same region or country can have the same time.

Some countries are so large that they are divided into more than one time zone. In the United States, for example, when it is noon in New York, it is 9:00 A.M. in San Francisco and 7:00 A.M. in Honolulu. The former Soviet Union was so large that it covered 11 time zones. When it was noon in Moscow, it was 11:00 P.M. on the Pacific coast of the Bering Strait, which was the easternmost territory of the Soviet Union. You will learn more about time zones when you read pages 350–351.

LESSON *1* REVIEW

THINK AND WRITE

A. What can we learn about the former Soviet Union from Humboldt's visit to the Russian empire?

B. What are the important bodies of water in the former Soviet Union?

C. Which two mountain ranges mark the boundary between Europe and Asia?

D. Describe the climate of the former Soviet Union.

E. What types of land cover the former Soviet Union?

F. How is the earth divided into time zones?

SKILLS CHECK

MAP SKILL

Use the map on page 287 to answer these questions: Which vegetation region of the former Soviet Union covers the largest land area? What type of vegetation region surrounds the Aral Sea?

The Lands of Eastern Europe

Find the countries of Eastern Europe on the inset map on page 285. What physical characteristics do you think these countries may have in common?

gorge   sanctuary

What kinds of lands could be seen on a trip down the Danube, Vistula, and Oder rivers?

A. One Continent, Two Regions

Europe   As you learned in earlier chapters, the continent of Europe was divided into Western Europe and Eastern Europe as a result of World War II. This political division between Western and Eastern Europe continued until 1989. In that year the Soviet government lost control of Eastern Europe, and new governments not tied to the Soviet Union came to power.

Because of these political changes, the distinction between Eastern and Western Europe will no longer exist someday. But for now, it is still convenient to consider the countries of Europe as part of these two regions.

The Trip Begins   It is easy to remember where the Danube River begins and ends. It flows from the Black Forest to the Black Sea. The Black Forest is in Germany. To travel from the Danube's source to its mouth—that is, from its beginning to its end—you would start out in Western Europe. But after passing through Germany

and Austria, you would travel between two countries of Eastern Europe, Czechoslovakia (chek uh sloh VAH kee uh) and Hungary. At the "elbow" of the Danube, you would turn sharply south as the river carried you through Hungary to its capital city of Budapest (BOOD uh pest).

Across Plains   Below Budapest you would follow the Danube across the Great Hungarian Plain. This gently rolling land is about the size of the state of Virginia. The Great Hungarian Plain extends from Hungary into the former Yugoslavia and Romania.

While traveling in Hungary, you might want to take a side trip to see Hungary's "Far West." It is here you could see longhorn cattle, cow ponies, and cowhands. As with American cowhands, pictures of the Hungarian cowhands usually

This Hungarian cowhand entertains tourists on the cattle range.
▶ How is this cowhand similar to an American cowhand?

The Iron Gate between Serbia and Romania is the deepest gorge in Europe.
▶ What river flows through it?

show them wearing broad-brimmed hats and very colorful clothing. Actually, one is more likely to see this sort of dress at horse shows staged for tourists rather than on the cattle range.

Once back on the Danube, you would go downstream to Belgrade, Serbia. The Danube flows through the area that was once Yugoslavia. Some of this area is part of the Great Hungarian Plain, but much of the area is mountainous. Along the Adriatic coast mountains and beaches attract many tourists.

Through Mountains Farther down the Danube the river forms the boundary between Serbia and Romania. Here you would come to the Iron Gate, a deep **gorge**, or a narrow passage through land. The Iron Gate is probably the most scenic section of the river. Here the Danube rushes through the gorge between the Carpathian (kahr PAY thee un) and Balkan mountains. This is the deepest gorge in Europe. At one time it was difficult to move boats through the Iron Gate. Now, dams and locks make it much easier.

Below the Iron Gate you would follow another national boundary. North of the river is Romania; to the south is Bulgaria.

The Trip Ends The Danube makes still more turns before it finally reaches its delta on the Black Sea. Recall that a delta is the built-up land at the mouth of a river. Just before its final turn toward the sea, the Danube touches the boundary of the former Soviet Union. As you can see from the map on page 285, a trip down the Danube would take you to many countries, several of them in Eastern Europe.

If you are interested in birds and animals, you would probably want to take a trip onto the Danube Delta. It is one of Europe's great wildlife **sanctuaries**. A sanctuary is a place where birds and animals are protected from hunters and others who would disturb them. More than 300 species of birds and many kinds of animals are found on the Danube Delta.

B. Travel to the Black Sea and the Baltic Sea

The Black Sea The Danube, Dnieper, and Don are among the Eastern European rivers that flow into the Black Sea. But the Black Sea has only one narrow outlet. This outlet passes through two straits, the Bosporus and the Dardanelles. The Bosporus links the Black Sea with the Sea of Marmara. The Dardanelles, called the Hellespont in ancient times, connects the Sea of Marmara with the Aegean Sea, which is an arm of the Mediterranean Sea. The straits serve as a narrow gateway not only to the countries located on the Black Sea but also to all the lands on the Danube.

The straits divide Europe from Asia, although it is now easy to cross back and forth between the two continents. A bridge spans the Bosporus, which is less than a half mile (1 km) wide at this point. The Turkish city of Istanbul, formerly Constantinople, stands on both sides of the Bosporus. Most of the city is in Europe, but part of it is in Asia.

The Baltic If you were to travel down the Vistula River, you would start in the Carpathian Mountains that stretch along Poland's southern border. On your journey to the river's mouth, you would never leave Poland. The Vistula is Poland's own river. It is also the longest river flowing into the Baltic Sea.

The Vistula begins as a rushing mountain stream, but it becomes a slow-moving lowland river as it makes its way to the sea. Although Poland is mountainous in the south, most of it is part of the North European Plain.

A trip down the Vistula would take you to Warsaw, Poland's capital, and several of the country's largest cities. The port

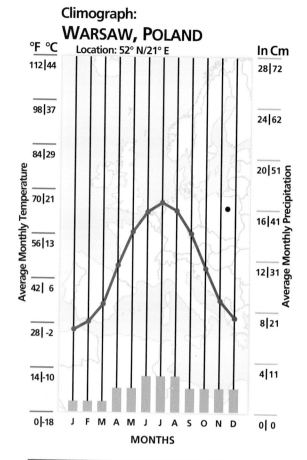

Climograph:
WARSAW, POLAND
Location: 52° N/21° E

This climograph is for Warsaw, which has a continental climate.
▶ About how cold is it in Warsaw during the month of February?

of Gdańsk (guh DAHNSK) is located at the mouth of the Vistula River. Gdańsk was once known as Danzig.

The Oder River is the second longest river flowing to the Baltic. Unlike the Vistula, the Oder is an international river. Its source is in the mountains of Czechoslovakia, but farther downstream the Oder River serves as the boundary between Germany and Poland. Canals connect the Oder and Vistula, so these rivers form part of a network of waterways in Germany and Poland.

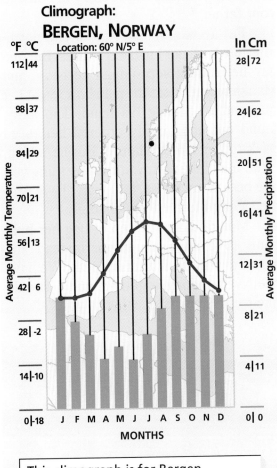

Climograph:
BERGEN, NORWAY

Location: 60° N/5° E

°F °C — In Cm

Average Monthly Temperature — Average Monthly Precipitation

MONTHS

J F M A M J J A S O N D

This climograph is for Bergen, which has a maritime climate.
► About how cold is it in Bergen during the month of February?

C. Eastern Europe's Continental Climate

If you want to take a trip down the Danube or Vistula, plan to go in the summer. Parts of the rivers freeze during the winter. Most places in Eastern Europe have a continental climate. Winters here are milder than in most of the former Soviet Union but colder than in Western Europe, which has a maritime climate.

The differences between maritime and continental climates can be seen by comparing average summer and winter temperatures of cities in Western Europe and Eastern Europe. Warsaw, on the Vistula, has colder winters than Bergen, Norway, even though Bergen is located much farther north. On the other hand, a July day in Warsaw will likely be warmer than one in Bergen. Warsaw also has much colder winters than London, although these cities are located at about the same latitude. Remember that Warsaw and London are both farther from the Equator than is northern Maine or North Dakota.

Places on the Baltic coast of Poland are somewhat warmer than inland cities, such as Warsaw. But these coastal cities still have cooler winters than cities of comparable latitudes on the Atlantic coast.

LESSON **2** *REVIEW*

THINK AND WRITE

A. What geographic features of Eastern Europe could you see on a trip down the Danube?

B. What rivers could you travel down to reach the Black Sea and the Baltic Sea?

C. Why do Budapest and Warsaw have colder winters than Brussels and London?

SKILLS CHECK

THINKING SKILL

Turn to the Atlas map on pages 616–617 and estimate the latitude of each of these cities: Budapest, Brussels, Warsaw, and London. Check your estimates by looking up the latitudes for these cities in the Gazetteer.

More Nationalities Than Countries

THINK ABOUT WHAT YOU KNOW

In the United States there are many citizens who originally came from other countries. What things can you think of that unite the citizens of the United States?

STUDY THE VOCABULARY

folk tale   **proverb**

FOCUS YOUR READING

What is the difference between country and nationality?

A. An Old Tale About a Clever Woman

Eastern Europe has a variety of nationalities. Indeed, some countries have more than one nationality. For example, the former Soviet Union was a country of diverse nationalities. Each of these nationalities valued its language, literature, beliefs, and traditions that had been handed down from generation to generation.

Folk tales, or stories handed down from one generation to another, often reflect ideas and traditions that a nationality values. Czechoslovakians have a folk tale about a woman named Manka.

According to the folk tale, Manka was the beautiful and clever daughter of a shepherd. She married a village judge. The judge loved his wife, but he warned her, "My dear Manka, you are not to use that cleverness of yours at my expense. I won't have you interfering in any of my cases. In fact, if ever you give advice to anyone who comes to me for judgment, I'll turn you out

of my house at once and send you home to your father."

For a time, Manka was careful not to interfere with her husband's cases. But one day he made a very unjust decision, and Manka secretly told the man how to get her husband to change his mind. The judge found out and angrily ordered her to go back to her father's house. But he added, "You may take with you the one thing you like best in my house, for I won't have people saying I treated you shabbily."

Manka did not weep or beg her husband to change his mind. Instead she asked to stay until after supper. "We have been very happy together, and I should like to eat one last meal with you."

The story of Manka, in this Czechoslovakian folk tale, has been handed down through many generations.
▶ In what way was Manka clever?

The judge agreed, and Manka prepared a fine supper of all the dishes she knew he liked best. The judge ate heartily and drank so much that he became drowsy and fell sound asleep in his chair. Manka had the servants carry him quietly to a wagon and drove to her father's house.

When the judge awoke in the morning, he rubbed his eyes in surprise and burst out, "What does this mean?" Manka smiled and answered sweetly, "You know you told me I might take with me the one thing I liked best in your house, so of course I took you!" The judge could not help but laugh, and he told his wife, "Manka, you're too clever for me. Come on, my dear, let's go home."

B. Other Parts of Nationality

Proverbs and History A **proverb** (PRAHV urb) is a short saying that expresses some truth or fact. Like folk tales, proverbs are handed down from one generation to another and reflect valued ideas. Almost every nationality has its own proverbs. Those given here are Russian.

> *A small hole can sink a big ship.*
> *Yesterday's storm causes no damage today.*
> *It does not help the mouse to say "meow" to the cat.*
> *Just because the child has lice, you need not cut off its head.*

Folk tales and proverbs that people have in common are not the only things that unite people as a nationality. Knowledge of history is usually very important in causing a group of people to feel that they are a nationality. Hungarians are said to remember the battle of Mohacs that cost Hungary its freedom, even though it took place more than 400 years ago. The Hungarians have a saying whenever things go wrong: "No matter, more was lost at Mohacs Field!"

Language Language is an important bond between people who belong to a nationality. A common language is a very strong tie between people. Most nationalities in the former Soviet Union and Eastern Europe have their own languages. A nationality is sometimes thought of as a group of people who share the same language.

Related languages are said to belong to the same family of languages. You read earlier about the Romance languages, which grew out of Latin, the language of the Romans. Most languages of Eastern Europe belong to the Slavic family of

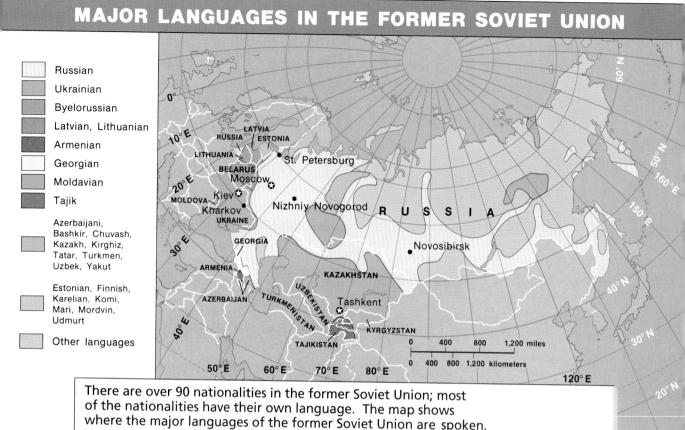

Russian
Ukrainian
Byelorussian
Latvian, Lithuanian
Armenian
Georgian
Moldavian
Tajik

Azerbaijani, Bashkir, Chuvash, Kazakh, Kirghiz, Tatar, Turkmen, Uzbek, Yakut

Estonian, Finnish, Karelian, Komi, Mari, Mordvin, Udmurt

Other languages

There are over 90 nationalities in the former Soviet Union; most of the nationalities have their own language. The map shows where the major languages of the former Soviet Union are spoken.
▶ What is the major language spoken in Moscow?

languages. They are related, although they differ from each other. The people who speak one of the Slavic languages as their native tongue are called *Slavs*.

C. Nationalities and Languages in the Former Soviet Union

The map above shows the many languages that are spoken in the former Soviet Union. The people do not use the same alphabet as that used for Western European languages. Instead they have an alphabet based on one invented during the Middle Ages by a Christian monk named Cyril. This alphabet is known as the Cyrillic (suh-RIHL ihk) alphabet.

When the Soviet Union existed, about half of the people who lived in that country were Russians. The Russians are the

largest Slavic nationality. Two other groups of Slavs, the Ukrainians and Belorussians, make up one fifth of the population of the former Soviet Union.

Not all the people in the former Soviet Union are Slavs. Other nationalities include the Armenians and Georgians, who live south of the Caucasus Mountains, and the Uzbeks, of Central Asia. Three nationalities living on the Baltic Coast—the Estonians, the Latvians, and the Lithuanians—had their own countries before they were taken over by the Soviet Union at the beginning of World War II.

All of the nationalities mentioned in this section became independent nations in 1991. Find these nations on the map above. Some names have changed slightly.

The lands of the former Soviet Union are home to many different nationalities. Most of the nationalities have their own language, culture, and way of life.

▶ What problems might arise from so many different nationalities?

THE FORMER SOVIET UNION AND EASTERN EUROPE: POPULATION DENSITY

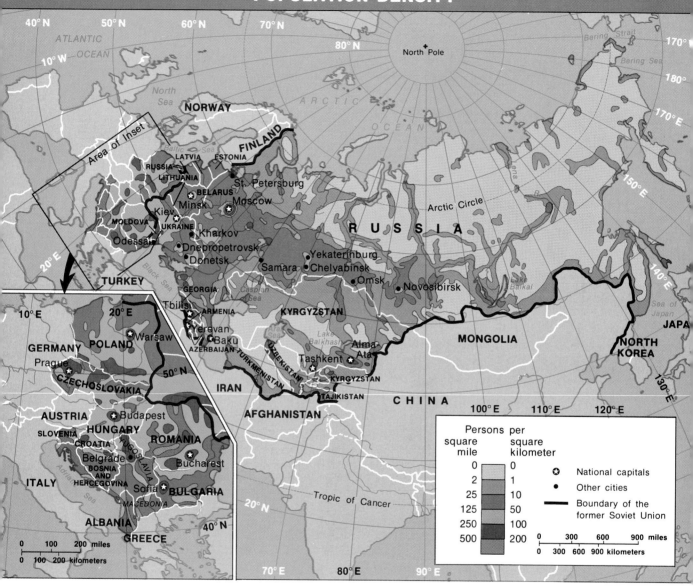

THE 24 LARGEST CITIES OF THE FORMER SOVIET UNION AND EASTERN EUROPE

Moscow (Russia) 8,527,000
St. Petersburg (Russia) 4,359,000
Kiev (Ukraine) 2,495,000
Budapest (Hungary) 2,080,000
Tashkent (Uzbekistan) 2,077,000
Bucharest (Romania) 1,976,000
Warsaw (Poland) 1,659,000
Kharkov (Ukraine) 1,567,000

Minsk (Belarus) 1,510,000
Belgrade 1,470,000
Novosibirsk (Russia) 1,405,000
Yekaterinburg (Russia) 1,315,000
Samara (Russia) 1,267,000
Prague (Czechoslovakia) 1,194,000
Sofia (Bulgaria) 1,183,000
Tbilisi (Georgia) 1,174,000

Dnepropetrovsk (Ukraine) 1,166,000
Yerevan (Armenia) 1,164,000
Odessa (Ukraine) 1,132,000
Omsk (Russia) 1,122,000
Baku (Azerbaijan) 1,114,000
Chelyabinsk (Russia) 1,107,000
Alma-Ata (Kazakhstan) 1,088,000
Donetsk (Ukraine) 1,081,000

Many cities in the former Soviet Union have over a million people.
▶ How many cities in Russia have more than one million people?

D. Nationalities in Other Eastern European Countries

Czechoslovakia, as the name suggests, is the country of both Czechs and Slovaks. Both speak a Slavic language, so both Czech and Slovak are official languages. Fortunately, the differences between these languages are not great, so a person who knows one of the languages can usually understand the other.

The former Yugoslavia, like the former Soviet Union, was made up of several nationalities. The Serbs were the largest single group. There were also Croatians (kroh AY shuns), Slovenians, Albanians, and other national groups. The Serbs and Croatians speak the same language, but they use different alphabets when writing. The Serbs, like the Russian people, use an alphabet based on the Cyrillic alphabet. The Croatians use the Roman alphabet, which is the alphabet we use.

Three Eastern European nations do not have a Slavic language. The language of most Hungarians is Magyar, which was brought to Europe by Asian conquerors during the Middle Ages. Romanian, as you have read, comes from the language of the Romans. The origins of Albanian, the language of mountainous Albania as well as parts of the former Yugoslavia, has long puzzled historians. It does not seem to be

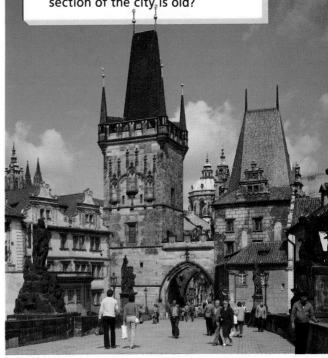

People cross the Charles Bridge towards the historic center of Prague, in Czechoslovakia.
▶ How can you tell that this section of the city is old?

related to any other European language. But like the other languages spoken in Eastern Europe and the former Soviet Union, Albanian is an important part of a nationality. Together, the nationalities of Eastern Europe and the countries that were once part of the Soviet Union help to make this region of the world a land of great diversity.

LESSON **3** *REVIEW*

THINK AND WRITE

A. How are folk tales related to the study of nationalities?

B. Besides folk tales, what things do people of the same nationality have in common?

C. What are some of the nationality groups who live in the former Soviet Union?

D. How do the languages of Hungary, Romania, and Albania differ from those of other Eastern European nations?

SKILLS CHECK

WRITING SKILL

Using the information in this lesson, describe the characteristics of a nationality.

299

USING THE VOCABULARY

On a separate sheet of paper, write the letter of the term that best matches each numbered statement.

a. tundra
b. permafrost
c. continental climate
d. taiga
e. steppe
f. time zone
g. gorge
h. sanctuary
i. folk tale
j. proverb

1. A narrow passage through land
2. Climate in which winters are cold and summers are hot
3. A story handed down from one generation to another
4. The treeless arctic region of the former Soviet Union
5. A place where birds and animals are protected
6. A layer of permanently frozen earth
7. A name for a treeless plain in the former Soviet Union
8. A short saying that expresses some truth or fact
9. One of 24 standard divisions of the earth
10. The northern coniferous forests of the former Soviet Union

REMEMBERING WHAT YOU READ

On a separate sheet of paper, answer the following questions in complete sentences.

1. Why was Alexander von Humboldt invited to Russia?
2. What river in the former Soviet Union is the longest river in Europe?
3. What is the name of the world's deepest lake?
4. What two mountain ranges form a boundary between Europe and Asia?
5. Why have the beaches of Crimea been called the Riviera on the Black Sea?
6. How many time zones were there in the former Soviet Union?
7. Through how many Eastern European countries does the Danube River flow?
8. What two straits serve as a gateway to countries located on the coast of the Black Sea?
9. What kind of climate do most places in Eastern Europe have?
10. To what family of languages do most Eastern European languages belong?

TYING LANGUAGE ARTS TO SOCIAL STUDIES

Try to write your own folk tale to describe a characteristic of your nationality. First think of an idea or a tradition that you feel is specific to your nationality. Then make up a story to try to explain how that idea or tradition developed.

THINKING CRITICALLY

On a separate sheet of paper, answer the questions below in complete sentences.

1. Would you have wanted to travel around the Russian empire with Alexander von Humboldt? Explain.
2. Why are wildlife sanctuaries important?
3. How accurate, do you think, are stories that are handed down from one generation to another?
4. What does the proverb "Yesterday's storm causes no damage today" mean?
5. Do you think every country should be divided into smaller countries on the basis of nationality alone?

SUMMARIZING THE CHAPTER

Copy this graphic organizer on a separate sheet of paper. Beside the main heading for each lesson, write three key words or phrases that support the main idea.

CHAPTER THEME

The former Soviet Union and the countries of Eastern Europe are lands of great diversity in both geography and the people who live there.

LESSON 1 **The former Soviet Union has various geographic characteristics.**

1. _____
2. _____
3. _____

LESSON 2 **The Danube, Vistula, and Oder rivers flow through the different types of lands in Eastern Europe.**

1. _____
2. _____
3. _____

LESSON 3 **In the former Soviet Union and each country of Eastern Europe, there are many different nationalities.**

1. _____
2. _____
3. _____

11 HISTORY OF RUSSIA AND EASTERN EUROPE

Outside influences shaped the history of this region, which was once part of large empires. As the result of a revolution in 1917, the Russian empire was reorganized. Small independent countries replaced old empires in Eastern Europe.

The Middle Ages in Russia and Eastern Europe

In Chapter 6 you read about some things that happened in western Europe during the Middle Ages. How did religion affect life in western Europe at that time?

STUDY THE VOCABULARY

schism

FOCUS YOUR READING

How did Constantinople and the Mongol Empire affect Russia and eastern Europe during the Middle Ages?

A. The Tale of Bygone Years

Princess Olga Nearly 900 years ago, Christian monks prepared the earliest written history of the Eastern Slavs, *The Tale of Bygone Years*. This work can be called a tale because it combines legend and history. As you know, we learn about people from their legends as well as from their history.

Among the stories told in *The Tale of Bygone Years* is that of Princess Olga, who lived more than a thousand years ago. Olga was the wife of a prince of Kiev (kee EV), a city located on the Dnieper River. When Olga's husband was killed in battle, she took over the city and led it to victory over its enemies.

Olga later journeyed to Constantinople, the gateway to the Black Sea and the capital of the Byzantine Empire. That empire had become far smaller by the time Olga went on her journey, but Constantinople was still the largest and richest city in Europe.

When Olga met the Byzantine emperor, he was struck by her beauty and her wisdom. In fact, he proposed marriage. Olga did not give him an answer; instead she asked to be taught about his religion, Christianity. People from Kiev were not Christians at that time. They worshiped a variety of gods and goddesses.

The emperor, eager to win Olga's hand, asked the patriarch to teach her. The patriarch was the head of the church at Constantinople. According to *The Tale of Bygone Years*, Olga took in the patriarch's teachings "like a sponge absorbing water." She accepted the Christian religion but turned down the emperor's offer of marriage. She returned to Kiev, where she tried without success to introduce the Christian religion among her people.

Vladimir of Kiev Olga's grandson Vladimir (VLAD uh mihr) became ruler of Kiev in A.D. 980. At first he supported the old religion, so the people could continue to worship the old gods and goddesses. Yet Vladimir was curious about other religions. When he questioned travelers who came to Kiev about the religions of their homelands, they each said that their religion was the best.

Vladimir asked his nobles what they thought about the different views. The nobles told Vladimir that if he wanted to learn about different religions, he should send "ten good and true men" to visit other lands and observe how people there worshiped. Vladimir did as the nobles suggested. When the ten advisers returned, they reported that Christian services in the city of Constantinople were by far the most beautiful.

Vladimir of Kiev became a Christian in the year 988. He directed that all statues

Grand Prince Vladimir of Kiev brought the Christian religion to his people in the year 988.
▶ How did the artist portray Vladimir in this drawing?

countries, followed the teachings of the church at Rome and accepted the pope as head of the church. The church at Constantinople was headed by the patriarch. The Bible and services of the Roman church were in Latin. The Bible and services of the church at Constantinople were in Greek.

Other differences between the church at Rome and at Constantinople led in time to a **schism** (SIHZ um), or division, between the eastern and western branches of the Christian Church. The western branch was called Roman Catholic; the eastern was known as Eastern Orthodox. The word *orthodox* means "having the right views," and the word *catholic* means "general" or "universal."

Orthodox Church The Eastern Orthodox Church spread Christianity throughout several eastern European countries as

and pictures of the old gods and goddesses be cut into pieces and burned. Vladimir ordered all the people in Kiev to come to the Dnieper River to be baptized as Christians. *The Tale of Bygone Years* would have us believe that the people of Kiev accepted Christianity gladly. Perhaps this is true, but one wonders if the monks' tale tells the full story.

B. The Christian Churches of Eastern Europe and Russia

Church Divisions Vladimir's advisers had observed Christian services in Germany as well as in Constantinople. There were important differences between the Christian Church in eastern Europe and that in western Europe. Christians in Germany, as in most of the western European

This cathedral was built as a place of worship for Russian Christians.
▶ How would you describe the domes of this church?

well as Russia. In time the church in Russia had its own patriarch and was known as the Russian Orthodox Church. A number of other eastern European nations also came to have their own churches, among them the Serbian Orthodox Church and the Romanian Orthodox Church.

The Christian Church, however, was not the only thing to affect Russia and eastern Europe during the Middle Ages. More than 200 years after Vladimir of Kiev accepted Christianity, conquerors from the steppes would invade Russia and eastern Europe, and bring much of this large territory under their control.

C. Conquerors from the Steppes

The Nomads The steppes that stretch from the Black Sea into central Asia were the home of nomadic tribes during the Middle Ages. These nomads had learned to live on the dry grasslands. They kept herds of horses, cattle, sheep, and goats. The nomads lived in tents so that they could easily pack up and move with their herds to better pastures. The animals provided milk and meat for food, as well as hides and wool for clothing.

Sometimes the nomads traded for certain goods; other times they raided settled areas and took what they wanted. The nomads looked down on anyone who sought safety behind town walls. The nomadic warriors were fierce fighters, and their small, tough, fast horses enabled them to cover long distances and catch their victims by surprise. Those victims even included other tribes of nomads until the people of the steppes were united under the leadership of the Mongols.

The Mongols lived in the land that is still called Mongolia. The chief of the Mongol tribe had a son who would come to be

Genghis Khan became ruler of the Mongols, who were known as marvelous horsemen and fierce fighters.
▶ What does Genghis Khan's name mean?

known as Genghis Khan (GENG gihs kahn). When the boy was 13 years old, his father died, leaving him at the mercy of his rivals. In spite of his youth, the boy outwitted those rivals and took his father's place as leader of the Mongol tribe. In the years that followed, Genghis Khan brought other tribes under his rule and thus earned his name, which means "mighty leader." By the year 1206, Genghis Khan was widely known as the undisputed master of the steppes.

Mongol Conquests Armies led by the Mongols began a rapid conquest of neighboring lands. They swept across Eurasia from China to eastern Europe. By 1240 the army of Batu Khan, grandson of Genghis Khan, reached Kiev. Batu sent word to the

305

prince of Kiev, "Give me one tenth of everything—one man in ten, and the tenth part of your wealth." To this demand the prince answered, "We will give you nothing: when we are dead, then you can have it all!"

These were brave words indeed, but words did not stop the Mongols. They broke down the gates of the city with a battering ram and launched a fierce attack. Kiev fell in five days, and a terrible slaughter followed. According to one famous account, "No eye was left open to weep for the dead."

The Mongols did not stop at Kiev. They pressed farther west, into Poland, where they defeated an army of heavily armed knights. The Mongols advanced south across the Great Hungarian Plain and crossed the Danube. They destroyed towns and villages throughout much of Russia and eastern Europe. People in western Europe shuddered fearfully when they heard about the Mongols and worried that these fierce warriors from the steppes would come farther west. Fortunately for the western Europeans, Batu Khan turned back to central Asia. When he later returned west, he made his empire's permanent capital on the lower Volga River.

The fast-riding Mongols conquered towns and villages throughout much of Russia and eastern Europe.
▶ What weapons did the Mongol forces use?

D. Paying the Golden Horde

The Mongols conquered a huge territory, creating the Mongol Empire—the largest empire the world has ever known. The Russians called the Mongols the Golden Horde. Gold was the color of Batu's tent. *Horde* comes from a Mongol word meaning "camp."

The Golden Horde did not directly govern the lands they conquered in Russia. They only wanted the conquered people to pay them money and to send laborers to serve them. The Mongols were quite willing to let the Russian princes continue governing their states as long as they paid money on demand. The princes in turn had to collect the money from their own people. Some princes collected more than they had to pay the Golden Horde, so they profited from the arrangement. It was the large number of peasants who carried the heavy burden. The Golden Horde would continue to control Russia in this way for many years.

A Russian prince is shown visiting the Mongol headquarters of Batu Khan. The Russians called the Mongols the Golden Horde.
▶ What decorated the Mongol headquarters?

LESSON **1** *REVIEW*

THINK AND WRITE

A. According to *The Tale of Bygone Years*, how was Christianity brought to Kiev?
B. What were the results of the schism between the eastern and western branches of the Christian Church?
C. Describe what areas the Mongol armies conquered.
D. What did the Golden Horde want from the Russians?

SKILLS CHECK

MAP SKILL

Locate Mongolia on the political map of Eurasia on Atlas pages 616–617. Then locate Mongolia on the physical map on pages 618–619. How does the land elevation of Mongolia differ from that of the area along the northern coast of the Caspian Sea?

In the Time of the Czars

Imagine that you will become the ruler of a nation on your thirteenth birthday. What methods will you use to govern your nation?

STUDY THE VOCABULARY

czar   coronation

FOCUS YOUR READING

How did important rulers change Russia in the time of the czars?

A. The Story of Three Ivans

Ivan I and Ivan III Three rulers named Ivan played parts in creating the Russian empire. Ivan I, later called Ivan Kalita, was the prince of Muscovy from 1328 to 1341. Muscovy was the Russian state ruled from Moscow. Ivan believed it was better to work for the Golden Horde than to oppose it. He collected money for the Mongols not only from the people in Muscovy but also from other Russian princes. This expanded the area that Ivan controlled. Also, in return for his services, the Mongols let Ivan keep a share of what he collected. He was an efficient collector and also very thrifty, so he did well through this arrangement. That was why people gave him the name Kalita, which means "moneybags."

Like Ivan I, later rulers gained more land for the state of Muscovy. But it was not until the reign of Ivan III that the Golden Horde lost its hold on Muscovy. Ivan III ruled Muscovy from 1462 to 1505. He was called Ivan the Great because he enlarged Muscovy's territory so that it was the largest Russian state at that time. The map on page 309 shows how much land

Ivan the Great gained control of during his reign. He eventually became so powerful that he simply refused to pay any money to the Golden Horde.

Ivan the Terrible Ivan IV took full control of the government in 1547 and ruled until 1584. He is known as Ivan the Terrible. That name tells something about him and his reign. Ivan the Terrible believed that people respected a ruler only when they feared that ruler. He inspired fear by such acts as having the tongue torn out of a man who had criticized him.

Ivan IV was born in 1530. Both of his parents were dead by the time he was eight years old. Ivan feared that the nobles who

Ivan IV, known as Ivan the Terrible, expanded Russia's territory and made Moscow his capital.
▶ What is shown in the background?

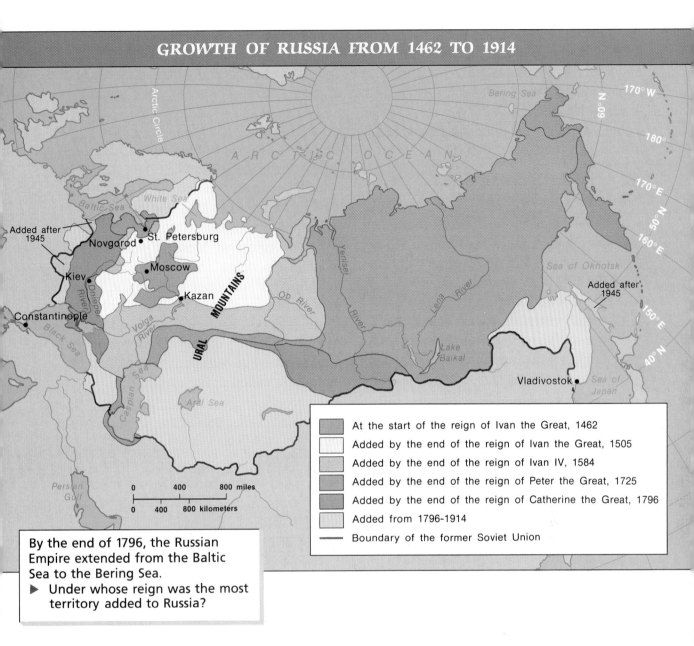

Arctic Circle

Bering Sea

170° W

180°

White Sea

Baltic Sea

170° E

50° N

160° E

Added after 1945

Novgorod

St. Petersburg

60° N

Moscow

Sea of Okhotsk

Kiev

Yenisei

Lena River

Added after 1945

Kazan

Ob River

URAL MOUNTAINS

150° E

Constantinople

Volga River

Dnieper River

Black Sea

Caspian Sea

River

Lake Baikal

40° N

Vladivostok

Sea of Japan

Aral Sea

Persian Gulf

| 0 | 400 | 800 miles |
| 0 | 400 | 800 kilometers |

At the start of the reign of Ivan the Great, 1462

Added by the end of the reign of Ivan the Great, 1505

Added by the end of the reign of Ivan IV, 1584

Added by the end of the reign of Peter the Great, 1725

Added by the end of the reign of Catherine the Great, 1796

Added from 1796–1914

—— Boundary of the former Soviet Union

By the end of 1796, the Russian Empire extended from the Baltic Sea to the Bering Sea.

▶ Under whose reign was the most territory added to Russia?

had taken control of the government would kill him before he could take power. When Ivan was 13, he decided to act first. He had his servants kill the leading noble. The other nobles, caught by surprise, were now afraid of the boy who had succeeded in issuing such an order. Thus, Ivan IV discovered the power of fear. It was a lesson he never forgot.

Ivan the Terrible has long puzzled historians. He was a harsh ruler, but he did

accomplish some great things. He defeated the Mongols in the lands along the Volga River. Russia was now an empire that extended to the Caspian Sea. He celebrated his victory over the Mongols by building the cathedral of St. Basil in Moscow, which is shown on pages 280–281.

Along with having a terrible temper, Ivan had a good mind. He read many more books than most rulers of his time. He had books imported from other lands and

309

brought the first printing press to Russia. Ivan had a great love of music and recommended that schools all over the land teach music. Perhaps if Ivan the Terrible had not learned about the power of fear as a boy, he might have been known as another Ivan the Great.

B. Why the Russian Rulers Were Called Czars

The Roman emperor Constantine had made Constantinople the second Rome. For that reason, later Byzantine emperors claimed that they held the same office as the rulers of ancient Rome. For more than a thousand years, they were called caesar, the title of the ancient Roman emperors.

Turkish Muslims conquered Constantinople and killed the last of the Byzantine emperors in 1453. Christian Constantinople was now ruled by people who followed another religion. You will read more about the Turkish Muslims and their conquests in a later chapter.

After the fall of Constantinople, some Russians said that Moscow had taken the place of Constantinople as the greatest of Christian cities. Constantinople had been the second Rome; Moscow, they argued, was the third Rome.

The rulers at Moscow accepted the idea of its being the third Rome. They adopted the title once held by the Roman and Byzantine emperors. They were called **czar** (zahr) — sometimes spelled *tsar* — the Russian form of the title *caesar*. Russia had a czarist government, or was ruled by emperors called czars, until 1917.

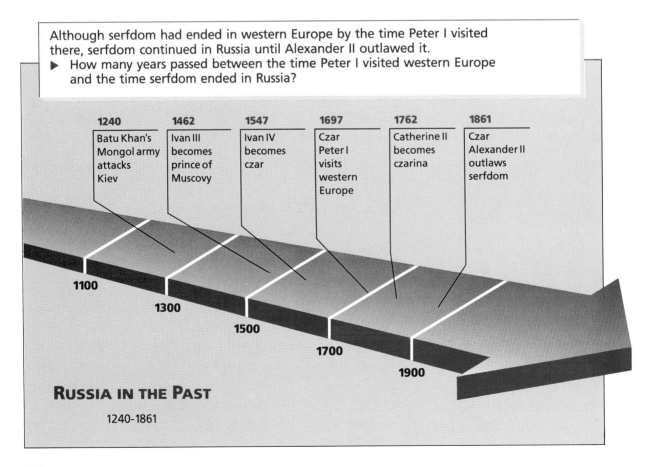

Although serfdom had ended in western Europe by the time Peter I visited there, serfdom continued in Russia until Alexander II outlawed it.
▶ How many years passed between the time Peter I visited western Europe and the time serfdom ended in Russia?

1240	1462	1547	1697	1762	1861
Batu Khan's Mongol army attacks Kiev	Ivan III becomes prince of Muscovy	Ivan IV becomes czar	Czar Peter I visits western Europe	Catherine II becomes czarina	Czar Alexander II outlaws serfdom

1100 1300 1500 1700 1900

RUSSIA IN THE PAST

1240-1861

Peter the Great visited a shipyard in western Europe.
▶ What are some of the tools used to build the ships?

C. Czar Peter I Learns About Western Europe

Two Czars at Once Peter I and his half brother Ivan V were both declared czars in 1682. At their **coronation**, or crowning ceremony, the two czars sat on a double throne. Concealed by a curtain behind the throne, their sister Sophia sat telling them what to say. Sophia had to prompt her brothers during the long ceremony because 16-year-old Ivan was sickly and Peter was only 10 years old.

In truth, Sophia ruled Russia for the next seven years. Ivan was not able to rule, and Peter was still thought to be too young. This left Peter free to follow his own interests.

What Peter Learned For the most part, Peter learned only what he wanted to learn. He never became a good speller, but he knew quite a lot of geography because he liked to look at a large globe that stood taller than a man. He also learned a great deal about army affairs by playing war games with a group of companions. They had uniforms, lived in barracks, and even spent a year building an earth and timber fort, which they bombarded with a cannon.

Peter's great curiosity led him to spend time talking with western Europeans who lived in one section of Moscow. He made friends with a Dutch merchant named Franz Timmerman. One day they found an old boat in a storage building on a royal estate. It was unlike any of the flat-bottomed riverboats that Peter had seen. Timmerman said it was a common western European boat that could sail against the wind as well as with it.

Peter insisted that the old boat be repaired and fitted with sails. Once he saw the boat sail a zigzag course against the wind, he decided that someday the people of Russia would learn how to build and sail such boats. Peter later called the small boat "the grandfather of the Russian navy." Today it is a prize exhibit in a Soviet naval museum.

When Peter was 17 years old, he sent Sophia away from Moscow and took the government into his own hands. Ivan lived for another seven years, but Peter was in fact the sole ruler of Russia.

Peter's Travels Peter strongly believed that Russia could learn a lot more than shipbuilding from the West. He decided to see for himself how western Europeans lived. In the spring of 1697, Czar Peter I and a party of 270 set out for western Europe. Peter did not travel as the czar. He posed as a sailor named Peter Mikhailov, but the disguise fooled no one.

When the party reached the Netherlands, Peter went to work in a shipyard. This excerpt from the book *Peter, the Revolutionary Tsar*, written by Peter Brock Putnam, describes what the experience was like for Peter.

> *Peter had come to Europe to learn, and the next few months were a period of intensive learning. At the simplest level, he studied shipbuilding. He and ten companions worked under the master shipwright, Gerrit Claes Pool. Peter enjoyed the physical labor and the experience of being treated as a workman.*

After several months, Peter received a certificate stating that he was a qualified shipwright. He was quite proud of it.

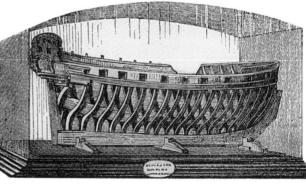

Peter the Great studied shipbuilding and made this model of a ship.
▶ Why is Peter dressed in a sailor's clothing?

D. Great Rulers Made Some Major Changes

Peter the Great Peter I wanted to make Russia a modern nation. He firmly believed that his empire was held back by its clinging to old customs. Peter had his greatest success in reforming the army and creating a navy. He also had canals built to connect some of the rivers. He attempted to establish modern industries like those he had seen in western Europe.

Peter insisted that the Russians change their ways of thinking and living. He ordered nobles to learn a western

Peter outlawed the traditional long coats and beards worn by many Russian men.
▶ Why is Peter cutting the sleeves of the man in this picture?

European language so that they could read the books of other nations. The czar thought that changing the appearance of his subjects would change their way of thinking. Peter ordered Russian men to shave their beards, since they were no longer the fashion in western Europe, and to change the way they dressed.

Peter built a new capital to take the place of Moscow. The capital was to be a modern city with buildings like those in western Europe. Peter believed that it was of greatest importance that Russia have an outlet to the sea and a "window on Europe," so the capital was built where the Neva River empties into the Baltic Sea. The city was called St. Petersburg to honor the saint for whom Peter was named. It would be renamed Petrograd at the beginning of World War I.

Peter tried to make many changes in Russia, but much remained unchanged. Russia was a large land, and even the most energetic czar could only do so much. But Peter did enough to be remembered as Peter the Great.

Catherine the Great Peter the Great died in 1725, and in the next 75 years, half of the Russian rulers were women. These empresses were called czarinas. Catherine II, the czarina from 1762 to 1796, came to be known as Catherine the Great.

Catherine added a large amount of territory to the Russian empire. Her armies conquered the Turks on lands north of the Black Sea. With the gain of these lands, Russia had outlets on both the Baltic Sea and the Black Sea. Catherine also added a large part of Poland to her empire. In North America the earliest Russian settlements in what is now Alaska were established during Catherine's reign.

Like Peter the Great, Catherine admired western Europe and wanted to make changes in Russia, but she did not intend to change its form of government. She believed, as Peter the Great had believed, that the power to rule must belong to the monarch alone.

Alexander II, known as "the reforming czar," abolished serfdom in Russia and freed peasants from the personal control of the nobles.
▶ How is Alexander portrayed?

E. How Serfs Lived in the Time of the Czars

Most of Catherine's subjects had very little freedom. More than half of the people were serfs. You learned in Chapter 6 that serfs were people bound to the land they worked. Serfdom had disappeared in most of Europe by the time Catherine died in 1796. But in Russia, serfs still worked the land of the nobles and czars.

Most serfs knew little about the world outside their own village. Few could read, and serfs could not leave their village without their master's permission. Some serfs on large estates worked as household servants. They served as cooks, maids, butlers, and carpenters. Great nobles took pride in having everything done by the people on their own estate. A wealthy master might have a personal tailor, cobbler, or piano tuner.

Serfdom in Russia was much like slavery. Masters could punish their serfs or sell them as if they were livestock. Serfdom in Russia lasted about as long as slavery in the United States. Czar Alexander II issued a law ending serfdom in 1861. That was four years before African-American slaves in the United States gained their freedom at the end of the Civil War.

Alexander's law gave the serfs their freedom. They could no longer be sold. But the serfs did not receive all the land to which they felt they were entitled. The nobles still held large estates, so freedom did not greatly change the ways the former serfs lived. Most were still poor and uneducated. They still lived in villages and worked as servants or on the land.

LESSON **2** REVIEW

THINK AND WRITE

A. Why was one Ivan called "Kalita," one called "the Great," and another called "the Terrible"?

B. Why were the Russian rulers called czars?

C. Why did Peter I visit western Europe?

D. What changes did Peter the Great and Catherine the Great make in Russia?

E. What was the life of a serf like?

SKILLS CHECK

WRITING SKILL

Which Russian ruler that you read about in this lesson was the best ruler? Write a paragraph explaining why you think he or she was the best.

The Russian Revolution

THINK ABOUT WHAT YOU KNOW

If you had been a Russian peasant after serfdom ended in 1861, what kinds of changes would you have wanted to occur in Russia?

STUDY THE VOCABULARY

anarchy   socialism
abdicate   communism

FOCUS YOUR READING

How did the revolution of 1917 affect Russia?

A. The Last of the Czars

Riots Begin   On a cold March evening in 1917, a train pulled into Pskov (puh-SKOF), a city southwest of Petrograd. The train carried Czar Nicholas II. He had been at the Russian army headquarters near where the battles of World War I were being fought. Now the czar was trying to get back to Petrograd because he had heard alarming news from the capital city.

There had been crowds marching in the streets of Petrograd, shouting "Bread, bread, give us bread!" Then the demonstrations had turned into riots. Worst of all, troops called out to control the crowds had joined them. Shop windows were smashed, prisons were broken open, buildings were set on fire. When firefighters tried to put out the flames, crowds of rioters stopped them. An official had telegraphed the czar with the warning, "There is **anarchy** in the capital." Anarchy is a complete lack of government and law.

Nicholas Gives Up   When Nicholas's train got within 100 miles (161 km) of Petrograd, he learned that armed men were blocking the route into the city. The czar then ordered the train to Pskov, where there was an army headquarters. There Nicholas received more bad news. The uprising had gone too far: it was now a revolution. Messages from Nicholas's army generals advised him to **abdicate**, or give up power. Nicholas realized that if the generals no longer supported him, he could not hope to put down the revolution. Thus on March 15, 1917, Nicholas II abdicated, and czarist rule in Russia came to an end.

Nicholas hoped that he and his family would be allowed to continue living in Russia or, if that was not possible, to go to England. But the revolutionary government arrested the former czar and his family. They were later sent to a town in the Ural Mountains, where they were killed in July 1918.

Czar Nicholas II abdicated the throne of Russia. Later he and his family were killed.
▶ Why did the czar abdicate?

B. Taking Control of the Russian Revolution

Different Ideas The uprising in the city of Petrograd was indeed the beginning of a revolution. For years many Russians had discussed the need for a major change in their country. But those who agreed that a change was needed had very different ideas about what the change should be.

Some Russians wanted a government like that of Great Britain. They wanted a limited monarchy, in which the monarch serves as head of state but does not govern. Other Russians wanted to follow the example of France or the United States. They wanted a democratic republic, in which the people elect those who make the laws and govern.

There were other Russians who believed that a revolution ought to change much more than the type of government. They wanted a revolution that would do away with the private ownership of land and industry. Some of these people favored **socialism**, a system in which the government not only rules but also owns all the land and industry. Some socialists followed the ideas of Karl Marx, a German writer who had died in 1883. Marx argued that the struggle between the rich and the poor would not end until a revolution brought about socialism.

Lenin's Ideas Vladimir Lenin was a Marxist, that is, he accepted the ideas of Karl Marx. Lenin's original name had been Vladimir Ulyanov (VLAD uh mihr ool YAH-nuf). His older brother had taken part in a plot to kill the czar. The plot failed, and the plotters were hanged. The czar's police suspected that Vladimir might also pose a threat. Their suspicions were right.

Vladimir had joined a group that was working to overthrow the czarist government. He was arrested and sent to Siberia for three years. It was after his release from exile that Vladimir Ulyanov adopted the name Nikolai Lenin to confuse the czar's police. However, the police were not fooled, so Lenin fled to western Europe.

Lenin was living in Switzerland at the time of the uprising in Petrograd. A new government had been formed by the time he returned to Russia. Lenin came not to support the new government but to overthrow it. He believed that only his small Marxist party could lead a true revolution. Lenin called his party the Communists because they believed in **communism**, the

Karl Marx believed that socialism could end the struggle between the rich and the poor.
▶ What were his followers called?

The Communists engaged in a bloody battle against government troops in 1918.
▶ Where did the battle take place?

common ownership of land and industry by the people as a group.

Lenin was a skillful leader willing to do anything to get power. He declared that the Communists alone acted for the soldiers and workers of Petrograd. Communist-led groups took part in a bloody struggle for control of the capital. By November 1917, Lenin and the Communists had seized power in Petrograd and declared that they were the true government of all Russia. Later they took control of Moscow and made it the capital.

Even though the Communists held Petrograd and Moscow, they did not yet control the whole country. It took two years of civil war before the Communists controlled all of Russia. The civil war caused much suffering. Many people were killed, and many more starved to death. The Russian people paid a heavy price for the revolution.

C. The Communist Control of Russia

Government Lenin did not believe in democracy as it is understood in western Europe and the United States. He claimed that most people did not know what was good for them and that the Communists acted for the good of the people. Lenin's way of thinking was much like that of the czars. They, too, said that they ruled for the good of the people.

Lenin controlled the Communist party, and the party controlled the government. Only Communist party members held positions of authority. Other political parties were outlawed. No one was allowed to speak out or print anything against the government. Indeed, control of the press was even tighter than it had been under the czars. The Communists created a secret police force that spied on anyone suspected of opposing Communist rule.

Other Takeovers Lenin strongly opposed religion, particularly the Russian Orthodox Church. The Communist government took over all church property and tried to discourage all religious beliefs, particularly among young people. At the time of the revolution, there were 454 churches in Moscow. Twenty years later, only 25 were still used for religious services. Some of the others had been destroyed or allowed to decay. Some were put to use as museums and other secular, or nonreligious, public places.

In the confused months after the fall of the czar, peasants began taking over the large estates. Groups of workers seized

This painting shows Lenin speaking to a group of workers in 1917.
▶ Does Lenin seem to have the support of his audience?

This monument in Moscow contains Lenin's tomb.
► Where are there monuments to honor American political leaders?

control of a number of factories. The Communists at first supported these takeovers. The Communists declared that the land belonged to the peasants, and that the factories belonged to the workers. The Communists issued an order that the local revolutionary governments could take over private homes, particularly those of rich people. But after the Communists were firmly in control of the country, they declared that all of the land and factories belonged to the state rather than to groups of people.

Lenin became seriously ill in 1922 and died two years later. But by that time those who held his views had a firm grip on the government. The Communists made Lenin the country's official hero. Lenin's picture became as common in schools and public places as those of the czars had been in earlier times. Lenin's body was preserved and put on display in a tomb in Moscow's Red Square. The city of Petrograd was renamed Leningrad in his honor. Today the city of Leningrad is called St. Petersburg.

LESSON 3 REVIEW

THINK AND WRITE

A. What events led to the end of czarist rule in Russia?

B. What kind of revolution did Lenin lead in Russia?

C. What methods did the Communists use to control Russia?

SKILLS CHECK

THINKING SKILL

Look up *Constantinople*, *Moscow*, and *Leningrad* in the Gazetteer to find the latitude and longitude for each city. Then make a table to show this information for the cities.

USING THE VOCABULARY

czar socialism
anarchy communism
abdicate

On a separate sheet of paper, write the word from above that best completes each of the sentences below.

1. The common ownership of land and industry by the people as a group is known as _____ .
2. To give up power is to _____ .
3. A complete lack of government and law is called _____ .
4. The Russian form of the title *caesar* is _____ .
5. A system in which the government not only rules but also owns all land and industry is called _____ .

REMEMBERING WHAT YOU READ

On a separate sheet of paper, answer the following questions in complete sentences.

1. What book tells the story of Princess Olga and Vladimir of Kiev?
2. What was the name of the eastern branch of the Christian Church?
3. What did Batu Khan and his armies do in Russia and eastern Europe?
4. Why was Ivan III called Ivan the Great?
5. What were some good characteristics of Ivan the Terrible?
6. What changes did Peter the Great make in Russia?

7. How was Catherine the Great similar to Peter the Great?
8. Why did Czar Nicholas II abdicate?
9. What kind of government did Nikolai Lenin want Russia to have?
10. How did the Communists honor Lenin after his death?

TYING ART TO SOCIAL STUDIES

You have learned that many peasants in Russia had to work for nobles and czars on large estates. Draw a picture of what you think one of these large estates might have looked like. You may want to include the workers in your drawing.

THINKING CRITICALLY

On a separate sheet of paper, answer the following questions in complete sentences.

1. What reasons might the Mongol armies have had for not advancing into western Europe?
2. Do you think Ivan Kalita was right to work for the Golden Horde rather than to oppose it? Explain.
3. How much do you think changing people's appearance changes their way of thinking?
4. What do you think would have happened in Russia if Nicholas II had not abdicated on March 15, 1917?
5. What advantages might there be to communism, or the common ownership of land and industry by the people as a group?

SUMMARIZING THE CHAPTER

On a separate sheet of paper, copy the graphic organizer shown below. Beside the main idea for each lesson, fill in each missing cause and effect. The first one has been done for you.

CHAPTER THEME

Many changes occurred in Russia and eastern Europe during the period from the Middle Ages to 1917.

	CAUSE	EFFECT
LESSON 1 Constantinople and the Mongol Empire affected Russia and eastern Europe during the Middle Ages.	Vladimir, the ruler of Kiev, was curious about different religions.	Christianity was accepted in Kiev in A.D. 988.
	There were important differences between the Christian Church in eastern Europe and that in western Europe.	
		The Russian people had to pay money and send laborers to the Golden Horde.
LESSON 2 Important rulers changed Russia in the time of the czars.		Russia became a large and powerful empire.
	Peter I greatly admired the culture of western Europe.	
	After serfdom ended, the nobles still held the land and large estates.	
LESSON 3 The revolution of 1917 affected Russia.		There was anarchy in the capital, and the czar was forced to abdicate.
		Vladimir Ulyanov adopted the name Nikolai Lenin and fled to western Europe.
	Lenin controlled the Communist party, and the party controlled the government.	

CHAPTER 12

THE FORMER SOVIET UNION AND EASTERN EUROPE TODAY

The former Soviet Union and the countries of Eastern Europe have undergone many political and economic changes since the end of the 1980s. The dismantling of Lenin's statue symbolizes the collapse of communism.

Communist Rule in the Soviet Union

THINK ABOUT WHAT YOU KNOW

Look up the term *republic* in the Glossary. Using what you have already learned about the former Soviet Union, discuss whether you think the country fit the definition of *republic*.

STUDY THE VOCABULARY

collectivism   central planning

collective farm   market economy

FOCUS YOUR READING

How did the Communist government reorganize industry and agriculture in the Soviet Union?

A. A Show Trial

This letter, written in 1928 by a 12-year-old boy living in the Soviet Union, appeared in *Pravda,* the official Communist party newspaper.

> *I denounce [speak against] my father as a whole-hearted traitor and enemy of the working class. I demand for him the severest punishment. I reject him and the name he bears. Hereafter I shall no longer call myself by his name.*

The boy's father was one of 53 mining engineers on trial before a court in the Soviet Union. The Soviet engineers were charged with trying to harm the country by wrecking the coal mines. They supposedly had broken machines, set fires, and flooded the mines.

The boy's letter was read in court, even though it offered no proof of guilt. In fact, no real proof was ever produced in court, since the trial was not an effort to decide if the charges were true. It was a "show trial," designed to show what would happen to anyone suspected of opposing Communist rule. In the end, five of the mining engineers were executed; the others were sent to prison.

The trial of 1928 was only one of the show trials staged by the Communist government during the years that Joseph Stalin ruled the Soviet Union. Stalin had gained control of the Communist party when Lenin died, in 1924, and control of the party guaranteed control of the government. Stalin's dictatorship lasted until his death, in 1953.

The Communists had renamed the Russian empire in 1922, calling it the Union of Soviet Socialist Republics. The name was usually shortened to Soviet Union or U.S.S.R. It was a huge area, about one sixth of the earth's land surface.

B. Revolutions in Agriculture and Industry

After the revolution of 1917, most Russian peasants believed they would finally be allowed to own the land they worked. After the Communists took power, however, the peasants discovered that their new rulers had very different plans.

The Communist party believed in ownership by all the people together, or **collectivism.** In practice this meant ownership by the state, or the central government, which Stalin controlled. The state forced peasants to combine their small farms to form large **collective farms**. Stalin thought that fewer people would now be needed to work the land, leaving more people free to work in mines and factories.

A collective farm sold everything it produced to the government.
▶ What crop is being harvested on this collective farm?

Members of a collective farm worked as a group. Some had specialized jobs, such as tractor mechanics; others did less skilled work in the fields. A collective farm rented the land from the Soviet government but owned its farm equipment and livestock.

A collective farm had to sell everything it produced to the government, so the farm had little control over the prices it received. Members of the collective farm were paid wages according to the kind of work they did. All these farm workers received a share of the profit from the sale of farm products.

State Farms The Communist government also formed state farms. An average state farm covered about 175 square miles (453 sq km) — about ten times the size of a collective farm. State farms were operated like factories. The land and products were owned by the government, and the workers were paid wages. But state farm workers did not share in a farm's profits, as collective farm workers did.

Small Plots The large collective and state farms produced most of the Soviet Union's potatoes, cotton, wheat, and sugar beets. But an important part of the Soviet food supply was grown on small plots, or sections of land. The government permitted people to grow vegetables and fruits on plots of land up to 1 acre (0.4 ha) in size. People who held these small plots could sell their crops in city markets. Prices in those "free" city markets were whatever the buyers were willing to pay.

Most peasants opposed collectivism. But Stalin insisted that there would be a "revolution in agriculture," whether or not the peasants wanted it. Many peasants who refused to give up their farms were arrested. Some were killed, and many others were sent to labor camps, where large numbers of peasants died. In fact, Stalin's revolution in agriculture cost millions of peasants their lives.

Natural Resources and Industries Before the 1917 revolution, Russia was largely an agricultural country, but it had most of the natural resources needed for modern industries. Forests that covered Russia and the rest of the U.S.S.R. made up a fourth of the world's timber reserves. The area was — and still is — rich in many minerals, including coal, iron ore, copper, and bauxite. The area also had — and still has — large amounts of oil and natural gas. The Communists declared that all of these resources belonged to the state. The government also took over the banks, mills, and factories. The former owners received nothing for the property that the government took away from them.

During the years of Communist rule, the Soviet Union grew into an industrial country. It became one of the world's leading producers of steel, oil, gold, and electricity. No longer were most of the people peasants, working the land. Instead, two thirds of the people lived and worked in urban areas.

Although the Soviet Union became an industrial country, it was lagging behind other countries by the 1980s. Soviet factories were inefficient as compared with those in Western Europe, the United States, and Japan. Equipment was out of date and wasteful. Many plants employed more workers than were needed.

Planners Set Goals The Communists established **central planning** for the state-owned industries. This meant that a government committee set production goals for each industry. For example, the central planners would tell a garment factory manager that the factory should produce a

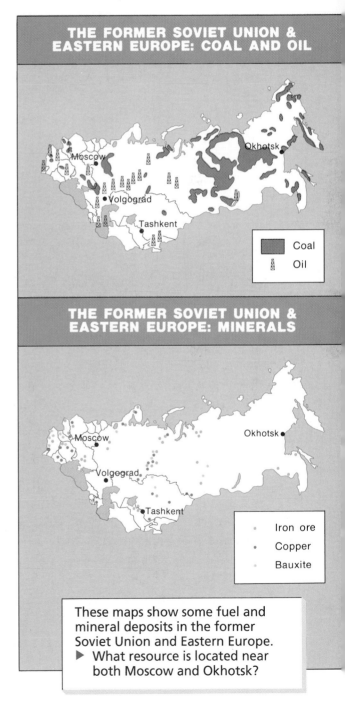

THE FORMER SOVIET UNION & EASTERN EUROPE: COAL AND OIL

Coal
Oil

THE FORMER SOVIET UNION & EASTERN EUROPE: MINERALS

Iron ore
Copper
Bauxite

These maps show some fuel and mineral deposits in the former Soviet Union and Eastern Europe.
▶ What resource is located near both Moscow and Okhotsk?

LEADING STEEL-PRODUCING COUNTRIES

This bar graph shows the world's leading steel-producing countries.
▶ About how many short tons of steel does the former Soviet Union produce?

THE FORMER SOVIET UNION AND EASTERN EUROPE: POLITICAL

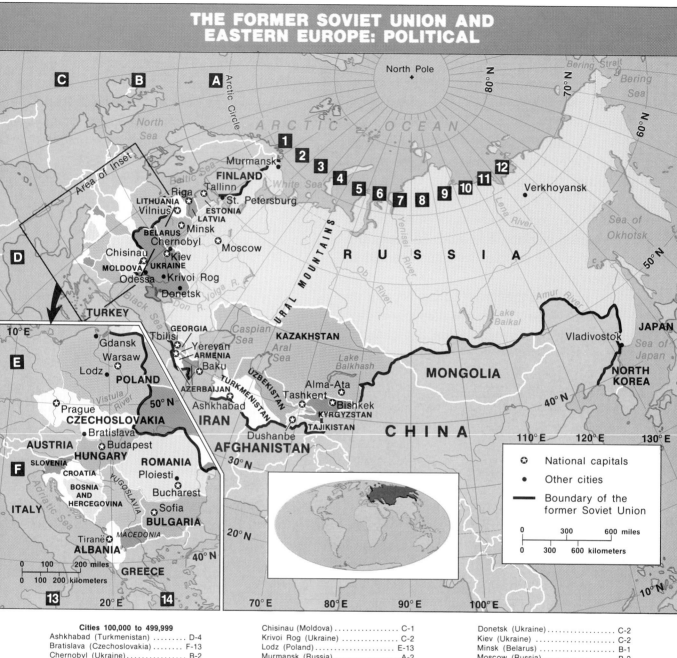

✪	National capitals
•	Other cities
▬	Boundary of the former Soviet Union

0   300   600 miles
0   300   600 kilometers

Cities 100,000 to 499,999
Ashkhabad (Turkmenistan) D-4
Bratislava (Czechoslovakia) F-13
Chernobyl (Ukraine) B-2
Ploiesti (Romania) F-14
Tallinn (Estonia) B-1
Tiranë (Albania) F-13
Verkhoyansk (Russia) A-12

Cities 500,000 to 999,999
Bishkek (Kyrgyzstan) C-6
Dushanbe (Tajikistan) D-5
Gdansk (Poland) E-13

Chisinau (Moldova) C-1
Krivoi Rog (Ukraine) C-2
Lodz (Poland) E-13
Murmansk (Russia) A-2
Riga (Latvia) B-1
Vilnius (Lithuania) B-1
Vladivostok (Russia) C-12

Cities 1,000,000 or more
Alma-Ata (Kazakhstan) C-6
Baku (Azerbaijan) D-4
Bucharest (Romania) F-14
Budapest (Hungary) F-13

Donetsk (Ukraine) C-2
Kiev (Ukraine) C-2
Minsk (Belarus) B-1
Moscow (Russia) B-2
Odessa (Ukraine) C-2
Prague (Czechoslovakia) E-13
St. Petersburg (Russia) A-1
Sofia (Bulgaria) F-14
Tashkent (Uzbekistan) C-5
Tbilisi (Georgia) C-3
Warsaw (Poland) E-14
Yerevan (Armenia) C-3

This map shows the boundaries of the former Soviet Union and the 15 independent countries that were Soviet republics until the U.S.S.R. was dissolved in 1991.
▶ How large is the population of the capital of Ukraine?

certain number of garments during the year. The manager would then tell each worker how much he or she must do to receive full pay. Because the goal — the number of garments produced — was the most important part to the planners, neither the manager nor the workers would pay much attention to the quality of the products.

Buyers' Choices The central planners based their decisions on what products they thought people should have, not on what people might actually want. The planned economy system in the U.S.S.R. differed greatly from the **market economy** that exists in the United States and Western Europe. In a market economy the buyers largely decide what items will be produced. The owners and managers of businesses try to find out what people want to buy and then produce the items. The goal is to make what will sell.

C. Soviet Influence Around the World

Soviet Communists believed that socialism would spread throughout the world. That is what a Soviet leader meant when he told an American president, "History is on our side. We will bury you."

Following World War II the Soviet Union worked to make sure that the Communist party won control of the countries

For about ten years, Soviet troops fought in Afghanistan.
▶ How do you think these troops felt as they left Afghanistan?

in Eastern Europe. The Soviet Union also provided arms and other support for revolutionary movements in Cuba, Central America, Vietnam, Africa, and elsewhere.

In 1979 a Soviet-backed government in the neighboring country of Afghanistan (af GAN ih stan) was threatened. The government had come to power by a revolution, but it was opposed by many Afghans. The Soviet Union sent an army into Afghanistan, and a long, bitter war followed. Not until May 1988 did the Soviet Union begin to withdraw its troops. By February 1989 more than 100,000 Soviet soldiers had left Afghanistan.

LESSON **1** *REVIEW*

THINK AND WRITE

A. What was the purpose of the show trial of 1928?

B. How does a planned economy differ from a market economy?

C. Why did the Soviet Union provide arms and other support to various countries?

SKILLS CHECK

WRITING SKILL

Look up the word *revolution* in the Glossary. Write a paragraph explaining why the Communist revolution was more than a change of governments.

The Collapse of Soviet Communism and the U.S.S.R.

Why, do you think, did people in the Soviet Union become discontented with Communist rule?

glasnost   **perestroika**

What changes took place in the Soviet Union during and after the mid-1980s?

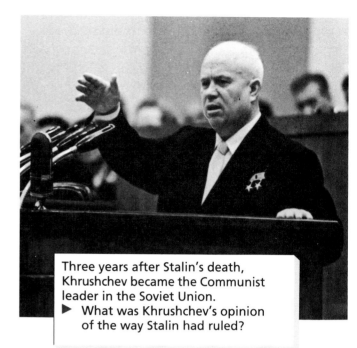

Three years after Stalin's death, Khrushchev became the Communist leader in the Soviet Union.
▶ What was Khrushchev's opinion of the way Stalin had ruled?

A. A Critical Look at Stalin

A Leader Speaks Out For many years loyal Soviet Communists never dared to criticize Stalin. He was praised as a great leader who did what was necessary to make the Soviet Union a socialist state. The Soviet silence about Stalin's dictatorship was not broken until 1956, three years after his death. By that time, Nikita Khrushchev (nih KEE tah KROO shawf) had become the leader of the Communist party in the Soviet Union. Khrushchev shocked many Communists with a speech condemning the wrongs committed during Stalin's rule.

Although he criticized Stalin, Khrushchev did not criticize socialism. Indeed, he boasted that the Soviet Union would become the model for the world in the future. It was he who had boasted to an American President, "History is on our side. We will bury you."

Not all the Communist party members approved of Khrushchev's attack on Stalin. They feared that the criticisms would weaken the Communist party. Finally, in 1964, Khrushchev's opponents forced him to retire from office.

Later Criticisms It was not until more than 20 years later that a Soviet leader spoke out in defense of Khrushchev and what he had said. In 1985, Mikhail Gorbachev (mee kah EEL GOR buh chawf) became the leader of the Soviet Communist party. He said that Khrushchev had shown courage in speaking out about Stalin's "enormous and unforgivable crimes." Gorbachev also said that the Soviet people should be proud of their socialistic society but that it was sometimes necessary to "examine our history with a critical eye."

Some Soviet writers went on to publish accounts admitting that millions of Soviet people had been killed under Stalin's rule. The secret police finally revealed that 787,000 people had been shot as "enemies of the state" during Stalin's rule.

This was not news to historians outside the Soviet Union. But it was the first time that these facts were printed openly within the Soviet Union.

B. Reforming the Government

The Need for Openness Mikhail Gorbachev was born 14 years after the Russian Revolution, so he had grown up under communism. However, he believed that some important changes were needed. Gorbachev called for **glasnost** (GLAHS-nust), which means "openness." Glasnost would result in less secrecy about public affairs.

The Communist policy had always been to keep secret any unfavorable news about the government, such as disagreements among the leaders. Newspapers did not print full accounts of natural disasters or accidents, such as the nuclear power plant accident in 1986. A nuclear plant in Chernobyl (chur NOH bul), a town in the Soviet Union, caught fire and melted down. Over 30 people were killed immediately, and radiation from the nuclear fuel in the plant leaked into the atmosphere. The Soviet government did not announce the accident until days later. This policy of secrecy allowed officials to hide their mistakes and flaws.

Under glasnost, the Soviet people were finally allowed to read books that had once been banned by the government. Television broadcasts showed Communist party conferences in which delegates were disagreeing. The Soviet government granted the Russian Orthodox Church permission to build the first new church in Moscow since the revolution.

As part of his political reform, Mikhail Gorbachev allowed free elections in the Soviet Union in 1989.
▶ How is Gorbachev voting?

End of One-Party Rule Along with promoting glasnost, Gorbachev spoke of the need for **perestroika** (per es TROI kuh), the reform of the government and economy. This was the most striking—and revolutionary—of Gorbachev's reforms. Gorbachev proposed that the Soviet people should have a voice in how their country was governed. To make this happen, he gradually introduced a number of changes.

These changes weakened the position of the Communist party, which had ruled the Soviet Union for so many years. In 1988, Gorbachev introduced a measure that allowed more than one Communist party member to compete in an election for a position. Two years later a more important change took away the Communist position as the only legal political party. Other parties could now be formed and could offer candidates in elections. This change was an important step toward giving people a real choice in elections, a right that is necessary for a democracy.

The first McDonald's restaurant in Moscow opened in 1990.
▶ How did this reflect an economic change in the Soviet Union?

C. Reforming Industry and Agriculture

Less Central Planning Because the Soviet economy was lagging behind the economies of other industrial countries, Gorbachev called for changes in industry and agriculture. He told the Communists that the country needed to encourage better work. Reforms were needed that would allow people to make profits. Socialism, Gorbachev insisted, should not prevent one individual from making more money than another. Perestroika must include reforms in the ways factories, farms, and mines were operated.

The first reforms reduced the amount of central planning and attempted to encourage competition in the Soviet economy. Industries would still belong to the government, but they must compete against each other in selling their goods. The managers of factories would try to make profits rather than to fulfill goals handed down by central planners.

The reforms would also allow some individuals to rent space in government-owned buildings so that they could establish their own businesses. Foreign companies would also be encouraged to set up enterprises within the Soviet Union.

Making Room for Competition Perestroika also included reforms for agriculture. The land would still belong to the state, but individuals could lease farms from the government for periods of 50 years. Farmers could work the land as individuals rather than as members of large collective groups. Like the holders of small plots, the individual farmers could grow crops for sale in the free markets.

Gorbachev introduced the reforms because he believed that complete state ownership had destroyed the people's willingness to work hard. In order to improve the economy, he said, the country must "make room for competition."

Many of the Soviet people agreed with Gorbachev at first. They supported reforms that gave the people a greater choice in government. They agreed that something had to be done to make the economy more productive. But, unfortunately, the economic reforms introduced by Gorbachev did not produce immediate benefits for most people. Indeed, daily life for many became worse rather than better. All too often, shelves in the stores were bare. People stood in long lines waiting to buy food and other necessities. Food prices in the free markets rose rapidly.

The first years of perestroika did not give people a higher standard of living, but glasnost made it possible for them to express their discontent. People who had supported Gorbachev at first began to criticize him. Some complained that his

Soviet people often had to wait in long lines to buy goods.
▶ What is the cause of these lines?

These women are selling produce in a free market in the Soviet Union.
▶ What type of reform does this indicate?

reforms did not go far enough. Some reformers wanted the country to move more rapidly to establish a market economy. A market economy is one in which choices about what is produced depend upon what people will buy. Goods are produced in order to make profits. In 1991 the Soviet government passed a law allowing the sale of state-owned businesses to private individuals and companies.

D. The Soviet Union Collapses

The Republics of the Soviet Union The old Russian empire extended from the Baltic Sea to the Pacific Ocean. When the Communists seized control of this vast land, they divided it into separate republics. Even though they were called republics, these divisions were not independent. The Communist party controlled all of them, and Communists in all parts of the U.S.S.R. followed orders from authorities in Moscow.

The Soviet Union was made up of 15 republics. As you can see on the map below, Russia was by far the largest republic. It contained over half of the Soviet population and three fourths of the territory. The Ukraine was the most thickly populated republic. It had a much smaller area than Russia, but its black soil belt supplied most of the Soviet Union's wheat.

Three republics—Estonia, Latvia, and Lithuania—were located on the Baltic Sea. They had been part of the old Russian empire, but they became independent after World War I. They remained free until World War II, when they were occupied and made part of the Soviet Union.

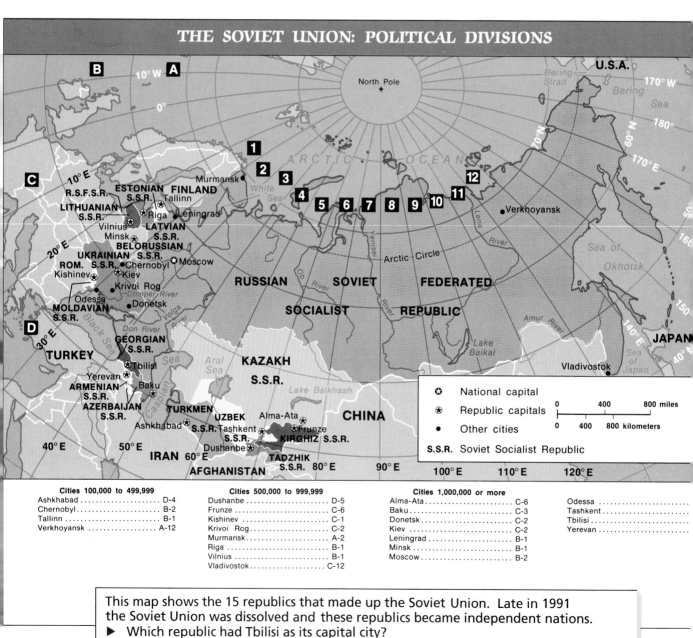

THE SOVIET UNION: POLITICAL DIVISIONS

Cities 100,000 to 499,999		Cities 500,000 to 999,999		Cities 1,000,000 or more		
Ashkhabad	D-4	Dushanbe	D-5	Alma-Ata	C-6	Odessa
Chernobyl	B-2	Frunze	C-6	Baku	C-3	Tashkent
Tallinn	B-1	Kishinev	C-1	Donetsk	C-2	Tbilisi
Verkhoyansk	A-12	Krivoi Rog	C-2	Kiev	C-2	Yerevan
		Murmansk	A-2	Leningrad	B-1	
		Riga	B-1	Minsk	B-1	
		Vilnius	B-1	Moscow	B-2	
		Vladivostok	C-12			

This map shows the 15 republics that made up the Soviet Union. Late in 1991 the Soviet Union was dissolved and these republics became independent nations.
▶ Which republic had Tbilisi as its capital city?

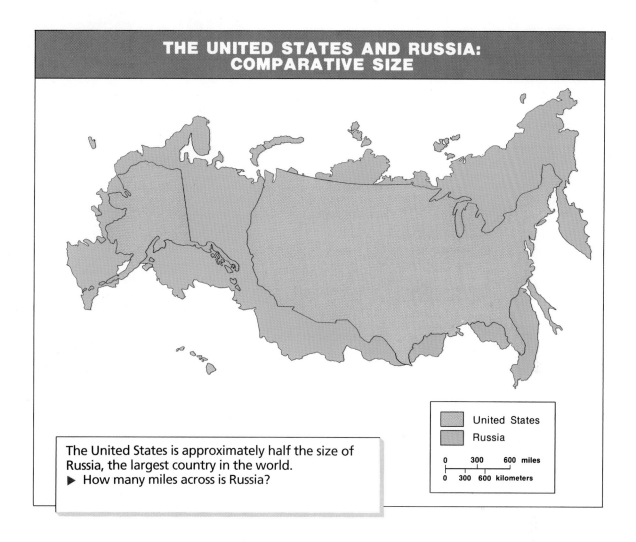

THE UNITED STATES AND RUSSIA: COMPARATIVE SIZE

The United States is approximately half the size of Russia, the largest country in the world.
▶ How many miles across is Russia?

United States
Russia

0   300   600 miles
0 300 600 kilometers

There were two other Soviet republics in Europe and five more in Central Asia. In addition, three Transcaucasian republics were located across the Caucasus Mountains, between the Black and Caspian seas.

Many Nationalities, Many Languages
Only about half of the people in the former Soviet Union were Russians. This huge country had more than a hundred different nationalities. Each republic contained more than one nationality. For example, the large Russian republic included areas inhabited largely by the Tatars. Tatars are

descendants of the Mongols, who once swept across Europe from Asia. Not all Russians lived in Russia. About half of the people in the Central Asian republic of Kazakhstan were Russians or Ukrainians. Even small republics usually had more than one nationality. Only half of Latvia's residents in 1990 were Latvians; a third of its people were Russians. The U.S.S.R. had been compared to a wooden doll that has within it dolls within other dolls.

Some of the different nationalities had their own languages. The Communist government did not try to prevent the use of these languages. But Russian was the official language of the central government

FIFTEEN NEW NATIONS

These nations once belonged to the Union of Soviet Socialist Republics.

	FLAG/CAPITAL	TOTAL AREA	POPULATION AND DENSITY	INDEPENDENCE DECLARED
ARMENIA	★Yerevan	11,306 sq mi 29,283 sq km	3,300,000 292 per sq mi 113 per sq km	September 21, 1991
AZERBAIJAN	★Baku	33,400 sq mi 86,506 sq km	7,000,000 210 per sq mi 81 per sq km	August 30, 1991
BELARUS [1]	★Minsk	80,200 sq mi 207,718 sq km	10,200,000 127 per sq mi 49 per sq km	August 25, 1991
ESTONIA	★Tallinn	17,413 sq mi 45,100 sq km	1,600,000 92 per sq mi 35 per sq km	August 20, 1991
GEORGIA	★Tbilisi	26,911 sq mi 69,699 sq km	5,500,000 204 per sq mi 79 per sq km	April 9, 1991
KAZAKHSTAN	★Alma-Ata	1,049,200 sq mi 2,717,428 sq km	16,500,000 16 per sq mi 6 per sq km	December 16, 1991
KYRGYZSTAN [2]	★Bishkek	76,642 sq mi 198,503 sq km	4,300,000 56 per sq mi 22 per sq km	August 31, 1991

[1] Formerly Byelorussia   [2] Formerly Kirghizia

and the language of the largest nationality. The authorities encouraged people to learn Russian as a second language. Many people belonging to other nationalities found it to their advantage to do so.

Independence for the Republics

Glasnost and perestroika brought some changes that Gorbachev did not expect or want. He expected that openness and reform would provide for greater freedom *within* the Soviet Union. But the republics came to demand freedom *from* the Soviet Union. They wanted independence.

When the reforms reduced the powers of the central government, "freedom fever" erupted in the U.S.S.R. Conflict broke out between the Transcaucasian republics of Armenia and Azerbaijan. In the Baltic republics a growing number of people

	FLAG/CAPITAL	TOTAL AREA	POPULATION AND DENSITY	INDEPENDENCE DECLARED
LATVIA	★Riga	24,695 sq mi 63,960 sq km	2,700,000 109 per sq mi 42 per sq km	August 21, 1991
LITHUANIA	★Vilnius	26,173 sq mi 67,788 sq km	3,700,000 141 per sq mi 55 per sq km	March 11, 1990
MOLDOVA [3]	★Chisinau	13,012 sq mi 33,701 sq km	4,300,000 330 per sq mi 128 per sq km	August 27, 1991
RUSSIA	★Moscow	6,592,800 sq mi 17,075,352 sq km	147,400,000 22 per sq mi 9 per sq km	December 8, 1991
TAJIKISTAN [4]	★Dushanbe	54,019 sq mi 139,909 sq km	5,100,000 94 per sq mi 36 per sq km	September 9, 1991
TURKMENISTAN [5]	★Ashkhabad	188,417 sq mi 488,000 sq km	3,500,000 19 per sq mi 7 per sq km	October 27, 1991
UKRAINE	★Kiev	233,100 sq mi 603,729 sq km	51,700,000 222 per sq mi 86 per sq km	August 31, 1991
UZBEKISTAN	★Tashkent	172,700 sq mi 447,293 sq km	19,900,000 115 per sq mi 44 per sq km	August 31, 1991

[3] Formerly Moldovia   [4] Formerly Tadzhikistan   [5] Formerly Turkmenia

began to openly speak out against Soviet control. They wanted to regain the freedom they had had before being taken over by the Soviet army. Early in 1990 the Lithuanians voted to withdraw from the Soviet Union. Gorbachev opposed Lithuania's effort to break away, but he failed to stop the movement for independence. The other two Baltic republics, Estonia and Latvia, voted to follow Lithuania's example. Other republics, including Ukraine, also declared their independence. Russia, the largest of the republics, took over functions that had belonged to the central government. As symbols of their independence, republics replaced the red Soviet flag with their own national flags. Russia brought back the old white, blue, and red flag used before the 1917 revolution. The Soviet Union was breaking apart.

Gorbachev tried to persuade the republics to form a federation of equal states. In the federation each republic would be free to run its own affairs, but the central government would control foreign affairs and certain other matters. Gorbachev faced two very different groups of opponents. One group of Communist leaders charged that his reforms were destroying the country. Another group was led by Boris Yeltsin (BOR ihs YELT sihn), president of the Russian Republic. Yeltsin declared that Gorbachev's reforms did not go far enough.

While Gorbachev was away from Moscow on vacation in August 1991, a group of Communist leaders who opposed the reforms attempted to take over the government. Yeltsin and his supporters opposed this attempt to seize power. Yeltsin was backed by large crowds of people who took to the streets in Moscow. Faced with such strong opposition, the attempt to take over the government failed. Gorbachev returned to Moscow, but Boris Yeltsin was now the leader of the reform movement.

On Christmas Day in 1991, Gorbachev resigned as president of the Soviet Union, which had already been dissolved.

This crowd assembled in Moscow to protest an attempted takeover in the Soviet Union in August 1991.
► Why, do you think, has a hole been cut in the Soviet flag?

The breakup of the Soviet Union was only one of the great changes taking place at that time. You are living in a time of many changes, and the future, no doubt, will bring still more changes—some expected, some not. In order to keep learning about the world and its peoples, you will need to follow the history of your times. You will find that history in newspapers, news magazines, and television and radio broadcasts.

LESSON 2 REVIEW

THINK AND WRITE

A. What was the importance of Khrushchev's and Gorbachev's views of Soviet history?

B. What changes did glasnost bring about in the Soviet government?

C. What changes did perestroika produce in Soviet industry and agriculture?

D. What factors contributed to the collapse of the Soviet Union?

SKILLS CHECK

MAP SKILL

The map on page 332 shows the republics of the former Soviet Union. Which was the largest republic? Which other republics were located south of 50°N latitude and east of 40°E longitude?

Poland and Czechoslovakia

THINK ABOUT WHAT YOU KNOW
If you had a choice between owning your own farm and working on a collective farm owned by the government, which one would you choose? Explain your reasons.

STUDY THE VOCABULARY
Solidarity   consumer goods

FOCUS YOUR READING
What are some major changes that have taken place in Poland and Czechoslovakia in recent years?

A. Communist Rule in Poland

Early Rule   After World War II ended the Soviet Union took over about 70,000 square miles (181,300 sq km) of eastern Poland. To make up in part for this loss, Poland was given about 40,000 square miles (103,600 sq km) of German territory. Ten million people, both Polish and German, were told they had to leave their homes. They were forced to relocate within the new boundaries.

The Soviet Union not only took a thick slice of Polish territory but also made sure that the Polish government was controlled by Communists. In the early years of Communist rule in Poland, the government followed Stalin's example. No open opposition to the government was allowed.

Demands for Freedom   In 1980, after years of Communist rule, shipyard workers led by a man named Lech Walesa (lekh vah WEN sah) went on strike. The workers demanded more freedom, particularly the freedom to form a union not controlled by the government. So many Poles supported the shipyard workers that the government agreed to their demand for a free union. No other Communist country allowed such freedom at that time.

Other Polish workers joined with the shipyard workers to form a large free union called **Solidarity**. The name means "strongly united." As the union grew, its leaders demanded that the Polish people be allowed to vote on whether the Communists should rule. The Communist leaders decided that the union had gone too far in demanding free elections. In 1981 the military took control of the country, and Solidarity was outlawed. Many union members, including Walesa, were arrested. Walesa was not released from jail until about a year later.

Polish Solidarity leader Lech Walesa helped to bring about free elections in Poland.
▶ How do you think these people feel about Walesa?

Reduced Controls Within a few years, however, the Polish government greatly reduced its controls over the nation. In April 1989, Solidarity was legalized. In June the government allowed a free election. For the first time in over 40 years, Poles could vote for candidates not chosen by the Communist party. Candidates representing Solidarity won a sweeping victory and went on to help elect a non-Communist prime minister for Poland. Solidarity's victory marked the beginning of the political revolution in Eastern Europe. In 1990, Lech Walesa, the Solidarity leader, was elected president of Poland by an overwhelming majority.

B. Farming and Industry in Poland

Economy Before World War II, Poland was largely an agricultural country. After the war, the Polish Communists tried to form collective farms but had little success. Today about 85 percent of the farmland is privately owned, and the farmers are free to sell what they grow. Poland ranks among the world's leading producers of potatoes. Other important crops grown in Poland include sugar beets and wheat. However, more people in Poland work in industry than in farming.

When the Communists came to power in Poland, they laid down a central plan for

THE FORMER SOVIET UNION AND EASTERN EUROPE: POTATO PRODUCTION

Production per year (in thousands of short tons)
- 0-500
- 501-3,900
- 3,901-10,900
- 10,901-43,000
- 43,001 or more

—— Boundary of the former Soviet Union

Farms in the former Soviet Union and in all countries of Eastern Europe produce potatoes.
▶ Which country is the second largest producer of potatoes in this region?

industry. This plan called for producing such things as steel, chemicals, and ships. Less attention was given to **consumer goods**, the products that people use in their daily lives.

Today there is a move toward a Western-style market economy. The Solidarity government hopes this will provide Poland with the economic growth that it did not achieve under communism.

A Polluted Land   In building large industries, the planners seem to have thought very little about pollution. But after Solidarity came to power, the government began to report that Poland was suffering from enormous environmental problems. For years, Poland's steel, chemical, and power plants used coal for power. But there were no regulations about how much coal smoke could be released. As a result, trees are dying from acid rain, and the air is heavy with coal dust.

C. Religion in Communist Poland

The Polish Communist government at first tried to discourage religious practices, but these efforts also failed. About 92 percent of all Poles are Roman Catholics, and the Church became the strongest non-Communist force in the country. In fact, Church holy days are national holidays on which even government offices are closed.

The Roman Catholic Church had chosen a Polish churchman as pope in 1978. Pope John Paul II was welcomed by huge, cheering crowds whenever he visited his homeland of Poland. During a visit in 1987, the pope spoke openly in favor of Solidarity, even though it had been outlawed by the Polish government.

Poland had been home to more than 3 million Jews before World War II. The

Friendly crowds greet Pope John Paul II when he visits Poland.
▶ What reasons can you give to explain why the pope is so popular in Poland?

Nazis killed a very large number of these people during the German occupation. The Nazis also transported Jews from other lands to the terrible death camps they built in Poland. Today there are very few Jews in Poland—perhaps only about 5,000.

D. Land of the Czechs and Slovaks

In 1948, Soviet-backed Communists took over the government of Czechoslovakia. Twenty years later these Communists tried to reform their socialist country to allow greater freedom. However, the Soviet Union sent an army into

These men are blowing glass in a factory in Eastern Europe.
▶ What makes the glass soft so that it can be shaped?

Czechoslovakia, sent in new Communist leaders, and put an end to the reforms.

In 1989, however, Soviet tanks did not enter Prague when people demonstrated for an end to communism. By year's end, the Communist party was out of power. The new government was headed by Vaclav Havel. At one time he had been jailed for asking for a democratic government; now he was the head of one.

Havel remained in office until 1992. He resigned after a vote in the Slovak Parliament made it probable that Czechoslovakia would be divided into two nations. One would be a Czech republic, the other a Slovak republic.

LESSON **3** *REVIEW*

THINK AND WRITE

A. Why was the Solidarity movement important?

B. What policies did the Polish Communists follow for farming and industry after World War II?

C. What was the Communist position on religion in Poland?

D. Why are 1948, 1989, and 1992 important dates in the history of Czechoslovakia?

SKILLS CHECK

THINKING SKILL
In the Gazetteer, find the entries for Prague and Warsaw. What do these two cities have in common?

Southeastern Europe

THINK ABOUT WHAT YOU KNOW

You have learned that the former Soviet Union was made up of different nationality groups. How do you think people of different nationalities might feel if they were forced to join together to form a new country?

STUDY THE VOCABULARY

ethnic group   **arable**
atheism

FOCUS YOUR READING

What are some ways in which changes in the governments of the countries of southeastern Europe were brought about?

A. Yugoslavia: Past and Present

Under Communist Rule   Yugoslavia was created after World War I when several **ethnic groups** were joined together in one country. An ethnic group is a nationality with its own special characteristics, such as language, customs, and religion. The ethnic groups in the new country spoke Slavic languages. The name Yugoslavia means "land of the South Slavs."

Communists led by Jospip Broz Tito (YOH seep brohz   TEE toh) took over Yugoslavia at the end of World War II. Tito had worked with the Soviet Communists before the war, but he refused to let the U.S.S.R. control his country.

Breakup of Yugoslavia   Under Tito's rule, Yugoslavia had a federal government made up of six republics: Serbia, Croatia, Slovenia, Bosnia and Hercegovina,

Macedonia, and Montenegro. Each republic had its own government as well as representatives in the central government. Each major ethnic group had its own republic, although individuals might live anywhere within the country.

In the 1990s conflicts arose between some ethnic groups which led to the breakup of the old federal government. Declarations of independence by Slovenia, Croatia, Bosnia and Hercegovina, and Macedonia set off a destructive civil war. At first Serbia supported the Serbs in the other republics, but in 1992 Serbia established a New Federal Republic of Yugoslavia. The new republic consisted of Serbia and Montenegro. It was only about half as large as the old Federal Republic.

THE NEW BALKAN STATES
(As of August 1992)

The new Balkan states were once part of the former Yugoslavia.
▶ Which of these Balkan states is bordered by Austria, Italy, Hungary, and Croatia?

In 1967, Albania outlawed religious groups and seized their property, for example, this Orthodox church.
▶ How can you tell that this building is a church?

B. Albania: A Country in Isolation

Land and Language Only the narrow Adriatic Sea separates Albania from Italy, and Albania's borders touch Yugoslavia and Greece. But in spite of this closeness to other countries, Albania has long been isolated from both Eastern Europe and Western Europe.

Albania is a rugged, mountainous land. It has no navigable rivers and had few good roads or railroads until recent times. Even language sets Albania apart from other nations. As you know, Albanians speak an ancient tongue not closely related to any other.

Communist Policy The Albanian Communist party ruled the country for years after World War II. The Albanian party quarreled with both Communist Yugoslavia and the Soviet Union, so Albania was cut off even from other Communist countries.

The Albanian Communist party strongly opposed religion and instead supported **atheism** (AY thee ihz um). Atheism is the belief that there is no God. The government declared Albania to be the first atheistic state in the world.

In 1990, changes in the rest of Eastern Europe affected Albania too. Its Communist rulers opened relations with the Soviet Union. They also allowed some religious observances. Other changes followed the next year. Demonstrations against the government forced the Communists to permit other political parties and to share power with them.

Economy Albania is a poor country—the poorest in Europe—but it does have some valuable resources. The mountains contain a variety of minerals, and mining is an important industry. The mountain streams are being used to produce electricity both for use in Albania and for sale to neighboring countries.

C. Changes in Hungary

Early Communism Communists supported by the Soviet Union took over Hungary in 1947. Large numbers of people who fought against the takeover were arrested, and some were executed. Nine years later an anti-Communist revolt broke out, but it was put down by the Soviet army. Many more Hungarians lost their lives, and more than 50,000 fled the country.

Freedom Increases The Communists continued to rule Hungary, but in 1968 they began to make some changes. The Hungarian government reduced the amount of central control. Industries and collective farms were allowed to make profits in which workers and farm members would share. Hungarians could own small businesses and also were encouraged to grow and sell crops from their own small plots of land.

More than half the land in Hungary is **arable**, that is, suitable for growing crops. Farmers there raise enough food to export to other lands. Factories turn out a variety of goods, many of which are exported. Mines produce coal and bauxite, the ore from which aluminum is obtained.

Along with the freedom to make profits, the Hungarians were allowed more freedom to speak out and express themselves than people in the Soviet Union were. In fact, by the late 1980s, Hungary was being described as the most reform-minded Communist country in Eastern Europe. Thus it was no surprise that Hungary was one of the first Eastern European countries to allow democratic elections in 1990. The elected Hungarian prime minister, Jozsef Antall, pledged that his democratic government would represent all of the Hungarian people. The non-Communist Hungarian Democratic Forum, the party that won the elections, also has called for quicker movement to a market economy.

Although some changes were made in the economy in 1968, the government of Hungary today continues to strive for a market economy.
▶ What kinds of produce is this man selling in the sidewalk market?

D. Romania's Ancient History

Outside Influences Romanians say that a Roman emperor began the conquest of their land in A.D. 101 and that the descendants of the Romans inhabited their country throughout the Middle Ages. It is for this reason that the land is called Romania, "land of the Romans." As you have already learned, the Romanian language comes from Latin and is written with the Roman alphabet.

The Soviet army helped to put a Communist government in power in Romania after World War II. Later differences between the Romanians and the Soviet Union did not result in more freedom for the Romanian people. The Romanian Communist government kept strict control over the Romanian people.

Romania, too, saw changes in its government. Unlike the other Eastern European countries, however, a bloody revolution was required to overthrow the Communist ruler, Nicolae Ceausescu (chou SHES koo). Thousands died as supporters of the government fired on unarmed citizens protesting Ceausescu's rule. Finally the army joined with the civilians and helped overthrow Ceausescu. A new government was elected in May 1990.

Economy Romania has good soil that produces crops of corn, wheat, potatoes, and sugar beets. However, more Romanians today are employed in industry than in farming. Romania produces petroleum and is a leading oil producer in Europe.

The Romanian government encourages tourists to come and spend money at resorts on the Black Sea coast. The government has also developed other tourist attractions, including an old castle restored as Dracula's castle. You can read a literature selection from Bram Stoker's famous novel *Dracula* on the next page.

E. Bulgaria's Ties with Other Nations

In the Past In Sofia, the capital city of Bulgaria, there is a church named after a Russian hero, Alexander Nevsky. The

THE FORMER SOVIET UNION & EASTERN EUROPE: WHEAT & COTTON

Moscow · Kazan · Kiev · Bishkek

• Wheat
· Cotton

THE FORMER SOVIET UNION & EASTERN EUROPE: SUGAR BEETS

Moscow · Kazan · Kiev · Bishkek

🌱 Sugar beets

Wheat, cotton, and sugar beets are grown in parts of the former Soviet Union and Eastern Europe.
▶ Which of these crops are grown in the area near Kiev?

FROM:

Dracula

By: Bram Stoker
Setting: Romania and England in the 1800s

Bram Stoker was born in Dublin, Ireland, in 1847. Stoker wrote stories in his spare time. *Dracula*, his most famous work, was first published in 1897 and is still a bestseller, more than 75 years after Stoker's death.

In *Dracula*, Stoker uses remote settings, an eerie atmosphere, and extraordinary events to tell a tale of horror. The novel is written in the form of the journals, diaries, and letters of characters whose lives are touched by Count Dracula — a vampire in human form.

The story begins in the Carpathian Mountains of Transylvania, a region in Romania. Jonathan Harker, a law clerk, has traveled to the count's castle to complete a business deal. The excerpt below is from an entry in Harker's journal.

A s I leaned from the window my eye was caught by something moving a storey below me, and somewhat to my left, where I imagined, from the order of the rooms, that the windows of the Count's own room would look out. The window at which I stood was tall and deep. . . . I drew back behind the stonework, and looked out.

What I saw was the Count's head coming out from the window. . . . I was at first interested and somewhat amused, for it is wonderful how small a matter will interest and amuse a man when he is a prisoner. But my very feelings changed to repulsion and terror when I saw the whole man slowly emerge from the window and begin to crawl down the castle wall over that dreadful abyss [cliff], face down with his cloak spreading out around him like great wings. At first I could not believe my eyes. I thought it was some trick of moonlight, some weird effect of shadow; but I kept looking, and it could be no delusion. I saw the fingers and toes grasp the corners of the stones, worn clear of the mortar by the stress of years, and by thus using every projection and inequality move downwards with considerable speed, just as a lizard moves along a wall.

What manner of man is this, or what manner of creature in the semblance [appearance] of man? I feel the dread of this horrible place overpowering me; I am in fear — in awful fear — and there is no escape for me. . . .

Bulgarians built the church more than a hundred years ago to show their thanks to the Russians for help in a war against the Turks. Bulgaria had been part of the Ottoman Empire for nearly five centuries. The armies of the Russian empire had helped Bulgaria win its freedom.

There were other ties between the Bulgarians and the Russians. Both groups of people spoke related Slavic languages and used the Cyrillic alphabet. The two nations also shared a religion. Most Bulgarians belonged to the Eastern Orthodox Church, as did the Russians.

In Recent Times Bulgaria's ties with its large neighbor have continued in more recent times. The Soviet Union supported the creation of the Bulgarian Communist government after World War II. For years the Bulgarian government closely followed the leadership of the Soviet Union.

Bulgaria also made many changes during the years 1989 and 1990. The ruling Communist party renamed itself the Bulgarian Socialist party. It also allowed free elections in June 1990. Even non-Communist parties were allowed to compete.

Economy About one third of Bulgaria is mountainous, but there is also level farm-

More than half of Bulgaria's land is used for raising livestock and for growing crops such as roses.
► What product is made from roses?

land. Bulgarians grow grain, vegetables, fruits, and tobacco. Roses are another important crop. The blossoms are pressed to make an oil used in perfume.

Like Romania, Bulgaria has fine Black Sea beaches. There are also mountains in the central and southern parts of Bulgaria. These beaches and mountains are the basis for the country's tourist industry.

LESSON **4** REVIEW

THINK AND WRITE

A. What major events took place in Yugoslavia in 1991?
B. Why is Albania isolated?
C. What changes were introduced in Hungary after 1968?
D. What does the name *Romania* tell you about that country's history and its language?

E. What ties did Bulgaria have with the Soviet Union and the earlier Russian empire?

SKILLS CHECK

MAP SKILL

Look at the Atlas map on page 614. List the national capitals of the following countries: Albania, Hungary, Romania, Bulgaria.

USING THE VOCABULARY

On a separate sheet of paper, write the letter of the term that best matches each numbered definition.

a. collectivism
b. glasnost
c. perestroika
d. collective farm
e. central planning
f. market economy
g. Solidarity
h. consumer goods
i. ethnic group
j. atheism

1. The Polish free union whose name means "strongly united"
2. A farm worked by members who share in the profits, but owned and controlled by the government
3. The products that people use in their daily lives.
4. The openness that Mikhail Gorbachev wanted in the Soviet Union
5. An economy in which the choices of buyers decide what is produced
6. Ownership by all the people together
7. A system in which the government decides what industries should produce
8. The belief that there is no God
9. A nationality with its own special characteristics
10. Gorbachev's proposed reforms for the Soviet government and economy

REMEMBERING WHAT YOU READ

On a separate sheet of paper, answer the following questions in complete sentences.

1. Which Soviet leader wanted collective farms as part of his revolution in agriculture?
2. Why were accounts of accidents or natural disasters not printed in Soviet newspapers before glasnost?
3. Why did the Soviet Union lag behind other industrial countries by the 1980s?
4. On what basis did central planners in the Soviet Union set production goals?
5. How did Boris Yeltsin become the leader of the reform movement in the Soviet Union?
6. Compare the demonstrations of 1948 and 1989 in Czechoslovakia.
7. What did Solidarity achieve in 1989?
8. In what ways is Albania isolated from other countries?
9. How did Hungary change between 1968 and 1990?
10. What tourist attraction do Romania and Bulgaria have in common?

TYING MATH TO SOCIAL STUDIES

Over eight years the former Soviet Union produced these amounts of potatoes, rounded to the nearest million tons: 100 million, 74 million, 79 million, 86 million, 91 million, 94 million, 80 million, and 96 million. What was the total amount of potatoes produced in the eight years? What was the average number of tons produced each year?

THINKING CRITICALLY

On a separate sheet of paper, answer the following questions in complete sentences.

1. Do you think a government is weakened when one of its leaders openly criticizes that government? Explain.
2. How does competition and the chance to make a profit encourage people to work harder and produce better products?
3. What consumer goods, or products used in daily life, would you be willing to give up? Explain.
4. What freedoms gained recently in the former Soviet Union and Eastern Europe are freedoms that we have in our country?
5. Why, do you think, was communism not exactly the same in all the countries of Eastern Europe?

SUMMARIZING THE CHAPTER

On a separate sheet of paper, copy the information from this graphic organizer. Next to each question, write four answers from the chapter.

CHAPTER THEME	Tremendous changes have occurred in the governments and economies of the former Soviet Union and the countries of Eastern Europe.

LESSON 1	**How did the Communist government reorganize industry and agriculture in the Soviet Union?**	1. ___ 2. ___ 3. ___ 4. ___
LESSON 2	**What changes took place in the Soviet Union during and after the mid-1980s?**	1. ___ 2. ___ 3. ___ 4. ___
LESSON 3	**What are some major changes that have taken place in Poland and Czechoslovakia in recent years?**	1. ___ 2. ___ 3. ___ 4. ___
LESSON 4	**What are some ways in which changes in the governments of the countries of southeastern Europe were brought about?**	1. ___ 2. ___ 3. ___ 4. ___

COOPERATIVE LEARNING

In the 1980s and early 1990s tremendous changes took place in the Soviet Union and Eastern Europe. During that time, people in this region worked for social reform, freedom, and independence. Some accomplished their goals through political means and legislation. Some used peaceful demonstrations and others resorted to bloody revolutions.

Who are some of the people who changed the course of history in the former Soviet Union and Eastern Europe? What methods did these people use to try to make reforms? Were the methods successful? You and a group of classmates can use information in Unit 3 to create a television talk show that answers these questions about the individuals who have made an impact on the former Soviet Union and Eastern Europe.

PROJECT

Meet as a group and decide which guests your talk show will feature. Everyone in the group should have a role to play on the show, including one person who will serve as the host. Choose the appropriate number of guests from among the following: Nikolai Lenin, Peter the Great, Catherine the Great, Nikita Khrushchev, Lech Walesa, Mikhail Gorbachev, and Boris Yeltsin.

Next select a host and decide which guest role each group member will play. Then discuss the questions the host will ask and the answers the guests will give. Your program should cover reasons for change, methods used, and the successes and failures of the individuals involved.

Each group member should write down the questions and answers that apply to the role he or she will play. Those of you who will be guests may need to do research to find answers to some of the host's questions.

PRESENTATION AND REVIEW

Your group should rehearse your talk show. Once you are sure all group members are prepared to play their roles, present the talk show to the class. The host might want to open the discussion to include questions and comments from the audience.

After the presentation, your group should meet to evaluate your talk show. Was each group member prepared? Did you teach your audience anything new about the leaders of the former Soviet Union and Eastern Europe? How might your project have been improved?

REMEMBER TO:
- Give your ideas.
- Listen to others' ideas.
- Plan your work with the group.
- Present your project.
- Discuss how your group worked.

A. WHY DO I NEED THIS SKILL?

As you know, the earth is constantly moving. It rotates on its axis from west to east. Because of this movement, the direct rays of the sun do not hit everywhere on the earth at the same time. While it is night in some parts of the world, it is daytime in other parts. In order to know the time it will be when you travel to a distant part of the world, you need to understand the world's time zones.

B. LEARNING THE SKILL

The earth is divided into 24 standard time zones, one for each hour of the day. The earth makes a complete 360° revolution in those 24 hours. Since 360 divided by 24 equals 15, each time zone is 15° wide.

Notice on the map below that the time zones zigzag in several places. This has been done so that people living in the same region or country can have the same clock time.

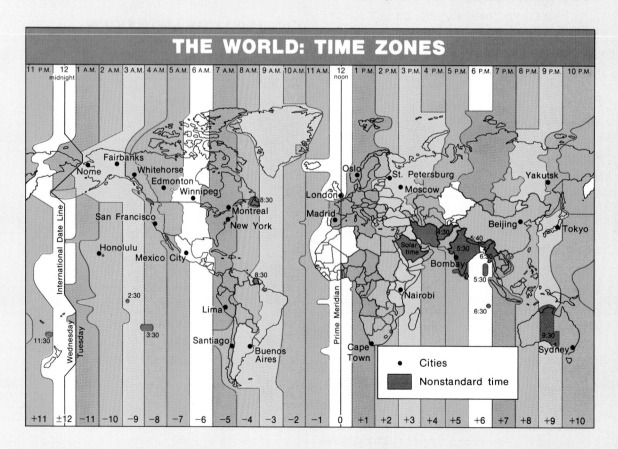

THE WORLD: TIME ZONES

Lines of longitude are sometimes called *meridians*. There are two meridians that are very important for understanding time zones. One is the *Prime Meridian*. It passes through Greenwich, England. By international agreement, time around the world is measured against the time in Greenwich.

As you can see on the map on the previous page, if it is 12:00 noon in Greenwich, the time in other zones is different, depending on how far east or west of the Prime Meridian they are. The time in the zone immediately to the east of the Prime Meridian time zone is 1:00 P.M. The time in the zone immediately to the west is 11:00 A.M.

The other important meridian is the *International Date Line*. It is exactly halfway around the world from the Prime Meridian. It is at the International Dateline that the day changes. For example, when it is Sunday east of the line, west of the line is Monday. If it is Sunday west of the line, it is Saturday east of the line.

What do A.M. and P.M. represent? A.M. stands for the Latin term *ante meridiem*, which means "before noon." P.M. stands for *post meridiem*, which means "after noon."

C. PRACTICING THE SKILL

1. Why are there different time zones?
2. How many time zones are there?
3. Which country has the most time zones?
4. If you are traveling from east to west on a Thursday, what day is it when you cross the Date Line?
5. What time is it in your town or city when it is noon in Greenwich, England?
6. When it is 3:00 P.M. in Moscow, what time is it in Mexico City?
7. If it is 2:00 P.M. in Greenwich, what time is it in Nairobi, Kenya?

D. APPLYING THE SKILL

Pick three places in the world that you would like to visit. Using the time zone map, figure out what time it would be in each of these places if it is 8:00 P.M. in Greenwich.

Suppose you were going to fly across the United States from New York City to San Francisco. If your plane left the airport in New York at 3:00 P.M. and the flight took five hours, what time would it be when you arrived in San Francisco?

Making SKILLBUILDER Comparisons

A. WHY DO I NEED THIS SKILL?

Writers sometimes organize ideas by making comparisons. Comparisons tell the reader how things are alike and different. If you are able to recognize and make comparisons, it will be easier for you to understand what you read.

B. LEARNING THE SKILL

Comparisons help us make sense of our world. For example, on page 286 in Chapter 10, you read that the peaks of the Caucasus Mountains are about three times as high as the Urals and are higher than the Alps. What if the author of this book told you only that the Caucasus peaks are high? This information would be correct, but by comparing the Caucasus with the Urals and the Alps, the author helps you better understand *how high* the Caucasus Mountains are. You will find many comparisons like this in your social studies textbook.

Sometimes comparisons are not stated directly. But by reading carefully, you will be able to make comparisons yourself. For instance, on page 288 you learned that the steppes have no trees. Earlier in the chapter, you read about another treeless region of the former Soviet Union, the tundra. However, you also learned that these two regions are different in that crops can be grown on the steppes but not on the tundra.

C. PRACTICING THE SKILL

One way for you to organize information and make your own comparisons is to make a comparison table like the one on page 353. The subjects that are to be compared are listed in the left-hand column; specific characteristics are listed in a row across the top of the table.

Each box in the table is to be filled in with a plus (+) or a minus (−). A plus is used when the subject has a particular characteristic; a minus is used when the subject does not have the characteristic. Once all the boxes have been filled in, you can look at the comparison table to see how the subjects are alike and different.

Copy this comparison table on a separate sheet of paper. Use the information in Chapter 10 to add more characteristics to the table and then fill in the rest of the boxes. Finally, review the table and note how the tundra, taiga, and steppes are alike and different.

COMPARING REGIONS OF THE FORMER SOVIET UNION				
	Grasses and low-growing plants	Farming	Permafrost		
Tundra	+	—			
Taiga	—	+			
Steppes	+	+			

D. APPLYING THE SKILL

Look for comparisons as you read the next chapter, which is about the geography of the Middle East and North Africa. Using the table above as a model, make some of your own comparison tables to show how the peoples and lands of these areas are alike and different.

Use this skill to compare peoples and lands of different regions of the Eastern Hemisphere that you will read about during the year. Remember, if you are able to recognize and make comparisons, it will be easier for you to understand what you read. Knowing how to make comparisons is an important skill to learn and to apply to all your reading.

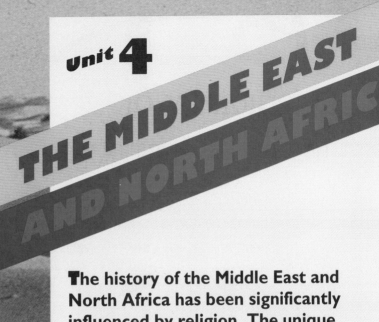

Unit 4

THE MIDDLE EAST AND NORTH AFRICA

The history of the Middle East and North Africa has been significantly influenced by religion. The unique geography of this region has also had a major impact on the people who live here.

▶ *The Sahara, the world's largest desert, is about the size of the United States and is nearly as large as the entire continent of Europe.*

Much of the region of the Middle East and North Africa is desert. The Sahara, which is nearly as large as the entire continent of Europe, extends across North Africa from the Atlantic coast to the Red Sea.

The Peoples of the Middle East and North Africa

THINK ABOUT WHAT YOU KNOW

In earlier chapters you learned about the ancient civilizations in the Middle East and North Africa. What peoples can you think of who were in these lands during ancient times?

STUDY THE VOCABULARY

migration   Bedouin
labor force

FOCUS YOUR READING

How are the peoples of the Middle East and North Africa alike, and how are they different?

A. Tales from Many Lands

The tales in *Arabian Nights* are among the world's best-known stories. These tales are supposed to be ones told by Scheherazade (shuh her uh ZAH duh), the clever wife of a cruel king. Scheherazade was by no means the first of the king's wives. He had had many wives, and he had distrusted them all. Every day he chose another wife and then had her head chopped off the following morning.

Scheherazade wished to escape the fate of the other wives, so she thought of a plan. On the night after her marriage, she started telling the king a story. The king became very interested in her marvelous tale, but just when she reached the most interesting part of the story, the sun came up. Scheherazade said that she would continue the story that night if the king would allow her to live. The king, eager to know how the story ended, let her live another day so that she could finish the tale.

That night, Scheherazade finished the first story and then began to tell an even more wonderful tale. But once again, dawn came before she finished, and the clever young woman said she would finish the story that night if the king let her live. Again the king said, "I will not kill her until I have heard the rest of this truly remarkable tale!" And so it went on, night after night. Finally the king realized that a wife who knew such stories was a true treasure. He never again threatened to take her life.

Some of the stories told by Scheherazade are very famous. You can read an excerpt from "The Voyages of Sinbad" on page 358. Not all the stories in *Arabian Nights* are Arabian. The book is, instead, a collection of

Scheherazade told her husband, the king, marvelous stories.
▶ In what book can we find some of these wonderful tales?

357

FROM: **Arabian Nights**

Translated by: Andrew Lang
Setting: A strange island

The *Arabian Nights*, or *The Thousand and One Nights*, is a collection of stories from many parts of the East. There were people long ago whose profession it was to amuse others by telling tales. At last, a storyteller wrote down the tales, which have since been translated into many languages.

Sinbad the Sailor, a famous character from an *Arabian Nights* tale, journeyed to unknown seas and adventures. He was shipwrecked seven times during his many voyages. In the passage below he describes an encounter with a creature during his third voyage.

𝐏ushing back the heavy ebony doors we entered the courtyard, but upon the threshold of the great hall beyond it we paused, frozen with horror, at the sight which greeted us. On one side lay a huge pile of bones—human bones, and on the other numberless spits for roasting! Overcome with despair we sank trembling to the ground, and lay there without speech or motion. The sun was setting when a loud noise aroused us, the door of the hall was violently burst open and a horrible giant entered. He was as tall as a palm tree, . . . and had one eye, which flamed like a burning coal in the middle of his forehead. His teeth were long and sharp and grinned horribly, while his lower lip hung down

upon his chest, and he had ears like [an] elephant's ears, which covered his shoulders, and nails like the claws of some fierce bird.

At this terrible sight our senses left us and we lay like dead men. . . . we lay shivering with horror the whole night through, and when day broke he awoke and went out, leaving us in the castle.

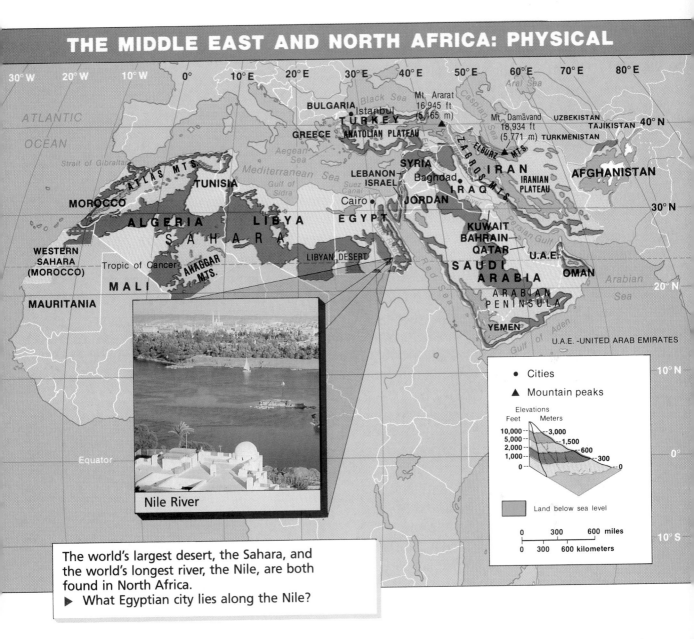

Nile River

The world's largest desert, the Sahara, and the world's longest river, the Nile, are both found in North Africa.
▶ What Egyptian city lies along the Nile?

tales from different lands and peoples. The word *Arabian* in the title refers to the Arabic language, the language in which the collected stories are written. The book was created about a thousand years ago.

B. Linking the Middle East with North Africa

Naming the Region The lands from which the *Arabian Nights* stories came are located in the Middle East and North Africa. The term *Middle East* was invented by western Europeans as a name for southwestern Asia. The Middle East and North Africa lie in the middle of a great land mass formed by three continents— Asia, Europe, and Africa. The region is called the Middle East to distinguish it from the Far East, a region that contains the lands of East Asia.

The history of the Middle East has been closely linked with that of North

Africa. These lands have similar climates, even though they stretch across two continents. The map on page 359 shows the two areas, which extend from Morocco in the west to Afghanistan in the east. Turkey is the northernmost country, and Yemen is the country farthest south.

The Region's History The Middle East and North Africa have a very long history. You have already read about the beginnings of civilization in Egypt and in Mesopotamia, which is now Iraq. You have also read that much of the Middle East and North Africa had been a part of the empires of the Roman emperors and of Alexander the Great. The land of Persia, which Alexander conquered, is now known as Iran. Some of the descendants of the ancient peoples still live in the region.

Like Europe, North Africa and the Middle East is a region with a variety of peoples and more than 20 nations. Over the centuries there has been a **migration** of peoples to this middle region from other parts of Asia, Europe, and Africa. Migration is the movement from one place to another. Some of the descendants of the peoples who migrated also make up part of the present-day population.

C. Where People Live and Work

City Dwellers At one time most people of the Middle East and North Africa were farmers or herders. Today the greater part of the population is urban. There are 17 cities that have a million or more people. Cairo in Egypt, Tehran in Iran, and Istanbul in Turkey rank among the world's largest cities. As you can see by looking at the population density map on the next page, some of the large cities in this region are very crowded.

Farmers Even though there are more city dwellers, many people still live in rural villages and work on the land, as did their ancestors. In Egypt, 40 percent of the **labor force**, the working population, works in agriculture. Farmers are a large part of the labor force in a number of countries in the region.

Nomads A very small part of the population are still nomadic herders. The nomads of the Middle East and North Africa are usually known as **Bedouins** (BED oo-ihnz), an Arabic term meaning "desert dwellers." The Bedouins live in tents so that they can easily move about on the desert and dry grasslands in the endless search for water and pasture for their herds of sheep, goats, and camels.

WORKERS IN THE MIDDLE EAST AND NORTH AFRICA

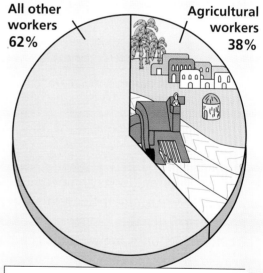

All other workers 62%

Agricultural workers 38%

This graph shows how much of the labor force in the Middle East and North Africa works in agriculture.
► What percentage of workers do not work in agriculture?

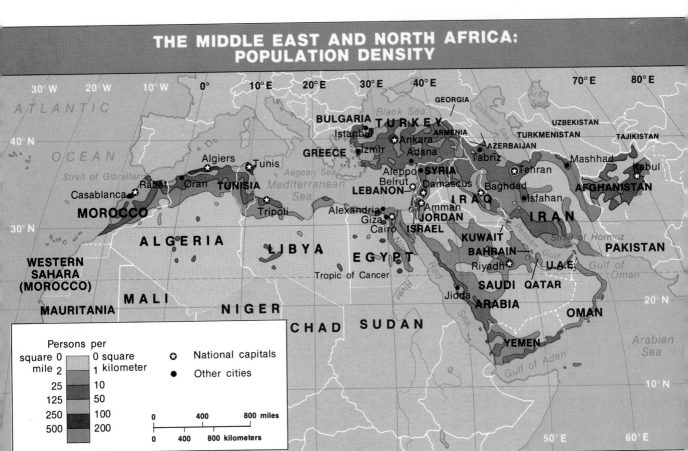

THE MIDDLE EAST AND NORTH AFRICA: POPULATION DENSITY

Persons per

square mile	square kilometer
0	0
2	1
25	10
125	50
250	100
500	200

✪ National capitals
● Other cities

THE 25 LARGEST CITIES OF THE MIDDLE EAST AND NORTH AFRICA

Cairo (Egypt) 6,205,000	Algiers (Algeria) 1,722,000	Isfahan (Iran) 1,121,000	Adana (Turkey) 776,000
Tehran (Iran) 5,752,000	Giza (Egypt) 1,608,000	Mashhad (Iran) 1,103,000	Oran (Algeria) 664,000
Istanbul (Turkey) 5,495,000	Beirut (Lebanon) 1,500,000	Kabul (Afghanistan) 1,036,000	Tunis (Tunisia) 597,000
Baghdad (Iraq) 4,649,000	Izmir (Turkey) 1,490,000	Riyadh (Saudi Arabia) 1,000,000	Rabat (Morocco) 519,000
Alexandria (Egypt) 2,821,000	Jidda (Saudi Arabia) 1,308,000	Tabrîz (Iran) 929,000	
Ankara (Turkey) 2,252,000	Damascus (Syria) 1,259,000	Tripoli (Libya) 859,000	
Casablanca (Morocco) 2,139,000	Aleppo (Syria) 1,173,000	Amman (Jordan) 800,000	

The area of highest population density in the Middle East and North Africa is found in Egypt.
▶ Along which river in Egypt is the population highest?

D. The Arabic Language and Alphabet

Arabic Alphabet Arabic is the language of most countries in the Middle East and North Africa. Arabic-speaking people are often called Arabs, even though most of them do not live on the Arabian Peninsula.

Arabic is written with an alphabet of 28 letters, which differ from those of the Roman alphabet. In Arabic the first line of a paragraph is indented on the right rather than on the left. This is because Arabic is written from right to left rather than from left to right, as are the words on this page.

361

This writing shows how Arabic letters differ from the letters in the Roman alphabet.

▶ Why is the first line of this paragraph indented on the right?

Spanish and Italian. The Arabic alphabet, too, is used for writing different languages. It is the second most widely used alphabet in the world. Both Persian and the language of Afghanistan are written with Arabic letters.

Arabic Language Written Arabic is much the same in all Arab countries, but the dialects, or forms of the same language, differ from one country to another. Some Arabic dialects differ so greatly that people who speak one dialect can hardly understand people who speak another. An English woman who had learned to read Arabic discovered that when she first visited an Arab country and listened to people talk, she "understood about one word in a hundred."

Not all peoples of the Middle East and North Africa speak Arabic. Hebrew is the language of the people of Israel. The Iranians speak Persian, and the people of Afghanistan speak a language closely related to Persian. The people of Turkey also have their own distinctive language. The Middle East and North Africa make up a large region that has a variety of languages, histories, as well as lands and resources, which you will read about later in this chapter.

As you have learned, an alphabet can be used to write more than one language. The Roman alphabet is used to write a variety of European languages, such as

---

LESSON **1** REVIEW

THINK AND WRITE

A. How did Scheherazade prevent the king from killing her?
B. Why is there a variety of peoples in the Middle East and North Africa?
C. Where do people live and work today in the Middle East and North Africa?
D. What alphabet and languages are used in the Middle East and North Africa?

SKILLS CHECK

MAP SKILL

Look at the population density map on page 361. What are the population and population density for the following cities: Rabat, Morocco; Alexandria, Egypt; Tripoli, Libya; Isfahan, Iran?

The Lands of the Middle East and North Africa

THINK ABOUT WHAT YOU KNOW
Imagine that you are standing in the middle of a desert. What five adjectives would you use to describe the desert?

STUDY THE VOCABULARY
wadi

FOCUS YOUR READING
What are the main geographical features of the region of the Middle East and North Africa?

A. From Deserts to Seas

Deserts Perhaps you think of a desert as a sandy wasteland where winds blow the sand into shifting dunes. Some deserts are like that, but less than a third of the world's deserts are sandy wastelands. Though many deserts are bare and rocky, some deserts have hardy plants that need little moisture.

Deserts are lands that average less than 10 inches (25 cm) of precipitation a year. Although precipitation is rare in deserts, rainstorms sometimes do occur. During one of these rare downpours, waters may rise rapidly in dry stream beds called **wadis** (WAH deez). Travelers who have carelessly camped in a dry wadi have been known to drown in the desert. Water can also be found in the desert in an oasis, which is a place where there is water from wells or springs.

Deserts make up a large part of the Middle East and North Africa. The Sahara, the world's largest desert, extends across North Africa from the Atlantic coast to the Red Sea. The Sahara is nearly as large as the entire continent of Europe. The Arabian Peninsula is not much more than the

These people are harvesting squash in the Sinai desert in Israel.
▶ How can farming be accomplished in a desert?

Arabian Desert. Although the Arabian Desert is not as large as the Sahara, it is more than four times the size of France.

Five Seas Just as there is an abundance of desert land within the Middle East and North Africa, there is an abundance of sea water around the region. This region is set among five seas: the Mediterranean, Black, Caspian, Arabian, and Red seas. All the countries in the region except Afghanistan have outlets to the sea.

Climate The coastal lands along the Mediterranean have a climate somewhat like that of the Mediterranean lands of Europe. Winters are cool and rainy; summers are hot and dry. The average January and July temperatures in Algiers, Algeria, in North Africa, are about the same as those in Athens, Greece. The beaches of Israel and Lebanon are much like the Mediterranean beaches of southern Europe.

B. The Anatolian and Iranian Plateaus

Anatolian Plateau The Anatolian (an uh-TOH lee un) peninsula is located between the Black and Mediterranean seas. It is also called Asia Minor. Look at the physical map on page 359. Notice that the Anatolian peninsula includes the country of Turkey and a small tip of southeastern Europe, where Istanbul is located.

Most of the Anatolian peninsula is a rugged plateau, from which rise hills and mountains. The highest part of the plateau

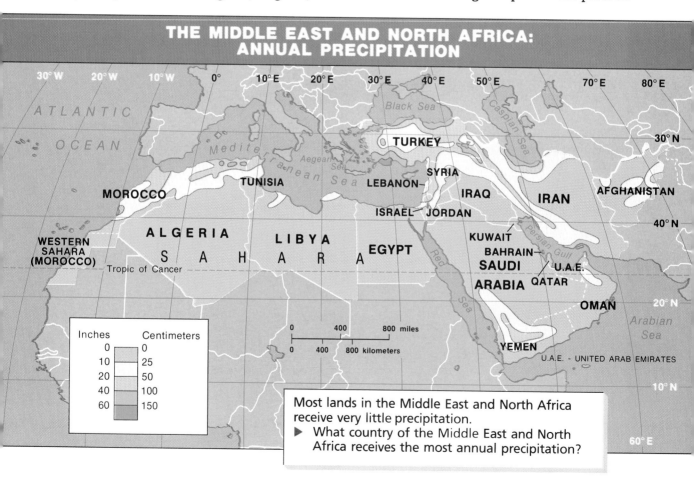

THE MIDDLE EAST AND NORTH AFRICA: ANNUAL PRECIPITATION

Inches	Centimeters
0	0
10	25
20	50
40	100
60	150

Most lands in the Middle East and North Africa receive very little precipitation.
▶ What country of the Middle East and North Africa receives the most annual precipitation?

Mount Damāvand, located in Iran, is the highest peak in the Elburz Mountains.
▶ How can you tell that the elevation has affected the climate on Mount Damāvand?

is in eastern Turkey. Mount Ararat is located on Turkey's eastern border. The Tigris and Euphrates rivers, the two great rivers of ancient Mesopotamia, rise from sources on the Anatolian plateau.

The lands along the western and southern coasts of the Anatolian peninsula have a climate greatly affected by elevation. Like southern Europe, these lands have a Mediterranean climate. The Black Sea coast is cool, but its climate is mild when compared with that of the high central plateau. Winters are cold and summers hot on the plateau. The land is dry although not dry enough to be called a desert.

Iranian Plateau Mountain ranges rise along the edges of the Iranian plateau, located south of the Caspian Sea. The Zagros (ZAG rus) Mountains separate the plateau

from the plain of the Tigris and Euphrates rivers to the west. The Elburz (el BOORZ) Mountains form a wall between the plateau and the narrow coastland along the Caspian Sea. Find these mountain ranges on the map on page 359.

The climb from the Caspian coast to the plateau is steep. The Caspian is an inland sea about 92 feet (28 m) below sea level. From its low-lying coast one can look up to Mount Damāvand (DAM uh-vand), which rises 18,934 feet (5,771 m) above sea level. Mount Damāvand is higher than Mont Blanc, the highest peak in the Alps.

Elevation greatly affects climate in the lands south of the Caspian Sea. The coast has very heavy summer rainfall, and much of the land is forested. The high plateau has very dry summers, and much of the land is barren desert.

The mountains and deserts of Afghanistan are located east of the Iranian plateau. The mountains in this rugged land are the highest in the Middle East.

C. The Lowest Place on the Earth's Surface

The Jordan River has the lowest elevation of all the world's rivers. It begins at the foot of a mountain in Syria, but it flows down through a valley that is below sea level. The Jordan empties into the Dead Sea, located between Israel and Jordan. The Dead Sea lies nearly one fourth of a mile (402 m) below sea level. It is the lowest place on the surface of the earth.

Because its elevation is so low, no water can drain out of the Dead Sea. But the hot desert sun evaporates the water about as fast as it flows in from the river. Evaporation leaves behind large deposits of salt and other minerals. The Dead Sea is about seven times saltier than are the oceans. If you completely evaporate a cup of Dead Sea water, you will have about one-fourth cup of dry salt left. People can easily float on the surface of this salty sea, but when they get out they have a salty crust left on their skin. The Dead Sea is so salty that fish cannot live in it. That is the reason for the name Dead Sea.

The photograph above shows salt columns in the Dead Sea, the saltiest body of water in the world.
▶ Why is there so much salt in the Dead Sea?

LESSON **2** REVIEW

THINK AND WRITE

A. What are the important deserts and seas of the Middle East and North Africa?

B. How does elevation affect the climates of the Anatolian and Iranian plateaus?

C. Why is the Dead Sea so salty?

SKILLS CHECK

THINKING SKILL

The Middle East and North Africa are set among five important seas: the Arabian, Black, Caspian, Mediterranean, and Red seas. Look in the Gazetteer to find out which of these seas is the largest in the world and which is the largest inland body of water in the world.

Resources of the Middle East and North Africa

THINK ABOUT WHAT YOU KNOW

Recall what you have learned about the natural resources of other countries. Can you name any natural resources that are found in the area where you live?

STUDY THE VOCABULARY

petroleum **ground water**
per capita income

FOCUS YOUR READING

What are the resources of the Middle East and North Africa?

A. In the Neighborhood of Oil

When Freya Stark, an English girl, was nine years old, her aunt gave her a copy of the *Arabian Nights.* For Freya the gift inspired a lifelong interest in the Middle East. She wanted to live and travel in the Middle East because, she explained,

§ *I thought the most interesting things in the*
§ *world were likely to happen in the neigh-*
§ *borhood of oil.*

When Freya Stark began her studies of Arabic in 1921, the Middle East produced only about 2 percent of the world's **petroleum**, or oil. She was not a geographer or a scientist, but she correctly guessed that the amount of oil discovered in the Middle East would increase greatly. She was exactly right. Today a large part of the world's petroleum supply comes from the Arabic-speaking lands of the Middle East and North Africa.

As Freya Stark guessed, the growing importance of oil caused interesting things to happen. Countries that had been poor desert lands in 1921 were rich by the 1970s. The **per capita incomes** in Saudi Arabia, Kuwait, and Bahrain were among the highest in the world. Per capita income is the amount of money that each person in the country would have if the country's total income were divided equally among all of its people.

Although petroleum has been found in a number of Middle Eastern and North African countries, it has not been found in every land. The resource map on page 369 shows where the oil fields are located.

The main source of the wealth in Saudi Arabia comes from the oil industry.
▶ Where in Saudi Arabia is this oil rig drilling for petroleum?

PRODUCTS OF THE DATE PALM TREE

Date Palm Fruit

Sugar

String and Rope

Bowls

Cooking Oil

Baskets and Mats

Animal Food

Medicine

Sandals

The date palm tree supplies many products to the people of the Middle East and North Africa.
▶ What are the food products that come from the date palm tree?

B. Making Use of the Dry Lands

Irrigating the Land Oil is not the only important resource of the Middle East and North Africa. Water is perhaps even more important in dry lands, which make up so large a part of this region. Kuwait, a small country on the Persian Gulf, has a lot of oil but almost no sources of fresh water. At one time, Kuwait imported river water from the nearby country of Iraq. Today Kuwait gets water from the world's largest factory for turning salty sea water into fresh water.

Much of the land in the Middle East and North Africa is too dry and too mountainous for growing crops. In some countries less than 5 percent of the land is arable, that is, suitable for cultivation.

Other countries have more arable land, but none have as much as do the Western European countries. Yet this dry part of the world is where people first learned to grow wheat, barley, peas, onions, and a variety of melons. Here people first cultivated fig and date trees. The chart above shows some products of the date palm tree. The largest part of the world's date supply still comes from the Middle East. Almonds were probably first raised in this region. English walnuts are probably more accurately called Persian walnuts, since the nuts were first cultivated in Persia.

People are able to grow crops in dry lands and deserts if they have water for irrigation. As you have read, the ancient Egyptians drew water from the Nile River to irrigate the desert. Modern Egyptians do the same. The resource map below shows areas of irrigated agriculture. Note that the two largest areas lie along the Nile and the Tigris and Euphrates rivers. You will also see that the map shows small areas of irrigated lands scattered across the Sahara and Arabian deserts. These are oases where people have learned to use **ground water** to grow crops. Ground water is water that has seeped below the ground during the occasional rains and has collected in layers of soil, sand, and rock. People tap this underground water by digging or drilling wells. In some lands, tunnels are dug to carry underground water from the highlands to lower valleys. In the past the digging of wells and the lifting of water was done by human muscle and by animals. Today machines and pumps are used for these tasks.

A Need for Water The population of the Middle East and North Africa has grown rapidly in recent years. As the number of people has increased, so has the need for water. In some places, ground water is being used more rapidly than it is being replaced. Consequently, the precious waters of the region's great rivers have become more and more polluted.

It has been difficult to make plans for the use of the rivers in the region, because the major streams run through more than

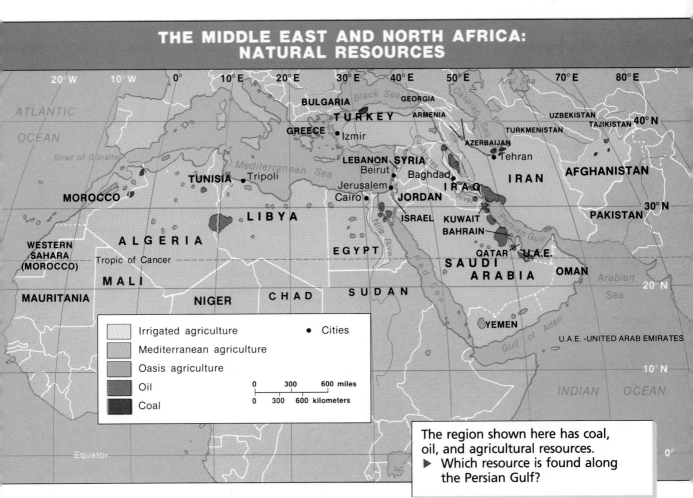

THE MIDDLE EAST AND NORTH AFRICA: NATURAL RESOURCES

Irrigated agriculture
Mediterranean agriculture
Oasis agriculture
Oil
Coal
• Cities

0   300   600 miles
0   300   600 kilometers

U.A.E. -UNITED ARAB EMIRATES

The region shown here has coal, oil, and agricultural resources.
▶ Which resource is found along the Persian Gulf?

one country. Although the source of the Jordan River is in Syria, it receives water from other rivers in Lebanon. The Jordan River flows to both the country of Israel and the country of Jordan. The Euphrates River rises in Turkey and crosses Syria before it finally reaches Iraq. All of the countries along these rivers depend on the water from them.

C. Animals for Dry Lands

Donkeys Long ago in the Middle East and North Africa, people domesticated, or tamed, animals for use in dry lands. The sturdy donkey was perhaps the first animal trained to carry loads. Donkeys are hearty

Camels are among the most useful animals in hot, dry lands, such as the Middle East and North Africa.
▶ What kind of camel is shown in the photograph below?

creatures able to survive in regions where vegetation and water are too scarce for most large animals to survive.

Camels It is believed that camels were also first used in the Middle East. Dromedary camels, those with one hump, were probably domesticated in the Arabian Peninsula. Bactrian camels, camels with two humps, were most likely first used in Bactria, a land now known as Afghanistan. Both of these camels are found mainly in central Asia.

Camels are very useful in dry lands. They can go without water for long periods of time. A camel may drink 15 to 25 gallons (57 to 95 L) of water at one time, and then not drink again for several days or longer. If a camel can find food, it can go for 20 days without water. Camels will eat various sorts of desert plants. They store the energy that they get from food in their humps, which are piles of fat under the skin. The stored energy makes it possible for camels to go without food for days.

Since camels can go without water and food for long periods, they can easily travel through a desert. Camels are able to carry loads and riders and can pull plows or wagons. At one time, camels provided the main form of transportation in the desert. Today they are raised for food and leather. Camel herds provide milk, meat, and hides. Camels are well suited to the Middle East and North Africa because they can be raised on land where cattle would starve.

Sheep and Goats Raising sheep and goats is also another way to make use of dry lands. Like camels, these animals can feed on desert plants. Since the plants are sparse in the desert, herds must travel over large areas in search of more plant life.

Long ago the mountainsides of Lebanon were covered with cedar forests.
▶ After looking at the photograph above, how would you describe the mountainsides of today?

D. The Lost Forests

Once, forests covered many of the hills and mountains throughout the Middle East and North Africa. The cedar forests of Lebanon were famous in ancient times. The Egyptian pharaohs imported cedar wood to make coffins for tombs. Solomon, king of ancient Israel, imported cedar wood from Lebanon to build a temple at Jerusalem. Today there are small remains of Lebanon's ancient forests. But like nine tenths of the forests in the Middle East and North Africa, the cedar forests were destroyed and never replaced. Trees grow slowly in the dry climate, and the forests were cut faster than they could grow.

Part of the reason the forests disappeared is that wood is such a useful resource. People used wood for buildings, furniture, and tools. Wood is also excellent fuel, so trees were cut to heat homes and cook meals.

People's need for wood was not the only reason for the destruction of forests. Herds of sheep and goats also did their part in destroying the forests. Since these animals eat such a wide variety of plants, they have stripped the ground of shrubs and young trees.

E. The Suez Canal Opens New Trade Routes

Difficult Trade Routes Because of its location the Middle East has had the advantage of being on major trade routes between three continents. In ancient times, traders brought silk from China by way of the long "Silk Road" across Asia. This high-priced cloth was then carried by ship from ports on the Mediterranean to Rome. Ships from East Africa and South Asia brought goods to ports on the Persian Gulf and Red Sea. From there camel caravans carried the goods to Mediterranean ports, where they could be reloaded onto ships bound for southern Europe.

Ships from East Africa and South Asia could not sail directly to Europe because the Isthmus of Suez blocked the way. The isthmus separates the Red Sea and the Mediterranean by a narrow strip of land that connects Africa and Asia.

The Suez Canal A canal across the Isthmus of Suez was not completed until 1869. The building of the canal at that time was partly the result of a friendship between Ferdinand de Lesseps, a French official, and a young Egyptian who liked macaroni. The friendship began when Lesseps was serving as the French representative in Egypt. At that time the Egyptian ruler had a teenage son named Said, who was somewhat overweight. Said's father decided that his son must do vigorous exercises and go on a strict diet.

Almost every day after doing his exercises, Said was very hungry, and he would go to the house of his French friend. There he would have the cook make him a large dish of macaroni, which was one of Said's favorite foods. The macaroni did not reduce Said's weight, but it strengthened his friendship with Lesseps.

Lesseps left Egypt in 1837. Seventeen years later, Said, now called Said Pasha, became the ruler of Egypt. He remembered his old friend and invited him to

The Suez Canal opened for use in November 1869.
▶ How has the Suez Canal served as an important resource for the Middle East and North Africa?

visit. Lesseps jumped at the chance to return to Egypt. He wanted to tell Said Pasha about a project he had in mind, the building of a modern ship canal across the Isthmus of Suez. A canal connecting the Mediterranean and Red seas would greatly shorten the route between Europe and Asia. When Lesseps explained his plan to Said Pasha, the ruler assured his friend, "I am convinced. You can count on me."

Improved Trade Routes Work on the Suez Canal began in 1859 and was completed ten years later. The completion of the canal put the Middle East and North Africa on one of the world's most important sea routes. Ships traveling from western Europe to East Africa or to South and East Asia could now go through the point where Africa and Asia met.

Other trade routes, which pass through the Middle East, have opened up between Europe and Asia. In 1973 a bridge was built across the Bosporus at Istanbul. A second bridge was completed in 1988. The bridges make it possible for large trucks to carry goods from Europe to cities in the Middle East. Now, as in ancient times, trade routes still pass through the Middle East and North Africa.

This bridge is one of two bridges that link the Asiatic and European sections of Istanbul.
▶ How have the bridges helped to increase trade?

LESSON **3** *REVIEW*

THINK AND WRITE

A. How did the demand for oil affect the Middle East and North Africa?

B. In what ways have people made use of land in the Middle East and North Africa?

C. Why are donkeys, camels, sheep, and goats useful in the Middle East and North Africa?

D. What happened to most of the forests in the Middle East and North Africa?

E. What changes in the Middle East and North Africa have resulted from the completion of the Suez Canal?

SKILLS CHECK

WRITING SKILL

Imagine that you are riding a camel across the Sahara. Write a short descriptive essay about your journey.

USING THE VOCABULARY

migration   petroleum
labor force   ground water
wadi

From the list above, choose a vocabulary term that could be used in place of the underlined word or words in each sentence. Rewrite the sentences on a separate sheet of paper.

1. During a rainstorm, water can rise quickly in a <u>dry stream bed</u> in a desert.
2. Over the centuries there has been a <u>movement</u> of people into the Middle East.
3. A large part of the world's <u>oil</u> is found in some of the countries in the Middle East and North Africa.
4. <u>Water that has seeped below the ground during the occasional rains and has collected in layers of soil, sand, and rock</u> is used to grow crops.
5. Much of the <u>working population</u> in Egypt works in agriculture.

REMEMBERING WHAT YOU READ

On a separate sheet of paper, answer the following questions in complete sentences.

1. Who tells the tales in the *Arabian Nights?*

2. The Middle East and North Africa lie in the middle of a landmass formed by what three continents?
3. What does the Arabic term *Bedouin* mean?
4. What is the language that most people of the Middle East and North Africa speak?
5. What is the world's largest desert?
6. Name the five seas that surround the Middle East and North Africa.
7. Explain why fish cannot live in the Dead Sea.
8. Why are camels useful animals in the desert?
9. What strip of land blocked the way for ships from Africa and South Asia to sail directly to Europe?
10. What improved trade routes for the Middle East and North Africa after 1869?

TYING MATH TO SOCIAL STUDIES

Figure out the per capita income of the fictitious countries of Northland and Southland, using the following information: Northland has a total income of $5,000,000 and a population of 10,000. Southland has a total income of $4,000,000 and a population of 20,000. What would be the per capita income if these two countries united?

THINKING CRITICALLY

On a separate sheet of paper, answer the following in complete sentences.

1. What are the advantages and disadvantages of people migrating to different countries?
2. Compare and contrast the Arabic alphabet and the Roman alphabet.
3. Why, do you think, do some countries in the Middle East, such as Saudi Arabia and Qatar, have among the highest per capita incomes in the world?
4. How do you think the Middle East and North Africa can conserve their ground water?
5. How would the economy of the Middle East and North Africa have been affected if the Suez Canal had not been built?

SUMMARIZING THE CHAPTER

On a separate sheet of paper, copy the graphic organizer shown below. Beside each main idea, write three statements that support the idea.

CHAPTER THEME	The people of the Middle East and North Africa have learned to use the gifts of nature to survive in their unique geographic environment.

LESSON 1

The peoples of the Middle East and North Africa are alike and different.

1. _____
2. _____
3. _____

LESSON 2

The Middle East and North Africa have many geographical features.

1. _____
2. _____
3. _____

LESSON 3

The Middle East and North Africa have many resources.

1. _____
2. _____
3. _____

The religion of Islam developed in the Middle East. Its culture has had a strong impact on many parts of the world. Beautiful houses of prayer, such as this one in Cairo, Egypt, are part of that Islamic culture.

Origins of the Muslim Religion

THINK ABOUT WHAT YOU KNOW

You have learned about the importance of religion in different cultures. Name some religious leaders that you have studied about in earlier chapters and tell to whom they were important.

STUDY THE VOCABULARY

shrine   pilgrimage

prophet

FOCUS YOUR READING

How did the Muslim religion begin?

A. How Muhammad Settled a Dispute

Rebuilding the Kaaba The Kaaba (KAH-buh) is a building in Mecca, a city located in the Arabian Desert. It is a simple stone structure built in the shape of a cube. In fact, the name *Kaaba* comes from the Arabic word for cube. Set in the wall at one corner of the Kaaba is a black stone encased in silver.

For centuries the Kaaba has been a religious **shrine**, a place considered holy. At one time, people came to the Kaaba to worship the images of gods and goddesses and to touch the black stone, which was considered sacred, or holy.

About 1,400 years ago one of the rare thunderstorms in the desert flooded Mecca. Rushing waters destroyed the walls of the Kaaba so that it had to be rebuilt. Men from all of the city's leading families took part in rebuilding the important shrine. At last all the stones were in place, except for the sacred black stone that the leaders of the four major families claimed the honor of putting back in the Kaaba. Since they could not decide who would replace the sacred stone, it was agreed upon to settle the dispute by chance. It was decided that the first man who walked through the gate would

People from all over the world journey to Mecca to pray at the Kaaba.
▶ What is the Kaaba?

choose the person to place the black stone in the wall.

Muhammad Enters As it happened, the first man through the gate was a respected merchant named Muhammad. When the dispute was explained to him, he asked for a large cloth. He spread the cloth on the ground and placed the black stone in the center. He then had the leading men from the four families each take hold of a corner of the cloth. He told them to lift the cloth and carry the stone to its place in the wall. The men did as the merchant directed. When they had raised the stone to the proper height, Muhammad pushed it into place. Muhammad's wise decision satisfied all four families. All had shared equally in the honor of restoring the black stone.

B. The Messages of Muhammad

A Young Boy The merchant later became the founder of the religion of the Muslims. Muhammad was born about A.D. 570 in Mecca. Muhammad's father had died before he was born. His mother died when he was about 6 years old, leaving his grandfather and an uncle to raise him.

The uncle was a merchant who took trading caravans to cities on the edge of the desert. When Muhammad was 12 years old, he persuaded his uncle to take him on a caravan trip to Syria. While on the trips, Muhammad met many different people. He talked with a Christian monk, who taught him about Jesus and Christianity, and with Jews, who taught him about the laws of Judaism.

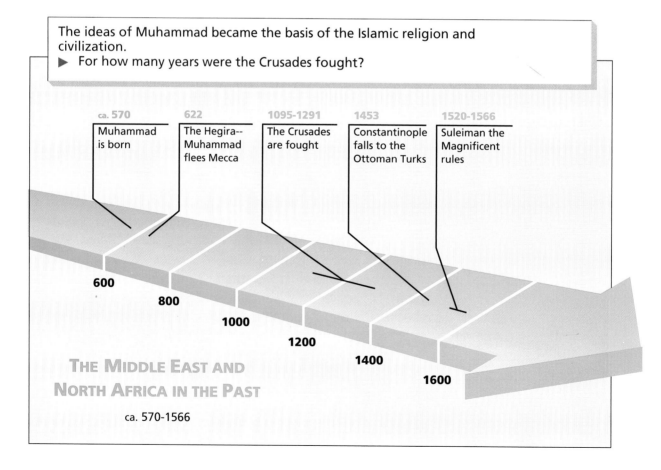

The ideas of Muhammad became the basis of the Islamic religion and civilization.
▶ For how many years were the Crusades fought?

ca. 570 — Muhammad is born

622 — The Hegira-- Muhammad flees Mecca

1095-1291 — The Crusades are fought

1453 — Constantinople falls to the Ottoman Turks

1520-1566 — Suleiman the Magnificent rules

600
800
1000
1200
1400
1600

THE MIDDLE EAST AND NORTH AFRICA IN THE PAST
ca. 570-1566

Muhammad is shown below receiving one of the many messages from the angel Gabriel.
► Which of the two figures depicted is Gabriel?

An Angel's Message After spending time traveling with his uncle, Muhammad returned to live in Mecca. Sometimes Muhammad would leave the crowded marketplace of the city and go into the desert to be alone. One night in a desert cave, Muhammad reported that an unusual thing happened. According to Muhammad's account, an angel appeared and told him that it was wrong to worship the images of gods and goddesses in the Kaaba because there was only one true God.

When Muhammad told others about the angel's message, he used the Arabic word *Allah* (AL uh), which simply means "the God." Muhammad reported that the angel said that Allah had sent earlier **prophets** but that he, Muhammad, was the last of them. A prophet is a religious leader who speaks out against wrongdoing and warns that punishments will come to those who break God's laws.

The Koran The message in the desert cave was the first of a number of messages that Muhammad said he received. He repeated the messages to others, who learned them by heart. Later, Muhammad's followers wrote down these messages and gathered them into a book called the *Koran*, an Arabic word meaning "the reading." The Koran, the holy book of the Muslims, contains many teachings, some of which you can read on page 380. Muhammad called his teachings *Islam*, which means "surrender to God." A person whose religion is Islam is known as a *Muslim*, "one who has surrendered to God."

THE TEACHINGS OF MUHAMMAD

Muslims believe that Muhammad was a prophet who served as God's messenger. The messages that Muhammad used as his teachings are contained in the Koran, the holy book of the Muslims. Here are translations of some passages from the Koran.

Muhammad is only a messenger, and many a messenger has gone before him.

Pay homage to God . . . and be good to your parents and relatives, the orphans and the needy and the neighbors who are your relatives, and the neighbors who are strangers, and the friend by your side, the traveler and your servants.

O believers, give in charity what is good of the things you have earned, and of what you produce from the earth; and do not choose to give what is bad as alms [donations], that is, things you would not like to accept yourself.

If you give alms openly, it is well; but if you do it secretly and give to the poor, that is better.

Be good to your parents. . . . say gentle words to them. And look after them with kindness and love. . . .

Give full measure when you are measuring, and weigh on a balanced scale.

You may dislike a thing yet it may be good for you; or a thing may haply [by chance] please you but be bad for you. . . .

God is with those who preserve themselves from evil and do the right.

Understanding Source Material

1. How would you rephrase the Koran's passage about not giving things you would not accept yourself?
2. The Koran's statement about measuring does not just apply to measuring that is done with a ruler, scale, or other instrument. To what other kinds of "measuring" do you think the statement could apply?

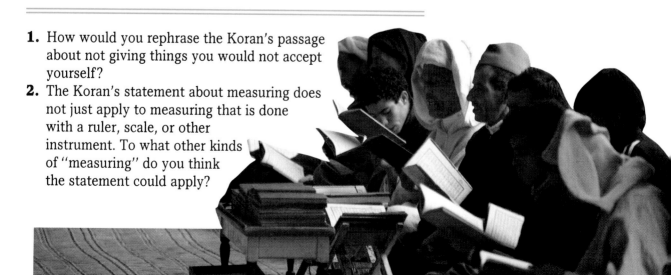

Muhammad is shown here completing the Hegira, the journey from Mecca to Medina.
► Why, do you think, are these people gathered around him?

C. Muhammad as a Leader

A Religious Leader At first only a few people in Mecca believed Muhammad's account of the angel's message. His wife, his cousin, and a freed slave were among the first to accept it. Most people mocked him. The leaders of Mecca believed that Muhammad had gone mad.

In spite of opposition, Muhammad began to preach about the messages. In time, Muhammad did win followers, and his opponents grew alarmed. They began to abuse and persecute those who believed Muhammad. Muhammad decided to seek safety in another city. So, in A.D. 622, Muhammad left Mecca and went to Medina. The journey from Mecca to Medina is called the *Hegira* (hih JYE ruh). Muslims number the years of their calendar from the Hegira, so that their year 1 is 622 on the Christian calendar.

Defeating Mecca Muhammad became the leader of Medina. When a war broke out between Medina and Mecca, Muhammad led his adopted city into battle and defeated Mecca. He assured the people of Mecca that they would not be harmed if they gave up their old religion.

Muhammad had the Kaaba cleared of the images of the gods and goddesses, but he saw to it that no harm was done to the ancient shrine. He declared that in the future the Kaaba would be dedicated to the worship of Allah. Muhammad instructed his followers to face toward the Kaaba in Mecca whenever they prayed. Muslims still do so today.

381

After the conquest of Mecca, other cities of Arabia accepted Muhammad as their leader. Ten years after the journey from Mecca, almost all of Arabia accepted Muhammad as both ruler and prophet.

D. Muslims in the World Today

There are millions of Muslims in the world today. Islam is the religion of most people in the Middle East and North Africa. It is also the faith of large numbers in other parts of Asia. Indeed, there are Muslims on all continents.

Muslims, like Christians, are divided into different groups, but all the Muslim groups share some beliefs. All accept the belief that there is only one God and that Muhammad was the last of the prophets. All regard the Koran as a holy book. Some Muslims memorize the entire Koran,

even though the book contains about 78,000 words.

Muhammad taught that faithful Muslims have certain duties. Muhammad said that all should declare their belief in one God and all should pray five times a day, while facing Mecca. Faithful Muslims who could possibly do so had a duty to make a **pilgrimage** to Mecca at least once in their lives. A pilgrimage is a journey to a shrine or other sacred place. Those who make such a journey are called pilgrims. Before pilgrims enter Mecca, they change to simple clothing so that rich and poor are dressed alike. The pilgrims go to the Kaaba, kiss the black stone, and walk around the sacred building seven times,

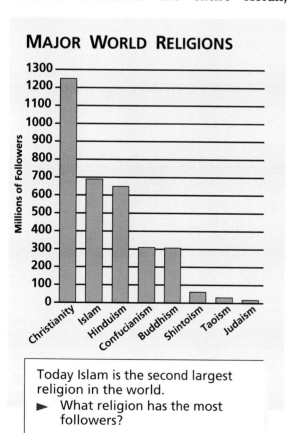

MAJOR WORLD RELIGIONS

Millions of Followers

Christianity, Islam, Hinduism, Confucianism, Buddhism, Shintoism, Taoism, Judaism

Today Islam is the second largest religion in the world.
► What religion has the most followers?

382

Each year thousands of Muslims from around the world make a pilgrimage to Mecca, Saudi Arabia, the birthplace of Muhammad.
▶ By what means do modern-day Muslims travel to their holy city of Mecca?

reciting prayers as Muhammad did. Each year large numbers of Muslims from many lands make the pilgrimage to Mecca.

Muhammad taught his followers that they had a duty to help the poor and others in need. He spoke particularly of helping widows and orphans. Perhaps he remembered that his mother had been a widow before he was born and that he became an orphan when he was very young.

LESSON **1** *REVIEW*

THINK AND WRITE

A. How did Muhammad settle the dispute about placing the black stone in the wall of the Kaaba?
B. According to Muhammad, what message did he receive in the cave?
C. What did Muhammad do after the conquest of Mecca?
D. What are important duties of Muslims?

SKILLS CHECK

MAP SKILL

Muhammad journeyed from Mecca to Medina to seek safety. Look in the Gazetteer for the coordinates of Medina. Then find Mecca on the political map of Eurasia in the Atlas. About how far did Muhammad travel?

383

CITIZENSHIP AND AMERICAN VALUES

WHAT MAKES A PERSON GREAT?

If you were to ask each person in your class what makes a man or woman great, you would probably get many different answers. These answers would show the different values of the members of your class.

You have just read about Muhammad, who has been called great by many people. All the persons described in the following paragraphs have been called great at one time or another. Of course, not all people have agreed that these persons were great. Do you think they were great? Read about each of them and then make up your mind.

Martin Luther King, Jr.

Martin Luther King, Jr., was born and raised in Atlanta, Georgia. He became a Baptist minister who preached nonviolence and racial integration. Dr. King received the Nobel Peace Prize in 1964 for his role in seeking racial equality and justice. He was assassinated in 1968, in Memphis, Tennessee.

Ludwig van Beethoven

Beethoven was a German composer who wrote some of the world's greatest music. Before he was 30 years old, Beethoven began to lose his hearing. He continued to write music even after he was completely deaf. Now, more than 150 years after Beethoven's death, his music is still enjoyed by many.

Thomas Edison

Thomas Edison, born in Ohio, was the inventor of the incandescent electric lamp and the phonograph. He also improved the inventions of other people, such as the telephone, the typewriter, and the motion picture. Many of Edison's important devices were invented at his workshop in Menlo Park, New Jersey. He was responsible for more than 1,000 inventions in his lifetime.

Sally Ride

Sally Ride, who was born in Los Angeles, California, became the first American woman to travel in space. In 1978 she was one of 35 people chosen from among 8,000 to train as astronauts. In June 1983, Sally Ride and four crew members made a six-day flight on the space shuttle *Challenger*. Ride was later a member of the presidential commission investigating the 1986 *Challenger* accident.

◀ Martin Luther King, Jr.

Thinking for Yourself

On a separate sheet of paper, answer the following questions in complete sentences.

1. Which of the people described do you consider to be the greatest? Explain your answer.
2. Which of the people described do you think least deserves to be called great? Explain your answer.
3. Name someone living today whom you would include in a list of great people. Why do you consider that person to be great?

◄ Ludwig van Beethoven

Sally Ride ►

Thomas Edison ►

Caliphs and Crusaders

THINK ABOUT WHAT YOU KNOW

Imagine that you had an opportunity to be part of the First Crusade. Why would or would you not decide to go?

STUDY THE VOCABULARY

caliph   **sultan**

FOCUS YOUR READING

What brought about the crusades, and what were the results?

A. The Empire of the Caliphs

Abu-Bakr When Muhammad fled Mecca, he was accompanied by his faithful friend Abu-Bakr (ah boo-BAH kur). After Muhammad's death in 632, his followers chose Abu-Bakr as the **caliph** (KAY lihf) of Muhammad. The title *caliph* means "one who comes after." The caliphs acted as religious and political leaders. They used the Koran as the basis for ruling the empire.

Abu-Bakr was a modest man. He is reported to have told the people who chose him caliph,

> *Obey me only so far as I obey God and the prophet [Muhammad]. If I go beyond these bounds, I have no authority over you. If I am wrong, set me right.*

Omar When Abu-Bakr died, the Muslims chose Omar as the caliph. Omar was another of Muhammad's old companions. He was a stern military leader who declared, "The Arabs are like an unruly camel, but I am he who can keep them on the right path." Omar led the Muslims to victories over their foes, but he warned that their triumphs should not make them lazy.

Muslim Empire Abu-Bakr and Omar were the first of a long line of caliphs. The Arabs, under the leadership of the caliphs, conquered a large empire, as shown by the map on page 387. The empire included all of North Africa and much of the Middle East. The Muslims also conquered all of the Iberian Peninsula, now divided into Spain and Portugal.

Muhammad and the first four caliphs ruled from the city of Medina, which is located in the heart of Arabia. The fifth caliph made the city of Damascus, in Syria, the capital of the Muslim empire. Damascus is believed to be the oldest existing city in the world.

Later caliphs moved the capital farther east to Baghdad, on the Tigris River in Iraq. At both Damascus and Baghdad, the

Abu-Bakr was a close friend and father-in-law to Muhammad.
► What title was Abu-Bakr given after Muhammad's death?

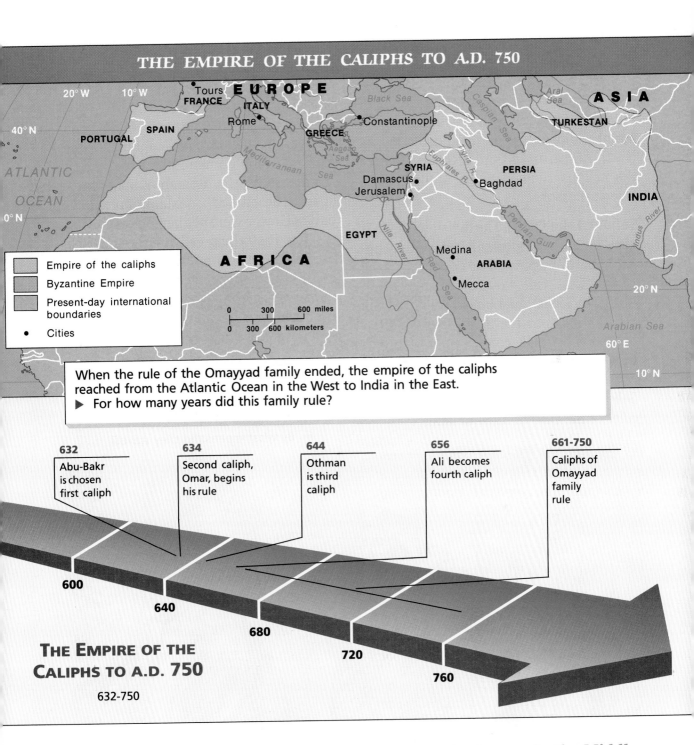

THE EMPIRE OF THE CALIPHS TO A.D. 750

Empire of the caliphs
Byzantine Empire
Present-day international boundaries
• Cities

When the rule of the Omayyad family ended, the empire of the caliphs reached from the Atlantic Ocean in the West to India in the East.
▶ For how many years did this family rule?

632
Abu-Bakr is chosen first caliph

634
Second caliph, Omar, begins his rule

644
Othman is third caliph

656
Ali becomes fourth caliph

661-750
Caliphs of Omayyad family rule

THE EMPIRE OF THE CALIPHS TO A.D. 750
632-750

caliphs built fine palaces. They and the people of their court enjoyed many luxuries. The later caliphs did not copy Omar's simple way of life. They lived more like kings than like successors to a prophet from the desert.

B. The Turks Appear in the Middle East

Caliphs' Rule Ends The lands conquered by the Muslims contained a variety of peoples. Many of these conquered peoples adopted the Muslim religion. Many spoke

Arabic, since this was the language of their conquerors. But the empire of the caliphs did not remain united. Many bitter disputes arose among different groups of Muslims. At one time there were three different caliphs, one in Baghdad, one in North Africa, and a third in Spain. Each of the caliphs claimed to be Muhammad's true successor.

Seljuks Take Over The divisions made it easy for Turkish-speaking tribes from central Asia to migrate, that is, move, to the Middle East. One group of Turks, the Seljuks (SEL jooks), had already adopted the Muslim religion. The Seljuks were skillful fighters who took control of the eastern Muslim lands. They did not replace the caliph at the capital city of Baghdad, but the Seljuk leader called the **sultan** became the ruler of the eastern Muslim lands.

The Seljuks conquered the Anatolian peninsula, which was ruled by the Christian emperor at Constantinople. As you have learned in an earlier chapter, Constantinople became the "new Rome." Constantinople became the capital of what was left of the Roman Empire. During the Middle Ages the Roman Empire broke apart. The city of Constantinople and a part of Greece were all that remained of the empire. Historians call this later Roman Empire the Byzantine Empire.

Turkish-speaking tribes other than the Seljuks migrated into Anatolia. In time the peninsula became known as Turkey —land of the Turks.

Turkish nomadic tribes known as the Seljuks migrated to western Asia. Their advance marked the start of Turkish power in the Middle East.
▶ By what means did they travel?

C. The Call for a Holy War

A Plea for Help After the Seljuk conquest of Anatolia, the Christian emperor at Constantinople sent a message to the pope at Rome asking for help. The emperor probably wanted trained fighting men to help his armies win back lost territory. But Pope Urban II, who received the appeal, had a much more far-reaching plan. The pope wanted to send an army to conquer and rescue from the Muslims the Holy Land, that is, the land where Jesus had lived. Above all, the pope wanted the Christians to capture the Holy City of Jerusalem.

In 1095, Pope Urban called on the knights of western Europe to join in a war against the Muslims. This war was the first of a series of wars that were later called Crusades—wars for the cross—between European Christians and Muslims in the Middle East. The pope declared,

> *It would be far better for the warlike knights of Europe to fight Muslims in the Middle East than to cut each other in pieces in wars at home.*

The pope charged that the Muslim Turks robbed and tortured Christian pilgrims journeying to the Holy Land. He said that Christian knights would win great glory by rescuing the Holy City from the Muslims. They could also win great wealth in the eastern lands. The Holy Land was "fruitful above others." The pope pointed out that the Bible called it a land "flowing with milk and honey."

People's Crusade Even before feudal lords and knights could organize an army, many people in western Europe answered Pope Urban's call for help. These people organized the People's Crusade and started for the Holy Land. The People's

Pope Urban II and Peter the Hermit preach to the crowd about going to war with the Muslims.
▶ How would you describe the reaction of the crowd?

Crusade was a crowd, not an army. Most of those who started for the Middle East were not trained fighters. Few of these crusaders had weapons or knew anything about warfare. The result was a disaster. Most of the first wave of crusaders were killed or captured.

D. European Colonies in the Middle East

First Crusade The official army of the First Crusade made up of knights and feudal lords reached Constantinople in 1097. Two years later, in 1099, the crusaders captured Jerusalem.

The fighting between Christians and Muslims was fierce, and neither side showed mercy. When the crusaders took

Jerusalem, they killed not only fighting men but also many of the women and children. A French priest who accompanied the crusaders later wrote, "War is not beautiful. It is hateful to the innocent and horrible to see."

The crusaders conquered a strip of territory along the eastern Mediterranean shore. There they established four colonies. The crusader colonies were governed like the feudal states in Europe. The largest state, which included the Holy City, was the kingdom of Jerusalem. Two colonies, Edessa and Tripoli, were called counties because they were ruled by counts. Antioch (AN tee ahk) had a prince, so it was a principality. Locate these four colonies on the map below.

Learning New Customs In their colonies the crusaders met people who had different customs and fashions than their own. At first these customs seemed strange, but in time many of the Europeans adopted some of the ways of the Middle East. Those who remained in the conquered lands began to dress in the Middle Eastern fashion. Some crusaders even learned to speak Arabic.

Crusaders who returned home had acquired a taste for Middle Eastern foods, particularly those sweetened with sugar and seasoned with spices. They took back to Europe fine cloth and swords manufactured in the workshops of the east. As Europeans learned more about the products of the Middle East, trade increased. Merchants from such Italian cities as Venice prospered through this trade.

E. Later Crusades

Second Crusade Western Europeans sent later Crusades to the Middle East to support their overseas colonies. When the Muslims recaptured the county of Edessa in 1144, the Second Crusade was organized. This time a fiery monk aroused support for the Crusade. He called upon Christians in France and Germany to leave their homes and go fight for their faith. Many did so, including the kings of France and Germany. Many of those crusaders who left on the Second Crusade never returned home. Both the French and German armies of crusaders were badly beaten by the Muslims.

The First Crusade had succeeded partly because the Muslims were divided. The situation was quite different a half

CRUSADER COLONIES IN THE MIDDLE EAST A.D. 1140

Black Sea
Constantinople
BYZANTINE EMPIRE
EMPIRE OF THE SELJUKS
Tigris River
KINGDOM OF ARMENIA
COUNTY OF EDESSA
• Edessa
Antioch
PRINCIPALITY OF ANTIOCH
Euphrates River
CYPRUS
COUNTY OF TRIPOLI
Tripoli
Mediterranean Sea
SULTANATE OF DAMASCUS
Damascus
KINGDOM OF JERUSALEM
Jerusalem

Crusader colonies
• Cities
0   100   200 miles
0   100   200 kilometers

One crusader colony, the county of Edessa, was not located along the Mediterranean Sea.
► To which two rivers did Edessa have direct access?

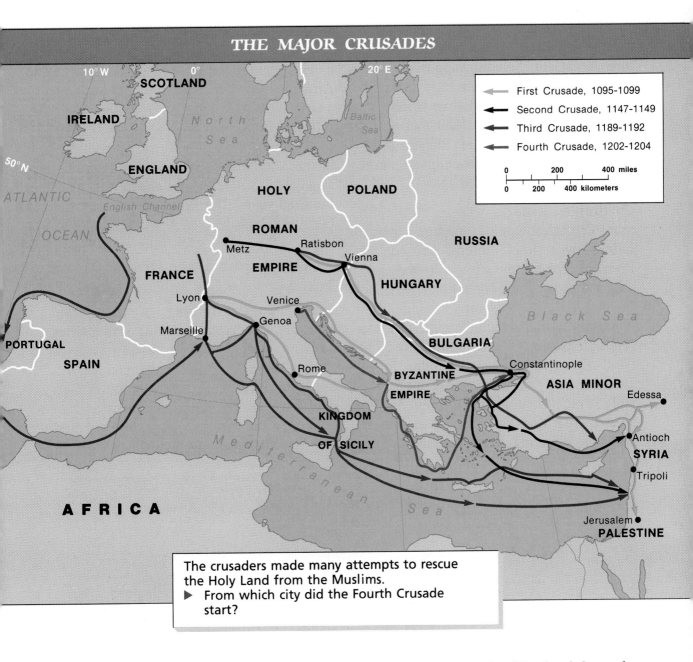

THE MAJOR CRUSADES

First Crusade, 1095–1099
Second Crusade, 1147–1149
Third Crusade, 1189–1192
Fourth Crusade, 1202–1204

The crusaders made many attempts to rescue the Holy Land from the Muslims.
▶ From which city did the Fourth Crusade start?

century later. A remarkable leader named Saladin (SAL uh dihn) had succeeded in uniting the Muslims under his rule. Like the Christian crusaders, Saladin believed that war for the faith was right. In 1187, Saladin's army captured Jerusalem.

Third Crusade News of the fall of Jerusalem shocked Europeans at home. Three kings, Frederick I of Germany, Philip II of France, and Richard I of England, formed a Third Crusade. Richard, well-known for his bravery in battle, was called Richard the Lion-Hearted.

Christians, although winning some battles, could not recapture Jerusalem. Richard and Saladin agreed to make peace for at least five years. Saladin still held the Holy City, but it was agreed that Christians were free to visit their shrines.

391

Richard sailed for Europe promising that he would return in five years to capture Jerusalem. Saladin supposedly said that if he ever did lose the city, he would rather lose it to Richard than to anyone else. But the two rulers never met again. Saladin died within a year. Richard faced so many problems at home that he never undertook another Crusade.

Children's Crusade There were still other Crusades. One of the strangest and saddest was the Children's Crusade. A French shepherd boy named Stephen and a German boy named Nicholas called upon the children to set out on a Crusade. Stephen said he had a vision in which he was told that children might capture the Holy Land through love rather than force. Thousands of girls and boys set out for the Holy Land, although most of them had no idea where it was. They made their way to seaports, thinking that someone would take them to Jerusalem. Some slave merchants promised to do so, but instead they carried them to the slave markets in North Africa. Few of the children who set out on a Crusade to conquer the Holy Land ever returned home.

In spite of later Crusades, the colonies in the Middle East were finally lost. The Muslims captured the last one in 1291, two hundred years after Pope Urban called for the First Crusade.

F. The Empire of the Ottoman Turks

Fall of Constantinople At about the time the last crusader colony was lost in 1291, a young Turkish warrior named Osman married a beautiful woman known as "Moon Bright." The descendants of that couple replaced the Seljuk Turks as the rulers of the Muslims. Those descendants are known as the Ottoman Turks. The

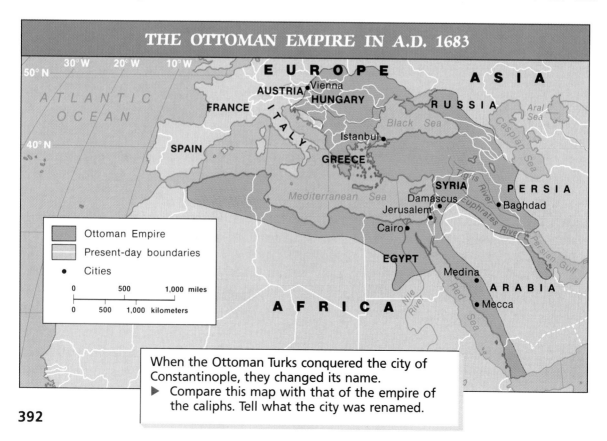

THE OTTOMAN EMPIRE IN A.D. 1683

When the Ottoman Turks conquered the city of Constantinople, they changed its name.
▶ Compare this map with that of the empire of the caliphs. Tell what the city was renamed.

The conquest of Constantinople left much of the city in ruins.
▶ How was the city of Constantinople destroyed?

Ottoman Turks were to build one of the largest and longest-lasting empires of all time.

One of the Ottoman sultans conquered the city of Constantinople in 1453. With the fall of the "city of Constantine," the Christian Byzantine Empire came to an end. The Muslim Ottoman conqueror changed the city's name from Constantinople to Istanbul.

Suleiman In 1517 the Ottoman sultan claimed the title of caliph—successor to Muhammad. One of the greatest leaders of the Ottoman Turks was Suleiman (soo lay-MAHN) the Magnificent—magnificent because of his great riches and power. Suleiman ruled not only much of the Middle East and North Africa but also a good part of southeastern Europe. During the reign of Suleiman, the Black Sea was a Turkish lake; that is, the Turks ruled almost all of its shores.

Ottoman power reached its greatest extent in Suleiman's time, but the Ottoman sultans continued in power for many years. Not until 1922 was the last descendant of Osman and Moon Bright forced from the throne when a group of army officers took over the government.

G. The Armenians

Invading Armenia In ancient time the region around Mount Ararat formed the kingdom of Armenia. It consisted of land that now forms parts of the countries of Turkey and Iran, and the former Soviet Union. A king of Armenia adopted Christianity in A.D. 301, making it the first Christian kingdom in the Middle East.

About 700 years later the Seljuk Turks invaded Armenia. The independent kingdom of Armenia disappeared, but the Armenian people survived. Even after the Turkish conquest of the Middle East, the

From 1894 to 1918 the Turks made many attacks on the Armenian people.
▶ By looking at this etching, what can you tell about the advantages the Turks had over the Armenians?

Armenians remained in their mountain homeland, holding onto their language and their Christian religion.

Armenian Massacres In the 1890s the Ottoman sultan became alarmed by the growth of national unity among the Armenians. Attacks were made on the Armenians in Turkey. Thousands were killed in what are known as the Armenian massacres. During the early part of World War I, many Armenians welcomed the Russian invasion of Turkey. The Ottoman government in turn drove Armenians from their homes. Again, many lost their lives. Most Armenians fled Turkey, so few remained in the ancient homeland near Mount Ararat. Many migrated to the Russian empire. When the Communists formed the Soviet Union, the Armenian territory within the Russian empire became the Armenian Soviet Socialist Republic. In 1991, this republic became the independent nation of Armenia.

LESSON 2 REVIEW

THINK AND WRITE

A. What lands were included in the empire of the caliphs?

B. Why were the Turks able to migrate to the Middle East?

C. Why did Pope Urban II call for a holy war?

D. What did the crusaders learn from the colonies they established in the Middle East?

E. What were the results of the later Crusades?

F. What changes took place during the rule of the Ottoman Turks?

G. What happened to the Armenians who lived within the Ottoman Empire?

SKILLS CHECK

WRITING SKILL

Imagine that you and some of your friends had joined the Children's Crusade. Write a paragraph or two describing your journey.

Art and Learning in the Muslim Lands

THINK ABOUT WHAT YOU KNOW

List the numbers from 1 to 10, using our system of Arabic numerals and then using Roman numerals.

STUDY THE VOCABULARY

calligraphy   **minaret**
mosque

FOCUS YOUR READING

What are the contributions of the people of North Africa and the Middle East?

A. Preserving the Learning of the Greeks

The Arabic language spread with the Muslim religion. Arabic was the language of the Koran and the language of the Muslim rulers. Students throughout the caliph's empire who wanted to get ahead in the world learned the Arabic language. As you have already read in an earlier chapter, Arabic became the language of many of the Middle Eastern and North African countries.

Arabic-speaking Muslims realized that there was much of value written in other languages, particularly in Greek. In order to preserve the learning of the Greeks, Muslim rulers encouraged the translation of Greek books into Arabic.

The caliph at Baghdad established a House of Wisdom, where the work of translation was carried on. The translations made it possible for Muslims to study the works of Greek philosophers, such as Plato and Aristotle, as well as the Koran. Muslim philosophers wrote books about

Greek thinkers that were later studied by Christians in Europe. Some Greek writings that were no longer known in Europe would have been lost had they not been translated into Arabic.

B. The Numerals Borrowed from India

Muslim traders and travelers visited India, and they discovered that the people of that land possessed valuable learning. A poet of Baghdad wrote that there were two things of which the Indians were justly proud: the game of chess and a numeral system that made use of zero.

One can write any number, no matter how large, with the ten digits of the Indian numeral system. It is far more convenient than the Roman system of numerals.

Arabic scholars learned from Greek writings.
▶ For what purpose was the House of Wisdom established?

COMPARING NUMERALS

Modern	Arabic	Greek	Roman	Chinese	Hindi
1	١	I	I	一	१
2	٢	II	II	二	२
3	٣	III	III	三	३
4	٤	IIII	IV	四	४
5	٥	Γ	V	五	५
6	٦	ΓI	VI	六	६
7	٧	ΓII	VII	七	७
8	٨	ΓIII	VIII	八	८
9	٩	ΓIIII	IX	九	९
10	١٠	△	X	十	१०

There are many similarities among the numerals shown in this table.

► Which numeral systems represented the number ten in the same way as the modern system does?

Arabic-speaking Muslims adopted the convenient system of Indian numerals, and Europeans later borrowed it from them. Because Europeans learned of these numerals from Arabic-speaking people, they called them Arabic numerals. You are familiar with these numerals. They are used in numbering the pages of this book.

Our way of writing the numerals differs somewhat from the Arabic form, as you can see by the chart on this page. It is easy to recognize the Arabic way of writing 1, 9, and 11. The 10 is simple once you understand that a point or dot is used for zero. How do you think 90 or 100 would be written in the Arabic script?

The system of Arabic—or Indian—numerals was one of the world's most important inventions. The system is so useful that it has been adopted all over the world. One historian calls it "the only real universal language."

C. Mathematics and Science Among the Muslims

Studying Math The name *Omar Khayyám* (kye YAHM) means "Omar the Tentmaker." But he is not remembered today for his tents—if indeed, he ever made any. Omar Khayyam is known as a poet. He was not only a poet but also an astronomer who studied the movements of the stars and other heavenly bodies. He also wrote an important book on algebra, a field of mathematics. The word *algebra* comes from Arabic. Arabic-speaking Muslims did much to develop this field during the Middle Ages.

As an astronomer, Omar Khayyám changed the Persian calendar.
► What tools and materials is he working with?

396

Studying Science Muslims also studied a number of sciences, particularly chemistry. It has been said that they originated this field of science. A sign of their influence is found in the number of Arabic words used in chemistry. For example, *alcohol* and *alkali* are Arabic words.

Studying Medicine The Christian crusaders reported that the Muslim doctors were more skillful than those from Europe in caring for wounds and setting broken bones. Muslim physicians had studied medicine by learning from the Greeks, but they also learned through their own observations. By carefully observing the symptoms, or signs, of a disease, Muslim physicians were able to identify diseases more accurately.

In about A.D. 900, a Muslim doctor learned by observation that smallpox and measles were different diseases. He wrote the first book in the world describing these diseases. Muslims also discovered that once a person had had the disease smallpox, he or she became immune to the disease, that is, the person would not get it again. Another doctor observed the diseases of the eye and wrote about them. Both of these books were translated into Latin and studied in western Europe. Careful observations also made it possible to discover the effects of different plants and other medicines in the treatment of diseases.

D. Handwriting as a Fine Art

Calligraphy (kuh LIHG ruh fee) is the art of beautiful handwriting. The Muslim belief that the Koran was a holy book encouraged the development of this art.

Pages from the Koran are decorated with borders and beautiful writing.
▶ What is the art of beautiful writing called?

The Granger Collection

Muslims believed that no other art could be so great as the making of beautiful copies of the Koran, which they held to be the word of God.

Copying the Koran was a religious act somewhat like saying a prayer or going on a pilgrimage. One man made 42 copies of the whole Koran. He worked with great care, using costly inks of different colors. He made one copy entirely in gold. The copies were not given to others to read but instead stored safely in a chest. The man had copied the Koran in order to show how much he loved the words of the holy book. When he died, all 42 copies were buried with him.

Calligraphers took as much care in writing a page as painters do in producing fine pictures. They used the finest materials and decorated the pages. The hand-copied books were bound in fine leather that was often decorated with gold, silver, and precious stones. Among the Muslims a beautifully copied book was considered a truly great work of art.

E. How the Muslim Religion Affected Other Arts

Decorating Buildings The Muslim religion affected other arts too. Strict Muslims believed it was wrong to make a picture or statue of any living thing. This rule was not in the Koran but came from an old account of Muhammad's teachings. It was said that the prophet had spoken against the making of pictures. He was supposed to have said that no one should try to copy what God has made.

Because of the rule against pictures, artists used other ways to decorate buildings and the things people used. Of course, words from the Koran could be placed on the walls of Muslim places of worship, called **mosques** (mahsks). Artists covered both inside and outside walls of buildings with colorful designs like those used in jewelry and pottery.

Carpets Carpetmaking was an important art in the Middle East. Carpets could be made with patterns that did not look like any living thing. Carpets are made by tying threads tightly together by hand. A carpet maker ties up to 320 knots for each square inch of carpet.

People in the Middle East sometimes used carpets in place of furniture. They sat on cushions or low carpet-covered platforms. Carpets covered the floors of mosques, which had no benches or seats. Instead worshipers sat and kneeled on the carpets. Before worshipers or visitors entered a mosque, they removed their shoes or sandals.

Mosques Mosques and religious shrines were among the most important buildings erected by the Muslims. Except for the Kaaba, the oldest existing shrine is the Dome of the Rock in Jerusalem. It was

This Persian carpet, woven in Tabriz, Iran, is characterized by flowing patterns that feature flowers and leaves.
► For what purposes are carpets used in the Middle East?

The Dome of the Rock is Jerusalem's holiest Muslim shrine.
▶ How is the shape of this shrine different from that of the Kaaba?

completed 1,300 years ago, and its gilded dome is still seen atop a hill in the old city.

Mosques did not have bell towers like those of many Christian churches. Instead, there were tall and slender towers with balconies, called **minarets**, where people would call others to prayer every day.

In spite of the rule against pictures, some artists did make paintings of living things. Particularly in Iran and Turkey, artists painted pictures not only of animals and plants but also of people. Even the strictest religious beliefs did not affect all of the arts.

LESSON **3** REVIEW

THINK AND WRITE

A. How did the Muslims preserve the learning of the Greeks?

B. Why are the numerals we use called Arabic?

C. What developments did the Muslims make in math, science, and medicine?

D. How did the Muslim religion encourage the development of handwriting as an art?

E. How did the Muslim religious beliefs affect other arts?

SKILLS CHECK

THINKING SKILL

Divide a sheet of paper into two columns, leaving space to the left of the columns. On the top of the paper, label one column *Arts* and the other column *Sciences.* Then skim through the lesson and list the contributions of the Muslims on the left side of the paper. Place a check in the column in which each contribution belongs.

USING THE VOCABULARY

shrine   caliph
prophets   minarets
pilgrimage

On a separate sheet of paper, write the word from above that best completes each of the sentences.

1. Muhammad's followers made Abu-Bakr the first _____ since he was the first "one who came after" Muhammad.
2. The _____ in Jerusalem is considered a holy place by Christians, Muslims, and Jews.
3. People throughout the world make a _____, or journey, to a religious site.
4. Mosques have tall and slender towers, or _____, instead of bell towers like those of many Christian churches.
5. The angel told Muhammad that he was the last of the _____, or religious leaders who speak out against wrongdoing and warn that punishments will come to those who break God's laws.

REMEMBERING WHAT YOU READ

On a separate sheet of paper, answer the following questions in complete sentences.

1. What is the Kaaba?
2. Who founded the Islamic religion?
3. What is the holy book of the Muslims?
4. What is the journey called that Muhammad made from Mecca to Medina?
5. What were the series of wars between European Christians and Muslims in the Middle East called?
6. Who built one of the largest and longest-lasting empires of all time?
7. What was the name of the city of Constantinople changed to after it was conquered by the Ottoman Turks?
8. What system did the Europeans borrow from the Arabic-speaking Muslims?
9. What field of science is believed to have been originated by the Muslims?
10. What are Muslim places of worship called?

TYING ART TO SOCIAL STUDIES

Muslims used calligraphy, a beautiful form of handwriting, to copy the Koran. They believed that a copied book was truly a great work of art. Look in an encyclopedia to find our alphabet written in calligraphy or look in the library for a book on calligraphy. Then copy a page from a book, newspaper, or magazine, using calligraphy. Be creative by using your imagination and different-colored inks to decorate the page.

THINKING CRITICALLY

On a separate sheet of paper, answer the following in complete sentences.

1. The Koran is the holy book for the Muslims. What are some holy books that are important to people of other religions?
2. Omar, the second caliph, said, "The Arabs are like an unruly camel, but I am he who can keep them on the right path." What did he mean by that?
3. Pope Urban II pointed out that the Bible called the Holy Land a land "flowing with milk and honey." What do you think that meant?
4. In your opinion, why did children join the Children's Crusade?
5. Muslims worship in mosques. What are some places of worship for other religions?

SUMMARIZING THE CHAPTER

On a separate sheet of paper, draw a graphic organizer like the one shown here. Copy the information from this graphic organizer on the one you have drawn. Under each main idea write three phrases that support it.

CHAPTER THEME

The Middle East has had an important place in the world's history not only because of the universal contributions its people have made but also because it was the birthplace of world religions.

LESSON 1

The Muslim religion began about 1,400 years ago.

1. _____
2. _____
3. _____

LESSON 2

The Crusades brought about many results.

1. _____
2. _____
3. _____

LESSON 3

The people of the Middle East and North Africa have made many contributions.

1. _____
2. _____
3. _____

15 THE MIDDLE EAST AND NORTH AFRICA TODAY

*F*requent conflicts threaten the region of the Middle East and North Africa. Oil has made a number of the countries in this region wealthy in recent years.

Iran, Iraq, and Afghanistan

THINK ABOUT WHAT YOU KNOW

Explain how you would feel if there were a dress code, or a law, in this country that stated what kind of clothing you could and could not wear. How could a law like that be good or bad?

STUDY THE VOCABULARY

shah	embassy
modernize	ambassador
mullah	hostage
ayatollah	crude oil

FOCUS YOUR READING

How is the recent history of the Middle East a continuation of many years of problems?

A. The Scorpion and the Frog: A Tale of the Middle East

A scorpion and a frog met on the banks of the Jordan River. The scorpion, who could not swim, asked the frog to carry him across the river to the other side.

The frog said, "Absolutely not! If I carry you on my back, you might sting me." The scorpion reassured the frog, "If I sting you while we are crossing the river, we will both drown."

The frog thought that the scorpion's argument made sense. Surely the two of them could work together. At last the frog agreed to help the scorpion.

Halfway across the river, the scorpion suddenly stung the frog. As they both started to sink beneath the water, the frog croaked, "Why did you do that? Now we are both going to die." The scorpion sighed and said, "Oh, well, that's life in the Middle East!"

This legendary tale suggests that the nations in the Middle East often find it difficult to get along with one another. Even though they may have many things in common, both old and new rivalries have often led to violence. The Middle East today is one of the most dangerously explosive areas in the world.

B. Two Revolutions in Iran

New Ways of Living The first revolution in Iran happened in 1921, shortly after World War I, when an army officer named Reza Khan overthrew the government. After Reza Khan was declared **shah**, or king, he announced that Iran must **modernize** — that is, adopt up-to-date ways of living. The new shah believed that his people must copy Western ways of thinking. He was convinced that the Muslim religious teachers, known as **mullahs**, encouraged people to cling to their old-fashioned ways. To lessen the influence of the mullahs, the shah established government schools to take the place of religious schools.

When Reza Khan's son, Muhammad Reza Pahlavi, took his father's place as shah, he pushed modernization even faster. He decided that the small villages where most people lived were far too small to have the benefits of modernization. He ordered that many villages be torn down in order to force the people to move to larger and better places.

Things changed very rapidly as a result of the first revolution in Iran. The shah proudly boasted that there had not been so much change in 3,000 years. However, some people did not think that the changes were all for the better.

The mullahs declared that the government schools weakened religion. Even some of the people who favored modernization disliked the shah's undemocratic methods. The shah had secret police who kept close watch on people. Those who spoke out against the government often ended up in prison.

The Second Revolution In 1979, discontent grew so strong that the shah was forced to give up the throne and flee the country. The leader of the revolution was a mullah named Ruhollah Khomeini (roo-HOH luh koh MAY nee), who was often called the **ayatollah** (eye yuh TOH luh), an honorary title for a religious leader in Iran.

C. The Islamic Republic of Iran

Islamic Ways After the revolution in 1979, Iran became an Islamic republic — that is, a government based on the Muslim religion. It had an assembly with a president and prime minister, but final authority rested with the chief religious official. Ayatollah Khomeini was chosen as chief religious official for life.

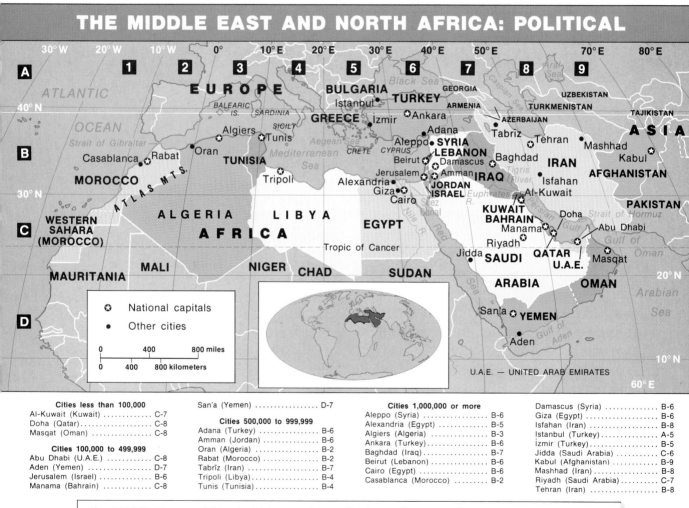

THE MIDDLE EAST AND NORTH AFRICA: POLITICAL

Cities less than 100,000	
Al-Kuwait (Kuwait)	C-7
Doha (Qatar)	C-8
Masqat (Oman)	C-8

Cities 100,000 to 499,999	
Abu Dhabi (U.A.E.)	C-8
Aden (Yemen)	D-7
Jerusalem (Israel)	B-6
Manama (Bahrain)	C-8

San'a (Yemen)	D-7

Cities 500,000 to 999,999	
Adana (Turkey)	B-6
Amman (Jordan)	B-6
Oran (Algeria)	B-2
Rabat (Morocco)	B-2
Tabriz (Iran)	B-7
Tripoli (Libya)	B-4
Tunis (Tunisia)	B-4

Cities 1,000,000 or more	
Aleppo (Syria)	B-6
Alexandria (Egypt)	B-5
Algiers (Algeria)	B-3
Ankara (Turkey)	B-6
Baghdad (Iraq)	B-7
Beirut (Lebanon)	B-6
Cairo (Egypt)	B-6
Casablanca (Morocco)	B-2

Damascus (Syria)	B-6
Giza (Egypt)	B-6
Isfahan (Iran)	B-8
Istanbul (Turkey)	A-5
İzmir (Turkey)	B-5
Jidda (Saudi Arabia)	C-6
Kabul (Afghanistan)	B-9
Mashhad (Iran)	B-8
Riyadh (Saudi Arabia)	C-7
Tehran (Iran)	B-8

The Middle East and North Africa are located where three continents come together.
▶ What three continents intersect to form the Middle East and North Africa?

In 1979, revolutionary supporters of the Ayatollah Khomeini seized the American embassy in Tehran, Iran.
▶ Who, do you think, is pictured on their signs?

In the Islamic republic, the mullahs supervised all education. Boys and girls attended separate classes. Students entering the universities had to pass a test on the Muslim religion. Rules laid down by the mullahs regulated all parts of life. Neither alcohol nor Western-style music was allowed. Men could not wear T-shirts, short-sleeved shirts, or neckties. Women and girls had to wear long dark garments that covered their hair and body. Anyone suspected of opposing the Islamic republic was severely punished.

The Iranian Islamic Republic did not have good relations with other countries. The ayatollah constantly attacked the United States in speeches. In November of 1979 the Iranian government permitted a group of revolutionaries to take over the American **embassy** in Tehran, the capital. An embassy is where **ambassadors** and their staffs live and work. Ambassadors are officials who represent their governments in foreign countries. The Iranians held more than 50 Americans as **hostages** for more than a year. A hostage is a person held captive until demands of the captor are met. Negotiations between the United States and Iran finally ended the hostage crisis in 1981.

Iran-Iraq War The United States was not the only country that Iran and the ayatollah had conflicts with. In 1980 Iran became involved in a costly war with the neighboring country of Iraq. The war began because of a dispute about the border. Many people, including many children, lost their lives in this struggle. In 1988, Iran and Iraq finally accepted a United Nations plan to end the war. The next year, the Ayatollah Khomeini died at age 89, and a struggle began to see who would lead Iran. Hashemi Rafsanjani (hah SHAYM ee rahf-sahn JAH nee) was elected president of that country in August of 1989.

405

D. People and Resources of Iran

Population The population of Iran has grown very rapidly in recent years. Even the war with Iraq did not slow the increase, partly because the war brought in large numbers of refugees from Iraq. Iran also received refugees fleeing from another war in the neighboring country of Afghanistan.

Most of Iran's people live in the northern and western parts of the country, near Tehran. The central region is sparsely populated, because salt deserts cover much of the land.

Land and Resources Iran has long seacoasts. One third of the country's boundaries are formed by the Caspian Sea, Persian Gulf, and the Arabian Sea, which is part of the Indian Ocean. Find the country of Iran on the map below.

Only about one tenth of Iran's land is arable, and much of this must be irrigated to grow crops. At one time Iran produced most of its own food. But the population has grown so much more rapidly than the food supply that the country depends partly on imports.

Iran's great wealth lies in its **crude oil** and natural gas deposits. Crude oil is oil that is found in its natural state — that is, oil that has not been refined, or purified. The war with Iraq greatly affected oil production, yet Iran remained the second largest producer in the Middle East. Iran also has valuable mineral deposits of copper, chromium, and coal.

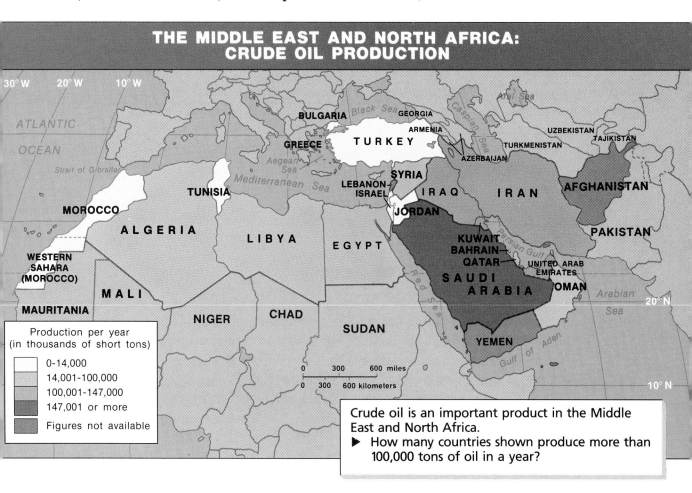

THE MIDDLE EAST AND NORTH AFRICA: CRUDE OIL PRODUCTION

Production per year
(in thousands of short tons)

	0-14,000
	14,001-100,000
	100,001-147,000
	147,001 or more
	Figures not available

Crude oil is an important product in the Middle East and North Africa.
▶ How many countries shown produce more than 100,000 tons of oil in a year?

E. Iraq Today

Oil and a Dictator   Modern Iraq includes ancient Mesopotamia, which you learned about as the land of early civilizations. The people of Mesopotamia depended on the waters of the Tigris and Euphrates rivers. So do the people of Iraq today. The rivers make it possible to irrigate the fields that produce beans, grains, and vegetables. But in recent years Iraq has depended on the sale of oil abroad.

Iraq is a republic, but it has only one political party. Saddam Hussein (sah DAHM hoo SAYN), who became president in 1979, rules as a military dictator. He built up a large army and used it to wage a war against Iran. The war dragged on for eight years and cost many lives.

The Persian Gulf War   The war with Iran left Iraq with enormous debts. Saddam needed funds to maintain the army, which he used to control his country. Neighboring Kuwait, on the Persian Gulf, is a very wealthy land. It has far fewer people than Iraq but nearly twice as much oil. Saddam declared that Kuwait had been wrongfully separated from Iraq after World War I. According to him, this oil-rich land was part of Iraq. On August 2, 1990, Iraqi troops invaded Kuwait and began taking over the country.

The United States and most other countries in the United Nations condemned Iraq's invasion. The United States and a number of other countries sent armed forces to the Persian Gulf. The United Nations repeatedly ordered Iraq to withdraw from Kuwait, but Saddam refused. On January 17, 1991, the United States and its allies began air raids on Iraq. Large ground forces attacked Iraq on February 23. It took the allies about 100

The Khyber pass is a major link between Afghanistan and Pakistan.
▶ Why, do you think, could travel on this pass be dangerous?

hours to defeat the Iraqi army. This was one of the shortest wars in history.

Before the Iraqi forces fled from Kuwait, they set fire to hundreds of oil wells. Firefighters from the United States and other countries were able to put these fires out more quickly than was expected. However, these oil fires have caused considerable damage to the environment.

Iraq suffered much during the Persian Gulf War and during the months that followed. Revolts broke out against the government. Saddam used what was left of his army to suppress these revolts.

F. Mountainous Afghanistan

Land and Resources   In ancient times the land routes across Asia from the Middle East passed through Afghanistan. One route led to China, in the Far East. Another led south to India, through the Khyber Pass. The caravans found it difficult crossing the mountainous country of Afghanistan. Even today, travel is not easy here. Afghanistan has no railroad. There are, however, some modern roads.

Afghanistan is a landlocked country—that is, it has no outlet to the sea. Almost the whole country is at an altitude of at least 2,000 feet (610 m). The Hindu Kush mountains rise much higher. Kabul, the capital, is more than a mile (2 km) above sea level. Throughout their history, the people of Afghanistan have depended on farming small plots of land. They also kept herds of cattle, goats, and sheep.

A Bloody War In 1979, a Communist group seized control of the government of Afghanistan. The Soviet Union sent troops to support the takeover. A bloody war broke out between the Soviet army and Afghans who opposed the Communists. Many people were driven from their homes and fled to Pakistan and Iran. After ten years of costly war, the Soviet troops withdrew. In 1991, in an effort to discourage further fighting in Afghanistan, the United States and the Soviet Union agreed to stop all military aid to either side. In 1992 Afghanistan's communist government collapsed. An alliance of rebels took power.

The Soviets had far better equipment and weapons than the Afghan soldiers.
► What weapon does this soldier have to protect himself?

Today the search for a just peace in all the countries of the Middle East continues. In 1991, the United States and the Soviet Union sponsored a Middle East peace conference in Madrid, Spain. Peace talks in Washington, D.C., and Moscow followed.

LESSON *1* REVIEW

THINK AND WRITE

A. What does the tale of the scorpion and the frog suggest about life in the Middle East?

B. What changes resulted because of the first revolution in Iran?

C. How did life in Iran change after the second revolution?

D. How did the war with Iraq affect Iran's population and resources?

E. How did the results of the Iran-Iraq War lead eventually to the Persian Gulf War?

F. What are some geographic features of Afghanistan?

SKILLS CHECK

THINKING SKILL

Make a time line for the period from 1975 to 1991. Show the following events: Ayatollah starts revolution in Iran; War breaks out between Afghanistan and Soviet Union; War breaks out between Iran and Iraq; Soviets withdraw troops from Afghanistan; the Persian Gulf War.

THINK ABOUT WHAT YOU KNOW
Israel has had many leaders throughout its history. What leaders can you name from ancient Israel?

STUDY THE VOCABULARY
Knesset   **fez**

FOCUS YOUR READING
What political and economic changes have taken place in Israel and Turkey since World War I?

A. The Creation of Modern Israel

Many Rulers   General Yigael Yadin was a leader in Israel's war of independence, in 1948. General Yadin was also an enthusiastic archaeologist, because he believed that ancient remains provided a link between modern Israel and the kingdoms of David and Solomon. As a soldier, Yadin helped win modern Israel's independence. As an archaeologist, he uncovered the remains of the city that Solomon had built in ancient Israel.

The region known today as Israel has had many rulers during its long history. When it was part of the Roman Empire, the Romans called the area *Palestine*. Then Arab caliphs and Ottoman sultans ruled the region throughout the Middle Ages. Palestine was still a part of the Ottoman Empire when World War I began in 1914.

Since Turkey was on the side of Germany during World War I, the British attacked Turkish-ruled lands in the Middle East. Some of the Arabs, wishing to be free of Turkey, helped the British. In return, the British promised that the Turkish Empire would be broken up. Since the majority of the peoples in the Turkish Empire were Arabs, the Arabs took this promise to mean that they would rule Palestine. But the British also made a promise to the Jews. The British said they supported the creation of a national home for the Jews in Palestine.

After World War I, the British took control of Palestine. At that time most of the inhabitants of Palestine were Arabs. But the number of Jews increased rapidly after Adolf Hitler rose to power in Germany in the 1930s. Many more Jewish settlers arrived after World War II. However, the Arabs in Palestine opposed the growing Jewish settlement.

Israel's Independence   In 1947, following World War II, the United Nations proposed to divide Palestine into two states,

Jews celebrated their independence in Israel in 1948.
▶ What is this girl holding in her right hand?

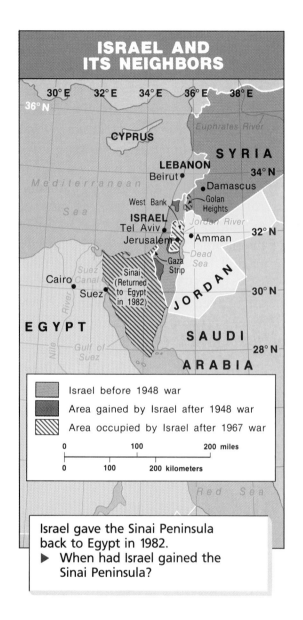

ISRAEL AND ITS NEIGHBORS

Israel before 1948 war

Area gained by Israel after 1948 war

Area occupied by Israel after 1967 war

Israel gave the Sinai Peninsula back to Egypt in 1982.

▶ When had Israel gained the Sinai Peninsula?

B. A Modern Country in an Ancient Land

Industry and Resources Israel is a small country—one of the smallest in the Middle East. It is even smaller than the state of Maryland. The southern half of the country, called the Negev, is very dry, but Israelis proudly say that they have "made the desert bloom." Water piped from the north, which has plentiful winter rainfall, is used for irrigation in the Negev. Israeli farmers grow about three fourths of the country's food, and they also produce citrus fruits, avocados, flowers, and other crops for export.

Israel earns more from its industries than does any other Middle Eastern country. Most Israeli industries require skilled workers, such as those who make scientific instruments and electronic equipment and those who cut diamonds. Israel is second only to Belgium in the cutting and polishing of diamonds, an industry that requires highly skilled people. Tourism is also an important industry in Israel. As you have learned, Israel is the Holy Land for Christians and Jews.

Israel is not a country rich in minerals, although it has some copper. There is some oil and natural gas, but not enough to supply the country's needs. The Dead Sea is an important source of minerals, which are used for such products as table salt and fertilizer.

Government Israel is a democratic republic governed by an elected assembly called the **Knesset** (KNES et). The members of the Knesset choose the president and the prime minister. One of the prime ministers, Golda Meir, had studied to be a school teacher in Milwaukee, Wisconsin, before she emigrated to Israel.

one Jewish and one Arab. The Arabs in Palestine and the neighboring Arab countries refused to accept the proposal, but the Jewish state of Israel declared its independence in 1948.

In the year that Israel declared independence, war broke out between Israel and the Arabs. Israel won its war of independence, but victory did not bring peace. There were other Arab-Israeli wars in 1956, 1967, and 1973. Israel won these wars, but there was still no peace agreement.

C. Modernizing Turkey

Abandoning a Custom For nearly a century, men in Turkey wore a type of hat called a **fez,** a felt hat with a flat top and no brim. The custom began when an Ottoman sultan ordered his soldiers and officials to wear fezzes. The lack of brims on fezzes made it easier for Muslim men to touch their foreheads to the ground when they prayed.

In 1925, Mustafa Kemal (MOOS tah-fah ke MAHL), the powerful president of the Turkish republic, appeared wearing a hat with a brim and other Western clothing. The president told all Turkish men that they, too, must wear such hats. To make sure that they did so, Kemal created a law forbidding the wearing of a fez.

The law against fezzes upset many Turks. They said that wearing a brimmed hat showed that a man had given up the Muslim religion. One man avoided wearing a hat by tying bandages about his head as if suffering great pain.

Turkish Women New laws also changed the lives of the women in Turkey. Turkish women wore veils to hide their faces in public places. But Kemal said that veils could no longer be worn.

Kemal wanted Turkish women to change more than the way they dressed. He said that in a modern nation men and women should be equal. In the past, girls in Turkey had not gone to school outside the home. Kemal ordered them to do so. Women got the right to take jobs in business and government. Women also were given the right to vote.

Mustafa Kemal changed the Turkish laws of dress.
▶ How is this woman's clothing different from the traditional clothing of Turkish women?

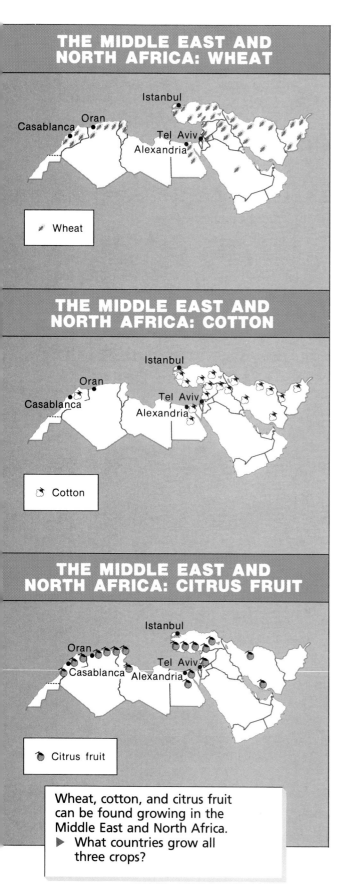

THE MIDDLE EAST AND NORTH AFRICA: WHEAT

Istanbul
Oran
Casablanca
Tel Aviv
Alexandria

✎ Wheat

THE MIDDLE EAST AND NORTH AFRICA: COTTON

Istanbul
Oran
Casablanca
Tel Aviv
Alexandria

🌣 Cotton

THE MIDDLE EAST AND NORTH AFRICA: CITRUS FRUIT

Istanbul
Oran
Casablanca
Tel Aviv
Alexandria

🍊 Citrus fruit

Wheat, cotton, and citrus fruit can be found growing in the Middle East and North Africa.
▶ What countries grow all three crops?

New Laws, New Ways Why all this fuss about fezzes and veils? It was part of the great changes taking place in Turkey after World War I. A revolution had ended the rule of the Ottoman sultans, and Turkey had become a republic. Mustafa Kemal insisted that Turkey do more than change its government. Turkey had to modernize. The fez was a sign of the past. The president thought that changing what men wore *on* their heads would help change what went on *in* their heads.

Adopting Western-style clothing was only one of the changes introduced by Mustafa Kemal. He moved the capital from Istanbul to Ankara. He introduced an alphabet based on the Roman alphabet used for western European languages. Three months after the introduction of the new alphabet, Kemal ordered all newspapers, books, and street signs to be printed in the new style.

D. Land and People of Turkey

Farming and Resources Even though much of the Anatolian peninsula, where Turkey is located, is dry and mountainous, about one third of the land is cultivated. Wheat and cotton are the largest crops, but Turkey also produces other crops such as citrus fruits, olives, and raisin grapes.

Turkey has the largest coal deposits in the Middle East. It also has other minerals, including chromium, which is used in making stainless steel. Turkey leads the world in the production of an unusual mineral called meerschaum (MIHR shum). It is an easily carved material, used mainly for making tobacco pipes.

Population Turkey lies in both Europe and Asia. Only about 3 percent of Turkey is in Europe, but that part includes its largest

Istanbul, Turkey's largest city, has been one of the world's important cities for hundreds of years.
► What building in the photograph symbolizes the city's culture?

city, Istanbul, which you learned used to be Constantinople. Turkey's population is spread unevenly over the Anatolian peninsula. The greater number of people live in western Turkey, and they feel they are more like Europeans than like peoples of the Middle East.

Government Mustafa Kemal came to be called Kemal Ataturk. *Ataturk* means "father of the Turks." His title was President of the Republic; but he was, in fact, a dictator. Although elections were held, only one political party was allowed to run for office.

Mostly because of political unrest, the control of Turkey's government has changed many times over the last five decades, since Ataturk's death in 1938. However, in 1982 a new constitution was adopted. Today the Turkish government is more like a republic of Western Europe, in which voters may choose candidates from among several parties.

LESSON *2* REVIEW

THINK AND WRITE

A. How was the dispute over Palestine after World War I resolved?
B. What are some of the ways the people of Israel make a living?
C. In what ways did Mustafa Kemal modernize Turkey?
D. What are some products produced in Turkey?

SKILLS CHECK

MAP SKILL

Turn to the map Israel and Its Neighbors on page 410, and answer the following questions: What body of water does Israel share with Jordan? What are the names of the three areas that Israel gained after 1967?

413

Other Countries of the Middle East

THINK ABOUT WHAT YOU KNOW

Think of different ways in which we use oil. Then describe why oil is such an important resource.

STUDY THE VOCABULARY

reserve   causeway
nonrenewable resource

FOCUS YOUR READING

What are some of the important characteristics of each of the Arab countries of the Middle East?

A. Jordan and Syria

Jordan   On the northern edge of the Arabian Peninsula are the countries of Jordan and Syria. Jordan was part of the Ottoman Empire before World War I. The British controlled Jordan after the war. Then, in 1928, Jordan gained some control over its own affairs, but Jordan did not get its complete independence until 18 years later, in 1946.

During the 1948 Arab war against Israel, Jordan won territory west of the Jordan River. In 1950 this area, known as the West Bank, became part of Jordan, even though most of the Arab people who lived there called themselves Palestinians. Since 1967, however, all of the West Bank has been under Israel's control. Many of the Arabs who lived on the West Bank fled to Jordan.

Jordan has remained a poor land with very few resources. It has some minerals, but no oil. The removal of minerals from the Dead Sea water is one of the country's important industries.

Only about 5 percent of Jordan's land is arable, yet agriculture is an important occupation. Most of its crops—such as grapes, olives, and citrus fruits—are grown on irrigated land.

Syria   Syria, Jordan's neighbor to the north, has some of the best land in the Middle East. About half of Syria's land is arable. When irrigated, the land produces crops of cotton, wheat, tobacco, and various vegetables. About one fourth of the land in Syria can be used for grazing sheep and goats.

Syria was part of the Ottoman Empire before World War I. France controlled the country between World War I and World War II, but Syria became independent in 1946. Although called a republic, Syria is a one-party state.

Crops such as these chili peppers grow well in the Jordan River valley.
▶ What, do you think, makes the Jordan River valley an important agricultural region?

Years of fighting have left many sections of Beirut in ruins.
▶ How are these people bringing supplies to their homes?

B. Divisions Within Lebanon

Religious Differences Lebanon is a small country—smaller than the state of Connecticut. But in spite of its small size, Lebanon has a varied geography and climate. Winter temperatures along the Mediterranean coast are warmer than those on the French Riviera. And, while basking in the sun on the beach, it is possible to see the snow-covered peaks of the Lebanon Mountains.

Differences in religion have divided the Lebanese people. Part of the population is Christian, and part is Muslim. When Lebanon became independent in 1943, the political offices were divided according to religion. The Christians were then in the majority, so it was agreed that the president would be a Christian and the prime minister, a Muslim. In more recent years, the Muslims say that they have become the majority, so they have demanded more political power.

A Civil War The dispute about the sharing of power led to civil war in the 1970s. Both Christians and Muslims formed fighting forces. The situation was made more difficult by large numbers of Palestinians who fled north during the Arab-Israeli conflict. The Palestinians had their own military forces and bases. Both of the neighboring countries of Syria and Israel became involved in Lebanon.

At one time a peacekeeping force made up of soldiers from the United States, Britain, France, and Italy was sent into the country of Lebanon. In spite of many efforts to make peace, the fighting in Lebanon continues. Thousands of people have been killed, and much property has been destroyed.

C. Saudi Arabia: Oil in the Desert

Land and Resources Saudi Arabia occupies most of the Arabian Peninsula. Even though Saudi Arabia has a very large land area, it has fewer people than the Netherlands. Saudi Arabia is a monarchy ruled by the Saud family, for whom the country is named.

The kingdom of the Saudis is truly a desert country. Only about 1 percent of the land is arable. Another 39 percent can be used by nomadic Bedouins as pasture for goats, sheep, and camels. But beneath the desert are enormous known oil **reserves**. Reserves are supplies of a natural resource that are known to exist but have not yet been used.

Oil is a **nonrenewable resource**— that is, a resource that cannot be replaced. The graphs below show important facts about the earth's known oil reserves. The greater part of these reserves are in the Middle East and North Africa, and Saudi Arabia has the largest reserves in that region. The largest of the Arabian oil fields is also the largest single reserve in the world.

Modernizing Oil has brought great wealth to Saudi Arabia in recent times. Much of the wealth has been used to modernize the country. The government has built modern schools, hospitals, roads, and airports. Some modern industrial plants have been erected, particularly chemical plants and others that make use of oil. The production of petroleum and petroleum products makes up about 70 percent of what Saudi Arabia produces. Look at the chart on page 418 to see some products that are made from petroleum.

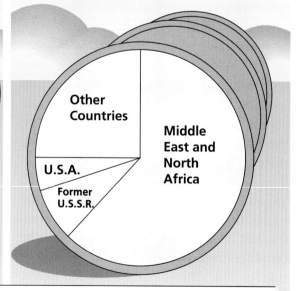

PROVEN OIL RESERVES IN THE MIDDLE EAST AND NORTH AFRICA

Other Countries
Libya
Iraq
Iran
Saudi Arabia
Kuwait

PROVEN OIL RESERVES IN THE WORLD

Other Countries
U.S.A.
Former U.S.S.R.
Middle East and North Africa

Most of the world's oil reserves are in the Middle East and North Africa.

► Which country in the Middle East and North Africa has about the same amount of oil reserves as does the United States, the former Soviet Union, and other countries in the world combined?

Oil has brought wealth to parts of the Middle East. Universities in Saudi Arabia can now buy computers.
▶ How has money helped these schoolchildren in Qatar?

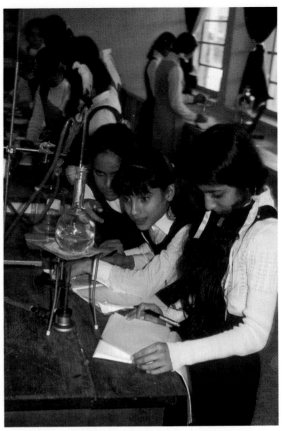

The Saudis also have used some of the money from oil to buy land and businesses in Europe and the United States.

Oil money has brought many other changes in Saudi Arabia. Pickup trucks have replaced camels among the Bedouins. Riyadh (ree YAHD), the capital, has grown into a modern city with over a million people. But the Saudi leaders do not believe that everything should change. As one Saudi official explained, hospitals and new industries are fine, but they cannot take the place of mosques, the Muslim places of worship. According to this official, "The price we will not pay for development is our religion."

D. Persian Gulf States

Kuwait Kuwait, located on the northwest coast of the Persian Gulf, is smaller than the state of New Jersey. Before 1940, pearls from the Persian Gulf were Kuwait's main export. The discovery of oil in the desert made Kuwait one of the world's richest countries.

It has been said that Kuwait has more oil than it has water. At one time, Kuwait had to import water by boat from Iraq. Kuwait has used part of its wealth to build the world's largest plant for changing sea water into fresh water.

The wealth from their country's oil has also been used to provide Kuwaitis with free education and medical care. As you have read, the desire for Kuwait's oil brought about an invasion by Iraq, which resulted in the Persian Gulf War.

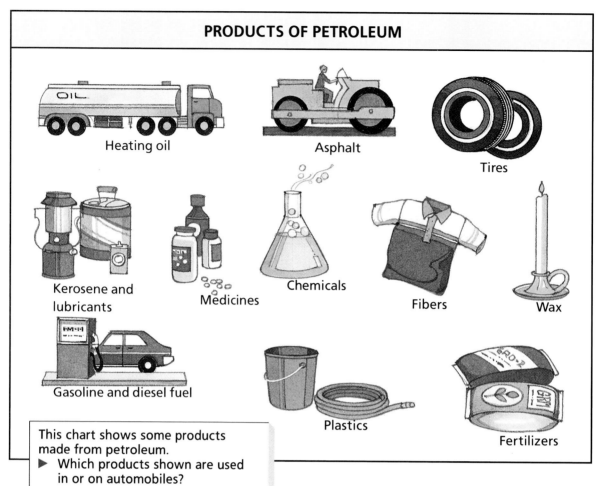

PRODUCTS OF PETROLEUM

Heating oil

Asphalt

Tires

Kerosene and lubricants

Medicines

Chemicals

Fibers

Wax

Gasoline and diesel fuel

Plastics

Fertilizers

This chart shows some products made from petroleum.
► Which products shown are used in or on automobiles?

Qatar and United Arab Emirates Qatar is on a peninsula that extends into the Persian Gulf from the Arabian Peninsula. Just to the south, also along the coast, is the state known as the United Arab Emirates. Both Qatar and the United Arab Emirates are sandy, stony deserts that have benefited from the discovery of oil.

Bahrain The countries of Bahrain and Oman are not as rich as are Saudi Arabia, Kuwait, Qatar, and the United Arab Emirates. Bahrain was the first Persian Gulf nation to produce oil, but by the 1970s its reserves were largely used up. Its refineries, however, still operate with oil carried by pipeline from Saudi Arabia.

Bahrain consists of a group of about 35 islands just north of Qatar in the Persian Gulf. A **causeway** connects the main island with the coast of Saudi Arabia. A causeway is a raised road across water or swampy land.

E. Oman and Yemen

Oman Ships entering and leaving the Persian Gulf must pass through the Strait of Hormuz (HOR muz). The territory of Oman includes land at the tip of a peninsula overlooking this passageway, which is 24 miles (39 km) wide at this point. Oman also consists of a large stretch of land that forms the southeastern corner of the Arabian Peninsula. Oil is the main source of wealth in Oman.

Yemen Another country on the Arabian Peninsula is Yemen, located at the southern end. Although Yemen does have some oil, its resources are small compared with those of other nations in the region. Unlike the oil-rich lands on the Persian Gulf, Yemen is one of the world's poorest countries. A large part of the population cannot read.

Before 1990, Yemen was divided into two countries—North Yemen and South Yemen. Today, the united country of Yemen is a republic controlled by military officers. San'a is the capital city.

Western Yemen includes highlands that rise sharply from the Red Sea. These highlands are said to enjoy the best climate on the Arabian Peninsula. Summers are warm with plenty of moisture. Winters are cool and rather dry. This is the region that produces the rich-tasting coffee called mocha, Yemen's most famous export. Other crops, such as grains, cotton, fruits, and vegetables, are also grown in western Yemen.

Part of eastern Yemen was the British colony of Aden before 1967. The port of Aden is near the narrow entrance to the Red Sea. Aden is on the sea route between the Mediterranean Sea and the Indian Ocean. Ships sailing by way of the Suez Canal and the Red Sea can dock at Aden.

The growing of coffee plants is important in western Yemen.
▶ Do you think these plants were planted by hand or by machine?

LESSON **3** *REVIEW*

THINK AND WRITE

A. What are some similarities and differences between Jordan and Syria?

B. What led to the civil war in Lebanon in 1970?

C. Why has Saudi Arabia been important in the world?

D. How did the discovery of oil affect Kuwait?

E. Why is Yemen one of the world's poorest countries but other countries in the region are considered wealthy?

SKILLS CHECK

THINKING SKILL

Look at the graphs on page 416. About how many of the proven oil reserves of the Middle East and North Africa do Libya, Iraq, Iran, and Kuwait have?

419

Countries of North Africa

THINK ABOUT WHAT YOU KNOW

Suppose your school is holding an international fair, and you are to plan an exhibit about Egypt. What are some things you would exhibit at the fair?

STUDY THE VOCABULARY

revenue   **phosphate**
terrorism   **asphalt**

FOCUS YOUR READING

How are the countries of North Africa similar and how are they different?

A. Egypt: A Crowded Country

Population   A travel guidebook warns people planning to visit Cairo, Egypt, that the central part of the city "is not for the faint-hearted." Egypt's capital is a very crowded city in a very crowded country — one of the most crowded in the world. Visitors must make their way through snarled traffic and packed crowds. The guidebook adds that although some visitors may find the bustle and confusion exciting, others may want to escape to quieter places.

Egypt has plenty of quiet places, but they are in the desert, where few people live. Most Egyptians today, as in ancient times, live along the Nile River and on the delta that has formed at the river's mouth. Egypt's population has grown very rapidly in recent years, but 99 percent of the people must still live on a scant 3.5 percent of the land. Cairo is on the banks of the lower Nile. Alexandria, Egypt's large Mediterranean port, is on the delta.

Government   Egypt was a monarchy before 1952, but in that year a group of army officers staged a revolt. They forced the king to leave the country, and they established a republic. Egypt today has an elected president and assembly.

Cairo, the capital of Egypt, has the largest population and also is the most densely populated city in the Middle East and North Africa.
▶ Why, do you think, do so many Egyptians live in Cairo?

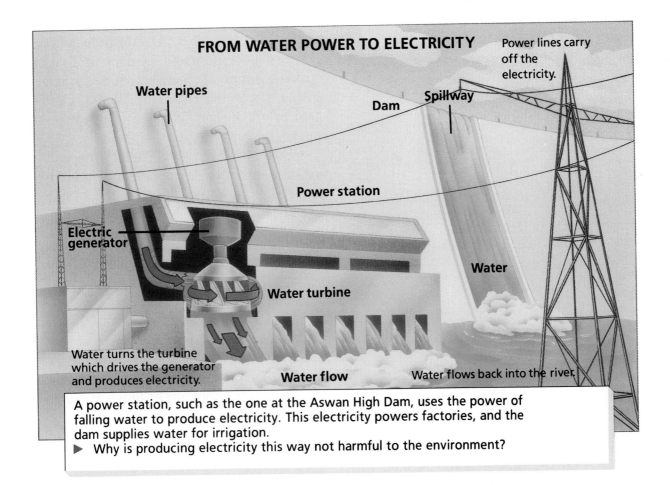

FROM WATER POWER TO ELECTRICITY

Water pipes

Dam

Spillway

Power lines carry off the electricity.

Power station

Electric generator

Water

Water turbine

Water turns the turbine which drives the generator and produces electricity.

Water flow

Water flows back into the river.

A power station, such as the one at the Aswan High Dam, uses the power of falling water to produce electricity. This electricity powers factories, and the dam supplies water for irrigation.

▶ Why is producing electricity this way not harmful to the environment?

B. Egypt's Resources

Aswan High Dam Egypt completed a high dam on the Nile south of the city of Aswan in 1970. The dam was built in order to provide water for irrigating new land and to provide power for making electricity. Electric power meant providing more industries and jobs for people.

The Aswan High Dam created both benefits and problems. It provided water for new agriculture, but the costs were far higher than expected. The dam also made it possible to grow an extra crop each year by holding back the summer flood that had covered lowlands downstream. But there had been some benefits from the yearly floods. The high water carried rich silt, which was left on the fields when the flood waters lessened. To replace the fertile silt, Egyptian farmers have had to apply expensive chemical fertilizers.

By forming Lake Nasser behind Aswan, the dam provided new fishing areas. But reducing the summer flood harmed fishing at the mouth of the river. The summer flood carried much plant material into the Mediterranean Sea. Fish fed on the plant material, so cutting down on the flood meant cutting down on the food supply for fish.

The beneficial and harmful effects of the Aswan High Dam show how hard it is to make great changes in a natural resource. Has the dam helped more than it has harmed? People still do not agree on the answer.

421

Suez Canal The Suez Canal is also an important Egyptian resource. Turn to the map on page 404 and find the Suez Canal. Fees paid by ships passing through this busy waterway provide **revenue,** or income, for the government.

Tourism Egypt has some oil, but its reserves are far less than those of the major Middle Eastern oil countries. However, Egypt has another valuable resource, as can be seen by a visit to the crammed museum in Cairo. The remains of Egypt's ancient civilization make up one of the country's resources. Thousands of tourists visit Egypt each year to see the pyramids, temples, tombs, and museums. Tourism is one of Egypt's important industries.

C. Libya: Oil in the Sahara

Industry Except for a strip of land along the Mediterranean coast, Libya lies within the huge desert called the Sahara. It is a country without a river, and only 2 percent of the land is arable. At one time most Libyans were nomadic herders or oasis farmers. But great changes occurred when it was discovered that Libya had a great deal of oil. In fact, it has the largest reserves in North Africa.

Some of the money gained from selling oil went to the development of modern industries. Now two thirds of the people live in or around cities. Tripoli, the capital, has a population of more than a million.

Government A revolution led by army officers in 1969 made Colonel Muammar al-Qaddafi (MOO uh mahr al-kuh DAH-fee) head of the Libyan government. Colonel Qaddafi is not called president but "leader of the revolution." He is a very strict Muslim, and the government bases its laws on the Muslim religion. For example, it is illegal to bring alcoholic drinks or pork into the country, since they are forbidden to

Colonel Qaddafi gained power after he helped overthrow Libya's monarchy.
▶ What charge do many governments make against Qaddafi?

The sunny beaches of Tunisia attract many tourists each year.
► What kind of climate does the coast of Tunisia have?

Muslims. All public signs, including those in airports, must be written in Arabic script only.

Relations between Libya and other countries have been stormy since Colonel Qaddafi came to power. The United States and other countries have charged that Libya has supported **terrorism**. Terrorism is the use of fear to threaten people or nations to make them do things that they do not want to do.

D. Tunisia: A Land with Variety

Language and Government Tunisia, Libya's neighbor to the west, is also a Muslim country. Arabic is the official language, but many people speak French. This land was part of the French empire before becoming an independent republic in 1957. For a number of years, Tunisia had a one-party government, but today other parties can run for office.

Climate and Land Tunisia is the smallest of the North African countries, yet it has a variety of lands and climates. Tunisia's Mediterranean coast has the same kind of climate as other Mediterranean lands — mild winters and hot summers. Tunisia's sunny Mediterranean beaches attract thousands of tourists, since Tunis, the capital, is only a short flight from Rome and other European cities.

In ancient times, Carthage was a powerful rival of Rome. Today, Carthage is a suburb of Tunis. Only a few ruins remain in modern Carthage to remind travelers that this was the city of Hannibal. You read about Hannibal and the wars of Rome and Carthage in Chapter 3.

Tunisia is basically an agricultural country. Northern Tunisia has forests and fertile farmlands. Farther south there are dry grasslands suitable for grazing sheep, goats, and camels.

Algiers is the capital of and the largest city in Algeria. The city has many valuable resources, including its harbor on the Mediterranean coast.
► How is the harbor in Algiers a valuable resource?

Tunisia has few minerals. The country has some oil and **phosphate** deposits. Phosphate is a mineral used for fertilizers and detergents.

E. Algeria: The Coast and the Desert

Land and Resources The Trans-Sahara highway runs from the Mediterranean coast of Algeria to Niger in West Africa. Even though it is called a highway, a trip across this desert road is not for your family car. The road has been partly paved with **asphalt**. Asphalt is a substance formed from a combination of oil, sand, and rock. The pavement on one long stretch is so badly broken up that it is better to drive alongside the highway rather than on it.

Algeria is a big country — the biggest in North Africa and the Middle East. Find it on the map on page 404. Part of Algeria is a strip along the Mediterranean coast where most people live. The climate and crops of this part of the country are typical of the Mediterranean lands. Mountains of the Atlas range separate the coastal strip from the Sahara, which makes up the larger part of the country.

Unlike Tunisia, Algeria has a number of valuable minerals as well as oil and natural gas fields. It is one of the leading natural gas exporters. The natural gas reserves are the fourth largest in the world.

Algeria's History The French began the conquest of Algeria in the 1830s. After they won control of the land, they encouraged French and other Europeans to settle there. The European settlers regarded Algeria as part of a Greater France. At one time the settlers made up 11 percent of the population. Most of the other Algerians did not think of their country as part of France. They were Muslims in religion, and most of them spoke Arabic.

A civil war broke out in the 1950s in which those who wanted independence for Algeria fought against those who wanted to remain with France. After 8 years of fighting, both sides settled the matter by a vote. The majority chose separation from France, and Algeria became an independent republic in 1962. Most of the European settlers left the country. The new government was controlled by one political party, so the people did not have a true choice in electing officials for the republic.

F. Morocco: The Land Farthest West

Land and Resources Morocco, located on the northwest corner of Africa, faces the Atlantic Ocean as well as the Mediterranean Sea. When the Arabs conquered Morocco, they called it "the land farthest west." Morocco is the most mountainous of the North African lands. It contains the highest mountains in the Atlas range. Some peaks are snow-covered from winter until well into the summer months. The high mountains and the Atlantic and Mediterranean beaches are the basis of Morocco's tourist industry.

About half of Morocco's land is arable, and many people depend on farming and herding for a living. The country has various minerals and possesses about two thirds of the world's known phosphate reserves. At present Morocco ranks third among the producers of phosphates.

Moroccan History The Arabs conquered Morocco in the Middle Ages, and Arabic is the official language of this Muslim land. But a third of the people are Berbers, who have a language of their own. The ancestors of the Berbers lived in this part of Africa long before the Arab conquest.

Only mountains separate the lush, fertile land of Morocco from the Sahara desert.
▶ What is this mountain range?

Although many Moroccan workers are turning to industry, handicrafts are still an important trade.
► What famous handicraft are these workers producing?

The French controlled most of Morocco from 1912 to 1956, but they never considered it a part of Greater France. Morocco became independent in 1956. Morocco has a king; it is the only monarchy in North Africa today.

Industry For centuries Moroccan craftspeople have been famous for producing fine carpets, metalwork, and leather goods made from goatskin. This leather is known all over the world. In recent years the country has created modern industrial plants that turn out such products as textiles, soaps, and canned foods. Moroccan workers now assemble automobiles. Morocco seeks to modernize. As you have learned in this chapter, modernization has been the aim of most countries of the Middle East and North Africa.

LESSON 4 REVIEW

THINK AND WRITE

A. Why, do you think, do most people of Egypt live along the Nile River valley and on the delta?
B. What benefits and problems were created by the Aswan High Dam?
C. How does Colonel Qaddafi run the government of Libya?
D. What types of land and climate does Tunisia have?

E. What was the result of the civil war in Algeria?
F. Name some of the ways in which Morocco differs from other North African countries.

SKILLS CHECK

WRITING SKILL

Write a paragraph or two telling whether, in your opinion, the Aswan High Dam has been more of a benefit or a problem to Egypt.

USING THE VOCABULARY

modernize	Knesset
mullah	fez
ayatollah	nonrenewable resource
embassy	terrorism
hostage	phosphate

On a separate sheet of paper, write the word or words from above that best complete the sentences.

1. The use of fear to threaten and manipulate people or nations is called _____ .
2. A _____ is a person held captive by someone who has demands.
3. The elected assembly of Israel, called the _____ , chooses the president and prime minister.
4. A resource that cannot be replaced, such as oil, is a _____ .
5. _____ is an honorary title for a religious leader in Iran.
6. A _____ is a mineral used for fertilizers and detergents.
7. An ambassador to a foreign country lives and works in an _____ .
8. A felt hat with a flat top and no brim, worn by men in Turkey, is called a _____ .
9. A Muslim religious teacher is called a _____ .
10. Many countries are trying to _____ , or use up-to-date ways of doing things.

REMEMBERING WHAT YOU READ

On a separate sheet of paper, answer the following questions in complete sentences.

1. Who was the leader of the second revolution in Iran?
2. Why has the population of Iran grown so rapidly in recent years?
3. In what year did the Jewish state of Israel declare its independence?
4. What issue has divided the people of Lebanon?
5. For whom is the country of Saudi Arabia named?
6. What do Saudi Arabia, Kuwait, Qatar, and the United Arab Emirates have in common?
7. What are the beneficial effects of the Aswan High Dam?
8. Who is the head of the Libyan government?
9. What is the biggest country in North Africa and the Middle East?
10. Which country is the only monarchy in North Africa today?

TYING LANGUAGE ARTS TO SOCIAL STUDIES

If you were in charge of writing a peace treaty to be signed by two warring nations, what terms would you include in the treaty? Try writing a one-page treaty that any two countries could follow to maintain peace.

THINKING CRITICALLY

On a separate sheet of paper, answer the following questions in complete sentences.

1. How do you think oil prices would be affected if oil were a renewable resource?
2. What nonviolent methods might successfully be used to prevent terrorism?
3. Why are the countries on the Arabian Peninsula of great importance to countries in other parts of the world?
4. Why do so many countries have to win their independence through revolution?
5. What kinds of jobs do you think people have in modern cities in the Middle East and North Africa?

SUMMARIZING THE CHAPTER

On a separate sheet of paper, draw a graphic organizer like the one shown here. Copy the information from this graphic organizer to the one you have drawn. Under the main idea for each lesson, write four statements that support the main idea.

CHAPTER THEME

Geography, resources, religions, and political policies and conflicts continue to have a strong influence on daily life in the Middle East and North Africa today.

LESSON 1

The recent history of the Middle East is a continuation of many years of problems.

1. _____
2. _____
3. _____
4. _____

LESSON 3

Important characteristics shape each of the Arab countries of the Middle East.

1. _____
2. _____
3. _____
4. _____

LESSON 2

Many political and economic changes have taken place in Israel and Turkey since World War I.

1. _____
2. _____
3. _____
4. _____

LESSON 4

There are many similarities and differences among the countries of North Africa.

1. _____
2. _____
3. _____
4. _____

COOPERATIVE LEARNING

In Chapter 14 you read about Muhammad and the spread of Islam. You learned that the Seljuk Turks conquered Jerusalem and the Holy Land. In 1095 Pope Urban called on the knights of western Europe to join in a war to gain control of the Holy Land and the Holy City of Jerusalem from the Muslims. This was the first of a series of wars that became known as the Crusades.

PROJECT

Work with a group of your classmates to create a board game in which teams of players try to gain control of the Holy Land, especially the Holy City of Jerusalem. Use information from Chapter 14 in your game. Be sure to include people such as Pope Urban, Peter the Hermit, Saladin, and Richard the Lion-Hearted. Think about other board games you have played and about how the boards are designed. Also decide how the pieces in your game will advance. Many board games use spinners, cards, or dice to determine how far a player will move. Sometimes, bonus cards give players extra turns and chances to move ahead; penalty cards cause players to lose turns or move backward. Once your group has discussed and chosen a design, each group member should work to construct part of the game. One person might sketch the board on butcher paper. Others might make the game pieces, dice, cards, or spinner. Each group member could write three bonus cards and three penalty cards.

Finally, your group should meet to put the game together. Don't forget to give it a name!

PRESENTATION AND REVIEW

Your group should test your game by playing it together. By testing the game, you will be able to find and fix any problems. When the group is pleased with the way the game works, present it to the rest of the class. Trade games with another group to see other ideas about how to learn about the Crusades. You might consider having groups each choose a representative for another group whose goal would be to select the best features of each of the game boards and try to put them together into one new game.

REMEMBER TO:
- Give your ideas.
- Listen to others' ideas.
- Plan your work with the group.
- Present your project.
- Discuss how your group worked.

A. WHY DO I NEED THIS SKILL?

The kinds of natural resources that countries have has much to do with what products those countries can make. Natural resources, then, are very important for the economies of nations. However, natural resources are not evenly distributed throughout the world. Countries that do not have certain natural resources have to gain them through trade with nations that do have those resources. This has a major effect on the way countries deal with one another. Resource maps show us the distribution of various natural resources in particular areas.

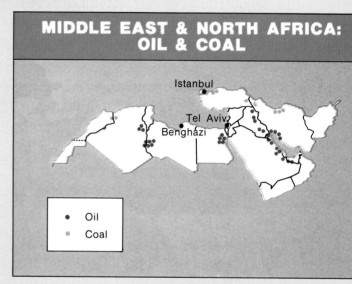

MIDDLE EAST & NORTH AFRICA: OIL & COAL

Istanbul
Tel Aviv
Benghâzi

● Oil
● Coal

B. LEARNING THE SKILL

At right is a resource map showing areas of coal deposits and oil fields in the Middle East and North Africa. There are a number of colored dots within many of the countries. The red dots represent the areas where oil fields are located. The green dots represent coal deposits.

By looking at this map, you can see that not all of the countries of the Middle East and North Africa have some oil fields. You can also see that only a few of the countries have some coal deposits. However, if you take a closer look at the map, you will learn a great deal of information. For example, some countries have oil fields and no areas of coal deposits. Other countries have coal deposits and no oil fields. Some countries have no coal or oil at all.

In addition to showing the distribution of natural resources, resource maps help us figure out what industries a country or region may have. For example, a country with oil fields may have oil refineries. If that is true, then that country might also have a well-developed system for exporting oil. Countries with large coal deposits may rely on coal for fueling their industries. These nations might then have problems associated with air pollution.

Answer the following questions by using the resource map on the opposite page and the map of the Middle East and North Africa in the Atlas of this book.

1. Which countries have oil fields?
2. List three countries that have no coal deposits or oil fields.
3. Which countries have both oil fields and coal deposits?
4. Is Saudi Arabia's oil in the western or eastern part of the country?
5. Which natural resource can be found in Morocco?

Answer the following questions by using the resource map on this page and the map of the Middle East and North Africa in the Atlas of this book.

1. Which two countries are leading producers of phosphates?
2. Name three countries that produce neither phosphates nor manganese.
3. Which countries produce manganese?
4. Which country in this region produces both phosphates and manganese?
5. Which is more abundant in this region — phosphates or manganese?

D. APPLYING THE SKILL

Find information about the leading natural resources in your state and where they are located. Next trace or draw a map of your state, then choose at least two of your state's resources and make your own state resource map, using the map below and the one on page 430 as examples. Remember to add a title and a key box to the map. Be creative by using different colors and symbols on your map. When you and the other class members have completed your maps, display them in the classroom.

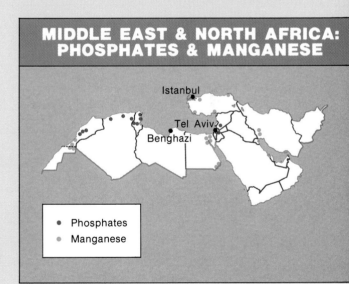

MIDDLE EAST & NORTH AFRICA: PHOSPHATES & MANGANESE

Istanbul
Tel Aviv
Benghazi

● Phosphates
● Manganese

A. Why Do I Need This Skill?

Sometimes your teacher may ask you to do special assignments, such as written reports or oral presentations, as a social studies project. The information you need to do these assignments may not be in your textbook. At other times you may have questions that cannot be answered by using your textbook. In these situations, you will need to use other resources. **Resources** are books, articles, and other materials you can use to find the information you need. Knowing how to select the right resources is an important social studies skill.

B. Learning the Skill

The table on page 433 shows some resources that may help you find information about social studies topics. Study the table on the next page carefully.

To select the most helpful resources, you need to ask yourself two questions: *What sort of information do I need? What resources might contain this information?* For example, if your teacher asked you to compute the distance of a journey from Athens, Greece, through the Suez Canal to Bombay, India, you would probably want to use an atlas. However, if you needed to know the depth of the Suez Canal, you could use an encyclopedia to find the information. To learn about the construction of the Suez Canal, you might look for books on the Suez Canal in the card catalog.

C. Practicing the Skill

Suppose your teacher has asked you to write a report about some important feature of the Middle East and North Africa. You have decided to write about the Aswan High Dam, in Egypt. On a separate sheet of paper, list the resources you would use to complete each of the following parts of the report.
1. Draw a map of Egypt and show the location of the Aswan High Dam.
2. Make a diagram showing the design of the dam.
3. Explain how the dam was constructed, who helped to pay for it, who worked on it, and how long it took to build the dam.
4. Compare the water capacity of the Aswan High Dam with that of other major dams in the world.
5. Find out about any recent events involving the Aswan High Dam.
6. Make a glossary of the new or important words used in the report.
7. Make a bibliography of various sources of information about the dam.

D. Applying the Skill

Finding information is easy when you know how to select resources. Use the table and ask yourself the two questions for selecting resources whenever you need information for social studies projects. In addition, you can use this skill when you do projects in other subject areas — or whenever you want some information.

RESOURCES FOR INFORMATION

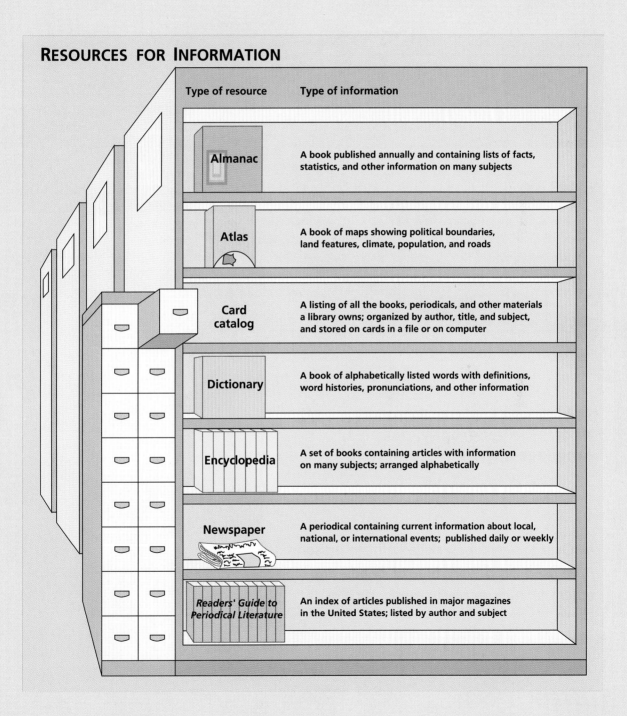

Type of resource	Type of information
Almanac	A book published annually and containing lists of facts, statistics, and other information on many subjects
Atlas	A book of maps showing political boundaries, land features, climate, population, and roads
Card catalog	A listing of all the books, periodicals, and other materials a library owns; organized by author, title, and subject, and stored on cards in a file or on computer
Dictionary	A book of alphabetically listed words with definitions, word histories, pronunciations, and other information
Encyclopedia	A set of books containing articles with information on many subjects; arranged alphabetically
Newspaper	A periodical containing current information about local, national, or international events; published daily or weekly
Readers' Guide to Periodical Literature	An index of articles published in major magazines in the United States; listed by author and subject

Unit 5

AFRICA SOUTH OF THE SAHARA

Africa south of the Sahara is a land of diverse geography, peoples, languages, and governments.

▶ *Over the centuries, skilled African artisans have used wood, ivory, bronze, beads, and other materials to create masks such as these.*

435

Africa south of the Sahara has many variations in land and climate. There are rain forests, grasslands, and deserts. People from all over the world come to see the region's variety of wildlife.

A Variety of Lands

THINK ABOUT WHAT YOU KNOW

Suppose you were invited to make a trip to Africa south of the Sahara. What would you expect to see?

STUDY THE VOCABULARY

savanna	tropics
Tropic of Cancer	equatorial
Tropic of Capricorn	river basin

FOCUS YOUR READING

What kind of variety is found in the land south of the Sahara?

A. A Change in Climate

Ancient Drawings It was something of a surprise to a French army officer in 1932 to discover a picture of an elephant on a canyon wall on the Tassili plateau in the heart of the Sahara. Searching further, he found drawings of hippopotamuses, giraffes, antelopes, rhinoceroses, wild oxen, baboons, and ostriches. None of these creatures can be seen today on the plateau. The rocky, windswept land receives little rain. There are no rivers for animals such as hippopotamuses, and elephants would certainly die of thirst. There were also pictures of people on the walls. Some were hunters; others were herders.

Change Over Time Who made these drawings, and how did they know about elephants and hippopotamuses? Scientists believe that the drawings were made by people who lived on the Tassili plateau between 6000 and 2000 B.C. The animals in the drawings also lived there 8,000 years ago. Then this part of Africa had a wetter climate. Trees, grass, and other vegetation grew on the land, and animals as large as

Rock paintings on the walls of caves were made by African people thousands of years ago.
► What is shown on this wall?

elephants could graze there. Later, herders brought cattle to feed on the plateau.

Sometime after 2000 B.C. the climate became drier. Rivers slowly dried up. Land once covered with grass became a desert, as it is today. No one knows for sure why the climate changed. But the Tassili rock paintings show that it did.

B. The Second Largest Continent

Africa is a large continent. It is two-thirds the size of Asia and three times as large as Europe. Africa's Mediterranean coast and its southern tip are about 5,000 miles (8,045 km) apart. They are nearly the same distance from the Equator, which crosses the continent. Both the northern coast and the southern tip have a Mediterranean climate, with cool, rainy winters and hot, dry summers.

The physical map on page 440 shows some important facts about Africa. Much of the land south of the Equator is a plateau that rises sharply from a narrow plain along the coast. Along the hump, or bulge, of West Africa, the lowland extends farther into the interior.

Although Africa is the second largest continent, it ranks behind Asia in population and Europe in population density. Asia has five times as many people as Africa, and Europe has over five times as many people per square mile.

C. Vegetation Regions

Deserts and Grasslands More than a fourth of Africa is desert. The Sahara is only one of three major deserts found in Africa. In southwest Africa are the Kalahari (kal uh HAHR ee) and Namib (NAHM-ihb) deserts. The Kalahari Desert is drier than the Sahara and covers an area about as large as the state of Oregon in the

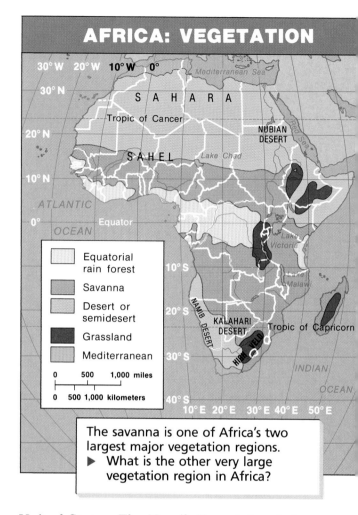

AFRICA: VEGETATION

Legend:
- Equatorial rain forest
- Savanna
- Desert or semidesert
- Grassland
- Mediterranean

0   500   1,000 miles
0   500 1,000 kilometers

The savanna is one of Africa's two largest major vegetation regions.
▶ What is the other very large vegetation region in Africa?

United States. The Namib Desert, located on Africa's southwest coast, is a cool desert. Find all three of these African deserts on the vegetation map on this page. The map shows the great extent of the deserts. These deserts do not support more than a sparse population.

As the map shows, much of the rest of Africa is **savanna**, or grassland with scattered trees and bushes. Herds of large animals, including elephants, giraffes, zebras, and wildebeests, graze here. Some of the savanna is now used for farming, although the soil is thin.

The savanna receives the most rain during the summer months. Winters are usually very dry. Rainfall varies each year.

The Sahel Between the Sahara and the savanna is a strip of land called the Sahel, which means "border" in Arabic. When rain is plentiful, cattle, sheep, and goats can graze on the Sahel. During times of drought, however, the Sahel has little to offer these herds.

Recently the desert has been advancing into the Sahel. When too many animals are allowed to graze on the dry grasslands, they destroy the vegetation, and the land is left bare. When people cut too many trees and bushes for fuel, this too robs the land of its cover. Strong winds carry away the thin topsoil, leaving stony land on which neither grass nor crops can grow.

Drought is a constant threat to farmers in nations of the Sahel.
▶ How has drought affected the land shown below?

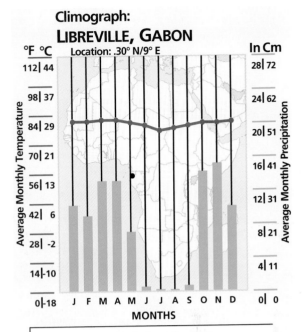

Climograph:
LIBREVILLE, GABON
Location: .30° N/9° E

Average Monthly Temperature / Average Monthly Precipitation

MONTHS

This climograph is for Libreville, Gabon, which is located in an eqatorial rain forest.
▶ On the average, which month receives the most rainfall?

D. Rain Forests and Snow-Covered Mountains

The Forests A large part of Africa lies on either side of the Equator between the **Tropic of Cancer**, at 23 1/2° north latitude, and the **Tropic of Capricorn**, at 23 1/2° south latitude. This region is known as the **tropics**. The lands along the Equator are called **equatorial**.

The equatorial parts of Central Africa and West Africa receive a lot of rain. Most areas average at least 50 inches (127 cm) of precipitation a year. Look at the climograph to see how much precipitation Libreville receives. The wet equatorial lands are covered by dense rain forests that produce valuable hardwoods such as ebony.

The Mountains The tallest mountains south of the Sahara are in East Africa. Mount Kenya is located on the Equator,

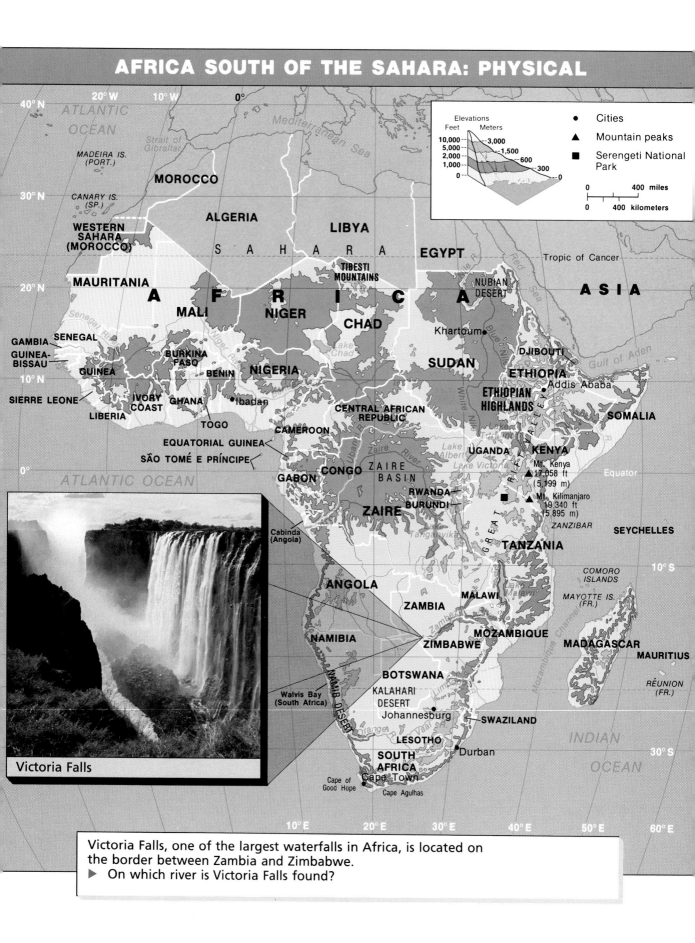

AFRICA SOUTH OF THE SAHARA: PHYSICAL

Elevations
Feet   Meters
10,000 — —3,000
5,000 — —1,500
2,000 — —600
1,000 — —300
0 — —0

● Cities
▲ Mountain peaks
■ Serengeti National Park

0   400 miles
0   400 kilometers

ATLANTIC OCEAN

Mediterranean Sea

MADEIRA IS. (PORT.)

Strait of Gibraltar

CANARY IS. (SP.)

MOROCCO

WESTERN SAHARA (MOROCCO)

ALGERIA

LIBYA

EGYPT

Tropic of Cancer

S   A   H   A   R   A

MAURITANIA

A   F   R   I   C   A

NUBIAN DESERT

ASIA

Senegal River

MALI

NIGER

Niger River

TIBESTI MOUNTAINS

CHAD

Lake Chad

Khartoum

Red Sea

Blue Nile R.

DJIBOUTI

Gulf of Aden

GAMBIA   SENEGAL
GUINEA-BISSAU
GUINEA
SIERRE LEONE
LIBERIA

BURKINA FASO

BENIN

NIGERIA

SUDAN

ETHIOPIA

ETHIOPIAN HIGHLANDS

Addis Ababa

SOMALIA

IVORY COAST   GHANA
•Ibadan
TOGO

CENTRAL AFRICAN REPUBLIC

White Nile R.

EQUATORIAL GUINEA
SÃO TOMÉ E PRÍNCIPE

CAMEROON

Ubangi R.

Zaire River

ZAIRE BASIN

Lake Albert

UGANDA

Lake Victoria

KENYA

▲ Mt. Kenya
17,058 ft
(5,199 m)

Equator

ATLANTIC OCEAN

GABON   CONGO

ZAIRE

RWANDA
BURUNDI

■ ▲ Mt. Kilimanjaro
19,340 ft
(5,895 m)

ZANZIBAR

SEYCHELLES

Cabinda (Angola)

Lake Tanganyika

GREAT RIFT VALLEY

TANZANIA

10° S

ANGOLA

ZAMBIA

MALAWI

Lake Malawi

COMORO ISLANDS

MAYOTTE IS. (FR.)

MADAGASCAR

MAURITIUS

NAMIBIA

Zambezi R.

ZIMBABWE

MOZAMBIQUE

Mozambique Channel

RÉUNION (FR.)

Walvis Bay (South Africa)

NAMIB DESERT

BOTSWANA

KALAHARI DESERT

Johannesburg

SWAZILAND

Limpopo R.

INDIAN OCEAN

Orange R.

Vaal R.

LESOTHO

Durban

30° S

SOUTH AFRICA

Cape Town

Cape of Good Hope

Cape Agulhas

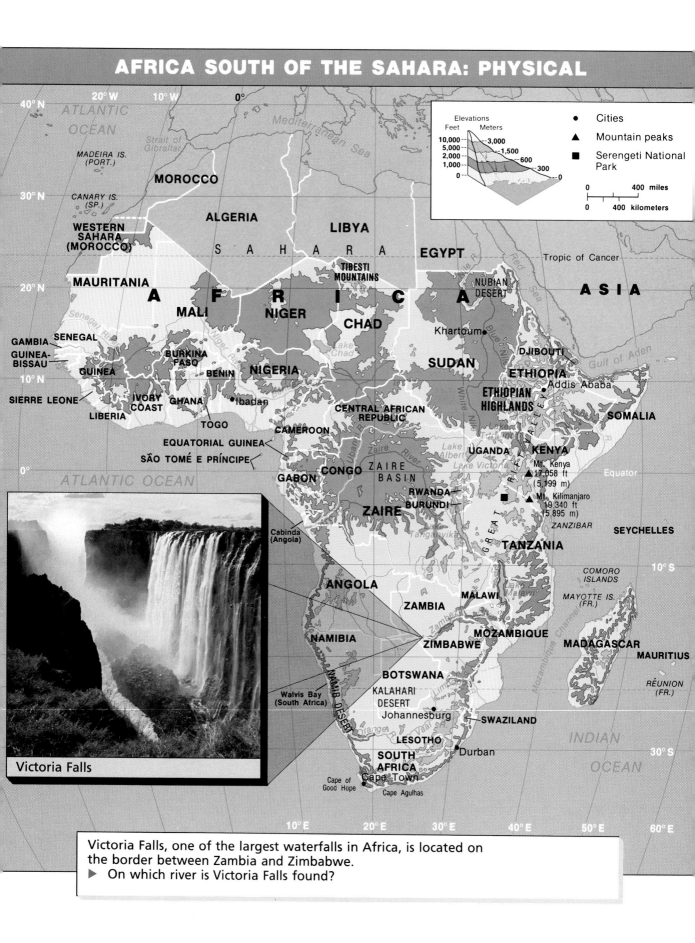

Victoria Falls

Victoria Falls, one of the largest waterfalls in Africa, is located on the border between Zambia and Zimbabwe.
▶ On which river is Victoria Falls found?

Mount Kilimanjaro, just south of the Equator, is the tallest mountain peak in Africa.
► Why is there snow covering the top of the mountain?

possible," flowing lazily through an overgrown swamp "in a what's-it-matter-when-it-comes-out style." Trace the river's course on the map on page 440. Note that its long route to the sea is also winding.

European explorers called the second longest African river the Congo. But to Africans it was known as the Zaire, or "big river." Note on the map on page 440 that the **river basin**, the area drained by the river, is crossed by the Equator.

The Zambezi River, in south central Africa, rises on the high plateau and flows over falls and rapids on its way to the Indian Ocean. The largest of the falls — Victoria Falls — is twice as wide and nearly twice as high as Niagara Falls, in North America.

yet snow covers its summit throughout the year because of its high elevation. Snow-peaked Mount Kilimanjaro (kihl uh mun-JAHR oh), just south of the Equator, is taller than any of the mountains in Europe.

E. Africa's Rivers and Lakes

The Rivers The Niger is the third longest river in Africa. The river rises in the highlands of Guinea and empties into the Atlantic Ocean. Near the Atlantic the Niger divides into many channels that crisscross each other.

Explorers had trouble finding the mouth of the Niger for just this reason. As an early traveler observed, the Niger "comes to sea with as much mystery as

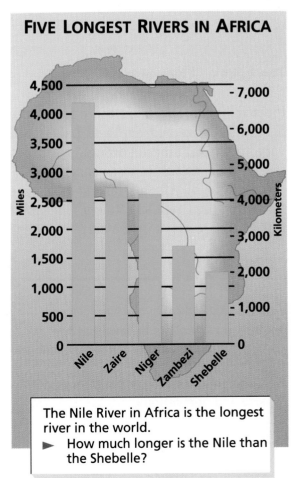

FIVE LONGEST RIVERS IN AFRICA

The Nile River in Africa is the longest river in the world.
► How much longer is the Nile than the Shebelle?

Lake Tanganyika is the second deepest lake in the world. Only Lake Baikal in Russia is deeper.

► Where is Lake Tanganyika located?

The Lakes Africa also has a number of lakes south of the Sahara. Lake Chad is located in the Sahel, on the edge of the desert. The size and depth of Lake Chad vary greatly. In times of drought it shrinks to one third its size in wet years.

Several of Africa's largest lakes are located in the Great Rift Valley. The Great Rift is a huge crack in the earth's surface that extends from East Africa into the Middle East. Lake Victoria, the largest of the African lakes, is here. It is one source of the Nile, Africa's longest river. Lake Tanganyika (tan gun YEE kuh), also in the valley, is deeper than any other lake on the continent. If you dropped a rock at the lake's deepest point, it would sink nearly a mile before reaching the bottom.

LESSON **1** REVIEW

THINK AND WRITE

A. Why do scientists believe that the climate in the Sahara is not the same as it once was?

B. Compare Africa to Asia and Europe in size and population.

C. Identify the Sahel and summarize how it is changing.

D. What type of vegetation is found in equatorial Africa?

E. Name three rivers and three lakes south of the Sahara.

SKILLS CHECK

MAP SKILL

Locate the Niger, Zaire, and Zambezi rivers on the physical map of Africa on page 440. List the countries through which each river flows or for which it forms a boundary.

A Variety of Peoples

Think about all the people you know. What different kinds of people live in our country?

multilingual

How do people south of the Sahara differ?

A. Some People Who Live in Africa

In Liberia Kama is a 12-year-old girl who lives with her grandmother in a village in Liberia, in West Africa. Kama's grandmother also takes care of Kama's brothers and one of her cousins.

Kama attends a school conducted by Muslims, although she and her family are Christians. Kama is especially interested in learning about faraway places. She has even borrowed an advanced geography book from her teacher to do extra reading.

Often in the evening Kama's grandmother gathers the children into the living room, and they sing songs and hymns. Some of the songs are in English, which is Liberia's official language. Others are in Kpelle, the language of Kama's own people. About 26 African languages are spoken by different groups within Liberia.

In Nigeria Binta also lives in West Africa. Her home is Kano, a large city in northern Nigeria. Even though Binta is only 11 years old, she goes out on the street early each morning to sell bean cakes made by her mother. Binta some-

times makes small pancakes to sell to other children.

For an hour or so each day, Binta goes to an Arabic school, where she studies the language of the Koran, which you learned is the holy book of Muslims. There are also public schools in Kano, where subjects are taught in English, the language of Nigeria. But Binta's family, like most people in Kano, are Muslims. They think it is more important for a girl to learn to read the Koran than English.

Binta's family are Hausas, one of the ethnic groups in Nigeria. Members of a particular ethnic group may share language, religion, and customs. In some ways an ethnic group is like a nationality. Most Hausas are Muslims. The Yorubas, Ibos, and Fulanis are other ethnic groups in Nigeria. Each of these ethnic groups has its own language.

People carry goods for sale along the streets of West Africa.
► What are these women carrying on their heads?

Children in schoolrooms in Kenya learn how to speak English.
► How can you tell that English is being taught?

In Kenya Mr. and Mrs. Munoru and their four children live in Kenya, in East Africa. They are Christians, like the majority of people in Kenya. Mr. Munoru raises coffee beans on a tiny plot of land he inherited. The plot is only half an acre (.2 ha), so it cannot support the family. But Mr. Munoru is a trained stone mason, and he works at his trade in a nearby town whenever he can get a job. Mrs. Munoru earns some money working on large farms.

Mr. and Mrs. Munoru work very hard because they are determined to give their children a good education. The children will learn English in school, although Swahili is Kenya's national language. The Munorus want their children to learn English so that they can get good jobs someday. Most government and business affairs in Kenya are carried on in English.

B. Many Countries, Many Languages

Ethnic Groups Kama, Binta, and the Munoru family are all Africans, but they are not alike. Africa is a huge continent with more than a half billion people. As you would expect, there are many differences among so many people. There are more countries in Africa than on any other continent. Within most of the countries there are different ethnic groups.

Some of the ethnic groups in Africa are descendants of people who came from other continents. In East Africa and South Africa there are people whose ancestors came from India. In South Africa about 18 percent of the people are descendants of Europeans who settled there.

Languages Because of the many different ethnic groups, a variety of languages are spoken in most countries south of the Sahara. At least 16 languages are used in Zaire, for example, and 15 in Tanzania. Because various languages are spoken in African countries, many people there are **multilingual**, or able to speak several languages. However, in most countries where there are many different languages the official language is that of the European country that ruled before the nation became independent. France once ruled Senegal, for instance, and French is the official language there.

In addition to being the language of the Muslim religion, Arabic has long been a language for traders in parts of Africa. It is also the official language of several countries. Swahili, an African language widely used in East Africa, includes many Arabic words and is written in Arabic script.

C. Wise Sayings, Works of Art, and Special Music

Proverbs Africans did not develop systems of writing for all the different languages. But they did create a rich variety of poems, songs, stories, and legends. These were passed on by word of mouth. Children learned them from their parents and grandparents, and taught their own children in turn.

Africans are fond of proverbs, or short wise sayings. Here are some samples.

> *He who cannot dance will say the drum is bad.*
> *A loose tooth will not rest until it is pulled out.*
> *He who talks all of the time talks nonsense.*
> *Not to know is bad; not to wish to know is worse.*
> *To try and to fail is not laziness.*

Art and Music One proverb points out that seeing is different from being told. The photograph below tells more than words can tell about the variety of art the peoples of Africa produce. It shows that African artists use all kinds of materials. Today, African artwork is found in museums in many parts of the world.

Africans developed a special style of music that makes use of many different rhythms, or beats. They invented a variety of musical instruments, including many different kinds of drums. One, known as the talking drum, makes sounds somewhat like those of the human voice. African musicians also use many different kinds of xylophones, string instruments, horns, and flutes.

Artists of Africa used antelope skin and other materials to create the ceremonial helmet shown in the photograph below.
► What other materials were used?

AFRICA SOUTH OF THE SAHARA: POPULATION DENSITY

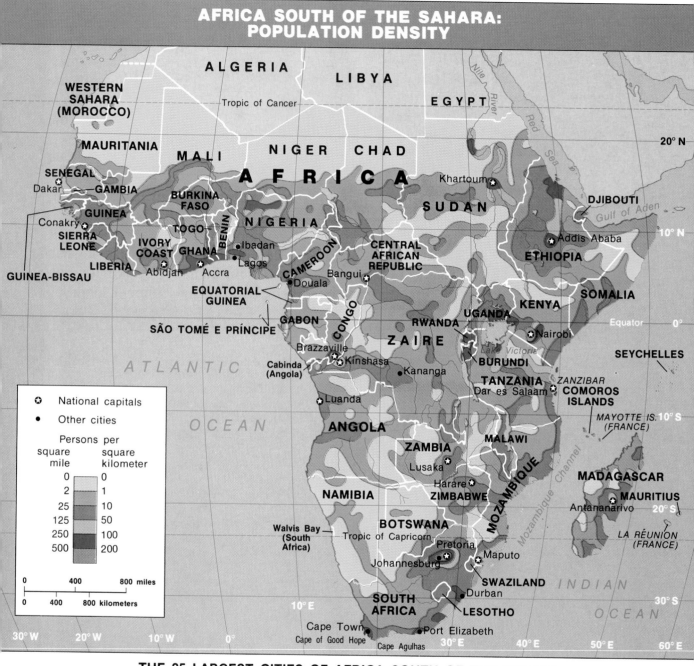

National capitals ✪

Other cities ●

Persons per
square mile	square kilometer
0	0
2	1
25	10
125	50
250	100
500	200

0   400   800 miles

0   400   800 kilometers

THE 25 LARGEST CITIES OF AFRICA SOUTH OF THE SAHARA

Kinshasa (Zaire) 2,778,000
Abidjan (Ivory Coast) 2,534,000
Johannesburg (S. Afr.) 1,536,000
Addis Ababa (Ethiopia) 1,412,000
Dakar (Senegal) 1,211,000
Nairobi (Kenya) 1,104,000
Lagos (Nigeria) 1,097,000

Antananarivo (Madag.) 1,050,000
Accra (Ghana) 860,000
Cape Town (S. Africa) 855,000
Ibadan (Nigeria) 847,000
Douala (Cameroon) 841,000
Dar es Salaam (Tanzania) .. 757,000
Maputo (Mozambique) 755,000

Kananga (Zaire) 704,000
Conakry (Guinea) 656,000
Harare (Zimbabwe) 656,000
Khartoum (Sudan) 557,000
Lusaka (Zambia) 538,000
Pretoria (South Africa) 528,000
Durban (South Africa) 506,000

Port Elizabeth (S. Africa)... 492,000
Brazzaville (Congo) 481,000
Luanda (Angola) 475,000
Bangui (C.A.R.) 474,000

Most Africans living south of the Sahara live
in rural areas rather than in cities.

▶ How many of the 25 largest cities have a
population of a million or more?

D. Villagers and City Dwellers

In the past most Africans south of the Sahara lived in small groups. They were villagers who farmed the land, herded livestock, hunted, and fished. Today a majority still live in villages, but the number of city dwellers has been growing rapidly. In some countries more than a fourth of the population is urban.

A number of African cities have more than a million inhabitants. Look at the population density map on page 446 to find out how many African cities south of the Sahara have a population of a million or more. These large cities, like those on other continents, have tall buildings, packed living quarters, and traffic jams. Lagos, Nigeria, has been called the most crowded city south of the Sahara. Its urban area sprawls through suburbs just like the urban areas of many cities in the United States. More people live in the suburbs than in Lagos itself.

The rapid growth of cities is one of the great changes taking place in the lands south of the Sahara. As more and more people live in cities, life in this part of Africa is becoming more like life in other parts of the world.

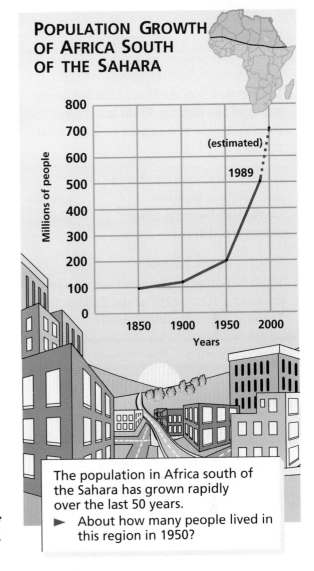

POPULATION GROWTH OF AFRICA SOUTH OF THE SAHARA

The population in Africa south of the Sahara has grown rapidly over the last 50 years.
► About how many people lived in this region in 1950?

LESSON 2 REVIEW

THINK AND WRITE

A. What are some of the differences between Kama, Binta, and the Munoru family?

B. Name some languages spoken south of the Sahara.

C. Give an example of a proverb, a piece of art, and a musical instrument from south of the Sahara.

D. How is African life south of the Sahara changing?

SKILLS CHECK

WRITING SKILL

The idea of a proverb can be stated in other words. For example, the idea behind "A proverb is the horse of conversation" is that a wise saying keeps the conversation going. In your own words, write the idea of each proverb given on page 445.

Making Use of Resources

THINK ABOUT WHAT YOU KNOW

In Lesson 1 you studied about the lands south of the Sahara. What natural resources would you expect to find in this region?

STUDY THE VOCABULARY

subsistence farming   **cacao**
slash-and-burn farming   **sisal**
commercial farm

FOCUS YOUR READING

What important natural resources are found in Africa south of the Sahara, and how are these resources used?

Gold mining is a major industry in South Africa.
▶ What are these miners wearing for protection?

A. Land of Gold and Other Minerals

Gold first attracted people from other lands to Africa. In early accounts the region south of the Sahara was called "the land of gold." One writer told of an African king who ate from plates of gold, and whose dogs had collars of gold.

Such early accounts no doubt stretched the truth a bit, but there was gold in Africa. There still is. Half of all the gold mined in the world between 1972 and 1987 came from Africa south of the Sahara.

Africa has other minerals that are more useful in the modern world. It is a major source of chromium ore and has one of the world's largest bauxite reserves. Africa also supplies the world with diamonds, uranium, iron, tin, and oil.

MINERAL PRODUCTION IN AFRICA SOUTH OF THE SAHARA

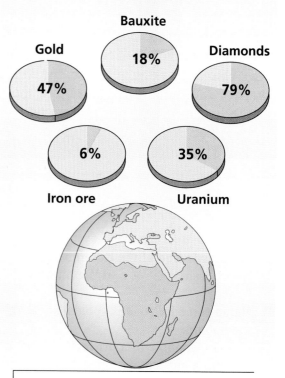

Gold 47%

Bauxite 18%

Diamonds 79%

Iron ore 6%

Uranium 35%

Africa south of the Sahara produces 79 percent of the world's diamonds.
▶ How much of the world's gold comes from this part of Africa?

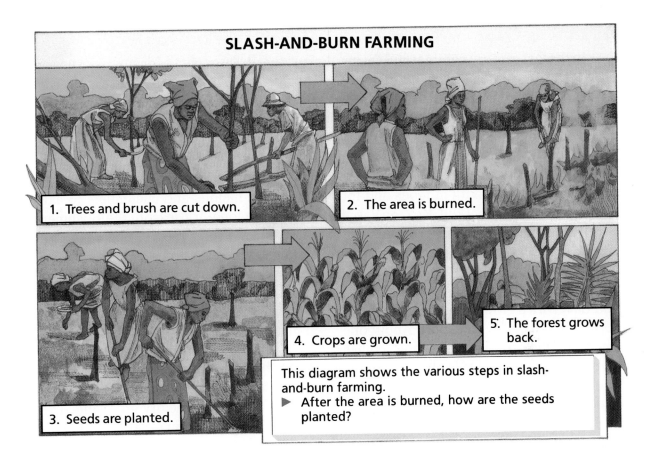

SLASH-AND-BURN FARMING

1. Trees and brush are cut down.

2. The area is burned.

3. Seeds are planted.

4. Crops are grown.

5. The forest grows back.

This diagram shows the various steps in slash-and-burn farming.
▶ After the area is burned, how are the seeds planted?

B. Growing Crops for Family Use

Farming Methods For many centuries **subsistence farming** was the main form of agriculture south of the Sahara. Subsistence farmers grow crops mostly for their own use rather than for sale. About two thirds of African cropland is still used in this way.

There are many small farms in the rain forests. Because these soils are not rich, farmers use **slash-and-burn farming**. First they slash, or cut, the trees and bushes on a patch of land. When the vegetation is dry, they set it on fire. After the fire ashes cover the soil. Farmers then break up the soil with hoes and plant their crops. The ashes serve as fertilizer.

Land Use Farmers in the rain forests plant different crops side by side. Corn,

beans, and peanuts might be grown in the same small field, for example. Africans also grow two important root crops, yams and cassava. The cassava plant, also known as manioc, has a large root that is ground into meal or flour.

Because the soil wears out very quickly, farmers must slash and burn new patches of land every few years. Trees and bushes are allowed to grow up again in the deserted fields. After 20 years or so, the land may be ready to be cut and burned again. In recent times, however, the African population has increased rapidly, and farmers have cut and burned land every few years instead of waiting longer periods. As a result, the soil in some areas has become so poor that it will support neither crops nor forest. Too much farming makes the land nearly useless.

449

C. Growing Crops for Export

In the last century **commercial farms** have taken the place of many subsistence farms. A commercial farm is one that produces crops for sale. Often the crops are exported to other countries.

Products from commercial farms in the rain forest include coconut and palm oils, which are used both in foods and for making soap. **Cacao** (kuh KAY oh) is a very important commercial crop in West Africa. Most chocolate is made from African cacao beans.

Commercial farms in southern Africa and East Africa grow crops such as wheat, corn, tea, and coffee for export. About one fourth of the world's coffee now comes from Africa. East Africa is also the source of **sisal**, a plant with strong fibers used to make rope.

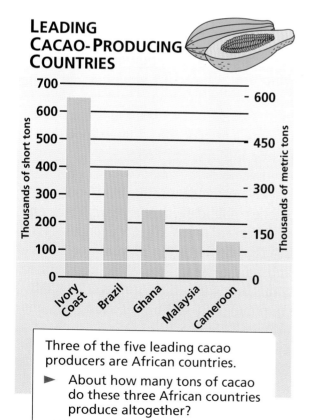

LEADING CACAO-PRODUCING COUNTRIES

Three of the five leading cacao producers are African countries.

► About how many tons of cacao do these three African countries produce altogether?

D. Using the Dry Lands

Survival in Deserts Africans make use of much land that is too dry for crops. The Bushmen long ago learned to live in the dry Kalahari. While many work for cattle ranches today, in the past they were food gatherers and hunters. At the end of the short rainy season, they would gather small wild melons and cucumbers to eat. During the long dry season, the Bushmen survived by eating roots. They knew, for instance, where to find a vine that stores water in its thick roots. The Bushmen's knowledge of such desert plants enabled them to stay alive where others would die of hunger and thirst.

Using the Grasslands Herders have long made use of the savanna. Their sheep and goats can graze on the dry grassland. The herders also keep some cattle, although Central Africa is not well suited for these animals because of the tsetse fly. The tsetse fly carries sleeping sickness, a disease that kills cattle.

Herds of cattle are raised on the East African plateau, however, which is largely free of the tsetse fly. The Masai people there depend largely on cattle. A family's wealth, in fact, is measured by the size of its cattle herds.

The Masai have permanent homes, and during the rainy season they are able to pasture their cattle near their villages. But when the dry season comes, the boys and men have to move about with the herds in search of grass for their cattle to eat. The Masai girls and women usually remain in the villages. They raise various vegetables and sorghum, which is a grain that can grow in fairly dry climates. Sorghum seed may be ground into meal for people or used as livestock feed.

E. Valuable Wildlife

Wildlife Resources Africa has a wide variety of wildlife. Elephants, giraffes, zebras, and many kinds of antelopes feed on the grasslands. There are big cats—lions, cheetahs, and leopards—that prey on other animals. Chimpanzees, baboons, gorillas, and a number of smaller monkeys add to the variety. Africa has an equally great variety of birds.

Wildlife is one of Africa's most valuable natural resources. For centuries, people hunted the wildlife for food, hides, and ivory. In recent times, wildlife has become valuable in another way. Animals and birds are the basis of a profitable tourist industry. Thousands of people visit Africa mainly to see the animals and birds in their natural setting.

Protecting Wildlife Yet at the same time that tourism has been growing in importance, the wildlife population has been on the decline. As the human population has increased, more and more forestland and grassland has been taken over for farms. Farmers do not want wild animals near their crops. Herders also have been driving wild animals away because they eat grass that cattle could graze on. In addition, although most African countries have laws

Wild animals roam freely in their natural setting in many parts of Africa.
► What animals are visible in this photograph?

protecting wildlife, poaching, or illegal hunting, continues.

Because of the declining wildlife population, there is a danger that some animals will become extinct, or die out. To protect this natural resource, game parks and reserves have been created.

LESSON **3** *REVIEW*

THINK AND WRITE

A. What are some of Africa's mineral resources?

B. Summarize why the soil in some areas of the rain forest has become too poor to support crops or forest.

C. What crops are grown on African commercial farms for export?

D. How have Africans made use of the dry lands?

E. Why is the African wildlife population declining?

SKILLS CHECK

THINKING SKILL

Look at the cacao graph on page 450. Which of the leading cacao-producing countries are African? What is the leading cacao-producing country in the world? About how many tons of cacao does it produce?

USING THE VOCABULARY

savanna
Tropic of Cancer
tropics
equatorial
river basin

multilingual
subsistence farming
commercial farm
cacao
sisal

From the list, choose a vocabulary term that could be used in place of the underlined word or words in each sentence. Rewrite the sentences on a separate sheet of paper.

1. A large part of Africa is in the <u>region that lies on either side of the Equator.</u>
2. About two thirds of African cropland is used for <u>the growth of crops mostly for the farmers' own use rather than for sale.</u>
3. The lands of Central Africa and West Africa that are <u>along the Equator</u> receive a lot of rain.
4. East Africa is a source of <u>a plant with strong fibers used to make rope.</u>
5. Between the Sahara and the <u>grassland with scattered trees and bushes</u> is a strip of land called the Sahel.
6. On the Zaire River the <u>area drained by the river</u> is crossed by the Equator.
7. The crops from a <u>farm that produces crops for sale</u> are often exported to other countries.
8. The beans from <u>a very important commercial crop in West Africa</u> are used to make chocolate.
9. A large part of Africa lies between the <u>latitude 23 1/2° north</u> and the Tropic of Capricorn.
10. Because so many languages are used in African countries, many people there are <u>able to speak several languages.</u>

REMEMBERING WHAT YOU READ

On a separate sheet of paper, answer the following questions in complete sentences.

1. Why were the pictures found on rocks on the Tassili plateau surprising?
2. What type of climate do the northern coast and the southern tip of Africa have?
3. What type of land makes up more than a fourth of Africa?
4. Which mountain in East Africa is higher than any mountain in Europe?
5. On which African river is Victoria Falls located?
6. What three things might members of an ethnic group have in common?
7. How are large cities on the African continent similar to large cities on other continents?
8. What is the difference between subsistence farming and commercial farming?
9. How do Africans make use of land that is too dry for farming?
10. What are African countries doing to try to protect the wildlife population?

TYING LANGUAGE ARTS TO SOCIAL STUDIES

Scientists have learned about the Tassili plateau from drawings that are about 8,000 years old. Write a paragraph or two describing what you would want scientists 8,000 years from now to know about the place where you live. You could also do a sketch of your ideas for scientists to discover.

THINKING CRITICALLY

On a separate sheet of paper, answer the following questions in complete sentences.

1. How will the lives of the people of the Sahel change if all the land there becomes desert?
2. Which of the African citizens you read about in Lesson 2 would you trade places with — Kama, Binta, or the Munoru family? Explain.
3. What problems might be created by the use of so many different languages in African countries?
4. How would you restate the proverb "He who cannot dance will say the drum is bad"?
5. What do you think is the most important resource in Africa south of the Sahara? Explain.

SUMMARIZING THE CHAPTER

On a separate sheet of paper, draw a graphic organizer like the one shown here. Copy the information from this graphic organizer to the one you have drawn. Under the main idea for each lesson, write five statements that support the main idea.

CHAPTER THEME

The many different landforms, climates, cultures, and resources found in Africa south of the Sahara affect the way people there live.

LESSON 1

There is much variety in the types of land found in Africa south of the Sahara.

1. _____
2. _____
3. _____
4. _____
5. _____

LESSON 2

Many different kinds of people live in Africa south of the Sahara.

1. _____
2. _____
3. _____
4. _____
5. _____

LESSON 3

Many important, useful natural resources are found in Africa south of the Sahara.

1. _____
2. _____
3. _____
4. _____
5. _____

CHAPTER 17

HISTORY OF AFRICA SOUTH OF THE SAHARA

The climate and land of the continent of Africa produced cultures rich in crafts, music, and dance. African trading states, such as Kilwa, developed in the region in earlier times.

West Africa

THINK ABOUT WHAT YOU KNOW

Some history, such as that of a family, is handed down by word of mouth. What kinds of things have you heard about that happened in your family before you were born?

STUDY THE VOCABULARY

oral history **plaque**

FOCUS YOUR READING

What was life like in the kingdoms of West Africa?

A. Sundiata, the African Alexander

Handing Down History Storytellers were the historians of Africa 700 years ago. Like the Greek poet Homer, they told about the heroes and kings of past times. The storytellers did not find their stories in books, however. Accounts of the past were handed down by word of mouth from one generation to another. Such knowledge is called **oral history**. For this oral history to be remembered, the storyteller had to be entertaining as well as informative. Some of the most famous of these African stories are the Anansi (ah NAHN see) tales. You can read an Anansi tale in the literature selection on page 456.

Stories of the past greatly interested a boy named Sundiata (sun JAHT ah), who was born the son of a king ca. 1210 in a West African village. Most stories Sundiata heard were about African rulers and heroes, but the storytellers also told about Alexander the Great. As you recall from Chapter 2, Alexander was the young king of ancient Macedonia who conquered Greece and other lands and formed an empire. The African storytellers called Alexander "the mighty king of gold and silver whose sun shone over half the world."

Sundiata's Kingdom Sundiata was also curious about faraway places. He liked to talk with travelers who came to his village and often questioned them about the lands on the other side of the Sahara. After Sundiata became king, ca. 1230, he conquered neighboring lands and created the Mali kingdom. The kingdom included most of the land between the Atlantic coast and the great bend of the Niger River. Today seven countries lie in this area.

In later times when storytellers told about Sundiata's kingdom, they called him "the king of kings." They compared him with Alexander the Great. One modern historian has even called Sundiata "the African Alexander."

B. The Wealth of Mansa Musa

Mansa Musa, a descendant of Sundiata, ruled the Mali kingdom from ca. 1307 to ca. 1332. The kingdom was rich in gold. The king of Mali rewarded officials and soldiers with beautiful gold collars, bracelets, and even trousers, much as governments today award medals.

Many of the people of the Mali kingdom followed the old African religions, but Mansa Musa was a Muslim. In 1324 he led a large group of his Muslim subjects on a pilgrimage to Mecca, the Muslim holy city in Arabia.

On the way, Mansa Musa and his party stopped in Cairo, Egypt. The people there were dazzled by Mansa Musa's great wealth, and they were awed by his generosity. Mansa Musa gave away so much gold that its price remained low in Cairo for several years.

FROM:
The Anansi Tales

By: Peggy Appiah
Setting: African forest

Anansi, the spider, sometimes called Kwaku (Uncle) Anansi, is the trickster hero of the Ashanti peoples of Africa. His adventures were passed down orally in the form of folk tales.

In the story "How Wisdom Was Spread Throughout the World," Anansi, sometimes spelled *Ananse*, was the only wise creature in the world. Being greedy, he wished to keep all this wisdom to himself. He asked his wife to store his wisdom in a big pot so he could hide it safely in a big tree in the forest.

Carrying the pot in front of him, he made his way through the forest, followed—unbeknown—by his small son Ntikuma. At last he reached the great tree and started to try climbing it. He hung the pot by a rope around his neck, with the stopper just below his nose so he could make quite sure it did not tip over.

Alas, try as he would, Kwaku Ananse could not climb the tree, for the pot got in the way of his arms and he found he was unable to grip the trunk. He tried, and he tried, and he tried. . . .

Ananse's son, watching from behind a tree, advised his father to tie the pot to his back to free his hands.

Ananse was furious. Here his small son was teaching him a lesson—a lesson which he realized was only too true. Shaking with anger and exhaustion he lifted the pot, meaning to take it off and chastise [scold] his son. His hands were slippery with sweat and the great pot was heavy. It slipped through his fingers and crashed to the ground.

The pot burst open and its contents were scattered far and wide. There was a storm coming, and the wind swept through the forest, lifting the wisdom and carrying it on its way. The rain poured down and swept the wisdom into the streams, which carried it into the sea. Thus was wisdom spread throughout the world. . . .

C. Centers of Trade and Learning

Trade Timbuktu was one of the most important cities of the Mali kingdom. An old saying described its location on the edge of the Sahara near the Niger River as "the meeting place for all who travel by camel and canoe."

Camel caravans crossed the desert, loaded with silks, brassware, steel weapons, and other goods from North Africa, Europe, and the Middle East. The caravans also carried blocks of salt from salt mines in the Sahara. Salt was scarce south of the Sahara. It was so valuable that in some places it was used for money. Traders exchanged these goods in Timbuktu for gold, copper, ivory, cotton cloth, and other products brought by boats on the Niger River.

Teachers and Students Timbuktu was known for its learned Muslim teachers as well as its traders. The city had several large mosques where people came to study. Because of the many students and teachers, traders brought bundles of books to Timbuktu. It was said that books sold for more money than any other goods.

Jenné was another center of trade and learning in the Mali kingdom. It was located farther upstream on the river.

D. Benin, Kingdom in the Forest

Farm and Town The kingdom of Benin (be NEEN) was located in what is now southern Nigeria. An early king named Ewuare made Benin the most powerful state in this part of Africa.

Most people in the kingdom were forest farmers. They used the slash-and-burn method as some farmers today still do. The king of Benin lived in a walled town. The houses of craftworkers and people who

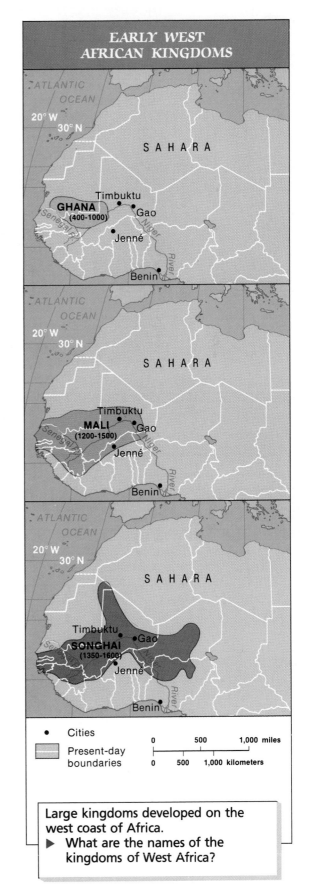

EARLY WEST AFRICAN KINGDOMS

- Cities
- Present-day boundaries

Large kingdoms developed on the west coast of Africa.
▶ What are the names of the kingdoms of West Africa?

served the king stood along the town's broad streets. The king and members of his household lived in an enclosed area in the middle of the town. Their houses had wooden pillars decorated with bronze **plaques**, or sheets of metal. The plaques showed kings, queens, hunters, soldiers, musicians, and acrobats. Figures of animals also decorated the plaques.

Ways of Learning The plaques were more than decorations, however. They served as historical records. Benin had no system of writing. Storytellers passed on accounts of the past, and the plaques served as reminders of those events.

In 1486, Portuguese traders visited Benin. They found that the king of Benin was as curious about Portugal as they were about Benin. When the Portuguese ships set sail, one of the king's advisers was on board. He was sent by the king to find out more about the kingdom of Portugal.

Artists from the kingdom of Benin were skilled in sculpting figures from bronze.
► Who do you think these bronze statues might depict?

LESSON 1 REVIEW

THINK AND WRITE
A. Why has Sundiata been called "the African Alexander"?
B. How would you describe what kind of person Mansa Musa was?
C. What were two important centers of trade and learning in Mali?
D. Give a brief summary of what most people in Benin did for a living.

SKILLS CHECK

THINKING SKILL
Make a time line showing the following events: the Magna Carta is signed, 1215; Sundiata becomes king, 1230; Mansa Musa goes to Mecca, 1324; Gutenberg develops new printing method, ca. 1455; Portuguese traders visit Benin, 1486; Columbus discovers America, 1492.

458

East Africa

THINK ABOUT WHAT YOU KNOW

If you were an archaeologist, what would you look for that would tell you about people who lived long ago?

STUDY THE VOCABULARY

dry stone   **monsoon**

FOCUS YOUR READING

What were some of the achievements of people living in East Africa?

A. Clues About the Past in Zimbabwe

Stone Ruins The remains of stone structures in southeast Africa provide many clues about the past. The most famous ruins are those at Great Zimbabwe (zihm BAHB way) National Park, in Zimbabwe. The structures there are the largest built south of the Sahara before modern times.

Huge boulders connected by stone walls cover a hill at Great Zimbabwe. At the foot of the hill is a walled enclosure with a cone-shaped tower inside. The enclosure walls are about 17 feet (5 m) thick at the base. The tower is about 34 feet (10 m) high, although it may once have been taller. All of the structures were built with **dry stones,** that is, stones held together without mortar.

Studying the Ruins Archaeologists who have studied Great Zimbabwe think that the largest stone structure there was built about 500 years ago. They believe it served as the residence of kings who ruled this part of Africa.

Archaeologists have recovered some objects at Zimbabwe that were used by the people who once lived there. They have found carved stone figures and gold ornaments made by African craftworkers. They have also uncovered glassware from the Middle East, and delicate porcelain, or very fine earthenware, from China.

Great Zimbabwe, now lying in ruins, was built by the Shona people.
▶ What material did the Shona use to build these walls?

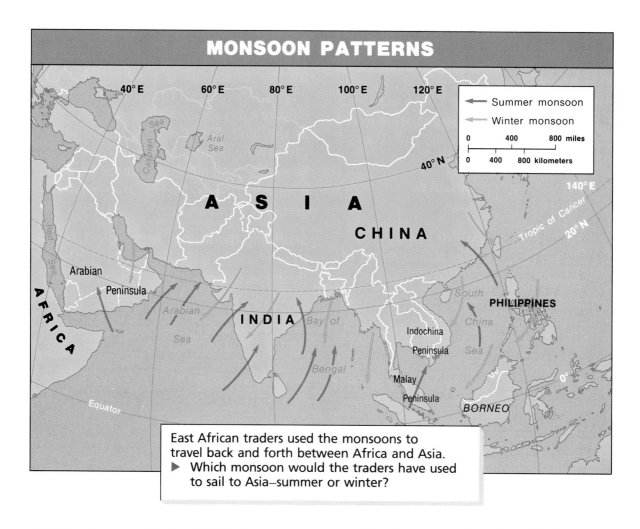

MONSOON PATTERNS

East African traders used the monsoons to travel back and forth between Africa and Asia.
▶ Which monsoon would the traders have used to sail to Asia—summer or winter?

B. Trade on a Path of Wind

Trade Grows Great Zimbabwe is more than 200 miles (322 km) from the sea. The porcelain found there must have been traded in cities on the East African coast. Goods from Asia came into these ports.

The trading ships often sailed with the seasonal winds of the Indian Ocean. These winds, called **monsoons**, change direction with the seasons. From May to September the summer monsoon blows from the southwest. By sailing with the wind, ships were carried from Africa to Arabia or even farther east to India. From November to March the monsoon blows in the opposite direction, so ships could sail from Arabia or India back to Africa. No

wonder that one writer described a monsoon as a "path of wind."

Ships coming from Arabia and India carried products from those lands and goods from still more distant places. In this way fine cloth from Persia and porcelain from China reached East Africa.

Cities Grow During the Middle Ages, trade increased and the coastal cities grew. When the Portuguese explorer Vasco da Gama reached East Africa, he was surprised to find such well-built cities. He reported that Kilwa had "good buildings of stone." Houses within that walled city rose to three and four stories and stood so close together that one could "run along the tops of them."

C. Ethiopia's Long History

Early Christianity The kingdom of Ethiopia was isolated compared with the trading cities on the coast. It was located on a mountainous plateau in East Africa. Because of its isolation it was able to keep its own language and beliefs.

The Ethiopian kings were Christians. They claimed to be the descendants of Solomon, king of ancient Israel, and Queen Makeda. In the Bible, Makeda is known as the queen of Sheba. The Ethiopian account of Solomon and Makeda is found in a book entitled *The Glory of Kings*.

According to the book, Makeda was an excellent queen. She heard of Solomon's great wisdom and decided to go to Jerusalem, Solomon's capital. Before leaving she told her people, "I am going to seek wisdom and learning. Learning is better than treasures of silver and gold, better than all that has been created on earth."

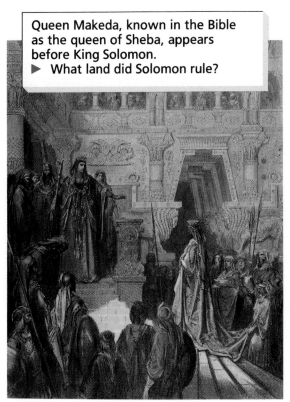

Queen Makeda, known in the Bible as the queen of Sheba, appears before King Solomon.
▶ What land did Solomon rule?

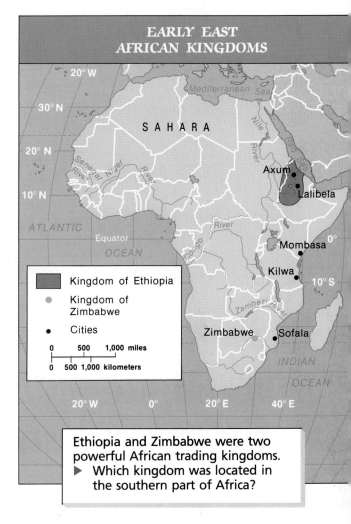

EARLY EAST
AFRICAN KINGDOMS

Kingdom of Ethiopia
Kingdom of Zimbabwe
Cities

Ethiopia and Zimbabwe were two powerful African trading kingdoms.
▶ Which kingdom was located in the southern part of Africa?

When Solomon met Makeda, he was struck by her beauty and fell in love with her. Makeda stayed with Solomon for a time and then returned to her country.

The Glory of Kings was written about 700 years ago and is one of the oldest Ethiopian books. Even so, it was written long after the time of Solomon. Most historians do not consider the story of Makeda and Solomon to be true history. They compare it with Homer's account of the Trojan War.

But Ethiopia does have a long history. Its beginnings go back at least as far as King Ezana, who came to power around A.D. 320. Ezana was the king who adopted Christianity as the religion of the kingdom.

461

This is the Church of St. George, which is located in Ethiopia.
► Into what shape was the solid stone church carved?

People and Churches During the Middle Ages most people in Ethiopia were either farmers or herders. The farmers lived in small villages, and the herders wandered with their animals. Even the king and his officials moved about the kingdom and lived in tents. There were no large cities.

Although the Ethiopians did not build large cities, they did create beautiful buildings. The Ethiopian king Lalibela had 11 churches carved—not built—from solid stone. Some of the churches were cut into the sides of rock cliffs. Others were shaped from layers of rock. Both the insides and outsides were decorated with carvings. Only highly skilled workers could have created these churches. A single mistaken blow with a hammer would have ruined the whole work. People still worship in the carved stone churches of Ethiopia.

LESSON *2* REVIEW

THINK AND WRITE

A. What can be learned from the ruins at Great Zimbabwe?
B. What are monsoons, and how did they affect trade in East Africa?
C. What lasting works did the Ethiopians create?

SKILLS CHECK

WRITING SKILL

Pretend that you are the first European to see the stone structures that are now part of Great Zimbabwe National Park. Write a two-paragraph essay describing what you see and your reaction to it. In writing your essay use both the information given in the text and your imagination.

Europeans South of the Sahara

THINK ABOUT WHAT YOU KNOW

Would you like to be an explorer? If you were one, where would you go? Why?

STUDY THE VOCABULARY

navigator   **missionary**
Boer

FOCUS YOUR READING

What role did Europeans play in Africa south of the Sahara?

A. Portuguese Exploration

Henry the Navigator   Prince Henry of Portugal was called "the Navigator." It was, perhaps, a strange title for a man who seldom went to sea. A **navigator** plans and steers a course through water or air, or on land. Yet although Henry remained in Portugal most of the time, he did plan the courses for the ships he sent to explore the west coast of Africa.

Henry the Navigator set up a school for sailors and explorers on the southwest coast of Portugal. He sent ships to explore the African coast. The captains recorded what they saw as they sailed farther south. Henry had maps for later expeditions made based on this information.

Exploration Continues   Prince Henry died in 1460, but the Portuguese continued to travel along the African coast. By 1482 a Portuguese ship had sailed as far south as the Equator. Six years later Bartholomeu Dias (bahr THAHL uh myoo DEE us) discovered the Cape of Good Hope at the southern tip of Africa. This discovery showed that it was possible to sail around Africa. A few years later, Vasco da Gama sailed around the Cape to the east coast.

Prince Henry sent out ships because he had great curiosity about Africa. Other Portuguese may have shared Henry's desire to know more, but it was not curiosity alone that caused them to explore the African coast. The Portuguese wanted to trade for Africa's gold, ivory, pepper, and slaves.

B. Kidnapped by Slave Traders

One Villager's Tale   Slave traders from other countries followed the Portuguese to the African coast. Over the next 350 years, millions of Africans were captured and transported to the Americas.

Prince Henry the Navigator of Portugal established a school for sailors and explorers.
► What is Prince Henry holding?

PRINCE HENRY OF PORTUGAL

Many African slaves died of disease or cruel treatment during voyages in overcrowded ships.
▶ How were the slaves mistreated?

A book written by an African named Olaudah Equiano (oh LOU duh ek wee-AHN oh) tells what it was like to be captured and sold as a slave. Equiano was born around 1745 in a village in Benin. As he remembered it, the village was a very pleasant place. The villagers raised their own food, built their own dwellings, and largely managed their own affairs. The village was far from the king's town and from the sea. Equiano wrote in his book that as a child he had "never heard of white men or Europeans."

The people of Equiano's village had a few slaves. It was the practice to enslave rather than kill persons captured in war. When European traders came to Africa, the demand for slaves increased. Slave traders kidnapped people and took them to the European trading posts, where they were sold and shipped to distant lands.

Sold into Slavery   When Olaudah Equiano was 12 years old, he and his sister were stolen from their African home. The kidnappers sold the two young captives to other slave traders, and they were passed from one owner to another. Olaudah was separated from his sister, and after about six months he was taken to the coast. Olaudah was put on board a slave ship, where he was roughly handled and mistreated by the sailors. Many years later, Equiano remembered how terrified he was that day he was carried on board.

I was now persuaded that I had gotten into a world of bad spirits and that they were going to kill me. Their complexions too differing so much from ours, their long hair and the language they spoke (which was very different from any I had ever heard) united to confirm me in this belief.

Equiano's fears increased when he was shoved below deck of the ship. After a time the badly frightened boy found some of his own people held in chains. From them he learned that "we were to be carried to these white people's country to work for them."

Equiano's Experiences The first stop was at Barbados, an island in the West Indies. Most of the captives were sold to planters in the islands. They were taken to work in the sugar fields. Equiano was put on another ship and taken to the British colony of Virginia, where he was sold to a planter. Later the planter sold him to a British naval officer.

Equiano served the officer for several years. Equiano had a quick mind, and he learned to speak English well. He also learned to be a barber. He was taken to London, where he found friends who enabled him to attend school for a short time. Equiano managed to make and save some money. When he was 21, he was able to buy his freedom.

As a free man, Olaudah Equiano tried to awaken people in Europe to the cruelty of the slave trade. He wrote the story of his life because he wanted to tell people about "the inhuman traffic of slavery."

C. European Footholds in Africa

In 1481 a large Portuguese fleet set sail from the port of Lisbon. It was headed for the African coast. This time, in addition to traders, it carried carpenters, stone

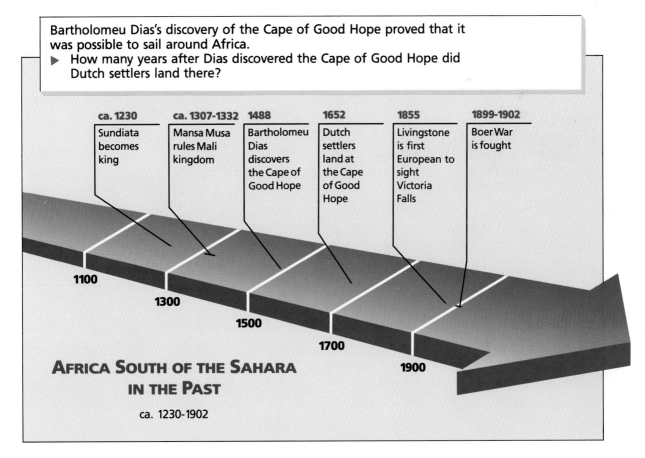

Bartholomeu Dias's discovery of the Cape of Good Hope proved that it was possible to sail around Africa.
▶ How many years after Dias discovered the Cape of Good Hope did Dutch settlers land there?

ca. 1230	ca. 1307-1332	1488	1652	1855	1899-1902
Sundiata becomes king	Mansa Musa rules Mali kingdom	Bartholomeu Dias discovers the Cape of Good Hope	Dutch settlers land at the Cape of Good Hope	Livingstone is first European to sight Victoria Falls	Boer War is fought

1100
1300
1500
1700
1900

AFRICA SOUTH OF THE SAHARA IN THE PAST

ca. 1230-1902

masons, and a company of soldiers. The fleet had orders to establish a fort and trading post on the coast.

The Portuguese built Fort St. George at Elmina, which is shown below, on the coast of what is now called Ghana. Later they established other permanent trading stations. One was located at Luanda, on the coast of modern Angola.

The Portuguese were not the only Europeans to seize footholds in Africa. The French built Fort St. Louis at the mouth of the Senegal River, in the country now called Senegal. The Dutch, Danes, and English also built fortified trading posts on African soil.

D. Europeans Settle in South Africa

Dutch Settlers Europeans did not settle in tropical Africa, partly because they were particularly susceptible to, or likely to catch, certain tropical diseases. So many of the early traders and explorers died of these diseases that Europeans called tropical Africa "the white man's grave." South of the tropics, however, at the Cape of Good Hope, Europeans found a land that did attract many settlers. The South African climate was very much like that of the Mediterranean lands.

A group of Dutch settlers landed at the Cape of Good Hope in 1652 and were there to stay. The Cape settlement was to

The fortress of St. George at Elmina, on the coast of what is now called Ghana, was built in 1482 at the order of the king of Portugal as a trading post and supply base for Portuguese navigators.
▶ What did the Portuguese build at their new settlement?

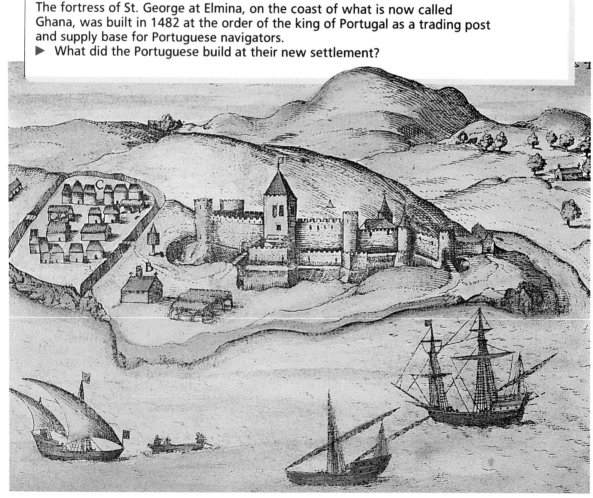

Dutch settlers, called the Boers, traveled across South Africa in search of land they could farm. They made the trip with large herds of cattle.
▶ What form of transportation did the Boers use to travel?

serve as a supply base rather than a trading post. It would be a place where ships making the long trip from Europe to India could find fresh food and water. The settlers called themselves **Boers** (boorz), a Dutch word meaning "farmers." The Boers planted crops, set out orchards and vineyards, and kept herds of cattle.

Taking Africans' Land South Africa was not an empty land when the Europeans first settled there. It was a homeland for several African peoples. But the settlers thought the land was little used because the Africans did not cultivate crops. Instead they depended on hunting, herding, and food gathering for their living.

The settlers pushed the Africans off some of the land. Fighting broke out between the two groups. African spears were no match for European guns, and soon parts of the African hunting grounds became settlers' farms. The Boers employed black workers on their farms. Many of them were slaves. Those who were free, however, were not treated much better than the slaves.

British Settlers Great Britain seized control of the Cape settlement from the Dutch during a war in 1795. The Boers disliked British rule, and they were outraged when the British abolished slavery within the British Empire in 1834. The British government paid owners for their slaves, but the Boers complained that the payments were far too little. As for the black slaves, they received their freedom but no land, so many of them still had to work for the white settlers.

Because of their differences with the British, a number of Boers left the Cape colony to settle farther inland. At the end of the century, however, the Boers went to war with the British again, over many of the same issues.

Henry Stanley was an American reporter who went to Africa in 1869 to find David Livingstone, a famous explorer of the time who was feared to be missing.
▶ Besides exploring, for what other work was Livingstone known?

E. A Missionary Explorer in Africa

David Livingstone David Livingstone did not come to South Africa from Scotland in 1841 to settle or trade. He was a doctor who was also a **missionary**, so he came to teach the African people about the Christian religion.

After arriving in Africa, Livingstone decided that he could best serve the Africans by helping open up the continent to the outside world. Livingstone respected the ways of the Africans. He lived among them and learned their languages and customs. But he was convinced that Africans needed to learn about modern science and business. He by no means gave up the hope of bringing Christianity to Africa. He simply decided that the faith could best be spread by Africans who knew more about the outside world.

To help open up Africa, Livingstone spent much of his life exploring the continent. He traveled hundreds of miles by boat and on foot, visiting lands no white person had seen. He explored the Kalahari, traveled to Africa's great lakes, and discovered Victoria Falls.

Teaching About Africa Livingstone not only taught Africans about the outside world, he also taught the outside world about Africa. He wrote books about his travels that were widely read in Europe and America. He told the world about the slave trade, which he called "the open sore of Africa."

Livingstone died in 1873 in a central African village in what is now Zambia. His African friends buried his heart in African soil before carrying his body to the coast to be sent back to Britain.

F. European Rule in Africa

Colonial Africa Europeans first established footholds in Africa so they could trade. They did not try to rule the continent. After 1880, however, European governments claimed large areas of Africa for their empires. Within a very short time, they had divided Africa into colonies.

The map on this page shows which countries ruled in Africa in 1920. Only two lands, Ethiopia and Liberia, were independent. Find these lands on the map below.

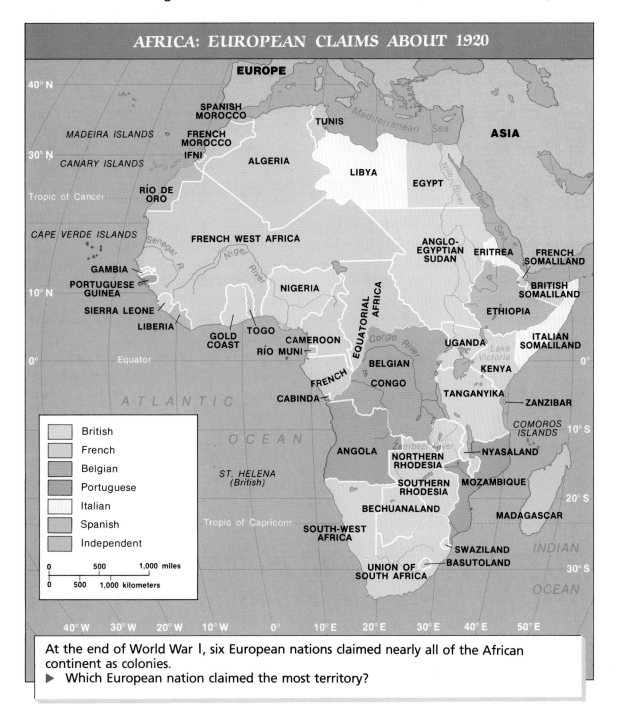

AFRICA: EUROPEAN CLAIMS ABOUT 1920

EUROPE

40° N

SPANISH MOROCCO

TUNIS

Mediterranean Sea

ASIA

MADEIRA ISLANDS

FRENCH MOROCCO

30° N

IFNI

ALGERIA

CANARY ISLANDS

LIBYA

EGYPT

Nile River

Red Sea

Tropic of Cancer

RÍO DE ORO

CAPE VERDE ISLANDS

Senegal R.

FRENCH WEST AFRICA

Niger River

ANGLO-EGYPTIAN SUDAN

ERITREA

FRENCH SOMALILAND

GAMBIA

PORTUGUESE GUINEA

10° N

NIGERIA

BRITISH SOMALILAND

SIERRA LEONE

EQUATORIAL AFRICA

ETHIOPIA

LIBERIA

GOLD COAST

TOGO

CAMEROON

ITALIAN SOMALILAND

RÍO MUNI

Congo River

UGANDA

0°

Equator

FRENCH

BELGIAN CONGO

KENYA

0°

CABINDA

TANGANYIKA

ZANZIBAR

ATLANTIC

COMOROS ISLANDS

10° S

OCEAN

British

French

ANGOLA

Zambezi River

NORTHERN RHODESIA

NYASALAND

Belgian

ST. HELENA (British)

SOUTHERN RHODESIA

MOZAMBIQUE

Portuguese

20° S

Italian

BECHUANALAND

MADAGASCAR

Spanish

Tropic of Capricorn

SOUTH-WEST AFRICA

INDIAN

Independent

SWAZILAND

0   500   1,000 miles

BASUTOLAND

0   500   1,000 kilometers

UNION OF SOUTH AFRICA

30° S

OCEAN

40° W   30° W   20° W   10° W   0°   10° E   20° E   30° E   40° E   50° E

At the end of World War I, six European nations claimed nearly all of the African continent as colonies.
▶ Which European nation claimed the most territory?

Portugal, Spain, and Italy Portugal was the first country to explore the African coast, and the first to establish colonies. Portuguese Guinea and Angola had grown from forts built to protect trade — particularly the slave trade. The Portuguese had acquired the coast of Mozambique by conquering the trading cities of East Africa. They later extended their control along the Zambezi. Spain's holdings were confined to northwest Africa.

Spain held Ifni and Río de Oro on the Atlantic coast of the Sahara desert. The name *Río de Oro* means "river of gold." The name went back to the time when caravan merchants traded gold from West Africa there.

Italy's largest colony, Libya, was directly across the Mediterranean in North Africa. Italy also held Eritrea on the Red Sea coast and Somaliland on the Horn of Africa, the peninsula on the east coast.

Britain and France Great Britain and France ruled the largest part of Africa. Before World War I some British leaders had dreamed that Britain would someday rule a strip of land "from the Cape to Cairo," that is, from South Africa to Egypt. This dream came true after World War I, when Britain acquired some German colonies. The British Empire also included Nigeria and other lands in West Africa. The name of one of these lands, Gold Coast, recalls why it was that Europeans first came to tropical Africa.

France held much of North Africa, ruling or controlling Algeria, Tunis, and most of Morocco. The French flag flew over a large part of the Sahara. South of the Sahara were several large French colonies, including French Equatorial Africa, which extended to the Congo River. France also ruled Madagascar, a large island off the East African coast.

The Foreign Legion is made up of volunteers from different countries. One of its original purposes was to assist in the conquest of Algeria. Later many of the Legion's units served in North Africa.
▶ Under which government do you think the Foreign Legion serves?

Belgium Belgium, one of Europe's smallest countries, ruled one of the largest colonies in tropical Africa. The Belgian Congo was 77 times as large as Belgium itself. Belgium had acquired this land because the Belgian king Leopold II had organized an international business company to develop the resources of the Congo Basin.

Although Leopold made a large fortune from ivory and rubber, he could not convince many Europeans to move to the Congo. Leopold used extreme cruelty in his attempt to get as much labor as he could from the people who lived in the Congo. Countries around the world loudly protested Leopold's methods. Largely due to the international pressure, the Belgian government took over the colony and made reforms. Today this area is the independent country of Zaire.

The division of Africa among European nations took place quickly, but the European countries did not hold on to their colonies long. The Gold Coast became independent in 1957 and took the name Ghana. Other African colonies soon gained their independence.

King Leopold's treatment of the Congo people angered many nations.
▶ How does the artist portray King Leopold?

LESSON **3** *REVIEW*

THINK AND WRITE

A. What reasons did the Portuguese have for exploring the coast of Africa?

B. What effect do you think Olaudah Equiano's book had on people during his lifetime?

C. What European countries built forts along the African coast?

D. Summarize the development of the colony in South Africa.

E. What effects did David Livingstone's mission in Africa have on Africans and Europeans?

F. How did European activity in Africa change after 1880?

SKILLS CHECK

MAP SKILL

Compare the map of European colonies in Africa, on page 469, with that of Africa today in the Atlas, on page 624. Write the modern name of each of these former colonies: Gold Coast, Belgian Congo, Bechuanaland, Southern Rhodesia, Tanganyika. Name at least three countries created out of what had been French West Africa.

USING THE VOCABULARY

oral history   monsoon
navigator   Boer
missionary

On a separate sheet of paper, write the word or words from above that best complete the sentences.

1. A Dutch farmer who settled at the Cape of Good Hope in the 1600s had the name _____ .

2. Prince Henry of Portugal was a _____ who planned the courses for ships he sent to explore the west coast of Africa.

3. The summer _____ on the Indian Ocean blows from the southwest.

4. An account of the past that African story-tellers handed down by word of mouth is called _____ .

5. Dr. David Livingstone was a _____ who went to Africa to teach people there about the Christian religion.

REMEMBERING WHAT YOU READ

On a separate sheet of paper, answer the following questions in complete sentences.

1. Where was Mansa Musa going when he stopped to spend time in Cairo, Egypt?
2. Why was the African city of Timbuktu important?
3. What were the purposes of the plaques on houses in the kingdom of Benin?
4. What objects have archaeologists found at Great Zimbabwe?
5. How did sailing ships from Africa make use of the monsoons to trade with Asian countries?

6. How did increased trade affect cities on the coast of East Africa during the Middle Ages?
7. Where did most people in Ethiopia live during the Middle Ages?
8. Why was Bartholomeu Dias's discovery of the Cape of Good Hope important?
9. Why did Olaudah Equiano write a book about his experiences?
10. What changes did European settlers make in Africa south of the Sahara?

TYING ART TO SOCIAL STUDIES

Use the maps and the information in this chapter to create a map showing goods that were traded in Africa south of the Sahara. First draw or trace the outline of the continent. Then design your own symbols for some of the traded goods and draw the symbols on your map to show areas where those goods were traded. Label any cities or countries in the appropriate areas of trade.

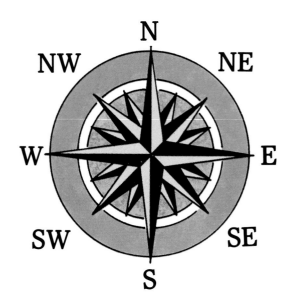

THINKING CRITICALLY

On a separate sheet of paper, answer the following questions in complete sentences.

1. What are some of the ways in which we have learned about earlier times in Africa south of the Sahara?
2. Why would people have paid more money for books than for any other goods traded in Timbuktu?
3. What do you think the cone-shaped tower at Great Zimbabwe might have been used for?
4. Why, do you think, did so many different countries come to explore Africa south of the Sahara?
5. Why, do you think, did David Livingstone want to teach people outside of Africa about this continent?

SUMMARIZING THE CHAPTER

On a separate sheet of paper, copy the graphic organizer shown below. Beside each question, write four answers from the chapter.

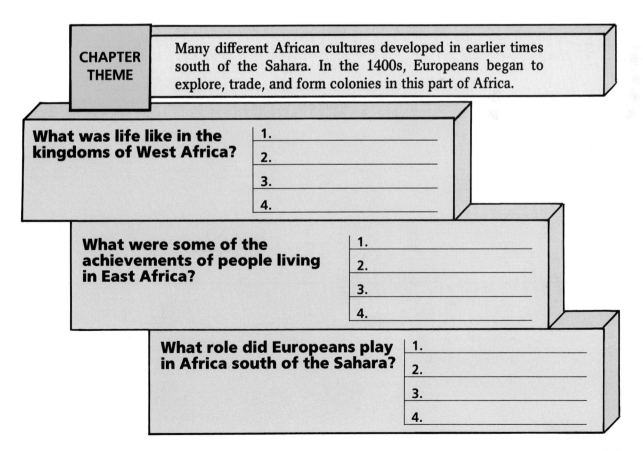

CHAPTER THEME

Many different African cultures developed in earlier times south of the Sahara. In the 1400s, Europeans began to explore, trade, and form colonies in this part of Africa.

What was life like in the kingdoms of West Africa?
1. _____
2. _____
3. _____
4. _____

What were some of the achievements of people living in East Africa?
1. _____
2. _____
3. _____
4. _____

What role did Europeans play in Africa south of the Sahara?
1. _____
2. _____
3. _____
4. _____

*T*he nations of Africa struggle to build strong economies despite differences in cultures, languages, and customs. Africa's cities, like big cities everywhere, have modern buildings, theaters, and museums.

West Africa

THINK ABOUT WHAT YOU KNOW

You will learn in this lesson that oil has had a great influence in the development of the country Nigeria. What other countries have you learned about that have prospered from oil?

STUDY THE VOCABULARY

economic boom   groundnut

FOCUS YOUR READING

What problems did West African countries face after independence?

A. Independent Ghana

At the time European countries ruled Africa, some Africans went to Europe or America for an education. Among them were Jomo Kenyatta (JOH moh ken YAHT-uh) and Kwame Nkrumah (KWAH mee un-KROO muh). Both returned to Africa to lead movements for African independence in the 1950s. Kenyatta was named the first president of Kenya. Nkrumah became Ghana's first president.

When Ghana became independent, it kept ties with Great Britain. English remains the official language, and Ghana is a member of the Commonwealth of Nations.

Nkrumah was not in office for very long. He grew impatient with those who opposed him and finally had himself declared president for life. In 1966, however, a group of army officers took over the government. Though it is called a republic, Ghana is still under military rule.

Ghana has remained an agricultural country, although the government has taken steps to develop industry. Cacao is the country's most valuable export. Ghana also sells electricity to neighboring countries. Electric power is produced at a large dam on the Volta River.

B. A Better Tomorrow for Nigeria

Independent Nigeria   The British invented the name Nigeria for the different regions along the Niger River that were part of their empire. When British rule ended, the African leaders had to create a Nigerian nationality. At one time it seemed that they might fail. A bloody civil war broke out between some of Nigeria's many ethnic groups in the 1960s. In the end, however, Nigeria remained one country. As a member of the Commonwealth of Nations, it has kept some ties with Britain.

Independent Nigeria has had several types of governments. There were two efforts to establish elected governments, but army officers seized power each time. In

Kwame Nkrumah (right) talks with Dwight D. Eisenhower, President of the United States from 1953–1961.
▶ Of what country was Nkrumah president?

Oil has had a great influence on Nigeria's development.
▶ What are these oil drillers wearing for protection?

C. Ivory Coast, Senegal, and Gambia

Ivory Coast Côte d'Ivoire (koht deev-WAHR) is the French name for "Ivory Coast" and the nation's official name. French is the official language in Ivory Coast, as it is in nine other West African nations that were once part of the French empire. Ivory Coast is a republic, but it has only one political party.

Good soil is the main natural resource of Ivory Coast, and most people work on farms or in the forests. Most of those who work in industry process agricultural and forest products. Ivory Coast leads the world in the export of coffee and cacao. It also exports pineapples, bananas, palm oil, and timber.

Senegal Senegal, another former French colony, kept close ties with France after

1989, however, the military rulers promised that there would be an elected government again in the future.

Nigeria's Economy Nigeria has rich soil, forests, and deposits of oil and natural gas. Oil has had the greatest influence on the country's development. When oil prices were high in the 1970s, Nigeria enjoyed an **economic boom**, a period of great prosperity. Many people left the farms to take higher-paying jobs in the cities. As a result, a land that had once fed itself had to import food. Nigeria borrowed large amounts of money from foreign banks, believing that oil prices would stay high or even rise.

The price of oil fell sharply in the early 1980s, however, and the boom was followed by hard times. Nigeria could not repay the foreign loans. In the meantime the population kept on growing, so the standard of living fell. But Nigeria's leaders have not given up hope. They believe "tomorrow can be better."

These children are working on a plantation in the Ivory Coast.
▶ What crop are the children harvesting?

476

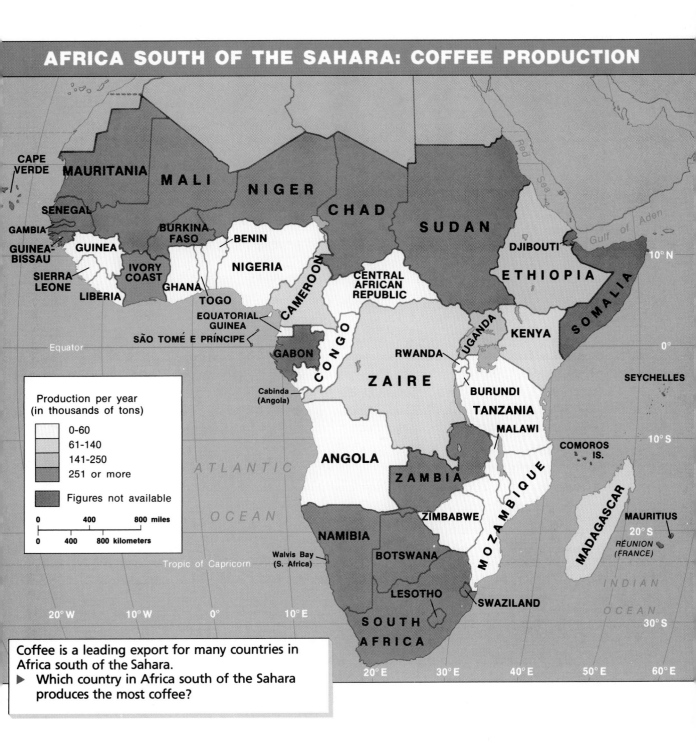

AFRICA SOUTH OF THE SAHARA: COFFEE PRODUCTION

Production per year (in thousands of tons)

- 0–60
- 61–140
- 141–250
- 251 or more

Figures not available

0   400   800 miles

0   400   800 kilometers

Coffee is a leading export for many countries in Africa south of the Sahara.

▶ Which country in Africa south of the Sahara produces the most coffee?

becoming independent. Dakar, the capital city, has been called the cultural center for all French-speaking West Africa.

Senegal is somewhat more democratic than many African states. It has a number of political parties. All but one,

however, are so small that they have never held power.

Gambia Gambia, the smallest African country, was once a British colony. English is the official language of Gambia. There are several parties in Gambia. One,

AFRICA SOUTH OF THE SAHARA: POLITICAL

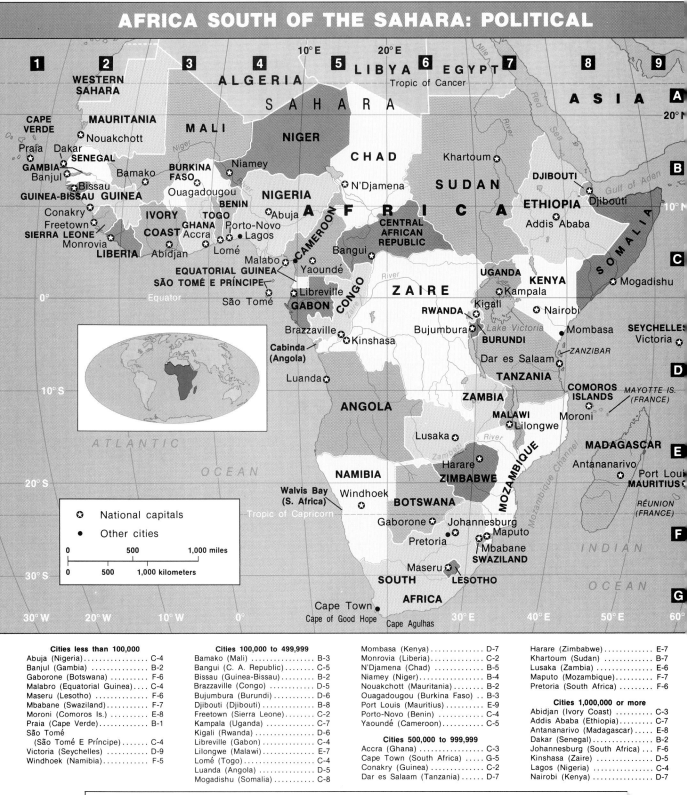

| 1 | 2 | 3 | 4 | 5 | 6 | 7 | 8 | 9 |

WESTERN SAHARA
ALGERIA
10°E 20°E
LIBYA
EGYPT
Tropic of Cancer
ASIA A
20°N

CAPE VERDE
MAURITANIA
⊛ Nouakchott
MALI
SAHARA
NIGER
CHAD
Khartoum ⊛
DJIBOUTI

Praia Dakar
SENEGAL
Niamey
SUDAN
Djibouti B
10°N

GAMBIA
Banjul
Bamako
BURKINA FASO
N'Djamena ⊛
ETHIOPIA

GUINEA-BISSAU GUINEA
Bissau
Ouagadougou
NIGERIA
Addis Ababa

Conakry
IVORY TOGO
BENIN
⊛ Abuja
A F R I C A
SOMALIA

Freetown
GHANA
Porto-Novo
CAMEROON
CENTRAL AFRICAN REPUBLIC
UGANDA
KENYA
⊛ Mogadishu C

SIERRA LEONE
COAST
Accra
• Lagos
Bangui
ZAIRE
Kampala ⊛

Monrovia
Lomé
Malabo
EQUATORIAL GUINEA
Yaoundé
CONGO
River
⊛ Nairobi
SEYCHELLES

LIBERIA Abidjan
SÃO TOMÉ E PRÍNCIPE
Libreville
GABON
RWANDA
Kigali
Victoria ⊛

Equator
São Tomé
CONGO
Brazzaville
Bujumbura
BURUNDI
Mombasa
ZANZIBAR

0°
Kinshasa
Dar es Salaam
TANZANIA

Cabinda (Angola)
Luanda ⊛
ZAMBIA
COMOROS ISLANDS
MAYOTTE IS. (FRANCE) D

10°S
ANGOLA
MALAWI
Lilongwe
Moroni

Lusaka ⊛
River
MADAGASCAR E

ATLANTIC OCEAN
NAMIBIA
ZIMBABWE
Harare
MOZAMBIQUE
Antananarivo
Port Louis
MAURITIUS

Walvis Bay (S. Africa)
Windhoek
Tropic of Capricorn
BOTSWANA
RÉUNION (FRANCE)

20°S
Gaborone ⊛
Johannesburg
Maputo
INDIAN F

Pretoria
Mbabane
SWAZILAND

⊛ National capitals
• Other cities

0   500   1,000 miles

0   500   1,000 kilometers

Maseru
LESOTHO
SOUTH AFRICA
OCEAN G

30°S
Cape Town
Cape of Good Hope
Cape Agulhas
30°E 40°E 50°E 60°E

30°W 20°W 10°W 0°

Cities less than 100,000

Abuja (Nigeria) C-4
Banjul (Gambia) B-2
Gaborone (Botswana) F-6
Malabro (Equatorial Guinea).... C-4
Maseru (Lesotho) F-6
Mbabane (Swaziland) F-7
Moroni (Comoros Is.) E-8
Praia (Cape Verde)............ B-1
São Tomé
   (São Tomé E Príncipe) C-4
Victoria (Seychelles) D-9
Windhoek (Namibia)........... F-5

Cities 100,000 to 499,999

Bamako (Mali) B-3
Bangui (C. A. Republic)........ C-5
Bissau (Guinea-Bissau)........ B-2
Brazzaville (Congo) D-5
Bujumbura (Burundi) D-6
Djibouti (Djibouti) B-8
Freetown (Sierra Leone)....... C-2
Kampala (Uganda) C-7
Kigali (Rwanda) D-6
Libreville (Gabon) C-4
Lilongwe (Malawi)............ E-7
Lomé (Togo).................. C-4
Luanda (Angola) D-5
Mogadishu (Somalia).......... C-8

Mombasa (Kenya) D-7
Monrovia (Liberia)............. C-2
N'Djamena (Chad) B-5
Niamey (Niger)............... B-4
Nouakchott (Mauritania)....... B-2
Ouagadougou (Burkina Faso) .. B-3
Port Louis (Mauritius) E-9
Porto-Novo (Benin) C-4
Yaoundé (Cameroon).......... C-5

Cities 500,000 to 999,999

Accra (Ghana) C-3
Cape Town (South Africa) G-5
Conakry (Guinea) C-2
Dar es Salaam (Tanzania) D-7

Harare (Zimbabwe)............ E-7
Khartoum (Sudan) B-7
Lusaka (Zambia) E-6
Maputo (Mozambique)......... F-7
Pretoria (South Africa) F-6

Cities 1,000,000 or more

Abidjan (Ivory Coast) C-3
Addis Ababa (Ethiopia) C-7
Antananarivo (Madagascar) E-8
Dakar (Senegal)............... B-2
Johannesburg (South Africa) ... F-6
Kinshasa (Zaire).............. D-5
Lagos (Nigeria) C-4
Nairobi (Kenya) D-7

Africa south of the Sahara extends from Senegal in the west to Somalia
in the east. It extends south from the Sahara to South Africa.
▶ Does the capital of Senegal have more than, or less than, 1 million people?

478

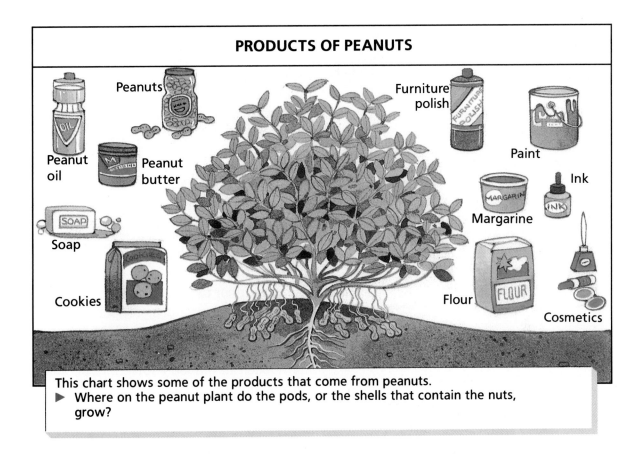

PRODUCTS OF PEANUTS

Peanuts

Furniture polish

Paint

Peanut oil

Peanut butter

Ink

Margarine

Soap

Cookies

Flour

Cosmetics

This chart shows some of the products that come from peanuts.
▶ Where on the peanut plant do the pods, or the shells that contain the nuts, grow?

however, has had more political power than the others.

Gambia's main export is peanuts. Peanuts are also called **groundnuts** because they grow underground rather than on trees or bushes. Groundnuts are an important crop in Senegal, too.

One village in Gambia is known to many through the book *Roots* by Alex Haley. The village of Juffere was the home of Haley's ancestor Kunta Kinte. Like Haley, other African Americans have looked for their ancestors' homelands.

Gambia and Senegal are separate countries, but they have joined to form the Confederation of Senegambia. Under this arrangement the nations have agreed to act together on defense and other matters.

LESSON **1** REVIEW

THINK AND WRITE
A. How did Ghana's government change after it became independent?
B. What problems did Nigeria face when British rule ended?
C. Summarize the similarities and differences between the governments of Ivory Coast, Senegal, and Gambia.

SKILLS CHECK

WRITING SKILL
Imagine that you have traveled to West Africa to find your "roots." Write a brief letter to a friend in the United States describing your emotions on discovering the village where your ancestors were born.

Central Africa

THINK ABOUT WHAT YOU KNOW

Most of the nations of Central Africa became independent around 1960. What problems, do you think, would a new country face?

STUDY THE VOCABULARY

Africanized   **cash crop**

FOCUS YOUR READING

What do the countries discussed in this lesson have in common?

A. Zaire: The Importance of Names

Zaire is one of the largest countries south of the Sahara. It is also one of the largest on the African continent. Because of its size, Zaire is easy to locate on a map of Africa. But you would not find Zaire on a map made in 1970. Instead you would see a land labeled *Republic of the Congo*. You would also discover cities with different names. Kinshasa (keen SHAH sah), which is the capital of Zaire today, was then called Léopoldville. Kisangani (kee sun GAYN ee) was Stanleyville.

The names of both the country and its cities were **Africanized**—changed to African forms. The African names were one way to show that the country was completely independent. The old names reminded people of a time when Europeans had ruled. Léopoldville was named after King Leopold II of Belgium. Stanleyville was named for Henry Stanley, the first white man to explore the Congo River, now known as the Zaire.

Even though place-names have been Africanized, French remains the official language in Zaire. It was used during the years of Belgian rule and is understood by leaders in all parts of the country. Zaire's different ethnic groups, however, have their own languages.

B. Different Ways of Life in Zaire

Zaire's Economy   The peoples of Zaire have varied ways of living. Most work on the land. Many are subsistence farmers; others grow **cash crops** such as cacao and peanuts. These crops are grown for sale rather than for the farmer's own use.

A number of people make their living as miners. Zaire produces copper, tin, zinc, and uranium. It is the world leader in the production of industrial diamonds, which are needed in industry for grinders, glass cutters, and oil drills.

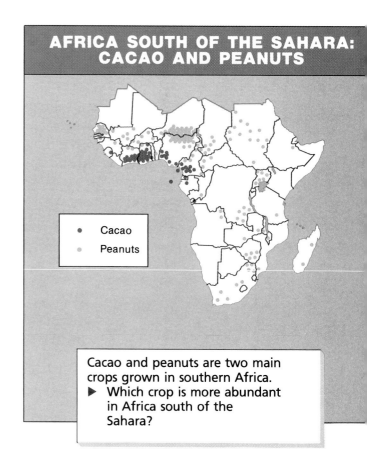

AFRICA SOUTH OF THE SAHARA: CACAO AND PEANUTS

- Cacao
- Peanuts

Cacao and peanuts are two main crops grown in southern Africa.
▶ Which crop is more abundant in Africa south of the Sahara?

The Mbuti of Zaire live by hunting and gathering in the rain forests.
▶ How would you describe the rain forests shown above?

City Dwellers and Forest Dwellers
About 44 percent of the people in Zaire live and work in cities. Very different from the city dwellers are a group of people who live in the rain forest. Outsiders have called these people Pygmies because adults in the group average between 4 feet and 5 feet (between 1 m and 1.5 m) in height. The people themselves consider the name Pygmy to be offensive and prefer to be called by the name of their ethnic group. These names include Mbuti (em BOOTEE) and Efe (AY fay).

These forest people live by hunting and food-gathering. Their size makes it easy for them to move through the thick tropical forest. They do not grow crops or have permanent villages. Instead they move from one forest camp to another.

Officials have encouraged these forest dwellers to adopt a more settled way of life, but with little success. The building of roads and the cutting of the forests make their way of life increasingly difficult. A member of one of these ethnic groups has observed, "When the forest dies, we die."

C. Cameroon: A Mountain and a Country

Cameroon's History Cameroon is one of five independent countries that were once French colonies in equatorial Africa. The country takes its name from Mount Cameroon, an active volcano on its coast. One side of this mountain is one of the wettest places on earth. It receives about 400 inches (1,016 cm) of rain a year. The southern part of Cameroon lies in the tropical rain forest. The north is dry savanna.

Germany ruled Cameroon before World War I. After Germany's defeat in the war, Great Britain and France divided the country. When Cameroon became independent, one part of the British territory chose to become part of neighboring Nigeria. The remainder of the British territory joined with the French territory to form one country. Both French and English are official languages in Cameroon.

Cameroon's Economy About eight out of ten people in Cameroon are farmers. Many are subsistence farmers. At one time, Cameroon supplied most of its own food. Now it depends partly on imports to feed its growing population. Some farmers in Cameroon produce crops for export. Among these cash crops are cacao, coffee, and rubber.

D. Congo, Gabon, Central African Republic

Congo Before 1960 two African states had the name Congo. One was the Belgian Congo, the other the French Congo. The first became Zaire; the other is still called Congo. Brazzaville, the capital of Congo, is located directly across the Zaire River from Kinshasa.

About half of the people in Congo now live in cities. Only a small part of the land is arable. Timber was once the principal export, but oil has replaced it in recent years.

Gabon Gabon (ga BOHN), like Congo and Cameroon, was created from French Equatorial Africa. Libreville, Gabon's capital, is located almost on the Equator. *Libreville* means "free town." It was established by the French about 150 years

Gabon became independent in 1960. Presidential Guard members celebrate Gabon National Day.
▶ To what American national holiday can this celebration be compared?

ago as a town for freed slaves. Another town in Gabon, Lambaréné (lahm buh RAY-nee), is known as the place where Albert Schweitzer, a Christian missionary, set up a hospital in 1913. It has room for 600 patients and their families. Schweitzer was a famous musician and philosopher in addition to being a medical doctor.

Gabon has forests, oil, and other mineral resources. Mining is the most important industry. About one fourth of the manganese used in the Western industrial countries is mined in Gabon. As you have learned in an earlier chapter, manganese is used to harden steel.

Central African Republic The Central African Republic is mostly savanna, although it has some forest. Diamonds are the leading export, but most people are employed in agriculture.

In 1976 a military leader had himself crowned emperor and changed the country's name to Central African Empire. But his empire did not last long. He was driven from power in 1979, and the nation again became a republic. The republic, however, has but one political party. Congo and Gabon are also one-party states.

The Granger Collection, NY

Albert Schweitzer is shown above working in his hospital office.
▶ Besides medicine, what other fields was Albert Schweitzer famous for?

LESSON **2** REVIEW

THINK AND WRITE

A. Why did the Republic of the Congo change its name and the name of its capital?
B. What are some different ways that people live in Zaire?
C. Which European countries ruled Cameroon at different times in the past?
D. What are the natural resources of Congo, Gabon, and the Central African Republic?

SKILLS CHECK

MAP SKILL

Gabon's capital, Libreville, is one of the three capitals of African countries that lies almost on the Equator. Look at the political map of Africa in the Atlas on page 624 and name the other two African capitals.

Southern Africa

THINK ABOUT WHAT YOU KNOW

Relations between different races are poor in many parts of Southern Africa today. What have you learned about the history of the region that would help to explain the racial situation there today?

STUDY THE VOCABULARY

apartheid   high veld

FOCUS YOUR READING

How have relations between different races affected the countries of Southern Africa?

A. Peoples of South Africa

Language and History Monuments usually honor great people or are set up in memory of great events. But in one of the nations of Southern Africa there is a monument to a language. The monument, which is in South Africa, honors Afrikaans (af rih KAHNZ), one of the two official languages of the country. The other official language is English. Afrikaans is based on the Dutch that was spoken by the earliest European settlers. It also includes many words from French, German, and a number of African languages.

The language monument was erected by Afrikaners, the descendants of the early settlers. The Afrikaners held fast to their own ways and language after the British acquired South Africa. Defeat in the Boer War only strengthened their desire to remain Afrikaners. The monument was a way to show pride in their culture. The majority of the white South Africans today are Afrikaners.

Whites are a minority in South Africa. Nevertheless, they have controlled the government. Only whites have had any real political power, although they make up just one-sixth of the population.

The white government of South Africa divided the population into four racial groups. The groups were white descendants of Europeans; black Africans; people of mixed race, called coloreds; and Asians, mostly of Indian descent.

The classification by race was used to keep whites in power and blacks powerless. More than two out of three South Africans are black, but they have had no voice in government. Coloreds and Asians have had only a limited part.

Apartheid laws restricted the freedom of blacks in South Africa.
▶ What people were permitted to use this beach?

484

B. History of Laws to Keep Races Separate

A Divided Nation In 1948 the South African government adopted a policy called **apartheid** (uh PAHR tayt). *Apartheid* means "apartness" or "separateness" in Afrikaans. The apartheid laws segregated people according to race. People of different races could not live in the same area, go to the same school, or eat in the same restaurant. Marriage between people of different races was illegal.

According to the white South African government, apartheid was supposed to provide for "the separate development of the races." Certain areas were set aside as "homelands" for blacks. But these areas were small, making up only 13 percent of the land. The large black majority could not possibly make a living there. Black people had to go to work on white-owned farms and in white-owned industries. As a result, many black workers have been forced to travel long distances to work each day. Some laborers, such as miners, have had to leave their families for long periods and live in camps near their jobs.

Protest In 1960 the South African government banned the African National Congress, the main black political party. Many people, however, continued to speak out against apartheid and were put in jail. One of the best known is Nelson Mandela. In 1962 he was sentenced to five years in prison. Later he was sentenced to life in prison.

Several black leaders urged black South Africans to use nonviolent protest to end apartheid. One of the most highly respected is Archbishop Desmond Tutu, who is now the leader of the Anglican Church in several African countries.

C. The Beginning of Change

Improvements Almost all blacks and some South African whites opposed apartheid. The policy was also condemned by people all over the world. Partly as a result of this condemnation, the South African government made some changes in the 1980s. Marriage between people of different races was no longer illegal. Segregated eating places were no longer required by law. Schools for blacks and whites were still separate, but funds for black schools were increased.

In 1990, the South African government realized it must do more to meet black demands. It lifted the ban on the African National Congress. It released Nelson Mandela from prison, a step that met with worldwide approval. The apartheid laws were finally repealed in 1991; but not all customs have changed. There is still much segregation in practice.

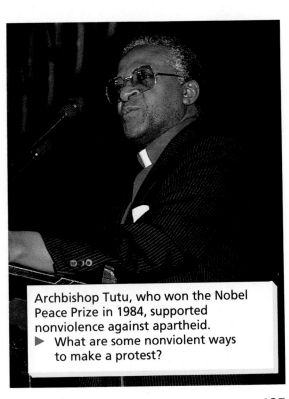

Archbishop Tutu, who won the Nobel Peace Prize in 1984, supported nonviolence against apartheid.
▶ What are some nonviolent ways to make a protest?

NELSON MANDELA: SYMBOL OF THE STRUGGLE AGAINST APARTHEID

"**O**ur march to freedom is irreversible. We must not allow fear to stand in our way." With those words, Nelson Mandela, a 71-year-old black South African leader was freed after almost 30 years in prison. In February of 1990 the South African government released Mandela. His freedom has raised the hope among millions of black South Africans living in that troubled country.

As you have just learned, the mostly-black nation of South Africa has been ruled by the white National Party for more than 40 years. This party began a system of apartheid, or apartness, where people of different races in South Africa have different rights.

Nelson Mandela, the son of a tribal chief who was born in a tin-roofed house, became involved with a black nationalist party called the African National Congress (ANC). The ANC and Mandela fought against the system of apartheid, starting with nonviolent demonstrations. Then, in 1960, after the police killed 69 peaceful demonstrators in the town of Sharpeville, the ANC saw that these peaceful demonstrations were not effective.

ANC leaders set off bombs in four cities and made plans to overthrow the government. The South African government banned, or outlawed, the ANC, and Mandela and others were arrested for trying to overthrow the government. Mandela was sentenced to life in prison.

For the first ten years of his confinement, Mandela broke boulders into gravel with a pick-ax. In later years, he woke up every morning at 3:30, exercised for two hours, and then spent the rest of the day studying. He took correspondence courses in law and read about economics and history. Mandela was a role model to the younger prisoners. People began to call the prison Mandela University.

In 1989 the people of South Africa elected a new president, F. W. de Klerk, who had promised in his campaign that he would work for change with black leaders. Mandela had repeatedly refused government offers of freedom on the condition that he leave the country or limit his activities against apartheid. After months of negotiations under the new president, Mandela was finally freed unconditionally, that is, without any reservations.

Nelson Mandela became a symbol of the struggle against the system of apartheid in South Africa. Mandela's release set off joyous celebrations among the blacks of South Africa. His dignity in his many years as a prisoner transformed him into a national figure who commands the respect of whites as well as blacks.

Thinking for Yourself

1. Why, do you think, has Nelson Mandela gained worldwide respect?
2. What characteristics does Mandela possess that helped him endure almost 30 years in prison?
3. Why, do you think, did Mandela become a symbol for the struggle against the policy of apartheid?

AFRICA SOUTH OF THE SAHARA: OIL, GOLD, AND DIAMONDS

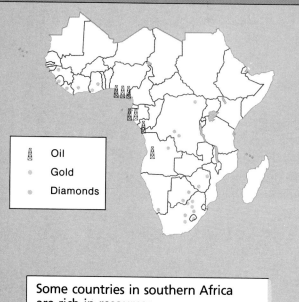

Legend:
- Oil
- Gold
- Diamonds

Some countries in southern Africa are rich in resources.
► What important energy resource is found in Africa south of the Sahara?

LEADING GOLD-PRODUCING COUNTRIES

Millions of troy ounces

(Bar chart with y-axis 0 to 24. Countries: South Africa, Former Soviet Union, Canada, United States, China)

South Africa is the world's leading producer of gold.
► About how much gold does South Africa produce?

C. South Africa's Resources

Valuable Minerals It is said that the discovery of diamonds in South Africa was an accident. Children playing on the banks of the Orange River in 1866 found some pebbles, which they took home. Later someone discovered that the pebbles would scratch glass. This is one way to test diamonds, which are the hardest of stones.

The discovery of diamonds, followed later by the discovery of gold, laid the foundation for South Africa's important mining industry. South Africa has half of the world's known gold reserves. It also has other minerals, including iron, chromium, nickel, tin, platinum, and coal.

Industry South Africa today is one of the continent's most industrialized countries. Its factories turn out automobiles, farm machinery, tires, and electrical equipment. Mining, agriculture, and industry all depend on black workers. Mining is a major South African industry, and most of the miners are black. They dig the country's gold, diamonds, copper, and other useful minerals. They do most of the heavy work in cities where whites live. This is one reason why complete separation of the races has not worked.

Tourism has also been an important industry. South Africa has a mild climate, striking scenery, beaches on two oceans, and large national parks where visitors can see animals in the wild. However, a number of people from other lands avoided going to South Africa because they disapproved of apartheid.

Agriculture South Africa is a major agricultural country in Africa. Early settlers discovered that the Mediterranean climate of the Cape colony was great for growing

The high veld is valuable grassland that helps to make South Africa one of the important agricultural countries of Africa.
▶ How can you tell from the photograph above that the high veld is an agricultural area?

wine grapes. When the settlers later moved out on the **high veld** (velt), they found land well suited for cattle and grain. The high veld is a region of open grassland with a good water supply and is similar to the Great Plains of the United States.

D. Zimbabwe: An Old Name Brought Back

Before it became independent, Zimbabwe was called Rhodesia. Then it was ruled by a very small white minority. When black leaders finally got control of the country in 1980, they proudly chose a name connected with Africa's past. The name Zimbabwe reminded the world that people in this land had built the stone structures of Great Zimbabwe long before white Europeans arrived in this part of Africa.

Many whites left the country after it became Zimbabwe. Today only about 1 percent of the population is white. Whites still own much of the best land. Some black families have received land from the government, but many are still waiting.

Harare (hah RAH ree), a large, modern city, is the capital and business center of Zimbabwe. The country has mines and some industrial plants, but agriculture is the most important industry. Zimbabwe usually produces enough food to feed its people and to export.

E. Botswana, Zambia, and Mozambique

Botswana Before winning its independence from Great Britain in 1966, Botswana (baht SWAH nuh) was called Bechuanaland (bech oo AHN uh land). A large part of the country is desert or dry grassland. Copper mining and cattle raising are the most important industries. Although it has had close economic ties with South Africa, Botswana has strongly disapproved of apartheid.

Zambia Zambia was Northern Rhodesia under British rule. The leaders of this land also chose an African name when the country became independent in 1964. Zambia takes its name from the Zambezi River, on which it is located. The country recently changed from a one-party government to a multiparty government.

Victoria Falls and copper are two of Zambia's natural resources. The great falls are a tourist attraction. Copper is the most valuable export.

Mozambique Mozambique, as you learned in Chapter 17, was once a Portuguese colony. Located on the Indian Ocean, it offers an outlet to the sea for both Zimbabwe and Zambia. Mozambique

This African worker is mining copper in Zambia, where copper is the most valuable export.
▶ What piece of equipment is he working with?

has rich agricultural land and deposits of diamonds, copper, lead, and tin. But a long civil war, combined with drought, makes it one of the world's poorest countries.

LESSON **3** *REVIEW*

THINK AND WRITE

A. Into what four groups do South African laws divide the population?

B. Summarize the purpose of apartheid.

C. What are some of South Africa's resources?

D. Why did Rhodesia take the name Zimbabwe when it became independent?

E. In your opinion, why might civil war and drought make a country poor?

SKILLS CHECK

WRITING SKILL

Imagine there was a law that separated students into different schools based on their hair color. Write a paragraph or two describing how that law would make you feel.

East Africa

THINK ABOUT WHAT YOU KNOW

Tourism is important in East Africa. What are some sights that tourists to your state visit?

STUDY THE VOCABULARY

pyrethrum   **teff**

FOCUS YOUR READING

In what ways are the East African countries described in this lesson alike?

A. Kenya on the Equator

Nairobi, the capital of Kenya, is located just south of the Equator, yet it has a mild climate. Even during the hottest months, temperatures are not as high as on most July days in New York or Boston. Nairobi has a mild climate because it is located in the Kenyan highlands.

The climate of the highlands attracted white European settlers to Kenya when it was part of the British Empire. Whites made up only a minority of the population, but a large area, called the White Highlands, was reserved for them.

The black majority in Kenya felt it was unfair that so much of the best land was reserved for the white settlers. Blacks rose up against white rule in the 1950s. Kenya became an independent republic in 1964. Kenya's first president, Jomo Kenyatta, urged all races to help build the new nation. He gave the country its motto, *Hamambee*, "Pull together!"

The new government invited European and American companies to establish businesses in Kenya. A number of foreign companies did so, but agriculture and cattle raising remain the main occupations in Kenya. Cash crops that are grown mainly for export include coffee, tea, cotton, and **pyrethrum**. Pyrethrum is a plant used to make insect poison.

B. Tourism and a Growing Population

Kenya is one of the most visited countries in Africa, so tourism is a big business. People come partly to see the scenery, but mainly to see the marvelous variety of African animals and birds there. Kenya has a

This plantation worker is picking tea on the highlands in Kenya.
▶ Why, do you think, is it useful for the worker to carry the basket on his back?

491

Many tourists go to Tsavo National Park to see the wildlife of Africa.
▶ What animal herd is shown below roaming the park?

number of parks. Tsavo National Park outside Nairobi is the largest national park in the world.

Kenya's population has been growing rapidly. More than twice as many people live in Kenya today as in 1964. The nation's population is also very young, with more than half under the age of 15. A young and growing population needs land and jobs. Farmland in Kenya is limited because more than half of the country is desert. The number of jobs in industry has grown, but not as fast as the population.

C. Two Countries Unite

When Tanganyika and the island of Zanzibar joined together to form one country in 1964, they took the name Tanzania.

Tanganyika was a German colony until Great Britain took it over after World War I. Zanzibar was already under British rule. Both countries had become independent in the early 1960s.

Farmers in Tanzania raise cotton, coffee, and sisal. Zanzibar and nearby islands are referred to as the Clove Islands because they produce that spice.

Mount Kilimanjaro, Africa's highest mountain, is in Tanzania. When the first European explorer to see it reported that there was a snowcapped mountain on the Equator, people did not believe him. Today large numbers of tourists travel to Tanzania to see the mountain and to visit the national parks. Almost one fourth of the country is parkland.

D. Changes in an Old Country

History and Economy   About 100 years ago, Menelik II, emperor of Ethiopia, lived on top of a mountain near the center of his empire. It was cold there, and Taitu, the empress, persuaded Menelik to build a new residence farther down the mountain, near a hot spring. This was the beginning of a city. Taitu called it Addis Ababa, or "Little Flower." Addis Ababa is now a city of more than a million people.

Ethiopia is largely an agricultural country. Coffee is its main export. A grass-like grain called **teff**, which is little known in other parts of the world, is another important crop. The Ethiopians make a thin, flat bread from teff, which is used to scoop up hot, spicy stews.

Famine and Civil War   In 1974 the last Ethiopian emperor, Haile Selassie (HYE lee suh LAS ee), was overthrown. Mengistu, a military leader, became president of Ethiopia. He was a harsh Communist ruler with ties to the Soviet Union. A long civil war against him ended in May 1991, when he was forced to flee the country. Drought conditions that have brought famine persist, but now that the war has ended, more food aid may get through to the people.

E. Sudan: A Meeting Place

Sudan is the largest country in Africa, extending from Zaire to Egypt. Here Africa south of the Sahara meets North Africa and the Middle East.

FROM BERRIES TO COFFEE

Berries are picked.

2. Berries are dried and sorted.

3. Beans are removed from the berries.

Coffee beans are roasted and ground.

5. Coffee is tested.

6. Coffee is packed for sale.

Unroasted coffee beans are often exported to the country where the final product will be sold.
► What is done to the unroasted beans before the product can be sold?

The White Nile and the Blue Nile join at the place shown here.
▶ What city is located where these rivers meet?

Northern Sudan, like Egypt, is desert. The climate is also similar to that of Egypt. Khartoum, the capital of Sudan, is located where the White Nile and Blue Nile flow together. The irrigated land between the rivers is Sudan's major agricultural region. Fine cotton is one crop grown there. In southern Sudan the desert gives way to savanna and woodlands.

People in north Sudan speak Arabic and are Muslims. Black Africans in the south have many languages. Some are Christians, but most follow African religions.

Blacks make up the largest group, but Arabic-speaking Muslims have controlled the government. When the government ruled in 1962 that the nation's laws would be based on Muslim laws, civil war broke out between the north and the south. To this day the meeting of Africa and the Middle East in Sudan has brought more conflict than understanding.

LESSON **4** *REVIEW*

THINK AND WRITE

A. What are the White Highlands, and why were they a cause of conflict?
B. How does Kenya's growing population affect tourism?
C. How does Tanzania's name explain the country's origin?
D. What problems did Ethiopia face after Haile Selassie was overthrown?
E. Why has Sudan been called a meeting place?

SKILLS CHECK

THINKING SKILL

You have learned that Mount Kilimanjaro is Africa's highest peak. In earlier chapters you have read about mountain peaks in other regions of the world. Look in the Gazetteer to find the heights for the following: Mount Kilimanjaro, Mount Olympus, Mont Blanc, Mount Ararat, and Mount Damāvand. Then make a graph using the information you found.

USING THE VOCABULARY

Africanized
cash crop
apartheid
high veld
teff

Each of the following sentences is an answer to a question about a term above. On a separate sheet of paper, write a question to go with each answer.

Example:
Answer: They are Gambia's main export.
Question: What are groundnuts?

1. This open grassland is well suited for cattle and grain.
2. Some African nations did this to their place-names to show independence.
3. Bread is made from this grasslike grain.
4. People throughout the world think this policy is unfair.
5. A profit can be made if this agricultural product is sold.

REMEMBERING WHAT YOU READ

On a separate sheet of paper, answer the following questions in complete sentences.

1. What two people led movements for African independence in the 1950s?
2. What caused the economic boom to end in Nigeria?
3. What is the principal natural resource of the Ivory Coast?
4. What two countries form the Confederation of Senegambia?
5. What is the largest country south of the Sahara?
6. Why have the names of many countries and cities been Africanized?
7. How do the Pygmies of Zaire live?
8. How did Cameroon get its name?
9. What three nations were created from French Equatorial Africa?
10. What two discoveries laid the foundation for South Africa's mining industry?
11. What was Zimbabwe called before it became independent?
12. Why is Kenya one of the most visited countries in the world?
13. What country did Tanganyika and the island of Zanzibar join to form in 1964?
14. Where is Mount Kilimanjaro located?
15. What caused civil war to break out in Sudan?

TYING LANGUAGE ARTS TO SOCIAL STUDIES

Imagine you are on a five-day photographic safari, taking pictures of African birds and animals. You will keep a journal of your trip. First, you need to do some reading about African wildlife. Now you are ready to begin your journal. Tell where in Africa you are. Write about some of the photographs that you take each day. You may choose to describe some of the animals, what they were doing, or what you think will make your photographs special.

THINKING CRITICALLY

On a separate sheet of paper, answer the following questions in complete sentences.

1. Why, do you think, were the countries of Europe interested in ruling African lands?
2. How can you explain the fact that cattle raising is one of Botswana's most important industries?
3. If the soil of the Ivory Coast were suddenly to become poor and unable to support plant life, how do you think that would affect the Ivory Coast's economy?
4. Which product of Gabon do you think is most important to Western countries? Explain why.
5. How do you think Kenya could resolve the conflict between its people's demand for land and its animals' need for land?

SUMMARIZING THE CHAPTER

On a separate sheet of paper, draw a graphic organizer like the one shown here. Copy the information from this graphic organizer to the one you have drawn. Under the main idea for each lesson, write three statements that support the main idea.

CHAPTER THEME Independence movements in Africa led to the end of European empires. Governments and economies are varied among African countries south of the Sahara.

LESSON 1

West African countries faced problems after gaining their independence.

1.
2.
3.

LESSON 2

The countries of Central Africa have many things in common.

1.
2.
3.

LESSON 3

Relations between different races have affected the countries of Southern Africa.

1.
2.
3.

LESSON 4

In many ways the countries of East Africa are alike.

1.
2.
3.

COOPERATIVE LEARNING

In Unit 5 you learned about the geography of Africa south of the Sahara. You also read about the economies, cultures, and governments of countries in this region.

A good way to present facts about these and other characteristics of a country is to make a bulletin-board display. Work with a group of classmates to design and make a bulletin-board display of information for one country you read about in Unit 5.

PROJECT

When your teacher assigns a country to your group, hold a group meeting to plan your bulletin board. Discuss what information you want to include in the display. As a group, decide what kinds of facts you think are most interesting and useful. You might want to do some research to add to information presented in your textbook.

After you have decided on the information to be included in the display, divide tasks among group members. Your group might divide tasks such as the following.

● One group member could draw and label a map of the country.

● Another group member could make a table or chart telling the country's size, population, chief exports, and capital city.

● One person could find magazine or newspaper articles about recent events in the country and write a one-page summary of these events.

● Another group member could research and write a one-page biography about the country's leader.

● A group member could draw some pictures illustrating interesting places in the country.

PRESENTATION AND REVIEW

When each person has finished his or her part of the project, hold another group meeting. Decide on a background color and talk about how you will arrange your bulletin board. Then set up your bulletin-board display in your classroom.

Look at the displays designed by the other groups in your class. Are the bulletin-board displays attractive and fun to look at? Do they present clear, interesting, useful facts about countries in Africa south of the Sahara? Could your group's display be improved?

REMEMBER TO:
- Give your ideas.
- Listen to others' ideas.
- Plan your work with the group.
- Present your project.
- Discuss how your group worked.

A. WHY DO I NEED THIS SKILL?

In Unit 5 you learned that the nations of Africa have undergone many changes in the twentieth century. Some of these changes are reflected on maps that show political divisions. By comparing political maps that show a particular region during different periods, you can quickly see how boundaries and other features of countries have changed over time. Comparing the political maps presented in your social studies textbook will help you remember some of the changes you have read about.

B. LEARNING THE SKILL

Political maps show the boundaries of countries within a region or the divisions within a country, such as states, countries, provinces, or republics. Countries and other divisions on a political map are usually shown in different colors so that the divisions can be easily distinguished from one another.

Political maps may also show cities within a political division. A symbol, usually a dot, is placed on a map to show where a city is located. A capital city may be indicated by a star within a circle. As on other types of maps, a map key on a political map often explains what particular symbols on the map stand for.

In Chapter 17 and Chapter 18, you read about changes that occurred in Africa. By comparing political maps that show Africa at different times in the twentieth century, you can see what some of those changes were.

The map on page 469 of Chapter 17 shows European claims in Africa in 1920. Turn to that page and study the map. The different colors on the map show the claims in Africa by various European colonial powers. Notice the colonial names of each area within the various claims.

Now turn to page 478 in Chapter 18 and study the map that shows Africa today. Flip back and forth between the two maps to see if you can notice any differences between what is shown on the maps. Which African countries retained the same name following the departure of the colonists? Which African countries were independent in 1920?

By comparing these two maps, you can see how the continent of Africa changed after these individual African countries became independent.

C. PRACTICING THE SKILL

On a separate sheet of paper, copy the table shown below. Next, turn to the map on page 469 and use it to find ten countries that existed in Africa in 1920. List the countries in the first column of the table. Then compare this map with the map on page 478. Indicate in the second column the present-day name of the country (in some cases there has been no change). In the third column list the empire of which the country was a part or with which it was associated. For example, if you listed Belgian Congo in the first column, you would write Zaire in the second column. In the third column you would write Belgian.

D. APPLYING THE SKILL

As you read this textbook, take the opportunity to compare political maps that show any particular region in different periods. Looking at the maps as you read about changes in the region will help you visualize the results of the changes. Looking back at the maps later on will help you recall the changes you have read about.

THE CHANGING MAP OF AFRICA		
African Countries in 1920	Present-day Country	European Empire

A. WHY DO I NEED THIS SKILL?

Sometimes as you read your social studies textbook, you may want to get an overview of a particular lesson or chapter. At other times you may be looking for a specific fact or idea. In these cases, you can use the skills of skimming and scanning to get the information you want. Knowing how to skim and scan will help you to do a better job of locating needed information and studying social studies materials.

B. LEARNING THE SKILL

Skimming is reading a selection quickly to get a general idea of what it is about. Skimming a selection before you read it carefully will help you identify the main ideas and most important information.

Scanning is looking quickly over a selection to find some specific information. Readers usually scan material after they have read it. Scanning is especially helpful when you must answer questions about what you have read.

The table on the next page lists five steps to follow when you skim through a reading selection and four steps to follow when you scan for information. Study the skimming and scanning table carefully.

C. PRACTICING THE SKILL

Turn to page 505 and skim through Lesson 1 of Chapter 19, "Geography of South and East Asia," to see if you can get a general idea of what it is about. Follow the five steps in the table. Write a sentence that tells the topic of the first lesson.

What did you write? Did you mention the variety of land areas in South Asia?

Now turn back to Lesson 1 of Chapter 16, "Geography of Africa South of the Sahara," to practice scanning. See if you can find the European name for the second longest river in Africa.

How did you do? Did you find on page 441 that the Europeans called this river the Congo? Did the heading "Africa's Rivers and Lakes" help you find this information?

Turn to Lesson 2 in Chapter 19. Skim the lesson, following the steps on the chart. What is the topic of Lesson 2?

Now scan all of Chapter 16 to answer these questions.

1. What is bauxite?
2. Where does sisal grow?
3. How is sleeping sickness spread?
4. What is the deepest lake in Africa?
5. In what part of Africa are its tallest mountains found?

D. APPLYING THE SKILL

Skimming and scanning are important reading skills that you can use as you continue reading your social studies textbook. Before you read any chapter, skim through it to get an idea of what the chapter is about. After you have read a chapter, scan it to find facts you need to answer questions and to remember the important topics in the chapter.

SKIMMING AND SCANNING FOR INFORMATION				
What?	**When?**	**Why?**	**How?**	
Skim	Usually **before** you read a selection	To get a general idea of what a selection is about	1. Read the lesson title and the FOCUS YOUR READING question. 2. Read the first paragraph of the lesson. 3. Quickly glance through the rest of the lesson. Read the first sentence in each paragraph.	4. Pay attention to boldfaced vocabulary terms, headings, and other key words in the lesson. 5. Read the last paragraph in the lesson and see if you can summarize the lesson in your own words.
Scan	Usually **after** you have read a selection	To look for specific information	1. Decide what question you have and what information you need to find. 2. Read through the section headings until you find a section related to information you need.	3. Move your eyes quickly through the section until you come to a key word related to your question. 4. Read the nearby text to try to find the answer to your question.

501

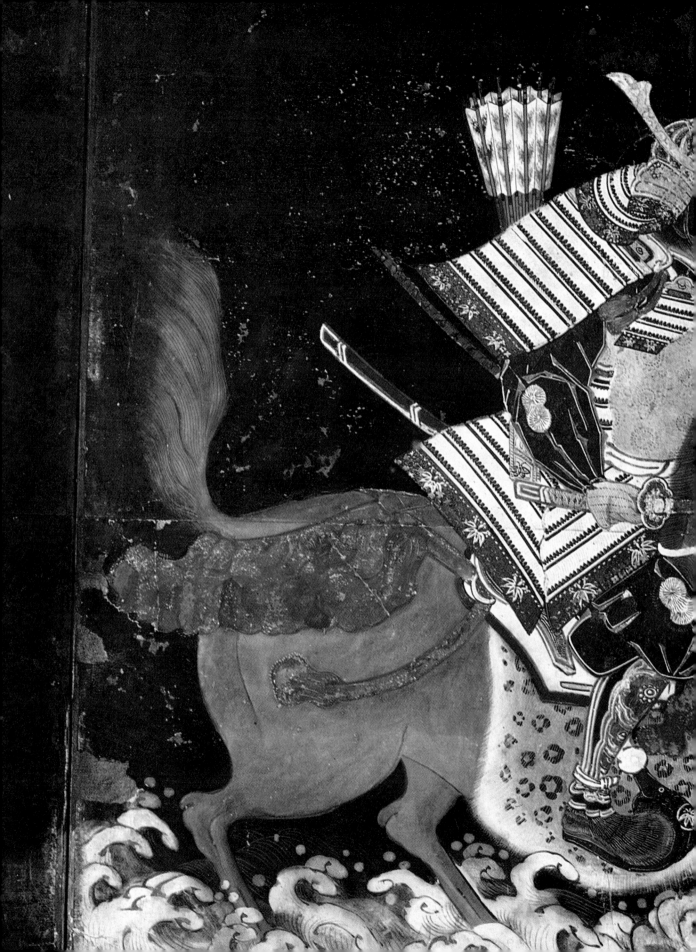

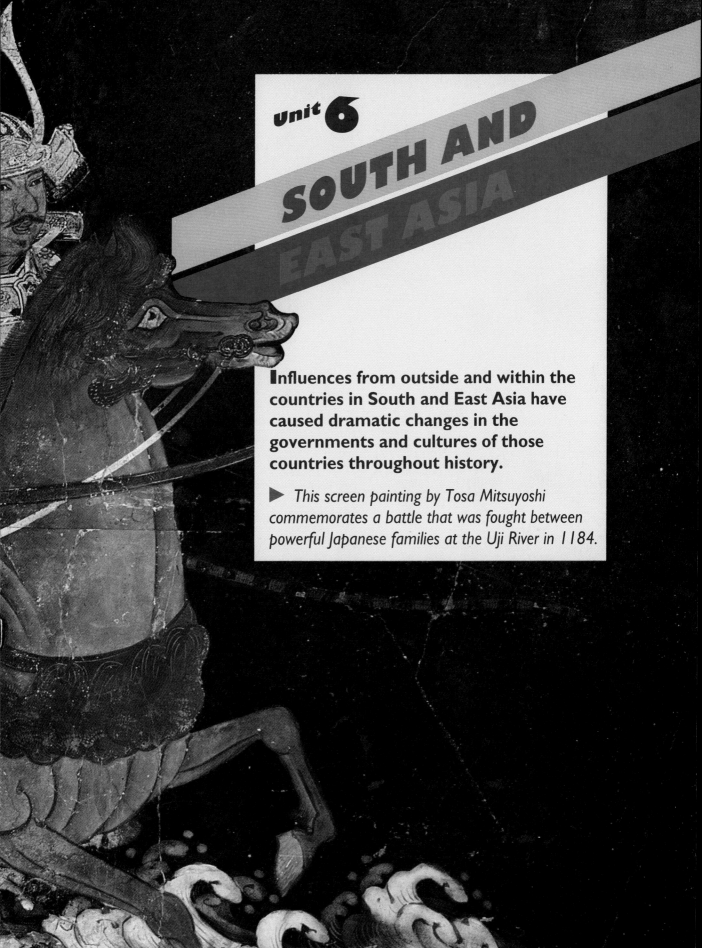

Unit 6

SOUTH AND EAST ASIA

Influences from outside and within the countries in South and East Asia have caused dramatic changes in the governments and cultures of those countries throughout history.

▶ *This screen painting by Tosa Mitsuyoshi commemorates a battle that was fought between powerful Japanese families at the Uji River in 1184.*

19

GEOGRAPHY OF SOUTH AND EAST ASIA

*S*outh and East Asia form a region of many geographic contrasts. Some parts are very rainy; others are deserts. The highest mountains in the world and some of the lowest delta lands are found in this region.

The South Asian Subcontinent

THINK ABOUT WHAT YOU KNOW

In an earlier chapter, you studied ancient India. Based on what you have already learned, what would you expect to see if you visited India?

STUDY THE VOCABULARY

Deccan

FOCUS YOUR READING

What are the principal geographical features of South Asia?

A. Around the World in 80 Days

A trip around the world in 80 days would not seem fast now. One could make the trip in far less time today by airplane. However in 1873, when author Jules Verne wrote a book entitled *Around the World in Eighty Days*, such a trip seemed an improbable adventure.

Phileas Fogg, the main character of Verne's book, and his servant, Jean Passepartout, use various modes of transportation on their round-the-world trip from London. They use a hot-air balloon to fly to the Mediterranean and then travel by steamship and railroad. Their trip would have been even shorter if they had been able to travel straight east across Europe and Asia. But in 1873 no railroad crossed Asia, the world's largest continent. In order to make the story believable, the author has Fogg and Passepartout use steamship and railroad routes that existed at the time. The travelers go through the Suez Canal and make their way along the southern and eastern edges of Asia.

Around the World in Eighty Days is a travel adventure book to be read with a map in hand. Fogg and Passepartout's route through Asia is accurately described. The travelers sail through the Red Sea and across the Indian Ocean to Bombay, on the west coast of India. They travel overland across India to Calcutta, on the Bay of Bengal. From there they take a ship to Singapore, in Southeast Asia. Another ship then takes them to Hong Kong, on the Chinese coast.

After a number of difficulties, the travelers reach Japan. They take a ship to the United States, travel across the country by rail, and eventually cross the Atlantic to London. To learn more about the adventures in Jules Verne's *Around the World in Eighty Days*, read the literature selection on the next page.

B. The Mountain Wall

In the story of Phileas Fogg's journey, Jules Verne describes India as a "great reversed triangle of land, with its base in the north and its apex [peak] in the south." A look at the map on page 508 explains why Verne describes India this way. The triangle is actually the South Asian subcontinent; India is only one country located on it. The other five countries are Pakistan, Bangladesh, Nepal, Bhutan, and the island of Sri Lanka. Locate these countries on the physical map on page 508. The subcontinent is part of Asia, but it is separated from the rest of the continent by a mountain wall formed by the Himalaya and Hindu Kush mountain ranges.

The Himalayas include 30 of the world's highest mountains. The name *Himalaya* means "abode, or home, of snow." Snow covers the high peaks throughout

FROM: **Around the World in Eighty Days**

By: Jules Verne
Setting: India

Even as a boy, Jules Verne dreamed of exciting voyages. At the age of 12, he stowed away on a ship bound for India. His father retrieved him, and from then on, Verne's adventures took place in his imagination. Verne researched his books carefully, blending fantasy with facts. Before writing *Around the World in Eighty Days*, he plotted realistic courses for his characters to take.

Phileas Fogg, the book's main character, bets his friends that he can travel around the world in eighty days. In the excerpt below, Fogg, his servant, Passepartout, and Sir Francis Cromarty, a passenger, are on a train traveling through India when it suddenly comes to a halt because the railway has ended.

*"**I** shall go afoot," said Phileas Fogg.*

Passepartout . . . said, "Monsieur, I think I have found a means of conveyance [transportation]. . . . An elephant! An elephant that belongs to an Indian who lives but a hundred steps from here."

. . . Kiouni—this was the name of the beast—could doubtless travel rapidly for a long time, and, in default of any other means of conveyance, Mr. Fogg resolved to hire him. But elephants are far from cheap in India, where they are becoming scarce. . . . When, therefore, Mr. Fogg proposed to the Indian to hire Kiouni, he refused point-blank. . . .

Finally, after Mr. Fogg made many offers to hire or to buy the elephant, the Indian sold the beast at a costly price.

*. . . **T**he elephant was led out and equipped. The Parsee, who was an accomplished elephant driver, covered his back with a sort of saddle-cloth, and attached to each of his flanks some curiously uncomfortable howdahs [seats].*

. . . While Sir Francis and Mr. Fogg took the howdahs on either side, Passepartout got astride the saddle-cloth between them. The Parsee perched himself on the elephant's neck, and at nine o'clock they set out from the village, the animal marching off through the dense forest of palms by the shortest cut.

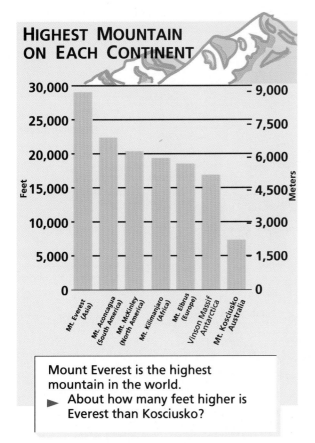

HIGHEST MOUNTAIN ON EACH CONTINENT

Feet	Meters
30,000	9,000
25,000	7,500
20,000	6,000
15,000	4,500
10,000	3,000
5,000	1,500
0	0

Mt. Everest (Asia), Mt. Aconcagua (South America), Mt. McKinley (North America), Mt. Kilimanjaro (Africa), Mt. Elbrus (Europe), Vinson Massif Antarctica, Mt. Kosciusko Australia

Mount Everest is the highest mountain in the world.
► About how many feet higher is Everest than Kosciusko?

(brahm uh POO truh). All three rivers have their sources in the high mountains and plateaus that set the subcontinent apart from the rest of Asia. The Indus and Brahmaputra both begin on the Tibetan plateau but flow to different sides of the continent. The Indus goes to the Arabian Sea. The Brahmaputra empties into the Bay of Bengal. The waters of the Ganges come from melting snow and ice high in the Himalayas. The river flows eastward across its broad plain and joins the Brahmaputra. The two rivers form a large delta in what is now the country of Bangladesh.

Islands are located near the southern tip of the subcontinent. Sri Lanka, the largest, was once called Ceylon. The Maldives are a chain of more than 1,000 small islands, located southwest of the South Asian subcontinent. Only about 200 of these islands are inhabited.

the year. Mount Everest, the tallest mountain in the world, is in the Himalayas. It rises 29,028 feet (8,848 m) above sea level. As the map on page 508 shows, Mount Everest is on the border between the countries of Nepal and China.

The southern part of the subcontinent contains a low plateau called the **Deccan**. Two mountain ranges, the Western Ghats (gawts) and the Eastern Ghats, form the edges of the Deccan Plateau.

C. Rivers and Islands

On their tour, Verne's characters travel along the plain of the Ganges River. The plain is a very fertile and densely populated region of the subcontinent.

The Ganges is one of the three longest rivers in South Asia. The other two rivers are the Indus and the Brahmaputra

This fertile plain runs along the Ganges River.
► How can you tell that people travel on the plain?

SOUTH AND EAST ASIA: PHYSICAL

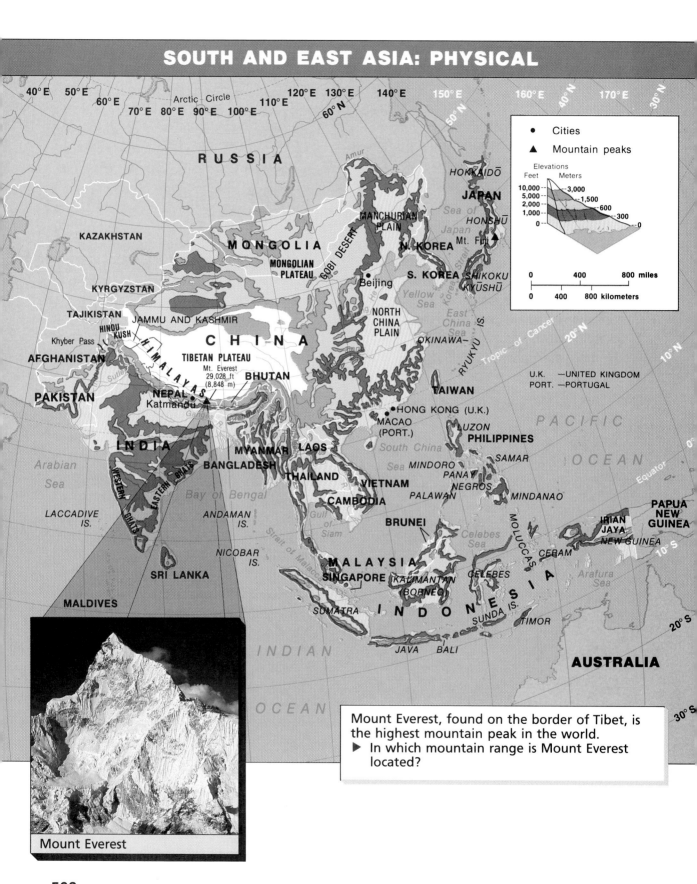

40°E 50°E 60°E 70°E 80°E 90°E 100°E 110°E 120°E 130°E 140°E 150°E 160°E 170°E

Arctic Circle

60°N

30°N

20°N

10°N

RUSSIA

KAZAKHSTAN

MONGOLIA

MONGOLIAN PLATEAU

GOBI DESERT

MANCHURIAN PLAIN

Amur R.

HOKKAIDŌ

JAPAN

Sea of Japan

HONSHŪ

Mt. Fuji

KYRGYZSTAN

TAJIKISTAN

JAMMU AND KASHMIR

HINDU KUSH

Khyber Pass

AFGHANISTAN

HIMALAYAS

CHINA

TIBETAN PLATEAU

Mt. Everest 29,028 ft (8,848 m)

BHUTAN

NEPAL

Katmandu

Sutlej

Ganges R.

PAKISTAN

INDIA

WESTERN GHATS

EASTERN GHATS

MYANMAR

BANGLADESH

LAOS

THAILAND

VIETNAM

CAMBODIA

N. KOREA

S. KOREA

Beijing

Yellow Sea

NORTH CHINA PLAIN

Korea Strait

SHIKOKU

KYŪSHŪ

East China Sea

OKINAWA

RYUKYU IS.

Tropic of Cancer

TAIWAN

HONG KONG (U.K.)

MACAO (PORT.)

LUZON

PHILIPPINES

MINDORO

SAMAR

PANAY

NEGROS

PALAWAN

MINDANAO

BRUNEI

PACIFIC OCEAN

U.K. —UNITED KINGDOM
PORT. —PORTUGAL

Arabian Sea

LACCADIVE IS.

ANDAMAN IS.

Bay of Bengal

South China Sea

Gulf of Siam

Strait of Malacca

NICOBAR IS.

SRI LANKA

MALDIVES

MALAYSIA

SINGAPORE

KALIMANTAN (BORNEO)

SUMATRA

INDONESIA

CELEBES

MOLUCCAS

CERAM

Celebes Sea

IRIAN JAYA

NEW GUINEA

PAPUA NEW GUINEA

Arafura Sea

SUNDA IS.

TIMOR

JAVA

BALI

AUSTRALIA

INDIAN OCEAN

Equator

10°S

20°S

30°S

Legend

- Cities
- ▲ Mountain peaks

Elevations

Feet	Meters
10,000	3,000
5,000	1,500
2,000	600
1,000	300
0	0

0   400   800 miles
0   400   800 kilometers

Mount Everest, found on the border of Tibet, is the highest mountain peak in the world.
▶ In which mountain range is Mount Everest located?

Mount Everest

508

D. How the Monsoons Affect Climate

Monsoon winds, which moved early sailing ships across the Indian Ocean from Africa, greatly affect the subcontinent's climate. Summer monsoons, blowing from the southwest, pick up moisture as they pass over the ocean. As the air moves over highlands and mountains on the subcontinent, it cools and drops moisture in the form of rain or snow. As you can see on the map at the right, heavy precipitation falls on the Western Ghats and Himalayas. Cherrapunji (cher uh PUN jee), in northeastern India, is 4,300 feet (1,311 m) above sea level and averages 450 inches (1,143 cm) of rainfall a year. Most of this rain falls between April and September. Delhi, on the central plain of the subcontinent, also receives most of its rain during the summer, but much less than Cherrapunji. You will note on the map above that Pakistan receives very little summer rain. Can you explain why?

The winter monsoons blow from the northeast, off the Asian continent. These winds bring dry, sunny weather to the subcontinent. Even Cherrapunji usually receives less than an inch of rain in January.

E. A Crowded Land

Asia is the home of most of the human race. About 60 percent of the world's people live in Asia. One third of Asia's population lives on the subcontinent.

The population of the subcontinent is growing rapidly. Between 1965 and 1990 the total number of people more than doubled. The population is spread unevenly over the land. There is a high density of population in the Ganges valley and delta and also along the southwestern coast of the subcontinent.

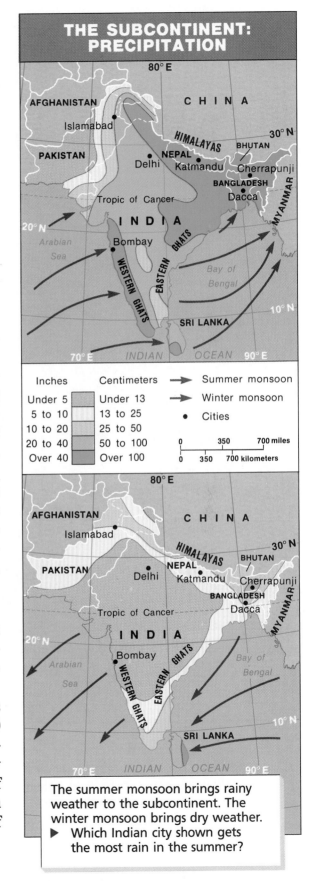

THE SUBCONTINENT: PRECIPITATION

Inches	Centimeters	
Under 5	Under 13	→ Summer monsoon
5 to 10	13 to 25	→ Winter monsoon
10 to 20	25 to 50	• Cities
20 to 40	50 to 100	
Over 40	Over 100	

0   350   700 miles
0   350   700 kilometers

The summer monsoon brings rainy weather to the subcontinent. The winter monsoon brings dry weather.
▶ Which Indian city shown gets the most rain in the summer?

SOUTH AND EAST ASIA: POPULATION DENSITY

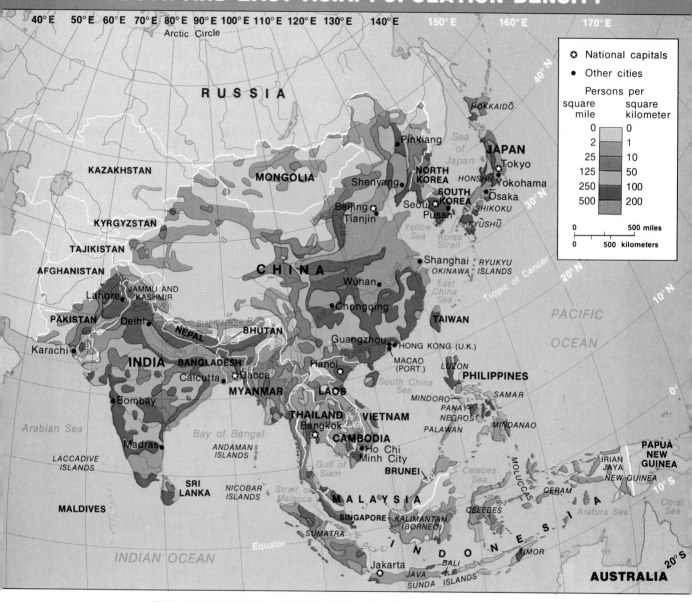

THE 25 LARGEST CITIES OF SOUTH ASIA AND EAST ASIA

Seoul (South Korea) 9,501,000
Tokyo (Japan) 8,355,000
Bombay (India) 8,227,000
Jakarta (Indonesia) 7,348,000
Shanghai (China) 6,881,000
Beijing (China) 5,755,000
Hong Kong (United Kingdom) . . . 5,553,000
Tainjin (China) 5,312,000
Karachi (Pakistan) 5,103,000

Bangkok (Thailand) 5,018,000
Delhi (India) 4,884,000
Shenyang (China) 4,135,000
Dacca (Bangladesh) 3,459,000
Ho Chi Minh City (Vietnam) . . . 3,420,000
Wuhan (China) 3,338,000
Calcutta (India) 3,305,000
Madras (India) 3,277,000
Guangzhou (China) 3,222,000

Pusan (South Korea) 3,160,000
Yokohama (Japan) 2,993,000
Lahore (Pakistan) 2,922,000
Chongqing (China) 2,734,000
Ōsaka (Japan) 2,636,000
Pinkiang (China) 2,592,000
Hanoi (Vietnam) 2,571,000

Some of the most populated cities in the world are in South Asia and East
Asia. China has many of the most populated cities in this region.
▶ How would you describe the difference in the population densities of
eastern and western China?

510

Calcutta, with a population of 11 million, is India's second largest city.

▶ By looking at the photograph above, how can you tell that this is a very crowded city?

The subcontinent's large population is made up of many ethnic, language, and religious groups. There are 14 major languages, plus hundreds of dialects. Each of the major languages is spoken by millions and has its own ancient literature. Differences between religious groups have had a great effect on the history of the subcontinent. You will read about some of these religious groups in Chapters 20 and 21.

LESSON *1* REVIEW

THINK AND WRITE

A. Why did Fogg and Passepartout not travel straight east across Europe and Asia?

B. What separates the South Asian subcontinent from the rest of Asia?

C. Name the three main rivers and some of the islands of South Asia.

D. Summarize how monsoons affect the climate of the subcontinent.

E. Why, do you think, is the population spread unevenly across the subcontinent?

SKILLS CHECK

MAP SKILL

Use the precipitation maps on page 509 to answer these questions: (a) How much rain does Delhi usually receive during the summer monsoon? During the winter monsoon? (b) Does Pakistan receive more or less rain than Bangladesh in the summer? (c) Which country receives about the same amount of precipitation in the winter as it does in the summer?

Southeast Asia

THINK ABOUT WHAT YOU KNOW

Suppose some students from Southeast Asia visited your class. What questions would you ask them? What kinds of questions do you think they would want to ask you?

STUDY THE VOCABULARY

archipelago   teak
terrace   latex

FOCUS YOUR READING

What variety can be found among the peoples and across the lands of Southeast Asia?

A. A Peninsula and Islands

Indochina Fogg and Passepartout traveled around the large peninsula formed by Southeast Asia. Because this peninsula lies between India and China, Europeans called it Indochina.

Indochina has many interesting sights, but Fogg did not care about that. He simply wanted to take the shortest sea route to the Chinese coast. If you look at the map on page 508, you can easily figure out the route the travelers took. From the subcontinent they sailed to Singapore. As the map shows, Singapore is located at the tip of the Malay Peninsula, which is part of the Indochina peninsula. It reaches almost to the Equator and is the southernmost part of the continent.

Tiny Singapore is only one of the countries of Indochina. Today the peninsula holds seven countries. Look at the physical map of South Asia and East Asia on page 508. Can you name the other six countries?

Southeast Asia's longest river, the Mekong, runs through all of these lands except Singapore. The sources of the Mekong are on the Tibetan plateau. As it nears the South China Sea, the Mekong River forms a large delta.

Malay Malay is also the name of an **archipelago** (ahr kuh PEL uh goh), or group of islands, off the coast of Southeast Asia. The Malay Archipelago is the world's largest group of islands. It extends more than 3,800 miles (6,114 km) along the Equator and includes thousands of islands. Some are very small and have no inhabitants. Others are among the largest islands in the world. New Guinea, for instance, the world's second largest island, is bigger than the state of Texas. Two of the world's largest islands belong to the Malay Archipelago.

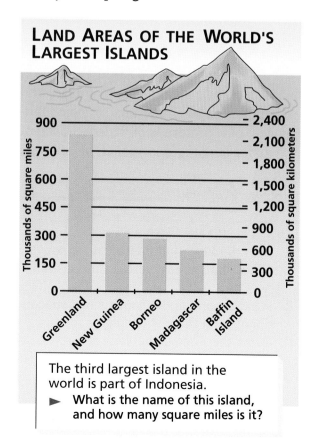

LAND AREAS OF THE WORLD'S LARGEST ISLANDS

The third largest island in the world is part of Indonesia.
► What is the name of this island, and how many square miles is it?

B. Many Peoples

Different Languages The Malay Archipelago of Southeast Asia is divided into four countries. Indonesia is the largest country. The others are the Philippines, Brunei, and part of Malaysia. These, added to those of Indochina, make up the 11 nations of Southeast Asia.

Each country has a variety of ethnic groups that speak different languages. Singapore has four official languages. English is one of the official languages in Singapore, the Philippines, and Brunei. Chinese is spoken throughout the region.

Many Religions A number of the world's major religions have followers in this part of Asia. Many of the people in Indochina are Buddhists. Indonesia is a Muslim country. In fact, it has more Muslims than any country in the Middle East or North Africa. On the Indonesian island of Bali the people are Hindus. Christianity is the religion of the large majority of people in the Philippines. Some of the people of Southeast Asia also hold to religious beliefs and practices that originated in the region.

C. Climate and Natural Resources

Farming Southeast Asia lies within the tropics and has a generally hot and humid climate. Yet the climate offers one great advantage: crops can be grown all year.

Much land is mountainous and hilly, although there is some flatland, such as that on the Mekong delta. Through hard work and skill, the people of Southeast Asia farm even steep mountainsides. They construct **terraces**, flat areas built up like steps on steep slopes. Crops are planted and tended on each terrace. Rice is Southeast Asia's most important crop, but farmers also grow sugarcane and fruits.

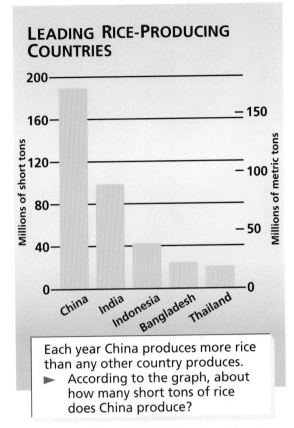

LEADING RICE-PRODUCING COUNTRIES

Each year China produces more rice than any other country produces.
► According to the graph, about how many short tons of rice does China produce?

This photograph shows rice terraces in the Philippines.
► How can you tell that this land is used for terrace farming?

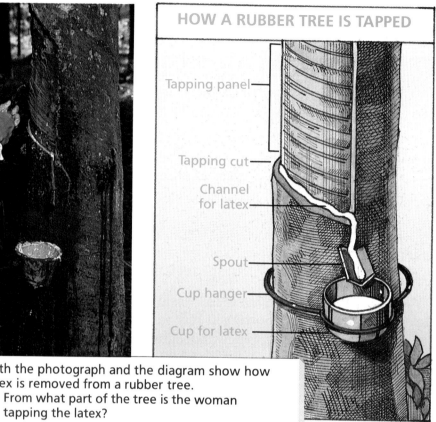

HOW A RUBBER TREE IS TAPPED

Tapping panel

Tapping cut

Channel for latex

Spout

Cup hanger

Cup for latex

Both the photograph and the diagram show how latex is removed from a rubber tree.
▶ From what part of the tree is the woman tapping the latex?

Valuable Resources Tropical forests cover much of the land that has not been cleared for crops. The forests provide valuable timber, such as **teak**, a hardwood once used for building ships. Teak is still used for making furniture.

Rubber trees were brought to Southeast Asia from Brazil, a country in South America. Natural rubber is produced by cutting slits in the bark of the rubber trees and collecting **latex**, the milky sap that drips from the cuts.

Southeast Asia also has oil and natural gas fields. In addition, important deposits of such minerals as tin, copper, lead, and iron are found in the region.

LESSON 2 REVIEW

THINK AND WRITE
A. Locate and describe the peninsulas and islands of Southeast Asia.
B. Why can it be said that no one person is typical of the people in Southeast Asia?
C. What climate and natural resources does Southeast Asia offer?

SKILLS CHECK
THINKING SKILL

Turn to the Countries of the Eastern Hemisphere charts on pages 32–43 and find the seven countries that make up the Indochina peninsula. Use the information on the table to answer the following questions: Which country is the largest? Which country has the highest population?

THINK ABOUT WHAT YOU KNOW

You have already learned about the three most important rivers in China in Chapter 4. Can you name them?

STUDY THE VOCABULARY

artery

FOCUS YOUR READING

What are the principal geographical features of East Asia?

A. Different Maps of the World

Matteo Ricci, a Roman Catholic priest from Italy, went to China in 1582. Father Ricci was a Christian missionary. He took some religious books with him, but he also took some works on science and a world map. When the Chinese first saw the map, they scarcely knew what to make of it. It was not that they had never seen a map before. The Chinese had made maps since ancient times, and they had mapped areas within China quite accurately. But the Europeans' map differed greatly from any world map they had ever seen.

The Chinese people called their land the Middle Kingdom. On Father Ricci's map, however, China did not appear in the middle, but was placed near the edge. The Chinese showed Ricci a map of their own, which was entitled *Picture of All Under Heaven.* It represented the world as a square, with China filling most of the square. Japan and Korea were squeezed into one corner, India and Arabia into another. All of the foreign lands put together were smaller than the smallest part of the Chinese empire.

Father Ricci explained that since the earth was a sphere, there really was no Middle Kingdom. A map drawn on a flat sheet could be made to show different parts of the world. He made a map locating China at the center of the page, with the Americas on the right and Europe and Africa on the left. The new map correctly showed that China was a large land, but smaller than all the other lands combined.

B. China's Lands

The Gobi China is by no means as large as it appeared on the Chinese map *Picture of All Under Heaven,* but it does make up the greater part of East Asia. It is more than twice as large as the South Asian subcontinent.

The world's second largest desert lies partly in northwestern China and partly in the neighboring country of Mongolia. It is a stony wasteland with very few shady

Nomads have set up camp here in the Gobi—a vast desert area.
► What homes of other groups of people are similar in shape to these houses?

areas. It is called the *Gobi*, which means "waterless place." It is well named. The Gobi has an extreme continental climate. Temperatures there may fall to −40°F (−40°C) in the winter and rise as high as 113°F (45°C) in the summer. Those who think that all deserts are sandy, hot lands would learn otherwise if they crossed the Gobi in January.

Tibetan Plateau   Only about one tenth of China is cultivated. Two thirds of the land is either mountainous or desert. Southwestern China consists of very high mountains and plateaus. The Tibetan plateau, called Zizang (shee SHAHNG) by the Chinese, rises as high as 15,000 feet (4,572 m). It is the highest inhabited plateau in the world.

C. China's Three Great Rivers

Huang He   All of China's large rivers flow from west to east. The Chang Jiang (chahng jee AHNG), formerly known as the Yangtze, and the Huang He (hwahng-hih) begin on the Tibetan plateau. They run down from the highlands and across the broad North China Plain. Both rivers carry silt to the plain. You may recall that silt is fine particles of soil carried by water. The Huang He flows through areas of yellow soil, and its muddy yellow water gives the river its name. *Huang He* means "Yellow River." The Huang Hai (hwahng hye), or "Yellow Sea," into which the river empties, also takes its name from the silt-filled water.

Chang Jiang   The course of the Chang Jiang runs south of the Huang He. After crossing the North China Plain, the Chang Jiang empties into the East China Sea. It is China's longest river and the world's fourth longest. The Chang flows for over 3,000 miles (4,827 km).

The Huang He, or Yellow River, is 2,903 miles (4,671 km) long.
▶ Why, do you think, is Yellow River a good name?

Xi Jiang   The Xi Jiang (shee jee AHNG), the third of China's great rivers, has its sources in the hills of southern China. The river is called *Xi Jiang*, which means "West River," because it flows from the west toward the South China Sea. The Xi Jiang is not as long as the other great rivers, but it serves as a main **artery**, or transportation route, for southern China. The important port of Guangzhou (GUAHNG joh), which was formerly known as Canton, is located on the delta formed by the Xi Jiang.

A very large part of China's population lives along or on the deltas of the three great rivers. The rivers are used for irrigation and for travel and shipping. They also flood from time to time and have destroyed many lives and much property. It is because of this that the Huang He is known as "China's sorrow."

D. The Korean Peninsula and Taiwan

The Korean peninsula juts out from the northern coast of China. It separates the Yellow Sea from the Sea of Japan, on the east. The Korean peninsula is mountainous, particularly in the east. Most of the level and rolling land is on the west side. Forests cover much of the mountainous land. At one time, overcutting nearly destroyed the forests. In more recent times the forests have been replanted and are carefully conserved.

The island of Taiwan lies about 90 miles (145 km) off the Chinese coast. When the Portuguese first arrived on this island in 1590, they called it *Formosa,* which means "beautiful." For many years the country was labeled *Formosa* on maps.

Taiwan, like Korea, has rugged mountains on its eastern side, with more gently sloping land on the west. Taipei, the capital, and Taiwan's other large cities are located on the western half of the island.

E. The Japanese Archipelago

Main Islands The Japanese archipelago stretches for 1,500 miles (2,414 km) along the coast of East Asia. There are four main islands and numerous smaller ones. Honshū, on which Japan's capital, Tokyo, is located, is the largest. It is a little larger than Utah. Hokkaidō, the second largest, has over one fifth of Japan's land but only one twentieth of its people. Many Japanese think of Hokkaidō as an "icebox" because it receives so much snow. Kyūshū is located farthest to the south and has the warmest climate. The smallest of the four main islands is Shikoku.

There are bridges and tunnels that now link the main islands of Japan. Trains glide 33.5 miles (54 km) through the tunnel between the islands of Honshū and Hokkaidō. A series of six bridges connect Honshū and Shikoku. Kyūshū and Honshū are joined by both a bridge and a tunnel.

This bridge links Kōbe, located on Honshū, with the island of Awaji.
► Why, do you think, is this bridge important to Awaji?

Mount Fuji is 12,388 feet (3,776 m) high. It was once a volcanic mountain but is no longer active. Its last eruption was almost 300 years ago.
▶ For what purpose is the land shown in the foreground of the photograph used?

Mountains Mount Fuji, in Japan, may well be the world's most-pictured mountain. It has been drawn, painted, and photographed countless times. Because it has been pictured so often, millions of people who have never been to Japan are familiar with Mount Fuji's snowy, cone-shaped peak. The cone was formed by the eruption of the volcano, which is no longer active. There are, however, a number of active volcanoes in Japan.

Mountains cover most of Japan, so only about 13 percent of the land is arable. This island country is slightly smaller than California, but its population is more than four times larger. Because space is so limited, the Japanese have learned to make use of every bit of land. The farmers carefully cultivate the small plots of arable soil. Well-managed forests, covering about two

thirds of the country, grow on the mountain slopes. The forests supply timber and bamboo. Bamboo is not a tree but a type of grass that, like trees, is used to make houses, furniture, and paper.

F. The Climates of East Asia

East Asia has many climates because the region covers such a large area. Hong Kong, on the coast of China, is located in the tropics, and Harbin, in northeastern China, is as far from the tropics as Minneapolis, Minnesota, is. A large part of China has a continental climate, but Japan and Taiwan have a maritime climate, one influenced by winds blowing from the sea.

The seasonal monsoon winds affect the climates of East Asia just as they affect those of the South Asian subcontinent. From May to October, winds generally

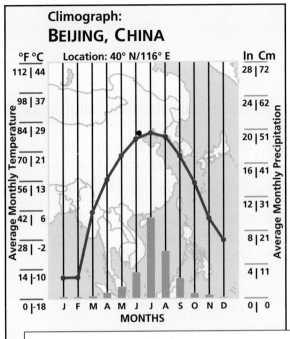

Climograph: BEIJING, CHINA

Location: 40° N/116° E

Average Monthly Temperature (°F °C): 112 | 44, 98 | 37, 84 | 29, 70 | 21, 56 | 13, 42 | 6, 28 | -2, 14 | -10, 0 | -18

Average Monthly Precipitation (In Cm): 28 | 72, 24 | 62, 20 | 51, 16 | 41, 12 | 31, 8 | 21, 4 | 11, 0 | 0

MONTHS: J F M A M J J A S O N D

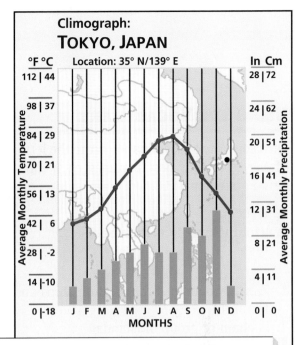

Climograph: TOKYO, JAPAN

Location: 35° N/139° E

Average Monthly Temperature (°F °C): 112 | 44, 98 | 37, 84 | 29, 70 | 21, 56 | 13, 42 | 6, 28 | -2, 14 | -10, 0 | -18

Average Monthly Precipitation (In Cm): 28 | 72, 24 | 62, 20 | 51, 16 | 41, 12 | 31, 8 | 21, 4 | 11, 0 | 0

MONTHS: J F M A M J J A S O N D

Although Beijing has a continental climate and Tokyo has a maritime climate, both cities are affected by seasonal monsoons.

► How does the temperature during the winter months in Tokyo differ from that of Beijing?

blow off the Pacific Ocean. These summer monsoons bring rain. In the northern part of the country, China's capital, Beijing (BAY JING), once known as Peking, receives most of its yearly rainfall in the summer.

The winter monsoon winds blow from the heart of Asia and bring cold, dry weather. Beijing receives little rainfall from October to May, but on the Japanese islands, the winter is neither as dry nor as cold. The winter winds from Asia blow over the Sea of Japan, which warms the air.

The monsoons affect all the climates of East Asia, but their effects vary from place to place. As a result, East Asia is a region not of one climate, but of many.

LESSON 3 REVIEW

THINK AND WRITE

A. Why did the Chinese think that Father Ricci's map was strange?

B. What is the difference between the climate on the Tibetan plateau and that in the Gobi?

C. What are the names and courses of the three great rivers of China?

D. In what way is the geography of the Korean peninsula like that of Taiwan?

E. What are the names of the four main islands of the Japanese archipelago?

F. What two factors explain the variety of climates in East Asia?

SKILLS CHECK

WRITING SKILL

Describe in a short paragraph why the Tibetan plateau has been called "the roof of the world."

519

USING THE VOCABULARY

On a separate sheet of paper, write the letter of the term that best matches each numbered statement.

a. Deccan
b. archipelago
c. teak
d. latex
e. bamboo

1. A hardwood used for building ships and furniture
2. A chain or group of islands
3. The milky sap that drips from slits cut into the bark of rubber trees
4. The low plateau that is located on the southern part of the South Asian subcontinent
5. A type of grass used to make houses, furniture, and paper

REMEMBERING WHAT YOU READ

On a separate sheet of paper, answer the following questions in complete sentences.

1. What book tells about Phileas Fogg and his worldwide travels?
2. What two mountain ranges separate the South Asian subcontinent from the rest of Asia?
3. Where is the tallest mountain in the world located?
4. What are the three longest rivers in South Asia?
5. Which is the largest island located off the tip of the subcontinent?
6. What kinds of winds greatly affect the climate of the subcontinent?
7. Where does about one third of Asia's population live?
8. How do the different groups that are part of the population of the South Asian subcontinent differ from each other?
9. What are the name and location of the world's largest group of islands?
10. What are some of the resources of Southeast Asia?
11. What country makes up the largest part of East Asia?
12. What is the name of the world's second largest desert?
13. Why is the Xi Jiang an important river in China?
14. How many main islands make up the country of Japan?
15. Why is East Asia a region of many different climates?

TYING SCIENCE TO SOCIAL STUDIES

Imagine that you are planning a trip around the world. Make a copy of a world map, or perhaps your teacher can provide a copy for you. Choose at least six countries that you would like to visit. Mark these locations on the map to show where you will stop on your trip. Then use an encyclopedia or another reference book to find the average temperatures and average precipitation levels for the time of year you plan to visit these countries. Indicate the temperature and rainfall levels on the map. Of all the countries you have chosen, which is the warmest? Which is the wettest? Which is the coldest?

THINKING CRITICALLY

On a separate sheet of paper, answer the following questions in complete sentences.

1. Why did so many people in 1873 find the book *Around the World in Eighty Days* exciting and interesting?
2. Why, in your opinion, is the population of the South Asian subcontinent spread unevenly over the land?
3. How do you suppose so many of the world's major religions came to have followers in the Malay Archipelago?
4. The Chinese had designed an incorrect map of the world. How would you explain this?
5. What differences are there between the Malay Archipelago and the Japanese archipelago?

SUMMARIZING THE CHAPTER

On a separate sheet of paper, draw a graphic organizer like the one shown here. Copy the information from this graphic organizer to the one you have drawn. Under the main idea for each lesson, write four statements that support the main idea.

| CHAPTER THEME | A variety of lands and climates exist in South Asia and East Asia. |

LESSON 1

South Asia has a variety of geographical features.

1. _____
2. _____
3. _____
4. _____

LESSON 2

Many differences can be found among the people and lands of Southeast Asia.

1. _____
2. _____
3. _____
4. _____

LESSON 3

East Asia has a variety of geographical features.

1. _____
2. _____
3. _____
4. _____

CHAPTER 20

HISTORY OF SOUTH AND EAST ASIA

Asia is the home of some of the world's oldest cultures. Inventions and ideas that were developed here have influenced all the world. Europeans came to South and East Asia to trade and to settle.

China

THINK ABOUT WHAT YOU KNOW

You have already read about the conquests of the Mongol emperor Genghis Khan. How, do you suppose, did life in early China change with the arrival of the Mongols?

STUDY THE VOCABULARY

cocoon

FOCUS YOUR READING

How did outsiders affect the development of China?

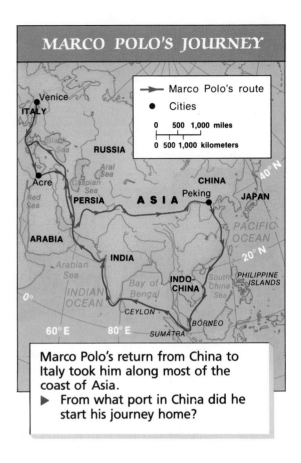

MARCO POLO'S JOURNEY

→ Marco Polo's route
● Cities

Marco Polo's return from China to Italy took him along most of the coast of Asia.
▶ From what port in China did he start his journey home?

A. Marco Polo Visits China

Kublai Khan's Empire When Niccolò and Maffeo Polo visited China in 1265, they were presented to the ruler Kublai Khan (KOO blye kahn). The Polo brothers had left their home in Venice, Italy, five years earlier. After many delays and difficulties, they had made their way overland across Asia to northern China.

Kublai Khan was the grandson of Genghis Khan, the Mongol chief whose armies had conquered the world's largest empire. Kublai Khan, also known as the Great Khan, conquered China. Kublai Khan had never met a European.

Marco Polo's Book Niccolò's son, Marco, accompanied the Polo brothers on their second trip to China, almost ten years later. Marco Polo set about learning the language of the Great Khan's people. This so pleased Kublai Khan that he took Marco into his service and sent him on missions to various parts of the empire.

Marco Polo served Kublai Khan for 17 years before returning to Venice. He took careful notes on his travels and later wrote

about them in a book now known as *The Travels of Marco Polo*.

Much of the book is about Kublai Khan. Marco Polo describes the Great Khan as the richest and most powerful ruler in the world. His empire was larger than any other, and his palace was the biggest ever known.

B. Chinese Discoveries and Inventions

Making Paper Europeans knew little about China in Marco Polo's day, but they did know about Chinese discoveries and inventions. Paper, as we know it today, was invented in China about A.D. 100, and knowledge of papermaking spread to the Middle East and to Europe. The first paper mills in Italy were being built about the time that Marco Polo arrived in China.

523

MARCO POLO DISCOVERS PAPER MONEY

Kublai Khan

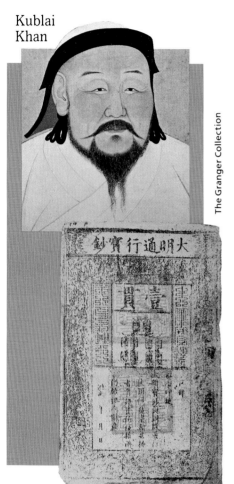

The Granger Collection

Marco Polo spent nearly two decades serving Kublai Khan. Polo spent much of that time traveling throughout the Mongol Empire. During his travels, Polo kept careful notes, which he later used to write *The Travels of Marco Polo*. In the following passage from his book, Polo describes how paper money is made and used in the empire.

> In this city of Kanbalu [now Beijing] is the mint of the Great Khan, who may truly be said to possess the secret of the alchemists, as he has the art of producing money. . . . He causes the bark to be stripped from . . . mulberry-trees. . . . This . . . is made into paper, resembling, in substance, that which is manufactured from cotton, but quite black. When ready for use, he has it cut into pieces of money of different sizes, nearly square, but somewhat longer than they are wide. . . . The coinage of this paper money is authenticated with as much form and ceremony as if it were actually of pure gold or silver; for to each note a number of officers, specially appointed, not only subscribe their names, but affix their seals also. . . . The act of counterfeiting it is punished as a capital offence. When thus coined in large quantities, this paper currency is circulated in every part of the Great Khan's dominions; nor dares any person at the peril of his life, refuse to accept it in payment. All his subjects receive it without hesitation, because, wherever their business may call them, they can dispose of it again in the purchase of merchandise they may require; such as pearls, jewels, gold, or silver. With it, in short, every article may be procured.

Understanding Source Material

1. How does the paper money that Polo described in his book compare with ours today?
2. How can you tell from the above passage that Kublai Khan was truly a powerful man?

Inventing Gunpowder When the Mongols invaded eastern Europe, they used gunpowder, which may have been another Chinese invention. Many historians believe that the Chinese had gunpowder by the tenth century. If so, they used it mainly for fireworks. Cannons and guns were probably invented later.

Making Silk Since ancient times the Chinese have known how to make silk cloth from fibers spun by silkworms. A silkworm is a caterpillar that spins an especially light, strong covering. This covering, which protects the silkworm while it is changing into a moth, is called a **cocoon.** The Chinese discovered how to unwind the thin fibers of cocoons, spin them into thread, and weave the thread into cloth. Silk cloth was valuable and easily transported. Passing from trader to trader, it was being carried across Central Asia 1,200 years before Marco Polo wrote his book.

C. European Traders Reach China

Chinese emperors after Kublai Khan did not welcome visitors from Europe and saw no reason for China to open its doors to foreign trade. They thought that China lacked nothing within its own borders.

One of the emperors, however, understood why foreigners wanted Chinese silk, tea, and porcelain. For this reason he permitted foreigners to enter the city of Guangzhou for limited trading.

The Chinese laid down strict rules for trading at Guangzhou. European traders had to come during the summer, and they could do business with only a few Chinese merchants. All Europeans had to stay within a district set aside for foreigners. The European traders were not supposed to mix with the Chinese.

SILK: FROM SILK MOTHS TO TIE

1. A silkworm moth lays hundreds of eggs.

2. Silkworms hatch from the eggs.

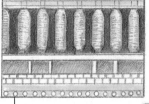
3. Silkworms spin cocoons of silk fibers.

4. The silk fibers are spun into yarn.

5. The yarn is woven into fabric.

6. A silk garment is made from the fabric.

Silk was first used by the ancient Chinese, who kept the secret of the silkworm for thousands of years.
► What happens after the silkworm moth lays its eggs?

D. The Opening of China's Doors

A Special Favor In 1793 the British sent a representative to Ch'ien Lung (chee UN lung), the Chinese emperor. The emperors had never received ambassadors, or official representatives, from European countries, but Ch'ien Lung agreed to do so as a special favor to the British.

The ambassador carried a message from the British king, George III. The king asked that the British be allowed to open an embassy in Peking and that there be freer trade between the two countries. In his reply to the king, Ch'ien Lung said that the Chinese did not need such contacts.

The Chinese officials thought the British were very rude to ask for more favors after the emperor had been kind enough to meet their ambassador. The British viewed Ch'ien Lung's refusal to allow an embassy very differently. They thought civilized countries exchanged ambassadors. But there were other differences between China and Britain. The British complained that the Chinese did not treat their merchants at Guangzhou fairly. The Chinese charged that British merchants broke Chinese laws.

China Defeated These quarrels led to a war in 1839, in which the British defeated the Chinese. Britain forced China to open

The British are shown here attacking the Chinese in the First Opium War, in 1839.
▶ What caused the war?

more of its ports to trade. The British also acquired Hong Kong, off the coast of southern China, where they set up a colony.

Once the British forced China to open its doors, other countries did the same. China was not divided up into colonies, as Africa was, but by 1900, European countries largely controlled the country.

LESSON *1* REVIEW

THINK AND WRITE

A. How was Marco Polo able to learn so much about Kublai Khan's empire?

B. What were some Chinese discoveries and inventions?

C. How did the views of Chinese emperors change regarding European trading in China?

D. Summarize the results of the quarrels between the Chinese and the British.

SKILLS CHECK

WRITING SKILL

Suppose you were a Venetian who listened to Marco Polo tell about his years in China. Write a letter to a friend, describing what you heard.

Korea and Japan

THINK ABOUT WHAT YOU KNOW

If you visited a class in North Korea or Japan and were asked to tell something about the history of your country, what would you talk about?

STUDY THE VOCABULARY

samurai   **typhoon**
shogun

FOCUS YOUR READING

How did Korea and Japan differ from China?

A. Korea and Chinese Civilization

The people of Korea have a proverb: After the house has burned, pick up the nails. By this they mean, if you suffer a loss, take what is left and start over. The Koreans have done this a number of times. The Korean peninsula, located between China and Japan, was occupied by both the Chinese and the Japanese at different times during Korea's long history.

In early times the Koreans borrowed many things from Chinese civilization. The Buddhist religion, which originated in India, was taken to Korea by the Chinese. The Koreans studied ancient Chinese writings, particularly those of Confucius. They also used the Chinese system of writing.

The Korean language is very different from Chinese, however. As long as the Koreans wrote with borrowed Chinese characters, only a few people could learn to read and write. Most people did not have time to memorize the thousands of different Chinese characters.

To solve this problem, in the mid-1440s the Korean king, Sejong (SAY ZHONG) introduced an alphabet of 28 letters. The alphabet represented the sounds of the Korean language and so provided a simpler way to write and read. Some officials who knew the Chinese characters continued to use them. Today, however, Korean students learn King Sejong's alphabet.

B. Japan and the Chinese

Chinese Influence   Japan was influenced by Chinese civilization, too. Buddhism was taken to Japan from China by way of Korea. Japanese nobles went to China to learn Chinese ways. Like the Koreans, Japanese scholars in early times wrote with Chinese characters and read Confucius. Later a simpler writing system was invented that was better suited to the Japanese language.

About 550 years ago, King Sejong introduced the Korean alphabet that is used today.
▶ Why did he invent the alphabet?

Ancient samurai warriors wore very elaborate suits of armor that were considerably lighter in weight than those worn by European knights.
▶ With what weapons are these samurai warriors equipped?

Feudalism Like China, Japan had emperors. But the Japanese government was much more like the feudal governments of the European countries during the Middle Ages. Real power belonged to the nobles, who had large estates. Each noble ruled the people who lived on his land. Many nobles had their own bands of fighting men called **samurai** (SAM uh rye). The most powerful of the nobles was a military leader called the **shogun**. For nearly seven centuries the shoguns held real power, although the emperors supposedly ruled.

Takeover Attempts When Kublai Khan ruled China, he heard tales about Japan's great wealth and decided to add Japan to his empire. He sent a message to the Japanese, demanding that they pay tribute to him. If they did not, he would invade their islands. When the Japanese refused, Kublai Khan sent a fleet to attack them. Fortunately for the Japanese, a storm wrecked part of the Mongol fleet, forcing it to return to the mainland.

Kublai Khan did not give up his dream of conquering Japan. In 1281 he sent an even larger force. Once again bad weather favored the Japanese. A **typhoon**, or severe hurricane, destroyed most of the Mongol fleet. Japan remained independent. Although the Japanese borrowed ideas and customs from China, Japan was never part of China's empire.

C. Japan Closes the Door to Foreigners

Japan's Fear Portuguese merchants and Christian priests were the first Europeans to visit Japan. At first the Japanese welcomed the Europeans, although they thought them rather rude. Japanese nobles bought European goods from merchants from the West. The nobles particularly liked clocks and musical instruments. Some bought European clothes to wear.

Christian priests reported that the Japanese were eager to hear about new things. They were especially interested in European science and geography. Some Japanese were interested in the Christian religion. By the 1630s the shogun in power became worried about the growing interest in European ways and ideas. He feared that Europeans who came to trade would later try to rule the country. He knew that European countries had established colonies on the subcontinent and in the Philippines.

Closing the Door The shogun decided that Japan should follow China's example and close the door to foreigners. Yet, although most Europeans had to leave the country, the shogun did agree to leave the door ajar. A few Dutch traders were allowed to stay at the port of Nagasaki. Rules for the traders at Nagasaki were much like those set by the Chinese for traders at Guangzhou.

The Japanese left this opening because they wanted to know what was going

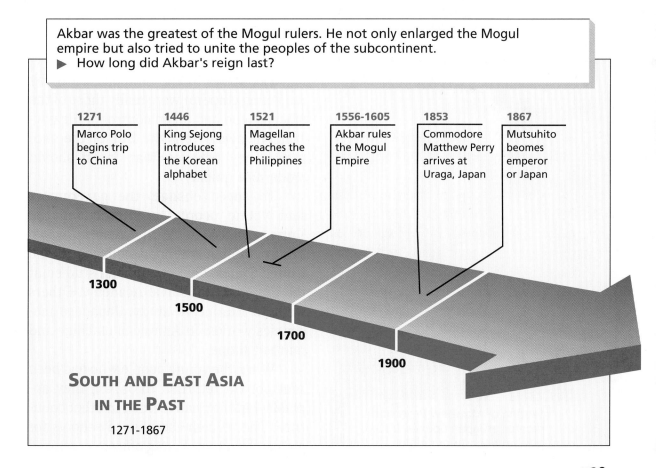

Akbar was the greatest of the Mogul rulers. He not only enlarged the Mogul empire but also tried to unite the peoples of the subcontinent.
▶ How long did Akbar's reign last?

1271	1446	1521	1556-1605	1853	1867
Marco Polo begins trip to China	King Sejong introduces the Korean alphabet	Magellan reaches the Philippines	Akbar rules the Mogul Empire	Commodore Matthew Perry arrives at Uraga, Japan	Mutsuhito beomes emperor or Japan

1300

1500

1700

1900

SOUTH AND EAST ASIA IN THE PAST

1271-1867

on in the world. Every year when a new Dutch officer came to take over the post at Nagasaki, he had to write a newsletter about the important events of the past year. The Dutch were required to supply the Japanese with European books, which a few Japanese could read.

D. The United States Navy Opens the Door

A few years after the British forced China to open its doors to trade, the United States sent a small fleet to Japan. Commodore Matthew Perry was in command of the fleet, which included the first steamships ever seen in Japan. Perry arrived at Uraga in 1853 with a letter from President Millard Fillmore to the emperor of Japan. The letter said that the United States wanted nothing more than friendship and trade between the two countries.

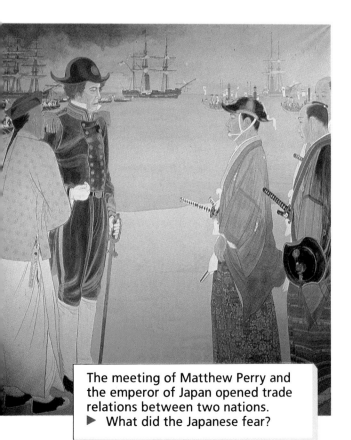

The meeting of Matthew Perry and the emperor of Japan opened trade relations between two nations.
▶ What did the Japanese fear?

Matthew Perry's visit was friendly. The Japanese feared, however, that in the future the fleets might be less peaceful. They knew that China had fought and lost against foreigners. Some Japanese leaders, however, believed that to remain independent, Japan had to learn from the Western countries.

E. "Knowledge from the Whole World"

A 15-year-old boy named Mutsuhito became the emperor of Japan in 1867. As emperor he became known as *Meiji*, which means "enlightened government." On taking the throne, Emperor Meiji read this statement:

My country is now undergoing a complete change from old to new ideas, which I sincerely desire. To speed the change people should seek knowledge from the whole world.

The views in the statement read by the young emperor were really those of the officials who had taken control of the government away from the last of the shoguns. They believed that Japan should modernize quickly.

To speed change, the government sent young people to Europe and the United States to learn Western ways. Young women attended colleges in the United States. One young man studied at the United States Naval Academy. Others went to Europe to study. Japanese mechanics worked in American machine and railroad shops.

When the young people who had been sent abroad returned to Japan, they applied what they had learned in other countries. The women established schools for girls and women. Young officers organized

高繩鉄道之圖

The Japanese built their first railway as part of their plan to modernize.
► Where did the Japanese learn to build locomotives?

and trained modern armed forces. Mechanics built modern locomotives.

How well the Japanese had learned their lessons became plain when Japan defeated the much larger country of China in 1895. Ten years later, Japan surprised the world by defeating the Russians in East Asia. These victories showed that Japan had become the most powerful country in all of East Asia.

LESSON **2** REVIEW

THINK AND WRITE

A. What did the Koreans borrow from the Chinese?

B. How was Japan like Europe during the Middle Ages?

C. Why did Japan not close the door to the West completely?

D. What did the United States want from Japan?

E. How did the Japanese promote change under Emperor Meiji?

SKILLS CHECK

THINKING SKILL

Make a time line for the years 1400–1900. Look in the lesson for the dates of the following events and show them on the time line: King Sejong introduces an alphabet; Japan closes the door to foreigners; Perry lands at Nagasaki; Emperor Meiji comes to the throne; Japan defeats China.

THINK ABOUT WHAT YOU KNOW

Europeans first went to South Asia seeking spices. Name some of the ways that spices are used today.

STUDY THE VOCABULARY

successor　　**free port**
mausoleum

FOCUS YOUR READING

How did people from outside the South Asian subcontinent and Southeast Asia affect these regions?

A. Newcomers Enter the Subcontinent

Vasco da Gama　In 1498 the Portuguese explorer Vasco da Gama landed on the west coast of the South Asian subcontinent. Da Gama erected a stone pillar as proof of Portugal's claim to the land. The people living there did not think that the newcomers had any claim to the land. But the Portuguese went on to take the port of Goa a few years later, declaring it a Portuguese colony. It was the first European colony on the subcontinent.

Mogul Invasions　Another group of newcomers entered the subcontinent through the Khyber Pass from Afghanistan. They were raiders led by Babur, a descendant of the Mongol conqueror Genghis Khan. People of the subcontinent called the invaders Moguls, their word for Mongols.

Babur's followers were fierce and skillful fighters. At first they came only to raid the land. Later, however, Babur decided he wanted an empire, and in 1526 he set out to win one.

On the subcontinent, Babur faced armies far larger than his own. His opponents had thousands of foot soldiers, many horses, and even war elephants. But Babur's men were better fighters and better armed. A Mogul could shoot a bow while riding at full speed. More important, Babur's men had cannons. Even if the cannonballs did not hit the elephants, the noise so frightened the large animals that they often trampled their handlers.

Babur conquered the northern part of the subcontinent. His **successors**, those who came after him, enlarged the empire. Mogul emperors, known as the Great Moguls, came to rule an empire that stretched from Afghanistan to the country now called Bangladesh.

Babur's army invaded the land of Afghanistan in 1507.
► What animals did the Moguls use in fighting?

Christian priests and Muslims are debating religion before Akbar ca. 1605.
▶ What books do you suppose are shown in this picture?

B. Akbar: Greatest of the Great Moguls

Akbar's Accomplishments Akbar, the grandson of Babur, was the greatest of the Mogul rulers. He ruled for 49 years, from 1556 to 1605. He not only enlarged the Mogul Empire, he also tried to unite the different peoples of the subcontinent. The peoples of the empire spoke different languages and followed different religions.

The Moguls were Muslims, but the majority of the people on the subcontinent were Hindus. Akbar took steps to win the support of the Hindus. He placed Hindus in high positions and arranged the marriage of his son to the daughter of a Hindu noble. He also did away with a special tax that people who were not Muslims had been forced to pay.

Akbar's Religion Religions greatly interested Akbar. He built a hall of worship to which he summoned teachers of different faiths. Among others, Akbar invited Christian priests from Goa. Akbar questioned the priests for hours, not only about their religion but also about Europe.

Akbar did not adopt any of the existing religions. Instead he invented a religion that borrowed ideas from other religions. Akbar thought that such a religion would help to unite the peoples of his empire. But when Akbar died in 1605, his new religion died too.

C. The Moguls and the Arts

Akbar encouraged artists, craftspeople, and writers. He set up studios for the artists and gave prizes for the best works.

The Taj Mahal stands at Agra, in northern India. It is made of white marble and was built by about 20,000 workers between 1630 and 1650.
▶ For what purpose was the Taj Mahal built?

Akbar's successors did the same. The Moguls also invited Persian artists and craftspeople to the subcontinent. Persian and subcontinental styles were often combined in the paintings.

These two styles can also be seen in one of the world's most famous buildings, the Taj Mahal. The Taj Mahal was built by Akbar's grandson, Shah Jahan, as a **mausoleum** (maw suh LEE um), or large tomb, for his beloved wife. Shah Jahan told the builders that he wanted a building "as beautiful as she was beautiful."

D. Trading Companies and Empires

Trading Posts Other Europeans followed the Portuguese to the subcontinent. Dutch, English, and French trading companies sought sugar, spices, cotton, yarn, and cloth.

Europeans went to trade rather than to settle, but they established permanent trading posts. The European companies needed places where their employees could live and do business. The first trading posts were enclosures with offices, warehouses, living quarters, and usually a chapel, or small church. As trade increased, the companies fortified their posts and hired troops to protect them. Although the officers of the troops were Europeans, most of the common soldiers were Asians.

British India As the power of the European companies increased, the power of the Moguls declined. After 1700 the Great Moguls lost control of the subcontinent. Wars broke out between local rulers, and the trading companies entered into these struggles with their armies.

French and British companies clashed on the subcontinent. This conflict was part of a much larger struggle between France and Britain, fought in Europe and North America. The British defeated the French and became even more powerful on the subcontinent. Although a Mogul remained on the throne until 1857, the subcontinent had become part of the British Empire and was known as British India.

E. Peoples of Southeast Asia

Peoples from China, from the subcontinent, and even from the Middle East went to Southeast Asia to trade and to settle. All of these groups had their own religions, languages, and customs.

Peoples from the subcontinent settled in many parts of the Indochina peninsula and the Indonesian archipelago. They spread Buddhism and Hinduism throughout these regions. Today, Buddhism is the main religion in Burma, Cambodia, and Thailand. Remains of famous Hindu temples in these countries show that Hinduism was once common there.

Chinese traders and settlers moved south along the coast of East Asia. They, too, spread their language and culture. The Vietnamese adopted Chinese characters to write their language. When Marco Polo visited Vietnam, he reported that although the country had its own king, it paid tribute every year to the Great Khan.

Arab leaders from the Middle East also journeyed to Southeast Asia. They introduced the Muslim religion, which largely replaced Hinduism and Buddhism on the Malay Peninsula, the Indonesian archipelago and in the Philippines.

Angkor Wat, a Hindu temple, was built in Cambodia in the 1100s.
▶ What does this ruin tell about the history of Cambodia?

F. Europeans in Southeast Asia

Portugal Europeans first went to Southeast Asia seeking pepper, ginger, nutmeg, and other spices. Spices were popular in Europe because they made food tastier and helped to preserve it.

The Portuguese were the first to arrive in Indonesia, where many of the spices grew. The Dutch later drove the Portuguese out. By 1750 the Dutch controlled the more important islands of Indonesia, which they called the Dutch East Indies. They were part of the Dutch Empire until after World War II. Locate the islands in the Dutch East Indies on the map.

Spain A Spanish fleet commanded by Ferdinand Magellan reached the Philippines in 1521. Magellan was attempting to sail around the world. He had sailed west from Europe, across the Atlantic, and around the tip of South America into the Pacific. Magellan did not complete his voyage though. He was killed in the Philippines. But one of his ships did make it back to Spain. It was the first ship to sail around the world.

The Spanish conquered the Philippines, which they named after their king, Philip II. The islands were under Spanish rule until after the Spanish-American

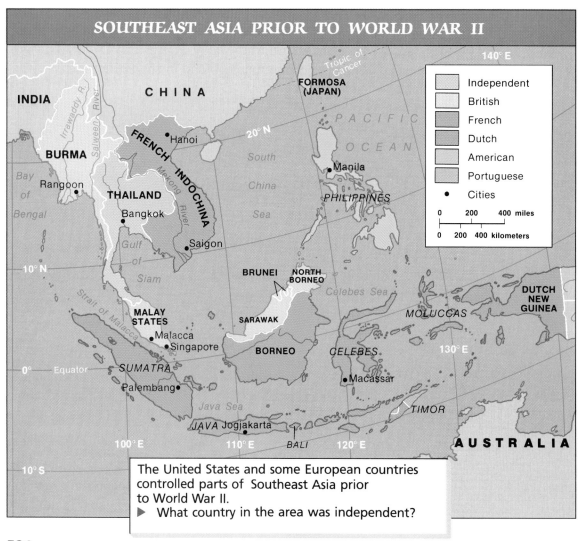

SOUTHEAST ASIA PRIOR TO WORLD WAR II

Legend:
- Independent
- British
- French
- Dutch
- American
- Portuguese
- • Cities

0   200   400 miles
0   200   400 kilometers

The United States and some European countries controlled parts of Southeast Asia prior to World War II.
▶ What country in the area was independent?

War, in 1898. At that time, Spain had to turn the islands over to the United States. The Philippines became independent in 1946, shortly after World War II.

Britain The British conquered Burma and ruled it as part of their empire in India. The British Empire also included Singapore, an island at the tip of the Malay Peninsula. At first, Singapore was the location of a British naval base. The naval base grew into a busy trading city, partly because it was a **free port**. A free port is one that does not collect taxes on goods landed there. Singapore became a profitable place to do business. The British also made the entire Malay Peninsula part of their empire. British rule of Singapore and the Malay Peninsula lasted until the late 1950s.

France French priests as well as traders went to Indochina more than 300 years ago. The priests went to teach people about the Christian religion. One priest also invented an alphabet that is still used today for the Vietnamese language. Between 1862 and 1893 the French conquered Vietnam, Laos, and Cambodia. These lands remained part of the French empire until after World War II.

British troops are shown here entering Singapore in 1824, making it part of their empire.
► By what means did they enter?

LESSON **3** REVIEW

THINK AND WRITE

A. How did the Portuguese and the Moguls establish their holds on the subcontinent?

B. How did Akbar attempt to unite the peoples of his empire?

C. Explain how the Moguls encouraged the arts.

D. Why did Europeans go to the subcontinent?

E. Why does Southeast Asia have so many different cultures?

F. What European countries had empires in Southeast Asia before World War II?

SKILLS CHECK

MAP SKILL

Singapore was a key port on a vital sea route. Use the map on page 536 to answer the following questions: What is the shortest sea route from the subcontinent to East Asia? Where is Singapore located in relation to this route?

USING THE VOCABULARY

On a separate sheet of paper, write the letter of the term that best matches each numbered statement.

    a. **cocoon**
    b. **samurai**
    c. **shogun**
    d. **typhoon**
    e. **mausoleum**

1. The strong, light covering that protects the silkworm while it changes into a moth
2. A large tomb
3. A military leader who was the most powerful noble in Japan
4. Bands of Japanese fighting men
5. A severe hurricane

REMEMBERING WHAT YOU READ

1. What did Marco Polo write about in his book?
2. What valuable cloth did the Chinese make?
3. What quarrels or conflicts led to a war between the Chinese and the British in 1839?
4. Who invented the alphabet that Korean students use today?
5. How long did the shoguns rule Japan?
6. Why did the shogun decide to close Japan's door to foreigners?
7. Who was the leader of the American fleet that visited Japan in 1853?
8. What was the name of the emperor who believed that Japan should be modernized?
9. What country established the first European colony on the subcontinent?
10. What group of raiders led by Babur invaded the subcontinent?
11. Why was Babur able to defeat his opponents, even though he faced armies far larger than his own?
12. Who was the greatest of the Mogul rulers?
13. Why was the Taj Mahal built?
14. From what country was the first ship to sail around the world?
15. What lands in Southeast Asia were part of the French empire until after World War II?

TYING SCIENCE TO SOCIAL STUDIES

What spice is used in your favorite food? Prepare an oral report to share with your classmates, telling about the spice in your favorite food. Use a reference book to find out what part of the plant the spice comes from, the country and climate in which the spice grows, and what other foods it is used to flavor. You could also show on a map where the spice is grown.

THINKING CRITICALLY

1. How do we know that Marco Polo was very impressed with Kublai Khan?
2. Do you think China was right to be fearful of visitors from Europe?
3. Why did Christian priests visit Japan?
4. Why have spices played an important role in history?
5. Do you think that countries have a right to claim other lands?

SUMMARIZING THE CHAPTER

On a separate sheet of paper, copy the graphic organizer shown below. Beside the main idea for each lesson, write four statements that support the main idea.

CHAPTER THEME

East Asia and South Asia were affected by new religions, trade, and empire builders from Europe, the Middle East, and from within the regions themselves.

LESSON 1

Outsiders affected the development of China.

1. _____
2. _____
3. _____
4. _____

LESSON 2

Korea and Japan differed from China.

1. _____
2. _____
3. _____
4. _____

LESSON 3

Newcomers affected the South Asian subcontinent and Southeast Asia.

1. _____
2. _____
3. _____
4. _____

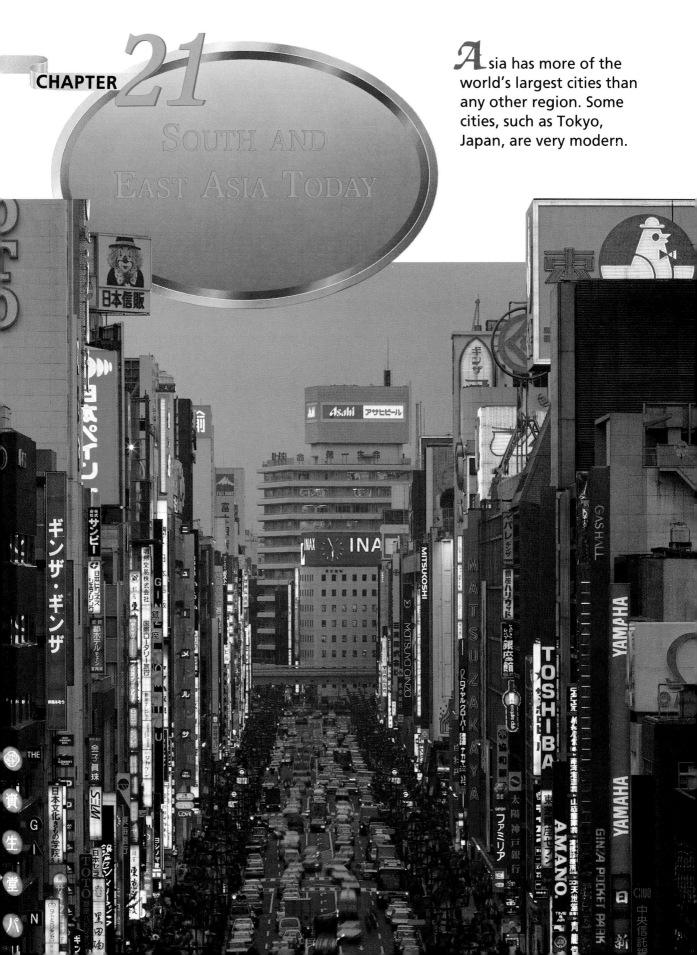

CHAPTER **21**

SOUTH AND
EAST ASIA TODAY

*A*sia has more of the world's largest cities than any other region. Some cities, such as Tokyo, Japan, are very modern.

China and Taiwan

THINK ABOUT WHAT YOU KNOW

In previous chapters you have read about revolutions in such places as England, France, and Russia. What are some changes that revolutions can bring?

STUDY THE VOCABULARY

warlord   **incentive**
commune

FOCUS YOUR READING

How have revolutions and civil wars affected China?

A. Revolutions and Civil Wars

China is about the same size as the United States, but it has four times as many people. About a billion people live in China. No other country in the world has such a large population.

The people of China have experienced many changes during the last century. A revolution forced the last of China's emperors, a 6-year-old boy, from the throne in 1912. A republic was established, but the new government was not able to control the land. Local rulers known as **warlords** held most of the country. The warlords had their own small armies, much like the feudal lords in Europe during the Middle Ages. Wars between the government and the warlords weakened China.

Japan took advantage of this weakness and invaded China in the 1930s. In 1941, Japan's war in East Asia became part of World War II. Peace did not come to China with the defeat of Japan in 1945, however. A civil war broke out between the Nationalists, who controlled the Chinese government, and the Communists.

By 1949 the Communists, who were led by Mao Ze-dong (mou DZU-doong), had control of the Chinese mainland. The Nationalists and their leader, Chiang Kai-shek (chang kye SHEK), fled to Taiwan.

B. The People's Republic of China

The Nationalists called their government, on Taiwan, the Republic of China. The Communists named their government, on the mainland, the People's Republic of China. Both the Nationalists and the Communists claimed that theirs was the lawful government of all China.

The Communists wanted to revolutionize the Chinese way of life. Loyalty to the state was to take the place of loyalty to family or friends. Neither families nor individuals could own land. Farmers had to join **communes**, farms on which people

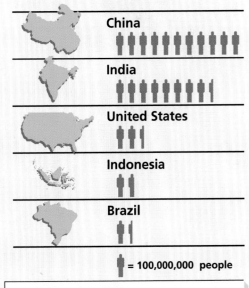

THE WORLD'S FIVE MOST POPULATED COUNTRIES

China

India

United States

Indonesia

Brazil

= 100,000,000 people

China is the most populated country in the world.
► About how many more people live in China than live in the United States?

lived and worked together. All people were to be equal. So, an individual farmer was not allowed to make a profit by growing and selling extra vegetables.

All industries became property of the state. Factory workers who worked hard and produced more were not paid more money. Instead they were awarded red stars and banners as symbols of China.

The Communist government under Mao Ze-dong crushed all opposition to the revolutionary changes. Special courts were set up to rid anyone thought to be against the revolution. These courts condemned many people. Thousands were killed; no one knows exactly how many.

C. Reforming the Revolution

Increasing Production The communes and state-owned factories failed, however, to produce the food and goods so badly needed by the large population of China.

After Mao Ze-dong's death in 1976, some of the Communist leaders decided that the revolution should be reformed. Under the leadership of Deng Xiaoping (dung shou-pihng), the government made use of **incentives** to increase production. Incentives are rewards for people who work harder or do more. For example, a farmer who grew extra food could sell it for a profit. Factory workers who produced more would be paid more. People could again own small businesses.

The offering of incentives did increase production. Both agricultural and industrial production rose. Farmers grew more when they could sell for a profit. Workers produced more when they could earn more. In some areas of China the peasants grew prosperous. Fortunately, China has an abundance of coal, which is used to fuel its industries. China is one of the world's leading producers of coal.

In December 1989, Brent Scowcroft, the United States National Security Adviser, met with Deng Xiaoping.
▶ Who is Deng Xiaoping?

SOUTH AND EAST ASIA: COAL PRODUCTION

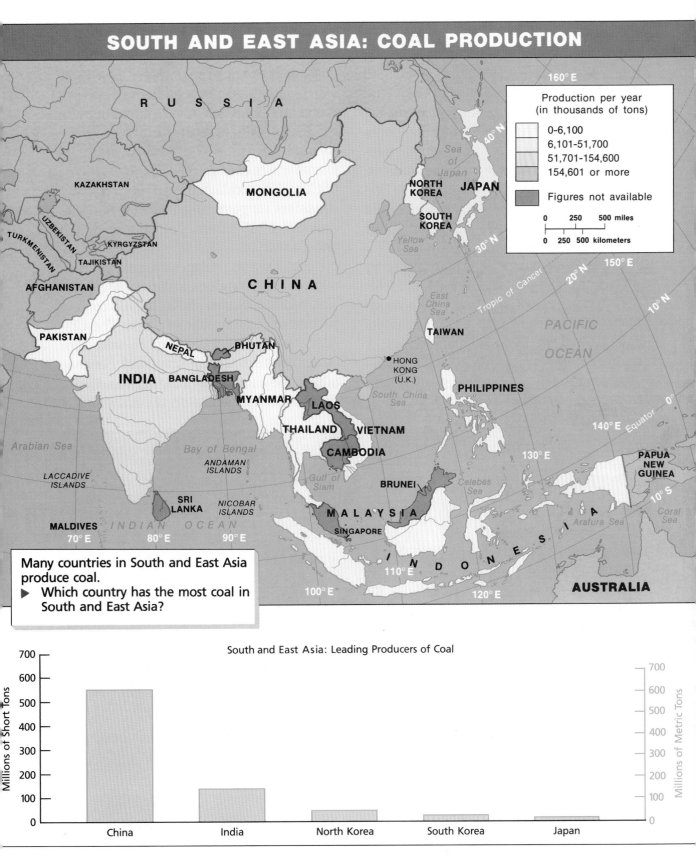

Production per year (in thousands of tons)

- 0–6,100
- 6,101–51,700
- 51,701–154,600
- 154,601 or more
- Figures not available

0   250   500 miles

0   250   500 kilometers

Many countries in South and East Asia produce coal.

▶ Which country has the most coal in South and East Asia?

South and East Asia: Leading Producers of Coal

(y-axis left: Millions of Short Tons; y-axis right: Millions of Metric Tons)

Countries: China, India, North Korea, South Korea, Japan

More Reforms   Reforms on the farms and in factories led to demands for other kinds of reforms. People not only wanted freedom to sell their goods, they also wanted freedom to speak out about what was on their minds. University students spoke of the need for democracy, the freedom of people to choose their government. In 1989 a large number of students in Beijing, the capital of China, demonstrated peacefully for more freedom. Other groups joined the student demonstrations.

The Communist government was by no means willing to allow this type of freedom and demonstration. The government used the army to clear the city's squares and streets of demonstrators. A number of people were killed, and the leaders of the demonstration were hunted down and arrested.

D. The Republic of China on Taiwan

The Nationalist Republic of China has continued to hold Taiwan since 1949. Taiwan appears small when compared with mainland China, but it has a larger population than many Western European countries. Both the Nationalists and the Communists consider the island to be part of China. As explained earlier, each group considers its government the lawful government of all China, both the mainland and Taiwan.

On Taiwan, businesses are privately owned. They produce a variety of goods. The United States is a major trading partner of the Republic of China. The Chinese on Taiwan export more and earn more than those on the mainland. Because of this, they also enjoy a higher standard of living than the people on the mainland.

These people are working in a factory in Taiwan.
▶ What product are the workers assembling?

SOUTH AND EAST ASIA: POLITICAL

KAZAKHSTAN

RUSSIA

7

6

5

4

3

1 **2**

UZBEKISTAN

TURKMENISTAN

TAJIKISTAN

KYRGYZSTAN

Ulan Bator ✪

MONGOLIA

HOKKAIDŌ

PACIFIC OCEAN

40° N

30° N

20° N

Tropic of Cancer

A

B

AFGHANISTAN

JAMMU AND KASHMIR

Islamabad ✪

PAKISTAN

TIBET

Delhi

New Delhi

NEPAL

Thimbu

Katmandu ✪ BHUTAN

Brahmaputra R.

C

CHINA

Great Wall

Beijing ✪

Huang He

Yellow Sea

Chang Jiang

Xi R.

Shanghai ●

Pyongyang ✪

Seoul ✪

SOUTH KOREA

NORTH KOREA

JAPAN

Tokyo ✪

HONSHŪ

SHIKOKU

Sea of Japan

East China Sea

RYUKYU IS.

Taipei ●

TAIWAN

Hong Kong (U.K.)

Macao (Port.)

LUZON

Manila ●

PHILIPPINES

MINDANAO

National capitals ✪

Other cities ●

0   400   800 miles

0   400   800 kilometers

Port. —Portugal
U.K. —United Kingdom

INDIA

Indus R.

Ganges River

Calcutta ●

BANGLADESH

Dacca ●

MYANMAR

Rangoon ●

LAOS

Hanoi ✪

Vientiane ✪

THAILAND

VIETNAM

Ho Chi Minh City ●

CAMBODIA

Bangkok ✪

Phnom Penh ✪

Bandar Seri Begawan ✪

BRUNEI

BORNEO

Bombay ●

Arabian Sea

Bay of Bengal

ANDAMAN IS.

NICOBAR IS.

Strait of Malacca

D

E

LACCADIVE IS.

SRI LANKA

Colombo ●

MALDIVES

Male ●

MALAYSIA

Kuala Lumpur ●

Singapore ✪

SUMATRA

INDONESIA

South China Sea

PALAWAN

Celebes Sea

CELEBES

MOLUCCAS

CERAM

IRIAN JAYA

NEW GUINEA

PAPUA NEW GUINEA

Coral Sea

Arafura Sea

F

INDIAN OCEAN

Jakarta ✪

JAVA

BALI

TIMOR

AUSTRALIA

Equator

20° S

10° S   0°   10° N

10° S

70° E   80° E   90° E   100° E   110° E   120° E   130° E   140° E

Cities less than 100,000
Bandar Seri Begawan (Brunei) E-5
Male (Maldives) E-1
Thimbu (Bhutan) C-2

Cities 100,000 to 499,999
Islamabad (Pakistan) B-1
Katmandu (Nepal) C-2
Macao (Portugal) C-5
New Delhi (India) C-1

Phnom Penh (Cambodia) D-4
Ulan Bator (Mongolia) A-4
Vientiane (Laos) D-4

Cities 500,000 to 999,999
Colombo (Sri Lanka) E-1
Kuala Lumpur (Malaysia) E-4

Cities 1,000,000 or more
Bangkok (Thailand) D-4

Beijing (China) B-5
Bombay (India) D-1
Calcutta (India) C-2
Dacca (Bangladesh) C-3
Delhi (India) C-1
Hanoi (Vietnam) C-4
Ho Chi Minh City (Vietnam) D-4
Hong Kong (United Kingdom) C-5
Jakarta (Indonesia) F-4

Manila (Philippines) D-6
Pyongyang (North Korea) B-6
Rangoon (Myanmar) D-3
Seoul (South Korea) B-6
Shanghai (China) B-6
Singapore (Singapore) E-4
Taipei (Taiwan) C-6
Tokyo (Japan) B-7

Asia has more of the world's largest cities than any other region.
▶ Which city in Myanmar has a population of 1,000,000 or more?

E. Three Territories

Hong Kong Great Britain and Portugal both hold land in China. As you recall, the British took over the island of Hong Kong in the 1840s. They later leased territory on the nearby Chinese mainland. Under British rule, Hong Kong grew into one of the great business centers of East Asia and world's major ports. Many of its people work in factories that make textiles and clothing.

The British lease on the mainland runs out in 1997. The British government and the Chinese Communist government agreed that Hong Kong would become part of China again in 1997. However, private businesses will be allowed to continue to operate there for 50 additional years.

Macao Near Hong Kong is the Portuguese colony of Macao (muh KOU), located on the mainland of China covering 6 square miles (16 sq km). The Portuguese have also reached an agreement with China about Macao's future. The territory will be given back to China in 1999, but, as in Hong Kong, private businesses can continue for another 50 years.

Tibet Tibet, which is located on a high plateau northeast of the South Asian subcontinent, has long been cut off from the outside world. The Chinese emperors claimed that Tibet was part of China, but Buddhist monks actually ruled the land. The leader of the Buddhists was known as the Dalai Lama (dahl EYE LAH muh).

Hong Kong is a center of international trade and finance.
▶ How can you tell that Hong Kong is a modern territory?

The Dalai Lama, spiritual leader of Tibet's Buddhists, accepted the 1989 Nobel Peace Prize for his nonviolent acts to free Tibet from China.
▶ How did the Dalai Lama escape the Communists?

After the Communists took over China, they occupied Tibet. The Communists attempted to destroy the Buddhist religion in Tibet. They wrecked monasteries and imprisoned monks and nuns. To escape the Communists, the Dalai Lama fled the country.

When the Communist leaders decided to reform their revolution, they realized that the old policy in Tibet had failed. The Chinese government still insisted that Tibet was part of China, but it released the monks and nuns. It also allowed some monasteries to be rebuilt.

LESSON *1* REVIEW

THINK AND WRITE

A. What changes took place in the government of China after 1912?

B. How did the Communists revolutionize China?

C. Summarize the kinds of reforms of the revolution that the Chinese did and did not allow.

D. How do businesses on Taiwan differ from most businesses on the Chinese mainland?

E. What is China's political position with regard to Tibet, to Hong Kong, and to Macao?

SKILLS CHECK

MAP SKILL

Look at the political map on page 545. Find the territories of Hong Kong, Tibet, and Macao on the map to answer the following questions. Which is landlocked? Which is under British rule? Which is at the mouth of the Xi Jiang?

YOU DECIDE: SHOULD PEOPLE HAVE THE RIGHT TO DEMONSTRATE AGAINST THEIR GOVERNMENT?

When Communist rule began in the People's Republic of China in 1949, the country was closed to the outside world. Things began to change in the 1970s. Foreigners were encouraged to visit China, and the Chinese people were allowed to travel to other countries. Many came to study in the United States.

As time went by, many people in China were inspired by the democratic ideas of other countries. These people felt they, too, should be able to participate in their own country's government and to express openly their desire for change.

Finally, in May 1989, thousands of students, workers, and other supporters of democracy gathered in Tiananmen Square, in Beijing, to show the government that the people of China wanted a change. As you read on page 544, the Chinese government eventually sent in the army to break up the demonstration. Why did the Chinese government react so strongly to a peaceful demonstration?

On the next page are two different points of view about the relationship between a nation's government and its citizens. Read both and decide for yourself whether people should have the right to demonstrate against their government.

The Government Must Be in Control

During the Renaissance, which you read about in Chapter 6, an important political thinker, Niccolò Machiavelli, wrote a book describing how leaders could build and maintain powerful nations. He said a healthy, powerful nation is one that is orderly and that is united under a strong government and ruler. Machiavelli went on to say that when the people of a nation are divided and order is disrupted, the government should use any means necessary—including force—to control the nation.

In the twentieth century, Niccolò Machiavelli's influence could still be seen in countries where success would be measured by the strength of the central government and its leaders. During the demonstration in Tiananmen Square in May 1989, China's premier, Li Peng, made the following statement to the demonstrators.

> *In the last few days, Beijing has fallen into a kind of anarchy [lack of government]. I hope you will think it over. What will result from the situation? China's government is responsible to the people. We will not sit idly by, doing nothing. We have to safeguard people's property and our students' lives. We have to safeguard our factories. We have to defend our socialist system. . . .*

The People Have a Right to Speak

During the seventeenth and eighteenth centuries, great thinkers such as John Locke, Thomas Jefferson, and Voltaire began to question old ideas about systems of government. The result was new ideas about "government by the people" and basic natural rights. Among these rights were those of freedom of thought and the expression of thought. These were revolutionary ideas that had significant effects on political revolutions and new governments.

The idea of a right to freedom made its way into the First Amendment of the United States Constitution.

> *Congress shall make no law . . . abridging the freedom of speech, or of the press; or the right of the people peaceably to assemble, and to petition the government for a redress of grievances.*

According to this amendment, the United States government cannot stop the American people from speaking or writing their thoughts. It also cannot stop people from demonstrating or sending petitions to let the government know what the people think.

Voltaire said, "Liberty of thought is the life of the soul." Today the right to free thought and expression is common to democratic societies and is a growing spirit in societies around the world.

Thinking for Yourself

1. Which is more important to the success of a nation—a strong government or personal freedom?
2. What examples of successful demonstrations against governments can you think of from history?

Japan and Korea

THINK ABOUT WHAT YOU KNOW

Name any products made in Japan or Korea that your family or friends use.

STUDY THE VOCABULARY

Diet	**finance**
gross national product	**literacy rate**

FOCUS YOUR READING

What changes took place in Japan and Korea after World War II?

A. Old and New in Government

Japan is by far the oldest monarchy in the world, with 125 emperors in the course of its long history. But the position of the emperor of Japan has changed greatly over the years. In the past it was said that the emperors were descendants of the Sun Goddess. In 1946, Emperor Hirohito informed his people that this was only a myth. "The emperor," he said, "is not a living god." Today the emperor of Japan is considered the symbol of the state. The emperor's position is similar to that of the British monarch.

After its defeat in World War II, Japan adopted a new constitution. The constitution was based on suggestions made by the Americans who occupied Japan for a time after the war. It provides for a prime minister as the head of the government. The prime minister is chosen by the **Diet**, a legislature made up of representatives elected by the people. The Diet is similar to Parliament in England.

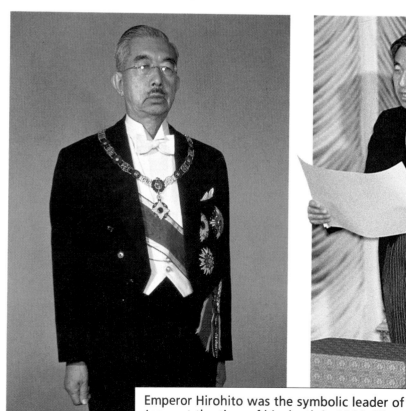

Emperor Hirohito was the symbolic leader of Japan at the time of his death in 1989. His son, Akihito, followed him to the throne.
► Who actually heads the Japanese government?

B. Japan's Economic Growth

Rebuilding Japan During World War II the Japanese suffered heavy losses. Firebombs destroyed almost half of the buildings in Tokyo and killed nearly 100,000 people. The atomic bombs dropped on the cities of Hiroshima and Nagasaki took even more lives.

With the help of the United States, the Japanese rebuilt the war-damaged cities and industries in a remarkably short time. Only eight years after the war ended, Japan was producing more goods than it had been producing when the war began.

Japanese Business Today, Japan is one of the world's richest countries. It produces and exports many different goods. Japanese automobiles, cameras, and television sets, for instance, are used in many parts of the world.

In fact, Japan has the second highest **gross national product** (GNP) in the world. A nation's gross national product is the total value of all the goods and services it produces in a year. We can use this figure to show economic growth from one year to the next. Only the United States has a larger GNP than does Japan.

Japan has also become a world leader in **finance**, or the management of money. Japanese banks lend money to foreign businesses. Japanese-owned companies have bought land and built industrial plants in a number of other countries, including the United States.

C. Literature and Sports

Poetry Although the Japanese have borrowed from others, they also cling to parts of their own culture. For example, the Japanese have long written and read *haiku* (HYE koo). A haiku is a three-lined poem

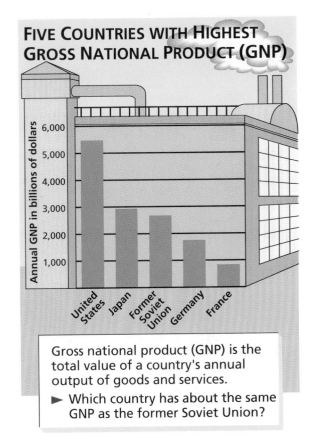

FIVE COUNTRIES WITH HIGHEST GROSS NATIONAL PRODUCT (GNP)

Annual GNP in billions of dollars: 6,000 / 5,000 / 4,000 / 3,000 / 2,000 / 1,000

United States, Japan, Former Soviet Union, Germany, France

Gross national product (GNP) is the total value of a country's annual output of goods and services.

▶ Which country has about the same GNP as the former Soviet Union?

that draws attention to something that has moved the poet. Here are some samples of translated Japanese haiku.

How the mulberry leaves
shine, as I trudge along the way
toward my parents' home!

Even the rabbit
droops one of her ears —
midsummer heat!

After killing
a spider how lonely I feel
in the cold of the night!

Baseball The Japanese have wisely followed Emperor Meiji's advice "to seek knowledge from the whole world." They have studied the sciences, business methods, and ways of other countries, and they have adopted what they like or find

Baseball is a favorite pastime in the United States and in Japan.
▶ How do Japanese fans differ from American fans?

D. How One Korea Became Two

Japan ruled Korea as a colony from 1910 until the end of World War II. When Japan surrendered, the United States occupied the southern part of the Korean peninsula, and the Soviet Union took over the north. The 38th parallel (38°N) served as a boundary between the occupation zones. No agreement was ever reached concerning the future of Korea, so two separate states were created in 1948. A Communist country was established in North Korea. South Korea became a republic.

North Korea invaded South Korea in 1950. The United Nations sent troops, most of them Americans, to help South Korea defend itself. Communist China sent troops to help North Korea, and the Soviet Union also gave support to North Korea. After more than three years, the fighting ended. Korea was still divided, and no permanent peace treaty was signed.

North Korea is called the Democratic People's Republic of Korea, but it is actually a Communist dictatorship. South Korea is a republic, but for years military leaders ran the government. In 1987 a free election was held. In 1991 the two Koreas signed agreements that may lead to a permanent peace treaty and eventual reunification.

E. Modernization in South Korea

Education South Korea has twice as many people as North Korea. South Korea's skilled and educated population is its main resource. Large numbers of South Koreans attend the country's modern schools and colleges. South Korea has a high **literacy rate**, or percent of the population able to read and write.

Industry When South Korea became independent, it was a land of peasant

useful. They have even made a foreign sport their own. That sport is baseball.

Japan now has both school and professional baseball teams. More than half of the Japanese are devoted baseball fans. Every year the winning teams in the two professional leagues play in the Japan Series. Some Japanese fans would like to see teams from around the world participate in the American World Series.

South Korea has one of the world's fastest-growing industrial economies. The United States is one of South Korea's main trading partners.
▶ In what type of industry are these South Korean people working?

farmers. Today it still grows much of its own food, but it also has modern industries that turn out automobiles, television sets, videocassette recorders, microwave ovens, and a host of other products.

South Korea's industrial success is due only in part to the education of its labor force. South Koreans also work longer hours than workers in most other industrial countries. For example, the average workweek in the United States is 40 hours, whereas, the average workweek in Korea is 54 hours. Yet, although incomes have risen rapidly in South Korea, wages are still lower than in Japan or the Western countries. By the late 1980s, Korean workers were demanding a larger share of the wealth they helped to create.

As a result of South Korea's shift from agriculture to industry, more Koreans live in cities today. Seoul, the capital, is one of the world's largest cities.

LESSON 2 REVIEW

THINK AND WRITE

A. How did the government of Japan change after World War II?

B. Summarize Japan's economic growth after World War II.

C. What does the popularity of baseball and haiku say about the Japanese?

D. Why is the Korean peninsula divided into two states?

E. Briefly explain the causes of South Korea's industrial success.

SKILLS CHECK

WRITING SKILL

Write a haiku that has three unrhymed lines. The first line should have five syllables, the second line seven syllables, and the third line five syllables.

The South Asian Subcontinent

A. The End of An Empire

Gandhi Before World War II the South Asian subcontinent was part of the British Empire. Britain also ruled the island of Ceylon, now called Sri Lanka, off the southern tip of the subcontinent. Within a few years after the war, all of these lands became independent nations.

Mohandas Gandhi (MOH hun dahs GAHN dee) was one of the leaders of the movement for India's independence. When Gandhi was a young man, he went to London to study law. He returned home after 3 years, and then he went to South Africa. Many other Indians had gone to live there. But they were treated unfairly by the white people who ruled that land.

Gandhi believed that British rule was unjust, but he did not call for an armed revolt. He strongly opposed the use of violence. Instead, Gandhi urged the use of **civil disobedience**. By this he meant that people should refuse to obey unjust laws, even if it meant going to prison. Gandhi set an example by cheerfully going to prison when he was convicted of refusing to obey laws he believed unjust.

Dividing the Subcontinent Most people on the subcontinent wanted an end to British rule, but they did not agree about what should take its place. The majority of people were Hindus, but there was a large Muslim minority. Some Muslim leaders feared that if the subcontinent became a single country, Hindus would have too much power. These leaders wanted to **partition**, or divide, the subcontinent into independent Muslim and Hindu countries. Hindu leaders did not want this but accepted it to secure independence.

Mohandas Gandhi led the movement for the independence of India.
▶ How are these people showing their respect for Gandhi?

This Hindu man is meditating, or reflecting, while sitting on a platform that overlooks the Ganges River.
▶ Why, do you think, did he choose this place to meditate?

The independent countries of Pakistan and India were created in 1947. Pakistan was made up of two regions. West Pakistan was on the Indus River plain; East Pakistan was located at the mouth of the Ganges and Brahmaputra rivers. A thousand miles (1,609 km) separated the two parts of Pakistan. The two regions were separated by more than distance, however. Although the majority of the people in the two regions were Muslims, they were of different ethnic groups and spoke different languages. These differences led to a civil war in 1971. East Pakistan won its independence and became the country of Bangladesh.

The island of Ceylon became independent in 1948. It later changed its name to Sri Lanka. The name *Sri Lanka* comes from a Hindu epic. India, Bangladesh, Sri Lanka, and Pakistan all chose to belong to the Commonwealth of Nations.

B. The People of the World's Largest Democracy

Religion and Language India is the largest country on the subcontinent. It is also the second most populous country on earth, with more people than any of the continents except Asia. Most people in India still work the land, but many live in the cities.

A variety of ethnic groups live in India, and the Indian people speak a number of languages. Both Hindi and English serve as official languages. There are also many different religions in India. The majority of people are Hindus, but Hinduism includes various beliefs and practices. Hindus are also divided into numerous castes. You learned earlier that a caste is a way of separating people into classes, or groups, based on birth. Castes have existed for centuries in India, but there are now many more than in ancient times.

One tenth of India's population is Muslim. There are also other religious groups, such as the Sikhs (seeks). The Sikh religion began as a movement to combine the Hindu and Muslim religions. Christians make up about 3 percent of the population of India.

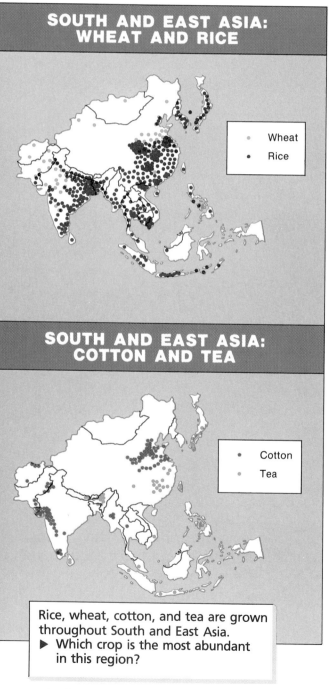

SOUTH AND EAST ASIA: WHEAT AND RICE

· Wheat
· Rice

SOUTH AND EAST ASIA: COTTON AND TEA

· Cotton
· Tea

Rice, wheat, cotton, and tea are grown throughout South and East Asia.
▶ Which crop is the most abundant in this region?

Government India is a republic made up of separate states. Voters elect the officials who govern. Indians enjoy freedom of religion, speech, and the press. They proudly point out that their country is the world's largest democracy. Yet, even though India is a democracy, one party has usually controlled the government.

Farming More than half of the Indian people still earn their living from agriculture. Rice is the most important crop. India is second only to China in rice production. Wheat and other grains are also major crops. India is a leading producer and exporter of spices, tea, and cashew nuts.

C. Pakistan and Bangladesh

Pakistan Pakistan is a poor country. Most people are farmers, although there is a limited amount of arable land. Many Pakistanis work in other countries and send part of their earnings home to their families. Pakistan is officially called an Islamic republic, and its laws are based on the Muslim religion. The name of the capital, *Islamabad,* means "city of Islam." Army leaders controlled the republic for years. In 1988, Benazir Bhutto (BOO toh), the daughter of a former prime minister, was elected prime minister. She was replaced by Nawaz Sharif in 1990.

Bangladesh Bangladesh is only about one-fifth the size of Pakistan, but it has a larger population. It is one of the most densely populated countries in the world, and one of the poorest.

Most of the land of Bangladesh is a delta, formed by the Ganges and Brahmaputra rivers. Farmers grow rice, vegetables, tea, and **jute** (joot) on this fertile land. The fibers of the jute plant are used for making rope, twine, and burlap fabric.

Tea is a major crop on the island country of Sri Lanka.
► How are these people carrying the tea that they picked?

D. Nepal, Bhutan, and Sri Lanka

Nepal and Bhutan are located in the Himalayas. Both are monarchies. Hinduism is Nepal's official religion, and Buddhism is the religion of Bhutan.

Few outsiders came to these lands before 1951 because they were so difficult to reach. Now roads and air flights connect both Nepal and Bhutan with India.

The island country of Sri Lanka has been influenced by the civilization of nearby India since ancient times. The ancestors of most Sri Lankans migrated from India. Sri Lanka's major languages are related to those of India. It is said that Buddhism, the religion of the largest part of the population, was brought to Sri Lanka by a son of Asoka, the ancient Indian emperor.

LESSON **3** *REVIEW*

THINK AND WRITE

A. Why was the subcontinent divided after British rule ended?
B. Describe the people and government of India.
C. How does Bangladesh differ from Pakistan?
D. What links do Nepal, Bhutan, and Sri Lanka have with India?

SKILLS CHECK

THINKING SKILL

After Gandhi was killed, the first prime minister of India told his people, "The light has gone out of our lives, and there is darkness everywhere." What do you think he meant by this?

Southeast Asia

THINK ABOUT WHAT YOU KNOW

Suppose you were going to take a trip to Southeast Asia. What kinds of clothing would you pack?

STUDY THE VOCABULARY

pagoda   **copra**

FOCUS YOUR READING

What changes has Southeast Asia undergone in the last half of this century?

A. Myanmar and Thailand

Changes on the Map Many changes have taken place in Southeast Asia. The country that was once called Burma is now called Myanmar. At one time it was part of British India. Today it is an independent state that does not even belong to the Commonwealth of Nations. Although it is called a republic, Myanmar has been controlled by army leaders.

Myanmar is a Buddhist country. Its most famous building is the gold-covered Shwe Dagon **pagoda** (puh GOH duh). A pagoda is a tower that serves as a religious building. The Shwe Dagon pagoda rises 326 feet (99 m) in the midst of Rangoon, Myanmar's capital city.

Except for the low-lying Irrawaddy River plain, most of Myanmar is mountainous. Rice is the main crop, and tropical forests provide valuable hardwoods, such as teak. The center of a teak log is so hard that even termites will not eat it. Teak beams in some Buddhist temples are more than 1,000 years old.

Thailand On old maps, Thailand appears as Siam. The name *Thailand* means "land of the free." The Thais are proud that their country was never a European colony, as were the other lands in Southeast Asia.

Thailand, like Myanmar, is a Buddhist country and has many famous shrines. The Thais have tried to preserve their ancient culture. Their alphabet was invented over 700 years ago by King Rama the Strong. Thailand still has a king, but the army has run the government in recent years.

Thailand has good farmland along its rivers and is a rice-exporting country. The Thais also export other resources such as hardwoods and tin. Thailand is the world's fifth leading producer of tin.

B. Malaysia and Singapore

Malaysia Malaysia appears as part of the British Empire on maps printed before 1963. It was in that year Malaysia became independent. The country includes the

The Shwe Dagon pagoda is the most famous Buddhist temple in Myanmar.
▶ With what material is the pagoda covered?

southern part of the Malay Peninsula and the northern coast of the island of Borneo. Nearly 400 miles (644 km) of ocean separate the two parts of Malaysia.

Malaysia's population is made up of several ethnic and religious groups. Over half of the people are Muslim Malays. A third of the population is of Chinese descent. There are also Hindus from India and Muslims from Pakistan. A variety of languages are spoken, but Malay is the official language.

Malaysia has valuable resources. More than half of its cultivated land is planted in rubber trees, making Malaysia the world's chief supplier of natural rubber. Malaysia produces more tin than any other country in the world. The country also exports considerable amounts of petroleum and palm oil, used as a preservative in many foods. Look at the distribution of tin, oil, and rubber in Malaysia on the map on this page.

Singapore Singapore was part of Malaysia before 1965. It is now an independent state, even though it is only a city built on islands off the tip of the Malay Peninsula. Singapore is the smallest independent country in Asia; it is also the most densely populated. Chinese make up the largest ethnic group in Singapore.

Singapore may be small, but it is not poor. It has one of the highest standards of living in Southeast Asia. Singapore makes good use of its two great resources: its location and its people. By taking advantage of its location on a major sea route, Singapore has become the largest port in Southeast Asia. It has also developed industries that make use of the skills of its people. Singapore manufactures goods that are exported to many parts of the world. It is a city that lives on trade.

SOUTH AND EAST ASIA: TIN AND OIL

- Tin
- Oil

SOUTH AND EAST ASIA: RUBBER

- Rubber

Tin, oil, and rubber can be found throughout South and East Asia.
▶ Which country produces the most tin?

C. Vietnam, Laos, and Cambodia

Vietnam After World War II, there was a long and costly struggle for control of Vietnam, Laos, and Cambodia. France withdrew from the area in 1954; however, a war continued between the Communist

559

Vietnamese government at the capital city of Hanoi in the north, and an anti-Communist government at the capital city of Saigon in the south. The Soviet Union and Communist China backed the north. The United States supported the south.

At first the United States sent only advisors and supplies, but then in 1965, American forces went to fight in Vietnam. At one time the United States had more than half a million troops in Vietnam. United States troops pulled out of Vietnam in 1973, but the war continued for another two years. North Vietnam finally conquered South Vietnam and brought the entire country under Communist rule.

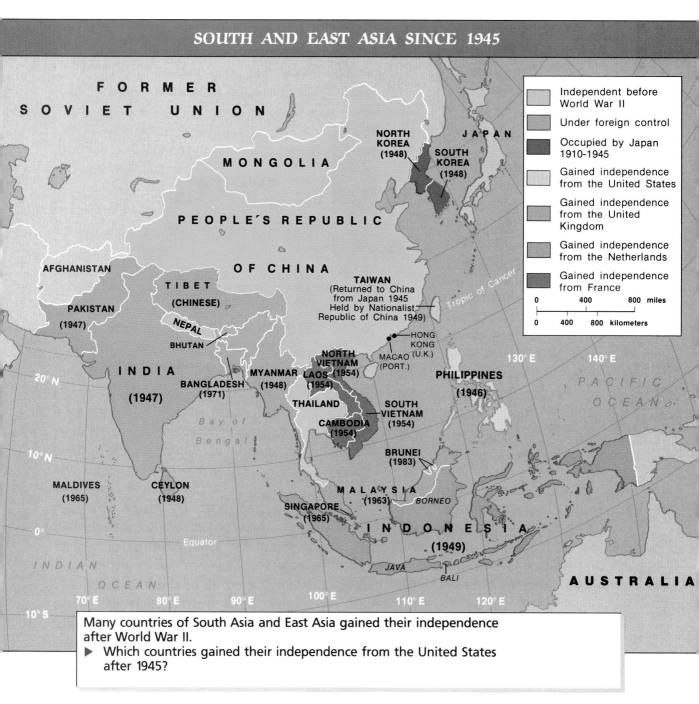

SOUTH AND EAST ASIA SINCE 1945

Legend:
- Independent before World War II
- Under foreign control
- Occupied by Japan 1910-1945
- Gained independence from the United States
- Gained independence from the United Kingdom
- Gained independence from the Netherlands
- Gained independence from France

0   400   800 miles
0   400   800 kilometers

FORMER SOVIET UNION

MONGOLIA

NORTH KOREA (1948)

JAPAN

SOUTH KOREA (1948)

PEOPLE'S REPUBLIC OF CHINA

AFGHANISTAN

TIBET (CHINESE)

TAIWAN (Returned to China from Japan 1945 Held by Nationalist Republic of China 1949)

PAKISTAN (1947)

NEPAL

BHUTAN

HONG KONG (U.K.)

MACAO (PORT.)

130° E   140° E

NORTH VIETNAM (1954)

PHILIPPINES (1946)

PACIFIC OCEAN

INDIA (1947)

MYANMAR (1948)

LAOS (1954)

BANGLADESH (1971)

THAILAND

SOUTH VIETNAM (1954)

Bay of Bengal

CAMBODIA (1954)

20° N

BRUNEI (1983)

10° N

MALDIVES (1965)

CEYLON (1948)

MALAYSIA (1963)

BORNEO

SINGAPORE (1965)

INDONESIA (1949)

0°

Equator

INDIAN OCEAN

JAVA

BALI

AUSTRALIA

70° E   80° E   90° E   100° E   110° E   120° E

10° S

Many countries of South Asia and East Asia gained their independence after World War II.
▶ Which countries gained their independence from the United States after 1945?

Laos and Cambodia Communists also took control of the countries of Laos and Cambodia. Thousands of people fled from the lands taken over by the Communists. Many came to the United States.

Even though Vietnam and Cambodia are both Communist-ruled lands, war broke out between them in 1978 when Vietnam invaded Cambodia. The world's two largest Communist states took different sides in this conflict. The Soviet Union supported Vietnam; Communist China helped Cambodia. The long years of war have left Vietnam, Laos, and Cambodia very poor.

D. Indonesia and the Philippines

Indonesia Indonesia and the Philippines are island countries. Indonesia consists of more than 13,000 islands, and there are more than 7,000 islands in the Philippines. Indonesia is about 50 times as large as the Netherlands. As you know, it was once part of the Dutch empire. Since becoming independent in 1949, Indonesia has been ruled by military leaders.

Among the countries of Asia, only China and India have more people than Indonesia. The island of Java is the most heavily populated Indonesian island. Jakarta, Indonesia's capital, is on Java.

Indonesia is the largest Muslim country in the world. It has more Muslims than Iran, Iraq, and Egypt combined. There were once important Buddhist kingdoms on the islands, and the remains of Buddhist temples may still be seen. Hinduism was also introduced into Indonesia in early times. It still survives on the island of Bali.

Indonesia is rich in resources. It has oil, natural gas, gold, tin, and tropical timber. Manufacturing has grown in importance, but most of the labor force is still employed in farming. Densely populated

This woman is planting rice seedlings in Java, Indonesia.
► What condition must the soil be in before planting?

Java is a very carefully cultivated food-producing island. Rice, coffee, and sugar are among the country's exports.

Philippines Spain established its rule in the Philippines 50 years after Ferdinand Magellan visited the islands in 1521. During the period of Spanish rule, Christianity spread. Today the Philippines is the only country of Southeast Asia in which Christianity is the main religion.

As you may recall, the United States acquired the Philippines as a result of a war with Spain in 1898. The United States controlled the Philippines for a much shorter time than Spain, but American influence has been important. English and Pilipino are both official languages. The

The Filipinos voted on a new constitution in 1987, which gave them more democracy and granted Corazon Aquino the presidency until 1992.
▶ In what year was Aquino elected?

Philippine government is similar to that of the United States. The president and the members of Congress are elected by the people. The Congress has a Senate and a House of Representatives. There is also a Supreme Court. In 1986, Filipinos elected their first woman president, Corazon Aquino (KOR uh zahn uk KEE noh). In 1992, Aquino was succeeded by Fidel V. Ramos.

The Philippine islands are mountainous, but about one third of the land is arable and produces sugar, rice, corn, and coconuts. Coconuts are exported largely in the form of vegetable oil or as **copra** (KAH-pruh), dried coconut. The country also manufactures products ranging from watches to clothing. The United States is its most important trading partner.

LESSON 4 REVIEW

THINK AND WRITE

A. Summarize the similarities and differences between Myanmar and Thailand.

B. How do the resources of Malaysia and Singapore differ?

C. What conflict developed in Vietnam after World War II?

D. Compare the religions and governments of Indonesia and the Philippines.

SKILLS CHECK

THINKING SKILL

Divide a sheet of paper into four vertical columns and five horizontal rows to make a chart. Assign each column one of the following religions: *Christianity, Buddhism, Hinduism, Muslim.* Assign each row one of the following Southeast Asian countries: *Myanmar, Thailand, Malaysia, Indonesia, Philippines.* Use a check (✔) in each row to show the main religion of each country.

USING THE VOCABULARY

warlord
civil disobedience
commune
partition
gross national
   product

jute
finance
pagoda
literacy rate
copra

From the list, choose a vocabulary term that could be used in place of the underlined word or words in each sentence. Rewrite the sentences on a separate sheet of paper.

1. Some Muslim leaders wanted to <u>divide</u> the subcontinent into independent Muslim and Hindu countries.
2. Farmers in Bangladesh grow <u>a plant that has fibers which are used for making rope, twine, and burlap fabric.</u>
3. <u>Refusing to obey unjust laws even if it means going to jail</u> is the opposite of violent opposition.
4. The <u>percent of the population able to read and write</u> is high in South Korea.
5. In China a <u>local ruler</u> had his own army.
6. The most famous building in Myanmar is the Shwe Dagon <u>tower</u>.
7. The Chinese Communists forced farmers to join a <u>farm on which people live and work together.</u>
8. The <u>total value of all the goods and services produced by a country in one year</u> is used to show the economic growth of a country from one year to the next.
9. Japan's banks and companies have helped Japan become a world leader in <u>the management of money</u>.
10. The Philippine Islands export coconuts in the form of <u>dried coconut</u>.

REMEMBERING WHAT YOU READ

On a separate sheet of paper, answer the following questions in complete sentences.

1. What weakened China and caused Japan to decide to invade China?
2. What did the Communists want to do in China?
3. What other kinds of reform do the people of China want in addition to reforms on the farms and in factories?
4. What is the agreement between Britain and the Communists about Hong Kong?
5. Explain how the government of Japan is organized.
6. What is South Korea's main resource?
7. How did Mohandas Gandhi encourage his followers to make changes in their government?
8. What religions exist in India?
9. What is the only country of Southeast Asia in which Christianity is the main religion?
10. How is the Philippine government similar to that of the United States?

TYING LANGUAGE ARTS TO SOCIAL STUDIES

Haiku is a lovely form of Japanese poetry that often deals with nature. Find a picture in a magazine that shows something from nature. Mount the picture on construction paper. Below the picture, write a haiku using these guidelines: The haiku has three lines. The first line has five syllables, the second line seven syllables, and the third line five syllables. Display your haiku in the classroom.

THINKING CRITICALLY

1. What do you think is the meaning of the term *Chinese mainland*.
2. What is your opinion of Emperor Meiji's advice to his country?
3. Why have many Pakistanis sought work in other countries?
4. What about Thailand's history makes it different from the other countries in Southeast Asia?
5. What has helped Singapore become the largest port in Southeast Asia?

SUMMARIZING THE CHAPTER

On a separate sheet of paper, draw a graphic organizer like the one shown here. Copy the information from this graphic organizer to the one you have drawn. Under the main idea for each lesson, write three statements that support the main idea.

CHAPTER THEME

The governments and economies of countries in South Asia and East Asia are varied.

LESSON 1

Revolutions and civil wars have affected China.

1. _____
2. _____
3. _____

LESSON 2

Many changes took place in Japan and Korea after World War II.

1. _____
2. _____
3. _____

LESSON 3

Independent countries were created on or near the South Asian subcontinent after World War II.

1. _____
2. _____
3. _____

LESSON 4

Southeast Asia has undergone changes in the last half of this century.

1. _____
2. _____
3. _____

COOPERATIVE LEARNING

In this unit you learned about important people, places, and events in South and East Asia. Sometimes, people, places, and events from history are the bases for works of literature, such as plays. Do you think you and your classmates could write a historical play?

PROJECT

Work with a group of classmates to plan, write, and perform a play about some real person, place, or event from South or East Asia. For example, a play could be written about Marco Polo's return to Venice. The characters in this play could be Marco, his father, and several Venetian nobles. The setting for your play could be a banquet hall in Venice, and the plot could tell how Marco and his father convinced the Venetians that their stories about China were true.

There are many other stories in Unit 6 that could be subjects of plays. Meet as a group and look through the chapters to select a subject for your play. Be sure to discuss each other's ideas politely and try to stay on the job.

Once you have chosen the subject for your play, discuss specific ideas for the characters, setting, and plot. Take notes to record each group member's ideas.

Once you have planned your play, the group is ready to begin writing. Divide the play's characters among the group members. Then as you write, each group member should suggest what lines his or her assigned character or characters might say. You may also want to write lines for a narrator to introduce and explain the action of your play. Give your play a title.

PRESENTATION AND REVIEW

When your play is written, decide together which group member will play each role. Rehearse your play. When you are ready, present your play in front of your classmates. Watch other groups' plays. Think about how plays can make history come to life.

Meet again with your group to evaluate your project. How well did your group members work together? How could your play have been improved?

REMEMBER TO:
- Give your ideas.
- Listen to others' ideas.
- Plan your work with the group.
- Present your project.
- Discuss how your group worked.

A. WHY DO I NEED THIS SKILL?

Each country has its own currency, or system of money. It is important when traveling and doing business with other countries of the world to know what the currencies are and how to exchange them with ours.

B. LEARNING THE SKILL

Each currency has its own monetary unit. For example, the dollar is the monetary unit for the United States. In this unit you have learned about South and East Asia. The chart below shows the monetary units for most of the countries in that region.

Country	Monetary Unit
India	Rupee
Pakistan	Rupee
Bangladesh	Taka
Sri Lanka	Rupee
China	Yuan
Taiwan	Dollar
Japan	Yen
South Korea	Won
Myanmar	Kyat
Thailand	Baht
Malaysia	Ringgit
Singapore	Dollar
Vietnam	Dong
Laos	Kip
Indonesia	Ruphiah
Philippines	Peso

The currency of each country has its own exchange rate. The exchange rate is the amount that the currency can be exchanged for in other currencies. Since exchange rates vary from day to day, it is important to check a newspaper for the exchange rate for a particular day. Banks and major hotels also have this information.

The following chart shows exchange rates for some of the currencies in South and East Asia on a particular day. For example, the chart shows that one United States dollar was worth 150 yen.

Monetary Unit	Monetary Unit per U.S. Dollar
Yen	150.00
Rupee	11.50
Won	668.00
Peso	21.60

C. PRACTICING THE SKILL

Use the tables on this page to answer the following questions on a separate sheet of paper.

1. If you exchanged 5 dollars for each of the currencies listed on the table above, how much would you receive? For example, multiply the exchange rate for 1 yen by 5: $150 \times 5 = 750$ yen.
2. What is the monetary unit for India?
3. What other countries use the same monetary unit that India uses?

4. What countries in Southeast Asia use the dollar as their monetary unit?
5. How many Indian rupees would you get by exchanging 100 United States dollars?
6. If you were in Japan and wanted to buy a product that cost 7,500 yen, how much would that be in United States money?
7. If wheat sold at 2.60 dollars a bushel and could be bought at the same price in South Korea, what would it cost?
8. What country uses the peso as its monetary unit?

9. According to the table, how many pesos would be exchanged for 2 United States dollars?
10. How many different monetary units are used in the South and East Asia region?

D. APPLYING THE SKILL

As you read a newspaper, check to see what the exchange rates are on a particular day. Check again a week later to see if there were any changes in those rates.

Making SKILLBUILDER Predictions

A. WHY DO I NEED THIS SKILL?

While you are reading a story, do you ever try to guess what will happen next in the story? If so, you are making a **prediction**. Trying to make predictions makes reading more interesting and enjoyable. Knowing how to make predictions will also help you understand the information you read in your social studies textbook.

B. LEARNING THE SKILL

You can use these four steps to make predictions when you read.

1. **Read** the first paragraph. As you read, think about what is happening and what might happen next.

2. **Predict** what will happen next or what additional information you might be presented with. You can try the following strategies to make predictions.

   - Think about what you already know about the subject of your reading.

   - Think about how events you have read about might cause something else to happen.

   - Think about people you have read about and how they might behave or what they might do next.

3. **Verify** your predictions. Continue reading to see if your guesses were correct.

4. **Change** your predictions or make new predictions if necessary. Then read on to verify them.

C. PRACTICING THE SKILL

Use the four steps for making predictions as you read the following selection from Chapter 22.

1. **Read** the beginning of the selection.

   When Elsie was eight years old, she went to a school run by Christian missionaries. She lived with other students in a building called a dormitory. She learned English and worked in the school garden. At first, Elsie hated school and living in a dormitory. She particularly disliked working in the garden. She thought it was far better to gather food in the bush [sparsely settled land], as her people had always done.

2. **Predict** what will happen next. Can you guess what might happen to Elsie? Are there any clues that her life might change? Write one or two predictions on a separate sheet of paper. Then read the next section.

   Later, Elsie changed her mind about school, at least partly. She grew to like life in the dormitory. She became a good runner and won prizes on school sport days. She never, however, learned to like working in the garden.
   The mission school closed during World War II, and Elsie, who was then 18, returned to her family. She now found life in the bush hard. When the school reopened after the war, Elsie went back to work there as a teacher's aide.

3. **Verify** your predictions. Were your guesses correct? Did you guess correctly about what life was like for Elsie? Were there any clues that helped you?

4. **Change** your predictions or make new ones. Can you predict what Elsie did after returning to the missionary school? Write down your new predictions. Now turn to pages 573–574 and read all of Elsie's story to again verify your predictions.

D. APPLYING THE SKILL

Use the four-step predicting strategy as you read all of Chapter 22. See if making predictions helps you to better understand what you read.

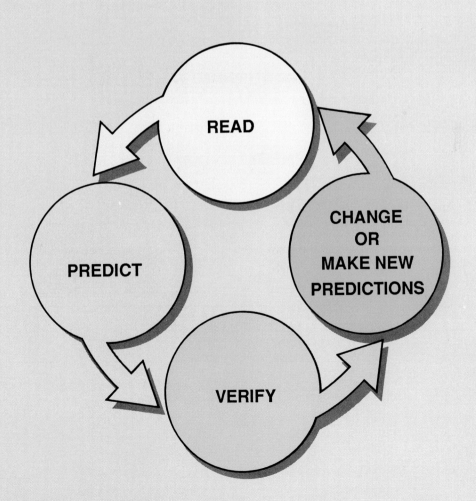

Unit 7
AUSTRALIA, NEW ZEALAND, AND THE PACIFIC ISLANDS

Australia, New Zealand, and the Pacific Islands make up a unique region, with a wealth of interesting peoples, animals, plants, and landforms.

▶ *Akaroa Harbor, which can be seen in the background, lies at the base of the lush hillsides of Banks Peninsula on New Zealand's South Island.*

CHAPTER

22

GEOGRAPHY OF AUSTRALIA, NEW ZEALAND, AND PACIFIC ISLANDS

*S*cattered across the Pacific Ocean are thousands of islands. They range in size from the continent of Australia to tiny islands so small that no one has ever lived on them. Mount Kosciusko is the tallest peak in the Australian Alps.

Australia

THINK ABOUT WHAT YOU KNOW
Suppose that you are going to take a vacation in Australia. What do you know about Australia that will make your visit there particularly interesting?

STUDY THE VOCABULARY
Aborigine   monolith
bush   coral reef

FOCUS YOUR READING
What are the characteristics of the Australian continent?

A. Australia's First Inhabitants

Bush Life The **Aborigines** (ab uh RIHJ uh-neez) are the earliest known inhabitants of Australia. They have lived on the continent for thousands of years. Today, however, Aborigines make up only a small part of Australia's population. White Australians form the large majority. Their ancestors started arriving in Australia from Europe 200 years ago.

Elsie Roughsey is an Aborigine. She was born in 1923 on Mornington Island, off the northern coast of Australia. As a child, Elsie lived with her family in the **bush**, which is what Australians call sparsely settled land far from any settlement. Elsie remembers these early years as a happy period, when her people spent their time "hunting, dancing, gathering for tribal meetings, [and] gathering together for great feasts."

New Ways When Elsie was eight years old, she went to a school run by Christian missionaries. She lived with other students in a building called a dormitory. She learned English and worked in the school garden. At first, Elsie hated school and living in a dormitory. She particularly disliked working in the garden. She thought it was far better to gather food in the bush, as her people had always done.

Later, Elsie changed her mind about school, at least partly. She grew to like life in the dormitory. She became a good runner and won prizes on school sport days. She never, however, learned to like working in the garden.

The mission school closed during World War II, and Elsie, who was then 18, returned to her family. She now found life in the bush hard. When the school reopened after the war, Elsie went back to work there as a teacher's aide. Elsie married a carpenter at the mission named Dick Roughsey. Dick was a skilled craftsperson who carved wood and painted pictures on bark in the Aboriginal fashion.

Although most Aborigines have adopted modern ways, some groups have kept their traditional culture.
▶ Why, do you think, is this Aborigine wearing paint?

Valuable Knowledge At the mission and in the cities that she and Dick visited, Elsie learned much about the ways of the white Australians. But she continued to respect the ways of her own people. She worried because the young Aborigines knew so little about their ancestors.

White Australians, Elsie knew, learned of their European ancestors through books that made "a history of the adventures of great men of the past [and] scenes of the past." Elsie's own people, however, did not pass on their knowledge in that way. Instead, she observed, they "sit in circles around the bush or camps and yarn about which is the right way to keep all their laws, customs, and legends and cultures." Since children rarely lived in the bush as she had done, they had little chance to learn about the "men and women of rich wisdom" among the Aborigines. To prevent all knowledge of her people from being lost, Elsie wrote a book about "some of the customs [that] were finally ruined and forgotten by [the Aborigines] when the white men came."

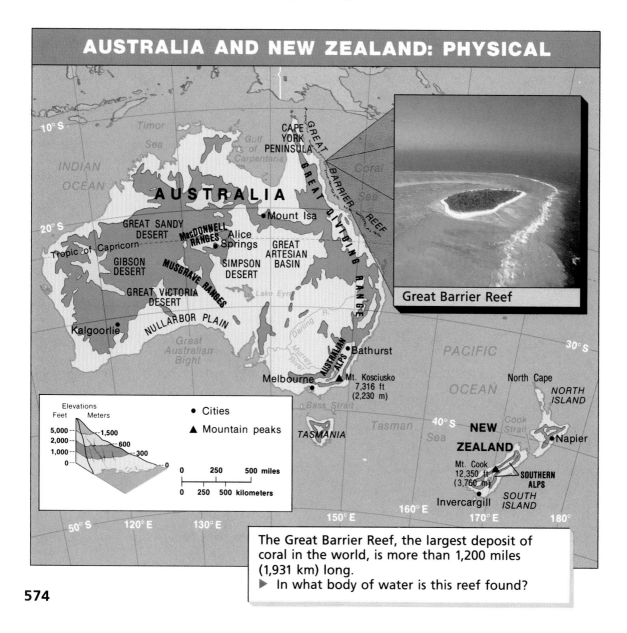

AUSTRALIA AND NEW ZEALAND: PHYSICAL

Great Barrier Reef

The Great Barrier Reef, the largest deposit of coral in the world, is more than 1,200 miles (1,931 km) long.
▶ In what body of water is this reef found?

Ayers Rock runs about 1 1/2 miles (2 km) long and rises to a height of 1,143 feet (348 m). It also has numerous small caves, many of which Aborigines covered with rock paintings long ago.

▶ Why, do you think, is Ayers Rock such a popular tourist attraction?

B. The World's Smallest Continent

Flat Land Australia, the land where Elsie Roughsey lives, is located south of the Equator, in the Southern Hemisphere. It is the smallest of the seven continents. It is about the size of the United States without Alaska and Hawaii. The distance from east to west across Australia is almost the same as the distance between the Atlantic and Pacific coasts of the United States. Australia has coasts on the Indian and the Pacific oceans.

Australia is also the flattest of the continents, although there are some mountains. The Great Dividing Range runs along the eastern and southeastern edges of the continent. Since this range rises from a coastal plain, it appears high and rugged. Part of the Great Dividing Range is even called the Australian Alps. But Mount Kosciusko (kahs ee US koh), the tallest peak, is less than half as high as the Alpine peaks in Europe.

Unusual Features Perhaps the most famous feature of Australia's landscape is Ayers Rock. Ayers Rock is a large mass of stone that rises 1,143 feet (348 m) above the desert in the center of the continent. It is said to be the world's largest **monolith**, or single stone. Ayers Rock is a sacred place for the Aborigines.

The Great Barrier Reef, the largest **coral reef** in the world, stretches more than 1,250 miles (2,011 km) along Australia's eastern coast. A coral reef is a ridge built up in shallow ocean water by the skeletons of countless tiny sea creatures.

575

C. A Mostly Dry Continent

Precipitation Australia is the second driest continent. Only Antarctica receives less precipitation. Two thirds of Australia is either desert or too dry to support any vegetation but scattered plants and dryland grass.

The eastern and southeastern parts of the continent receive the most moisture, and it is there that most people live. The center of the continent is very dry and thinly populated. The northern coast has a tropical climate; the southwestern coast has a Mediterranean climate.

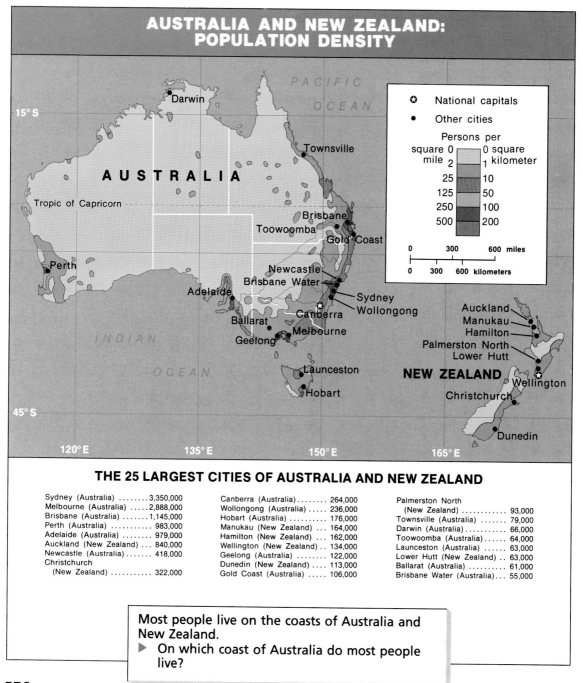

AUSTRALIA AND NEW ZEALAND: POPULATION DENSITY

Persons per	
square mile	square kilometer
0	0
2	1
25	10
125	50
250	100
500	200

✪ National capitals
● Other cities

THE 25 LARGEST CITIES OF AUSTRALIA AND NEW ZEALAND

Sydney (Australia) 3,350,000
Melbourne (Australia) 2,888,000
Brisbane (Australia) 1,145,000
Perth (Australia) 983,000
Adelaide (Australia) 979,000
Auckland (New Zealand) ... 840,000
Newcastle (Australia) 418,000
Christchurch
   (New Zealand) 322,000

Canberra (Australia) 264,000
Wollongong (Australia) 236,000
Hobart (Australia) 176,000
Manukau (New Zealand) ... 164,000
Hamilton (New Zealand) ... 162,000
Wellington (New Zealand) .. 134,000
Geelong (Australia) 122,000
Dunedin (New Zealand) 113,000
Gold Coast (Australia) 106,000

Palmerston North
   (New Zealand) 93,000
Townsville (Australia) 79,000
Darwin (Australia) 66,000
Toowoomba (Australia)...... 64,000
Launceston (Australia) 63,000
Lower Hutt (New Zealand) .. 63,000
Ballarat (Australia) 61,000
Brisbane Water (Australia)... 55,000

Most people live on the coasts of Australia and New Zealand.
► On which coast of Australia do most people live?

576

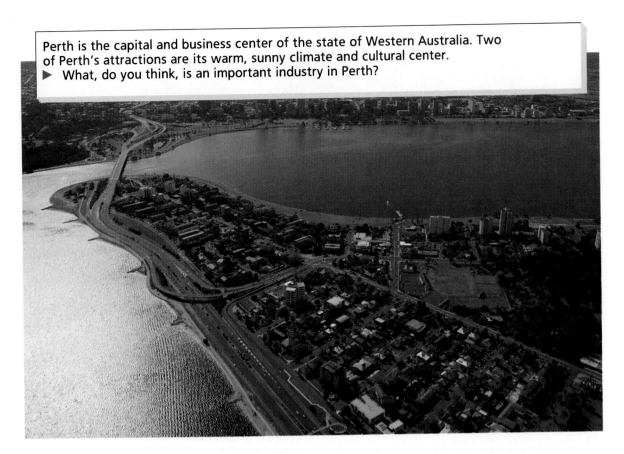

Temperature Southern Australia has a cooler climate than northern Australia because it is farther from the Equator. But no part of the continent has a truly cold climate. The coldest areas are in the high elevations of the Australian Alps. One range within the Alps receives enough snow to be called the Snowy Mountains.

Climate has greatly affected the locations of Australia's cities. As you can see on the map on page 576, there are no large cities in the dry interior. The five largest cities are on the coastal rim. Four of the five are on the eastern and southeastern coasts. Perth, the fifth, is in the southwest.

D. Australia's Animals and Birds

Unique Creatures The animals and birds of Australia differ from those found elsewhere because Australia is an island and was cut off from the other six continents. One European explorer noted that the kangaroo "bears no sort of resemblance to any European animal I ever saw." Another European said of a large kangaroo, "It is as tall as a man with a head of a rabbit [and] a tail as big as a bed-post." Actually, not all kangaroos are nearly so large. There are more than 47 different kinds of kangaroos, some smaller than a rabbit.

A number of other Australian animals appeared strange to European eyes. There are gliders, sometimes called "flying possums," which have flaps of skin between their front and hind legs. When they spread their legs, they can glide for long distances between the tops of trees. The small, furry koalas (koh AH luhz) look like tiny bears, although they are not related to bears at all.

Egglayers The so-called duckbill platypus (PLAT ih pus) is one of Australia's most unusual animals. The nickname duckbill is given to the platypus because it

Australia has some unique birds and animals, including the kookaburra (top left), the emu (bottom left), and the koala bear (right).
► Which of these creatures resembles an ostrich?

has webbed feet and a bill like that of a duck. Its tail is similar to a beaver's, and it has poison spurs on its hind feet. The platypus is a mammal, but it lays eggs. The echidna, also called the spiny anteater, is another Australian animal that lays eggs.

Europeans discovered that some of Australia's birds were unusual. The emu is a large flightless bird that looks similar to an ostrich. European settlers called the kookaburra, another Australian bird, "the laughing jackass" because of its hoarse cry.

LESSON *1* REVIEW

THINK AND WRITE

A. Briefly describe how life among Aborigines in the bush in Australia differs from life in the cities and other settled areas.
B. How does Australia compare in size and surface with other continents?
C. What kinds of climates does Australia have?
D. What unusual animals and birds are found in Australia?

SKILLS CHECK

THINKING SKILL

Find Australia and New Zealand on the charts on pages 32–43. Notice the land area and population of these two countries. Considering that Australia has almost 30 times the amount of land that New Zealand has, how can you explain why Australia only has about five times the number of people that New Zealand has?

New Zealand

THINK ABOUT WHAT YOU KNOW

Like Australia, New Zealand is separated from other lands. What does this suggest to you about the kinds of animals that are found in New Zealand?

STUDY THE VOCABULARY

geothermal energy   **temperate climate**

FOCUS YOUR READING

What are the main geographical features of New Zealand?

A. The Islands of New Zealand

High Land Abel Tasman, a Dutch explorer, discovered New Zealand in 1642. Tasman named New Zealand after a province in the Netherlands. The two Zealands are different from each other. The province in the Netherlands is low and flat; New Zealand is hilly and mountainous.

New Zealand appears small when compared with Australia, but it is actually larger than the United Kingdom. Like the United Kingdom, New Zealand is an island country. No part of it is more than 70 miles (113 km) from the sea. Its two main islands are North Island and South Island. South Island is larger in area, but North Island has a larger population. Both Auckland, the largest city, and Wellington, New Zealand's capital, are on North Island.

Both North Island and South Island are mountainous, but the highest and most jagged peaks are on South Island. Some are snow-covered all year. At 12,349 feet (3,764 m), Mount Cook is the highest peak and can be seen from the sea. There are also large glaciers on South Island.

Natural Resources The Hot-Water Belt, an area where heat from within the earth is close to the surface, is located on North Island. Water seeping into the hot earth there boils and turns to steam. The steam escapes through cracks in the earth's surface. Hot springs flow from other openings, and geysers shoot steam into the air. People in this region are able to heat their homes with the steam by driving pipes deep into the earth. The underground steam is also piped to a powerhouse and used to generate electricity. Heat from within the earth is called **geothermal energy**. It is one of New Zealand's natural resources.

Forests once covered the greater part of New Zealand. There are still forests, but much of the land has been cleared and turned into pastures for sheep and cattle to graze. New Zealand has far more sheep than people.

Hot springs create geysers that shoot steam into the air.
► How are geysers useful natural resources in New Zealand?

B. A Land Set Apart

People New Zealand and Australia are neighbors, but they are not close to each other. About 1,200 miles (1,931 km) of ocean lies between them. Today that distance can be flown in a short time, but for centuries, New Zealand was isolated from other lands. Few plants or living creatures from other places reached the islands.

When Europeans arrived in New Zealand, the Maoris (MAH oh reez) inhabited the land. The Maoris were the first inhabitants of New Zealand. They had been living in New Zealand long before any Europeans had reached the island. Europeans knew almost nothing about the Maoris. Today, historians believe that the Maoris originally came to New Zealand by way of sea from other Pacific Islands. You will read and learn more about the Maoris in Chapter 23.

Wildlife The first Europeans in New Zealand found few living creatures they recognized except the small dogs of the Maoris. Later the Europeans discovered that there were some bats and one kind of rat inhabiting the islands. But they found no other animals like those on other continents.

There were, however, large numbers of birds, including some that lived on the ground and could not fly. The largest of these birds, the moa, had already been killed off by the Maori people, but there were still kiwis. A kiwi is about the size of a chicken. Some kiwis still survive, but they are not often seen, because they feed at night and spend the day in their burrows, or underground homes.

Seagulls (top left), wallabies (bottom left), possums (top right), and kiwis (bottom right) live in New Zealand.
► Which belongs to the kangaroo family?

South Island has a mostly mild climate as well as sufficient precipitation throughout the year.
► Why, do you think, are there snowcapped mountains in South Island if the climate there is generally mild?

C. New Zealand's Climate

Mostly Mild The country of New Zealand has a **temperate climate**, one that is neither very hot nor very cold. North Island is generally warmer than South Island. Look at the map on page 574. Can you explain why this is so?

No part of New Zealand is within the tropics. New Zealanders call the peninsula north of Auckland, on North Island, "the winterless north." It is warm enough there to grow oranges and other citrus fruits.

Winters are also mild elsewhere on the islands except in the mountains.

Enough Rain New Zealand has no deserts. The whole country generally receives adequate rainfall, which is distributed throughout the year. Snow is not common except on South Island's high peaks.

The plain on the eastern side of South Island, around the city of Christchurch, is one of the drier parts of the country. Most of New Zealand's wheat is grown here.

LESSON **2** *REVIEW*

THINK AND WRITE

A. Describe the two main islands of New Zealand.
B. How did New Zealand's location affect plant life and wildlife there?
C. What sort of climate does New Zealand have?

SKILLS CHECK

MAP SKILL

Find the latitude of Wellington in the Gazetteer. Turn to the map on page 620 in the Atlas and find a city in North America that is located at about the same latitude north of the Equator.

LESSON 3

The Pacific Islands

THINK ABOUT WHAT YOU KNOW

On the basis of what you have already learned about volcanoes, describe how you think a volcanic eruption might result in the formation of an island.

STUDY THE VOCABULARY

atoll

FOCUS YOUR READING

What are the land and the climate of the Pacific Islands like?

A. Stories About the Pacific Islands

Many stories have been told about the Pacific Islands. One story was written by Herman Melville about 150 years ago. As a young man, Melville lived for a time on a Pacific island. Afterwards he painted a very favorable picture of island life in a book called *Typee* (tye PEE). Melville wrote that the island was a place of delightful beauty. He describes one scene here.

> *As the ship approached the beach, the crew saw a stirring of the water. At first I imagined it to be a shoal [large group] of fish sporting on the surface, but our friends assured us that it was a shoal of young girls, who in this manner were coming off from the shore to welcome us. As they drew nearer, and I watched the rising and sinking of their forms . . . I almost fancied they could be nothing else than so many mermaids.*

The Pacific Islands were enchanting to Melville. It should be noted that writers sometimes exaggerate when telling of faraway places. They often draw more from their imagination than from memory.

B. How the Islands Were Formed

Island Groups The Pacific Ocean is the world's largest body of water. It contains thousands of islands, many uninhabited. Geographers divide the islands located within the tropics into three large groups: Polynesia, Micronesia, and Melanesia.

Polynesia, which means "many islands," extends from New Zealand to the Hawaiian Islands, in the central Pacific. Read the literature selection on the next page to learn about Tahiti, a Polynesian island. Micronesia, meaning "small islands," is an area in the western Pacific, north of the Equator. Melanesia, or "black islands," is south of the Equator and west of Polynesia. Europeans gave Melanesia its name because of the dark skin of most islanders in that region. Melanesia includes New Guinea, the largest of the Pacific Islands and the second largest island in the world.

Tahiti is one of the scenic islands of French Polynesia.
▶ What makes this island so picturesque?

FROM: # Kon-Tiki
Across the Pacific By Raft

By: Thor Heyerdahl
Setting: Tahiti

In 1947, Thor Heyerdahl and five companions sailed on a balsa-wood raft named *Kon-Tiki* from Peru, South America, to the Tuamotu Archipelago, in eastern Polynesia. They made the voyage to test Heyerdahl's theory that the islands of Polynesia could have been settled centuries ago by Indians from South America. Heyerdahl tells of the voyage in his book *Kon-Tiki.* In this literature selection, Heyerdahl describes the island of Tahiti.

*F*our days later Tahiti rose out of the sea. Not like a string of pearls with palm tufts. As wild jagged blue mountains flung skyward, with wisps of cloud like wreaths round the peaks.

As we gradually approached, the blue mountains showed green slopes. Green upon green, the lush vegetation of the south rolled down over rust-red hills and cliffs, till it plunged down into deep ravines and valleys running out toward the sea. When the coast came near, we saw slender palms standing close packed up all the valleys and all along the coast behind a golden beach. Tahiti was built by old volcanoes. They were dead now and the coral polyps had slung their protecting reef about the island so that the sea could not erode it away.

Early one morning we headed through an opening in the reef into the harbor of Papeete. When we came into the harbor, the population of Tahiti stood waiting. . . . The pae-pae [raft]

which had come from America was something everyone wanted to see. The Kon-Tiki *was given the place of honor alongside the shore promenade, the mayor of Papeete welcomed us, and a little Polynesian girl presented us with an enormous wheel of Tahitian wild flowers. . . . Then young girls came forward and hung sweet-smelling white wreaths of flowers round our necks as a welcome to Tahiti, the pearl of the South Seas.*

Some coral reefs (inset) form ringlike islands, called atolls. The French Polynesian island of Motu, shown, is an atoll.
▶ How did the coral reef form the atoll?

Island Types Most Pacific islands were formed by volcanoes. Eruptions on the floor of the ocean threw up lava, which rose above the surface. In time, seeds brought by birds or washed up by the sea took root and grew in the volcanic soil. The Hawaiian Islands and Tahiti are volcanic. Some of the island volcanoes are still active and erupt from time to time.

Some islands were formed partly by coral reefs. The reefs were built up slowly in the shallow water along the edges of volcanic islands. Later, pressures under the ocean's floor caused shifts on the surface. The centers of some islands sank, and the surrounding reefs were thrust up. These coral rims formed ringlike islands, called **atolls** (A tawlz). A number of islands in Micronesia are coral islands.

C. The Climate of the Islands

There is no winter season in the tropical islands of the Pacific. High and low temperatures are about the same throughout the year. For example, the daily high in the Gilbert Islands usually reaches 88° or 90°F (31° or 32°C). The low is about 75° or 74°F (24° or 23°C). Freezing weather is unknown in the Pacific.

Rain falls throughout the year, but all the islands have much sunshine. Rains usually come in short, heavy showers, even during the rainy seasons.

Although the islands are very warm and humid, daytime ocean breezes make the air comfortable. Sometimes the islands are hit by very strong winds. Typhoons, as hurricanes are called in the Pacific, sometimes sweep over the islands.

west set their watches back an hour when they enter another time zone, because they gain an hour. People traveling east do the opposite. They set their watches ahead one hour when they enter another time zone, because they lose an hour. If one circles the entire earth from east to west, one will cross all 24 zones and gain 24 hours — a whole day.

Date Change So that everyone gains or loses a day at the same place, it has been agreed that the 180th meridian serves as the International Date Line. This imaginary line runs from the North Pole to the South Pole, through the Pacific Ocean. As you can see on the map on page 350, in some places the date line runs east or west of the 180th meridian so that neighboring regions will have the same date. Note that the date line is halfway around the world from the Prime Meridian.

People going west across the International Date Line gain a day. For example, if it is Sunday east of the line, it is Monday west of the line. Those going east across the line lose a day. If it is Sunday west of the date line, they go back to Saturday when they cross.

D. The International Date Line

Time Zones You have already learned that the earth is divided into 24 time zones. The time changes when one travels from one time zone to another. People traveling

---

LESSON **3** *REVIEW*

THINK AND WRITE

A. What led Melville and others to write stories about the Pacific Islands?
B. What are two ways that some of the Pacific islands were formed?
C. What kind of climate do the Pacific Islands have?
D. What is the International Date Line, and what happens there?

SKILLS CHECK

WRITING SKILL

Use your imagination to write a two-paragraph story about an experience in the Pacific Islands. You may also draw on the photographs and text of the lesson for material for your story.

USING THE VOCABULARY

bush
monolith
geothermal energy
temperate climate
atoll

On a separate sheet of paper, write the word or words from the above list that best complete the sentences.

1. Ayers Rock, the world's largest _____, is a sacred place for Aborigines.
2. _____, or heat from within the earth, is one of New Zealand's natural resources.
3. A country that has weather that is neither very hot nor very cold has a _____.
4. The Australian word for "sparsely settled land far from any settlement" is _____.
5. An _____ is a ringlike island that has formed from coral reefs.

REMEMBERING WHAT YOU READ

On a separate sheet of paper, answer the following questions in complete sentences.

1. Who are the earliest known inhabitants of Australia?
2. Where is Australia located?
3. How does the size of Australia compare with that of the United States?
4. What is the most famous feature of Australia's landscape?
5. What is the name of the largest coral reef in the world?
6. Where are the five largest cities in Australia located?
7. Why are the animals and birds of Australia different from the animals and birds found in other parts of the world?
8. What are the two main islands that make up the country of New Zealand?
9. How do the people in the Hot-Water Belt region of North Island heat their homes?
10. How were most of the Pacific Islands formed?
11. Which season of the year does not exist in the tropical islands of the Pacific?
12. What makes the air comfortable in the tropical islands of the Pacific, even though the climate is warm and humid?
13. How does the time change when a person travels from one time zone to another time zone?
14. Why has everyone agreed on the location of the International Date Line?
15. From what two points does the International Date Line run?

TYING ART TO SOCIAL STUDIES

The Great Barrier Reef is known around the world for the beauty of its animal life. Billions of coral animals live on top of the skeletons of the coral animals that have died there. Corals grow in many brilliant colors. Giant clams, sea turtles, and exotic fish and birds also inhabit the Great Barrier Reef. Find a science book or another reference book that has photographs of the Great Barrier Reef. Then, paint a picture that shows the beautiful underwater sea life of the Great Barrier Reef.

THINKING CRITICALLY

On a separate sheet of paper, answer the following questions in complete sentences.

1. What did Elsie Roughsey think that the Aboriginal children were in danger of losing?
2. What, do you think, is most unusual about the duckbill platypus?
3. If you lived on a Pacific island, would the climate there affect any of your favorite activities?
4. Coconut palm trees grow on tropical islands. These trees often lean out over the water's edge. Why, do you think, do the trees grow this way?
5. Where do the International Date Line and the Prime Meridian meet?

SUMMARIZING THE CHAPTER

On a separate sheet of paper, draw a graphic organizer like the one shown here. Copy the information from this graphic organizer onto the one you have drawn. Under the main idea for each lesson, write four statements that support the main idea.

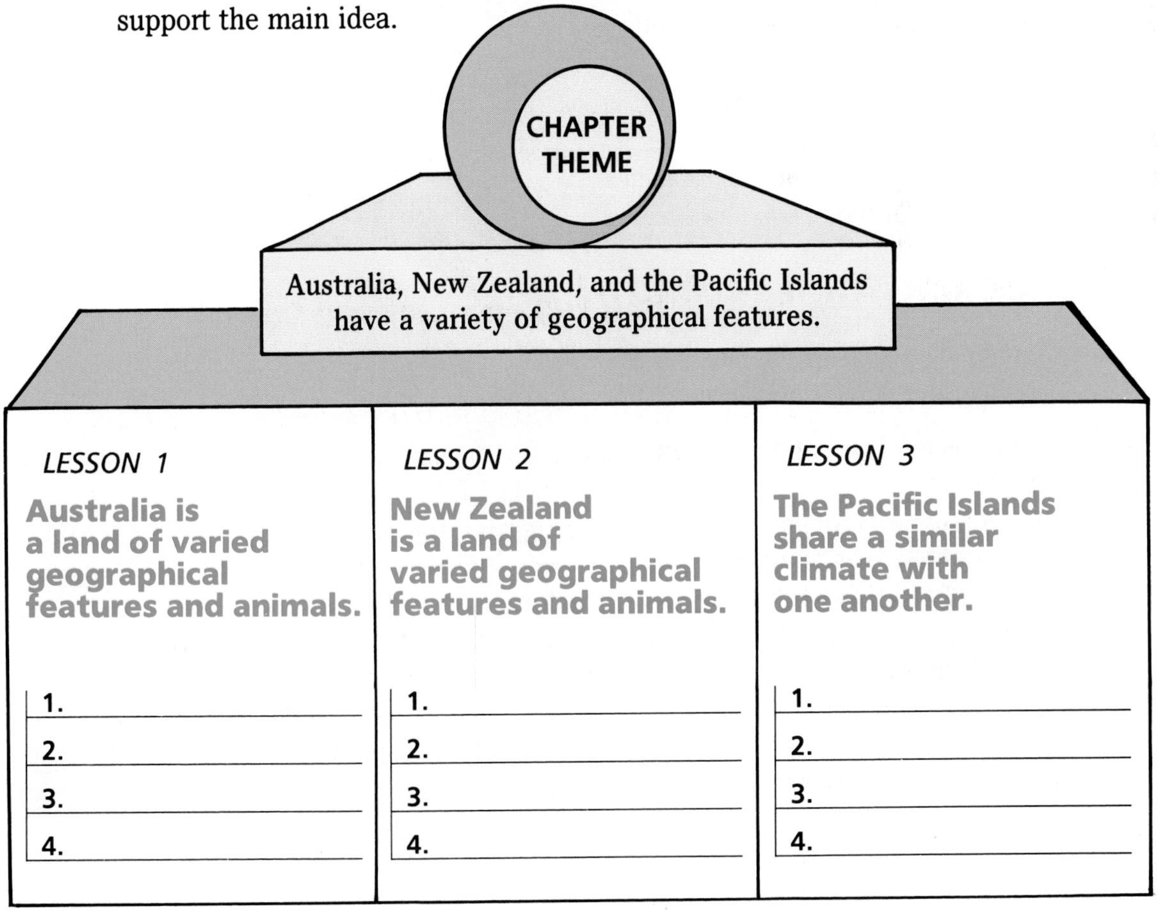

CHAPTER THEME

Australia, New Zealand, and the Pacific Islands have a variety of geographical features.

LESSON 1	LESSON 2	LESSON 3
Australia is a land of varied geographical features and animals.	New Zealand is a land of varied geographical features and animals.	The Pacific Islands share a similar climate with one another.
1.	1.	1.
2.	2.	2.
3.	3.	3.
4.	4.	4.

23

PAST AND PRESENT IN AUSTRALIA, NEW ZEALAND, AND THE PACIFIC ISLANDS

Most of the islands in this region are either independent or mostly self-governing. The isolated location of this region attracts many tourists from other lands.

Australia

THINK ABOUT WHAT YOU KNOW

Europeans regarded Australia as an "empty continent." What have you learned about Australia that would explain this point of view?

STUDY THE VOCABULARY

boomerang   **smelting**
food processing

FOCUS YOUR READING

How has Australia changed since Europeans arrived on the continent?

A. Aborigines and Europeans Meet

The Dutch As you know, the Aborigines had been living in Australia for thousands of years when the Europeans arrived. The Dutch explored the north and west coasts of Australia and called the land New Holland. But they did not establish colonies. They were interested only in trade.

William Dampier, an English seafarer who landed on the west coast of Australia in 1688, had an unfavorable view of the continent. He wrote that the land was barren and that the Aborigines were "the miserablest people in the world."

English Explorers In 1770, the English explorer Captain James Cook landed on the southeast coast. Cook had read Dampier's description of Australia, so he was surprised and pleased to find "a green and woody land." It should be noted, however, that Cook arrived in the fall, the wettest season of the year in southeastern Australia. Cook also found the Aborigines to be different from Dampier's description. Cook observed that the Aborigines were

"far happier than we Europeans," taking "all things necessary for life" from the earth and sea.

Cook named the place where he landed New South Wales and claimed the east coast for Great Britain. In 1803 another English explorer, Matthew Flinders, sailed around the continent and mapped much of the coast. He suggested that New Holland might better be called Australia, which means "southern land."

B. European Settlement

The first group of Europeans who came to Australia did not want to come. They were convicts sent to work far from home as punishment for breaking the law. The first fleet carrying convicts, together with marines to guard them, reached New South Wales in January 1788.

January is summer in Australia. It was a dry summer, so the country did not appear as green as Cook had described it. The convicts were made to plant crops, but because of the dry conditions, they had little success. They nearly starved during the first year. The convicts were also set to work constructing the buildings of the first settlement, which was named Sydney.

Other Europeans besides convicts eventually came to Australia. Many wanted to own farms. The discovery of gold in 1851 brought more immigrants. Some who failed to strike it rich in the 1849 California gold rush came to try their luck in Australia. Many gold seekers stayed.

C. Settlers Change a Continent

Land Use The Europeans brought animals, seeds, tools, ideas—and diseases— to Australia. All of these changed the continent and greatly affected the lives of the Aborigines. The settlers turned cattle and sheep loose on the grasslands. The Europeans used steel axes and plows to clear the land and plant crops.

The European settlers' farms and ranches occupied lands where the Aborigines had hunted and gathered food. When troubles broke out between settlers and Aborigines, the settlers used their guns. Guns were far more deadly than the Aborigines' spears and their throwing sticks, called **boomerangs**.

Imported Problems Europeans did not intend to bring diseases to Australia, but they did. Some diseases, such as smallpox, wiped out a large part of the Aboriginal population. The settlers also brought animals they would rather have left behind. Mice and rats arrived on European ships and escaped when the ships were in port.

Europeans did bring some animals on purpose, however. Camels were imported to pull wagons in dry areas where horses could not survive. Settlers brought wild animals that they could hunt for sport. In 1859 a man turned 24 English rabbits loose on his estate. Since there were no foxes or other beasts of prey, the number of rabbits increased rapidly. The 24 rabbits quickly became a horde of rabbits.

The rabbits spread over the country and destroyed crops, orchards, and even pastures. In dry years the rabbits strip the land of its cover. Then winds blow away the topsoil. Various methods have been used to control the rabbit population, but not with complete success.

D. The Commonwealth of Australia

Government The British established separate colonies in Australia. In 1901 the colonies united to form the independent Commonwealth of Australia. Each colony became a state in a federal government somewhat like that of the United States.

There are six states: New South Wales, Victoria, South Australia, Queensland, Western Australia, and Tasmania. The thickly populated Northern Territory has self-government, but it is not a state. The national capital, Canberra, is not located within any state but in a federal territory, like Washington, D.C.

The governments of the Commonwealth and the states are elected by the people. Australia has chosen to remain a member of the Commonwealth of Nations, the organization of countries that were once part of the British Empire. Queen Elizabeth II of the United Kingdom, who is head of the Commonwealth of Nations, is also queen of Australia. However, she serves only as the symbol of government.

Canberra was chosen as the site for Australia's federal capital in 1909.
▶ How is Canberra similar to Washington, D.C.?

AUSTRALIA, NEW ZEALAND, AND THE PACIFIC ISLANDS: POLITICAL

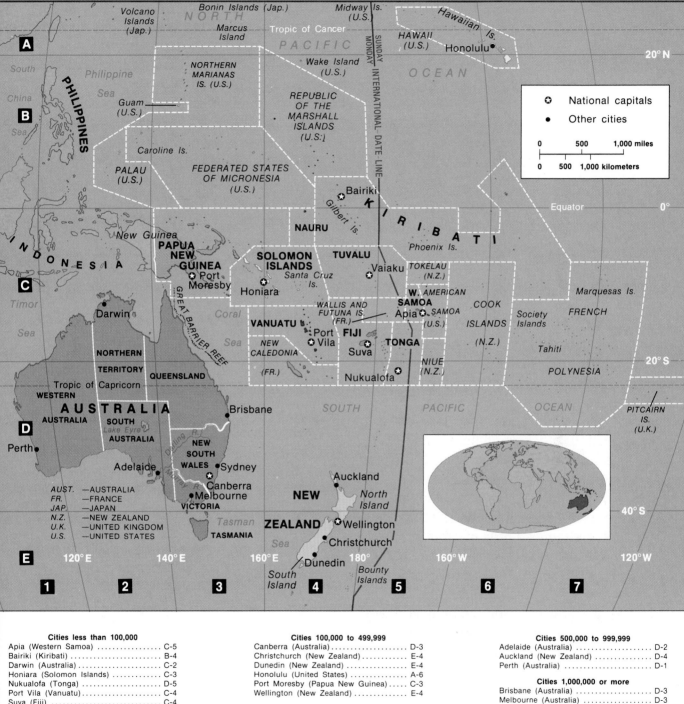

Cities less than 100,000
Apia (Western Samoa) C-5
Bairiki (Kiribati) B-4
Darwin (Australia) C-2
Honiara (Solomon Islands) C-3
Nukualofa (Tonga) D-5
Port Vila (Vanuatu) C-4
Suva (Fiji) C-4
Vaiaku (Tuvalu) C-4

Cities 100,000 to 499,999
Canberra (Australia) D-3
Christchurch (New Zealand) E-4
Dunedin (New Zealand) E-4
Honolulu (United States) A-6
Port Moresby (Papua New Guinea) C-3
Wellington (New Zealand) E-4

Cities 500,000 to 999,999
Adelaide (Australia) D-2
Auckland (New Zealand) D-4
Perth (Australia) D-1

Cities 1,000,000 or more
Brisbane (Australia) D-3
Melbourne (Australia) D-3
Sydney (Australia) D-3

There are more than 20,000 islands scattered across the Pacific Ocean.
▶ Which islands are included in the territory of French Polynesia?

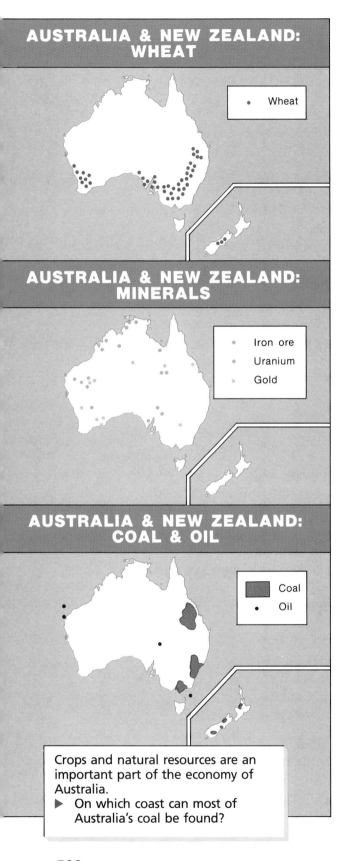

AUSTRALIA & NEW ZEALAND: WHEAT

• Wheat

AUSTRALIA & NEW ZEALAND: MINERALS

• Iron ore
• Uranium
• Gold

AUSTRALIA & NEW ZEALAND: COAL & OIL

■ Coal
• Oil

Crops and natural resources are an important part of the economy of Australia.
► On which coast can most of Australia's coal be found?

Population Most of the early settlers in Australia came from the British Isles. Later groups came from other European countries, such as Germany, Italy, and Greece. In recent years a growing number have come from Asia. Today, people of Asian descent outnumber the Aborigines.

Most Australians live in towns and cities. Most of the Aborigines are now city dwellers. Sydney, the oldest city, is also the largest. Other large cities are Melbourne, Brisbane, Adelaide, and Perth. Locate these cities on the map on page 591.

E. Australia's Economy

Crops European settlers introduced crops they had known at home — wheat, barley, oats, potatoes. Wheat is the largest export crop today. Australia also produces other grains, including corn and rice.

Sugarcane and various kinds of tropical fruit are grown in Queensland. In the southeast, wine grapes and other fruit have become important products.

Industry Although Australia's agricultural exports are numerous, more people work in factories and mines than on farms or ranches. Many workers have jobs in **food processing**. They can or freeze agricultural products. Others work in manufacturing, turning out machinery, electrical equipment, and other goods.

Mining and **smelting** make up a number of jobs in Australia. Smelting is the process of separating a metal from other materials in its ore. Gold is still mined, as are a number of other minerals. The continent has large deposits of coal, iron, copper, and bauxite. The world's most productive silver and lead mine is in Australia. Almost all opals, beautiful gemstones, come from this continent.

PRODUCTS OF SHEEP

PRODUCTS:

1. Wool for clothing and blankets
2. Food
3. Leather
4. Soap
5. Tennis racket strings
6. Fertilizer
7. Glue

Thirty percent of all the world's wool comes from Australia. Wool is used to make clothing.
▶ What sheep product besides wool can make something people wear?

Livestock The early settlers found that raising sheep was a profitable way to make use of the land. There were few predatory animals; Australia had no wolves or bears. Herding required fewer laborers than did farming. It was easier to export wool than food products. The first Australian wool was shipped to England in 1812.

The use of refrigerators on ships opened new markets. Frozen meat was first shipped to England in 1879. Australia now leads the world in the export of beef, and it ranks second after New Zealand in shipping mutton, or meat from sheep.

LESSON **1** REVIEW

THINK AND WRITE

A. How did Dampier's and Cook's views of the Aborigines differ?

B. What different reasons did Europeans have for coming to Australia?

C. What intended changes and what unplanned changes did European settlers make in Australia?

D. Summarize how the government of Australia is like that of the United States.

E. What are some of Australia's products?

SKILLS CHECK

WRITING SKILL

Write a letter to an Australian student, telling about your country and the place where you live. Point out similarities to and differences from Australia.

593

New Zealand

THINK ABOUT WHAT YOU KNOW

Australia and New Zealand are sometimes referred to as lands "down under." Try to explain this reference on the basis of what you know about the location of Australia and New Zealand.

STUDY THE VOCABULARY

heritage

FOCUS YOUR READING

How did the Maoris and the European settlers affect New Zealand?

A. The People of New Zealand

Maoris The Maoris tell a story about a great chief named Kupe who sailed in a large canoe to New Zealand from one of the Polynesian islands. Kupe later returned home and gave his people directions for sailing to Aotearoa, the Maori name for New Zealand.

Historians believe that the story of Kupe is a legend, but it is a legend partly based on fact. The ancestors of the Maoris did come to New Zealand by canoe from Polynesia about a thousand years ago.

Europeans The Dutch explorer Abel Tasman arrived in New Zealand long after the first Maoris. Although Tasman found the islands beautiful, he thought they had little value for Europeans. Captain James Cook, who arrived in New Zealand in 1769, had a different view. He thought it would be a good place for settlers.

After 1790 many Europeans found their way to New Zealand. Whaling ships stopped there. Some hunted seals along the coasts. A few convicts from Australia escaped to the islands. Other Europeans traded with the Maoris, who wanted guns.

Missionaries came to teach the Maoris about the Christian religion. Since the Maoris had no system of writing, the missionaries introduced the alphabet and printed the New Testament of the Bible in the Maori language.

The Maori people today use canoes as their ancestors did about a thousand years ago, when they came to New Zealand.
▶ What do you think the man at the front of the canoe is doing?

USING SOURCE MATERIAL

CAPTAIN JAMES COOK'S JOURNAL

In 1769 Captain James Cook became the first European to visit New Zealand. The next year he explored the east coast of Australia. British claims to both New Zealand and Australia were based on his expeditions. This passage about the Maoris of New Zealand is from Cook's journal.

The natives of this country are a strong, raw-boned, well-made, active people rather above than under the common size especially the men. They are all of a very dark brown color with black hair, thin black beards and white teeth. . . . They seem to enjoy a good state of health and many of them live to a good old age. . . .

Whenever we were visited by any number of them that had never heard or seen anything of us before, they generally came off in the largest canoes they had. . . . In each canoe were generally an old man, in some two or three, these used always to direct the others, and generally carried a halberd or battle ax in their hands. . . . As soon as they came within about a stone's throw of the ship, they would there lay and call out, . . . come ashore with us and we will kill you with our patoos [fighting axes]. . . . Musketry they never regarded unless they felt the effect, but the great guns they did because these threw stones farther than they could comprehend. After they found that our arms were so much superior to theirs and that we took no advantage of that superiority, . . . they ever after were our very good friends and we never had an instance of their attempting to surprise or cut off any of our people when they were ashore. . . .

Understanding Source Material

1. Do you think Captain Cook was favorably impressed by the Maoris? Explain.
2. Why, do you think, did the Maoris become friends with Captain Cook and his crew?

595

Great Britain made New Zealand part of the British Empire in 1840. The Maoris were promised protection of their lands if they accepted British authority, or rule. Conflicts arose between the Maoris and the government, in spite of this promise. The Maoris felt that they were being cheated. The European settlers thought that the Maoris stood in the way of the development of New Zealand. These conflicts led to warfare in which the Maoris were defeated.

Ancestry The Maoris make up about 12 percent of New Zealand's population. A number of New Zealanders have both Maori and European ancestors. Modern New Zealand has a double **heritage** (HER-ih tihj), that is, a culture handed down from the past.

Many immigrants in recent years have come from Polynesia, as the ancestors of the Maoris did long ago. A large number of these recent immigrants have settled in Auckland, which is called the largest Polynesian city in the world.

B. People Change the Land

Forest Fires Both the Maoris and the Europeans changed the New Zealand landscape. The Maoris set fires in the forest to drive out the birds they hunted and to clear the land for planting. Perhaps as much as one third of the forests in New Zealand had been cleared by fire before the Europeans arrived there.

The European settlers also used fire to clear the forests. Much of what is now green pasture was once covered with trees.

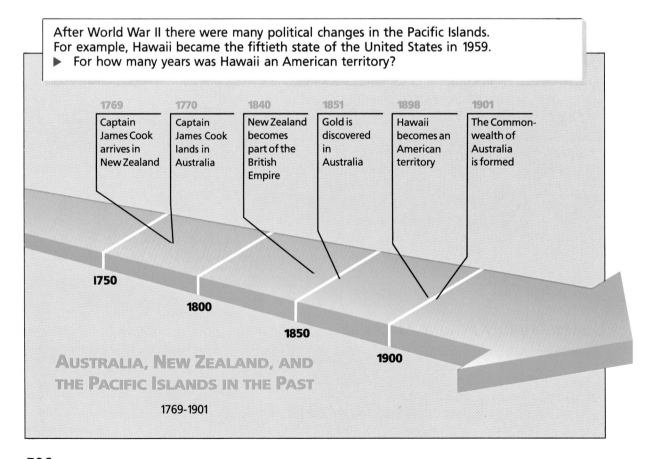

After World War II there were many political changes in the Pacific Islands. For example, Hawaii became the fiftieth state of the United States in 1959.
▶ For how many years was Hawaii an American territory?

1769	1770	1840	1851	1898	1901
Captain James Cook arrives in New Zealand	Captain James Cook lands in Australia	New Zealand becomes part of the British Empire	Gold is discovered in Australia	Hawaii becomes an American territory	The Commonwealth of Australia is formed

1750   1800   1850   1900

AUSTRALIA, NEW ZEALAND, AND THE PACIFIC ISLANDS IN THE PAST

1769-1901

European Imports Like the Europeans who settled in Australia, settlers in New Zealand brought animals, seeds, and tools, as well as ideas and diseases. Diseases killed off at least half of the Maoris in the 1840s and 1850s. In addition to farm animals, the settlers brought birds and wild animals from Europe. They thought the songs of familiar birds would make them feel more at home. They introduced grouse, rabbits, pheasants, and deer for hunting. They even imported fish for the streams.

Almost all the food grains and vegetables grown in New Zealand today were brought by early settlers. Even many of the plants sown for pasture, such as white clover, were imported. The settlers also brought bees to fertilize the clover.

Sheepherding is still an important industry in New Zealand.
▶ Why, do you think, does the shepherd use a motorcycle to do his job?

C. New Zealand Today

Government Today, New Zealand is an independent member of the Commonwealth of Nations. As in Australia, Queen Elizabeth II is the symbolic head of state, but she does not rule.

New Zealand is governed by a one-house parliament elected by the people. New Zealand was the first country in the world to allow women to vote in national elections. The women of New Zealand have been voting for nearly a century.

Economy New Zealand's main exports come from its farms and ranches, although 85 percent of the people live in cities and towns. Wool, meat, dairy products, and fruit are leading exports. New Zealand is known for the kiwi fruit. Its name supposedly comes from its shape, which is like that of the flightless bird called the kiwi.

LESSON **2** *REVIEW*

THINK AND WRITE

A. Explain New Zealand's double heritage.
B. How did the Maoris and the European settlers change New Zealand?
C. Describe the government and economy of New Zealand.

SKILLS CHECK

THINKING SKILL

Compare the flags of Australia and New Zealand, found on the charts on pages 32–43, with the flag of the United Kingdom also found on these charts. What element do the flags share? Why do they have this common element?

YOU DECIDE: SHOULD THE LAWS OF A COUNTRY REPLACE ITS TREATIES?

You learned in Chapter 23 that New Zealand is a relatively small island country in the Pacific Ocean. It is about 1,000 miles (1,609 km) southeast of Australia and 6,500 miles (10,500 km) away from the United States. During the days of the British Empire, New Zealand was a British colony. It gained its independence in 1907.

New Zealand fought on the side of the Allies during World War II. About 140,000 troops traveled all over the world to fight the enemy.

Following World War II, New Zealand, Australia, and the United States signed the Australia–New Zealand–United States (ANZUS) defense treaty. The name combines the first letter of each word in the names of the member countries. This treaty recognized that an armed attack on any of the nations would be dangerous to them all.

The government of New Zealand adopted a new policy in 1984, which later became a law. This law banned nuclear weapons and ships powered by nuclear energy from the nation's ports and territorial waters. On the next page are two different points of view about whether New Zealand has the right to deny the United States and Australia access to its shores if their ships are carrying nuclear weapons or are powered by nuclear energy. Read them both and decide for yourself.

New Zealanders Have the Right to Protect Their Country from Nuclear Weapons

Based on the provisions of the ANZUS treaty, the United States Navy and United States ships were free to move about the waters and ports of New Zealand. However, New Zealanders began to object to visits by American ships that carried nuclear weapons or were powered by nuclear energy.

Relations between the United States and New Zealand became strained when, in 1985, New Zealand's Prime Minister, David Lange, denied a United States destroyer access to a New Zealand port. Lange issued the denial after United States officials refused to give assurances that the ship carried no nuclear weapons. According to reports, the Prime Minister had the support of the people of New Zealand.

Polls have shown decided support for the antinuclear ships policy, although most New Zealanders, like their government, prefer to keep ANZUS intact.

The Security of New Zealand Cannot Be Guaranteed

The United States government was very unhappy with these developments. United States officials argued that the country cannot announce whether its ships do or do not carry nuclear weapons. That would expose its operations to the enemy. "An alliance partner," they said, "cannot pick and choose the nature of its contributions." Also, since 40 percent of the United States Navy is nuclear powered, it would be very impractical to comply with New Zealand's demands.

The United States government reacted very strongly to the position of New Zealand. Because of the policy, the United States announced in 1986 that it would no longer guarantee the security of New Zealand under the ANZUS treaty. In other words, the United States broke the alliance and isolated New Zealand as an ally.

Thinking for Yourself

1. Do you think New Zealanders had the right to keep United States ships from visiting their ports?
2. Do you think the United States should isolate New Zealand as an ally because of government policies?

The Pacific Islands

Most of the Pacific Islands are small and located in the tropics. What, do you think, would be the advantages and disadvantages of living on a small tropical island?

protectorate

How did the governments of the Pacific Island countries change after World War II?

A. Empires in the Pacific

Foreign Possessions In 1838, Queen Pomare of Tahiti sent a message to Queen Victoria of Great Britain, asking for protection. Queen Pomare made the request because a French warship had delivered a message demanding that the French be allowed to settle in Tahiti.

Victoria replied that Great Britain could not defend Tahiti at that time. In the meantime a French representative managed to get four Tahitian chiefs to sign a request that Tahiti be made a French **protectorate** (proh TEK tur iht). A protectorate is a land at least partly controlled by a stronger country. Queen Pomare protested the French action, but in the end, Tahiti became a French protectorate.

Between 1850 and World War I, many Pacific Islands were taken over by France, Great Britain, Germany, and the United States. Some islands became colonies in large empires. The United States took over the island of Hawaii in 1898 and declared it an American territory.

Independence World War I had little effect on the Pacific Islands. Major battles, however, were fought in the Pacific during World War II.

After the war there were great changes in the political status, or situation, of the Pacific Islands. Hawaii became the fiftieth state of the United States in 1959. A number of islands became independent, or self-governing.

B. Countries of Melanesia

Papua New Guinea is the largest of the Pacific Island countries, occupying the eastern half of the island of New Guinea. It became independent in 1975.

Much of Papua New Guinea is mountainous and heavily forested. Since becoming independent the country has changed rapidly. The discovery of gold and

In the mid-1800s, Queen Pomare tried to protect Tahiti from becoming a French protectorate.
► How can you tell that she was a queen?

oil has speeded change. One government official noted, "In the 14 years since independence, our people have gone from village huts and caves to skyscrapers."

Fiji was a British colony for nearly a century before it became independent, in 1970. Years ago, people were brought from India to work in the sugar fields. Today, Indians outnumber Fijians.

Other independent countries in Melanesia include the Solomon Islands, Tonga, and Vanuatu. These three countries and Papua New Guinea are members of the Commonwealth of Nations.

C. Countries of Polynesia

The island country of Tahiti is no longer a French protectorate. Tahiti and 130 other countries make up the French overseas territory of French Polynesia. As

Papua New Guinea lies on the eastern half of the second largest island in the world.
▶ To what island group does Papua New Guinea belong?

an overseas territory, French Polynesia has its own elected assembly.

The Samoan Islands were divided by Germany and the United States in 1900. The eastern islands, known as American Samoa, are a territory of the United States. The people elect a governor and legislature. Western Samoa became independent in 1962.

Tuvalu is one of the smallest states in Polynesia. It is less than half the size of Manhattan Island in New York City, yet it is an independent country.

601

D. Countries of Micronesia

Micronesia is truly a vast region of small islands. Some are independent countries. Tiny Nauru has an area of only 8 square miles (21 sq km). The center of the island is a deposit of high-grade phosphate rock. Phosphate is a valuable fertilizer. The country has been living by exporting parts of itself. Over the years many millions of tons of phosphate have been mined and shipped abroad. Nauru is now independent, but it has close ties with Australia.

Kiribati was once a British colony called the Gilbert Islands. The country consists of 33 coral islands that rise no more than 12 feet (4 m) above sea level. The islands of Kiribati are scattered over about 2 million square miles (5 million sq km) of the Pacific Ocean. Kiribati has been independent since 1979.

The United States has ties with several groups of islands in Micronesia. These include the Commonwealth of Northern Mariana Islands, the Federated States of Micronesia, the Republic of the Marshall Islands, and the Republic of Palau. All are self-governing, but the United States is responsible for their defense.

Phosphate mining is an important industry on the island of Nauru.
► What equipment is used to mine the phosphate?

LESSON 3 REVIEW

THINK AND WRITE

A. Which countries took over Pacific Islands before World War I?

B. Briefly describe the following five countries of Melanesia: Papua New Guinea, Fiji, the Solomon Islands, Tonga, and Vanuatu.

C. What is the difference in the political status of Tahiti, American Samoa, Western Samoa, and Tuvalu?

D. Why, do you think, is Micronesia an appropriate name for the island group in the Pacific?

SKILLS CHECK

MAP SKILL

Locate the following Pacific Islands on the Atlas map on pages 610–611: Hawaiian Islands, Fiji Islands, Tokelau Islands, Western Samoa, Nauru, Pitcairn Island. Determine whether each is independent or a possession of another country.

USING THE VOCABULARY

boomerang   heritage
food processing   protectorate
smelting

On a separate sheet of paper, write the word or words from the list above that best complete the sentences.

1. Many people in Australia have jobs in _____, the procedure in which agricultural products are canned or frozen.
2. The Maoris and the Europeans have given New Zealand a double _____, or culture handed down from the past.
3. Tahiti is no longer a French _____, a land at least partly controlled by a stronger country.
4. An Aborigine used a throwing stick, called a _____, for defense.
5. Mining and _____, which is the process of separating a metal from other materials in its ore, provide Australians with many jobs.

REMEMBERING WHAT YOU READ

On a separate sheet of paper, answer the following questions in complete sentences.

1. Why did the Dutch come to Australia?
2. What name did the Dutch give the land that we now know as Australia?
3. Who were the first group of Europeans to settle in Australia?
4. What did the Europeans bring to Australia that changed the continent?
5. Why did trouble break out between the Aborigines and the settlers?
6. What weapons did the Aborigines use to fight the Europeans?
7. Explain how the government of Australia is organized.
8. What is the oldest and largest city in Australia?
9. What animal did the early settlers make good use of in Australia?
10. What industries provide jobs for people in Australia?
11. What promise did the British authorities make to the Maoris?
12. What products do the farms and ranches of New Zealand produce?
13. What happened to many of the Pacific islands in the time period between 1850 and World War I?
14. What is the largest of the Pacific Island countries?
15. What islands of Polynesia are a territory of the United States?

TYING MATH TO SOCIAL STUDIES

You read that 24 English rabbits were released in Australia in 1859. If 50 percent of those rabbits were does, or female rabbits, how many does were released? A female rabbit usually produces about 20 young a year. How many baby rabbits could the does have produced in one year? In two years? In three years?

THINKING CRITICALLY

On a separate sheet of paper, answer the following questions in complete sentences.

1. Do you think there are any similarities between how Aborigines were treated in Australia and how Native Americans were treated in America?
2. How did the invention of refrigerated ships help the economy of Australia?
3. If you had been an explorer, do you think you would have agreed with Abel Tasman's view of New Zealand or with Captain James Cook's view of New Zealand? Explain your answer.
4. Why, in your opinion, would some Pacific Island countries choose to become independent, or self-governing?
5. What reasons could the United States have for maintaining ties with several island groups in Micronesia?

SUMMARIZING THE CHAPTER

On a separate sheet of paper, copy the graphic organizer shown below. Beside the main idea for each lesson, write four statements that support the main idea.

CHAPTER THEME	There are close economic and political ties between Australia, New Zealand, the islands of the Pacific, and other nations.

LESSON 1 **Australia has changed since Europeans arrived on the continent.**	1. _____ 2. _____ 3. _____ 4. _____
LESSON 2 **The Maoris and the European settlers have affected New Zealand.**	1. _____ 2. _____ 3. _____ 4. _____
LESSON 3 **The governments of the Pacific Island countries changed after World War II.**	1. _____ 2. _____ 3. _____ 4. _____

REVIEW

COOPERATIVE LEARNING

In Unit 7 you learned about Australia, New Zealand, and the Pacific Island nations. Each area has unique characteristics.

A report is a beneficial way for your group to learn more about a country or island.

PROJECT

Work with a group of classmates to write a report about a country or island in Unit 7. The purpose of the report will be to learn more about a certain place and teach the other students in your class.

The first step in the project will be brainstorming. Hold a group meeting to talk about all the interesting and exciting material about your area. Try to come up with at least ten different ideas. Choose one member to write down all your group's ideas. When you are finished brainstorming, the person should read the list aloud and ask group members to vote on what they think are the five best ideas to research.

After you have decided on the five best ideas to write about, divide the tasks among group members.

● One group member will be the presenter. This leader will gather all the information from the others and present the report to the class.

Each member in the group will gather information. Information can be found in your textbook and different encyclopedias.

● One person should draw and label the location studied. This could be the cover for the report.

● One group member will be responsible for writing or typing the report.

● One person should gather interesting photographs for the report.

PRESENTATION AND REVIEW

The group leader will present the report to the class. The students in other groups should ask questions based on the report. The members of the group will answer these questions.

After the presentation is over, your group should meet to evaluate your project. The following questions will help you in your evaluation: How well did your group's members work together? How could your project have been improved? Did everyone in the group do his or her job?

REMEMBER TO:
- Give your ideas.
- Listen to others' ideas.
- Plan your work with the group.
- Present your project.
- Discuss how your group worked.

A. WHY DO I NEED THIS SKILL?

Your social studies textbook contains so much information that it would be impossible for you to remember it all. Therefore, it is important for you to remember the main points of your reading. One way to do this is to write a **summary**. A summary is a short way of stating, in your own words, the important ideas from a piece of writing.

B. LEARNING THE SKILL

It would be very difficult to summarize all the information in this book in just a few sentences or even in a few pages. Such a summary would leave out many important ideas. This is why you need to break the material you are summarizing into manageable pieces. A good way of doing this is to summarize one section of a lesson at a time.

To write a summary for a section of a lesson in your social studies textbook, follow these steps.

1. Write the section heading as the title for your summary.
2. Decide what the main idea is for each paragraph in the section. Write the main ideas under the summary title.
3. Read through your section summary. Take out any information that is not important. Add any important ideas that you left out.

Here is a summary for the section of Chapter 23 called "New Zealand Today." Reread the section, found on page 597, and then compare it with this summary. Notice that the summary includes the title and the main ideas of the section.

New Zealand Today

- New Zealand is part of the Commonwealth of Nations, with Queen Elizabeth II serving as the symbolic head of state.

- New Zealand is governed by a one-house parliament elected by the people.

- Although most New Zealanders live in cities, farming and ranching are very important; the country's main exports come from farms and ranches.

Certain information in this section of the book has been left out of the summary. For example, the information that you read about the kiwi is interesting, but it is not the main idea for the paragraph. A summary contains only the most important information.

C. PRACTICING THE SKILL

On a separate sheet of paper, write a summary for the section called "Australia's

Economy," found on pages 592–593, in Chapter 23. The summary title and the first main idea have been written for you. Copy the parts of the summary shown and then write the main ideas for the rest of the section.

Australia's Economy
- Growing crops is an important industry in Australia, which is a leading exporter of such products as wheat, other grains, and fruit.

D. APPLYING THE SKILL

You can also summarize larger sections in your social studies textbook. For example, you can summarize an entire lesson by writing one or two sentences that tell the main ideas in each section. Try writing a summary of the first lesson in Chapter 23, which begins on page 589. See if making a summary helps you remember the main points in the lesson. Then try writing a summary of the entire chapter.

A. WHY DO I NEED THIS SKILL?

Two writers describing the same person or event may create two totally different impressions of that person or event. This is because writers each have their own beliefs and feelings that may be reflected in their writing. These beliefs and feelings are a writer's point of view. You, too, have your own point of view. As a reader, you need to be aware of any writer's point of view so that you can decide how much of what you read is strictly factual and how much is the writer's own beliefs and feelings. From there, you can decide if you agree with the writer's point of view.

B. LEARNING THE SKILL

Writers often express a point of view when they write to persuade—that is, to get the reader to feel a certain way, to believe in something, or to buy something. A letter to an editor, an editorial, and an advertisement are examples of persuasive writing.

Writers may also express a point of view when they write to inform, or give information about a topic. Your social studies textbook is an example of something written to inform. However, writers generally try to just present facts, not a point of view, when they write to inform.

When you read, your job is to try to decide if what you are reading reflects facts and reason rather than the writer's own point of view. A point of view may be based on emotions or faulty arguments and may not be logical. The table on the next page describes four steps to follow to recognize and understand a point of view.

In Chapter 22 you read, "A number of other Australian animals appeared strange to European eyes." Do you think this statement is the writer's point of view alone or is it factual as well? Turn back to pages 577 and 578 and reread the selection "Australia's Animals and Birds." Use the steps in the table as you read.

Does the textbook author express a particular point of view? If so, does the author also provide facts to support that point of view? Do the quotes from European explorers describing kangaroos express a point of view? Do those quotes support what the author has written?

C. PRACTICING THE SKILL

Using the steps in the table, try to determine if there is a point of view expressed in the following paragraph, which is related to early European settlement in Australia.

The first group of Europeans who reluctantly came to Australia did not want to come. They were savage convicts sent to do backbreaking work far from home as harsh punishment for breaking the law. The first fleet carrying villainous convicts, together with law-abiding marines to guard them, reached New South Wales in January 1788.

On a separate sheet of paper, answer the following five questions in complete sentences.

1. What point of view does the writer express?
2. What words or phrases are clues that the writer has a point of view?
3. What reasons might the writer have for expressing that point of view?
4. What, if any, facts are there to support the writer's point of view?
5. Do you agree with the writer's point of view?

Now turn back to Chapter 23 and read the first paragraph in the section called "European Settlement," on page 589. Does your textbook author express a point of view? If so, how does it differ from that expressed in the paragraph that you read on page 608?

D. APPLYING THE SKILL

Whenever you read, try to determine if the writer is expressing a point of view. Remember, it is all right for a writer to express a point of view. Just be certain that you recognize a point of view and try to determine if there are facts that support it. Then you can decide for yourself if you agree or disagree with the point of view.

POINT OF VIEW
Steps for Understanding Point of View
1. As you read, look for descriptive words or phrases that may express a particular belief or feeling.
2. Think about how those words and phrases tell what the writer's attitude toward a person, event, or topic may be.
3. Determine if any facts are presented to support the writer's point of view.
4. Decide if you agree or disagree with the writer's point of view.

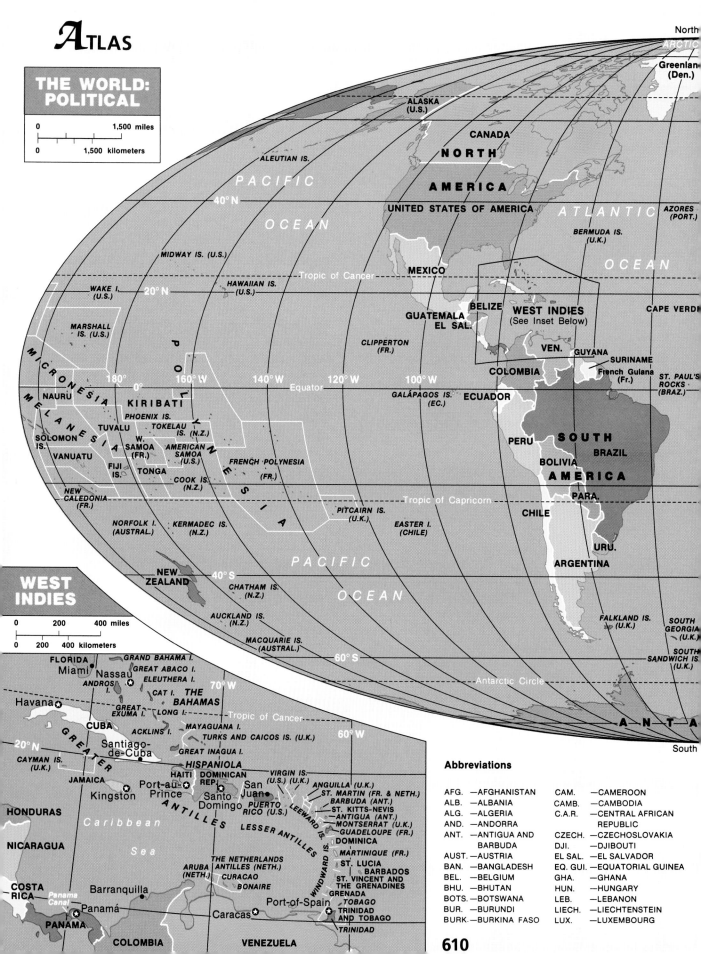

ATLAS

THE WORLD: POLITICAL

0 — 1,500 miles
0 — 1,500 kilometers

North

ARCTIC

Greenland (Den.)

ALASKA (U.S.)

CANADA

NORTH

ALEUTIAN IS.

PACIFIC

AMERICA

UNITED STATES OF AMERICA

ATLANTIC

AZORES (PORT.)

OCEAN

40°N

BERMUDA IS. (U.K.)

OCEAN

MIDWAY IS. (U.S.)

Tropic of Cancer

MEXICO

CAPE VERDI

WAKE I. (U.S.)

20°N

HAWAIIAN IS. (U.S.)

BELIZE

WEST INDIES (See Inset Below)

MARSHALL IS. (U.S.)

GUATEMALA EL SAL.

CLIPPERTON (FR.)

VEN.

GUYANA

SURINAME

French Guiana (Fr.)

ST. PAUL'S ROCKS (BRAZ.)

M I C R O N E S I A

180°

160°W

140°W

120°W

100°W

COLOMBIA

NAURU

P O L Y N E S I A

0°

Equator

GALÁPAGOS IS. (EC.)

ECUADOR

KIRIBATI

MELANESIA

PHOENIX IS.

TOKELAU IS. (N.Z.)

PERU

S O U T H

BRAZIL

TUVALU

SOLOMON IS.

W. SAMOA (FR.)

AMERICAN SAMOA (U.S.)

FRENCH POLYNESIA (FR.)

BOLIVIA

A M E R I C A

VANUATU

FIJI IS.

TONGA

COOK IS. (N.Z.)

Tropic of Capricorn

PARA.

NEW CALEDONIA (FR.)

NORFOLK I. (AUSTRAL.)

KERMADEC IS. (N.Z.)

PITCAIRN IS. (U.K.)

EASTER I. (CHILE)

CHILE

URU.

ARGENTINA

NEW ZEALAND

40°S

CHATHAM IS. (N.Z.)

PACIFIC

AUCKLAND IS. (N.Z.)

OCEAN

FALKLAND IS. (U.K.)

SOUTH GEORGIA (U.K.)

MACQUARIE IS. (AUSTRAL.)

60°S

SOUTH SANDWICH IS. (U.K.)

Antarctic Circle

A N T A

South

WEST INDIES

0 — 200 — 400 miles
0 — 200 — 400 kilometers

FLORIDA

Miami

GRAND BAHAMA I.

GREAT ABACO I.

Nassau

ELEUTHERA I.

ANDROS I.

CAT I.

THE BAHAMAS

70°W

Havana

GREAT EXUMA I.

LONG I.

Tropic of Cancer

CUBA

ACKLINS I.

MAYAGUANA I.

60°W

Santiago- de-Cuba

G R E A T E R

TURKS AND CAICOS IS. (U.K.)

20°N

CAYMAN IS. (U.K.)

GREAT INAGUA I.

HISPANIOLA

VIRGIN IS. (U.S.) (U.K.)

ANGUILLA (U.K.)

JAMAICA

HAITI

DOMINICAN REP.

San Juan

ST. MARTIN (FR. & NETH.)

Kingston

Port-au- Prince

Santo Domingo

PUERTO RICO (U.S.)

ST. KITTS-NEVIS

ANTIGUA (ANT.)

HONDURAS

A N T I L L E S

LEEWARD IS.

MONTSERRAT (U.K.)

GUADELOUPE (FR.)

LESSER ANTILLES

DOMINICA

Caribbean

MARTINIQUE (FR.)

NICARAGUA

THE NETHERLANDS ANTILLES (NETH.)

ST. LUCIA

Sea

ARUBA (NETH.)

CURACAO

BONAIRE

BARBADOS

ST. VINCENT AND THE GRENADINES

GRENADA

WINDWARD IS.

COSTA RICA

Barranquilla

Panama Canal

Panamá

Port-of-Spain

TOBAGO

TRINIDAD AND TOBAGO

PANAMA

Caracas

TRINIDAD

COLOMBIA

VENEZUELA

Abbreviations

AFG.	—AFGHANISTAN	CAM.	—CAMEROON
ALB.	—ALBANIA	CAMB.	—CAMBODIA
ALG.	—ALGERIA	C.A.R.	—CENTRAL AFRICAN
AND.	—ANDORRA		REPUBLIC
ANT.	—ANTIGUA AND	CZECH.	—CZECHOSLOVAKIA
	BARBUDA	DJI.	—DJIBOUTI
AUST.	—AUSTRIA	EL SAL.	—EL SALVADOR
BAN.	—BANGLADESH	EQ. GUI.	—EQUATORIAL GUINEA
BEL.	—BELGIUM	GHA.	—GHANA
BHU.	—BHUTAN	HUN.	—HUNGARY
BOTS.	—BOTSWANA	LEB.	—LEBANON
BUR.	—BURUNDI	LIECH.	—LIECHTENSTEIN
BURK.	—BURKINA FASO	LUX.	—LUXEMBOURG

610

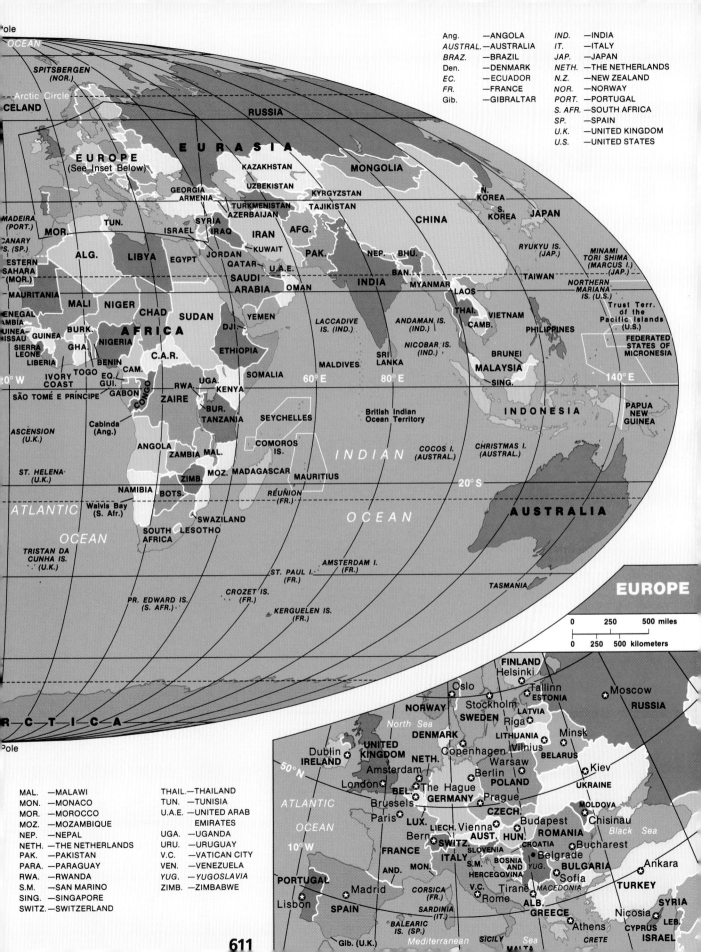

THE WORLD: PHYSICAL

Elevations
Feet | Meters
10,000 — 3,000
5,000 — 1,500
2,000 — 600
500 — 150
0 — 0

Land below sea level

Land under ice

North

ARCT

PACIFIC

OCEAN

40° N

NORTH
AMERICA

ROCKY MOUNTAINS

APPALACHIAN MTS.

ATLANTIC

OCEAN

Tropic of Cancer

20° N

ANDES MTS.

SOUTH
AMERICA

ANDES MOUNTAINS

160° E   180°   160° W   140° W   120° W   100° W   40° W

0°

20° S

Tropic of Capricorn

PACIFIC

40° S

OCEAN

60° S

Antarctic Circle

A—N—T

South

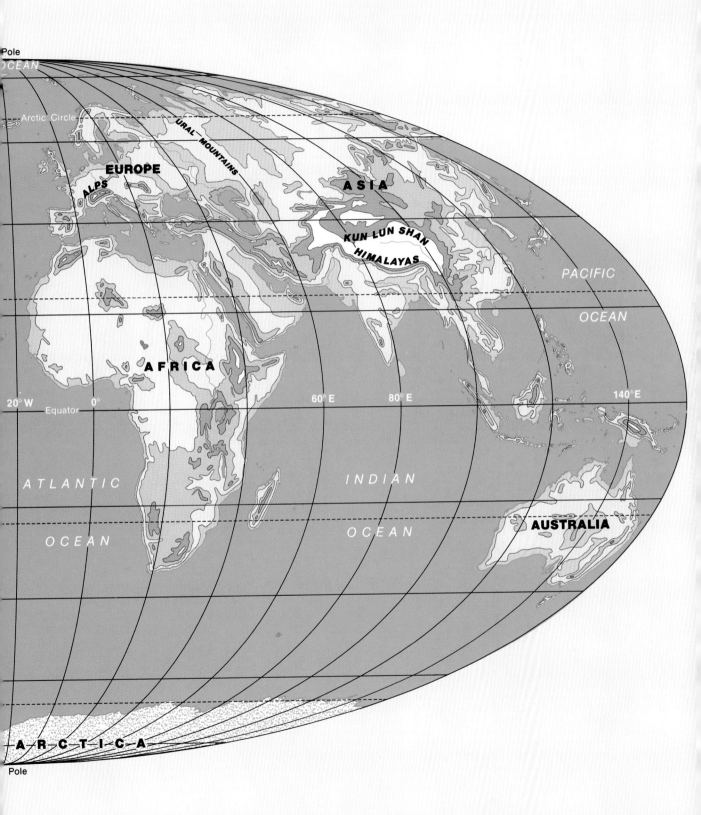

Pole

OCEAN

Arctic Circle

URAL MOUNTAINS

EUROPE

ASIA

ALPS

KUN LUN SHAN

HIMALAYAS

PACIFIC

OCEAN

AFRICA

20° W   0°   60° E   80° E   140° E

Equator

ATLANTIC   INDIAN

OCEAN   OCEAN   AUSTRALIA

A-R-C-T-I-C-A

Pole

613

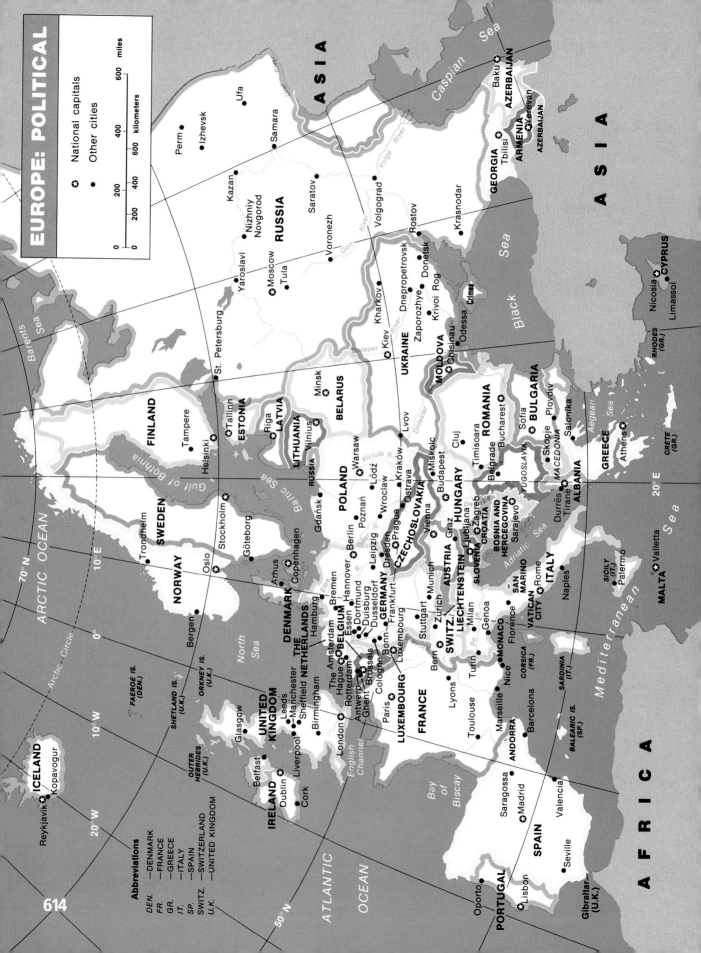

EUROPE: POLITICAL

⊕ National capitals
• Other cities

miles
0   200   400   600
0   200   400   600   kilometers
0   200   400   600   miles

Abbreviations

DEN. —DENMARK
FR. —FRANCE
GR. —GREECE
IT. —ITALY
SP. —SPAIN
SWITZ. —SWITZERLAND
U.K. —UNITED KINGDOM

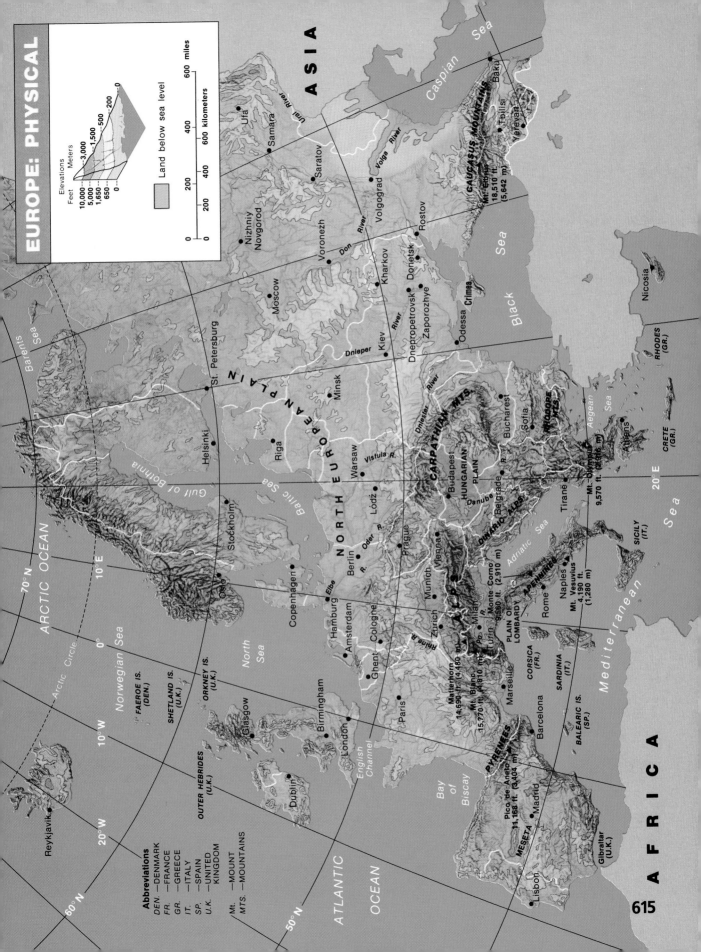

EUROPE: PHYSICAL

Abbreviations
DEN.—DENMARK
FR.—FRANCE
GR.—GREECE
IT.—ITALY
SP.—SPAIN
U.K.—UNITED
KINGDOM

Mt.—MOUNT
MTS.—MOUNTAINS

Elevations
Feet   Meters
10,000 — 3,000
5,000 — 1,500
1,650 — 500
650 — 200
0 — 0

Land below sea level

0   200   400   600 miles

0   200   400   600 kilometers

ASIA

Caspian Sea

Baku

CAUCASUS MOUNTAINS
Mt. Elbrus
18,510 ft.
(5,642 m)

Tbilisi
Yerevan

Ufa
Samara
Saratov

Volga River
Ural River

Volgograd
Rostov
Don River

Voronezh

Moscow

Nizhniy
Novgorod

Kharkov
Donetsk
Dnepropetrovsk
Zaporozhye
Odessa
Crimea

Black Sea

Nicosia

RHODES
(GR.)

Kiev
Dnieper River

Minsk

St. Petersburg

NORTH EUROPEAN PLAIN

Riga

Warsaw
Vistula R.
Dniester River

CARPATHIAN MTS.

Bucharest
Sofia

RHODOPE MTS.

Aegean Sea

CRETE
(GR.)

20° E

Athens

Mt. Olympus
9,570 ft. (2,916 m)

Helsinki

Gulf of Bothnia

Baltic Sea

Lódz
Prague
Oder R.
Elbe R.

Berlin

Budapest
HUNGARIAN PLAIN
Danube R.
Belgrade

DINARIC ALPS

Tiranë

Adriatic Sea

SICILY
(IT.)

Mediterranean Sea

Stockholm

Copenhagen
Hamburg
Amsterdam
Ghent
Cologne

Munich
Vienna

Zurich
Turin
Monte Corno
9,560 ft. (2,910 m)
Milan
Po R.
PLAIN OF
LOMBARDY

APENNINES

Naples
Mt. Vesuvius
4,190 ft.
(1,280 m)
Rome

CORSICA
(FR.)
SARDINIA
(IT.)

Oslo

Matterhorn
14,690 ft. (4,480 m)
Mt. Blanc
15,770 ft. (4,810 m)
Rhine R.

Paris

Marseille

Barcelona

BALEARIC IS.
(SP.)

Arctic Circle

70°

ARCTIC OCEAN

Reykjavik

60° N

Barents Sea

Norwegian Sea

FAEROE IS.
(DEN.)

SHETLAND IS.
(U.K.)

ORKNEY IS.
(U.K.)

OUTER HEBRIDES
(U.K.)

North Sea

Glasgow
Birmingham
London
English Channel

Dublin

Bay
of
Biscay

ATLANTIC
OCEAN

50° N

0°
10° W
20° W
10° E

PYRENEES
Pico de Aneto
11,168 ft. (3,404 m)

MESETA

Madrid

Lisbon

Gibraltar
(U.K.)

A F R I C A

615

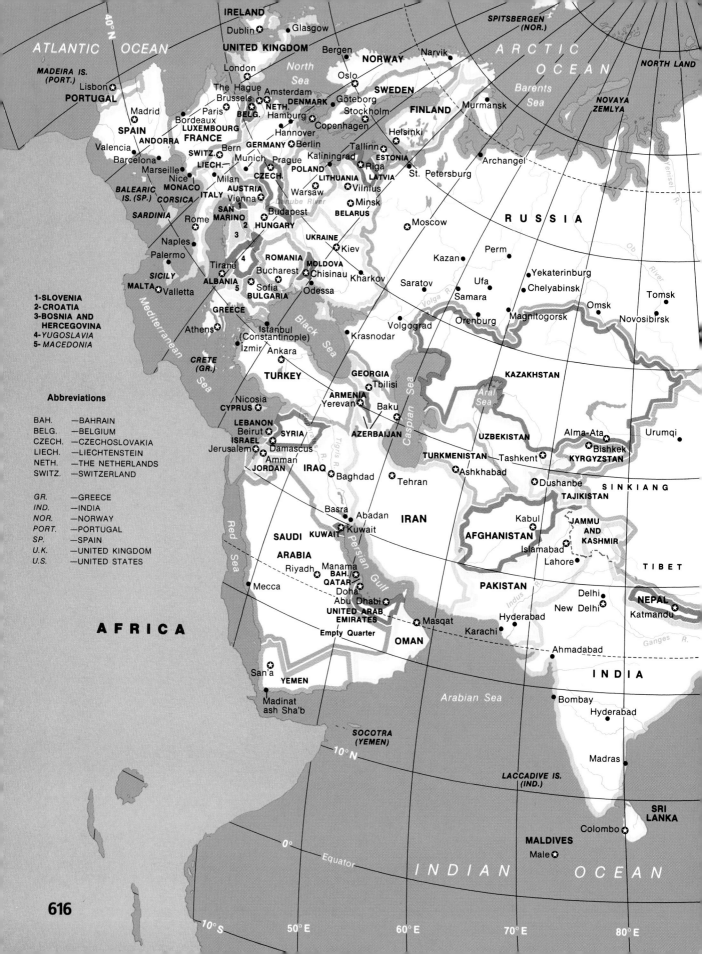

NEW
SIBERIAN
IS.

Bering Sea

*ALEUTIAN IS.
(U.S.)*

40°N

30°N

Magadan

*Kamtchatka
Peninsula*

S I B E R I A

Yakutsk

*Sea of
Okhotsk*

Lena R.

R U S S I A

SAKHALIN

KURIL IS.

20°N

Krasnoyarsk

Khabarovsk

Irkutsk

Amur

MANCHURIA

Harbin

Vladivostok

Sapporo

*Sea
of
Japan*

JAPAN

Tokyo
Yokohama

✪ Ulan Bator

Fushun
Shenyang

MONGOLIA

INNER
MONGOLIA

N. KOREA
✪ Pyongyang
Dalian

Kyōto   Nagoya
Kōbe   Ōsaka

Great Wall

✪ Beijing

Seoul
S. KOREA

Pusan

Tianjin

He

Kitakyūshū

Taiyuan

Lanzhou

Nanjing

Shanghai

Qingdao

Huang

*East
China
Sea*

RYUKYU IS. (JAPAN)

P A C I F I C

10°N

Xi'an

Wuhan

C H I N A

Chang   *Jiang*

Chengdu

Chongqing

Taipei

TAIWAN

O C E A N

Tropic of Cancer

FEDERATED STATES OF MICRONESIA

Lhasa

BHUTAN
✪ Thimbu

Guangzhou
Hong Kong
Macao   (U.K.)
(Port.)

Brahmaputra R.

Kunming

BANGLADESH
✪ Dacca   Mandalay
Calcutta

Hanoi

*South
China
Sea*

0°

MYANMAR

LAOS

✪ Vientiane

Hue
Da Nang

Manila

PHILIPPINES

Equator

*Bay
of
Bengal*

Rangoon

THAILAND

VIETNAM

Bangkok
CAMBODIA
Phnom
Penh

Ho Chi Minh
City

Davao

Djajapura

Lae

*ANDAMAN
IS. (IND.)*

Bandar
Seri
Begawan

Manado

IRIAN
JAYA

PAPUA NEW GUINEA

✪ BRUNEI

NEW GUINEA

Port Moresby

*NICOBAR
IS. (IND.)*

M A L A Y S I A

BORNEO

CELEBES

Coral Sea

Medan

✪ Kuala Lumpur

Samarinda

Arafura Sea

✪ Singapore

Pontianak
Bandjermasin

Ujung
Pandang

SUMATRA

I N D O N E S I A

TIMOR

617

Palembang

JAVA   Surabaja

A U S T R A L I A

Jakarta
✪ Bandung

90°E   100°E

EURASIA: POLITICAL

✪ National capitals

● Other cities

0   400   800 miles

0   400   800 kilometers

EURASIA: PHYSICAL

Elevations
Feet   Meters
10,000 --- 3,000
5,000 --- 1,500
2,000 --- 600
1,000 --- 300
0 --- 0

Land below sea level

0 — 400 — 800 miles
0 — 400 — 800 kilometers

Laptev Sea
NEW SIBERIAN ISLANDS
Peninsula
CHERSKI RANGE
VERKHOYANSK RANGE
KOLYMA RANGE
ALEUTIAN ISLANDS
Bering Sea
Kamtchatka Peninsula
CENTRAL RANGE

CENTRAL SIBERIAN PLATEAU
Lena River
Aldan River
Sea of Okhotsk
KURIL ISLANDS

S I B E R I A
Lower Tunguska R.
Angara River
Shilka River
Amur River
SAKHALIN
Shika River

SAYAN MTS.
Lake Baikal
Yenisei River
MONGOLIAN PLATEAU
MANCHURIA PLAIN
Harbin
HOKKAIDŌ

GREAT KHINGAN MTS.
Shenyang
HONSHŪ
Sea of Japan
Tokyo
Mt. Fujiyama
12,388 ft.
(3,776 m)

_ MTS.
THE GOBI
Great Wall
Beijing
Dalian
Tianjin
Yellow Sea
Korea Strait
Kyōto
SHIKOKU
KYŪSHŪ

NAN SHAN
NORTH CHINA PLAIN
Huang He
RYUKYU ISLANDS

OF ETI
SHAN
Shanghai
Chang Jiang
East China Sea
OKINAWA

Y A
Chongqing
BOREA HILLS
TAIWAN
Philippine Sea
PACIFIC

Brahmaputra River
Xi River
Ghuangzhou
Hong Kong
Luzon Strait
PHILIPPINE ISLANDS

Calcutta
HAINAN
LUZON
Manila
OCEAN

Salween River
Irrawaddy River
Mekong River
SAMAR
ADMIRALTY ISLANDS
NEW IRELAND

Bay of Bengal
South China Sea
MINDORO
PANAY
NEGROS
MINDANAO
NEW BRITAIN

Indochina Peninsula
PALAWAN

ANDAMAN ISLANDS
Gulf of Siam
Ho Chi Minh City
Celebes Sea
HALMAHERA
NEW GUINEA
SNOW MTS.

Andaman Sea
MOLUCCAS
ARU ISLANDS
Arafura Sea
Coral Sea

NICOBAR ISLANDS
NATUNA ISLANDS
CERAM
BURU

BORNEO
CELEBES

SUMATRA
MENTAWAI ISLANDS
Strait of Malacca

BANGKA
SUNDA ISLANDS
Java Sea
FLORES
TIMOR
619

Jakarta
BALI
JAVA
LOMBOK
SUMBAWA
SUMBA
AUSTRALIA

40° N
30° N
Tropic of Cancer
10° N
0°
90° E
100° E

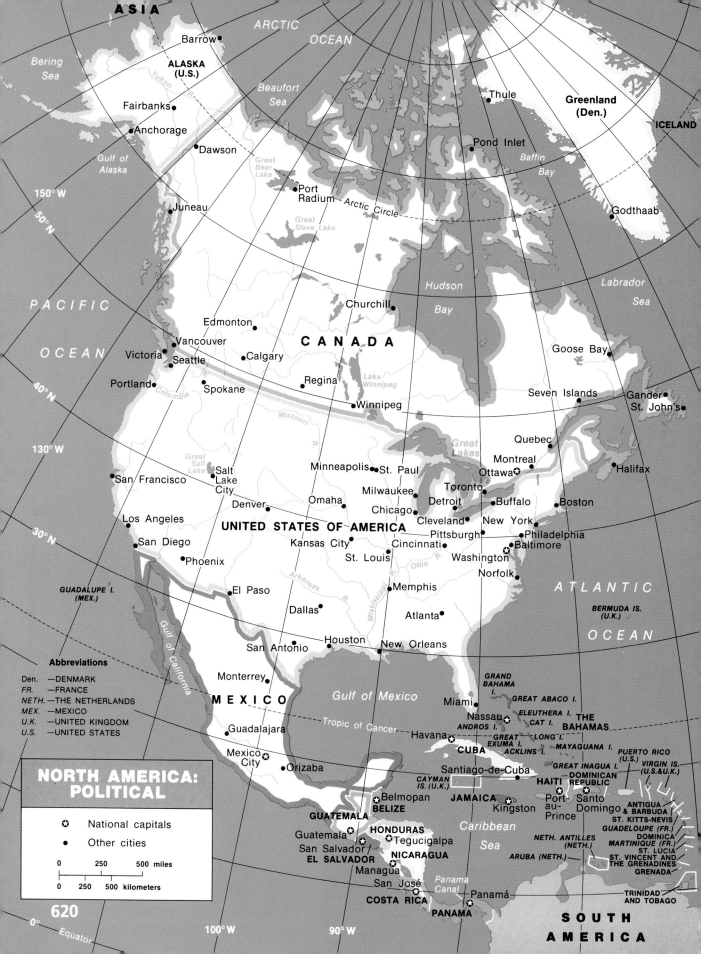

ASIA

ARCTIC OCEAN

Bering Sea

Barrow •

ALASKA (U.S.)

Beaufort Sea

Thule •

Greenland (Den.)

ICELAND

Fairbanks •
• Anchorage

Pond Inlet •

• Dawson

Gulf of Alaska

Great Bear Lake

Baffin Bay

150° W

• Port Radium

Arctic Circle

Godthaab •

50° N

• Juneau

Great Slave Lake

PACIFIC OCEAN

Hudson Bay

Labrador Sea

Churchill •

CANADA

Edmonton •

Vancouver

Goose Bay •

Victoria •
Seattle •

• Calgary

Gander •
St. John's •

40° N

Portland •

Regina •

Lake Winnipeg

Seven Islands •

130° W

Spokane •

Columbia R.

• Winnipeg

Missouri R.

Great Lakes

Quebec •

Halifax •

Montreal •
Ottawa ✪

San Francisco •

Great Salt Lake

Salt Lake City •

Minneapolis • • St. Paul

Toronto •
Buffalo •

Boston •

30° N

Los Angeles •

Denver •

Omaha •

Milwaukee •
Chicago •

Detroit •

New York •

San Diego •

UNITED STATES OF AMERICA

Cleveland •

Philadelphia •

• Phoenix

Kansas City •

Cincinnati •

Pittsburgh •

Baltimore •

St. Louis •

Ohio R.

Washington ✪

ATLANTIC OCEAN

GUADALUPE I. (MEX.)

El Paso •

Arkansas R.

Memphis •

Norfolk •

Dallas •

BERMUDA IS. (U.K.)

Gulf of California

San Antonio •

Houston •

Atlanta •

New Orleans •

OCEAN

Abbreviations

Monterrey •

Gulf of Mexico

Miami •

GRAND BAHAMA I.

GREAT ABACO I.

Den. —DENMARK
FR. —FRANCE
NETH. —THE NETHERLANDS
MEX. —MEXICO
U.K. —UNITED KINGDOM
U.S. —UNITED STATES

MEXICO

Tropic of Cancer

Nassau ✪

ELEUTHERA I.
CAT I.

THE BAHAMAS

ANDROS I.

Havana ✪

GREAT EXUMA I.

LONG I.

MAYAGUANA I.

PUERTO RICO (U.S.)

Guadalajara •

CUBA

ACKLINS I.

VIRGIN IS. (U.S.&U.K.)

Mexico City ✪

• Orizaba

Santiago-de-Cuba •

GREAT INAGUA I.

DOMINICAN REPUBLIC

CAYMAN IS. (U.K.)

HAITI

Santo Domingo

NORTH AMERICA: POLITICAL

Belmopan ✪

JAMAICA ✪

Port-au-Prince

ANTIGUA & BARBUDA

BELIZE

Kingston •

ST. KITTS-NEVIS

✪ National capitals

GUATEMALA

GUADELOUPE (FR.)

• Other cities

HONDURAS

Caribbean Sea

DOMINICA

Guatemala ✪

• Tegucigalpa

NETH. ANTILLES (NETH.)

MARTINIQUE (FR.)

0 250 500 miles

San Salvador

NICARAGUA

ST. LUCIA

0 250 500 kilometers

EL SALVADOR

ARUBA (NETH.)

ST. VINCENT AND THE GRENADINES

Managua ✪

GRENADA

San José ✪

Panama Canal

Panamá •

TRINIDAD AND TOBAGO

620

COSTA RICA

PANAMA ✪

SOUTH AMERICA

0°

Equator

100° W

90° W

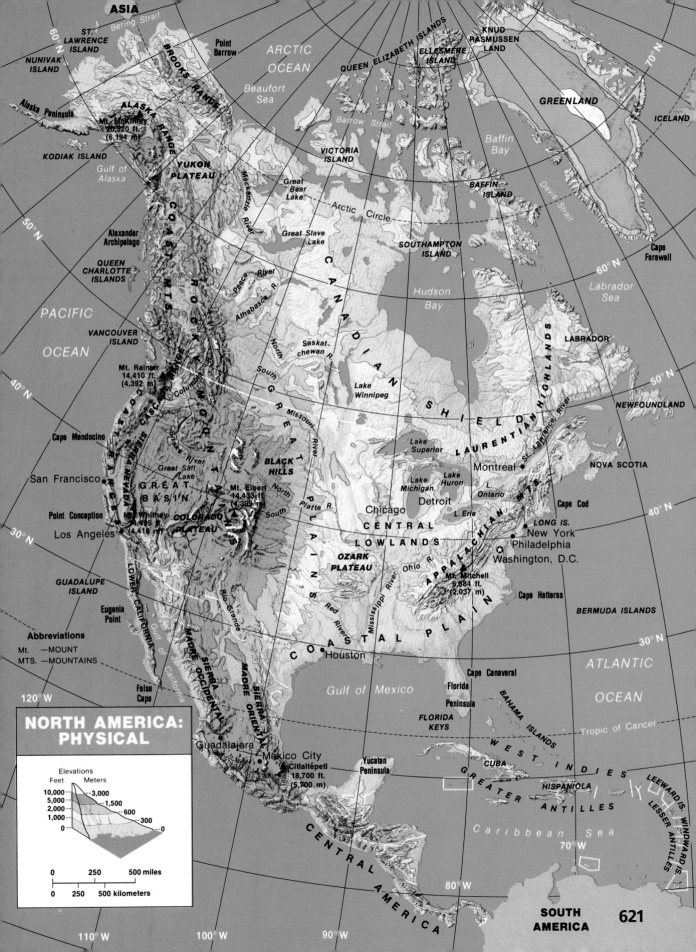

NORTH AMERICA: PHYSICAL

ASIA

Bering Strait

ST. LAWRENCE ISLAND

NUNIVAK ISLAND

Point Barrow

ARCTIC OCEAN

Beaufort Sea

QUEEN ELIZABETH ISLANDS

ELLESMERE ISLAND

KNUD RASMUSSEN LAND

GREENLAND

ICELAND

Alaska Peninsula

ALASKA RANGE

Mt. McKinley
20,320 ft.
(6,194 m)

BROOKS RANGE

Barrow Strait

VICTORIA ISLAND

Baffin Bay

Cape Farewell

KODIAK ISLAND

Gulf of Alaska

YUKON PLATEAU

Mackenzie River

Great Bear Lake

Arctic Circle

SOUTHAMPTON ISLAND

BAFFIN ISLAND

Davis Strait

Alexander Archipelago

Great Slave Lake

Labrador Sea

QUEEN CHARLOTTE ISLANDS

Peace River

Athabasca R.

C A N A D I A N   S H I E L D

Hudson Bay

LABRADOR

PACIFIC OCEAN

VANCOUVER ISLAND

North Saskatchewan R.

Saskat- chewan R.

Cape Mendocino

Mt. Rainier
14,410 ft.
(4,392 m)

Columbia R.

South Saskatchewan R.

Lake Winnipeg

NEWFOUNDLAND

Snake River

Missouri River

BLACK HILLS

Lake Superior

LAURENTIAN HIGHLANDS

St. Lawrence River

NOVA SCOTIA

San Francisco

Great Salt Lake

GREAT BASIN

Mt. Elbert
14,433 ft.
(4,399 m)

North Platte R.

Lake Michigan

Lake Huron

Montreal

Cape Cod

Point Conception

Mt. Whitney
14,495 ft.
(4,418 m)

COLORADO PLATEAU

South Platte R.

Detroit

L. Ontario

L. Erie

LONG IS.

Los Angeles

Chicago

C E N T R A L

New York

Philadelphia

Washington, D.C.

OZARK PLATEAU

Ohio R.

L O W L A N D S

APPALACHIAN

Mt. Mitchell
6,684 ft.
(2,037 m)

GUADALUPE ISLAND

Rio Grande

Red River

Mississippi River

Cape Hatteras

BERMUDA ISLANDS

Eugenia Point

C O A S T A L   P L A I N

Abbreviations

Mt. —MOUNT
MTS. —MOUNTAINS

False Cape

Gulf of California

LOWER CALIFORNIA

Houston

Cape Canaveral

ATLANTIC OCEAN

Florida

Gulf of Mexico

Florida Peninsula

Tropic of Cancer

SIERRA MADRE OCCIDENTAL

SIERRA MADRE ORIENTAL

FLORIDA KEYS

BAHAMA ISLANDS

W E S T   I N D I E S

Guadalajara

Mexico City

Citlaltépetl
18,700 ft.
(5,700 m)

Yucatan Peninsula

CUBA

GREATER ANTILLES

HISPANIOLA

LEEWARD IS.

WINDWARD IS.

LESSER ANTILLES

C E N T R A L   A M E R I C A

Caribbean Sea

Elevations

Feet	Meters
10,000	3,000
5,000	1,500
2,000	600
1,000	300
0	0

0   250   500 miles

0   250   500 kilometers

SOUTH AMERICA

MALPELO I.
(COL.)

Barranquilla
Cartagena
Maracaibo
Cúcuta
San Cristóbal
Medellín
Bucaramanga
Bogotá
Cali

Valencia
Caracas
Barquisimeto

VENEZUELA

Georgetown
Paramaribo
Cayenne
**French
Guiana
(Fr.)**

GUYANA

SURINAME

COLOMBIA

Quito

ECUADOR

Guayaquil
Iquitos

P E R U

Trujillo

Callao
Lima
Cuzco
Lake Titicaca
Arequipa
La Paz

BOLIVIA

Sucre

Chuquicamata

Antofagasta

Manaus

Belém
São Luis

Fortaleza

B R A Z I L

Recife
Maceió

Salvador

Brasília
(Federal District)

Belo Horizonte

Rio de Janeiro
São Paulo
Niterói
Curitiba
Santos

PARAGUAY

Asunción

Tucumán

Pôrto Alegre

P A C I F I C

O C E A N

SAN FELIX I.
(CHILE)
SAN AMBROSIO I.
(CHILE)

C H I L E

A T L A N T I C

Córdoba
Santa
Fe
Paraná
Rosario
Buenos Aires
La Plata

URUGUAY

Montevideo

O C E A N

JUAN FERNÁNDEZ IS.
(CHILE)

Valparaiso
Santiago
Concepción

A R G E N T I N A

Bahía Blanca
Mar del Plata

Rio de la Plata

FALKLAND IS. (U.K.)
(MALVINAS IS.)

Strait of
Magellan

Punta Arenas

Equator

Tropic of Capricorn

10° N

0°

10° S

20° S

30° S

40° S

50° S

90° W

80° W

60° W

50° W

40° W

30° W

Abbreviations

COL. — COLOMBIA
Fr. — FRANCE
U.K. — UNITED KINGDOM

**SOUTH AMERICA:
POLITICAL**

⊛   National capitals

•   Other cities

0   500 miles

0   500 kilometers

622

Caribbean Sea

Guajira Pen.

MARGARITA I.

Caracas

Orinoco River Delta

10° N

L. Maracaibo

Orinoco R.

GUIANA HIGHLANDS

Angel Falls

DEVILS I.

C. Orange

Abbreviations

ARCH.	—ARCHIPELAGO
C.	—CAPE
G.	—GULF
Mt.	—MOUNT
Pen.	—PENINSULA
Pt.	—POINT
U.K.	—UNITED KINGDOM

G. of Panama

Mt. Tolima 18,425 ft. (5,616 m)

Bogotá

Magdalena R.

Meta R.

LLANOS

Orinoco R.

Amazon River Delta

MALPELO I.

Caqueta R.

Rio Negro R.

MARAJÓ I.

0°

AMAZON

Japura R.

Amazon R.

Equator

Mt. Chimborazo 20,561 ft. (6,267 m)

R.

BASIN

Tapajóz R.

Xingu R.

Tocantins R.

Parnaiba R.

C. São Roque

Gulf of Guayaquil

Marañón R.

Juruá R.

R.

Araguaia R.

São Francisco R.

Aguja Pt.

Purus R.

Madeira R.

Tocantins R.

Mt. Huascarán 22,205 ft. (6,768 m)

Ucayali R.

Beni R.

10° S

Lima

Mamoré R.

MATO

Lake Titicaca

GROSSO

Brasília

Mt. Ancohuma 21,490 ft. (6,612 m)

L. Poopó

PLATEAU

BRAZILIAN

ANDES

GRAN

Paraguay R.

R.

HIGHLANDS

Mt. Bandeira 9,495 ft. (2,894 m)

ATACAMA DESERT

Pilcomayo R.

20° S

Tropic of Capricorn

CHACO

Paraná R.

São Paulo

SAN FELIX I.

SAN AMBROSIO I.

R.

Salado R.

R.

C. Frio

Rio de Janeiro

ATLANTIC

Mt. Aconcagua 22,834 ft. (6,960 m)

Paraná R.

Uruguay R.

30° S

PACIFIC

Santiago

MOUNTAINS

Buenos Aires

Montevideo

OCEAN

JUAN FERNÁNDEZ IS.

PAMPAS

Rio de la Plata

OCEAN

Colorado R.

40° W

30° W

Blanca Bay

San Matías Gulf

SOUTH AMERICA: PHYSICAL

Elevations

Feet	Meters
10,000	3,000
5,000	1,500
2,000	600
1,000	300
0	0

0 ——— 500 miles

0 ——— 500 kilometers

CHILOÉ I.

Valdés Pen.

CHONOS ARCH.

Gulf of San Jorge

Taitao Pen.

C. Tres Puntas

PATAGONIA

40° S

FALKLAND IS. (U.K.) (MALVINAS IS.)

Grande Bay

Strait of Magellan

Strait of Magellan

TIERRA DEL FUEGO

90° W

80° W

70° W

60° W

50° W

50° S

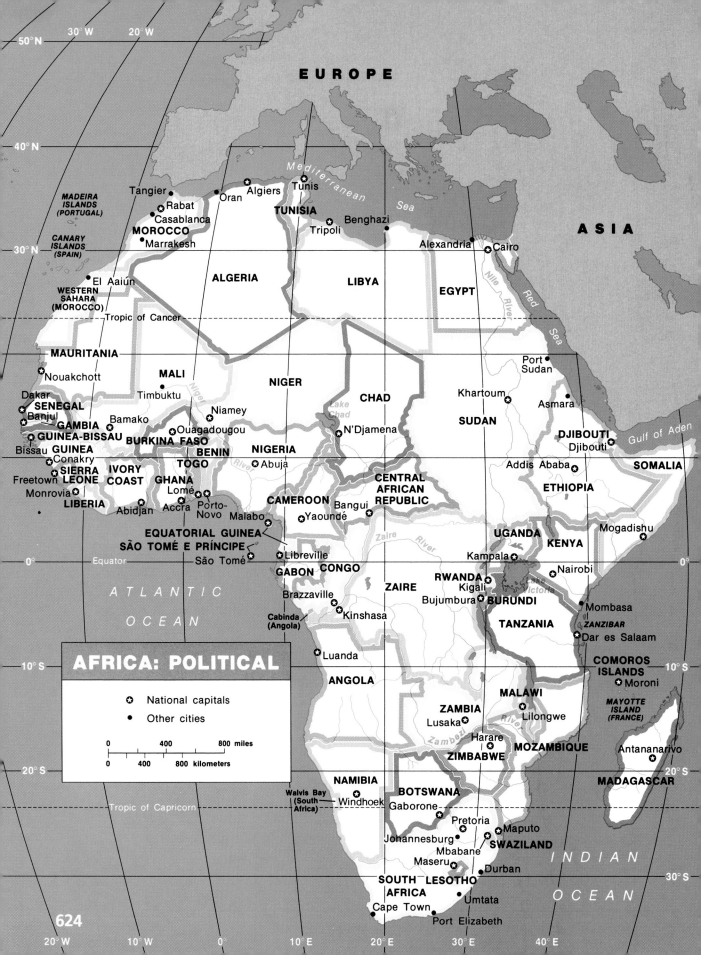

AFRICA: POLITICAL

EUROPE

ASIA

Mediterranean Sea

Tangier • Rabat
MADEIRA ISLANDS (PORTUGAL)
⊕ Algiers ⊕ Tunis
Oran • TUNISIA
Casablanca ⊕
MOROCCO
• Marrakesh
Benghazi •
Tripoli ⊕
Alexandria • ⊕ Cairo

CANARY ISLANDS (SPAIN)

30° N

El Aaiún •

ALGERIA

LIBYA

EGYPT

Nile River
Red Sea

WESTERN SAHARA (MOROCCO)

Tropic of Cancer

MAURITANIA

Nouakchott ⊕

MALI

Timbuktu •

NIGER

CHAD

Port Sudan •

Khartoum ⊕

Asmara •

Niger River

Dakar ⊕
SENEGAL
Banjul ⊕
GAMBIA
Bissau ⊕
GUINEA-BISSAU
Conakry ⊕
GUINEA
SIERRA LEONE
Freetown ⊕
Monrovia ⊕
LIBERIA

Bamako ⊕
Niamey ⊕
BURKINA FASO
Ouagadougou ⊕
BENIN
TOGO
IVORY COAST
GHANA
Lomé ⊕
Accra ⊕
Abidjan •
Porto-Novo ⊕
Malabo ⊕

N'Djamena ⊕

NIGERIA

Abuja ⊕

SUDAN

DJIBOUTI
Djibouti ⊕

Addis Ababa ⊕

SOMALIA

CAMEROON

Bangui ⊕
Yaoundé ⊕

CENTRAL AFRICAN REPUBLIC

ETHIOPIA

Mogadishu •

EQUATORIAL GUINEA
SÃO TOMÉ E PRÍNCIPE
São Tomé ⊕
Libreville ⊕
GABON
CONGO
Brazzaville ⊕
Cabinda (Angola)
Kinshasa ⊕

ZAIRE

Zaire River

UGANDA
Kampala ⊕

KENYA

Nairobi •

RWANDA
Kigali ⊕
Bujumbura ⊕
BURUNDI

Lake Victoria

Mombasa •

Equator

ATLANTIC OCEAN

Luanda ⊕

TANZANIA

ZANZIBAR
Dar es Salaam •

10° S

ANGOLA

ZAMBIA
Lusaka ⊕

MALAWI
Lilongwe •

COMOROS ISLANDS
Moroni ⊕

MAYOTTE ISLAND (FRANCE)

Zambezi River

Harare ⊕
ZIMBABWE

MOZAMBIQUE

Antananarivo •

MADAGASCAR

National capitals ⊕
Other cities •

0   400   800 miles
0   400   800 kilometers

NAMIBIA

Walvis Bay (South Africa)
Windhoek ⊕

BOTSWANA
Gaborone •

Tropic of Capricorn

Pretoria ⊕
Johannesburg •
Maputo ⊕
SWAZILAND
Mbabane ⊕
Maseru ⊕
Durban •

INDIAN OCEAN

SOUTH AFRICA
LESOTHO
Cape Town •
Umtata •
Port Elizabeth •

30° S

624

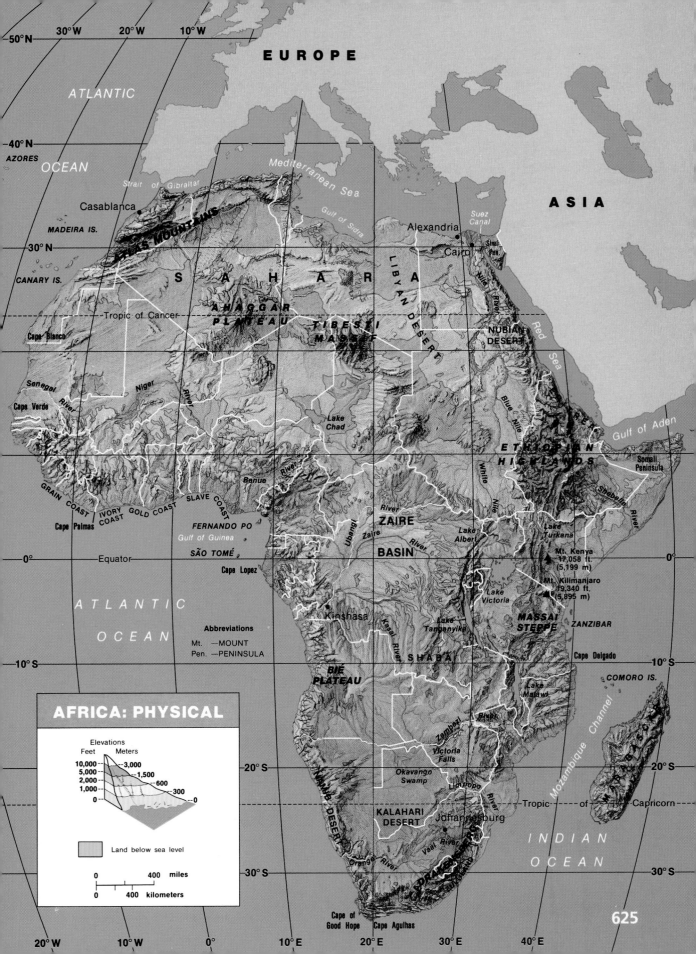

AFRICA: PHYSICAL

EUROPE

ATLANTIC

OCEAN

Mediterranean Sea

ASIA

AZORES

Strait of Gibraltar

Gulf of Sidra

Casablanca

MADEIRA IS.

ATLAS MOUNTAINS

Alexandria

Suez Canal

Cairo

Sinai Pen.

CANARY IS.

S A H A R A

L I B Y A N   D E S E R T

Nile River

Red Sea

Tropic of Cancer

AHAGGAR PLATEAU

TIBESTI MASSIF

NUBIAN DESERT

Cape Blanco

Senegal River

Niger River

Lake Chad

Blue Nile

Gulf of Aden

Cape Verde

ETHIOPIAN HIGHLANDS

Somali Peninsula

GRAIN COAST

IVORY COAST

GOLD COAST

SLAVE COAST

Benue River

Ubangi River

Zaire River

White Nile

Shebelle River

Cape Palmas

FERNANDO PO

Gulf of Guinea

SÃO TOMÉ

ZAIRE

BASIN

Lake Albert

Lake Turkana

Mt. Kenya
17,058 ft.
(5,199 m)

Equator

Cape Lopez

Kasai River

Lake Victoria

Mt. Kilimanjaro
19,340 ft.
(5,895 m)

A T L A N T I C

O C E A N

Kinshasa

Lake Tanganyika

MASSAI STEPPE

ZANZIBAR

Abbreviations

Mt. —MOUNT
Pen. —PENINSULA

SHABA

Cape Delgado

BIÉ PLATEAU

Lake Malawi

COMORO IS.

Zambezi River

Victoria Falls

Okavango Swamp

Limpopo River

Mozambique Channel

MADAGASCAR

Tropic of Capricorn

Elevations

Feet	Meters
10,000	3,000
5,000	1,500
2,000	600
1,000	300
0	0

Land below sea level

KALAHARI DESERT

Johannesburg

NAMIB DESERT

DRAKENSBERG

Orange River

Vaal River

INDIAN

OCEAN

| 0 | 400 miles |
| 0 | 400 kilometers |

Cape of Good Hope

Cape Agulhas

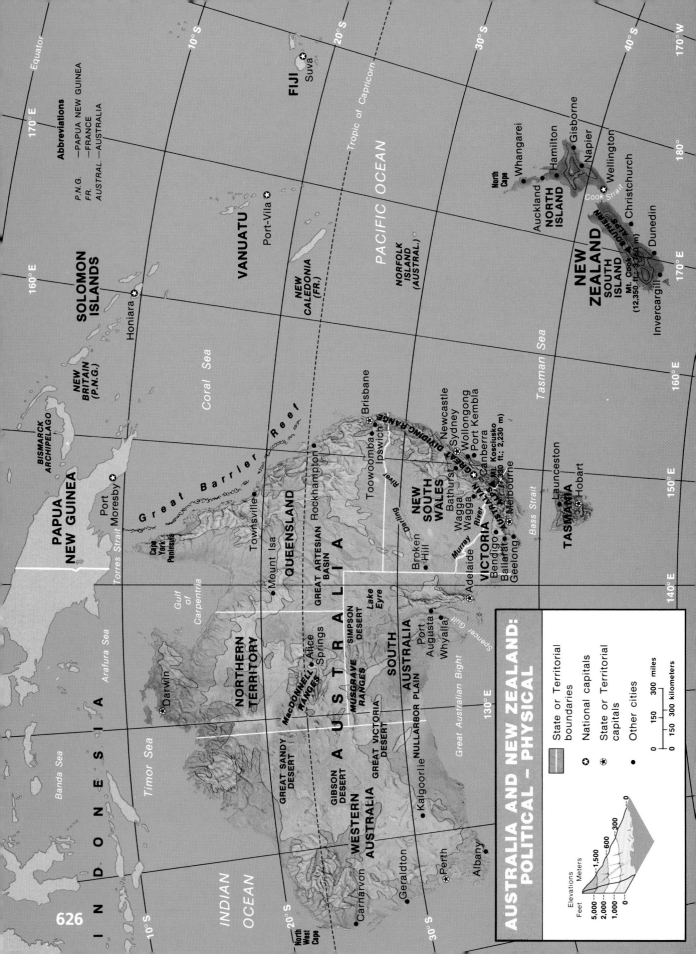

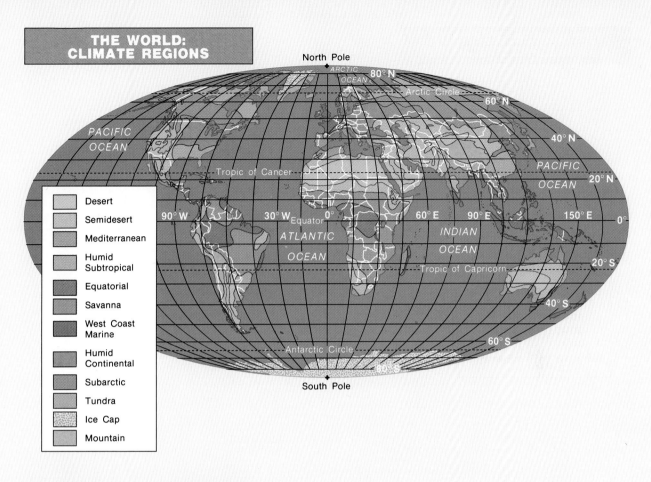

THE WORLD: CLIMATE REGIONS

- Desert
- Semidesert
- Mediterranean
- Humid Subtropical
- Equatorial
- Savanna
- West Coast Marine
- Humid Continental
- Subarctic
- Tundra
- Ice Cap
- Mountain

North Pole
ARCTIC OCEAN
80° N
Arctic Circle
60° N
40° N
PACIFIC OCEAN
PACIFIC OCEAN
20° N
Tropic of Cancer
90° W
30° W
Equator
0°
60° E
90° E
150° E
0°
ATLANTIC OCEAN
INDIAN OCEAN
Tropic of Capricorn
20° S
40° S
Antarctic Circle
60° S
80° S
South Pole

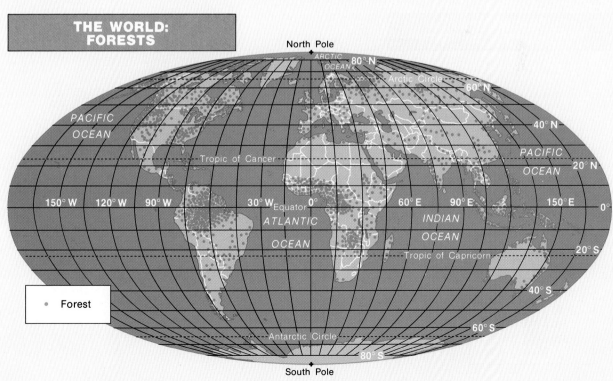

THE WORLD: FORESTS

- Forest

North Pole
ARCTIC OCEAN
80° N
Arctic Circle
60° N
40° N
PACIFIC OCEAN
PACIFIC OCEAN
20° N
Tropic of Cancer
150° W
120° W
90° W
30° W
Equator
0°
60° E
90° E
150° E
0°
ATLANTIC OCEAN
INDIAN OCEAN
Tropic of Capricorn
20° S
40° S
60° S
Antarctic Circle
80° S
South Pole

627

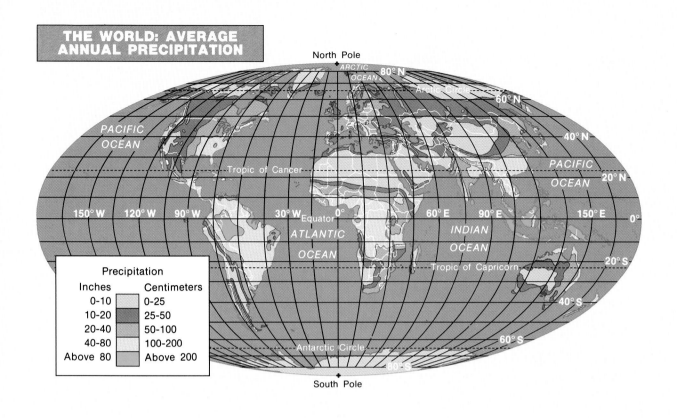

THE WORLD: AVERAGE ANNUAL PRECIPITATION

North Pole

ARCTIC OCEAN

80° N

Arctic Circle

60° N

40° N

PACIFIC OCEAN

Tropic of Cancer

PACIFIC OCEAN

20° N

150° W   120° W   90° W   30° W   Equator   0°   60° E   90° E   150° E   0°

ATLANTIC OCEAN

INDIAN OCEAN

20° S

Tropic of Capricorn

40° S

Precipitation

Inches	Centimeters
0-10	0-25
10-20	25-50
20-40	50-100
40-80	100-200
Above 80	Above 200

Antarctic Circle

60° S

80° S

South Pole

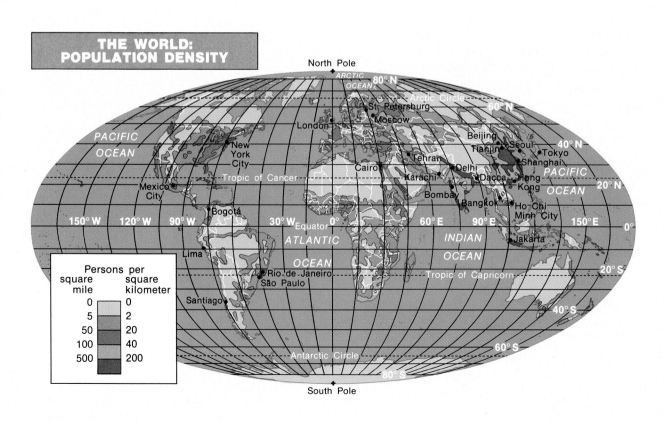

THE WORLD: POPULATION DENSITY

North Pole

ARCTIC OCEAN

80° N

Arctic Circle

60° N

St. Petersburg
Moscow
London

Beijing
Tianjin   Seoul
New York City   Tehran   Delhi   Shanghai
Cairo   Karachi   Dacca   Hong Kong
Mexico City   Bombay   Bangkok

40° N

PACIFIC OCEAN

Tropic of Cancer

PACIFIC OCEAN

20° N

Bogotá

Ho Chi Minh City

150° W   120° W   90° W   30° W   Equator   0°   60° E   90° E   150° E   0°

Lima

ATLANTIC OCEAN

INDIAN OCEAN

Jakarta

Rio de Janeiro
São Paulo

Tropic of Capricorn

20° S

Santiago

40° S

Persons per

square mile	square kilometer
0	0
5	2
50	20
100	40
500	200

Antarctic Circle

60° S

80° S

South Pole

628

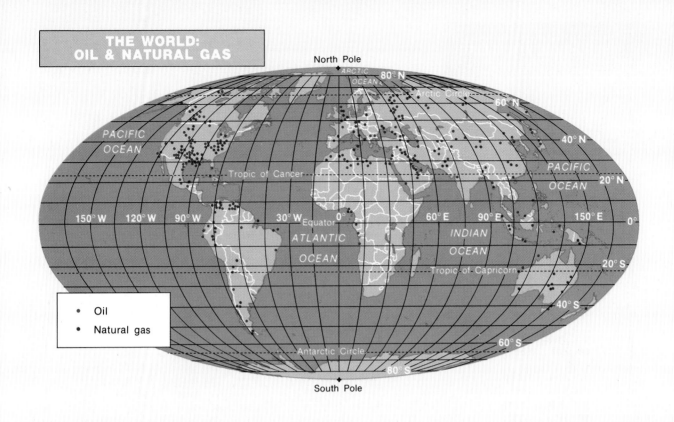

THE WORLD: OIL & NATURAL GAS

- Oil
- Natural gas

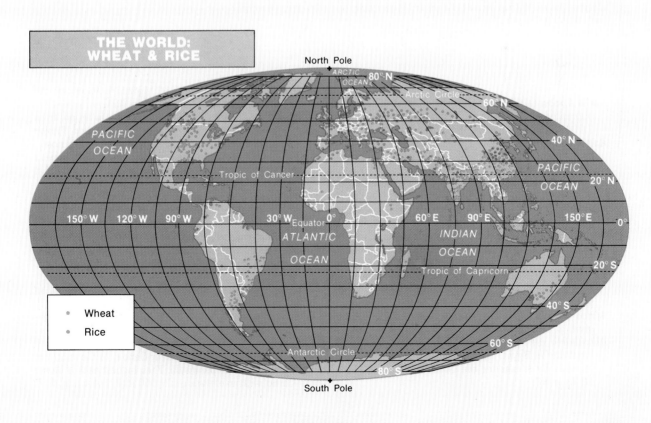

THE WORLD: WHEAT & RICE

- Wheat
- Rice

Some words in this book may be new to you or difficult to pronounce. Those words have been spelled phonetically in parentheses. The syllable that receives stress in a word is shown in small capital letters.

For example: **Chicago** (shuh KAH goh)

Most phonetic spellings are easy to read. In the following Pronunciation Key, you can see how letters are used to show different sounds.

PRONUNCIATION KEY

a	after	(AF tur)	oh	flow	(floh)	ch	chicken	(CHIHK un)
ah	father	(FAH thur)	oi	boy	(boi)	g	game	(gaym)
ai	care	(kair)	oo	rule	(rool)	ing	coming	(KUM ing)
aw	dog	(dawg)	or	horse	(hors)	j	job	(jahb)
ay	paper	(PAY pur)	ou	cow	(kou)	k	came	(kaym)
						ng	long	(lawng)
e	letter	(LET ur)	yoo	few	(fyoo)	s	city	(SIH tee)
ee	eat	(eet)	u	taken	(TAY kun)	sh	ship	(shihp)
				matter	(MAT ur)	th	thin	(thihn)
ih	trip	(trihp)	uh	ago	(uh GOH)	thh	feather	(FETHH ur)
eye	idea	(eye DEE uh)				y	yard	(yahrd)
y	hide	(hyd)				z	size	(syz)
ye	lie	(lye)				zh	division	(duh VIHZH un)

The Gazetteer is a geographical dictionary. It shows latitude and longitude for cities and certain other places. The page reference at the end of each entry in the Gazetteer gives the page on which the entry is shown on a map.

A

Addis Ababa (AD ihs AB uh buh). Capital of and most populated city in Ethiopia. Located at an elevation of 7,900 ft (2,408 m). (9°N/39°E) p. 478.

Adelaide (AD ul ayd). Capital of the Australian state of Victoria. Located near a gulf of the Indian Ocean. (35°S/139°E) p. 591.

Aden (AHD un). Port city in Yemen. Located on the Gulf of Aden. (13°N/45°E) p. 404.

Adriatic Sea (ay dree AT ihk see). Arm of the Mediterranean Sea, between Italy and the Balkan Peninsula. p. 157.

Aegean Sea (ee JEE un see). Part of the Mediterranean Sea, between the eastern coast of Greece and the western coast of Turkey. Bounded on the north by the Greek mainland and on the south by Crete. p. 77.

Africa (AF rih kuh). The earth's second largest continent. p. 23.

Alexandria (al ihg ZAN dree uh). Second most populated city in Egypt. Located in the Nile Delta. It was founded by Alexander the Great in 332 B.C. (31°N/30°E) p. 87.

Algiers (al JIHRZ). Capital of Algeria. Located on the Mediterranean Sea. (37°N/3°E) p. 361.

Alps (alps). Mountain system extending in an arc from the Mediterranean coast between Italy and France through Switzerland and Austria and into the northwest coast of the former Yugoslavia. The highest peak is Mont Blanc, with an elevation of 15,771 ft (4,807 m). p. 157.

Amsterdam (AM stur dam). Capital of the Netherlands. Connected to the North Sea by a canal. (52°N/5°E) p. 166.

Anatolian plateau (an uh TOH lee un pla TOH). Plateau on which Asian Turkey is located. This plateau lies between the Black and the Mediterranean seas. p. 359.

Ankara (ANG kuh ruh). Capital of Turkey. Located in central Anatolia. (41°N/33°E) p. 361.

Antarctica (ant AHRK tih kuh). The earth's third smallest continent. p. 23.

Apennines (AP uh nynz). Mountains in Italy, extending from northwestern Italy, near Genoa, to the southern tip of the Italian peninsula. Their highest peak is Monte Corno, with an elevation of 9,560 ft (2,914 m). p. 157.

Arabian Peninsula (uh RAY bee un puh NIHN suh luh). Large peninsula located east of the Red Sea. p. 359.

Arabian Sea (uh RAY bee un see). Arm of the Indian Ocean, between India and the Arabian Peninsula. p. 359.

Aral Sea (AR ul see). Inland body of salt water in the southwestern Asian area of the former Soviet Union, east of the Caspian Sea. p. 285.

Arctic Circle (AHRK tihk SUR kul). Line of latitude located at 66 1/2° north latitude. p. 10.

Arctic Ocean (AHRK tihk OH shun). Large body of water north of the Arctic Circle. p. 285.

Asia (AY zhuh). The earth's largest continent. p. 23.

Asia Minor (AY zhuh MYE nur). Asian peninsula on which most of Turkey is located. It is bounded on the north by the Black Sea, on the west by the Aegean Sea, and on the south by the Mediterranean Sea. p. 77.

Aswan (ahs WAHN). City on the Nile River. Site of Aswan High Dam. (24°N/33°E) p. 51.

Athens (ATH unz). City-state in ancient Greece. Today it is the capital of and largest city in Greece. (38°N/24°E) p. 166.

Atlantic Ocean (at LAN tihk OH shun). Large body of water separating North America and South America from Europe and Africa. p. 23.

Atlas Mountains (AT lus MOUNT unz). Mountains located in Morocco, Algeria, and Tunisia, along the northern edge of the Sahara. The highest peak is Jebel Toubkal, with an elevation of 13,665 ft (4,165 m). p. 359.

Auckland (AWK lund). Seaport in northern New Zealand. (37°S/175°E) p. 576.

Australia (aw STRAYL yuh). The earth's smallest continent. p. 23.

Australian Alps (aw STRAYL ee un alps). Mountain range in southeastern Australia. The southern end of the Great Dividing Range. p. 574.

B

Babylon (BAB uh lun). Ancient city in the country of Mesopotamia. Located on the Euphrates River. The city's ruins are near the present-day city of Baghdad, Iraq. (33°N/44°E) p. 51.

Baghdad (BAG dad). National capital of and most populated city in present-day Iraq. Located on the Tigris River. One-time capital of the empire of the caliphs. (33°N/44°E) p. 359.

Bali (BAH lee). Island of Indonesia, east of Java. p. 508.

Balkan Peninsula (BAWL kun puh NIHN suh luh). Peninsula in southeastern Europe, between the Adriatic and Ionian seas on the west and the Aegean and Black seas on the east. Usually thought to consist of Greece, Albania, Bulgaria, Romania, the former Yugoslavia, and European Turkey. p. 157.

Baltic Sea (BAWL tihk see). Arm of the Atlantic Ocean, south and southeast of Sweden. p. 157.

Barbados (bahr BAY dohs). Country that is the easternmost island of the West Indies. pp. 610–611.

Barcelona (bahr suh LOH nuh). Large port city in northeastern Spain, on the Mediterranean Sea. (41°N/2°E) p. 166.

Bay of Bengal (bay uv ben GAWL). Arm of the Indian Ocean, between the eastern coast of India and the Malay Peninsula. p. 508.

Beijing (BAY JING). Capital of China. Formerly known as Peking. (40°N/116°E) p. 545.

Belfast (BEL fast). Seaport and the capital of Northern Ireland. (55°N/6°W) p. 255.

Belgrade (BEL grayd). Capital of Serbia. Formerly capital of Yugoslavia. Located where the Sava River joins the Danube River. (45°N/21°E) p. 326.

Benin (be NEEN). Former native kingdom located in what is now southern Nigeria. p. 457.

Bering Strait (BER ihng strayt). Narrow body of water that connects the Arctic Ocean and the Bering Sea. Separates Asia from North America. p. 285.

Berlin (bur LIHN) The capital of Germany. Formerly a divided city located in East Germany. East Berlin was the capital of East Germany. West Berlin, although surrounded by East Germany, was a part of West Germany. (53°N/13°E) p. 228.

Black Sea (blak see). Large sea located on the southern divide between Europe and Asia. p. 285.

Bombay (bahm BAY). City in western India. (19°N/73°E) p. 510.

Bonn (bahn). City in Germany; located on the Rhine River. Formerly capital of West Germany. (51°N/7°E) p. 249.

Borneo (BOR nee oh). Large island in the East Indies, southwest of the Philippines. p. 508.

Boston (BAWS tun). Capital of and most populated city in Massachusetts. Located on Massachusetts Bay. (42°N/71°W) p. 620.

Brahmaputra River (brahm uh POO truh RIHV ur). River that rises in southwestern Tibet. Joins the Ganges River near Dacca, India, before flowing into the Bay of Bengal. p. 508.

Brazzaville (BRAH zuh vihl). Riverport and capital of the Congo. (4°S/15°E) p. 446.

Brisbane (BRIHZ bayn). Capital of the Australian state of Queensland. Port city located on the east coast of Australia. (28°S/153°E) p. 591.

British Isles (BRIHT ihsh EYE ulz). Group of islands northwest of France. Includes Great Britain, Ireland, and several smaller islands. p. 255.

Brussels (BRUS ulz). Capital of Belgium. (51°N/4°E) p. 249.

Budapest (BOOD uh pest). Capital of Hungary. Located on both sides of the Danube River. (48°N/19°E) p. 326.

C

Cairo (KYE roh). Capital of Egypt. Most populated city in Africa. Located on the eastern side of the Nile River. (30°N/31°E) p. 404.

Calcutta (kal KUT uh). City in northeastern India, on the Hooghly River. (23°N/88°E) p. 510.

Canberra (KAN bur uh). Capital of Australia. Located in southeastern Australia. (35°S/149°E) p. 591.

Cape of Good Hope (kayp uv good hohp). Cape located on southeast coast of South Africa. (31°S/23°E) p. 440.

Carpathian Mountains (karh PAY thee un MOUNT unz). Mountains that stretch from the Alps in the west to the Balkans in the east. Highest peak is Gerlachovka Peak, with an elevation of 8,737 ft (2,663 m). p. 285.

Carthage (KAHR thihj). Ancient city and nation on coast of North Africa, near present-day city of Tunis, Tunisia. (37°N/10°E) p. 110.

Caspian Sea (KAS pee un see). Largest totally inland body of water in the world. Except for its southern shore, which borders Iran, the Caspian Sea is completely within the former Soviet Union. p. 285.

Caucasus Mountains (KAW kuh sus MOUNT unz). Very high mountains in the former Soviet Union. They form part of the southern divide between Europe and Asia. Highest peak is Mount Elbrus, with an elevation of 18,481 ft (5,633 m). p. 285.

Central America (SEN trul uh MER ih kuh). The narrow part of America between Mexico and South America. Central America includes Guatemala, Belize, El Salvador, Honduras, Nicaragua, Costa Rica, and Panama. pp. 610–611.

Chang Jiang (chahng jee AHNG). One of the world's longest rivers. Rises in Tibet and flows into the East China Sea near Shanghai, China. Formerly called Yangtze River. p. 508.

Cherrapunji (cher uh PUN jee). Village in northeast India. One of the wettest places on earth. Averages 450 in. (1143 cm) of rain a year. (25°N/92°E) p. 509.

Christchurch (KRYST CHURCH). City in New Zealand. Located on South Island. (44°S/173°E) p. 576.

Congo River (KAHNG goh RIHV ur). River that rises in southeastern Zaire as the Lualaba River. Flows into the Atlantic Ocean at Matadi, Zaire. One of the world's longest rivers. Former name of the Zaire River. p. 461.

Constantinople (kahn stan tuh NOH pul). City built by Emperor Constantine in A.D. 325 on the site of the ancient Greek city of Byzantium. Renamed Istanbul in 1930. (41°N/29°E) p. 390.

Copenhagen (koh pun HAY gun). Capital of and largest city in Denmark. Important port. (56°N/13°E) p. 249.

Corsica (KOR sih kuh). French island in the Mediterranean, southeast of France. p. 157.

Crimea (kry MEE uh). Peninsula in the Black Sea. Located in Ukraine. p. 285.

Cyprus (SYE prus). Country on an island in the Mediterranean, south of Turkey. p. 157.

D

Dakar (duh KAHR). Capital and seaport of Senegal, in western Africa. (15°N/17°W) p. 478.

Damascus (duh MAS kus). Capital of Syria. (34°N/36°E) p. 404.

Danube River (DAN yoob RIHV ur). Second longest river in Europe. It begins in the Alps and in Romania and flows into the Black Sea. The Danube passes through or borders many European countries. p. 285.

Dardanelles (dahr duh NELZ). Narrow strait in Turkey. Connects the Sea of Marmara and the Aegean Sea. Called the Hellespont in ancient times. p. 77.

Dead Sea (ded see). Salt lake located on the border between Israel and Jordan. (32°N/36°E) p. 65.

Deccan Plateau (DEK un pla TOH). Most of the peninsula of India, south of the Narbada River. pp. 618–619.

Delhi (DEL ee). City in India. Located on the Jumna River. Once the capital of Mogul India. (29°N/77°E) p. 510.

Dnieper River (NEE pur RIHV ur). Located in Russia. Rises in the Valdai Hills and flows into the Black Sea. p. 285.

Don River (dahn RIHV ur). Located in the former Soviet Union. Rises south of Moscow and flows into the Sea of Azov, which is part of the Black Sea. Connected by canal to the Volga River. p. 285.

Dublin (DUB lun). Seaport and capital of Ireland. Located on the Irish Sea. (53°N/6°W) p. 255.

E

East China Sea (eest CHYE nuh see). Arm of the Pacific Ocean, east of China and west of Kyūshū, Japan, and the Ryukyu Islands. pp. 618–619.

Eastern Ghats (EES turn gawts). Mountains located along the eastern coast of India. Highest peak is Mount Doda Betta, at an elevation of 8,640 ft (2,633 m). p. 508.

Eastern Hemisphere (EES turn HEM ih sfihr). The half of the earth east of the Prime Meridian. p. 9.

Edessa (ee DES uh). Greek city in western Macedonia. A capital of Macedonian kings in ancient times. (41°N/22°E) p. 391.

Edinburgh (ED un bur uh). The capital of Scotland. Located in the southeastern part of Scotland. (56°N/3°W) p. 255.

Elbe River (EL buh RIHV ur). Flows 724 miles (1,165 km), mostly through Germany, and empties into the North Sea. p. 285.

Elburz Mountains (el BOORZ MOUNT unz). Mountain range located in northern Iran. Separates the Plateau of Iran from the Caspian Sea. p. 359.

English Channel (IHNG glihsh CHAN ul). Arm of the Atlantic Ocean, between southern England and northwestern France. p. 157.

Equator (ee KWAYT ur). 0° latitude. A line drawn on maps that circles the earth halfway between the North Pole and the South Pole. p. 8.

Euphrates River (yoo FRAYT eez RIHV ur). River that rises in mountains in eastern Turkey and flows through Syria into Iraq, where it joins with the Tigris River near Al-Qurna to form the Shatt-al-Arab, which flows into the Persian Gulf. p. 51.

Eurasia (yoo RAY zhuh). Name often given to the total area covered by Europe and Asia. pp. 616–617.

Europe (YOOR up). The earth's second smallest continent. p. 23.

F

Florence (FLOR uns). City in Italy, located on the Arno River at the base of the Apennines. (44°N/11°E) p. 249.

G

Ganges River (GAN jeez RIHV ur). Sacred river of India. Rises in the Himalayas. Joined by the Brahmaputra River near Dacca before flowing into the Bay of Bengal. p. 129.

Gaul (gawl). Historical name for area that consisted of northern Italy and part of southern France. p. 110.

Gdańsk (guh DAHNSK). City in Poland. Located on Baltic Sea. Formerly known as Danzig. (54°N/19°E) p. 326.

Genoa (JEN uh wuh). City in Italy. One of the most important Italian seaports. (44°N/9°E) p. 166.

Gilbert Islands (GIHL burt EYE lundz). Group of islands in the west central Pacific Ocean. p. 591.

Gobi, The (GOH bee). The world's second largest desert. Located in northwestern China and Mongolia. p. 508.

Gold Cost (gohld kohst). Former British territory located along the Gulf of Guinea. Named for large amounts of gold once mined in the area. p. 469.

Great Barrier Reef (grayt BAR ee ur reef). World's largest deposit of coral. Located in the Coral Sea, off the northeast coast of Australia. p. 574.

Great Dividing Range (grayt duh VYD ihng raynj). Mountain area of Australia. Extends from north to south near most of the east coast. Highest peak is Mount Kosciusko, at 7,305 ft (2,226 m). p. 574.

Great Hungarian Plain (grayt hung GER ee un playn). Plain located mostly in Hungary. The Danube River crosses this plain. p. 285.

Great Lakes (grayt layks). Chain of five large lakes in central North America. Except for Lake Michigan, the lakes are on the Canada–United States boundary. p. 620.

Great Plains (grayt playnz). Large plain area located in the western part of the Central Plains of the United States. p. 621.

Great Rift Valley (grayt rihft VAL ee). Huge crack in the earth's surface that runs about 4,000 mi (6,436 km) from the Middle East into East Africa. p. 440.

Greenland (GREEN lund). Large island off the coast of northeastern North America belonging to Denmark. It is the largest island in the world with the exception of the continent of Australia. p. 21.

Greenwich (GREN ihch). Place in London, England, designated as 0° longitude. The Prime Meridian runs from the North Pole through Greenwich to the South Pole. (51°N/0°long) p. 9.

Guangzhou (GUAHNG joh). Large seaport city in southeastern China. Formerly known as Canton. (23°N/113°E) p. 510.

Gulf of Mexico (gulf uv MEKS ih koh). Large bay of the Atlantic Ocean. Bounded by Mexico on the west and south, Cuba on the east, and the United States on the north. p. 162.

Gulf Stream (gulf streem). Warm ocean current, about 50 mi (80 km) wide, that flows from the Gulf of Mexico along the United States coast and across the Atlantic to Europe. p. 162.

H

Hague, The (hayg). City in western Netherlands and capital of South Holland province. (52°N/4°E) p. 249.

Hamburg (HAM burg). Busy port city in Germany, on the Elbe River. (54°N/10°E) p. 157.

Hanoi (hah NOI). Capital of Vietnam. Located on the Red River. (21°N/106°E) p. 545.

Harappa (huh RAP uh). Site of ancient city in the Indus Valley. (31°N/73°E) p. 129.

Harare (hah RAH ree). Capital of Zimbabwe, in southern Africa. (18°S/31°E) p. 478.

Harbin (HAHR bihn). City in northeastern China, on the Songhua River. (46°N/127°E) p. 617.

Hawaiian Islands (huh WAH eeun EYE lundz). Group of islands in the North Pacific Ocean that together form a state of the United States. p. 591.

Hellespont (HEL us pahnt). Historical name for the Dardanelles, a strait in Turkey. p. 77.

Himalayas (hihm uh LAY uz). World's highest mountain system. Located in central Asia. Mount Everest, at 29,028 ft (8,848 m) the highest peak in the world, is located in the Himalayas. p. 508.

Hindu Kush (HIHN doo kush). Mountain range located mostly in Afghanistan. Its highest point, Tirich Mir, has an elevation of 25,260 ft (7,699 m). p. 129.

Hokkaidō (hoh KYE doh). Northernmost of the four main islands of Japan. p. 508.

Hong Kong (HAHNG KAHNG). British colony in southeastern China. (22°N/114°E) p. 508.

Honolulu (hahn uh LOO loo). Capital of and most populated city in Hawaii. Located on the island of Oahu. (21°N/158°W) p. 591.

Honshū (HAHN shoo). Largest of Japan's four major islands. p. 508.

Huang He (hwahng hih). River in north central and eastern China that flows into the Yellow Sea. p. 508.

Iberian Peninsula (eye BIHR ee un puh NIHN suh luh). European peninsula southeast of the Pyrenees. Spain and Portugal are on this peninsula. p. 157.

Iceland (EYE slund). Island between the Atlantic and Arctic oceans and between Norway and Greenland. p. 157.

Indian Ocean (IHN dee un OH shun). Large body of water between Africa, Asia, Antarctica, and Australia. p. 508.

Indonesia (ihn duh NEE zhuh). Island group located between Southeast Asia and Australia. Made up of Java, Sumatra, most of Borneo, and other islands. p. 545.

Indus River (IHN dus RIHV ur). River that arises in Tibet and flows into the Arabian Sea in Pakistan, near the border with India. p. 129.

Ireland (EYE ur lund). Large island west of Great Britain. An independent country, the Republic of Ireland, takes up most of the island, but a small part in the north (Northern Ireland) is a part of the United Kingdom. p. 157.

Iron Gate (EYE urn gayt). Gorge, or pass, between the Carpathian and the Balkan mountains, through which the Danube River flows. (45°N/23°E) p. 283.

Islamabad (ihs LAHM uh bahd). Capital of Pakistan. (34°N/73°E) p. 545.

Istanbul (ihs tan BOOL). Most populated city in Turkey. Located on both sides of the Bosporus. Part of the city is in Europe, and part is in Asia. Formerly known as Constantinople. (41°N/29°E) p. 361.

Ivory Coast (EYE vuh ree kohst). Country in western Africa, along the Gulf of Guinea. p. 478.

J

Jakarta (juh KAHR tuh). Capital of Indonesia. One of the world's most populated cities. Located on the northwest coast of Java. (6°S/107°E) p. 545.

Java (JAV vuh). Island that is part of Indonesia. Located between the Java Sea and the Indian Ocean. p. 508.

Jerusalem (juh ROOZ uh lum). Capital of Israel. Holy city for Jews, Christians, and Muslims. (32°N/35°E) p. 404.

Jordan River (JORD un RIHV ur). River that rises in Syria and flows south through the Sea of Galilee and into the Dead Sea. p. 51.

Jutland Peninsula (JUT lund puh NIHN suh luh). Peninsula located between the North and Baltic seas. Denmark and part of Germany are located on it. p. 157.

K

Kabul (KAH bool). Capital of and most populated city in Afghanistan. (35°N/69°E) p. 361.

Kalahari Desert (kal uh HAHR ee DEZ urt). Dry plateau region located in Botswana, South Africa, and Namibia. p. 440.

Khartoum (kahr TOOM). Capital of Sudan, on the Nile River. (16°N/33°E) p. 478.

Khyber Pass (KYE bur pas). Narrow pass through the Hindu Kush, along the border between Pakistan and Afghanistan. (34°N/71°E) p. 129.

Kiev (kee EV). Capital of Ukraine. Located on the Dnieper River. (50°N/31°E) p. 296.

Kilwa (KIHL wah). Ancient town on a small island off the coast of Tanzania. Known for its excellent harbor. (9°S/39°E) p. 461.

Kinshasa (keen SHAH sah). Capital of Zaire. Located on the Zaire River. Formerly known as Léopoldville. (4°S/15°E) p. 478.

Kyūshū (kee OO shoo). Most southern of the four main islands of Japan. p. 508.

L

Lagos (LAY gahs). Most populated city in Nigeria. Formerly the capital. Located on the Gulf of Guinea. (6°N/3°E) p. 478.

Lake Baikal (layk bye KAWL). The world's deepest lake. It is 5,712 ft (1,741 m) deep. Located in Siberia, in Russia. p. 285.

Lake Chad (layk chad). Lake located on the borders between Niger, Chad, Nigeria, and Cameroon. The size of this lake varies, depending on the season. p. 440.

Lake Superior (layk suh PIHR ee ur). Lake located along the boundary between Canada and the United States. Largest of the five Great Lakes. Its coastline is in Minnesota, Wisconsin, and Michigan. p. 621.

Lake Tanganyika (layk tan gun YEE kuh). Lake in east central Africa. Four African nations—Tanzania, Zaire, Zambia, and Burundi—have coastlines on this lake. p. 440.

Lake Victoria (layk vihk TOR ee uh). One of the largest bodies of fresh water in the world. Located in eastern Africa. Kenya, Uganda, and Tanzania all have coastlines on this lake. p. 440.

Leningrad (LEN un grad). *See* St. Petersburg.

Libreville (LEE bruh veel). Seaport and capital of Gabon, in western equatorial Africa, on the Gulf of Guinea. (0°lat./9°E) p. 478.

Liechtenstein (LIHK tun styn). Country in west central Europe, on the Rhine River. p. 157.

Lisbon (LIHZ bun). Capital of Portugal. Mainland Europe's westernmost port city. (39°N/9°W) p. 249.

London (LUN dun). Capital and most populated city in the United Kingdom. Located on the Thames River. (52°N/0°long.) p. 157.

Luanda (loo AHN duh). Capital of and seaport in Angola, in southwestern Africa (9°S/13°E) p. 478.

M

Macedonia (mas uh DOH nee uh). Part of ancient Greece, once ruled by Alexander the Great. It was located in northern Greece. p. 77.

Madagascar (mad uh GAS kur). Island located in the Indian Ocean, off the southeast coast of Africa. Excluding Australia, it is the world's fourth largest island. The nation of Madagascar is on this island. p. 440.

Madrid (muh DRIHD). Capital of Spain. Second most populated city in Europe. (40°N/4°W) p. 249.

Malta (MAWL tuh). Country on a group of islands in the Mediterranean, south of Sicily. p. 157.

Manchester (MAN ches tur). City in northwestern England. (54°N/2°W) p. 255.

Manila (muh NIHL uh). Capital of and most populated city in the Philippines. Located on Manila Bay, on the island of Luzon. (15°N/121°E) p. 545.

Mecca (MEK uh). Birthplace of Muhammad. Holy city for Muslims. Located in Saudi Arabia. (21°N/40°E) p. 392.

Medina (muh DEE nuh). City in Saudi Arabia. Muhammad's trip from Mecca to Medina in A.D. 622 is called the Hegira. (24°N/40°E) p. 392.

Mediterranean Sea (med ih tuh RAY nee un see). Large body of water surrounded by Europe, Africa, and Asia. It is the largest sea in the world. p. 157.

Mekong River (MAY kahng RIHV ur). River in Southeast Asia. Rises in Tibet. Forms most of the boundary between Thailand and Laos. Flows into the South China Sea in southern Vietnam. p. 508.

Melanesia (mel uh NEE zhuh). Group of islands in the South Pacific, northeast of Australia. pp. 610–611.

Melbourne (MEL burn). Capital of the Australian state of Victoria. Located in southeastern Australia, near the coast. (38°S/145°E) p. 591.

Mesopotamia (mes up puh TAY mee uh). Region between the Tigris and Euphrates rivers. p. 51.

Micronesia (mye kruh NEE zhuh). Group of islands in the Pacific, east of the Philippines. pp. 610–611.

Milan (mih LAN). Industrial city in northern Italy. Second most populated city in Italy. (45°N/9°E) p. 166.

Minneapolis (mihn ee AP ul ihs). Most populated city in Minnesota. Located on the Mississippi River. (45°N/93°W) p. 162.

Mohenjo-Daro (moh hen joh DAHR oh). Site of an ancient city in the Indus plain. (28°N/69°E) p. 129.

Mongolia (mahng GOH lee uh). Country in east central Asia, north of China. p. 508.

Mont Blanc (mohn blahn). Highest peak in the Alps. Located in the French Alps, near the border with Italy. Elevation is 15,771 ft (4,807 m). p. 157.

Moscow (MAHS koh). Capital of Russia. Former capital of Soviet Union. The most populated city in Europe. (56°N/38°E) p. 326.

Mount Ararat (mount AR uh rat). Highest point in Turkey, at 16,945 ft (5,165 m). (40°N/44°E) p. 359.

Mount Cook (mount kook). Peak in west central South Island. The highest peak in New Zealand, with an elevation of 12,349 ft (3,764 m). (44°S/170°E) p. 574.

Mount Damāvand (mount DAM uh vand). Highest peak in Iran. Located in the Elburz Mountains. Elevation is 18,934 ft (5,771 m). (36°N/52°E) p. 359.

Mount Elbrus (mount EL broos). Peak in the Caucasus Mountains. Highest peak in Europe, with an elevation of 18,481 ft (5,633 m). (43°N/42°E) p. 285.

Mount Everest (mount EV ur ihst). Highest peak in the world. Located in the Himalayas, with an elevation of 29,028 ft (8,848 m). (28°N/87°E) p. 508.

Mount Fuji (mount FOO jee). Highest peak in Japan. Located on Honshū island. Elevation is 12,388 ft (3,776 m). (35°N/138°E) p. 508.

Mount Kenya (mount KEN yuh). Peak in central Kenya. Second highest point in Africa, with an elevation of 17,058 ft (5,199 m). (0° lat./37°E) p. 440.

Mount Kilimanjaro (mount kihl uh mun JAHR oh). Highest mountain peak in Africa, with an elevation of 19,340 ft (5,895 m). Located in northeastern Tanzania, near the Kenyan border. (3°S/37°E) p. 440.

Mount Kosciusko (mount kahs ee US koh). Highest peak in the Australian Alps. Located in southeastern Australia. Elevation is 7,316 ft (2,230 m). (36°S/148°E) p. 574.

Mount Olympus (mount oh LIHM pus). Highest peak in Greece, with an elevation of 9,570 ft (2,917 m). In ancient Greek mythology it was supposed to be the home of the gods. (40°N/22°E) p. 77.

Mount Vesuvius (mount vuh SOO vee us). Only active volcano on the European mainland. Located near Naples, Italy. (41°N/14°E) p. 110.

Murray River (MUR ee RIHV ur). Most important river in Australia. Rises in the Great Dividing Range and flows into the Indian Ocean near Adelaide. p. 574.

N

Nairobi (nye ROH bee). Capital of and most populated city in Kenya. (1°S/37°E) p. 478.

Namib Desert (NAHM ihb DEZ urt). Dry area along the coast of Namibia. p. 440.

Naples (NAY pulz). Important port city in Italy. Located on the Tyrrhenian Sea, which is part of the Mediterranean Sea. (41°N/14°E) p. 166.

New Delhi (noo DEL ee). Capital of India. Located on the Jumna River. (29°N/77°E) p. 545.

New Guinea (noo GIHN ee). Large island north of Australia. The western half is part of Indonesia; the eastern half is the country Papua New Guinea. p. 508.

New South Wales (noo south waylz). State of southeastern Australia. p. 591.

New York City (noo york SIHT ee). Most populated city in the United States. Located at the mouth of the Hudson River, in the state of New York. (41°N/74°W) p. 621.

Nice (nees). Resort city on Mediterranean coast of France. (44°N/7°E) p. 249.

Niger River (NYE jur RIHV ur). River that rises in southern Guinea, near the Sierra Leone border. Flows into the Gulf of Guinea in Nigeria. p. 440.

Nile River (nyl RIHV ur). Longest river in the world. Flows into the Mediterranean Sea at Alexandria, Egypt. p. 359.

Nineveh (NIHN uh vuh). Ancient capital in northern Mesopotamia, on the Tigris River. (36°N/43°E) p. 51.

North America (north uh MER ih kuh). The earth's third largest continent. p. 23.

North China Plain (north CHYE nuh playn). Large plain located in eastern China. p. 508.

Northern Hemisphere (NOR thurn HEM ih sfihr). The half of the earth that is north of the Equator. p. 8.

North European Plain (north yoor uh PEE un playn). Large area of flat land stretching from southwestern France through Belgium, the Netherlands, Germany, and Poland into the former Soviet Union. The southeastern part of the United Kingdom is also part of this plain. p. 285.

North Island (north EYE lund). Northernmost of the two major islands of New Zealand. p. 574.

North Pole The most northern place on the earth. Located at 90° north latitude. p. 8.

North Sea (north see). Part of the Atlantic Ocean between Great Britain and the European continent. p. 157.

O

Ob River (ohb RIHV ur). River that rises in the Altai Mountains and flows north into the Arctic Ocean. Located in Russia. p. 285.

Oder River (OH dur RIHV ur). River that flows north through Poland. In Germany, it is joined by the Neisse River. It then flows north to the Baltic Sea, forming the boundary between Poland and Germany. p. 249.

Olympia (oh LIHM pee uh). City in ancient Greece. Located in western Peloponnesus. Site of the ruins of the temple of Zeus. Ancient Greeks held their Olympian Games here every four years. (38°N/22°E) p. 77.

Orange River (OR ihng RIHV ur). Longest river in South Africa. Part of the river forms the boundary between South Africa and Namibia. Flows into the Atlantic Ocean at Alexander Bay. p. 440.

Oslo (AHS loh). Capital of Norway. Located on Oslo Fjord. (60°N/11°E) p. 249.

P

Pacific Ocean (puh SIHF ihk OH shun). The earth's largest body of water. Stretches from the Arctic Circle to Antarctica and from the western coast of the Americas to the eastern coast of Asia. p. 23.

Palestine (PAL us tyn). Region on the eastern coast of the Mediterranean. It was the country of the Jews in biblical times and is now divided into Arab and Jewish states. p. 391.

Paris (PAR ihs). Capital and river port of France. (49°N/2°E) p. 249.

Pennines (PE nynz). Range of mountains in northern England, extending from the Cheviot Hills southward to Derbyshire and Staffordshire. p. 255.

Persia (PUR zhuh). Ancient kingdom in the area that today is called Iran. p. 87.

Persian Gulf (PUR zhun gulf). Arm of the Arabian Sea. Separates Iran and Saudi Arabia. Connected with the Gulf of Oman and Arabian Sea by the Strait of Hormuz. p. 359.

Perth (purth). Capital of the Australian state of Western Australia. Located on the southwest coast of Australia. (32°S/116°E) p. 591.

Philippines (FIHL uh peenz). Country in the Pacific, north of Indonesia, made up of more than 7,000 islands. p. 508.

Polynesia (pahl uh NEE zhuh). Scattered group of many islands in the central and southern Pacific, including Hawaii and Tahiti. pp. 610–611.

Pompeii (pahm PAY ee). Ancient Roman city at the base of Mount Vesuvius. Destroyed in A.D. 79 by an eruption of Mount Vesuvius. (41°N/15°E) p. 110.

Po River (poh RIHV ur). Longest river in Italy. Starts in the Alps and flows into the Adriatic Sea south of Venice. p. 157.

Prague (prahg). Capital of Czechoslovakia. Located on the Vltava River. (50°N/14°E) p. 326.

Prime Meridian (prym muh RIHD ee un). 0° line of longitude that passes through Greenwich, England. It divides the earth into the Eastern Hemisphere and the Western Hemisphere. p. 9.

Prussia (PRUSH uh). Former state of northern Germany. p. 226.

Pyrenees (PIHR uh neez). Mountains along the border between France and Spain. Highest peak is Pico de Aneto, at 11,168 ft (3,404 m). p. 157.

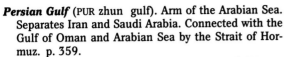

Rangoon (ran GOON). Capital of and most populated city in Myanmar. Located on the Rangoon River. (17°N/96°E) p. 545.

Red Sea (red see). Large sea separating part of eastern Africa from Asia. p. 359.

Rhine River (ryn RIHV ur). River that starts in the Alps in Switzerland. Flows north through the Netherlands into the North Sea. p. 157.

Rhone River (rohn RIHV ur). River that starts from a glacier in the Alps in Switzerland and flows through France and into the Mediterranean Sea near Marseilles, France. p. 157.

Riyadh (ree YAHD). Capital of Saudi Arabia. (25°N/47°E) p. 404.

Rocky Mountains (RAHK ee MOUNT unz). Longest mountain chain in Canada and the United States. Stretches from Alaska to Mexico. Its highest peak in Canada is Mount Robson, British Columbia, with an elevation of 12,972 ft (3,954 m). p. 621.

Rome (rohm). Capital of and most populated city in Italy. Located on the Tiber River. Most important city in the Roman Empire. (42°N/12°E) p. 249.

Rotterdam (RAHT ur dam). Seaport in the southwestern Netherlands (52°N/4°E) p. 166.

S

Sahara (suh HAR uh). Largest desert in the world. Located in North Africa. p. 359.

Saigon (SYE gahn). Seaport in South Vietnam. Saigon was the capital of South Vietnam when Vietnam was a divided country. The new name is Ho Chi Minh City. (11°N/107°E) p. 536.

St. Petersburg (saynt PEET urz burg). City in Russia built by Peter the Great in 1703. Located on the mouth of the Neva River. At different times known as Petrograd and Leningrad. Today it is the second most populated city in Russia. (60°N/30°E) p. 326.

Salamis (SAL uh mihs). Greek island in the Saronic Gulf, near Piraeus. Ancient Greeks won an important naval battle near here against the Persians in 480 B.C. (38°N/23°E) p. 77.

San'a (sah NA). Capital of Yemen. (15°N/44°E) p. 404.

Sarajevo (sar uh YAY voh). City in Bosnia and Hercegovina. Site of 1984 Winter Olympics. (44°N/18°E) p. 228.

Sardinia (sahr DIHN ee uh). Italian island in the Mediterranean. It is just south of the island of Corsica. p. 157.

Scandinavian peninsula (scan duh NAY vee un puh NIHN suh luh). Large peninsula in northern Europe, consisting of Norway and Sweden. p. 157.

Sea of Japan (see uv juh PAN). Arm of the western Pacific Ocean, between Japan and eastern Asia. p. 508.

Sea of Marmara (see uv MAHR muh ruh). Body of water between European Turkey and Asian Turkey. Connects the Bosporus and the Dardanelles. (41°N/28°E) p. 77.

Senegal River (sen ih GAWL RIHV ur). River that rises in Guinea and flows into the Atlantic Ocean at Saint-Louis, Senegal. Forms boundary between Senegal and Mauritania. p. 440.

Seoul (sohl). Capital of South Korea. One of the world's most populated cities. (38°N/127°E) p. 545.

Serbia (SUR bee uh). State in the eastern part of the former Yugoslavia. Formerly a kingdom. p. 228.

Shikoku (SHEE koh koo). Smallest of the four main islands of Japan. p. 508.

Siberia (sye BIHR ee uh). Region mostly in Russia, covering much of the area between the Ural Mountains and the Pacific Ocean. p. 285.

Sicily (SIHS ul ee). Largest island in the Mediterranean Sea. Part of Italy. p. 157.

Singapore (SIHNG uh por). City on the island of Singapore. Also the capital of the nation of Singapore. One of the world's busiest ports. Located on Singapore Strait. (1°N/104°E) p. 545.

Sofia (SOH fee uh). Capital of Bulgaria. (43°N/23°E) p. 326.

South America (south uh MER ih kuh). The earth's fourth largest continent. p. 23.

South China Sea (south CHYE nuh see). Arm of the Pacific Ocean, west of the Philippines and Borneo. p. 508.

Southern Hemisphere (SUTH urn HEM ih sfihr). The half of the earth that is south of the Equator. p. 8.

South Island (south EYE lund). Largest of New Zealand's islands. p. 574.

South Pole (south pohl). The most southern place on the earth. Located at 90° south latitude. p. 10.

Sparta (SPAHRT uh). City-state in ancient Greece. Today a small town on the Eurotas River, on the southern part of the Peloponnesian peninsula. (37°N/22°E) p. 74.

Sri Lanka (sree LAHNG kuh). Country in the Indian Ocean, off the southern tip of India. At one time called Ceylon. (7°N/81°E) p. 508.

Stockholm (STAHK hohm). Capital of Sweden. On the Baltic Sea. (59°N/18°E) p. 166.

Strait of Gibraltar (strayt uv jih BRAWL tur). Narrow neck of water separating the Iberian Peninsula from North Africa. Connects the Mediterranean Sea with the Atlantic Ocean. p. 157.

Strait of Hormuz (strayt uv HOR muz). Narrow body of water connecting the Persian Gulf and the Gulf of Oman. (27°N/56°E) p. 361.

Suez Canal (soo EZ kuh NAL). Waterway that joins the Red and Mediterranean seas. Construction started in 1859 and was completed in 1869. (30°N/33°E) p. 359.

Sydney (SIHD nee). Capital of the Australian state of New South Wales. Most populated city in Australia. Port city located on Tasman Sea, which is part of the Pacific Ocean. (34°S/151°E) p. 591.

T

Tahiti (tuh HEET ee). French island in the South Pacific, south of Hawaii. (18°S/149°W) p. 591.

Taipei (tye PAY). Capital of and most populated city in Taiwan. (25°N/122°E) p. 545.

Taiwan (tye WAHN). Island off the southeastern coast of China. This island country is called the Republic of China. p. 508.

Tashkent (tash KENT). Capital of Uzbekistan. (41°N/69°E) p. 326.

Tasmania (taz MAY nee uh). Island off the coast of Australia. Also, one of Australia's states. p. 574.

Tehran (te RAHN). Capital of Iran. Located at the base of the Elburz Mountains. (36°N/51°E) p. 404.

Thames River (temz RIHV ur). River in Great Britain on which London is located. p. 157.

Thebes (theebz). City-state in ancient Greece. (38°N/23°E) p. 77.

Thermopylae (ther MAHP uh lee). Narrow pass in eastern Greece, where ancient Greeks fought Persians in 480 B.C. (39°N/23°E) p. 77.

Tiber River (TYE bur RIHV ur). River in Italy. It rises in the Apennines and flows through Rome to the Mediterranean Sea. p. 110.

Tibet (tih BET). High mountainous area in western China, north of India and Nepal. p. 545.

Tigris River (TYE grus RIHV ur). River that rises in Turkey and flows into Iraq, where it joins with the Euphrates River near Al-Qurna to form the Shatt-al-Arab, which flows into the Persian Gulf. p. 51.

Timbuktu (tihm buk TOO). Town in central Mali, near the Niger River. (17°N/3°W) p. 457.

Tokyo (TOH kee oh). Capital of Japan. Located on the island of Honshū on Tokyo Bay. Second most populated city in the world. (36°N/140°E) p. 545.

Tripoli (TRIHP uh lee). Capital of Libya. Port city on the Mediterranean Sea. (33°N/13°E) p. 404.

Tropic of Cancer (TRAHP ihk uv KAN sur). Line of latitude located at 23 1/2° north latitude. p. 21.

Tropic of Capricorn (TRAHP ihk uv KAP rih korn). Line of latitude located at 23 1/2° south latitude. p. 21.

Troy (troi). Ancient city on the coast of Asia Minor. (40°N/26°E) p. 77.

Tunis (TOO nihs). Capital of Tunisia. Seaport located on the Mediterranean Sea. (37°N/10°E) p. 361.

U

Uruk (OO ruk). Ancient Sumerian city in southern Babylonia, on the Euphrates River. (31°N/45°E) p. 51.

Ural Mountains (YOOR ul MOUNT unz). Mountains located in Russia. They form the east-west divide between Asia and Europe. p. 285.

V

Vatican City (VAT in kun SIHT ee). Independent state inside the city of Rome, with the pope as its head. (42°N/12°E) p. 157.

Venice (VEN ihs). City in Italy. (45°N/12°E) p. 224

Victoria (vihk TOR ee uh). State in the southeastern part of Australia. p. 591.

Victoria Falls (vihk TOR ee uh   fawlz). Falls located on the Zambezi River, on the boundary between Zambia and Zimbabwe. More water flows over these falls than over any others in Africa. (18°S/26°E) p. 440.

Vienna (vee EN uh). Capital of and largest city in Austria. Located on the Danube River. (48°N/16°E) p. 249.

Vistula River (VIHS choo luh   RIHV ur). Longest river in Poland. Rises in the Carpathians and flows into the Baltic Sea near Gdańsk. p. 285.

Vladivostok (vlad ih VAHS tahk). City in Russia. Eastern end of the Trans-Siberian Railroad. Located on the Sea of Japan. (43°N/132°E) p. 285.

Volga River (VAHL guh RIHV ur). Longest river in Europe. Rises in the Valdai Hills of Russia and flows into the Caspian Sea. p. 285.

W

Wales (waylz). One of the four major political divisions of the United Kingdom. p. 255.

Warsaw (WOR saw). Capital of Poland. Located on the Vistula River. (52°N/21°E) p. 326.

Washington, D.C. (WAWSH ing tun   dee see). Capital of the United States. Located on the Potomac River. (39°N/77°W) p. 620.

Waterloo (WAWT ur loo). Village in Belgium where Napoleon met his final defeat, in 1815. (51°N/4°E) p. 218.

Wellington (WEL ing tun). Capital of New Zealand. Located on North Island and Cook Strait. (41°S/175°E) p. 591.

Western Ghats (WES turn   gawts). Mountains located along the western coast of India. Highest peak is Anai Mudi, at an elevation of 8,841 ft (2,695 m). p. 508.

Western Hemisphere (WES turn   HEM ih sfihr). Hemisphere in which all of South America and North America are located. The half of the earth west of the Prime Meridian. p. 9.

X

Xi'an (SHEE AHN). Capital of the Shaanxi province in east central China, on the south bank of the Wei River. Formerly called Sian. (34°N/109°E) p. 617.

Xi Jiang (shee   jee AHNG). River in southeastern China. Formerly known as Hsi Chiang. p. 144.

Y

Yenisei River (yen uh SAY   RIHV ur). River in Russia. One of the world's longest rivers. Rises in the Sayan Mountains and flows into the Kara Sea, which is part of the Arctic Ocean. p. 285.

Z

Zagros Mountains (ZAG rus   MOUNT unz). Mountains that stretch from northwestern Iran to near the southern end of the Persian Gulf. Highest peak is Zardeh Kuh, with an elevation of 14,921 ft (4,548 m). p. 359.

Zanzibar (ZAN zuh bahr). Island belonging to Tanzania. Located in the Indian Ocean, off the coast of Tanzania. Also the name of the chief city on the island. (6°S/39°E) p. 440.

A

abdicate (AB dih kayt). To give up a position of power, such as a kingship. p. 315.

Aborigine (ab uh RIHJ uh nee). A member of the first inhabitants of Australia. p. 573.

acid rain (AS ihd rayn). Rain or snow that has a high amount of certain acids due to air pollution. p. 271.

Africanized (AF rih kuh nyzd). Changed to reflect African names. p. 480.

alliance (uh LYE uns). An agreement by persons, groups, or nations to act together for some special purpose or benefit. p. 80.

altitude (AL tuh tood). The height above sea level. p. 14.

ambassador (am BAS uh dur). An official who represents his or her government in a foreign country. p. 405.

amphitheater (AM fuh thee ut ur). A large open-air theater built in a semicircular pattern, with ascending rows of seats built into a hillside. p. 95.

anarchy (AN ur kee). The complete lack of government or law. p. 315.

ancestor (AN ses tur). A person from whom a family or a group of people descends. p. 65.

anno Domini (AH noh DOH mee nee). Latin words that mean "in the year of the Lord." Usually shortened to the letters A.D., the term is used to mark the years after the birth of Jesus. p. 27.

apartheid (uh PAHR tayt). The policy of racial segregation that the Republic of South Africa had until 1991. Apartheid means "apartness." p. 484.

apprentice (un PREN tihs). A person learning a trade or an art. p. 182.

aqueduct (AK wuh dukt). A structure or an artificial channel used to transport water. p. 114.

arable (AR uh bul). Suitable for growing crops. p. 343.

archaeologist (ahr kee AHL uh jihst). A scientist who studies objects, ruins, and other evidence of human life in the past. p. 49.

archipelago (ahr kuh PEL uh goh). A group of islands. p. 512.

armistice (AHR muh stihs). A halt to fighting by agreement between warring nations. p. 230.

artery (AHRT ur ee). A main road or channel. p. 516.

ascetic (uh SET ihk). A person who chooses to live without the comforts of life, especially one who lives this way for religious reasons. p. 132.

asphalt (AS fawlt). A substance formed from a combination of oil, sand, and rock. p. 424.

assassination (us sas sih NAY shun). The murdering of someone by secret or sudden attack. p. 107.

astronomy (uh STRAHN uh mee). The scientific study of the sun, moon, planets, and stars. p. 201.

atheism (AY thee ihz um). The belief that there is no God. p. 342.

atlas (AT lus). A collection of maps. p. 22.

atoll (A tawl). A ring-shaped coral island enclosing or partly enclosing a lagoon. p. 584.

axis (AK sihs). The imaginary rod around which the earth turns. p. 4.

Axis (AK sihs). The name given to Italy, Japan, and Germany, the countries that fought against the Allies in World War II. p. 241.

ayatollah (eye yuh TOH luh). An honorary title for a Muslim religious leader in Iran. p. 404.

B

Bedouin (BED oo ihn). A wandering Arab herder. p. 360.

bilingual (bye LIHNG gwel). Having two languages. p. 267.

Blitzkrieg (blihts KREEG). A war conducted with great speed. From German words meaning "lightning" and "war." p. 236.

Boer (boor). An early Dutch settler in South Africa; Dutch word for "farm worker." p. 467.

boomerang (BOOM ur ang). A bent throwing stick that can be thrown in such a way that it comes back to the thrower. p. 590.

Brahman (BRAH mun). A class of priest under the Aryans' caste system. p. 134.

bush (boosh). Sparsely settled land far from any settlement. p. 573.

C

cacao (kuh KAY oh). The tree and the seeds from which cocoa and chocolate are made. p. 450.

caliph (KAY lihf). The Arabic title given to Muslim religious leaders. p. 386.

calligraphy (kuh LIHG ruh fee). The art of handwriting. p. 397.

capital (KAP ut ul). Wealth in the form of goods or money used for making more goods. p. 210.

cartographer (kahr TAHG ruh fer). A person who makes maps. p. 16.

cash crop (kash krahp). A crop grown for sale. p. 480.

caste (kast). A class or group into which people are separated based on birth. p. 134.

causeway (KAWZ way). A raised roadway across a body of water. p. 418.

central planning (SEN trul PLAN nihng). A system in which the government decides what and how much should be produced by industries. p. 325.

century (SEN chu ree). A period of 100 years. p. 28.

circa (SUR kuh). The Latin word meaning "about" or "approximately." Used to refer to dates. p. 28.

city-state (SIHT ee stayt). A state made up of an independent city and the nearby countryside, as in ancient Greece. p. 78.

civil disobedience (SIHV ul dihs oh BEE dee uns). Nonviolent opposition to a government law by refusing to obey the law. p. 554.

civilization (sihv ul luh ZAY shun). The stage of cultural development marked by the presence of cities, trade, government, art, writing, and science. p. 48.

civil war (SIHV ul wor). A war between two or more groups of people within a country. p. 107.

climate (KLYE mut). The kind of weather a place has over a long period of time. p. 24.

climograph (KLYE muh graf). A graph that shows both the average temperature and the average precipitation for a certain place over a period of time. p. 161.

cocoon (kuh KOON). The silky case, or covering, that caterpillars spin to shelter themselves while they are changing into butterflies or moths. p. 525.

collective farm (kuh LEK tihv fahrm). A farm that a group of people operate together to produce and to share the products. p. 323.

collectivism (kuh LEK tuh vihz um). A system of ownership by all the people together. p. 323.

colony (KAHL uh nee). A settlement in one land ruled by the government of another land. p. 86.

commercial farm (kuh MUR shul fahrm). A farm that produces crops for sale. p. 450.

Commonwealth of Nations (KAHM un welth uv NAY shunz). An association of countries that were once part of the British Empire. p. 258.

commune (KAHM yoon). Land that is worked together by a team of people. p. 541.

communism (KAHM yoo nihz um). A social and economic system in which most property is owned by the government and shared by the governed. p. 316.

Confucianism (kun FYOO shun ihz um). A religion based on the teachings of the philosopher Confucius. Confucianism teaches respect for the past and one's ancestors and stresses the importance of having only superior people rule a well-ordered society. p. 141.

coniferous (koh NIHF ur us). Having cones. p. 160.

constitutional monarchy (kahn stuh TOO shuh nul MAHN ur kee). A kind of government in which the monarch's powers are limited by a constitution. p. 213.

consul (KAHN sul). The annually elected chief magistrate of the Roman republic. The magistrate was given the powers of a king. p. 102.

consumer goods (kun SOOM ur goodz). Things that are grown or made by producers and used by people. p. 389.

continental climate (kahn tuh NENT ul KLYE mut). A climate with extreme changes of temperature, and with hot summers and cold winters. p. 287.

contour line (KAHN toor lyn). A line that is used to show elevation on a topographical, or physical, map. p. 15.

convent (KAHN vunt). A building or buildings in which a group of nuns live. p. 180.

copra (KAH pruh). Dried coconut meat. p. 562.

Coptic (KAHP tihk). An Egyptian language no longer used except in the services of the Egyptian Christian Church. p. 59.

coral reef (KOR ul reef). A line or ridge of coral lying at or near the surface of the water. p. 575.

coronation (kor uh NAY shun). The crowning of a king or queen. p. 311.

crest (krest). The highest point. p. 286.

crude oil (krood oil). Oil in the form in which it comes from the earth, before impurities are removed. p. 406.

Crusade (kroo SAYD). A Christian military expedition to take control of the Holy Land from the Muslims. p. 178.

culture (KUL chur). The way of life of a group of people, including their customs, traditions, and values. p. 88.

cuneiform (kyoo NEE uh form). A form of writing with wedge-shaped symbols that was used in Mesopotamia. p. 49.

current (KUR unt). A stream that flows in the ocean. p. 162.

czar (zahr). The title of any of the former emperors of Russia. p. 310.

D

decade (DEK ayd). A period of 10 years. p. 28.

Deccan (DEK un). A low plateau occupying most of the peninsula of India. Two mountain ranges, the Western Ghats and the Eastern Ghats, form the edge of the Deccan. p. 507.

deciduous (dee SIHJ oo us). Dropping off; losing leaves at the end of a growing season. Oak and maple trees are deciduous. p. 160.

delta (DEL tuh). The land formed by mud and sand in the mouth of a river. p. 55.

democracy (dih MAHK ruh see). A government in which power is held by the people. p. 78.

depression (dee PRESH un). An economic condition in which business is very bad and large numbers of people are unemployed. p. 233.

despot (DES put). A person who rules with total and unlimited control. p. 77.

dialect (DYE uh lekt). A form of a language that is used only in a certain place or among a certain group. p. 138.

dictator (DIHK tayt ur). One who has absolute power of rule in a country. p. 102.

Diet (DYE ut). The legislature of Japan. The Diet is made up of representatives elected by the people and is similar to Parliament in England. p. 550.

dike (dyk). A wall or bank built to control or hold back the water of a river or sea. p. 51.

distortion (dih STOR shun). A twisting or stretching out of shape. p. 20.

divine right (duh VYN ryt). A belief during the Middle Ages that kings received their powers from God. p. 195.

dry stone (drye stohn). A stone held together with another stone without the use of mortar. p. 459.

E

economic boom (ek uh NAHM ihk boom). A period of great prosperity. p. 476.

economy (ih KAHN uh me). The way in which natural resources and workers are used to produce goods and services. p. 175.

elevation (el uh VAY shun). The height of something. The elevation of land is its distance above or below sea level and is usually measured in feet or meters. p. 14.

embassy (EM buh see). The buildings where the ambassador of a country lives and works. p. 405.

emperor (EM pur ur). A supreme ruler of an empire. p. 109.

epic (EP ihk). A long narrative poem about great heroes and their deeds. p. 71.

equatorial (ee kwuh TOR ee ul). Near the Equator. p. 439.

ethnic group (ETH nihk groop). A group of people who share many traits and customs. p. 341.

explorer (ek SPLOR ur). A person who searches for new things and places. p. 190.

export (EKS port). **1.** Something that is sent to another country, usually for sale there. **2.** To send something to another country for sale. p. 257.

ex post facto law (eks pohst FAK toh law). The rule that no law can be used to punish a person for something done before the law was made. p. 121.

F

factory (FAK tuh ree). An industrial plant. p. 207.

Fascist (FASH ihst). A member of a group that believes in a political system that supports a single party and a single ruler, and involves total government control of political, economic, cultural, religious, and social activities. p. 232.

feudalism (FYOOD ul ihz um). The system of mutual rights and duties between lords and vassals. The system existed in the Middle Ages. p. 174.

fez (fez). A felt hat with a flat top and no brim once worn by Turkish men. p. 411.

fief (feef). Land granted by a lord to his vassal in return for military service. p. 174.

finance (FYE nans). The management of money. p. 551.

fjord (fyord). A long, narrow, often deep inlet of the sea, lying between steep cliffs. p. 261.

folk tale (fohk tayl). A story handed down from one generation to another that often reflects the ideas and traditions that a nationality values. p. 294.

food processing (food PRAH ses ihng). The canning, freezing, or drying of agricultural products. p. 592.

forestry (FOR ihs tree). The science and work of planting and taking care of forests. p. 160.

free enterprise (free ENT ur pryz). A type of economy in which people have many choices about how to make and spend their money. p. 211.

free port (free port). A port or place with no taxes on imports or exports. p. 537.

G

genocide (JEN un syd). The planned killing of a whole group of people because of their race, religion, or nationality. p. 239.

geothermal energy (jee oh THUR mul EN ur jee). The heat from within the earth. p. 579.

geyser (GYE zur). An underground stream that sends forth a gush of hot steam or hot water. p. 262.

gladiator (GLAD ee ayt ur). A person who fought another person or an animal for the entertainment of an audience in ancient Rome. p. 115.

glasnost (GLAHS nust). A policy of "openness" in the former Soviet Union, which resulted in less secrecy about problems and weaknesses of Soviet society. p. 329.

gorge (gorj). A narrow passage through land. p. 291.

grid (grihd). A network of lines that form a pattern of crisscrosses. p. 8.

gross national product (grohs NASH uh nul PRAHD ukt). The total value of all the goods and services produced in a year by a nation. p. 551.

groundnut (GROUND nut). Nuts that grow underground, rather than on trees or bushes. p. 479.

ground water (ground WAWT ur). Water that has seeped below the ground and has collected in layers of soil, sand, and rock. p. 369.

guild (gihld). An organization of people in a craft or trade. p. 182.

guillotine (GIHL uh teen). A machine for beheading people that was introduced in France during the French Revolution. p. 217.

Gulf Stream (gulf streem). The currents that flow north and east from the Gulf of Mexico. p. 162.

H

hemisphere (HEM ih sfihr). Half of a sphere, or ball. Half of the earth. p. 5.

heritage (HER ih tihj). Ways and beliefs handed down from one generation to the next. p. 596.

hieroglyphics (hye ur oh GLIHF ihks). A form of picture writing used by the early Egyptians. p. 60.

high veld (hye velt). The upland grassland area of South Africa. p. 489.

historical source (hihs TOR ih kul sors). A person or thing that tells about the past. p. 116.

Holocaust (HAHL uh kawst). The destruction of more than 6 million European Jews by the Nazis. p. 239.

hostage (HAHS tihj). A person held captive until demands of the captor are met. p. 405.

humidity (hyoo MIHD uh tee). The amount of water or dampness in the air. p. 24.

I

incentive (ihn SENT ihv). Anything that makes a person work harder or do more. p. 542.

Industrial Revolution (ihn DUS tree ul rev uh LOO shun). The period of great change in the way people worked and lived, brought about by the invention of power-driven machines. p. 207.

Inquisition (ihn kwuh ZIHSH un). A special court of the Roman Catholic Church, established in the thirteenth century. p. 204.

International Date Line (ihn tur NASH uh nul dayt lyn). The line at roughly 180° longitude that marks the place where each day begins. p. 9.

irrigate (IHR uh gayt). To bring water to crops, usually through canals, ditches, or pipes. p. 51.

isthmus (IHS mus). A narrow strip of land connecting two larger bodies of land. p. 23.

J

jury (JOOR ee). A group of people called into court to give a verdict, or decision, in a dispute. p. 80.

jute (joot). A plant, raised mostly in the Ganges Delta, from which the fiber for burlap and twine is obtained. p. 556.

K

Knesset (KNES et). The Israeli parliament. p. 410.

knight (nyt). A warrior of the Middle Ages. p. 174.

L

labor force (LAY bur fors). The working population. p. 360.

landlocked (LAND lahkt). Not having a seacoast. p. 248.

latex (LAY teks). The milky sap that drips from cuts made in the bark of rubber trees. p. 514.

latitude (LAT uh tood). The distance measured in degrees north and south from the Equator to the earth's poles. Lines of latitude are imaginary lines used to locate places on the earth. p. 8.

League of Nations (leeg uv NAY shunz). An international organization, formed after World War I, of nations interested in preventing war. p. 231.

legend (LEJ und). A story handed down from earlier times, which may be no more than partly true. p. 103.

literacy rate (LIHT ur uh see rayt). The percentage of the population able to read and write. p. 552.

longitude (LAHN juh tood). The distance measured in degrees east and west of the Prime Meridian. Lines of longitude are used to locate places on the earth. p. 8.

M

manor (MAN ur). A large medieval farm. p. 175.

maritime climate (MAR ih tym KLYE mut). A climate influenced by winds blowing off the sea. p. 256.

market economy (MAHR kiht ih KAHN uh mee). An economy in which the choices of buyers decide what shall be produced. p. 327.

mausoleum (maw suh LEE um). A large tomb. p. 534.

Mediterranean climate (med ih tuh RAY nee un KLYE mut). A warm, temperate climate occurring on the western margins of continents in the latitudes 30° to 40°. It is marked by hot, dry, and sunny summers and moist, warm winters. p. 264.

meridian (muh RIHD ee un). Another name for a line of longitude. p. 8.

metropolitan area (me troh PAHL ih tun ER ee uh). An area made up of a large city or several large cities and the surrounding towns, cities, and other communities. p. 167.

migration (mye GRAY shun). The movement of people from one place to another. p. 360.

minaret (mihn uh RET). A tall, slender tower, with a balcony, on a mosque. p. 399.

missionary (MIHSH un er ee). A person who tries to spread his or her religion. p. 468.

modernize (MAHD urn eyes). To change over to the use of up-to-date ways of doing things. p. 403.

monarchy (MAHR ur kee). A government headed by one ruler, usually a queen or a king. p. 78.

monastery (MAHN uh ster ee). Building(s) where monks live together. p. 179.

monolith (MAHN uh lihth). A large block of stone, or a statue or monument carved from a single large stone. p. 575.

monopoly (muh NAHP uh lee). The exclusive possession or control of a commodity or service. p. 182.

monsoon (mahn SOON). A seasonal wind that blows from the land to the water in one season and from the water to the land in the other. p. 460.

mosque (mahsk). A Muslim place of worship. p. 398.

mullah (MUL uh). A Muslim religious teacher. p. 403.

multilingual (mul tih LIHNG gwel). Having several languages. p. 445.

mummy (MUM ee). A body treated for burial with preservatives to keep it from decaying. p. 55.

myth (mihth). An ancient story that usually explains something in nature. p. 71.

N

nationalism (NASH uh nul ihz um). A feeling of loyalty and devotion to one's country. p. 223.

natural resource (NACH ur ul REE sors). Something useful to people that is supplied by nature, such as land, minerals, water, and forests. p. 160.

navigator (NAV uh gayt ur). A person who plans and steers a course through water or air or on land. p. 463.

nomad (NOH mad). A person who moves from place to place. p. 129.

nonrenewable resource (nahn rih NOO uh bul REE sors). A resource that will not be replaced by nature, such as oil. p. 416.

North Atlantic Drift (north at LAN tihk drihft). A large movement of water made up of the Gulf Stream and other warm currents. p. 162.

O

oasis (oh AY sihs). A green place in a desert where wells provide water. p. 55.

odometer (oh DAHM ut ur). An instrument that tells how far one has traveled. p. 11.

oligarchy (AHL ih gahr kee). A government by a few. p. 78.

oral history (OHR ul HIHS tuh ree). The history or tradition of a people handed down from one generation to another by word of mouth. p. 455.

orbit (OR biht). The path that one body travels as it goes around another body, such as the path of the earth around the sun. p. 4.

P

pagoda (puh GOH duh). A tower that serves as a religious building. p. 558.

papyrus (puh PYE rus). A tall reed that grows in the Nile Valley. The pith (spongy center part) was used to make a paperlike substance. p. 61.

parable (PAR uh bul). A short, simple story that teaches a moral lesson, as in the teachings of Jesus. p. 117.

parallel (PAR uh lel). An imaginary line of latitude running in an east-west direction on a map. p. 8.

Parliament (PAHR luh munt). The lawmaking body of the United Kingdom. p. 212.

partition (pahr TIHSH un). A division into parts. p. 554.

patrician (puh TRIHSH un). A member of one of the original citizen families of ancient Rome. A member of the upper class. p. 101.

peninsula (puh NIHN suh luh). A piece of land almost surrounded by water and connected to a large body of land. p. 102.

per capita income (per KAP ih tuh IHN kum). The amount of income (money received) that each person in a country would have if the country's total income were divided equally among all of its people. p. 367.

perestroika (per es TROI kuh). The reform of government and economy in the former Soviet Union. p. 330.

permafrost (PUR muh frawst). Permanently frozen ground. p. 286.

petroleum (puh TROH lee um). An oily liquid found in the earth, from which gasoline and many other products are made. p. 367.

pharaoh (FAR oh). A ruler of ancient Egypt. From the Egyptian word for "Great House." p. 55.

philosophy (ful LAHS uh fee). The study of human behavior, thought, and knowledge. The word *philosophy* originally meant "the love of wisdom." p. 90.

phosphate (FAHS fayt). A mineral used in making fertilizers and detergents. p. 424.

pictograph (PIHK toh graf). A kind of graph that uses symbols, instead of numbers, to represent fixed amounts of a particular thing. p. 50.

pilgrimage (PIHL grihm ihj). A journey to a shrine or other sacred place. p. 382.

Pinyin (pihn YIHN). A system of spelling and writing Chinese words, using the Roman alphabet. p. 138.

plaque (plak). A thin, flat piece of metal or wood with decoration or lettering on it. p. 458.

plateau (pla TOH). A large, high, rather level area that is raised above the surrounding land. p. 248.

plebeian (plee BEE un). One of the common people in any country, such as in ancient Rome. p. 101.

pollution (puh LOO shun). The unclean condition of the earth's soil, air, and water. p. 251.

population density (pahp yoo LAY shun DEN suh tee). The average number of people living in a unit of land area. p. 25.

precipitation (pree sihp uh TAY shun). Moisture that falls on the earth's surface: rain, snow, sleet, and hail. p. 24.

Prime Meridian (prym muh RIHD ee un). The line of 0° longitude that passes through Greenwich, England. p. 9.

prime minister (prym MIHM ihs tur). The chief official of a country. p. 224.

principality (prihn suh PAL uh tee). A territory ruled by a prince. p. 254.

profit (PRAHF iht). The gain made from selling a product or service over the cost of producing or purchasing the product or service. p. 211.

projection (proh JEK shun). The representation on a map of all or part of the earth's grid system. p. 19.

prophet (PRAHF ut). A person who was believed to have a message from God. p. 379.

protectorate (proh TEK tur iht). A place or country under the protection of another country. p. 600.

proverb (PRAHV urb). A short saying that expresses some truth or fact. p. 295.

province (PRAHV ihns). A division of a country. p. 106.

pyramid (PIHR uh mihd). A massive four-sided structure built on a broad base and narrowing gradually to a point at the top. p. 58.

pyrethrum (pye RETH rum). A plant used to make insect poison. p. 491.

R

raw material (raw muh TIHR ee ul). A natural material that can be processed into finished products. p. 251.

Reformation (ref ur MAY shun). The religious movement during the sixteenth century that aimed at reforming the Roman Catholic Church and resulted in establishing the Protestant churches. p. 192.

Renaissance (ren un SAHNS). The great revival of art and learning in Europe in the 1300s, 1400s, and 1500s. The word **Renaissance** means "a new birth." p. 184.

republic (rih PUB lihk). A government in which citizens choose representatives to run the country. p. 101.

reserve (rih ZURV). A reserve is a supply of a natural resource that is known to exist but has not yet been used. p. 416.

revenue (REV uh noo). Income. p. 422.

revolution (rev uh LOO shun). **1.** A complete change in the way a country is governed. p. 201. **2.** The movement of the earth around the sun. One complete *revolution* takes 365 1/4 days. p. 201.

river basin (RIHV ur BAYS un). The area drained by a river. p. 441.

Romance language (roh MANS LANG gwihj). Any language that grew out of Latin: Spanish, Portuguese, French, Italian, and Romanian. p. 122.

rural (ROOR ul). Having to do with the countryside; nonurban. p. 167.

S

samurai (SAM uh rye). The military class in feudal Japan. p. 528.

sanctuary (SANGK choo er ee). A place where birds and animals are protected from hunters and others who would disturb them. p. 291.

satellite (SAT uh lyt). An object made to go around the earth. p. 18.

savanna (suh VAN uh). Land covered with coarse grass and, sometimes, scattered trees and bushes. p. 438.

scale (skayl). The relationship between real size and size used on a map or model. Also, the line, drawn on maps, that shows this relationship. p. 12.

schism (SIHZ um). A split or division between the members of a church or other group when they no longer agree on what they believe. p. 304.

scribe (skryb). A person who copied manuscripts and records and wrote letters. p. 61.

Senate (SEN iht). An assembly or council, as in ancient Rome. Only patricians could be part of the Roman Senate. p. 102.

serf (surf). A person who lived and worked on a manor. p. 175.

service industry (SUR vihs IHN dus tree). A business that provides some kind of useful work for another business or a person. p. 257.

shah (shah). A Persian word meaning "king." p. 403.

shogun (SHOH gun). A military leader in feudal Japan. p. 528.

shrine (shryn). A place considered to be holy. p. 377.

silt (sihlt). Fine particles of earth that are carried and deposited by water and wind. p. 55.

sisal (SYE sul). A plant with strong fibers used for making rope. p. 450.

slash-and-burn farming (slash un BURN FAHRM ihng). A system of farming in which farmers slash, or cut, tree branches and other plant growth and let the vegetation dry so that it will burn. Then the farmers burn the dried vegetation, clearing the ground and enriching the soil at the same time. After this, they plant crops. p. 449.

smelting (SMELT ihng). The process of separating a metal from other materials in its ore. p. 592.

socialism (SOH shul ihz um). A system that calls for ownership of land and industry by the government. p. 316.

Solidarity (sahl uh DAR uh tee). The large free union of Polish workers. The word *solidarity* means "unity." p. 337.

sphere (sfihr). A three-dimensional figure that is round or nearly round. p. 4.

standard of living (STAN durd uv LIHV ihng). A measure of how well people live. p. 210.

steppe (step). One of the belts of grassland in Europe and Asia, somewhat like the prairie of North America. p. 288.

strait (strayt). A narrow waterway connecting two larger bodies of water. p. 78.

subcontinent (SUB kahnt un unt). A landmass of great size but smaller than the continents. p. 127.

subsistence farming (sub SIHS tuns FAHRM ihng). The growing of crops by farmers for their own use rather than for sale. p. 449.

successor (suk SES ur). A person who succeeds, or follows, another. p. 532.

sultan (SULT un). A ruler of a Muslim country. p. 388.

T

taiga (TYE guh). The great coniferous forest region of the northern and western parts of the former Soviet Union. p. 287.

tax (taks). Money paid to a ruler or government and spent on providing government services. p. 173.

teak (teek). A hard wood used in building ships and furniture. p. 514.

teff (tef). A grasslike grain native to northern Africa and grown for its edible seeds. p. 493.

temperate climate (TEM pur iht KLYE mut). A climate that is moderate, neither very hot nor very cold. The temperate zones of the earth are usually called the middle latitudes. p. 581.

terrace (TER us). A flat shelf of land, arranged like a wide step on a mountainside. p. 513.

terrorism (TER ur ihz um). Surprise violent attacks against people's lives. p. 423.

time line (tym lyn). A line representing a period of time, on which dates and the order of events are shown. p. 28.

time zone (tym zohn). A geographic region where the same standard time is used. p. 289.

tributary (TRIHB yoo ter ee). A stream or river that flows into a larger body of water. p. 284.

Tropic of Cancer (TRAHP ihk uv KAN sur). A line of latitude that circles the earth at 23 1/2° north latitude. p. 439.

Tropic of Capricorn (TRAHP ihk uv KAP rih korn). A line of latitude that circles the earth at 23 1/2° south latitude. p. 439.

tropics (TRAHP ihks). The zone between the Tropic of Capricorn and the Tropic of Cancer. p. 439.

tundra (TUN druh). A rolling plain without trees, found in the Arctic area of the high latitudes. p. 286.

typhoon (tye FOON). A tropical storm accompanied by strong winds and heavy rain. p. 528.

U

unification (yoon uh fih KAY shun). The uniting of separate regions and cities into one nation. p. 223.

United Nations (yoo NYT ihd NAY shunz). An organization set up to settle disputes between nations. p. 242.

urban (UR bun). Having to do with a town or city. p. 167.

V

volcano (vahl KAY noh). An opening in the earth, usually at the top of a cone-shaped hill or mountain, out of which steam and other gases, stone, ashes, and melted rock may escape from time to time. p. 112.

W

wadi (WAH dee). The bed of a stream that is dry most of the time. p. 363.

warlord (WOR lord). A general who controls an area by force. p. 541.

Z

ziggurat (ZIHG oo rat). A platform in the form of a terraced pyramid, with each story smaller than the one below it. p. 52.

INDEX

CREDITS

Front cover: *Background* © The Telegraph Colour Library/FPG; *insets b.l., b.r.* FourBy-Five/SuperStock.

Back cover: *t., b.* SuperStock; *m.* Ron Chapple/FPG.

Country charts: Scott Wilson

Maps: Maryland Cartographics, Inc.

Graphs: Richard Puder Design/JAK Graphics, Ltd.

Contributing artists: Anthony Accardo: 61, 72; Ray Dallasta: 175; Bert Dodson: 456; Len Ebert: 66, 479; Dan Fiore: 208, 230, 449; Phil Jones: 202; John Less: 292–293, 357, 388, 506; Gabriel Nunzione: 66–67; Tom Powers: 50, 93, 137 *b*; Leslie Stall: 136; Wayne Anthony Still: 368, 584, 593; Gary Torrisi: 421; Jean and Mou Sien Tseng: 140.

All photographs by Silver Burdett Ginn (SBG) unless otherwise noted.

Map Skills Handbook 3: David G. Fitzgerald/After Image. 7: The Bridgeman Art Library. 15: David G. Fitzgerald/After Image. 18: © Photo Researchers, Inc. 19: *t., b.* Culver Pictures. 22: David Falconer/After Image. 26–27: Baseball Hall of Fame.

Unit 1 opener 44–45: Lee Boltin Picture Library.

Chapter 1 46: Kurt Scholz. 49: Mary Evans Picture Library. 52: *t.* Robert Harding Picture Library. 53: Giraudon/Art Resource. 57: *l.* Lee Boltin. 58: Robert Frerck/The Stock Market. 59: *t. inset* Culver Pictures. 62: British Museum, London/The Bridgeman Art Library. 64: North Wind Picture Archives.

Chapter 2 70: H. Sutton/H. Armstrong Roberts. 73: Culver Pictures. 75: North Wind Picture Archives. 76: Peter Connolly. 78–79: North Wind Picture Archives. 80–81: Historical Pictures Service, Chicago. 82–83: Paul Conklin. 84–85: Scala/Art Resource. 86: Historical Pictures Service, Chicago. 88: Giraudon/Art Resource. 90: Scala/Art Resource. 91: Art Resource. 92: *b.* J. Snyder/The Stock Market. 94: Michael Holford. 95: © 1991 William Hubbell/Woodfin Camp & Associates.

Chapter 3 98: Scala/Art Resource. 100: Giraudon/Art Resource. 101: Ted H. Funk/FPG International. 102: Scala/Art Resource. 103: *t.* The Bettmann Archive; *b.* Historical Pictures Service, Chicago. 107: Giraudon/Art Resource. 108: North Wind Picture Archives. 109: Art Resource. 111: Ara Gulor. 112–113: The Bettmann Archive. 113: *inset* Scala/Art Resource. 114: Shostal/SuperStock; *inset* Art Resource. 115: North Wind Picture Archives. 123: Robert Frerck/Odyssey Productions.

Chapter 4 126: Henebry Photographs. 128: *bkgd.* © Paolo Koch/Photo Researchers, Inc.; *l.* Karachi Museum/Art Resource; *t.r., b.r.* Lee Boltin. 131: C.M. Dixon. 133: *bkgd.* Historical Pictures Service, Chicago; *t.* Robert Frerck/Odyssey Productions. 134: Michael Holford. 138: Werner Forman Archive. 139: Historical Pictures Service, Chicago. 142: *bkgd.* China Pictorial; *inset* © An Keren/Photo Researchers, Inc. 143: *t.* The Ancient Art and Architecture Collection; *b.* Nawrocki Stock Photos.

Unit 2 opener 152–153: Michael Holford.

Chapter 5 154: J. Messerschmidt/Bruce Coleman. 156, 158: Yves Ballu. 159: C.M. Dixon. 160: Eric and Maureen Carle/SuperStock. 163: Chris Hugh/TSW-Click, Chicago. 164: Historical Pictures Service, Chicago. 167: Frances Bannett/DPI, Inc. 169: Bruno Barbey/Magnum.

Chapter 6 172: FPG International. 174: North Wind Picture Archives. 175: *r.* Art Resource. 176: North Wind Picture Archives. 178: Mary Evans Picture Library. 179: Art Resource. 180: Eric Crichton/Bruce Coleman. 181: Scala/Art Resource. 182: North Wind Picture Archives. 183: Historical Pictures Service, Chicago. 184: FPG International. 185: *r.* Art Resource. 186: Art Resource. 187: Giraudon/Art Resource. 188: *t.* Historical Pictures Service, Chicago; *b.* North Wind Picture Archives. 189: *t.l.* The Bettmann Archive; *t.r.* The Granger Collection; *b.l.* Aldus Archive/Syndication International; *b.r.* Tom Tracy/The Stock Market. 190: Historical Pictures Service, Chicago. 191: Museum of London/The Bridgeman Art Library. 192, 195: Art Resource. 196: *t.* Walter Rawlings/Robert Harding Picture Library; *m.* © L. West/Photo Researchers, Inc.; *b.* Peter Le Grand/TSW-Click, Chicago.

Chapter 7 200: Galerie Dijol, Paris/The Bridgeman Art Library. 203: The Bettmann Archive. 204: Private collection/The Bridgeman Art Library. 205: The Bettmann Archive. 206, 209: North Wind Picture Archives. 210: Historical Pictures Service, Chicago. 212: North Wind Picture Archives. 213: Photoworld/FPG International. 215: *l.* Scala/Art Resource; *r.* Giraudaon/Art Resource. 216: Musée Carnavalet, Paris/The Bridgeman Art Library. 217: Giraudon/Art Resource.

Chapter 8 222: Keith Ferris. 223: Scala/Art Resource. 225: *t.* North Wind Picture Archives. 227: Historical Pictures Service, Chicago. 229: U.S. Army. 232: Mary Evans Picture Library. 233, 234: Photoworld/FPG International. 235: The Bettmann Archive. 236: Robert Harding Picture Library. 237: *t.* Augustus Upitis/SuperStock; *m.l.* SuperStock; *m.r.* Mike Wells/Aspect Picture Library; *b.* Rentmeester/The Image Bank. 239: FPG International. 240: The Bettmann Archive. 242: UPI/Bettmann Newsphotos. 243: Jon Riley/TSW-Click, Chicago.

Chapter 9 246: Tony Craddock/TSW-Click, Chicago. 248: John and Dallas Heaton/After Image; *inset* Luis Castaneda/The Image Bank. 249: J. Messerschmidt. 250: FourByFive/SuperStock. 251: Chip Hires/Gamma-Liaison. 253: Sygma. 253: Chip Hires/Gamma-Liaison. 254: Robert Harding Library. 256: Steve Vidler/Leo deWys. 258: Richard Gorbun/Leo deWys; *inset* T. Graham/Sygma. 259: © Linda Bartlett/Photo Researchers, Inc. 261: FourByFive. 262: *l.* Sunak/ZEFA/H. Armstrong Roberts; *r.* Eichhorn/ZEFA/H. Armstrong Roberts. 263: Stephen Johnson/TSW-Click, Chicago. 264, 266: M. Thonig/H. Armstrong Roberts. 267: Mike Howell/Leo deWys. 268, 269: Shostal/SuperStock. 271: Douglas Dickens. 272: Robert Harding Picture Library.

Unit 3 opener 280–281: FourByFive/SuperStock.

Chapter 10 282: A. Tessore/SuperStock. 283: Emil Schulthess/Black Star. 284: Peter Arnold. 286: Karl Heinz Jorgens/Robert Harding Picture Library. 286–287: Burt Glinn/Magnum. 288: © 1991 Adam Woolfitt/Woodfin Camp & Associates. 289: Vander Vaeren/The Image Bank. 295: *t.l.* © 1991 Howard Socharek/Woodfin Camp & Associates; *m.l., t.m.* Eastfoto/Sovfoto; *b.l., m.r., b.r.* Tass/Sovfoto; *t.r.* © 1991 G. Ludwig/Woodfin Camp & Associates; 297: Robert Everts/TSW-Click, Chicago.

Chapter 11 304: *t.* The Bettmann Archive; *b.* SuperStock. 305, 306: North Wind Picture Archives. 307: Tass/Sovfoto. 308: The Bettmann Archive. 311: Mary Evans Picture Library. 312: *l.* Michael Holford; *r.* North Wind Picture Archives. 314: The Bettmann Archive. 315: Culver Pictures. 316, 317: Mary Evans Picture Library. 318: The Bettmann Archive. 319: Van Phillips/Leo deWys.

Chapter 12 322: Epix/Sygma. 324, 327, 328: Tass/Sovfoto. 329: Novosti/Sygma. 330: Sipa-Press. 331: *t.* Ricki Rosen/The Picture Group; *b.* Richard Quataert. 336: A. Hernandez/Sipa-Press. 337: Weslowski/Sygma. 339: G. Giansanti/Sygma. 340: © 1991 John Eastcott/Momatuik/Woodfin Camp & Associates. 342: © Paolo Koch/Photo Researchers, Inc. 343: Owen Franken/Stock, Boston. 345: Peter Baker/Leo deWys. 346: © 1991 Adam Woolfitt/Woodfin Camp & Associates.

Unit 4 opener 354–355: © Alain Bordes/Photo Researchers, Inc.

Chapter 13 356: Richard Steedman/The Stock Market. 358: *The Arabian Nights Entertainments,* selected and edited by Andrew Lang, illustrated by H.J.Ford, Shocken Books, NY. 359: Robert Maust/Photo Agora. 363: Alon Reininger/Leo deWys. 365: Nick Faridani/TSW-Click, Chicago. 366: Peter Carmichael/Aspect Photo Library. 367: Thain Manske/The Stock Market. 370: H. Armstrong Roberts. 371: Inge Morath/Magnum. 372: Hubertus Kanus/SuperStock. 373: ZEFA/H. Armstrong Roberts.

Chapter 14 376: Steve Vidler/SuperStock. 377: Abu Hander/Firth Photobank. 380: © 1991 Craig Aurness/Woodfin Camp & Associates. 381: Culver Pictures. 382–383: Shostal/SuperStock. 384: UPI/Bettmann Newsphotos. 385: *l.* ARCHIV/Photo Researchers, Inc.; *m.* The Granger Collection; *r.* NASA. 386, 393: Historical Pictures Service, Chicago. 394, 396: Culver Pictures. 398: Art Resource, N.Y. 399: SuperStock.

Chapter 15 402: © Paolo Koch/Photo Researchers, Inc. 405: Abbas/Magnum. 407: © Emil Muench/Photo Researchers, Inc. 408: D. Aubert/Sygma. 409: Robert Capa/Magnum. 411: Wolfgang Kaehler. 413: © 1991 R & S Michaud/Woodfin Camp & Associates. 414: Jane Taylor/Sonia Halliday. 415: Assem Cherib/Gamma-Liaison. 417: *l.* Randa Bishop/DPI, Inc.; *r.* Bernard Gerard/Joe Viesti Associates. 419: F. Jackson/Bruce Coleman. 420: © 1991 Robert Frerck/Woodfin Camp & Associates. 422: *t.* FourByFive; *b.* A. Nogues/Sygma. 423: Steve Vidler/Leo deWys. 424: Shostal/SuperStock. 425: M. Thonig/H. Armstrong Roberts. 426: SuperStock.

Unit 5 opener 434: Gill C. Kenny/The Image Bank. 435: © 1993 Marc and Evelyne Bernheim/Woodfin Camp & Associates.

Chapter 16 436: SuperStock. 437: Eric Lessing/Magnum. 439: Georg Gerster/Comstock. 440: Mark N. Boulton/Bruce Coleman. 441: R.S. Virdee/Grant Heilman Photography. 442: Kim Naylor/Aspect Picture Library. 443: Harvey Lloyd/The Stock Market. 444: Victoria Southwell/Robert Harding Picture Library. 445: Michael Holford. 448: Dieter Blum/Peter Arnold. 451: Galen Rowell/After Image.

Chapter 17 454: © 1991 Marc and Evelyne Bernheim/Woodfin Camp & Associates. 458: Michael Holford. 461: The Granger Collection, New York. 462: Georg Gerster/Comstock; *inset* Lawrence Manning/TSW-Click, Chicago. 468: Mary Evans Picture Library. 470: Hulton/The Bettmann Archive. 471: By courtesy of the Crown Estate Commissioners, London/The Bridgeman Art Library.

Chapter 18 474: Comstock. 475: AP/Wide World Photos. 476: *t.* Mike Wells/TSW-Click, Chicago; *b.* © 1991 Marc and Evelyne Bernheim/Woodfin Camp & Associates. 481: Frans Lanting. 482: Bruno Barbey/Magnum. 483: The Granger Collection. 484: A. Tannenbaum/Sygma. 485: Frank Trapper/Sygma. 486: AP/Wide World Photos. 487: Peter Turnley/Black Star. 489: Keith Gunnar/FPG International. 490: © John Moss/Photo Researchers, Inc. 491: Robert Frerck/Odyssey Productions. 492: Meier/ZEFA/H. Armstrong Roberts. 494: Robert Caputo/Stock, Boston.

Unit 6 opener 502–503: Michael Holford.

Chapter 19 504: Art Wolfe/AllStock. 507: Jagdish Agarwal/DPA. 508: J. Hiebeler/Leo deWys. 511: Cary Wolinsky/Stock, Boston. 513: ZEFA/H. Armstrong Roberts. 514: *l.* Cameraman International. 515: © Elisabeth Weiland/Photo Researchers, Inc. 516: Henebry Photography. 517: Steve Vidler/After Image. 518: Raga/The Stock Market.

Chapter 20 522: FourByFive. 524: *b.* The Bridgeman Art Library. 527: Lee Eung Jun. 528: Robert Harding Picture Library. 530: U.S. Naval Academy Museum. 531: Historical Pictures Service, Chicago. 532: Victoria and Albert Museum/Michael Holford. 533: Robert Harding Picture Library. 534: Hilaire Kavanaugh/TSW-Click, Chicago. 535: Manley/SuperStock. 537: Historical Pictures Service, Chicago.

Chapter 21 540: Raga/The Stock Market. 542: Anderson/Gamma-Liaison. 544: Robin Moyer/Gamma-Liaison. 546: E. John/Bruce Coleman. 547: Anderson/Gamma-Liaison. 548: Charlie Cole/Sipa Press. 550: *l.* U. Gosset/Sygma; *r.* AP/Wide World Photos. 552: © Minori Aoki/Photo Researchers, Inc. 553: Neveu/Gamma-Liaison. 554: Mary Evans Picture Library. 555: Jonathan T. Wright/Bruce Coleman. 557: © 1991 Robert Frerck/Woodfin Camp & Associates. 558: Jean-Paul Nacivet/After Image. 561: David Austen/Stock, Boston. 562: Diana Walker/Gamma-Liaison.

Unit 7 opener 570–571: Andrea Pistolesi/The Image Bank.

Chapter 22 572: © Bill Bachman/Photo Researchers, Inc. 573: Dallas and John Heaton/Stock, Boston. 574: Australian Picture Library. 575: Brian Lovell/Nawrocki Stock Photos. 577: Peter Walton/Firth Photobank. 578: *l.* Russ Kinne/Comstock; *t.r.* TSW-Click, Chicago; *b.l.* SuperStock. 579: Steve Vidler/Nawrocki Stock Photos. 580: *t.l.* Jean-Paul Nacivet/Leo deWys; *t.r., b.l.* Dave Watts/TOM STACK & ASSOCIATES; *b.r.* Shostal/SuperStock. 581: Dallas and John Heaton/TSW-Click, Chicago. 582: Joe Carini/Bear Productions. 583: Thor Heyerdahl. 584–585: Jean-Paul Nacivet/Leo deWys. 585: *inset* Brian Parker/TOM STACK & ASSOCIATES.

Chapter 23 588: Paul Steel/The Stock Market. 590: David Ball/The Stock Market. 594: Robin Smith/SuperStock. 595: The Bettmann Archive. 597, 598: Robert Frerck/Odyssey Productions. 599: Kirby Harrison/Blue Yonder. 600: Historical Pictures Service, Chicago. 601: Bob and Ira Spring. 602: © 1991 Michael Friedel/Woodfin Camp & Associates.

660